THE JESUS DEBATE

THE JESUS DEBATE

A Survey and Synthesis

by
William M. Thompson

Paulist Press • *New York* • *Mahwah*

All biblical citations are from *The New American Bible,* copyright © 1970 by the Confraternity of Christian Doctrine, Washington, D.C.

Citations from the apocalyptic literature are from R.H. Charles, ed., *The Apocrypha and Pseudepigrapha of the Old Testament* (Oxford: Clarendon, 1913), Volume 2.

The publisher is grateful for permission either to quote from the following or to reproduce the following works:

The Christ of Velazquez by Miguel de Unamuno. © Johns Hopkins University Press, 1951. Reprinted by permission of the publisher.

Night by Elie Wiesel. Translated from the French by Stella Rodway. © Les Editions de Minuit, 1958. English translation © MacGibbon & Kee, 1960. Reprinted by permission of Hill and Wang, a division of Farrar, Straus & Giroux, Inc.

Psychoanalysis and Religion by Erich Fromm. © Yale University Press, 1950. Reprinted by permission of the publisher.

The Theology of Christ: Sources by Vincent Zamoyta. © Bruce, 1967. Reprinted by permission of Glencoe Publishing Co.

Christ Crucified by St. John of the Cross. © Washington Province of Discalced Carmelites, Inc., 1964. Reproduced by permission of the Institute of Carmelite Studies.

Guernica, by Pablo Picasso. © S.P.A.D.E.M., Paris/V.A.G.A., New York, 1984. Reproduced by permission.

Shroud of Turin. © Vernon Miller, Brooks Institute, 1978. Reproduced by permission.

Library of Congress
Catalog Card Number: 84-61490

ISBN: 0-8091-2666-4

Published by Paulist Press
997 Macarthur Boulevard
Mahwah, N.J. 07430

Printed and bound in the United States of America

Contents

PART TWO: LEADING INTERPRETATIONS OF NEW TESTAMENT CHRISTOLOGY

PART THREE: JESUS IN THOUGHT AND PRACTICE AFTER THE NEW TESTAMENT

"So we make up and supplement each other.
We give and others give to us."

". . . behind every saint stands another saint. . . ."
                                        —*Friedrich von Hügel*

Abbreviations

CT = *The Church Teaches: Documents of the Church in English Translation*, translated by John F. Clarkson et al. (St. Louis, Mo.: B. Herder, 1955).

DS = *Enchiridion Symbolorum*, eds. H. Denzinger and A. Schönmetzer (Freiburg: Herder, 1965).

NH = *The Nag Hammadi Library*, ed. James M. Robinson (New York: Harper and Row, 1977).

Preface

This book hopes to be an introductory survey and interpretation of current developments in the study of Jesus. Because it is only *introductory*, a certain degree of depth is necessarily sacrificed for the sake of breadth. The primary audience to which this book is addressed is educated beginners in the study of Jesus. This audience dictates the introductory nature of the work to a great extent. But my own limitations also dictate this, for the study of Jesus carries one into so many complex areas that no one person can really hope to be master of them all.

Because this book is a *survey* of current trends, it will attempt to put the student in touch with what the author thinks are the major developments taking place right now. Many fine works have appeared on Jesus from various points of view. This author feels it is time to try to integrate these into an introductory survey so that the interested reader can begin to sketch a preliminary map of the complex terrain.

Because this work is an *interpretation*, it will attempt some kind of critical integration of the varied currents taking place. In a sense, every work represents the author's own personal evaluation. This cannot be avoided, and admitting it perhaps makes both me and the reader somewhat more critical. But this author also feels it is time to attempt some kind of more formal integration. The various currents now developing are very rich and have much to contribute to one another.

From the very beginning let me say that this is a *theological* introduction to the study of Jesus. Theology has its own modest role to play in developing both our critical understanding of Jesus and our critical practice of the Christian life. If a theological book is written well, it can even inspire the reader psychologically and aesthetically. But we theologians need to be humble and recognize that the arts also have their important role to play in matters religious. This book simply needs to be complemented by some of the great literary works on Jesus, as well as the great artistic masterpieces. Van Gogh, Endo, Kazantzakis, Solzhenitsyn, and many more might fruitfully be consulted along with this book. They will help the reader respond to the Jesus event existentially, affectively, and even aesthetically in a way that no merely theological work can do. Between us, theologians and artists, perhaps the "whole person" will be motivated to make the kind of response to Jesus that he deserves.

1

Author's Note

The Carroll College Community in Helena provided me with the support that I needed to bring this project to its completion, especially President Francis J. Kerins and the Vice President for Academic Affairs, Sister Mary Sarah Fasenmyer. My special thanks to them. My very special thanks, too, to the many scholars mentioned throughout this work with whom I have tried to dialogue, sometimes in more personal conversations, but always through the written text. A project like this can also be somewhat stressful for a family; my special thanks to my wife and children for their support and patience.

This work is the completion of my original project in Christology undertaken some years ago with my *Christ and Consciousness* and *Jesus, Lord and Savior*. In those works I attempted to explore Christology and soteriology in an experiential-symbolic manner, hoping to make some helpful contribution to the theological task of mediating the tradition to modernity. But those works were only helpful first statements, whose tentative insights needed a more extended conversation with a more representative range of modern theologians and scholars. That is what I have attempted in this survey and synthesis. I am especially glad that I was able to incorporate the rich experiential insights and symbols of the martyrs, saints, and mystics into this new study. Readers will also note the new and more prolonged dialogue with literary critics and methodologists, with political-practical theologians, and with the venerable religions of the world. All of this has resulted in some new corrections, emphases, and sometimes in entirely new horizons of thought and practice. While this work can only be another tentative synthesis, still it is time to bring my original project to a close. In the end, this study not only "finishes" my project. It is an entirely new statement of Christology and soteriology in its own right.

1

A Proposal

Christianity is a Jesus-centered religion. Let me begin this book with some preliminary observations on what this means. I recently attended a symposium of scholars, during which a Jewish theologian maintained that what seemed to divide Christianity from its mother Judaism was the belief in the mediatorship of Jesus. As he explained it, over against Judaism's belief in direct access to the Divine for every individual Jew(ess), Christianity opts for access to the Divine through the mediation of Jesus of Nazareth.

What struck me about that view was the inattention to the "mediated" character of much of Judaism. Granted, few Jews look to Jesus for their access to God. Yet they believe that the divine self-revelation occurred through the saving events of Jewish history: the exodus, the revelation to Moses, the entry into Palestine, the formation of the covenant, even the dispersal of the exiles. Some of them maintain that that divine self-revelation continues to occur through other, more recent events, especially the horrible holocaust and the building up of a liberated and secure state of Israel. In a real sense, Judaism knows the reality of "mediated" access to the Divine. Jews not only "know" God as isolated individuals, but much more through their participation in the ongoing covenant of the Jewish people as a whole.

The mediated nature of Christianity and Judaism corresponds to what we can call a structural constant of human life. What we are and become as human beings seems to be something co-mediated to us by our culture and tradition, by other human beings, even by the ecological network of our body and its physical environment. The existence of isolated individuals who achieve human growth on their own seems largely a product of our imagination. The very ability to be isolated presupposes a human community over against which one rebels and from which one withdraws in isolation. In reality we seem to develop along with and through other persons, things, and events. Our very sense of self-worth, or the lack of it, is largely a product of either being respected and loved by others or rejected by them. The questions we ask, the hopes we entertain, the faults and limitations of which we are aware, our health or lack of it, the language we speak and which we use to try to understand ourselves and our world, even our awareness of and language for the Divine—all are at least partially mediated to us through others. In complex intersection with them, we forge our personalities.

What appears to be true of us as individuals seems also true of whole human communities. They, too, are mediated realities. Judaism looks to the exodus and the great events connected with it. Those events are what found and fund and thus mediate the reality of Judaism to subsequent Jewish believers. In intersection with those events Judaism forges out of many individuals a common exodus-identity which unites at a profoundly deep level all Jewish believers. We Americans look back to the founding mothers and fathers of the American way of life—Washington, Jefferson, Hamilton, Madison, Franklin, Lincoln, Elizabeth Cady Stanton, Susan B. Anthony, Sarah and Angelina Grimke, Martin Luther King, Chief Joseph. Through them we are Americans, sharing a common identity through participating in their struggle for life, liberty, and the pursuit of happiness. Even the self-proclaimed isolated rationalists who claim to rely upon their autonomous reason in reality rest upon the earlier historical foundations of humanity's development of reason, particularly as it found expression through the great philosophers of the classical age and through the lesser lights of the modern Enlightenment.

If all of this be true, then the crucial issue for us humans does not appear to be whether we should choose between a mediated or a non-mediated form of existence. Some form of mediation is the only choice we have. The really pertinent choice would seem to be to opt for the mediator(s) that will promise us the greatest liberation of our human potential. Not whether there should be mediation, but who/what should do the mediating—that seems the critical issue before us.

In reality, of course, there appear to be many kinds of mediators, ranging from our ecological habitat, through our families and teachers, to significant friends and great figures of the past. For the purposes of this book, let me suggest the simple distinction between minor mediators and the great breakthrough mediators. The latter would be distinguished by the fact that they discover and illuminate whole crucial areas of human existence which, apart from them, would remain unmined. It is the assumption of this book, and the belief of the Christian tradition, that Jesus is such a breakthrough mediator who makes a unique and decisive contribution to our common human existence. Without him, the liberation of our human potential would be decidedly lessened.

In exploring this theme throughout this book, I would propose that we probe Jesus' contribution to four cardinal dimensions of our common human life: (1) our relation to the Divine, (2) our vision and praxis as individuals, (3) our network of social relationships, ranging from the more interpersonal kinds of family, marriage, and friendship, to the less personal kinds characteristic of our larger political, economic, and cultural environment, and (4) our relationship to the natural environment and our very material body which positions us within this ecological habitat. I did not arrive at these four poles of human life by accident. As I hope to illustrate throughout this book, it seems that every human being is an intersection between these four poles. There is a kind of quaternion structure to our human existence. Furthermore, it seems as if the poles are interrelated, so that oscillations in any one of the poles seem to reverberate upon the others. For example, if something is wrong with pole #3 (our network of social relationships)—perhaps we might be living in a repressive society or even contributing to social oppression—this has consequences for the other three poles of our lives. If the problem is that we dwell within an oppressive regime, then perhaps our relationship with God will take the active form of a trust in a transcendent Power who summons us to struggle actively against oppression. Our vision and praxis of ourselves— our image of what we want to be—may correspondingly take the form of striving to be in solidarity with those in misery. Our relationship with the natural world might take on the form of a stewardship of the fruits of the earth, so that the oppressed can share equally with us in its life-giving power.

The above is only one example, but it does illustrate how the four poles of our common human existence are interrelated. If something is askew in one of the poles, the probability is that something will be askew in the other poles too. Conversely, healthiness in one of the poles will contribute toward the healthiness of all of the poles. The simple aim of this book is to explore Jesus' contribution to this quaternion structure of our common human life. This might be a helpful way, in our times, to learn anew why Christians consider him to be a breakthrough mediator who uniquely alters the total fabric of our human existence. What vision and praxis of the Divine, of ourselves, of our society, and of our bodily habitat does he empower and disclose? That is what we will be seeking to explore.

By way of a brief preview to the total argumentation to follow, I would ask the reader prayerfully to consider the following biblical passages. They will provide you with a first, tentative "feel" for the kind of mediator this book believes Jesus to be. I will add a brief commentary to each passage, hoping in this way to prepare you for what is to come.

God

> My command to you is: love your enemies, pray for your persecutors.
> This will prove that you are sons of your heavenly Father, for his sun
> rises on the bad and the good, he rains on the just and the unjust. If you
> love those who love you, what merit is there in that? Do not tax collec-
> tors do as much? And if you greet your brothers only, what is so praise-
> worthy about that? Do not pagans do as much? In a word, you must be
> made perfect as your heavenly Father is perfect (Mt 5:44–48).

Apparently the real secret of what Jesus is about is his discovery of a
transcendent power of love, justice, and peace, a power which somehow
flows through him and agitates him in such a way that he tries to embody
a form of universal love and justice which characterizes this divine reality
itself. This source and secret of Jesus is a universal Lover who breaks down
distinctions, and, in so doing, creates a more just form of human life. Notice how Jesus' love command is rooted in the Divine: this is the source.
Notice the analogy with the sun and the rain: like those natural realities,
the divine love is permanent, stable, and accessible to all. The motive of
this love is unconditional: it is not based on preference. Unlike the Stoics,
who called for non-retaliation of the enemy because of their freedom from
the passions which rule the masses, this love does not flow from a sense of
superiority to others. Unlike some of the intertestamental literature of the
time, which called for non-retaliation as a means of survival in a difficult
situation, and out of a belief that the Divine would take vengeance in the
end, this love flows from a God whose nature is permanently love. Jesus'
vision and praxis of the divine presence is one of unqualified love and love's
social embodiment, justice and peace.[1]

Self

> If a man wishes to come after me, he must deny his very self, take up his
> cross, and follow in my steps. Whoever would preserve his life will lose
> it, but whoever loses his life for my sake and the gospel's will preserve
> it (Mk 8:34–35).

Linked with Jesus' new vision and praxis of the divine presence is an
equally new vision and praxis of human person-making. The divine power
of justice, love, and peace agitates the self in such a way that selfhood now
becomes a project of struggling for justice, love, and peace. The self that
is denied is a self unattuned to Jesus and the Gospel. The new self that is
affirmed is a self who takes up the cross, that is, who painfully struggles on
behalf of unqualified love, justice, and peace. This is one of Jesus' pro-

verbial sayings, and like most of them, it is shocking because it entails a reversal of the commonly accepted wisdom. The "normal" vision and praxis of person-making is reversed.

Society

> On their journey Jesus entered a village where a woman named Martha welcomed him to her home. She had a sister named Mary, who seated herself at the Lord's feet and listened to his words. Martha, who was busy with all the details of hospitality, came to him and said, "Lord, are you not concerned that my sister has left me to do the household tasks all alone? Tell her to help me." The Lord in reply said to her: "Martha, Martha, you are anxious and upset about many things; one thing only is required. Mary has chosen the better portion and she shall not be deprived of it" (Lk 10:38–42).

Much of our tradition has seen in this story Jesus' upholding of the contemplative life as the highest ideal (= Mary), over against the active life (= Martha). William Johnston, an expert in spiritual theology, tells us that Clement of Alexandria, Origen, and Augustine thought that "Mary, the repentant sinner who sits silently, lovingly and mystically at the feet of Jesus, is singled out as the model of Christian perfection while busy Martha is something of a second-class citizen."[2] Johnston claims that the mystical masterpiece *The Cloud of Unknowing* bases its distinction between those called to perfection (= the Mary types) and those called only to salvation (= the Martha types) on just such an interpretation.

Recently I have become dissatisfied with this traditional interpretation. It seems to project a later monastic distinction between contemplatives and actives onto the thought world of a Jesus who himself was quite active and believed that God could be equally encountered in moments of prayer and in busy worldly activity. Under the influence of some of my women friends I have come to see in the text an example of how Jesus related to first century Jewish women. Note that Jesus commends Mary for doing the sort of thing that only men were supposed to do within Jewish society: "Mary has chosen the better portion. . . ." Presumably in that culture women already knew a lot about serving men. The virtue of service is not one that they were particularly in need of developing. Perhaps that accounts for Jesus' rebuke of Martha, who seems content with the traditional kitchen chores of Jewish women. As feminist theologian Rosemary Ruether puts it, "By vindicating Mary's right to join the circle of disciples and students of the Teacher, Jesus overthrows the traditional concept of women's place as upheld by Martha."[3] In essence, what Jesus seems to be mediating to Mary is the possibility of her fuller development. Jesus appears to be not so much a feminist, but a liberator who is attempting to rectify the limited possibilities of development available to the women of his culture.

Now let us turn to the story in which James and John ask to sit at the right and left of Jesus when he comes into his glory. Jesus responds by telling them that they do not know what they are asking.

> You know how among the Gentiles those who seem to exercise authority lord it over them; their great ones make their importance felt. It cannot be like that with you. Anyone among you who aspires to greatness must serve the rest; whoever wants to rank first among you must serve the needs of all. The Son of Man has not come to be served but to serve— to give his life in ransom for the many (Mk 10:42–45).

Note, now, that Jesus is speaking to men, and the ideal he holds out to them seems to be similar to the ideal held out by Martha: service. Presumably James and John did not need prestige, importance, and power. In their culture that was available to them already. What they lacked is precisely what Jesus offered them: service. Again we see that Jesus seems to be a liberator intent on aiding people to develop their fuller potential.

Taken together these two texts introduce us to a "feel" for the kind of society Jesus struggled to bring about. Fueled by his discovery that the deepest Source of life is a mystery of unconditional love, justice, and peace, and likewise fueled by his discovery that human selfhood is a project of realizing a similar love, justice, and peace, he now proposes a novel experiment in social relations. Society in its deepest core is rooted, not in blood, or race, or national origin, or sex, but in a love, justice, and peace which breaks down those kinds of limiting distinctions. A society of love, justice and peace means that Mary has chosen the better portion; it also means that James and John need to learn how to serve. Here we see how the oscillations in the divine pole and self-pole of Jesus are of a piece with the oscillation in his social pole. What seems to be oscillating is a current of unconditional love, justice, and peace.

Nature/World

> He proposed still another parable: "The reign of God is like a mustard seed which someone took and sowed in his field. It is the smallest seed of all, yet when full-grown it is the largest of plants. It becomes so big a shrub that the birds of the sky come and build their nests in its branches" (Mt 13:31–32).

One of the significant elements in this parable of Jesus is his appeal to nature. Apparently Jesus holds a high view of nature. This is why nature itself has something to teach us about the reign of God. There is a surprising mystery at work in nature too: notice the surprise element involved in the smallest seed of all becoming the largest of plants. What is the surprise? The mystery at work in nature is a mystery of mutual support and interdependence: the birds of the sky can build their nests in the largest of shrubs. Mutual support and interlocking dependence is what nature can teach us about the reign of God. If you will, there is an ecological sensitivity in Jesus. Nature is not an object to be used and abused by humans, but an interlocking network of mutuality and support which in some respects teaches humans about a deep mystery. The fact that Jesus appeals to nature so often when he talks about his message of the reign of God illustrates not only his high regard for nature but his awareness of how nature and humans are interconnected in his vision and praxis. Again, the realization dawns upon us that the oscillating current which flows through Jesus' divine, personal, and social poles also flows through the pole of his interconnectedness with nature. A new experiment in relations with nature is beginning.

By now it will have dawned upon the reader what the overall argumentation of this book will be. The divine love, justice, and peace current flowing through Jesus makes of him a mediator from whom flows a love-, justice-, and peace-reordering of our relationships to God, to self, to society, and to nature. Such is what I believe the various currents in the present study of Jesus collectively argue. Now it is time to begin our deeper look into this fascinating man from Nazareth.

Notes

1. Cf. Pheme Perkins, *Love Commands in the New Testament* (New York: Paulist, 1982), pp. 27–41.

2. William Johnston, *The Inner Eye of Love: Mysticism and Religion* (New York: Harper and Row, 1978), p. 25.

3. Rosemary Radford Ruether, *New Woman/New Earth: Sexist Ideologies and Human Liberation* (New York: Seabury, 1975), p. 66.

PART ONE

An Overview of
Contemporary Approaches to Jesus

The New Interest in Jesus

An interest in Jesus runs deep today. This is true of the West primarily, but Shusaku Endo's *A Life of Jesus,* which is a best-seller in Japan, indicates a certain interest even in the Orient.[1] What accounts for this new
interest, and what really makes it new? I would suggest, on the broad
level, that three great turning points or transitions in our modern history
largely account for this new interest.

The First Transition

I will call our first transition a new fascination for human experience.
A good case can be made that many of us sense that we are living in a new
epoch in human history. We are conscious of a certain break with prior
ages. Of course, human history is continuous and all attempts at historical
periodization are limited, needing to be refined as history proceeds and as
we gain a different perspective on our past. Yet I agree with James Livingston's judgment that "there is more in common between the world
views of the thirteenth and sixteenth centuries than between those of the
sixteenth and nineteenth"[2]—at least in the West. This means that the Reformation is not the watershed inaugurating the modern West. Livingston
speaks of a "revolution" in human self-understanding occurring. This is
perhaps too strong. But I think we can speak of the beginnings of a change
in self-understanding, first articulated by a few, and then gradually dis-
seminated up into our present. The image of a rock cast into a pond, with
its ever widening ripples—or perhaps of a boulder!—might be helpful.

What were some of the factors bringing about this new fascination for
human experience? One was clearly the new quest for discovery and
travel, beginning in earnest in the sixteenth and seventeenth centuries. As
Europeans began to discover other cultures and histories, their horizons
were widened. At times this could cause theological problems, for the discovery of other cultural histories could call into question the up-to-then accepted biblical portrait of human history. For example, Voltaire said, in
reference to what was being learned about China: ". . . authentic histories

15

trace this nation back . . . to a date earlier than that which we normally attribute to the Flood."[3] The widening of the experiential horizon brought a challenge to the inherited biblical framework of Europe.

Also emerging was an increasing tendency for philosophers to distinguish themselves from theology, as Machiavelli, Hobbes, Descartes, Locke, Hume, Kant, Hegel, and Spinoza illustrate. The new fascination for experience brought a new fascination for reason as the human instrument whereby experience is investigated. Theology was thought of more as the guardian of the past than as the investigator of present experience.

A new critical study of ancient texts also emerged. Tradition (the Scriptures, the classical authors) increasingly lost its force because of its antiquity and was critically scrutinized in the light of reason and the emerging historical sciences. The past was beginning to be studied in the light of the lessons of contemporary experience. And allied with this, of course, were the developments in the natural sciences, which were quite literally exploding after the period of the Reformation. Newton, representative of many, illustrates the new fascination for experience in his emphasis upon experimental verification. As he put it, "In experimental philosophy we are to look upon propositions inferred by general induction from phenomena as accurately or very nearly true, notwithstanding any contrary hypotheses that may be imagined, till such time as other phenomena occur, by which they may either be made more accurate or liable to exception."[4]

We should not exaggerate the novelty of what was happening. To some extent trends already begun in the classical Greek period and continued by the medieval Scholastics were only being intensified in the modern period: the new interest in nature, the fascination for human knowing/reason, the democratization of education through the emergence of a middle class. But the explosion of historical and scientific materials did initiate a sense of novelty and a new, more critical commitment to human experience as a guide for human knowledge.

This new fascination for experience sums up a complex movement in modernity which still continues today. It manifested itself in various ways, and continues to do so. One such manifestation, and a rather radical one at that, has come to be called "The Enlightenment," a designation coined by Immanuel Kant. "Enlightenment" was humanity's release from a self-incurred tutelage, the daring ability to use one's own reason, according to Kant.[5] Enlightenment thinkers were literally fascinated by the new powers of human reason. Although most of them remained believers, their God was the God of Deism, a divine reality which remained aloof from human affairs, thus allowing history to be subject to the guiding hand of human reason. Other Enlightenment thinkers were even more radically anti-religious. Eric Voegelin characterizes their thinking in this way: the "center is shifted from the sacred to the profane," initiating a process of secularization "in which history, including the Christian religious phenomena, is conceived as an inner-worldly chain of human events"; the whole is a "theogonic process" (god-creating process) which deifies reason, intellect, and the animalistic in humanity.[6]

But the modern period is a much wider phenomenon than the Enlightenment of the eighteenth century. The Enlightenment perhaps reflected in an extreme form the new fascination for experience, but it was only one reflection of a much wider maturation of the West. To some extent the more traditional culture of Germany mitigated the anti-religious tendencies of the Enlightenment. The same is true of the United States. The new stress on experience and reason was appealing to America's practical founders, but the strong religious traditions in America blunted the more radical anti-religious tendencies.[7]

The New Stress on Experience

What were some of the new interests beginning to manifest themselves in the modern period, and how do they link up with the new interest in Jesus? Let me begin with the new stress on experience. In a real sense we can speak of the modern period as initiating a new critical interest in experience, human and natural, as a norm for human knowing. The stress should fall upon the word "critical." Quite clearly people of previous ages had turned to experience, too, but not, I think, with the same self-conscious sensitivity as many do today. The latter evidence an almost unmitigated tendency to distinguish fact from fiction, unhistorical myth from historical reality, opinions from science, "dogma" from "reason," etc. Recall Newton's stress on experiential verification, cited earlier.

The new stress on experience is ambiguous. One unfortunate legacy of the Enlightenment has been a flattening out and restriction of the notion of experience, particularly owing to the new fascination for the natural sciences. These sciences, simply by virtue of their method, aim so to objectify experience that it no longer contains any personal or inward elements. Because these sciences are concerned to guarantee, through their objectivity, that their "experience" can be repeated by everyone and so be verifiable, they tend to abolish the personal and inward dimensions of human experience. In the end they restrict experience to the sense perception of objects. Louis Dupré[8] would view this as an extreme legacy of early Greek science, the so-called "slide into objectivism," setting in with the Greeks of the sixth century B.C. Through their fascination for *physis*, for the intrinsic nature of things, the capacity to be interested in the world as it *is* emerged. In the main, this resulted in a lack of attention to the human subject who does the perceiving. The focus was object-centered rather than subject-centered. With this tends to run a denigration of religious experience—the inner experience of transcendence—which presupposes more than sense experience, demanding an inward capacity to grasp the underlying depth and foundation of our sense experience of the world. Hence the anti-religious tendencies of the Enlightenment and many of its modern heirs in science, psychology (behaviorism), and philosophy (logical positivism, language analysis, etc.).

Human experience, however, need not be so restrictively conceived. Dante Germino, an important political philosopher, writes: "Human experience has many levels, and it is no less real or factual for being inner experience instead of external observation or sensory response to a physical stimulus." He goes on to maintain that when one restricts experience only to the sense perception of objects, "other dimensions of experience, apprehended through the *nous* or eye of the mind instead of the eye of the physical body, are treated as subjective because they are not as universally shared and readily communicable as experiences on the level of physical sensation." Inner human experience normally requires "laborious formation of character," but the vast majority of people "are able without comparable effort to verify" propositions based simply upon sense perception. In the end, this means that the "people of the meanest capacities" end up determining what constitutes the true field of human experience.[9]

Germino is arguing for a more expansive notion of human experience, one that is capable of being religiously sensitive, or "warm," as Friedrich Schleiermacher would put it. On this view experience must be broadened to encompass the full range of capacities and realizations of the human self. Experience is much more plastic than some imagine. Most importantly, this view would be open to religious experiences which seem to reveal the human subject as a "transcendent self," oriented to and open to an infinite Horizon which religious people call God. In confrontation with the Enlightenment, Schleiermacher and the very attractive theologian Friedrich von Hügel battled mightily for this more expansive notion of experience. "Philosophies," von Hügel tells us, "that leave no room for prayer, adoration, sin, forgiveness, redemption, may be excellent in many other directions, and also as criticisms and stimulants of religious thought; but as would-be adequate theories of religion, they cannot fail more or less to misconceive and to explain away facts of inexhaustible vitality."[10]

In any case, modernity's heightened stress on experience is a fact. Contemporary science, both physical and human, contemporary philosophy, and many forms of modern theology are based upon it. The axiom—

that we learn from experience—seems the ultimate court of appeal today. I also think that, on the deepest level, it is this new stress on experience that largely accounts for the new interest in Christology and the many developments that are taking place in that field. Perhaps we could say that to the extent that modernity falls under the influence of the axiom of experience, to that extent modern religion must return to the experiential foundations of its faith. For Christians, that means to the experience of Jesus, in an effort to retrieve as carefully and critically as possible the contours of their foundational experience. At least in part the new interest in Christology should be seen as a reaction to a religious faith which has grown abstract and reified, only ambiguously in touch with its experiential basis. Contemporary Christians increasingly need to know how the many doctrines of their faith are truly rooted in the experience of Jesus and in their own experience as followers of Jesus.

As we proceed we will also notice that the two traditions of the meaning of experience—sense experience vs. the more expansive notion—have greatly determined the image of Jesus put forward by various authors. If I may put it this way, to the extent that thinkers work under the influence of the model of sense experience, to that extent they are much more austere and agnostic in what they say. The so-called divine dimension of Jesus, together with miracles, prayer, the resurrection, etc.—all these remain, by and large, question marks for those thinkers. To the extent that thinkers move toward the more expansive model of experience, a greater inclusion of these elements seems noticeable.

A New Personalism

A second characteristic of modernity is a new critical interest in the personal. And again, the stress should fall upon the word "critical." We seem to be witnessing a new sensitivity to the personal. The new stress upon reason and the turn to experience brings with it a heightened experience of the human self as free, as personal, as autonomous, not simply subject to the past and its traditions, or to the present and its authority structures. This need not mean "doing as one pleases." Rather it means acting in accord with reason and experience.

Again we are confronting an ambiguous phenomenon. On the one hand, the stress on personalism can degenerate in a number of ways. For example, if pushed far enough, it can create a bias against tradition. Instead of viewing the individual as someone who develops his or her personality through and along with the inheritance of the past, tradition can be belittled in favor of the so-called enlightened individual. At its best, the

Enlightenment did not seek to ignore the tradition, even religious tradition. It was against the imposition of authority arbitrarily from without:
"Authority now depends on its inherent ability to produce rational conviction," says Livingston about the Enlightenment thinkers in the main.[11]

Personalism can also degenerate into individualism and narcissism.
The heightened awareness of the self's freedom can become a fascination
for the ego at the center of the self. Allied with this and at its most extreme,
personalism can become the deification of the self. The shift of center from
the sacred to the profane reality of the self can occur. This is why Voegelin
speaks of the Enlightenment as fostering a shift from the symbols of open
existence—the *nous* of inward experience, the divine Beyond, humble
openness to human limitations—to those of closed existence, namely, the
self-saving ego and an immanently explained cosmos. As a corrective and
balance to this problematic side of the modern spirit, one really ought to
read and study Voegelin's stunning critique of the Enlightenment.[12]

Still, the new personalism, properly assessed and balanced, has been
a real gain for modernity, for it brings with it a new reverence for the person, for freedom, for individual worth and striving. The great stress on toleration, characteristic of a thinker like John Locke (cf. his *Letters on
Toleration,* 1689), shows a profound exhaustion after the many religious
wars of the Reformation period, and evidences a new sense of human
worth which ought to be reverenced. From the religious point of view one
cannot but think that this new personalism has been a key ingredient in the
new interest in Jesus. Just as the experiential roots of Christianity are
found in Jesus, so, too, its personal roots are disclosed there. Not a little of
the perennial attractiveness of Jesus is found in the way in which he embodies, like Francis of Assisi after him, a highly personalized form of religious experience. His relationship with the Divine expressed in the very
personal and intimate name of Abba/"Daddy," his astounding freedom
with respect to the inherited traditions and institutions of authority in his
day, his love ethic in a society dominated by exploitative power, his relationship with the oppressed of his time, especially women—these are but
some of the attractive personal traits of Jesus which make him highly persuasive to and needed by the modern person. Here, too, we will notice as
we proceed that authors in Christology vary according to the manner in
which they preserve the balance between the individual and the social.
Those tending toward an individualistic, anti-tradition view of the personal
tend to project these features onto Jesus: he becomes the lone individual
struggling against the weight of tradition. Those writers preserving the
balance tend to think of Jesus as an individual, to be true, but an individual
in debt to his Jewish inheritance, and attempting to bring about a social
community of people in his present.

Affirming the World

A new affirmation of the world can serve as a third characteristic of the modern spirit. It is a widely held conviction that the medieval period denigrated the material in favor of the spiritual. Aleksandr Solzhenitsyn, in his prophetic address "The Exhausted West," speaks of this period as one in which our physical nature is cursed.[13] Even Albert Schweitzer characterized the medievals as ruled by the attitude of a "rejection of the world and life because the interest of Christianity at this time concentrated upon other-worldly things."[14] Certainly other-worldliness was a strain in medieval thought, but the bodiliness of Gothic architecture, the this-worldliness of the Aristotelianism of the Scholastics, and the emergence of the new middle class of craftspeople cautions us against excessively grand generalizations.[15] But be that as it may, the modern period is widely thought to have initiated a new world-orientation and affirmation. The new stress upon human and natural experience, human freedom, the new curiosity in nature, the new appreciation of commerce and finance—all are evidence of this.

Again we are confronting an ambiguous reality. World-affirmation can become mere materialism. An appreciation for commerce can end in the rapacious exploitation of the finite resources of the earth. These are all tendencies that need to be held in check by spiritual values—but only held in check, not smothered. Both dimensions—world-affirmation and spiritual values—are found in Jesus. Here we have another reason for the modern attraction to Jesus. The strain of world-affirmation we have already partly seen: his personalistic view of the Divine as a Being who responds to people personally, without violating them; his sense of autonomy and freedom, and his offer of the same to the people of his day. To this we could add Jesus' new interest in people and their struggles: he does not seem to be simply an other-worldly ascetic, but someone who holds out a new offer of inclusion in society, a new sense of joy and purpose, a new experience of love and justice. He dines and drinks with gluttons, drunkards, and tax collectors (Lk 7:34). There is even a kind of exaltation of nature in Jesus' parables—crops, leaves, mustard seeds, pearls, and nets mediate the presence of the Divine (cf Mt 13). "God clothes in such splendor the grass of the field" (Lk 12:28). Even the worth of the political realm ("Then give to Caesar what is Caesar's"—Mt 22:21) and of the commercial realm ("Those who have will get more until they grow rich, while those who have not will lose even the little they have"—Mt 25:29) finds a place in Jesus' ethic.

But the other critical strain of the priority of spiritual values is needed to perspectivize Jesus' affirmation of the world. "I repeat what I said: it is easier for a camel to pass through a needle's eye than for a rich man to enter the kingdom of God" (Mt 19:24). "Thus the last shall be first and the first shall be last" (Mt 20:16). "Do not lay up for yourselves an earthly treasure. . . . Make it your practice instead to store up heavenly treasure, which neither moths nor rust corrodes nor thieves break in and steal. Remember, where your treasure is, there your heart is also" (Mt 6:19–21). One feels that our heightened appreciation of the ecological crisis, of the world's poverty, of the plight of the oppressed, and of the threat of nuclear destruction gives a contemporaneity to this critical strain in Jesus, making it even more appealing than the strain of world-affirmation.

A New Sense of History

A new interest in history moves us into a fourth characteristic of the modern ethos. I think that the new return to Jesus can be directly linked to the new awareness of history which has emerged in our time. The many lives of Jesus, each purporting to reveal to us the historical Jesus, are a small indication of the new historical interest and its linkage with Jesus (cf. Albert Schweitzer's *The Quest of the Historical Jesus*[16]).

Briefly, our new awareness of history has produced two basic results. First, it has made us conscious of the fact that we humans are historical creatures through and through. What we are is co-mediated to us through our historical inheritance. Paying attention to the lessons of experience again and again has taught us this. Genetically and physically our body is literally the result of millions of years of biological evolution. Culturally, too, we are the result of thousands of years of human cultural experimentation. The Christian return to Jesus is simply a more specific manifestation of the return to experience under its historical guise, an awareness that whatever else makes up Christian revelation, surely its historical character must be one of the crucial elements involved. Owning up to the Jesus of history is owning up to our own historical makeup, an affirmation of the thoroughly historical character of our faith too.

Second, though, our new historical sensitivity has increasingly made us critical of our inherited biblical and post-biblical traditions about Jesus. We have become aware of the historical character, and thus culturally-conditioned character, of our Jesus traditions. Thus a good deal of the modern interest in Jesus has shown itself in an attempt to treat the biblical text truly critically, with not a little pain caused for those who have not developed an historical sensitivity. This painful process is of a piece with our attempt to own up to the necessarily historical character of our faith.

Of course, our new historical-critical sensitivity is as ambiguous as are all the other traits of the modern ethos. On the one hand, awareness of cultural-conditioning can create a needless bias against everything traditional and historical, a sort of deification of everything modern and denigration of everything old. But on the other hand it promises us the possibility of a more genuine recovery of the authentic experience going forward in Jesus and the Christian movement. To the extent that Christians become historically conscious and so aware of how much in debt they are to the inheritance of the past, to that extent they will be brought back to a new appreciation of the role of Jesus as the historical mediator and founder of the faith. A truly critical retrieval of Jesus need not land us in a useless bias against everything old. It can also teach us how much in debt we are to the legacy of the past, how relevant much of it still is, how foundational to our own experience it still is.

A New Artistic Search for Beauty

Finally, in its artistic form the new interest in human experience can take the form of a search for beauty, the search for the meaningful as it finds expression in the sensuous. Let this serve as our fifth characteristic of the modern spirit. Art has always been the attempt to find meaning in the mode of the sensuous (either through the colorful and imaginative images of novels, or through the more "hard" media of colors, stones, musical sounds, etc.). But our age is characterized by a celebration of the sensuous, which is the artistic way of speaking of a celebration of experience. More traditionally religious periods viewed art as the visual key to divine grace and revelation. Religious motifs and especially representations of Christ predominated in the artistic works of earlier periods. Since the time of Rembrandt, however, and increasingly today, the explicitly religious motifs have receded from art and it seems as if artists are searching for a new capacity to disclose meaning through sensual media.

On a general level, I think we can speak of two general tendencies among artists today. On the one hand, we have the heavily empirical tradition of art, which possibly begins with Dante's fascination for and even exaggeration of the immediately empirical, extends through to the modern impressionists, and finds expression today in the cult of the absurd in theater and art. This tradition is under the influence of the narrow view of sense experience as embracing the totality of the real. Art's function becomes that of celebrating this empirical reality—the world of "hard facts"—and denying the possibility of the disclosure of a deeper meaning in our human experience. T. S. Eliot characterized this mentality in his *The Waste Land:* "A heap of broken images, where the sun beats, And the dead tree gives no shelter, the cricket no relief; And the dry stone no sound of water."[17]

Over against this we seem to have the reaction of the post-impressionists (Cézanne, Gauguin, and Van Gogh), who sought to revitalize the experience of art as a disclosure of the humanly significant, of the meaning to be found within and through the sensuous. In some sense this seemed to continue the earlier tradition of religious art, but widened it, by attempting to find meaning not only in explicitly religious art, but in human experience at large. Ultimately, this artistic trend was recovering a more holistic notion of human experience, one which possesses religious and transcendent depth. A good illustration of this is Cézanne's *Sainte-Victoire Seen from the Lauves.* Here the structural forms of nature reveal a world which implies a "transcendent order and harmony apprehended by the painter."[18] The same is true of Van Gogh's *Crows over the Wheatefield.* Although the black birds, the wheat ready for the harvest, and the dark sky express loss and waste, still "three paths organizing the picture space in the form of a cross hint at a transcendent resolution, glimpsed beyond suffering."[19]

I think there is a link between the new discernment of meaning and depth found among the post-impressionists and the new interest in Jesus. For the Christian tradition has always maintained that the incarnation is precisely the celebration of the Transcendent as it discloses itself through the form of the sensuous. The belief in the divine-human Jesus implies an intersection between transcendence and sensuousness that seems to resonate well with the artistic intuitions of a Cézanne and Van Gogh. An interpreter of the Van Gogh painting alluded to above even explicitly brings out this Christological element in his commentary on that painting: "The unseen head of the painter-Christ lies at the convergence of the horizontal and vertical axis outside the painting, looking to heaven."[20] Perhaps artists are a symbol of a modern humanity's search for the signals of transcendence and religious meaning within human experience which is making Jesus an ever more intriguing question to us all.

The Second Transition

If our first transition can be characterized as a new fascination for experience, this second one can be seen as a somewhat more tentative struggle with experience's underside. Readers will perhaps not be as reflectively aware of this second transition through which modern humanity is passing, probably because it concerns itself with the shadow side of human existence, a shadow side requiring a certain struggle on our part.

What are some of the factors sensitizing modern humanity to the dark side of human experience? One was clearly the discrediting of the optimism of many of the early Enlightenment thinkers. The era of mass enlightenment had failed to transpire, and this caused some thinkers to suspect that factors other than rational were at work among human beings. The emotional, the social, the irrational all needed recognition and critique. The experiment of the French Revolution had ended in a bloody dictatorship. Further, industrialization was beginning to bring about massive and painful changes in European and American society. The First World War further called any excessive optimism into question, and the problems of our own times intensify this: World War II, Vietnam, the ecological crisis, the nuclear threat, etc. Of course, it is important not to exaggerate the novelty of this new sensitivity. The biblical sources, Plato, even Machiavelli, Hobbes, and Rousseau produced stunning analyses of the devastating effects of the human passions. One might even mention the Christian mystics as another source for the analysis of human pathology. Yet our age, to the extent that many thinkers have passed through our second transition, has produced a new concentration upon the irrational and a rather sophisticated attempt to come to terms with it.

One manifestation of this new sensitivity to evil has been called "The Second Enlightenment," a period which is usually associated with the generation of thinkers who wrote between 1890 and 1930: Freud, Marx, Jung, Durkheim, Weber, Dilthey, and Troeltsch, to name only some of the better known figures.[21] Karl Marx and Sigmund Freud have become something of a symbol for the work of this generation. Ernest Becker characterizes them as focusing upon the reverse side of the earlier Enlightenment—namely, upon human darkness, blindness, the forces which hinder illumination (= enlightenment). They view human enlightenment more critically and tentatively, for they grasp how difficult it is to achieve. There seems no direct route to reason—one must move via a long and painful detour of grappling with the irrational. Perhaps the mystics had something similar in mind when they spoke of the dark night of the senses and the soul.

For Freud, the new critical awareness took the form of a focus upon the process of social disruption in miniature, in the individual psyche. His various theories all attempt to show how different individuals use various techniques to ward off anxiety and maintain self-esteem. Trapped by these defense mechanisms, we are blinded from what truly is transpiring within us. The best short explanation of what Freud was up to has been provided us by Erich Fromm, one of Freud's disciples:

> . . . to recognize the *truth* is a basic aim of the psychoanalytic process. Psychoanalysis has given the concept of truth a new dimension. In pre-analytic thinking a person could be considered to speak the truth if he believed in what he was saying. Psychoanalysis has shown that subjective conviction is by no means a sufficient criterion of sincerity. A person

can believe that he acts out of a sense of justice and yet be motivated by
cruelty. He can believe that he is motivated by love and yet be driven
by a craving for masochistic dependence. A person can believe that duty
is his guide though his main motivation is vanity. In fact most rationalizations are held to be true by the person who uses them. He not only
wants others to believe his rationalizations but believes them himself,
and the more he wants to protect himself from recognizing his true motivation the more ardently he must believe in them. Furthermore, in
the psychoanalytic process a person learns to recognize which of his
ideas have an emotional matrix and which are only conventional clichés
without root in his character structure and therefore without substance
and weight. The psychoanalytic process is in itself a search for truth. The
object of this search is the truth about phenomena not outside of man
but in man himself. It is based on the principle that mental health and
happiness cannot be achieved unless we scrutinize our thinking and
feeling to detect whether we rationalize and whether our beliefs are
rooted in our feeling. [22]

Exactly! Despite the exaggerated claim for novelty—after all, the prophets
of Israel, Jesus, and the mystics knew a good deal about the destructive
role that unconscious motivations can play; so, too, did Plato—Fromm has
given us a masterful summary of Freud's contribution. At his best, Freud
was an archaeologist of the irrational.

Marx, it is widely believed, did for social analysis what Freud initiated
for the analysis of individuals: he tried to uncover the sources of human
destructiveness on the level of large-scale social institutions. He primarily
concentrated upon an analysis of capitalism and labor and the many ways
in which they alienate human beings. Others have looked for the sources
of human alienation in more than simply economic factors: Max Weber and
Emil Durkheim generally give equal stress to cultural factors, the network
of values promoted by various cultures through religions and other agen-
cies.

But, again, the modern critical sensitivity to evil is a phenomenon
larger than Freud, Marx and their heirs, and embraces all who have been
chastened by the horrors of evil in our time. As a matter of fact, the influence of Freud and Marx has been rather minimal in the United States. If
you will, they lack "carriers" for their ideas, except perhaps a minority of
intellectuals and leftist political movements which have never found a
large following here. This is probably related to a number of factors: their
anti-religiousness is not congenial to the majority of Americans; Marx's
anti-capitalism and socialism have historically been anathema here, etc.
Furthermore, the American political tradition has its own unique sources
for the study of evil passions, reaching back to the liberal tradition in

Hobbes, Locke, and Hume and to the classical tradition of Plato and Aristotle.

Furthermore, the religiously sensitive thinker needs to be cautious with Freud and Marx, even while learning from them. In some respects they have been excessively hard on religion and theology. The anti-religious bias of the earlier Enlightenment thinkers surfaces in Freud and Marx, too, only in a deepened form. For them, at least in their general orientation, religion is often on the side of the alienating factors in individual or society. Religion becomes either an infantile projection (Freud) or some kind of opiate-like consolation arising from and masking the injustices of society (Marx). This is surely a needed corrective to some forms of religion and theology—the mystics and prophets already knew of such dehumanizing forms of religion. But as a general characterization of all religion, it cannot carry the day. In many respects, this general characterization is an unfortunate legacy of the earlier Enlightenment's bias against all forms of religious experience. As such, we are back with the unnecessary restriction of human experience to simply sense experience.

A New Sensitivity to Evil

Let me turn, now, to some of the more specific contributions of the new sensitivity to human pathology and their linkage with the new interest in Jesus. The first would have to be the new sensitivity to evil. Surely this is the most basic reality that our new sensitivity is on to, in both its individual manifestations in the many human disorders and in its more public and social manifestations in society, the Churches, and public institutions. This is surely a contribution of the first order, and the many horrible events of our immediate period have greatly legitimated this concern for evil.

At this point it would be well for the readers to take time out to immerse themselves in some of the literature which will bring home for them the really massive evil of our times. One might begin with a meditation on Pablo Picasso's painting *Guernica*. Copies of it are easily available, and I find that Picasso expresses visually much that contemporary theologians are trying to say more didactically about the horror of evil (cf. the photo and explanation). This painting is a refusal to forget the reality of evil, particularly that of the suffering of the innocent. It is a kind of "dangerous memory" in visual, sensuous form, able to appeal to and penetrate the spectator's entire being, not just his or her mind. It is "dangerous" because it stimulates the spectator to experience both disgust and protest simultaneously, yet not without a certain inner calm. Interestingly Picasso's work shows how the artistic search for beauty—for signals of transcend-

Picasso's Guernica

This is Pablo Picasso's artistic rendering, to some extent into Christ figures, of several victims of the cruel bombing of non-combatants residing in the Basque village of Guernica during the Spanish civil war. Guernica was the traditional capital of the Basque country, and thus a symbol of resistance to the fascists. The bombing, by Nazi Luftwaffe, occurred on April 26, 1937. Probably close to one thousand were murdered.

"Considered to be the most poignant anti-war statement in this century, 'Guernica' is understandably seen only as a symbolic expression of 'man's inhumanity to man' and animal. The neighing horse, the panic-stricken faces, the disembodied hand with two broken swords, the human tongues in the form of spikes, the anguished dying mothers with their babes in arms, the infernal atmosphere of demonic darkness—all these elements coalesce to give exquisite expression to the artist's towering rage over the ineffable horror of modern warfare. Picasso's protest is seen earlier in his painting of Christ on the cross and of bulls dying by the matador's sword."

If viewed against the background of Picasso's other works, one can see earlier influences and styles reasserting themselves: classical Greek (minotaurs and centaurs), Roman (the rape of the Sabines), aboriginal masks, Mediterranean. Picasso was particularly open to a non-Western stress on the continuity between the human and the animal. He wants to overcome the boundaries between nature, animals, and humans. He thus challenges our way of perceiving, especially with *Guernica*, where he wants "to put us inside the event while we see it from the outside."

Neil Hurley especially notes the subliminal but real "Christomorphic quality" of the painting. " 'Guernica' is war projected by a visionary who can see Christ as sent into an arena to fight valiantly against overwhelming odds in a contest doomed to failure. . . . Picasso paints Christ with taut, outstretched arms, with a brutish up-turned head, mouth agape. He is seen as an animal—more like a dying bull than a sacrificial lamb." The triangular (Trinitarian?) quality of the painting, the light bulb (the Divine in judgment?), the horse (the white horse of Rev 19:11?), the eye movement of all toward the bull at the left/top (sacrificial?)—all perhaps reinforce the Christ-quality which Hurley is pointing to. Perhaps most poignantly of all we have the lily at the bottom/center—is this a struggling affirmation of the resurrection, of the presence of transcendence via the detour of evil?

The painting illustrates the need for sensitivity to evil. It is a remembrance of the victims, together with a protest. Paul Tillich called it the most "Protestant" of all modern paintings. It reminds us that negative experiences are often the path to God. It perhaps (?) shows God participating with us in our evil, actually co-entering the arena with us. Yet the Divine is also judging the evil (the light bulb) and salvaging something from it (the lily). One is reminded of Wiesel: Where is the Divine? "Here—hanging here on this gallows!"

ence and meaning in and through the sensuous—likewise has had to make the detour through struggling with evil before finding a reservoir of meaning in human existence.

Then I would suggest that the reader move to Elie Wiesel's *Night* and Aleksandr Solzhenitsyn's three-volume *Gulag Archipelago*. The first recounts Wiesel's experience of suffering through the Nazi holocaust; the second, the experience of the slave labor camps, which perhaps murdered eighty million people from the time of Lenin to that of Stalin. Finally, because all of these events can be somewhat "removed" from the American reader, I would recommend John Hersey's *Hiroshima* as a way of bringing home to Americans their involvement in the massive human suffering of our time.[23]

Guernica, Auschwitz, Gulag, Hiroshima and Nagasaki are but a mere sampling of the horrors of the twentieth century which bring home to us the legitimacy of the modern and critical concern for the irrational and shadow side of human existence. To these could be added the horrible suffering and genocides now occurring in Asia, Africa, India, and South America; the undercurrent of greed and narcissism now appearing in Western capitalistic societies; the dehumanizing totalitarianism of the communist nations; the sufferings of the blacks and Indians in the United States; the long history of suffering of women throughout the globe, and of the unprotected children. Perhaps most acutely, the possibility of a nuclear holocaust of humanity needs to be mentioned. Unlike previous horrors of the irrational, this last would be total—there would be no "safe" island on which the human experiment could continue.

In what way does this new sensitivity to evil link up with our concern for the new interest in Jesus? First of all, it provides us with a corrective to a naive and overly positive view of religious experience and of Christol-

ogy. It is a reminder of what really ought to be obvious, but isn't—namely,
that many if not perhaps most of us must struggle through to a faith in the
Divine. Religious experience is not only positive, but negative; faith is not
always a joyful affirmation of our ecstatic openness to the divine Beyond,
but a struggling capacity to protest against evil and to long for a better,
more serene future. The Second Vatican Council had this in mind when it
said: "The call to grandeur and the depths of misery are both a part of human experience."[24] In this sense the new sensitivity to evil makes us discover and appropriate with a new sense of relevancy the fact that many of
the great foundational experiences of our faith were primarily negative experiences. For example, we are aided in demystifying and de-etherealiz-
ing the exodus event: it was quite really a profound struggle against slavery
and oppression. Through that misery Moses discovered a new, Yahweh-
given, capacity to protest and move toward a better future. So, too, with
the two Jewish exiles to Assyria and Babylonia. It is no accident that the
great prophets worked out their profoundly ethical view of Judaism at the
time they did—they were searching for a more humane alternative to the
misery of the exiles they saw around them. "Tremble, you who are complacent! Shudder, you who are overconfident! . . . Justice will bring about
peace; right will produce calm and security" (Is 32:11, 17), says Isaiah in
the wake of the Assyrian exile of the eighth century B.C.

Most importantly, as many liberation theologians are bringing home,
we gain a new sense of the relevancy of much of Christology, some of
which a more positive age would either downplay or ignore. "Son though
he was, he learned obedience from what he suffered; and when perfected,
he became the source of eternal salvation for all who obey him" (Heb 5:8).
"He entered [the sanctuary] . . . with his own blood, and achieved eternal
redemption" (Heb 9:12). In other words, the cross of Jesus is recaptured
in its profound, symbolic importance and poignancy for us. Just as Solzhenitsyn could speak of the Gulag as a "Golgotha," [25] so Christians need
to think through the role that the cross plays in the life and work of Jesus.
A view of Jesus which bypasses the cross strips him of much of his relevancy to us today, robbing him of his profound commitment to struggle
against the irrational and dehumanizing in history. After all, Jesus did not
die a natural death, through heart failure or disease. He did not commit
suicide. He was executed by public powers, because what he was about
inevitably brought him into conflict with the irrational powers of his day.

Furthermore, I think that we gain a new appreciation for the so-called
"apocalyptic dimension" so present in the preaching of Jesus. As we shall
see, scholarship has had a difficult time coming to terms with this element
in Jesus' ministry. Either scholars have ignored apocalyptic altogether, because it won't "fit" the sentimentalized and romanticized picture of Jesus

so beloved to many, or even when its presence is acknowledged, scholars often don't know what to do with it. Apocalyptic becomes an unfortunate and outmoded inheritance of an all too Jewish Jesus. What, after all, does one make of a Jesus who preaches a soon-to-arrive Kingdom of God, whose arrival will entail horrible tribulations, divisions, anguish, judgment for the evil, and resurrection to joy for the good? "My mission is to spread, not peace, but division" (Mt 10:34), Jesus tells us. The reader ought to study Mark 13 and Matthew 10 to gain at least a preliminary acquaintance with this apocalyptic dimension in Jesus. What I would want to underscore now is this. If there is cogency to the view that the late Jewish apocalyptic mentality and literature arises as both a protest against the miseries suffered by late Judaism and a dreaming of a better, alternative future of peace, justice, and love (= the longed-for Kingdom), then again we are able to reappropriate with a new sense of urgency this element of the Jesus tradition.[26] Our new sensitivity to evil and longing for peace renders the apocalyptic persuasive once again! Like Jesus, we too all too often find ourselves struggling against and longing for . . .

Something similar could be said for the symbolism of the satanic and demonic so pervasive in the tradition of Jesus: "But if it is by the Spirit of God that I expel demons, then the reign of God has overtaken you" (Mt 12:28). Perhaps we need to reappropriate this a little more realistically too, viewing the satanic as the symbolism which provokes from us a horror at all that bruises and dehumanizes: the anti-kingdom to Jesus' Kingdom, the movements on the side of death and oppression rather than life and liberation.[27] Again, our new sensitivity to evil, by correcting our naive view of religious experience and Christology, makes an old symbolism take on new life once again!

The saving work of Jesus—what theologians call the soteriological thrust of the Jesus event—also thrusts itself into the awareness of people stunned by the horror of evil. Perhaps people naively unaware of evil's massiveness or inflated by their own hubris, the one the reverse of the other, might find no relevance in the image of Jesus the Savior. But not so the person humbled and hurt by suffering. The symbolism of a Savior Jesus, which either explicitly or implicitly dots the entire New Testament, seems exceedingly relevant for minds and hearts that are so chastened.

Secondly, our new sensitivity to evil engages us in something a bit more complicated than simply reminding us of the role that negative experiences play in our Christological past. Here I must struggle with what I want to say: whatever insights might emerge have only slowly and gropingly emerged! In a sense, we can also view negative experiences not only as a complement and corrective to an overly positive view of Christology and religious experience, but as a necessary detour. As such, they force us to rethink the very make-up of religious experience in general, and Christology in particular. Just as the mystics spoke of the need to enter the purifying and scorching fires of the dark night in order properly to open oneself to the Divine, so I would suggest that we need to descend into negativity if we are properly to glimpse authentic Christian experience. "To come to possess all, desire the possession of nothing," said John of the Cross. The dark night taught him that! Solzhenitsyn seems to have learned this lesson in Stalin's slave camps. And it would seem that our new awareness of evil is pushing others, especially liberation theologians, to learn this anew, and through it all to rediscover a new persuasiveness in Jesus. Through the purifying fire of negativity—the detour through evil and suffering—many are learning a lesson similar to Solzhenitsyn's: one's "conscience, like a clear mountain lake, shines in your eyes. . . . your eyes, purified by suffering, infallibly perceive the least haze in other eyes." What emerges is a "capacity of ours to see with the eyes of truth."[28]

For now, let me mention two lessons which the descent into negativity might have to teach us. These two lessons are also two ways in which the Jesus event takes on a special contemporaneity for us. One is that perhaps the cruel suffering of the innocent forces us to rethink our theodicy, our inherited understanding of the Divine. It is the old but relevant question of how there can be a God when there is so much evil? We are all familiar with the verbal attack: "If there is a God, evil cannot exist. But evil exists. Therefore, there is no God." The traditional response is to argue that the Divine permits evil for some reason: to allow us our freedom, to build character, to test and purify us, etc. But surely the murdering of the innocent victims cries out for more of a response than this. Something seems wrong with this view of the Divine—this traditional view seems to let God off the hook too quickly. Innocent sufferers cannot believe in an aloof deity that passively sits by while untold millions suffer.

Faced with questions like the above, many people under the pressure of the horrors of our time are discovering a renewed interest in the view of the Divine that seems to flow from the Jesus event. The detour through evil is helping us renew our appreciation for what Jesus reveals about God. I am referring to the"kenoticism" or "self-emptying" view of God present in the Greek Scriptures. The Divine does not remain aloof, but self-empties himself, to participate with us in our struggle (cf Phil 2:6–11).

Elie Wiesel was on to this, I think, in that remarkable and oft-quoted story from his *Night:*

One day, the electric power station at Buna was blown up. The Gestapo, summoned to the spot, suspected sabotage. They found a trail. It eventually led to the Dutch Oberkapo. And there, after a search, they found an important stock of arms.

The Oberkapo was arrested immediately. He was tortured for a period of weeks, but in vain. He would not give a single name. He was transferred to Auschwitz. We never heard of him again.

But his little servant had been left behind in the camp in prison. Also put to torture, he too would not speak. Then the SS sentenced him to death, with two other prisoners who had been discovered with arms.

One day when we came back from work, we saw three gallows rearing up in the assembly place, three black crows. Roll call. SS all around us, machine guns trained: the traditional ceremony. Three victims in chains—and one of them, the little servant, the sad-eyed angel.

The SS seemed more preoccupied, more disturbed than usual. To hang a young boy in front of thousands of spectators was no light matter. The head of the camp read the verdict. All eyes were on the child. He was lividly pale, almost calm, biting his lips. The gallows threw its shadow over him.

This time the Lagerkapo refused to act as executioner. Three SS replaced him.

The three victims mounted together onto the chairs.

The three necks were placed at the same moment within the nooses.

"Long live liberty!" cried the two adults.

But the child was silent.

"Where is God? Where is He?" someone behind me asked.

At a sign from the head of the camp, the three chairs tipped over.

Total silence throughout the camp. On the horizon, the sun was setting.

"Bare your heads!" yelled the head of the camp. His voice was raucous. We were weeping.

"Cover your heads!"

Then the march began. The two adults were no longer alive. Their tongues hung swollen, blue-tinged. But the third rope was still moving; being so light, the child was still alive. . . .

For more than half an hour he stayed there, struggling between life and death, dying in slow agony under our eyes. And we had to look him full in the face. He was still alive when I passed in front of him. His tongue was still red, his eyes not yet glazed.

Behind me, I heard the same man asking: "Where is God now?"

And I heard a voice within me answer him:

"Where is He? Here He is—He is hanging here on this gallows. . . ."

That night the soup tasted of corpses.[29]

That the Divine is hanging there on the gallows is an intuition that brings one to the cross and the kind of divinity disclosed there. Perhaps just how that might be so is the most profound lesson that Jesus has to teach modernity. But it has taken someone like an Elie Wiesel to help us Christians reappreciate that. In any case, what Wiesel describes is a kenotic God, and that kind of a God has a stinging contemporaneity for us today.

A second lesson from the descent into negativity runs like this: as with God, so with us. Or, the disciple is not above his or her master. By this I mean that the descent into horror teaches us that religious experience involves struggle against oppression, striving to overcome the vicious circle that continually makes today's oppressed into tomorrow's oppressors. Here we discover another reason for the new interest in Jesus. Certainly his continual preference for the oppressed in the Sermon on the Mount presents us with a figure willing to enter the struggle. But he goes beyond simply elevating the oppressed. He seems to know that once they come into power, they too can become tomorrow's oppressors, taking vengeance upon their erstwhile torturers. That is why he calls for a conversion of the inward part of the self, the heart. Unless the heart is transformed, the vicious circle will continue. "What emerges from within a man, that and nothing else is what makes him impure" (Mk 7:20), Jesus tells us. Perhaps his own temptations were just such an attempt to purify his own heart (Mk 1:13).

The Importance of the Political, Economic, Cultural, and Ecological

A second characteristic of our new sensitivity to human pathology is a heightened emphasis upon the big and the large, the collective as over against the individual. What many are increasingly onto is the way in which social collectivities form people, for better or for worse. The importance of the social is an insight as old as political theory, but our age has given a new prominence to it in the form of a more sustained and systematic analysis of society. What this comes down to is the fact that our humanity is a mediated humanity—all that we are is co-mediated to us by the opportunities and lack of opportunities present in our social matrix. I say co-mediated, for there is also the reality of human individuality and autonomy (the special insight of our first transition), which personalizes and integrates the social, and sometimes even transcends it. Furthermore, Christians believe in a transcendent, divinely given capacity to transcend and perspectivize our cultural conditioning. Something of this was present in the prophets and Jesus, in their remarkable ability to call their society to judgment in the name of their higher vision. But still there is the reality of the social, and to varying degrees we are all limited by the constraints which it places upon us.

This new sensitivity has enabled us to approach the social dimension within Jesus' ministry with new eyes, grasping its relevance in a new way. Of course, Jesus does not rob the individual of his or her autonomy—we have already noted his stress on the importance of the inner dimension of people (cf Mk 7:20). He does not reduce the individual to a mere echo of society. Thus he can call people to account and to conversion. But this stress on interiority has perhaps overshadowed the equal presence of the social in Jesus' ministry. After all, the very symbol of the"Kingdom of God," the central image of Jesus' message, derives from the social and political experience of Jewish life, not from the individual's private, interior experience. It seems to be derived from the apocalyptic sphere of influence, and we have already suggested how apocalyptic seems to reflect a politico-religious protest against misery. Jesus, too, is dedicated to the establishment of a new socio-religious reality—we might say "community" today—which promises an overcoming of the oppression of his times.

Many of Jesus' favored images pack a socio-religious punch too: he speaks of a wedding feast (Mk 2:18f), of a state of affairs when the poor will no longer experience poverty (Mt 5), of the Kingdom as a social banquet which overcomes harmful social separation (Mk 14:25), and of the blessedness of peacemakers (Mt 5:9). He knows how to mobilize people for action: he calls followers (Mt 4:18–22), he engages in a kind of consciousness-raising by enabling the oppressed to imagine themselves as liberated (Mt 11:19), he confronts the authority structures of his time (Mt 21:12–17—the temple cleansing). He has political "savvy" too: "You must be clever as snakes and innocent as doves" (Mt 10:16). He uses power: "I have come to set a man at odds with his father, a daughter with her mother, a daughter-in-law with her mother-in-law: in short to make a man's enemies those of his own household" (Mt 10:35–36).

Of course, it is the *divine* Kingdom to which Jesus is dedicated. He does not divorce religion from politics, but tries to refashion society through his religious vision. However the social is very much there. Jesus paid attention to the social! There is something political in his message, for he wants to bring about a new kind of community which frees the oppressed and overcomes the oppressor-oppressed dialectic. There is at least an implicit economic dimension involved, for he wants to overcome poverty in all its forms (cf Mt 5). The cultural dimension is present in his attempt to articulate the moral-religious foundations of his community through his preaching of the Kingdom. The ecological dimension also sur-

faces, both in his high view of nature as a locus for the presence of the Kingdom (Mt 13:31–32), and in his ethics of self-limiting love and respect for
creation (Mt 5:45).

In short, Jesus seems very contemporary to those of us who have become sensitized to the import of the social in our lives—yet without utopianism and fanaticism. Without utopianism, for he neither knows when
the Kingdom will be realized (Mk 13:32), nor whether we can do any better
for now than partially and fragmentarily work for its emergence (cf Mt 13,
the parables of the seed, weeds, mustard seed, and leaven). Without fanaticism, for he knows his own temptations toward exploitation and struggles against them (Mt 4:1–11), he warns his disciples against the same (Mk
7:20), and he possesses a profound trust which seems to fill him with a remarkable calm and gentleness: "Stop worrying. . . . Your Father knows
that you need such things" (Lk 12:29–30).

The Importance of the Practical

From what we have said so far it emerges that people who are
undergoing the purification of our second transition place a great stress
upon the practical: the reality of evil in its many forms; the realities of the
political, economic, cultural, and ecological as they impinge on human individuals and communities for better or worse. In this respect, those chastened by our second transition think that the first transition is too
theoretical, too abstracted from the social matrix and the vortex of the irrational. If you will, it seems to dwell upon experience in the mode of
meaning and truth, rather than in the mode of practice and action. There
are now many thinkers who, under the influence of the second transition,
see a need to work out their theoretical understanding of human existence
through a constant and critical attention to the lessons to be derived from
practice/action. They call for a kind of dialectical going back and forth between practice and theory, where theory partially derives from practice,
then enriches practice, and yields further theory.

To some extent, this is something novel. If we glance back at the interrelationship between theory and practice, we find that it has been an
uneven one.[30] Broadly speaking we can imagine a first phase, during which
theory and practice were not treated as equal partners within a reciprocal
relationship. Each, theory and practice, more or less followed its own
path. The reasons for this seem somewhat obvious upon reflection. "Theory" in our modern sense as a theoretical activity requiring mental effort—
thus quite different from "everyday knowledge" gained through routine
experience—was born about the sixth century B.C. with the advent of

Greek philosophy. In general the early philosophers were spellbound by their new theoretical knowledge, except perhaps for an elite few who followed Plato's attempt to combine theory with spiritual formation and civil renewal. Besides, theory was just not felt to be all that relevant to the practical side of life. "Practical knowledge"—tilling the soil, growing cereals, casting metals, building, etc.—was gained largely without the aid of theory, through repeated experience, habit, know-how passed from father to son, mother to daughter, skilled craftsperson to apprentice, intuitive hunches, etc.

Relatively recently a second phase has emerged, during which the interrelationship between theory and practice has become more even, reciprocal, and dialectical. With the advent of modern physical sciences, the relevance of theory to practice and vice versa becomes more obvious. Production methods based upon mathematics, physics, chemistry, and biology have resulted in a technical efficiency unheard of in earlier times. What the physical sciences did for industry, many thinkers now want to do for human society as a whole: combine theory and action in a productive relationship and mutual engagement. We can call this attempt the third characteristic of our second transition.

Americans ought to be relatively comfortable with this new stress upon practice/action. We are often characterized as a practical people, and we are the homeland of pragmatic philosophy (think of John Dewey and William James, for example). The latter, at their best, sought to engage theory and practice, if we can believe their modern interpreters. Abraham Lincoln is one of the best examples of the combination of the two. His remarkable understanding (= theory) of democracy grew out of his struggle with the attempt to practice it (think of his struggle over the slavery issue). Christians, too, should be comfortable with this. In the Scriptures, just as ordinary knowing involves doing (Adam "knew" Eve—Gn 4:1), so knowing the Lord involves practicing the obligations of the covenant (Dt 11:2; Is 41:20; Hos 11:3f) and obedience (Ps 119:71). As the prophet Jeremiah put it, "Because he dispensed justice to the weak and the poor, it went well with him. Is this not true knowledge of me? says the Lord" (Jer 22:16). Jesus, too, links knowing with doing (love). This is a constant in the Jesus tradition (cf Mt 1:25; Lk 1:34). To know the Lord is to love the Lord: "The man without love has known nothing of God" (1 Jn 4:8); "The way we can be sure of our knowledge of him is to keep his commandments" (1 Jn 2:3). Like Jesus, even Plato seems to link theory with practice, for he speaks of both "loving truth" and "doing all for the sake of truth." Aristotle, too, closely interrelates theory and praxis.[31]

Thus the tradition, Jewish and Christian and classical, knows some-

thing of the modern desire to engage theory and practice in a mutual relationship. Thinkers try to work this out rather more self-consciously now,
but still the basic insight is present within the tradition. The tradition
rather more emphatically also preserves the religious dimension of the
practical: the Divine is somehow encountered in our practical life too.
Something else we learn from the tradition is that it is not wise to reduce
theory to practice, or vice versa.

Historical experience seems to be against too simple an understanding of the relationship between theory and practice. While they are clearly
intertwined and inseparable, they are also distinct. Knowledge cannot be
reduced to action, for often we know more than we can actualize. Action
cannot be reduced to theory, for often our theory hasn't caught up with our
action. Reduce theory to practice and you ultimately rob your practice of
any critical and reflective dimension. Action can then easily turn into an
oppressive demon, with no checks and balances. But reduce practice to
theory, and you ultimately run the same danger with your theory: lacking
the correction that flows from practice it can become either abstract or utopian, or demonic and fanatic. It is this latter charge that thinkers influenced by our second transition hurl at the first transition!

This new stress upon the practical again throws renewed light upon
Jesus and reinforces his potential significance for us today. Of course, Jesus
wasn't a theoretician in the strict sense; he was rather more of a visionary.
But there is a theoretical component to his life found in his vision of the
Kingdom of God. But what needs equal stress is how Jesus remained in
touch with the practical: he sought to learn from it and to enrich it simultaneously. He was not an armchair philosopher, but someone who was responding to the crisis of his times. We seem to find in him a remarkable
sensitivity to both vision/theory and practice. He preaches the Kingdom,
but he also embodies it in his actions. He summons his disciples to do the
same. The Kingdom is not merely visionary: it demands conversion and
practice within a new kind of community without exploitative relationships. Neither is it merely action: the Kingdom has not fully come, it is not
fully embodied, it remains ahead of us as an inspiring and summoning vision (cf Mt 13). This remarkable balance is another attractive feature in Jesus for many of us today.

At times, Jesus attacks the visions/theories of others because they are
out of touch with people's real practical needs (cf his attack on the law in
Mt 5). At times he attacks people's practice, because it seems guided by a
faulty vision (cf Mt 6:1–18, the attack on hypocritical forms of prayer, fast-
ing, and almsgiving). He seems to move out of an equitable interrelation
between practice and vision: "Anyone who hears my words and puts them
into practice is like the wise man who built his house on rock" (Mt 7:24).

The Third Transition

Let me now briefly treat the third transition which humanity only now seems to be entering. I am referring to a phenomenon variously called "world unification," or "planetization," or "globalization," even "transculturalization" and "cosmification." The philosopher Karl Jaspers put it this way:

> What is historically new and for the first time in history decisive about our situation is the real unity of mankind on the earth. The planet has become for man a single whole dominated by the technology of communications; it is "smaller" than the Roman Empire was formerly.[32]

The technical interdependence of the planet, through communications media, is quickly bringing with it a number of other interdependencies: economic, political, and cultural (including religious). In a sense we are being dragged into becoming one world in some manner—and perhaps eventually, through space technology, one entire creation spanning many solar systems. The Picasso painting was an artistic indication of this new globalization: glance back at that picture and note the "ecumenical" use of different cultural art forms found in that art work.

Presently world globalization is in its preliminary phases. Perhaps this phase of the human experiment will not be successful. We just do not know. Our technological and economic interdependence is not matched by our political and cultural interdependence. The reality of the two world wars, and the possibility of another, illustrates our failure, thus far, to achieve a viable union on the political and cultural planes. Capitalism vs. socialism, communism, and totalitarianism; Christianity vs. other religious faiths; pre-industrial vs. industrial societies—all these clashes are only too well known. Even our economic interdependence brings with it a desire to control the world's resources for oneself.

Thus, a kind of global anxiety exists, indicating that we need to achieve a new understanding and praxis on a worldwide scale. This anxiety is then ambiguous: it may herald the birth pains of a new, more mature and transcultural humanity; it may also result in regressive movements, such as neo-nationalisms, religious neo-conservatisms, the seeking out of scapegoats to blame, totalitarianisms, etc. Even the Churches, Christian and otherwise, can regress to a kind of religious provincialism in the face of the challenges they are forced to face.

The issue for the religions is what globalization entails for them. What changes may/should they undergo? What contribution can they make to this phase of the human experiment? The answers to both questions seem to go hand in hand. As the Churches undergo change and gradually become more transcultural, the more they can guide the human community toward a new balance between the local and the universal, the provincial and the global. I take it that we have learned from experience that we must avoid two extremes. No reflective persons desire a globalism which destroys ethnic and cultural particularity—that is simply another way of describing totalitarianism. Neither do they want an ethnic particularity which destroys globalism—that would be simply a form of narcissism on a large scale.

So far the Churches have been primarily in a learning phase: simply discovering one another. In a highly engaging study written some time ago, Friedrich Heiler pointed out how the religions, at least on the scholarly level, have moved through three phases: first, an awareness of simply the wealth that each religion preserves; second, an "esteem" for that wealth; third, an acknowledgement of the falsity of many of the accusations that each makes against the other.[33] An interesting example of the last is Heiler's assertion that Tertullian and many Christians are quite wrong to believe that ". . . it is peculiar to Christians alone to love those that hate them." "All high religions of the earth . . . know the commandment to love the enemy," he claims. "A tree does not withhold its shade even from those who come to cut it down," says the Mahābhārata.[34] Probably as the various religions work together on the practical level they will discover a new standpoint toward one another. Oftentimes such global practical experience is even more powerful than the work of scholars in fostering change.

Clearly all of this raises questions for the Christian and once again brings Jesus front and center in our new global imagination. Lucien Richard illustrates what I mean in a recent work, *What Are They Saying about Christ and World Religions?* As Richard expresses it, "the major obstacle" to the cross-fertilization of the religions "remains Christianity's claim to uniqueness and normativeness." He poses the question: "Is it possible to believe simultaneously that God has acted decisively and for the salvation of all in the person of Jesus Christ and that Jews, Hindus, Muslims and Buddhists are warranted in remaining who they are and in following their own different ways to salvation?"[35] This kind of questioning becomes inevitable, I think, once Christians begin to allow their global experience of humanity to penetrate and confront their Christian faith. The other religions, too, are now undergoing a similar process of questioning.

So far no theologian or Church on the Christian side has won a consensus on proposed answers to Richard's question. We seem to be confronted with a case of our theory not yet catching up with our practice! Yet if Christology today is to be adequate to its task, it cannot allow our global

THE THREE GREAT TRANSITIONS

- which promote a new interest in Jesus
- which influence the nature of modern Christologies

TRANSITION I	brings a new stress on:	relation to Jesus:
a new emphasis upon human experience and its lessons as a norm for human knowing	1. experience	1. recapturing our experiential roots in Jesus
	2. personalism	2. renewing emphasis upon how Jesus embodies a personalistic form of religion
	3. world-affirmation	3. Jesus as a this-worldly reformer
	4. the role of history	4. appreciating the role of Jesus as an historical mediator
	5. artistic search for meaning within sensuous experience (= beauty)	5. gives new meaning to incarnation as the intersection between the sensuous and the Transcendent
TRANSITION II		
a new sensitivity to the forms of human pathology, both individual and collective	1. a new sensitivity to evil	1. recapturing the role of negative experiences in Christology; a new sense of the relevancy of apocalyptic, the demonic, the cross, kenoticism, and Jesus' saving work (soteriology)
	2. importance of the political, economic, cultural, and ecological	2. recapturing the social/political and ecological dimensions in Christology
	3. importance of praxis or action	3. Jesus critically combines vision with practice
TRANSITION III		
the beginnings of the experience of globalization	How can humanity combine particularity with universalism, the provincial with the global?	What can we make of our traditional claims for Jesus in a global age? How might Christianity and other religions critically enrich each other?

41

anxiety to serve as an excuse for the failure to confront what Richard is asking. One of the key tasks of this introductory book must be an honest grappling with this issue. Still, just as our other two transitions brought out the contemporaneity of Jesus, this one does too, only this time Jesus appears, not so much relevant to our times, as a question mark to an age which is moving into globalization. What can we make of him and our traditional claims for him in an age when we are being summoned to respect and learn from the possible religious wisdom found outside the Christian orbit?

These three transitions are but a sampling of the reasons for a new interest in Jesus. Hopefully the reader will resonate with one or several of the factors alluded to here. But as we proceed the reader will note that what characterizes modern Christologies is the influence, in varying degrees, of these three transitions. In fact, I have come to believe that this influence is what makes modern Christologies modern. And we might also add that the adequacy of modern Christologies seems dependent upon their ability adequately to come to terms with the lessons of our three transitions. But that brings us to the story of our next chapter, and indeed of the remainder of the book.

Notes

1. (New York: Paulist, 1978; Japanese edition, 1973).

2. James C. Livingston, *Modern Christian Thought: From the Enlightenment to Vatican II* (New York: Macmillan, 1971), p. 8.

3. As cited in Norman Hampson, *The Enlightenment* (Baltimore: Penguin, 1968), p. 26.

4. As cited in Stanley L. Jaki, *The Relevance of Physics* (Chicago: University of Chicago, 1966), p. 64.

5. See the actual citation in Livingston, *op. cit.*, p. 1.

6. Eric Voegelin, *From Enlightenment to Revolution*, John H. Hallowel, ed. (Durham, N.C.: Duke University, 1975), pp. 6–12.

7. See the important study of Henry F. May, *The Enlightenment in America* (New York: Oxford University, 1976).

8. Louis Dupré, *Transcendent Selfhood: The Loss and Recovery of the Inner Life* (New York: Seabury, 1976), pp. 1–17.

9. Dante Germino, *Beyond Ideology: The Revival of Political Theory* (New York: Harper and Row, 1967), p. 6, p. 183.

10. Baron Friedrich von Hügel, *The German Soul* (New York: E. P. Dutton, 1916), p. 209.

11. Livingston, *op. cit.*, p. 3.

12. See note 6. Also cf Leo Strauss, "The Three Waves of Modernity," in his *Political Philosophy: Six Essays* (Indianapolis: Pegasus/Bobbs-Merrill, 1975), pp. 81–98.

13. Cf Aleksandr Solzhenitsyn, *Detente: Prospects for Democracy and Dictatorship* (New Brunswick: Transaction Books, 1980), pp. 17–18.

14. Albert Schweitzer, *Out of My Life and Thought* (New York: Mentor, 1963), p. 120.

15. Cf M.-D. Chenu, *Nature, Man, and Society in the Twelfth Century* (Chicago: University of Chicago, 1968).

16. (New York: Macmillan, 1961).

17. As cited in Aidan Nichols, *The Art of God Incarnate: Theology and Image in Christian Tradition* (New York: Paulist, 1980), p. 9.

18. *Ibid.*, p. 11.

19. *Ibid.*, p. 12.

20. *Ibid.*

21. For an overview, see H. Stuart Hughes, *Consciousness and Society: The Reorientation of European Social Thought: 1890–1930* (New York: Vintage, 1958).

22. Erich Fromm, *Psychoanalysis and Religion* (New York: Bantam, 1950), pp. 74–75. Cf Ernest Becker, *The Structure of Evil: An Essay on the Unification of the Science of Man* (New York: George Braziller, 1968), pp. 120–142 (on Freud and Marx).

23. The interpretations of Picasso's *Guernica* are from Neil Hurley, "Meditation on Picasso's 'Guernica,'" *Theology Today* 37 (1980), 364–366, at 364 and 365; more detailed and equally stimulating is Frank D. Russell, *Picasso's Guernica: The Labyrinth of Narrative and Vision* (Montclair: Allanheld and Schram, 1980). The literature of horror is quite extensive; some examples: Herbert Rutledge Southworth, *Guernica! Guernica! A Study of Journalism, Diplomacy, Propaganda, and History* (Berkeley: University of California, 1977); Elie Wiesel, *Night* (New York: Avon, 1971); Lucy S. Davidowicz, *The War Against the Jews 1933–1945* (New York: Holt, Rinehart and Winston, 1975); Alexsandr Solzhenitsyn, *The Gulag Archipelago*, 3 vols. (New York: Harper and Row, 1973–1978); Georges Nivat, "The Cultural Influence of Solzhenitsyn," *Concilium* 141 (1981), 12–18; Philip Yancey, "Lessons from the Camps: Isolating the Human Spirit," *Christianity Today* 23 (1979), 855–859, 924–928; John Hersey, *Hiroshima* (New York: Bantam, 1946).

24. *Pastoral Constitution on the Church in the Modern World*, 13, *The Documents of Vatican II*, Walter M. Abbott, ed. (America Press, 1966), p. 212.

25. Solzhenitsyn, *The Gulag Archipelago*, 1, *op. cit.*, p. 499.

26. See, at this point, George W. E. Nickelsburg, *Jewish Literature Between the Bible and the Mishnah: A Historical and Literary Introduction* (Philadelphia: Fortress, 1981), esp. p. 5: "One important factor that holds together the largest part of this corpus of literature is its common setting in hard times: persecution; oppression; other kinds of disaster; the loneliness and pressures of a minority living up to its convictions in an alien environment. Within this context these writings may be read and appreciated as a sometimes powerful expression of the depths and the heights of our humanity and of human religiousness and religious experience."

27. For a preliminary insight see Trevor Ling, *The Significance of Satan: New Testament Demonology and Its Contemporary Relevance* (London: SPCK, 1961).

28. Solzhenitsyn, *The Gulag Archipelago*, 2, *op. cit.*, p. 598. The citation from St. John of the Cross: *The Ascent of Mount Carmel*, 1, 11 (*The Collected Works of St. John of the Cross*, Kieran Kavanaugh and Otilio Rodriguez, trans. [Washington, D.C.: Institute of Carmelite Studies, 1973], p. 103).

29. Wiesel, *Night, op. cit.*, pp. 75–76.

30. For an overview, see Paul Ricoeur, *Main Trends in Philosophy* (New York: Holmes and Meier, 1978), pp. 320–327.

31. *Philebus*, 58d (*The Collected Dialogues of Plato*, Edith Hamilton and Huntington Cairns, eds., Bollingen Series LXXI [Princeton, New Jersey: Princeton University, 1982], p. 1140); Aristotle, *Ethics*, 1139a16-b2, 1140a24-b12, 1181a12-b10 (*The Ethics of Aristotle*, J. A. K. Thomson, trans. [New York: Penguin, 1976], p. 205, p. 209, p. 341).

32. Karl Jaspers, *The Origin and Goal of History* (New Haven: Yale University, 1953), p. 126.

33. Friedrich Heiler, "The History of Religions as a Preparation for the Co-operation of Religions," *The History of Religions: Essays in Methodology*, M. Eliade and J. M. Kitagawa, eds. (Chicago: University of Chicago, 1959), pp. 132–160. For a similar view, see Raimundo Panikkar, "The Emerging Myth," *Monchanin* 8 (1975), 8–11.

34. Cited in *ibid.*, p. 147. For Tertullian, see *To Scapula*, 1 (*The Ante-Nicene Fathers*, 3 [Grand Rapids, Michigan: Wm. B. Eerdmans, 1957], p. 105).

35. (New York: Paulist, 1981), p. 3.

3

Finding Our Way Among Modern Christologies

The Nature of Modern Christologies

The word "Christology" is derived from the two Greek words *Christos* (= the Christ, anointed one) and *logos* (= the study or intellectual analysis of something). Thus, Christology is the study of how and why Jesus is believed by Christians to be the Christ. It is an activity as ancient as the New Testament itself, for all the New Testament writings are in a real sense various attempts to understand (= *logos*) who and what Jesus is and what he has done for humanity (= *Christos*). Throughout this book we will be looking at the New Testament contribution in more detail. For now we want to concentrate upon modern Christologies.

I would suggest that what makes Christologies "modern" is the fact that they are all in various ways influenced by one, two, or all of the three great contemporary transitions which we briefly considered in the previous chapter. All are in some vital way conscious of the "break" in human history when thinkers began to turn to human experience in a new, more critical, and more radical manner. It is not that pre-transition Christologies (whether biblical, patristic, medieval, or reformed) did not try to apply a critical reason to their grapplings with the Christ. Again, we do not want to exaggerate the novelty of the contemporary. But the "Christian ethos" was largely "in possession" for past epochs. The broad presuppositions of Christianity were shared by all Christian parties: that there is a God, that this God revealed himself in the history of Jesus of Nazareth, and that this revelation was good news for humanity, initiating a process of redemption which frees humans from their sins and other evils. The Christian debates about Jesus, such as they were, were largely about implications flowing out of these broad presuppositions. Typical questions were not "Is there a God?" but "What is the nature of the Divine?" Not "Does Jesus reveal God?" but "How does Jesus disclose the Divine?" Not, "Is salvation a fact realized in history?" but "What are salvation's precise benefits?"

Even when Christianity came into conflict with the non-Christian religions, as it did twice—in the early period, with Judaism and the Greco-Roman religions; in the medieval period, with Islam—still the debate did not become all that radical. Greeks, Romans, Jews, and Muslims all shared a religious view of the world. Reality was sacred for them, packed with a divine meaning and many divine mediators. The issue with Christians was over which divine mediator, not whether there was a mediator. Listen to what the early Christian writer Justin Martyr says in an open letter he penned around the year 150 to the Roman emperor Antoninus Pius. He complains that Christians are unjustly persecuted "even though we say the same things [about Jesus] that the Greeks [say about their gods/goddesses]." And he goes on:

> When we say that the Word (*Logos*), who is the firstborn of God, was born for us without sexual union . . . and that he was crucified and died and after rising again ascended into Heaven, we introduce nothing new beyond (what you say) regarding those whom you call sons of Zeus. . . . When we say that Jesus was born of a virgin, you should consider this something in common with Perseus. When we say that he healed the lame, the paralyzed, and those born blind, and raised the dead, we seem to be talking about things like those said to have been done by Asklepios.[1]

Here we see how Justin shares some rather large religious presuppositions with his non-Christian contemporaries. A similar agreement on broad presuppositions also lies behind what has come to be called the classic statement on Christology, the creed produced by the ecumenical Council of Chalcedon of 451. This Council tried to sum up earlier views about Jesus proclaimed at other councils: at Nicaea (325) and at Ephesus (431) especially. In doing so, it settled upon the classical formula for the doctrine of the incarnation: "God became man in Jesus of Nazareth."

The Chalcedonian approach is often called a "high Christology," or a "Christology from above," because it emphasizes the "high" or divine status of Jesus. The Divine has come down into history and become a human being in Jesus of Nazareth in order to save humanity. To be sure, Jesus remains a human being for Chalcedon. The intuition of the Church was that unless Jesus was truly human, we couldn't say that the Divine had really entered into the human plight as we know it and filled it with the divine, saving power. But the focus and marvel for Christians was on the *Divine*—it was the *Divine* which had descended. Here we encounter another designation for the classical Christology: it is a "Christology of descent" on the part of the Divine.

Readers may note a similarity in tone between the incarnation doctrine as we meet it in Chalcedon and the Gospel of John. I recommend that you take time out to familiarize yourself with the first chapter (or prologue) of that Gospel. The "high Christology" of the early Church was often legitimated by an appeal to this prologue: "In the beginning was the Word; the Word was in God's presence, and the Word was God. . . . The Word became flesh and made his dwelling among us. . ." (Jn 1:1, 14). The Chalcedonian Church was in dialogue with the Greco-Roman world of thought, and it was probably the Greek-sounding character of John's Gospel—note the *Logos* or Word beloved of Greek philosophy—which made it popular in the early Church. Eventually John's "descent Christology" became the dominant one in the Church.

Of course, there were disputes in the early Church among Christians about who this Jesus was with which the *Logos* united. Was he merely flesh ruled by the Divine? Was he fully human, possessed of a human intellect and will? But regardless, all agreed on the starting point: there is a Divine reality whom we believe we know. Most also agreed that this Divine reality had descended into Jesus. There were also disputes with non-Christian Greeks about whether the Divine could actually embroil itself so fully in the imperfections of human weakness, but note that here too the fundamental reality and nature of the Divine was assumed.

Modern Christologies, arising as they do after the break of the great transitions, tend to be more radical than the traditional Christologies. This does not necessarily mean that they are governed by a lack of belief in the reality of the Divine. Rather it means that they are influenced by that turn to experience as a guide for human knowing which we described earlier. They are conscious of the fact that modern men and women find it increasingly difficult to affirm anything, even in belief, that cannot be validated in some way by experience. As we shall see, even modern fundamentalists are conscious of the turn to experience and must grapple with it in a way uncharacteristic of the classical Christologies.

For example, the inherited Christology of Chalcedon takes Jesus' divinity for granted. This was meaningful enough in a God-centered age, surely. But this is just the issue that many moderns find hard to negotiate. This doesn't mean that we have to opt for atheism in order to be modern. It does mean that today's thinker must grapple with the experiential foundations of belief in the Divine as present in the man Jesus. What is an experience of the Divine? What are its characteristics? How is such an experience discerned? Would the distinction we made earlier—between a narrow view of experience as simply "sense experience" and a wider notion of "inward and religious experience"—be of any help here? Grappling with such questions is rather typical of modernity and untypical of the classical inheritance.

Something else the traditional Christologies tend to assume is the humanity of Jesus. There is a lot of wisdom about Jesus' humanity to be found in the tradition. But most theologians will unhesitatingly agree that the greater danger throughout Christian history has been one of subordinating the humanity to the divinity of Jesus. This danger is often called "monophysitism," after the ancient Christian heresy of swallowing up Jesus' humanity into his one divine nature (*monos* = one; *physis* = nature). The new personalism of our contemporary period leads people to wonder about Jesus' humanity—his birth, education, sexuality, ministry, death, temptations, etc. For many, only a truly human Jesus is credible. And even fundamentalists must struggle with this one: if they think that Jesus "departs" from our normal humanity, this must be explained for the modern mind. The resurrection also raises questions. Presumably this is an aspect of Jesus' humanity, for the Divine need not rise from the dead! The Chalcedonian Christology doesn't even mention the resurrection, yet St. Paul considers it the heart of the Christian message: our faith is empty without it (cf 1 Cor 15:14). Moderns are puzzled by the resurrection. In what way can we credibly believe in this and come to terms with it? Is this a genuinely human possibility?

Again, the traditional Christologies seem a good deal more certain about who God is than modernity does. The way scholars speak of this is to say that Chalcedon supposes an *a priori* notion of what the Divine must be like (*a priori* = assumed from the first). Moderns tend to be more experiential, more *a posteriori* (= after learning from experience). Fundamentalists at least often show a querying attitude, untypical of an earlier time. Many find themselves drawn toward probing the lessons of experience, historical and contemporary, for clues about who the Divine really is. This openness to learning from experience, this willingness to suspend our inherited ideas of what the Divine must be like—all of this is rather typical of the modern mind. Either that, or at least an honest attempt is made to meet the objections of modernity, if one is a modern fundamentalist.

Also, Chalcedon only sparingly touches on the saving significance of the Jesus event. To be sure, the Chalcedonian decree begins with the creed of Nicaea, which confessed that Jesus was born "for us men and for our salvation." And it re-emphasized the same toward the end of its decree: ". . . for our salvation [born] of Mary. . . ." Clearly it presupposes the reality of salvation as the basic context in the light of which the incarnation should be viewed. In our efforts to make a case for modern Christologies we have no need to deny this. The early Fathers of the Church were deeply aware of this: "The Word of God speaks, having become man, that such as you may learn from man how it is even possible for man to become a god," Clement of Alexandria tells us. But many moderns need this spelled out more fully, or are at least puzzled.[2]

In what way do we humans need salvation? We no longer live in an age which takes the need for salvation for granted. Much around us hammers home the notion that we save ourselves, through reason, through social and political betterment, through scientific discoveries and improvements, etc. Further, many feel the need to query just what kind of salvation we are talking about and how that is related to a Jesus who lived some two thousand years ago. Are we speaking of a so-called spiritual regeneration, or also of a bodily, political and social liberation? How can we credibly say that Jesus even now brings this about? Is our salvation in some sense unfinished, given our historical experience of tyranny and evil throughout the ages? These are but a sampling of the questions that our contemporary experience brings to the belief in Jesus the Savior.

Finally, the classical Christology omits an exploration of the kinds of concerns which flow from our second and third transitions. What is the practical "punch" of the Jesus event? What are its political, social, and ecological implications? How is the divine descent into Jesus related to the possible descent of the Divine into other, non-Christian religious figures? Such are some of the new questions, giving rise to a kind of Christology that can be called distinctively "modern." And, as we will see shortly, although modern fundamentalists won't generally embrace the modern experiential turn in the way we have described it here, still that experiential turn largely determines the questions grappled with even by those fundamentalists. They are also under the influence of experience and in a posture of struggle with it. Today's fundamentalist Christologies are peculiarly modern, because they reflect our great transitions.

A Sampling of Modern Christologies

Tradition and Contemporary Experience as the
Two Poles of Theology and Christology

Modern Christologies, I suggested, are all in some conscious way influenced by one, two, or all of the great transitions: the modern fascination for experience, the critical sensitivity to evil, and globalization. But they are not all influenced in the same way. In what follows I would like to acquaint the reader with some of the broad tendencies that seem to be at work among modern theologians. My aim is partly expositional: much of what follows will be a helpful background for this entire book. But my aim is also partly methodological: faced with all of the varied Christologies of

today, how might the thoughtful person go about sifting his or her way
through all of these, learning from them, yet perhaps rejecting some of
their positions, all the while remaining open to whatever fresh insights
some of them may have to offer?

Broadly speaking we can propose that Christian theology (including
Christology) is governed by a reciprocal relationship between the two
poles of tradition and contemporary experience. Modern Christologies can
be helpfully diagnosed by the attitudes they take toward each of these two
poles. The tradition pole should be somewhat obvious. Christianity is tradition-bound, for it maintains that divine revelation has somehow been
disclosed to us through creation, through history (especially that of the
Jewish people), and through the events in and surrounding Jesus of Nazareth. This tradition-bound character of Christianity is simply a specific example of the more general axiom we mentioned earlier—namely, that all
that we are as humans is co-communicated to us through history. Because
we are historical creatures, not isolated entities, we must pay attention to
tradition. Properly speaking, there is no gap between tradition and ourselves. Rather than a gap, we should speak of a relationship between tradition and the present within which we live and which takes various
shapes. Thus, the Christian today must still say with St. Paul, "I handed
on to you first of all what I myself received" (1 Cor 15:3). The Greek for "I
handed on to you" (= *paredoka*) is the origin of our Latin *tradere* (= "to
hand on"), from which our term "tradition" derives.

Catholics and Protestants will be somewhat familiar with what I mean
by the tradition pole, given the great debates that occurred during the Reformation on the nature of tradition. As is well known, the Catholic position
was hammered out at the famous Council of Trent in its decree of 8 April
1546. Against its view of the Reformers as reducing Christian revelation to
the Scriptures, the Council held that while the Gospel is the "source of all
living truth," still that revelation is "contained" not simply in the written
Scriptures but also in the unwritten traditions of the Church (cf *DS* 1501–
1508). The Reformers, perhaps influenced by the development of printing
and their own reformist desire to free Christianity from its more questionable traditions, appealed to Scripture alone "as the infallible and sufficient
authority in all matters pertaining to salvation, to which all human traditions should be subjected."[3]

This looks as if Protestants reduce revelation to the Scriptures, while
Catholics make room for a non-scriptural tradition. But the issue is
somewhat more complex. First, let us look at the Catholic position.
While Catholicism surely emphasizes, with Eastern Orthodoxy, a relative
independence of non-scriptural traditions (namely, liturgies, customs,
doctrines, sacred art, the experience of saints, martyrs, mystics, theolo-

gians, and the faithful), still the overwhelming majority of Catholic scholars today would hold that all the doctrines and valid customs of the Church
have emerged through reflection upon and the practical living out of the
Scriptures. The former are in some way a legitimate expression of the revelation witnessed to in the Scriptures. As one Catholic scholar, Gerald
O'Collins, puts it: "Given the organic life of the Church in which Scriptures and the whole traditionary process . . . function together as a living
unity, it seems highly implausible to hold for some . . . teaching mediated
to us neither through the New Testament nor through the traditional
interpretation of the Scriptures but somehow reaching us on its own."[4]
This is certainly the view of the Church before Trent, and Trent itself
leaves this an open question. Thus, Catholicism can be comfortable with
saying that "tradition" gives expression to the Scriptures and carries them
forward. The case for a valid tradition independent of the Scriptures is an
enormously weak one in the Catholic view.

What about the Protestant position? While it is true that the Reformers (Luther, Calvin, etc.) insisted upon the Scriptures as the final judge of
all traditions within the Church, it is becoming clearer to us that Reformation theology was not opposed to a legitimate place for some traditions.
The sixteenth century reformer Martin Chemnitz was only opposed to traditions which could find no scriptural basis. He was not opposed to all
forms of tradition.[5] If this is representative of mainline Protestantism, then
the case for a view of the Scriptures as independent of tradition is a weak
one on the Protestant side. It would seem that both traditional Protestantism and Catholicism, together with Eastern Orthodoxy, share a more
organic and unitary view of Scripture and tradition than later ages would
care to admit.

Then what happened? From the Catholic side I would suggest that a
certain argumentative attitude began to prevail in the post-Trent Church.
The polemicist tends to exaggerate differences of accent into absolute differences. Perhaps this is the case with those authors who argued that there
were valid Catholic traditions totally independent of the Scriptures. Such
would be a way of highlighting Catholicism's differences from Protestantism. Again, Catholics tended to exaggerate the power of their Church authorities, as if they were completely independent of the Scriptures. As the
same argumentative attitude took root among Protestants, we witnessed a
similar blurring of the place for tradition. Instead of being a book produced
by tradition and read in tradition's light, Scripture became something to
be read privately and autonomously.

Today Catholics and Protestants are moving toward a new consensus.
Increasingly Protestants recognize the role of tradition. Its place is well attested in the pre-Trent Church and in the thought of the Reformers. Be-

sides, on simple philosophical grounds, we humans are creatures of
tradition through and through. Even the Bible itself is a product of tradition: not only was it preserved through tradition, but also the choice of canonical writings was a decision of the tradition. And, finally, how can we
make the Scriptures relevant to succeeding generations? If there is no tradition to "hand on" and interpret the Scriptures, then they become a dead
letter.

   Catholics, on the other hand, are reappreciating the role of the Scriptures. They are rediscovering the teaching of the ancient Church that authentic tradition was in some real sense an authentic interpretation and
continuation of Scripture, a view which has come to be called the "material
sufficiency" of Scripture. If we further think of Scripture as a witness to
Jesus and his work, rather than a listing of dogmatic propositions, then the
material sufficiency of Scripture is even more greatly accentuated. It
seems as if Scripture and tradition are both witnesses in different forms of
the one revelatory event of Jesus of Nazareth.

   Perhaps we can generalize this growing agreement into more theoretical terms. Might we not distinguish between "Tradition," understood
as the "handing on" process of enabling each succeeding generation to appropriate the revelation event of Jesus (= the *actus tradendi*), and "tradition" (now with a small "t") understood as the results of that handing on
process (= the so-called *tradita*: Scripture and non-scriptural traditions
[prayer, liturgy, art, doctrine, Christian experience in general, etc.])? In
schematic form:

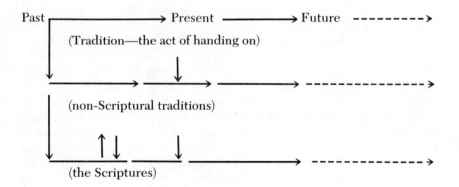

   Here we see how divine revelation occurs through the traditionary or
"handing on" process: God intersects with human experience and is known
through the ongoing human experience. The schema also illustrates, with
the ancient Church, the organic unity between Scripture and other tra-

ditions by illustrating that both are a witness to and sediment of the traditionary process. The tradition pole of Christian theology, then, can be summed up as the entire handing on process as expressed through both Scripture and other non-scriptural traditions.

Now let us move to the other pole of Christian theology and Christology, namely, contemporary experience. I have already prepared for this by proposing that Tradition shades off into contemporary experience. Because we are historical creatures, we are always linked with our past and somehow in dialogue with it. There is no gap between past and present, but various forms of dialogue between them. Tradition as a handing on process implies this linkage with the present. What this comes down to is the recognition that we humans and Christians are not only past-bound, but present- and future-bound. For better or worse we exist in a present moving into the future, and the only way in which the Christian past can become contemporary for us is if it finds an echo within our own experience. A kind of ongoing and reciprocal dialogue between tradition and contemporary experience seems a good way, then, to describe theology and Christology.

It is through that dialogue that the traditionary process occurs, through which a sifting of the false from the true or more adequate takes place. Incorporating a "contemporary experience pole" should not be surprising. The Scriptures are already an excellent example of this interpenetration between past and present. When Paul tells us that he hands on the Jesus tradition (1 Cor 15:3), he does so in the Greco-Roman terms intelligible to the contemporary experience of his audience. Of course, we need to think of experience here in its wider sense as embracing inward, religious experience. Revelation cannot find an echo in our contemporary experience unless we humans really do enjoy religious experiences through which the Divine can truly intersect with us.

Christologies of the Far Right and the Far Left

Now it seems to me that modern Christologies can be characterized by the attitudes they take to each of the two poles of Christian theology. Let me paint in broad strokes and distinguish three large postures among modern Christologians. We can speak first of all of fundamentalist Christologies. I borrow the designation "fundamentalist" from the well-known position among Protestant believers which seems to have arisen at the turn of the century. It was a reaction to the so-called modernists and liberals, who believed that Christian teachings (including biblical ones) should be viewed in the light of current intellectual progress. Thus, the modernists stressed the need to employ current historical methods in interpreting the

Scriptures. They also tried to bring out the relevance of the Scriptures to modernity, showing an openness to modern theories of evolution and technological progress.

The fundamentalists believed that the modernization process threatened the "very fundamentals" of Christianity. Hence their name. The term "fundamentalist" was probably first used in 1920 as a positive label for this reaction movement. The fundamentalists' main line of defense was the authority of the Scriptures: these were verbally inerrant. To some extent the emergence of American fundamentalism can be explained as a result of America's painful shift from a more conservative agrarian to a more liberal and industrial society. The fundamentalists perhaps felt this shift most painfully. But it was also a theological and religious movement, a kind of fusion between older American Protestant sectarians and some sophisticated "modern" theologians at Princeton Seminary in the 1800's.[6]

Fundamentalism continues today. In fact, if we think of it as a basic attitude, its roots extend far back into our Christian past and beyond that into our present among both Protestants and Catholics. The changes in thinking current at the turn of the century have only intensified today. An uneasiness with this change is a good breeding ground for fundamentalism. Whether we speak of Protestant fundamentalists, who rest their case on verbally inerrant Scriptures, or of Catholic and Eastern Orthodox fundamentalists, who rest their case on supposedly inerrant traditions, still both are united in their opposition to modernity's influence upon theology.

Father Raymond E. Brown, the noted biblical scholar, recently spoke of Catholic fundamentalists as the "Catholic right." He characterized some of their Christological positions in the following way. He points out that the "Catholic center" and the "Catholic right" both believe in the two natures of Jesus as human and divine, but they radically differ on how they understand their belief. "Often the Catholic right will insist that the divinity of Jesus means that there could have been no limitations during his earthly life, i.e., in his humanity he knew the future in detail, he could express fully his own divine identity and he could define all the doctrines of Christian revelation (e.g., Trinity, sacraments)."[7] What Father Brown calls the "Catholic center" rather tends not to see any contradictions between an affirmation of Jesus' divinity and an equal affirmation of his human limitations, sin excepted. This would mean that Jesus grew and developed, that he was tempted, that he shared many of the views current in his own time, and that he need not have known either the general human future or the future course of doctrinal development.

What is the basic attitude of the fundamentalist to the two poles of

Christian theology? It seems, first, one of resistance, hostility, suspicion, and often rejection of contemporary experience, at least as understood by our three great transitions. The turn to experience, to personalism, to history are often viewed as an assault on the autonomy of revelation and revelation's freedom from the limitations of human existence. But this attitude toward the present colors the fundamentalist's approach to the other pole of theology, the tradition. By rejecting an historical and experiential approach to tradition, fundamentalists run the danger of reading the tradition uncritically. Sometimes this means that they end up projecting their own biases onto the tradition, instead of grasping what the tradition actually means in the historical sense. Or it might mean that they possess no norm for discriminating between true and false traditions. By rejecting any appeal to contemporary experience as a norm for truth, they can only rest their case on their supposedly "inspired conscience." But how do we know that this is inspired? Lacking discriminating norms, fundamentalists leave themselves open to the wildest flights of the imagination. What perhaps could save them from this last possibility is their willingness to submit to some powerful authority figure. If you will, the authority of someone recognized in the fundamentalist movement becomes a kind of surrogate conscience or norm for the followers. But this is perilous too. On what grounds is this "leader" to be judged adequate? What if he or she is equally blinded and biased? The great danger of such leaders is blind fanaticism and totalitarianism.

If we were to go further and extend these general observations in a more theological direction, what could we say? Ultimately, fundamentalism tends toward denying that the Divine is somehow to be experienced in the present. The Divine is Lord, however, not only of the past, but also of the present. And if that is true, then contemporary experience should not be rejected out of court as a source for our religious and theological thinking. Christologically speaking, I believe Father Brown put the matter very well:

> The rightist theory of unlimited knowledge greatly reduces the *kenosis* or emptying involved in the incarnation. Uncertainty about the future and about how some of the most urgent issues in life will turn out is one of the greatest agonies of being human. The Jesus who knew exactly what would happen becomes almost a play actor on the stage of time, unaffected by vicissitudes. He is a Jesus who should not have feared death in Gethsemane since he knew exactly how he would triumph, and he should not have found it necessary to pray that this cup pass from him. One may ask whether he would have been truly human like us in all things but sin (Council of Chalcedon).[8]

Fundamentalism seems to end up as a form of what we earlier called "monophysitism," a kind of swallowing up of the humanity into the divinity of Jesus. Of course, the thoughtful Christian should pay attention to fundamentalism. We should try to learn from it and view it as a kind of critical conscience which forces us to ask whether we might not be too rash, too uncritical in our acceptance of modernity. But as a self-consistent position it just will not hold up.

If fundamentalism is to the far right, we can also speak of Christologies which tend toward the far left. If fundamentalism be characterized as an uncritical rejection of modernity, then we could name this next option an uncritical acceptance of modernity. This stance has definitely come under the influence of one, two, or all of our great transitions, but in a problematic manner as far as the Christian theologian is concerned.

For example, let us dwell for a moment upon a representative thinker influenced mainly by the first Enlightenment. As we saw earlier, this was a period when thinkers were beginning to turn to experience as a norm for human and religious knowing. For Christology the early Enlightenment initiated an intensive rethinking of the Church's traditional Christology. Herman S. Reimarus (d. 1768) is often credited with being the first to engage in this new critical thinking in his little work, *Fragments*. Because, for him, religion is recast, in good Enlightenment terms, into the pursuit of high moral ideals, then the Jesus which Reimarus considers authentic is the Jesus who is a "moral enlightener." Because the miraculous and supernatural do not fit into the rationally derived laws of nature as understood in the Enlightenment, then the Gospel miracles must have been fabricated by Jesus' disciples, especially the incredible resurrection stories. Jesus' apocalyptic message cannot be excised from the Gospels (it is too prevalent), but it is irrelevant and crude to the rationalist, and thus of no enduring value. In all of this, a particular kind of thinking characteristic of the Enlightenment seems to dominate: the "unerring signs of truth and falsehood are clear, distinct consistency and contradiction," he tells us. A sure "sign that a doctrine or history possesses no depth of authenticity . . . is . . . to resort to miracles in order to prove its truth."[9]

Reimarus' Christology is a good example of a low Christology. Jesus is quite radically de-divinized and de-supernaturalized. At most, Reimarus is a Deist, who will tolerate an inactive divine reality who won't interfere with humans. He tells us that "the goal of Jesus' sermons and teachings was a proper, active character, a changing of the mind, a sincere love of God and of one's neighbor, humility, gentleness, denial of the self, and the suppression of all evil desires. . . . These are nothing other than moral teachings and duties intended to improve man inwardly and with all his heart. . . ."[10]

Something similar to Reimarus shows up, but even more radically, in Paul van Buren's well known *The Secular Meaning of the Gospel*. Arguing that God-talk is quite literally meaningless to the modern mind, he holds that at least Christians still have the Jesus of history, a man quite remarkable in his freedom, in his love, and in the sincerity and creativity of his life. This kind of life was truly "contagious" and helped transform Jesus' erstwhile non-believing disciples.[11] Reimarus, Van Buren (in the above work), and thinkers like them represent in varying degrees the narrowly empirical strain of the early Enlightenment as applied to the issues of Christology.

The later Enlightenment (one of the manifestations of our second transition) has also generated its share of Christologies. As we remember, the agnostic strain of the later Enlightenment tended to reduce religion to some kind of infantile projection (Freud) or to a kind of opiate consolation caused by and legitimating social misery (Marx). So far as I know, Freud and Marx do not say much about Jesus, but some of their disciples do. Erich Fromm, for example, a kind of critical disciple of Freud and Marx, had written already in 1930 an extensive paper, "The Dogma of Christ." In it he proposed that the hopelessness of ever realizing their dreams for liberation from Roman oppressors led the early Christians "to formulate the same wishes in fantasy."[12]

Now, what was the nature of that fantasy? Ultimately it is rooted in the oedipal complex described by Freud. Every individual experiences both protection from his or her father and a hidden hostility for him, for the father breaks the child from the protective "womb" of the mother. Similarly, the God-belief arises from our need to project our father's protection and care into a cosmic form: God becomes a "father projection." But we harbor a hidden hostility for this cosmic father too. Now from this arises the "Christ fantasy": "he was a symbol of their unconscious hostility to God the Father, for if a man could become God, the latter was deprived of his privileged fatherly position of being unique and unreachable."[13] Elevating a man to divine status expresses an unconscious wish to remove the divine Father.

Later, as Christianity became the religion of the successful rather than the oppressed, the sense of hostility toward the Father evaporated. Why be hostile when you no longer feel oppressed? Accordingly, the Christ fantasy changed. Jesus now was not thought to have become God. Rather, he was always God: "Now . . . it was not a man, but his only begotten Son, existing before all creation, who was beside him."[14] God the Father was not dethroned, for Jesus now was always a component of God. Again, this new belief expresses the social change that occurred in Christianity: "Far from being a religion of rebels and revolutionaries, this reli-

gion of the ruling class was now determined to keep the masses in
obedience and lead them."[15]

In a later writing, Fromm has argued that not all forms of religion are
infantile and regressive projections. He holds respect for a humanistic religion "centered around man and his strength."[16] If this latter kind of religion uses theistic language, its true meaning is only humanistic. "God,"
for example, symbolizes "man's own powers which he tries to realize in his
life."[17] And Fromm thinks that the Jesus of history (not the Christ of
dogma!) was clearly humanistic, for his precept that "the Kingdom of God
is within you" clearly respects the dignity of man and avoids the authori-
tarianism of dehumanizing forms of religion.[18] Similar interpretations of
Jesus have been put forward by followers of C. G. Jung and Karl Marx, ev-
idencing a respect for Jesus and a desire to understand him through the
prism of psychoanalytic and Marxist categories. Thus, for example, Christ
can become variously the symbol of the fully integrated individual (for
Jungians) or the example of the social liberator of the oppressed (for Marx-
ists).[19]

Fromm is also influenced by our third major transition of globalization. His *Psychoanalysis and Religion* manifests an awareness of the religious wisdom of the great religions. He thinks that the distinction between
infantile/regressive religion and humanistic religion cuts across the various
religious divides. Not only Jesus, but other religious founders manifest a
humanizing trend. Buddha, for example, "calls upon every man to make
use of his own reason and to see the truth which he was only the first to
find."[20] Abraham Maslow has offered a similar analysis. The core of every
known high religion, he tells us, are "peak-experiences," types of personal
illumination about life's meaning. While these experiences have been explained "in terms of supernatural revelation, it is very likely, indeed almost certain," that they were, "in fact, perfectly natural, human peak-
experiences of the kind that can easily be examined today, which, however, were phrased in terms of whatever conceptual, cultural, and linguistic framework the particular seer had available in his time." And
Maslow claims that to the extent that these peak-experiences are the same
in essence, then "all religions are the same in their essence and always
have been."[21]

What, now, is the basic attitude of leftist Christologies to the two
poles of Christian theology? It seems basically one of simple acceptance of
the religiously critical strains of early and late Enlightenment thought. The
turn to contemporary experience in its more limited meaning of sense experience, or at least to a view of experience as excluding any properly religious element, is what governs the thought of these various thinkers.
Inward human experience, as including genuinely religious experiences

through which humans intersect with the Divine, is excluded. And as with the fundamentalists, this attitude toward contemporary experience governs the way in which these authors reappropriate the Christological tradition. The tradition is interpreted in purely naturalistic and humanistic categories. If you will, Jesus the human is accepted; Christ, the divine, is either rejected or simply humanized. Theologically speaking, the issue seems to be the narrowed view of human experience, which tends toward eliminating any presence of the Divine in human history. Christologically speaking, we have a kind of monophysitism in reverse: the divine nature of Jesus is swallowed up within the human. Even the properly religious dimension of non-Christian religions is reinterpreted in a simple, humanistic direction.

For the religious thinker, the difficulty is the extremely austere notion of human experience. As we will see, the witness of the varied religious traditions as well as some important contemporary work among philosophers and theologians is calling this narrow notion of human experience into question. Still, this does not mean that the thoughtful Christian hasn't much to learn from the leftists. It has been largely through an ongoing dialogue with them that we have been able to hammer out the next position to which I will shortly turn. And, further, few among us would want to deny the stress of the leftists upon grounding religious and Christological assertions within human experience. The difficulty is in discovering the correct texture of human experience, one which is holistic enough to incorporate the religious dimension of human existence. Finally, the stress of late Enlightenment thinkers on pathological forms of religious belief is a real gain for our growing understanding of the ambiguity of human experience. Surely Freud and Marx can be questioned on the total adequacy of their religious views. But that they have much to teach us about distorted forms of religious behavior few among us would wish to deny.

Centrist Christologies

"Centrist" Christologies, to borrow Raymond Brown's term, are Christologies which have attempted to learn from the thought of the far right and left, seeking to avoid their extremes, yet incorporating a number of their emphases and concerns. They are truly in dialogue with one, two, or all of our three great transitions, but, I think, in a more critical manner than the far right and left. Their attitude to the Christological tradition is an open yet critical one. They recognize that we are a tradition-bound religion and that we live in various degrees of dependency upon it, especially since we believe that the Divine manifests itself within the traditionary process. The tradition has much to teach us, especially because it witnesses to profound depths of human and religious experience—in the prophets, in Jesus, in the mystics and saints, in the non-Christian sages—which perhaps we have failed to realize in our own lives.

Yet that openness to tradition is matched by a critical sense: not everything the tradition has handed down is to be greeted with open arms. While the tradition witnesses to great depths of human and religious experience, it also witnesses to depths of human depravity and evil. Albert Schweitzer, among others, pointed out this ambiguity of the Christian tradition some time ago: "For centuries it treasured the great commandment of love and mercy as traditional truth without recognizing it as a reason for opposing slavery, witch burning, torture, and all the other ancient and medieval forms of inhumanity."[22]

Centrist Christologies also seem to maintain an equally open and critical attitude toward contemporary experience, our other pole of Christian theology—open because, like other modern thought, they are governed by the turn to experience. They seek to ground religious beliefs within human experience, recognizing that we can only affirm and somehow understand what forms a part of our genuine human experience. A supposed revelation which does not intersect with our human experience is simply unknowable in any sense. Engaging in this kind of project was first begun by Protestant liberal theology and Catholic liberal and modernist theology at the turn of the century. At least in intention Friedrich Schleiermacher, Adolf Harnack, Ernst Troeltsch, Albert Schweitzer, George Tyrrell, Baron Friedrich von Hügel, Maurice Blondel, and others among the so-called liberals were seeking the experiential grounds of our Christian belief, even if they may not have succeeded adequately in every case.[23] Their project continues today among centrist theologians and Christologians.

Yet centrists are also critical of the modern turn to experience. They recognize the ambiguities and limitations of every age. Our own present experience is also "fallen" and not always fully developed or grasped in its full potential. This is one of the reasons for deepening our ties to tradition: by remaining open to it we can perhaps discover depths of human potential or depravity which our own age has forgotten. The so-called neo-orthodox thinkers who reacted to what they regarded as the excessive optimism of the early liberals were on to this ambiguity of human experience, chastened by two world wars, the breakdown of the older European regimes, and the atrocities of Nazism, as they were. The two Niebuhrs, H. Richard and Reinhold, Karl Barth, Paul Tillich, Emil Brunner, Rudolf Bultmann, and perhaps even Hans Urs von Balthasar were all aware of the sinfulness and evil present within human experience and needing to be recognized. Their project continues today among centrists, even if many centrists might not so radically accept the neo-orthodox stress on the opposition between the Divine and a fallen humanity.[24]

Perhaps the two most promising developments for centrist Christologies are (1) the recovery of a more holistic notion of human experience, one which is religiously sensitive, and (2) the recovery of the ambiguity of human experience, its brokenness and fallenness, what we called earlier the negative dimension of human and religious experience. The recovery of religious experience as a genuine dimension of human experience has come from a number of quarters. Let us look at some of them.

Language philosophers, who remind us of the linguistic nature of human experience, argue that there are multiple uses of language, not only scientific, but also moral, aesthetic, and religious. This implies a break away from simple sense experience, used in scientific discourse, as the only valid form of human experience. Human experience is wide and complex, and our multiple language games reflect this. "God-talk" implies a depth to human experience, not apparent on the merely sense level. It affirms the meaningfulness of human existence, of the human possibility of faith.

"Phenomenologists" have developed a careful method of suspending our inherited prejudices about reality ("phenomena"), particularly our tendency to reduce experience to only the sense level. They have brought to light neglected phenomena of experience. Among these are experiences of transcendence in which humans seem to be open to an unlimited horizon of meaning. Others have analyzed the experiences of the mystics, discovering that they witness to the fact that the human self is more than the simple ego of sense perception. The mystics know a deeper or transcendent self. This latter seems to hold us together, despite sleep, amnesia, or comas. Through the difficult project of suspending the ordinary operations of their reason, the mystics seem to become aware of "this inner ground of the soul" through which they experience themselves as related to and supported by a divine Beyond. All of these exemplify a recovery of a wider, more religiously open notion of human experience.

This recovery of the religious depths of human experience makes it possible to explore, in a more disciplined and contemporary manner, what it means to affirm an intersection between Divine Presence and human experience. Human experience appears as theandric, a divine-human duality, an openness to a transcendent dimension. Christologians can build upon these insights, using them as models for clarifying what the tradition affirms about Jesus as a man in whom divinity shines through. These insights seem to promise a new ability to ground Christological beliefs within the contours of human experience.

But to all of the above should be added the equally crucial recovery of the ambiguity and negativity of human experience. As we noted earlier, humans know both the heights of grandeur and the depths of depravity and misery. Religious experiences are not always positive ones of transcendence into joy and bliss, but negative ones of human brokenness, limitations, dependency, protest, and struggling. A fully practical description of human experience simply cannot ignore this reverse side of what happens in our human experience. Through these negative experiences we humans somehow discover a transcendent capacity both to trust and to protest—to trust that evil will not have the last word, to protest against that evil. These, too, are experiences of transcendence, but in their negative form. Somehow, through them, we become aware of social/collective experiences of transcendence too—for example, whole social movements of protest. This reminds us that religious experience, even of a positive kind, can take a social form.

Again, the recovery of this negative dimension of religious experience is a helpful aid to theologians who attempt to ground Christology within human experience. They can use these experiences as models and guides for exploring some of the more salient features of our Christological beliefs. For example, the central image of the Kingdom of God can gain new relevance as a possible expression of Jesus' own divinely-inspired protest against human misery and his longing for a new kind of community where this misery is decisively overcome. The cross can perhaps be analogously seen as the negative religious experience *par excellence* of the Christian tradition.[25]

Thus, centrist Christologies try to engage reciprocally their open but critical attitude toward tradition with their open but critical attitude toward contemporary experience. From this critical dialogue, they hope, will flow a balanced Christology for today which remains in basic continuity with the Christologies of the past. Let me now highlight some of the major trends among our centrists. The remainder of this book will attempt to put their contributions to work in more detail.[26]

First of all, centrist Christologies are pluralistic. There is no one governing approach to the study of Jesus, but a variety of methods and views, in varying degrees under the influence of the three great transitions which we sketched in the previous chapter. This is a part of our complex situation presently, and it presents us with a much more radical variety than the past Christian tradition knew. The increasing specialization of the human and physical sciences (including theology), the complex historical research into Christian origins currently emerging, the variety of cultural and methodological backgrounds of various scholars—all of this presents us with a terribly complex situation.

Centrist Christologies frankly recognize the fact of theological pluralism. While it is messy and confusing, it also promises a greater depth in our Christological thinking. This new pluralism forces theologians to develop a more dialogical approach to their task. Because no one person can master all the materials alone, each theologian must strive to remain in contact with a wide variety of thinkers. Critical dialogue is the only way to avoid both narrowness of viewpoint and a crippling relativism which escapes into the patently discredited idea that every view is equally good. Out of this pluralism emerges the differing perspectives among the centrists.[27]

Second, some among the centrists, probably most, dwell upon Christological questions which primarily flow from the concerns of our first great transition sketched above. The contemporary turn to experience, to personalism, to nature, and to history are overriding concerns of these thinkers. Armed with these particular sensitivities, they attempt to rethink Christology in a creatively contemporary manner. A first example of these theologians is found among those centrists who concentrate upon the modern turn to experience and seek to ground Christological beliefs in a philosophically analyzed view of human experience. Sometimes this trend is called a "Christology from below," because it attempts to make sense of the Christological tradition from our human point of view by developing a view of human experience which can throw light upon Jesus.

The designation "from below" is somewhat misleading, for usually these thinkers work from a religious view of experience, according to which the Divine is somehow present within our human existence. Because of this, the "Above" (= the Divine) is also "below," within the human. In other words, a Christology from below is not a reduction of Christology to some form of secular humanism, as some writers seem to suggest.

Perhaps the most well known example of this trend is the brilliant thought of the German Jesuit Karl Rahner. Using a kind of phenomenological analysis of human existence (= hermeneutics), he has developed, quite plausibly, a view of the human person as a living response to the Unlimited Mystery of God which forms the horizon of every human person. Paraphrasing Rahner, we are all in our very beings "potential hearers of the Word." Our humanity is developed and actualized to the degree that we open ourselves to this mysterious horizon of our lives. One of the famous Rahnerian formulas brings this out well: human actualization develops in direct, not inverse, proportion to our relationship with the Divine. Rahner proposes that what we encounter in Jesus is the greatest instance of human actualization: his humanity is a supreme embodiment of our common human openness to the Divine Mystery.

Other thinkers may use different philosophical tools, but in every in-

stance the dominant concern is to cast light upon Jesus from the point of
view of a philosophically analyzed view of human experience. A further example is the German Protestant Wolfhart Pannenberg, who bases his work
upon an evolutionary philosophy, partly indebted to Hegel. History is
viewed as constantly moving into the future, and the Divine is seen as the
foundation and goal of history, the "Absolute and Final Future." Pannenberg then creatively recasts Christology in the light of this philosophy: Jesus becomes the one through whom the Absolute Future breaks into
history and reveals, proleptically, history's ultimate goal. The ultimate key
to history's meaningfulness is preliminarily disclosed within history
through the life, death, and resurrection of Jesus.[28]

Let me mention Hans Urs von Balthasar's project as a final example
of the attempt to recast Christology in the light of a philosophically analyzed view of human experience. While Rahner turns to a phenomenological analysis of human experience, and Pannenberg to an evolutionary
analysis of history, Von Balthasar turns to the rich realm of aesthetic experience. Perhaps more than anyone else he has tried to revitalize the significance of the experience of beauty for theology. The two poles of
love/charity and the perception of divine glory/radiance form the bases of
his rich Christology, and he sees these bases analogously reflected in our
common experience of beauty. For the splendor of an object can only at-
tract the beholder through some form of eros, which is a pull of attraction
of love. But simultaneously the object of our love must appear wonderful
and glorious for this erotic pull to occur. The experience of beauty is an
intersection between human love (eros) and transcendent glory, and this
is precisely what comes to expression in the Jesus event.

Drawing upon the Gospel of John, Von Balthasar proposes that Jesus
unites the two poles of love and glory: he is at once a fullness of mercy
and love, and yet the presence of divine glory. He is, at once, a human
loving openness to divine glory. "And we have seen his glory: the glory of
an only Son coming from the Father, filled with enduring love" (Jn 1:14).[29]
Just as in art the form or work strikes us as radiant and splendid because of
the beauty of the reality which offers itself to us, so Christ becomes the
form through which we are ravished by the radiance of the Divine.
Through the medium of Jesus our eyes are empowered with a new light by
which we see the glory of the Divine. We become enraptured, carried outside of ourselves to the transcendent glory experienced in the form of
Jesus.[30]

Von Balthasar has a predilection for the analogy with aesthetic experience, because it intensifies the transcendent dimension disclosed in the
Jesus event:

When one experiences startling beauty . . . what confronts us is over-
powering, like a miracle . . . just as in love I encounter the other *as* the
other in all his freedom, and am confronted by something which I cannot
dominate in any sense, so in the aesthetic sphere, it is impossible to attribute the form which presents itself to a fiction of my imagination.[31]

Here I would read Von Balthasar as a corrective to the possible tendency
to reduce revelation to simply a human-made reality: ultimately the Jesus
event is an experience of transcendent glory. As he further expresses it,
the object of our love, in the realm of aesthetic experience,

always appears wonderful and glorious to us; and objective glory attracts
the beholder only by being some sort of eros. . . . The two related poles
were surpassed in Revelation where the divine Logos descends to manifest and interpret himself as love, as *agape,* and therein as the Glory.[32]

So far Von Balthasar's project remains incomplete. Building upon his
theological aesthetics, he has worked out a "theological dramatics," in
which he examines the life and thought of significant saints and mystics
who have been profoundly ravished by the Radiance of Jesus. This dramatics illustrates his contention that a true Christian praxis or ethics must
flow from a conversion to the beauty of the Jesus event. In this respect,
Von Balthasar links up with the concerns of practical theologians, to which
we will come shortly. In a further "theological logic" he hopes to explore,
somewhat like Rahner and Pannenberg, the philosophical and theological
implications of the beauty of the Jesus event.[33]

Other scholars, reflecting the new historical consciousness characteristic of our first great transition, seek to employ the methods and concerns
of the historical sciences in an attempt to render Christology more meaningful for today. If the thinkers we have just mentioned concentrate upon
the contemporary experience pole of Christology, these scholars dwell
upon the tradition pole. Like the philosophical approach just sketched
above, it would seem that the historical avenue into Christology attempts
to perform two services. On the one hand, it attempts to enable us to
achieve a more adequate or "appropriate" understanding of what our
Christological tradition really is. For example, biblical historians will attempt to reconstruct the most authentic texts of the New Testament from
the varied and competing manuscripts. This is a first presupposition for
any adequate interpretation of this phase of our tradition. Further, these
scholars will attempt to reconstruct the events and meanings of the New
Testament witness to Jesus, thus clarifying for us what it is precisely that
the New Testament proclaims about Jesus.

On the other hand, the historical approach in Christology can be used to correct apparent inadequacies in the tradition in the light of our contemporary understanding. Here, as David Tracy helpfully points out, the issue is not an appropriate interpretation of the tradition's own self-understanding, but a correction or new interpretation of the tradition in the light of our ongoing research. This function of the historical method deals more with questions of "intelligibility" for modern twentieth century people who have developed a critical historical consciousness.[34] For example, Tracy points to the emergence of evolutionary theories which challenged a literal reading of Genesis. He also points to how the emerging historical study of the New Testament has challenged the view of the Gospels as simple "biographies" in our modern sense. As we will see in the next chapter, the quest for the historical Jesus is also a modern attempt to make the historical Jesus credible to modern critical people, and to show how the New Testament is an adequate "interpretation" of who Jesus really was. In this way, historical interpretation or hermeneutics protects our biblical and Christological heritage in a highly critical age.[35]

Allied with, and I think complementary to, the philosophical and historical approach to Christology is an emerging literary-critical avenue of approach to the Christological tradition. Like those other approaches, this one too serves both to facilitate an appropriate interpretation of the tradition's self-understanding, and to correct that tradition in the light of our developing understanding. It helps us arrive at a more appropriate interpretation of the tradition's own self-understanding in various ways. It reminds us, for example, that our New Testament is first of all a text, composed of various literary genres and images and symbols structured by those genres. An understanding of the letter genre, or the story-narrative genre of the Gospels, is essential for coming to grasp the meaning of the New Testament. An appreciation of the "mythical" nature of the "Kingdom of God" language in the New Testament or of the metaphorical nature of the Gospel parables can aid us in appropriately interpreting the Scriptures.

Literary-critical analysis can also correct the tradition's self-understanding by proposing new interpretations in the light of our current understanding. For example, a literary-critical analysis of the nature of myth can help the modern critical person to overcome the prejudice against myth as a false, outdated interpretation of reality. Armed with a new appreciation of myth as a colorful and imagistic expression of authentic experiences, the modern reader can approach the rich mythical symbolism of New Testament Christology with new meaning. In this respect, literary-critical analysis deals with questions of intelligibility for modern people and renders an essential service in a highly critical age.

Perhaps alone among modern theorists, Paul Ricoeur stands out as an enormously impressive thinker who has attempted to develop a literary-critical approach to tradition which is in genuine conversation with other, alternative methods. Because of the integrative nature of his project, I think that his general interpretation theory could serve as an appropriate model which unites the authentic concerns of the emerging methods of Christology into a kind of critical synthesis. Let me sketch at this point some of the more fundamental elements of his theory. Then in my own proposal for a Christological method I will return to him.

Perhaps most importantly, Ricoeur's interpretation theory or hermeneutics bases itself upon a theory of the text. This is not without significance for those of us working in Christology, for our primary traditional sources are texts, particularly the great text of the Scriptures. Especially key is the distinction between a "speech-event" or "performance" of past agents and authors, and "textual meaning and truth." While history-oriented theologians tend to dwell upon the attempted reconstruction of the former, Ricoeur's literary-critical analysis dwells upon the latter. The text possesses meaning and truth precisely because it transcends an original speech-event by fixing meaning and truth textually. As David Tracy, who is deeply influenced by Ricoeur at this point, explains it,

> What we write is the meaning, the *noema* of our speech-events, not the event itself. Once I write, it is my text alone which bears the meaning; not my intention in writing it; not my original audience's reaction to it.[36]

The text's meaning and truth, then, is ideal (or "noematic"): "What happens in writing is . . . the detachment of meaning from the event."[37] As such, the text becomes "distanciated"[38] from just those features that are usually of primary interest to the historical critic: the author's intentions, the audience addressed, the reconstruction of events and personal stances "before" the text, etc. Thus, for literary criticism, the method of interpretation of meaning and truth is primarily semantic and literary. The literary interpreter will dwell upon the meaning and truth ideally present in a work's genres (letters, stories, myths, etc.) and in its leading images and symbols which are structured by those genres ("Kingdom of God," "Abba," etc., in the case of the New Testament).

A further important element for Ricoeur is the distinction between a text's "sense" and its "reference." Since this distinction is rather crucial, let me quote Ricoeur himself:

> *Sinn* [sense] is the ideal objective content of a proposition; *Bedeutung* [reference] is its claim to truth. . . . Meaning is what a statement says,

> reference is *that about which* it says it. What a statement says is imma-
> nent within it—it is its internal arrangement. That with which it deals is
> extra-linguistic. It is the real insofar as it is conveyed in language; it is
> what is said about the world.[39]

Here Ricoeur relies upon his view that the function of language is "to articulate our experience of the world, to give form to this experience."[40]
The interpretation process, then, does not stop with the "sense" found immanently within the text. Interpretation must wrestle with the reference,
the potential disclosure of the world of reality which the work opens up to
the reader "in front of the text." The reference is "the disclosure of a possible way of looking at things."[41]

At this point let me interject a point of some interest to Christology.
Ricoeur's stress upon the "reference" of the (biblical) text is of special interest to a religion like Christianity which is rooted in the historical reality
of the Jesus event. Literary-critical analysis does not deny that this historical reality may be one of the more important "references" of the biblical
text. This seems worth emphasizing, since there are literary critics who
needlessly confine criticism to a text's sense (its immanent meaning), ignoring its referential power (the world of reality about which it "speaks").
In fact, some writers have spoken of the unique character of the biblical
texts which flow from Christianity's and Judaism's historical origins. Hans
Frei, for example, speaks of the history-like character of the biblical narratives. They are "realistic" narratives. Thus, in the New Testament attention is paid to personalities, and to the interaction between characters and
events. This "history-like" character of the biblical narratives illustrates
that a part of the referential power of the Scriptures is to raise questions
about the nature of historical reality itself.[42] This would seem sufficient to
protect literary-critical analysis from the charge of denying the historical
roots of our faith.

A further feature of literary-critical analysis is its avoidance of the
"psychologism" of some forms of textual and historical interpretation. Psychologism refers to the tendency to view textual interpretation as the art
of one ego (the interpreter's) trying to plumb the depths of another's ego
(namely, the author of the text). Literary-critical analysis aims for something quite different, and more attainable. For the interpreter, the aim is
not to "master" another ego through some sort of re-enactment of that
ego's intentions. The aim is to break free of one's ego and open oneself to
a text. The goal is not the intentionality of an author "behind" a text, but
openness to the "world of the text" itself. This is how Ricoeur puts it:

> Are we not putting the meaning of the text under the power of the sub-
> ject who interprets it? This objection may be removed if we keep in

mind that what is "made one's own" is not something mental, not the intention of another subject, presumably hidden behind the text, but the project of a world, the pro-position of a mode of being in the world that the text opens up in front of itself by means of its non-ostensive references. Far from saying that a subject already mastering his own way of being in the world projects the *a priori* of his self-understanding on the text and reads it into the text, I say that interpretation is the process by which disclosure of new modes of being . . . gives to the subject a new capacity for knowing himself.[43]

If I read him correctly, Ricoeur is arguing that all forms of interpretation, even historical interpretation, do not properly psychologize. One does not try to peek, psychologically, behind the text, but one opens oneself to the world of the text. All forms of interpretation attempt to appropriate the world opened up in front of the text. In this way, we are following the natural movement which conveys meaning to us: "the movement of the internal structure of the work toward its reference, toward the sort of world which the work opens up *in front of* the text."[44]

Ricoeur's form of literary-critical analysis is a needed corrective to other forms of analysis currently being employed in Christology. Its corrective function lies in its greater attentiveness to the texts of our tradition, which philosophical and historical forms of analysis tend to bypass too quickly. The latter forms of analysis tend to leave us with abstractions from the texts, rather than with the rich and diverse world of images and genres characteristic of the texts themselves. The Gospels and epistles are much more rich and diverse than we have been led to believe. Furthermore, the richly "poetic" and metaphorical language of the Bible protects the religious and transcendent dimension of the Jesus-event in a way that philosophical and historical abstractions cannot.

But literary-critical analysis, at least as practiced by Ricoeur, is complementary to other forms of analysis. As we will see in our brief chapter on a proposed method for Christology, Ricoeur thinks that there is a place for other methods in our attempt to interpret the meaning (sense and references) of the great texts of our tradition. All methods can play a role as ways of refining the "world opened up to us in front of the text."

A third trend among centrist Christologians is characterized by the attempt to learn from the lessons of our second great transition, and to apply these to Christology. This means that they pay attention to the reality of evil and human pathology, to the reality of the psychosocial and political, and to the reality of human practice, seeking clues for a revitalized Christology for today. What are the varied ways in which centrists reflect these concerns?

Some centrists seek to correct the historical approach to the tradition by bringing out the psychosocial dimensions of the past, a concern often ignored by more traditional historical approaches. Again, as was the case with our other approaches, psychosocial criticism aids us both in achieving a more appropriate view of the tradition's self-understanding and in correcting the tradition in the light of new data and concerns. It provides us with a more appropriate/adequate view of the tradition when it helps us appreciate the social-political-psychological concerns opened up by the text itself. For example, through this kind of analysis we can begin to appreciate how the New Testament is a response to the political calamities brought on by the tension between the Jewish culture and the occupation of Palestine through the Roman Empire. This aids us in reappropriating the social punch and relevance of the New Testament message as a real response to human crises.

Psychosocial criticism can also aid us in correcting or challenging the tradition in the light of new sensitivities revealed by our modern situation. For example, feminist theologians have steadily revealed the dominant patriarchalism of the biblical heritage and the tendency of the tradition to suppress the important role that women played in Christian history. Political and liberation theologians have challenged the tradition's loss of the political and social relevance of the Jesus event and have attempted to work out a Christology more sensitive to these concerns. Theologians influenced by contemporary psychological theories have attempted to recapture the healing/therapeutic dimensions of the Jesus event. Theologians in dialogue with the Frankfurt School have tried to develop a hermeneutics of suspicion, enabling them to locate destructive trends in both tradition and contemporary Church and society. I would be inclined to place the possible theological use of the deconstructionist trend in criticism here too. This trend seems to intensify the negative/critical element in criticism: it suspects every text and every tradition and every interpreter. It tries to hinder premature and naive analyses, much as a hermeneutics of suspicion. Insofar as its negativity is a moment within a simultaneously positive approach to tradition and experience, I would expect to see a deconstructionist trend more fully emerging in Christology. All of these approaches indicate that psychosocial criticism is quickly becoming a new and important partner in the theological task, which seeks to combine theory and praxis in a new dialogical relationship.[45]

A special contribution of psychosocial writing in Christology is that of revitalizing an interest in soteriology (= Jesus' saving work) and the need to highlight the interconnection between Christology and soteriology. Schillebeeckx' work is a fine recent example of the conviction, shared by all psychosocial critics, that Christology emerges out of soteriology or at least alongside of it: it is because people find in him a saving answer to their needs, struggles, failures, and sins that they develop a fascination for Jesus. Some theologians of a more traditionally philosophical or historical orientation have not ignored soteriology, but it is a peculiar emphasis of praxis-oriented work in Christology. In this sense, this new orientation in theology is aiding us in recovering the fuller contours of the Jesus event as a salvific experience on behalf of the needs of persons other than Jesus.

Fourth, some few centrists are turning their attention to the concerns which flow from our third great transition of globalization. Their sensitivity to this issue has caused them to ask whether our Christological work has not been too provincial, too isolated, and too Western. On the one hand, this new "global horizon" can aid us in achieving a more appropriate interpretation of the tradition's own self-understanding. For example, we can begin to reappreciate the fact that our Christological tradition is in some real sense a "global" tradition. The New Testament is not simply Jewish and Christian, but a confluence of Near Eastern, Greco-Roman, and perhaps even Far Eastern traditions. But, on the other hand and more commonly, global analysis serves to correct and challenge the tradition's self-understanding in the light of new sensitivities. It forces us to recognize that divine revelation is not simply the preserve of an isolated Jewish-Christian tradition. As one of the great global theologians of our times, Eric Voegelin, puts it: we need to come to terms with the Christ "in a Babylonian hymn, or a Taoist speculation, or a Platonic dialogue, just as much as in a Gospel." And he adds that we cannot "let revelation begin with the Israelite and Christian experiences, when the mystery of divine presence in reality is attested as experienced by man, as far back as ca. 20,000 B.C., by the petroglyphic symbols of the Palaeolithicum."[46] Needless to say, this forces modern Christologians to be more cautious in the judgments they make about the Christ who is Jesus.

Global analysis in Christology is in its infancy presently. In this particular work, I will try to be sensitive to it by attempting to place the Jesus event within the general context of humanity's global history. This will force the reader to query the possible relationship between the Jesus event and other great breakthroughs in revelation which have occurred within history. And this will prepare a context for a consideration of the uniqueness of Jesus, a question which, from the Christian side, seems to be a first hurdle we need to consider before we can be freed for a more extensive dialogue with the religions of our one common earth.

Fifth, centrist Christologies are conflictual. It should be evident from the above that not only are centrists pluralistic, they are also in varying degrees of competition and conflict with one another. Often they agree neither in their starting points nor in their conclusions. This, too, is a reflection of our contemporary situation, in which no one authority is able to dictate a Christological consensus. While this breeds confusion and complexity, it is a necessary consequence of the free competition of ideas and practices, and that free competition is the best safeguard against a narrow theological totalitarianism and a crippling relativism.

Ideas and practices compete: they must legitimate themselves before other scholars and their concerns. This conflictual character perhaps shows up most clearly between political theologians who stress the social punch of the Jesus event, and more philosophical theologians who are content with rather more abstract formulations of the Jesus event. But it also shows up all along the line: theologians will not agree on the philosophical theories which are most promising for a renewed Christology; historians will not agree on the factual details of the tradition; literary analysts will not agree upon the most promising methods of literary analysis; political theologians will not agree upon the political and economic visions which are in accord with a reformulated Christology. Paul Ricoeur will call this the "conflict of interpretations," and what can save each approach from narrowness is a free and public dialogical competition among scholars. That the outcome of this free "competition" will not be sterile is a hope that I think is warranted, for centrists do seem agreed upon the general model for a renewed Christology: a critical correlation between tradition and experience.

Finally, centrists seem to cut across the varied denominational divides. They seem to represent a newly emerging post-ecumenical form of theology. A sampling of the references I have provided for each of these trends would quickly confirm this. This is also reflective of our modern times. As scholars recognize that it is not Church authorities as such but the two poles of tradition and experience which constitute the basis of theology, then theology inevitably becomes ecumenical and global. For tradition and experience obviously cut across the Churches and are a preserve of all of them.

Protestants, it seems, recognized the ecumenical nature of theology quite early, for they were the first among the Churches to tangle with the new turn to experience brought on by our first great transition. But Catholicism, too, has joined ranks with them. *The Dogmatic Constitution on Divine Revelation* of the Second Vatican Council very clearly affirmed the ultimate authority of our two poles: the "teaching office is not above the word of God, but serves it, teaching only what has been handed on, listening to it devoutly, guarding it scrupulously, and explaining it faithfully. . . ." And the important document *Mysterium Ecclesiae*, the 1973 declaration of the Roman Doctrinal Congregation, clearly affirmed the need to be open to the lessons of ongoing experience. For it held that the past teachings of the Church are "formulated in terms that bear traces of 'the changeable conceptions of a given epoch' and solve only certain questions and then incompletely."[47]

Eastern Orthodoxy, too, is increasingly finding its place among the ranks of the centrists, particularly among its theologians of the Orthodox "diaspora." As the diaspora theologians confront the problems characteristic of our great transitions, their contributions become more self-critical. On the other hand, Western theologians have much to learn from the Orthodox. Their great appreciation for the patristic tradition is an antidote to the tendency to shrink the Christian tradition down to simply the Scriptures. Their profoundly mystical understanding of experience has enabled them to avoid the damaging post-Enlightenment temptation of narrowing human experience to only sense experience. Their Christological contribution promises to be a creative rethinking of the heritage of the Fathers and a renewed emphasis upon its spiritual and mystical meaning for modern humanity.[48]

A special problem for the Christologian is presented by the varied Christian "sects"—namely, the Jehovah's Witnesses, Quakers, Hutterites, Christian Scientists, Mormons, etc. For the most part these sects remain fundamentalists; they can hardly be said to be centrist. Still, there is much to be gained from a critical dialogue with them. Often they represent an important critique of the "underside" of the other, more "established" denominations, a protest against their narrowness. Their experience of alienation, breaking away, and critique has enabled them to discover a dimension of Jesus left underdeveloped by the "greater Churches." I am thinking of the sects' critique of the excessive hierarchical structure of the Churches, their stress upon equality and community, sometimes even their stress upon the full equality of women with men within the Churches. Frequently we find among them a recovery of the apocalyptic message of Jesus as an expression of their own yearning for a more equitable future. All of these insights are rooted in their understanding of the Jesus event, and today's Christologies should learn how to reappropriate them as they attempt to revitalize Christology for today.[49]

This completes our short sketch of the main trends among Christologians today. Hopefully the reader will have gained a perspective for "placing" the various writers who are currently engaged in the Christological task. In the next chapter I will make an attempt to integrate the varied centrists into a unified and dialogical approach to the study of Jesus, an approach which I hope to put to good use throughout the remainder of this book.

MODERN CHRISTOLOGIES

varied reactions to the three great transitions: the turn to experience, the awareness of human pathology, today's global horizon

Leftists	Centrists	Rightists
• accept the anti-religious strain of the Enlightenment	• open and critical with respect to tradition and contemporary experience	• tend to resist the modern turn to experience
• tend to deny the divine elements in their reading of the Christological tradition	• varied trends	• tend to be uncritical in the study of Christology
• Jesus tends to be simply humanized; Christology becomes a projection/fantasy to be explained psychologically or sociologically	(1) dwell upon first transition issues -philosophical explorations of the experiential foundations of Christology -use of historical sciences to appropriate and correct Christological tradition -use of literary-critical analysis to appropriate and correct Christology (2) dwell on second transition issues: psycho-social analysis to interpret and critique (3) sensitivity to today's global horizon	• result in a fundamentalist monophysitism which undervalues Jesus' humanity

Notes

1. As cited in David R. Cartlidge and David L. Dungan, *Documents for the Study of the Gospels* (Philadelphia: Fortress, 1980), p. 16; cf *The Apology*, I.21,22.

2. For the decree, see: *The Christology of the Later Fathers* (London: SCM, 1950), pp. 372–373; for Clement, *The Exhortation to the Greeks*, 1, 8 (G.W. Butterworth, trans. [New York: G.P. Putnam's Sons, 1919], p. 23).

3. *The Fourth World Conference on Faith and Order, Montreal, 1963*, P.C. Rodgers and L. Vischer, eds. (New York: Association Press, 1964), p. 51.

4. Gerald O'Collins, *Fundamental Theology* (New York: Paulist, 1981), p. 221.

5. Cf James P. Mackey, *Tradition and Change in the Church* (Dayton, Ohio: Pflaum, 1968), pp. 133–134.

6. See Ernest R. Sandeen, *The Origins of Fundamentalism*, Facet Books #10, Historical Series (Philadelphia: Fortress, 1968).

7. Raymond E. Brown, "The Importance of How Doctrine Is Understood," *Origins* 10 (1981), 739; cf 738–743 (for the whole).

8. *Ibid.*, 741.

9. *Reimarus: Fragments*, Charles H. Talbert, ed. (Philadelphia: Fortress, 1970), p. 234.

10. *Ibid.*, pp. 69–70.

11. (New York: Macmillan, 1963), p. 103, p. 155. Cf Paul M. van Buren's *Discerning the Way: A Theology of the Jewish-Christian Reality* (New York: Seabury, 1980) for changes in his thinking toward a more centrist position.

12. Erich Fromm, *The Dogma of Christ and Other Essays on Religion, Psychology and Culture* (Greenwich, Conn.: Fawcett, 1963), p. 49; cf pp. 15–93 (for the whole).

13. *Ibid.*, p. 54

14. *Ibid.*, p. 68.

15. *Ibid.*, p. 69.

16. *Psychoanalysis and Religion, op. cit.*, p. 36.

17. *Ibid.*, p. 37.

18. *Ibid.*, p. 47; he has not apparently changed his mind: cf the 1963 foreword to *The Dogma of Christ, op. cit.*, p. 11.

19. See, for example, Edward F. Edinger, *Christ as Paradigm of the Individuating Ego* (New York: Analytical Psychology Club of New York, 1966). The best study on Jung that I have seen is Robert M. Doran, "Jungian Psychology and Christian Spirituality," *Review for Religious* 38 (1979), 497–510, 742–752, 857–866. For a positive neo-Marxist analysis of Jesus, see M. Machovec, *A Marxist Looks at Jesus* (Philadelphia: Fortress, 1976).

20. Fromm, *Psychoanalysis and Religion, op. cit.*, p. 37.

21. Abraham H. Maslow, *Religions, Values, and Peak-Experiences* (New York: Viking, 1964), p. 20.

22. *Out of My Life and Thought, op. cit.*, p. 183.

23. For surveys of these engaging thinkers, see James Livingston, *op. cit.*, pp. 245–270, 271–300, 418–445. Schleiermacher (among Protestants) and Von Hü-

gel (among Catholics) were perhaps the greatest and most balanced. See Martin Redeker, *Schleiermacher: Life and Thought* (Philadelphia: Fortress, 1973), and Joseph P. Whelan, *The Spirituality of Friedrich von Hügel* (New York: Newman/Paulist, 1971).

24. For surveys, see Livingston, *ibid.*, pp. 301–344, 345–384, 446–477 (for the neo-Orthodox). They were called "neo-Orthodox" because they were open to modernity in secular matters (hence, "neo"), but stressed, like the Orthodox, the radical otherness of the Divine and the fallenness of humanity. Thus they tended to use paradoxical, dialectical, and antagonistic language: the Divine is over-against and paradoxical to human wisdom. For Von Balthasar, see Medard Kell and Werner Löser, eds., *The Von Balthasar Reader* (New York: Crossroad, 1982).

25. The literature is enormous. For language analysis, see Terrence W. Tilley, *Talking of God: An Introduction to Philosophical Analysis of Religious Language* (New York: Paulist, 1978); for phenomenology, see Langdon Gilkey, *Naming the Whirlwind: The Renewal of God-Language* (Indianapolis and New York: Bobbs-Merrill, 1969), pp. 241–246, 276–284; for the mystics, see Louis Dupré, "The Mystical Experience of the Self and Its Philosophical Significance," *International Philosophical Quarterly* 14 (1974), 495–511; for the recovery of negative experiences, see Johann Baptist Metz, *Faith in History and Society: Toward a Practical Fundamental Theology* (New York: Seabury, 1980).

26. For another helpful survey, I recommend Francis Schüssler Fiorenza, "Christology after Vatican II," *The Ecumenist* 18 (1980), 81–89.

27. See Karl Rahner's breakthrough writings on pluralism and the new form of theological dialogue this calls for: "A Small Question Regarding the Contemporary Pluralism in the Intellectual Situation of Catholics and the Church," and "Reflections on Dialogue within a Pluralistic Society," *Theological Investigations* VI (Baltimore: Helicon, 1969), pp. 21–30, 31–42; "Pluralism in Theology and the Unity of the Creed in the Church," *Theological Investigations* XI (New York: Seabury, 1974), pp. 3–23. Cf also Bernard Lonergan, *Doctrinal Pluralism* (Milwaukee: Marquette University, 1971).

28. See Leo J. O'Donovan, ed., *A World of Grace: An Introduction to the Themes and Foundations of Karl Rahner's Theology* (New York: Seabury, 1980); Wolfhart Pannenberg, *Jesus—God and Man: An Essay in Christology* (Philadelphia: Fortress, 1971). Other representative philosophical approaches: American process theology, Bernard Lonergan's transcendental theology, Walter Kasper's historical-idealist theology, etc.

29. For his summary of his project, see *Love Alone* (New York: Herder and Herder, 1969), esp. pp. 43–50.

30. Cf Aidan Nichols, *op. cit.*, p. 137, for a helpful application of Von Balthasar.

31. Von Balthasar, *Love Alone, op. cit.*, pp. 44–45.

32. *Ibid.*, p. 45.

33. His *Herrlichkeit: Eine theologische Ästhetik*, 6 volumes (Einsiedeln: Johannesverlag, 1961–1969), treats his aesthetic starting point; his praxis is found in *Theodramatik*, 3 volumes (Einsiedeln: Johannesverlag, 1973–1978); his "theological logics" is yet to be finished.

34. For the helpful distinction between an "appropriate" interpretation of the tradition's self-understanding and a corrective interpretation in the light of the needs of contemporary intelligibility, see David Tracy, *The Analogical Imagination: Christian Theology and the Culture of Pluralism* (New York: Crossroad, 1981), pp. 237–241.

35. Representative history-oriented theologians: Walter Kasper, *Jesus the Christ* (New York: Paulist, 1976), combined with philosophical analysis; Edward Schillebeeckx, *Jesus: An Experiment in Christology* and *Christ: The Experience of Jesus as Lord* (New York: Seabury, 1979, 1980), combined with philosophical and political analysis; George H. Tavard, *Images of the Christ: An Enquiry into Christology* (Washington D.C.: University Press of America, 1982), combined with philosophical analysis; my own *Jesus, Lord and Savior: A Theopathic Christology and Soteriology* (New York: Paulist, 1980), combined with philosophical analysis. Hans Küng's *On Being a Christian* (Garden City, New York: Doubleday, 1976), in its Christological section, pp. 119–457, is primarily historical in method.

36. David Tracy, *Blessed Rage for Order: The New Pluralism in Theology* (New York: Seabury, 1975), p. 75. Cf. Paul Ricoeur, *Interpretation Theory: Discourse and the Surplus of Meaning* (Fort Worth, Texas: Texas Christian University, 1976), esp. pp. 75–76, for Tracy's inspiration: "Here perhaps my opposition to Romanticist hermeneutics is most forceful. . . . The Romanticist forms of hermeneutics overlooked the specific situation created by the disjunction of the verbal meaning of the text from the mental intention of the author. The fact is that the author can no longer 'rescue' his work. . . . His intention is often unknown to us, sometimes redundant, sometimes useless, and sometimes even harmful as regards the interpretation of the verbal meaning of his work. In even the better cases it has to be taken into account in light of the text itself. . . . understanding takes place in a non-psychological and properly semantical space, which the text has carved out by severing itself from the mental intention of its author." Cf Hans-Georg Gadamer, *Truth and Method* (New York: Seabury, 1975), p. 357, for a similar view of the distanciation of the text.

Helpful here on Ricoeur is Mary Gerhart, *The Question of Belief in Literary Criticism: An Introduction to the Hermeneutical Theory of Paul Ricoeur* (Stuttgart: Hans-Dieter Heinz, 1979), and John W. Van Den Hengel, *The Home of Meaning: The Hermeneutics of the Subject of Paul Ricoeur* (Washington, D.C.: University Press of America, 1982).

37. Ricoeur, *ibid.*, p. 25.

38. For this notion, see Paul Ricoeur, "The Hermeneutical Function of Distanciation," *Philosophy Today* 17 (1973), 129–141. Also *Interpretation Theory, ibid.*, pp. 25–37. Some of what is implied here: (1) the author's meaning/truth now takes on a new form in the text as a potential source of meaning; (2) spoken discourse is local; but a text is potentially universal and creates its own public; (3) the works of language become as self-contained as sculptures; the text's meaning is freed from its situational limits.

39. Paul Ricoeur, "Biblical Hermenutics," *Semeia* 4 (1975), 81.

40. *Ibid.*

41. *Interpretation Theory, op. cit.*, p. 92.

42. Cf Hans W. Frei, *The Eclipse of the Biblical Narrative: A Study in Eighteenth and Nineteenth Century Hermeneutics* (New York: Yale, 1974), esp. pp. 1–16, and Erich Auerbach, *Mimesis: The Representation of Reality in Western Literature* (Garden City, N.Y.: Doubleday, 1957).

43. *Interpretation Theory, op. cit.*, p. 94.

44. Ricoeur, "Biblical Hermeneutics," *art. cit.*, 82. Cf Mary Gerhart, "Imagination and History in Ricoeur's Interpretation Theory," *Philosophy Today* 23 (1979), 51–68, and Van Den Hengel, *op. cit.*, pp. 140–142. Gadamer, *op. cit.*, shares a similar view, pp. 299–305. For a beginner's application of literary analysis to Scripture, see William A. Beardslee, *Literary Criticism of the New Testament* (Philadelphia: Fortress, 1970).

45. Some representative examples: Howard Clark Kee, *Christian Origins in Sociological Perspective* (Philadelphia: Westminster, 1980); Jon Sobrino, *Christology at the Crossroads* (Maryknoll: Orbis, 1978); Rosemary Radford Ruether, *New Woman/New Earth: Sexist Ideologies and Human Liberation, op. cit.*; Bernard J. Tyrrell, *Christotherapy: Healing Through Enlightenment* (New York: Seabury, 1975), and *Christotherapy II: A New Horizion for Counselors, Spiritual Directors and Seekers of Healing and Growth in Christ* (New York: Paulist, 1982); and Robbin Scroggs, "Psychology as a Tool To Interpret the Text," *The Christian Century* 99 (1982), 335–338; Matthew L. Lamb, *Solidarity with Victims: Toward a Theology of Social Transformation* (New York: Crossroad, 1982), for a creative adaptation of the Frankfurt School; Jonathan Culler, *On Deconstruction: Theory and Criticism after Structuralism* (Ithaca, New York: Cornell University, 1982); Mark C. Taylor, *De-constructing Theology* (New York and Chico, Cal.: Crossroad and Scholars Press, 1982); Thomas J.J. Altizer, *Total Presence: The Language of Jesus and the Language of Today* (New York: Seabury, 1980).

46. Eric Voegelin, "Response to Professor Altizer's 'A New History and a New But Ancient God?' " *Journal of the American Academy of Religion* 43 (1975), 766, 777. A good recent example of global analysis is John B. Cobb, Jr., *Beyond Dialogue: Toward a Mutual Transformation of Christianity and Buddhism* (Philadelphia: Fortress, 1982).

47. N. 10 (*The Documents of Vatican II, op. cit.*, p. 118), and Brown, *art. cit.*, citing the declaration, 740.

48. Cf John Meyendorff, *Living Tradition: Orthodox Witness in the Contemporary World* (Crestwood, N.Y.: St. Vladimir's Seminary Press, 1978).

49. For a creative appropriation of the sects, see Rosemary Radford Ruether, *The Church Against Itself* (New York: Herder and Herder, 1967). A helpful overview: Donald F. Durnbaugh, *The Believers' Church: The History and Character of Radical Protestantism* (New York: Macmillan, 1968).

4

A Possible Method for Christology

Now that we have noted the various trends among centrist Christologies, let us try to formulate a method that will help us to be open to and critical of each of their concerns—open to them, because out of their creative correlation between tradition and contemporary experience the best prospects for a renewed Christology seem to emerge; critical of them, because they are conflictual, and we cannot necessarily agree with every possible insight each of them has to offer. What follows is a sketchy formulation of a method which students can use to sift their way through the complicated labyrinth of today's centrist thinkers. It will also be the method which this book employs as it weaves its way through the central issues of today's Christology. I would place this approach within the hermeneutical tradition, because that tradition has been concerned with the appropriation of meaning, truth, and practice in a highly reflective way. Thus, I rely greatly upon Paul Ricoeur's interpretation theory, using especially its integrative openness. Hans-Georg Gadamer, Eric Voegelin, and David Tracy have also been particularly influential over this approach, and Karl Rahner and Bernard Lonergan have exercised influence in a more general way. "Hermeneutics," in general, simply refers to the study of interpretation.

(1) First, as we have indicated, a renewed Christology will flow from a creative engagement between the two poles of Christian theology—namely, tradition and contemporary experience. Tradition, because Christianity is tradition-bound. It believes that divine revelation has been communicated to us through history, especially through the events of Jesus and his work. Contemporary experience, because the tradition has to be appropriated anew in each age, made "actual" in each age; otherwise, it remains a dead letter.

It is important to recognize that this creative engagement is truly a two-way process. The tradition provokes questions to our present concerns, but our present concerns also raise questions of the tradition. Through this creative engagement, sometimes we will find that our two poles of theology are in agreement; sometimes tradition critiques and enriches our present, but also sometimes our present critiques and enriches our tradition.

(2) We can better understand the creative engagement between tradition and contemporary experience in the light of the model of a "genuine conversation." True conversation, in distinction to talking past one another, involves a back and forth, to-and-fro movement between the partners to the conversation, as illustrated so well for us in the great dialogues of Plato. The key to true conversation is a willingness to allow the question or the subject matter to assume the primacy. This involves a willingness to listen and reflect and be open to correction, from both sides. Counterfeit conversation is always one in which one or both of the partners are "controlled" by their own biases or fears, and not by the question before them. Thus, we must open ourselves to the great mystery of existence, in which we participate, and which raises questions to us. For Ricoeur, our "participation" in reality and the questions it raises for us is the primordial beginning point for all interpretation. For Voegelin, "there is no answer to the Question other than the Mystery as it becomes luminous in the acts of questioning."[1]

However, the model of conversation can be misleading if we forget that we are trying to enter into conversational dialogue with the world of the texts of our tradition. We no longer have two interlocutors sharing a common situation in the here and now, but only the textual tradition and ourselves. This means, partly, that we must allow the "world which the text opens up before us" to guide us and question us. As Ricoeur puts it, "Thus I exchange the 'I', master of itself, for the *self*, disciple of the text."[2] But, partly too, the world of the text is rendered open to communication and correction from our side, the world of the interpreter. Both the text and the interpreter are embraced in the larger reality of the "Question" to which each belongs.

(3) This back and forth movement of genuine conversation between the tradition's texts and our contemporary experience is a dialogical process of interpretation or hermeneutics which moves, as Ricoeur thinks, from (a) understanding to (b) explaining, and from explaining to (c) comprehension. First, (a) "understanding" involves our attempt to come to terms with the questions put before us through the conversation. It is based upon our own concerns, questions, presuppositions, hopes, fears, faith, spirituality, opinions, formation in various communities, practical modes of behavior, etc. In short, understanding embraces all that we are up to the point of our conversation as it begins to unfold. It is in the light of our understanding as men and women influenced by modernity that we approach the texts of our tradition and attempt to come to grips with the world that they open up before us.

In other words, "understanding" is a kind of first "guess" on our part of the meaning of the text. We must guess, for the text is mute. The text is only a potential source of meaning awaiting our interpretation. Because interpretation begins with our understanding, this means that there is a kind of anticipatory ability on our part to be ready for the Question put before us by the text.

But this recreating or guessing of the meaning of the tradition's texts needs refinement through methods of (b) "explanation." Our anticipatory understanding yields only a vague and too subjective interpretation unless it receives continual refinement through more precise methods of explanation. In Ricoeur's view, explanation is not a simple matter of rules for interpretation: "There are no rules for making good guesses."[3] Understanding must accompany explanation and envelop it. Still, explanation attempts to be methodic, to refine our guesses, and to move us toward ever more probable interpretations.

It is at this point of "explanation" that I would integrate the various trends among centrist Christologies into this general interpretation theory. At this point a truly genuine theological interpretation must take the hard and long detour of the "conflict of interpretations" stemming from diverse, critical, and hopefully complementary methods of explanation. Following David Tracy, I would suggest that all methods of explanation attempt two functions: on the one hand, to provide us with an "appropriate" interpretation of the tradition's own self-understanding, and, on the other, to correct and challenge the tradition in the light of our contemporary experience. In other words, each explanatory method concerns itself with issues of "appropriateness" and issues of "intelligibility."

Literary-critical analysis would seem the logical method of explanation with which to begin. In this way, as Ricoeur indicates, we would be following the natural movement of the text, from the sense to the reference which the text opens up to us *in front of the text*. Literary-critical analysis also reminds us that divine revelation always occurs through the mediation of language/the word. The mythical, symbolic, and analogical language through which revelation leaves traces of itself in tradition protects the "transcendent" nature of revelation and is an important corrective to the theologian's arrogant attempt to forget this. All theological interpretation must respect this fact, and literary analysis is the best way to do this, for it always roots the theologian in the originative and symbolic language of religious experience.[4]

Thus, a literary-critical analysis can help us move toward an appropriate understanding of the textual tradition's own self-understanding through a careful exploration of the key symbols or metaphors of the Scriptures and a study of the literary genres (narratives/stories, epistles, doctrines, myths, etc.) through which those symbols are structured and transformed. Literary analysis can also challenge and correct our understanding of the Scriptures through proposing new and more adequate ways in which we should understand the nature of symbolism, metaphor, myths, literary genres, etc.

A helpful, preliminary example of how literary-critical analysis works is provided us by David Tracy's insightful analysis of the narrative nature of the Gospels. "The Gospels share the prejudice of life for narrative as a key to lived experience," he tells us.[5] Human experience seems to demand the narrative form, for human experience is a "plot," an unfolding movement from beginning, through a middle, to an ending. The narrative genre "alone provides us with some fuller way to order and unify our actual lived experience with its tensions and surprises, its reversals and triumphs, its experience through memory of a past and, through anticipation and hope, of a future. . . ."[6] The crucial issues of the human drama—real tension, struggle, possibility, tragedy, resignation, hope, etc.—find a much greater disclosive power in the narrative-story than in more abstract, philosophical or historical modes of reflection. The narrative genre is not an accidental vehicle for expressing a human journey: only through it can the real pathos and drama of lived experience find disclosure. And so, as Tracy continues:

> When we approach these confessing narratives *as narratives*, therefore, with the aid of literary-critical methods, we can begin to sense their fuller religious and existential significance. We sense that significance by studying the dangerous memory of Jesus in the form that best reveals it: the narratives disclosing a person, a life, and thereby disclosing through the narrative form what a human life can be.[7]

This is but a small example of the wealth that awaits us from this new literary-critical turn in contemporary theology.

Historical-critical methods of explanation also have their contribution to make to the appropriation of the world disclosed to us *in front of the text*. Although literary-critical analysis relativizes the hegemony that historical-critical analysis has enjoyed in theology and Christology, it by no means dispenses with the role of history and the possible power of the text to open up a new world of historical reality. For Ricoeur, historical-critical methods function as a kind of protest against any tendency to lock the text up in itself and to forget that language is always an expression of our lived, historical experience.[8] Thus, like our other methods, historical-analysis can move us toward a more appropriate interpretation of the world of the texts (viz., helping us to reconstruct the primary apostolic witness of the

Gospels), and it can challenge and correct the tradition (viz., the Gospels are not simple biographies, there are historical inconsistencies, etc.).

Psychosocial-critical methods function in the same two ways: they aim for appropriateness and contemporary intelligibility. For example, the recovery of the dominant patriarchalism of our textual world is both a more appropriate understanding of our tradition and a challenge to move toward a more equitable interrelation between women and men in the Christian world. These methods also function as a kind of protest against the human and institutional pathology which pollutes our tradition and cries out for redress.[9] They are a hermeneutics of suspicion or deconstruction, if you will.

Philosophical-theological methods of explanation likewise have their crucially important role to play in our interpretation work. Ricoeur has expressed himself on this in a rather important manner:

> It is the task of theology to coordinate the experience articulated by the Biblical text with human experience at large and as a whole. . . . this polarity is required by the very nature of religious experience and discourse, inasmuch as it claims to describe—or redescribe!—the whole experience of man and the experience of all men.[10]

But today this takes place within the context of a conflict of interpretations, and therefore "we must assume that this mutual relation expresses in a formal way a full range of existential situations, from harmony to open warfare, by way of practical coexistence."[11] David Tracy will speak of the philosophical moment in interpretation as one of investigating the conditions of possibility within human experience of the world opened up to us in front of the text.[12] Voegelin will speak of all interpretation as remaining unintelligible to modernity unless it can "stir up parallel experiences as the empirical basis for testing the truth of theory." And he continues: "Unless a theoretical exposition activates the corresponding experiences at least to a degree, it will create the impression of empty talk or will perhaps be rejected as an irrelevant expression of subjective opinions."[13] And so in this book we will make an effort to explore the experiential foundations of the world opened up to us by the Christological texts of our tradition.

Finally, some form of "global analysis" is now entering into our conflict of interpretations and indicates a new frontier in interpretation whose outcome we cannot yet predict. In its most comprehensive sense, global analysis would mean that the theologian must enter into critical dialogue with scholars in comparative religions and the history of religions, with experts in oral cultures, and with representatives of the venerable religious traditions of today. Throughout this work I will try to be sensitive to these varied fields, but from a limited perspective and end in view. On the one hand, I will try to help the reader in Christology gain a more appropriate view of the tradition by pointing to the global horizon in the light of which our tradition should be understood. Specifically, this means that I will make some preliminary attempt to situate the Jesus event in the global context of a universal history of religion. On the other hand, I will try to show how our new global sensitivity challenges us to come to a more adequate understanding of the specialness/uniqueness of the Jesus event. This is a limited perspective, but I think these issues are a logical *sine qua non* for the next stage of the dialogue between the religions which might lead to a mutual transformation.

Each of these methods of explanation must work together dialogically and simultaneously critique and enrich one another. Only all of them in critical confrontation can help us approach anything like a probable and adequate interpretation of the Christological tradition in the light of our experience. Each method appeals to criteria appropriate to it: literary, to textual warrants; historical, to plausible historical hypotheses in the light of the evidence; psychosocial, to the warrants of praxis (psychological, political, economic, and cultural data); philosophical, to some form of experiential analysis of the conditions of possibility of Christological beliefs; global, to the evidence of humanity's global religious tradition. A convergence of results from all of these methods and criteria enables us to move toward ever more probable conclusions in our "explanation."

Understanding and explanation, finally, promote (c) "comprehension." The ongoing end product within this dialogical process is what Hans-Georg Gadamer calls a "fusion of horizons" between the world of the interpreter and the world opened up to us in front of the texts. Van Den Hengel even translates this term of Gadamer's (*Horizontverschmeltzung*) as a "wiping away of horizons"; through it we are enabled to move beyond our previous boundaries and limits toward a world of new possibilities projected in the texts.[14] The total being of the interpreter, theoretically and practically, is transformed. What the interpreter has learned is digested and results in a new being. One is *com*-prehended, in other words.

(4) What are some implications which flow from this sketch of a theological method? Here let me simply list some of the more promising features. (a) It unites a sensitivity to the tradition with a sensitivity to contemporary experience in its major dimensions (literary, historical, psychosocial/practical, philosophical, and global). Neither is idolized, neither is denigrated. Every person is in varying degrees a product of tradition, and nowhere is this more apparent than in Christology. Yet tradition is open to critique: we live in the present, which enables us to approach the

tradition in a distanciated way, with a critical distance. It is in the critical fusion of tradition and contemporary experience that we have our best hopes for a renewed theology and Christology.

(b) This method tries to avoid both dogmatism and relativism. Dogmatism occurs when one considers either tradition or contemporary experience to be beyond critique. In this case, no genuine conversation can occur. But relativism (as well as skepticism) equally inhibits genuine conversation, for it denies the primacy of the subject matter in which we participate and which can guide, enrich, and correct us. Relativism only allows for autonomous opinions which see no need to open themselves to correction. Because it denies the primacy of "The Question," which is placed before us by tradition and experience, it finally leaves only naked power as the means of adjudicating conflicts. Either that, or it ends in indifference to truth and practice.

(c) This style of hermeneutical theology is attuned, if I may use the classical terminology, to the true, the good, and the beautiful. To the true, because it seeks through varied methods to appropriate the meaning and truth that is opened up to us through a critical correlation between tradition and experience. To the good, because it seeks primarily through psychosocial-critical methods the practical and ethical implications of Christology. To the beautiful, because it seeks through literary-critical analysis to disclose the "medium" of the texts of our tradition and the text of our narrated and present experience[15] through which meaning, truth, and praxis are communicated to us.

The "truth" of this kind of theology is a truth which is verified by its adequacy to the *trivium* of the true, the good, and the beautiful as these three mutually critique, refine, and transform one another in the work of the theologian. David Tracy's "transformational model" of truth seems, perhaps, the most adequate present formulation of the theory of truth underlying this style of theological methodology.[16]

(d) Finally, this method attempts to preserve the continuity of the Christian and global tradition, which is finally based upon the continuity between the one God of the past and the same God of the present. The Divine is faithful, we trust, even if in surprising ways. This method tries to reflect that fact. But because we are dealing with a surprising fidelity, which takes on radically diverse forms throughout history, this method recognizes that "continuity" is an exceedingly complex reality. Sometimes it is simply logical: drawing further conclusions from the premises of the tradition. Sometimes it is much more subtle: making explicit what remains only implicit within tradition, grasping meaning and truth in a more complex, less one-sided manner and so correcting inadequacies within our past or present, etc.[17]

A HERMENEUTICAL METHOD FOR CENTRIST CHRISTOLOGIES

TRADITION ←——————————————→ CONTEMPORARY
(texts)   conversation, the to-and-fro move- EXPERIENCE
ment, maintaining openness to
the subject matter or "The Question"

        ↓   ↑

1. understanding

        ↓   ↑

2. explanation:
   -literary-critical methods (or
   aesthetic methods)
   -historical-critical methods
   -psychosocial methods
   -philosophical methods
   -global analyses

        ↓   ↑

3. comprehension

86

Notes

1. Eric Voegelin, *Order and History* 4, *The Ecumenic Age* (Baton Rouge, Louisiana: Louisiana State University Press, 1974), p. 330; see the section on the symbolism of "The Question," pp. 316–335. Cf Eugene Webb, *Eric Voegelin: Philosopher of History* (Seattle: University of Washington, 1981). Voegelin employs the model of the to-and-fro movement between traditional texts and contemporary experience throughout his *Order and History*. For Ricoeur, see *Interpretation Theory, op. cit.*, pp. 71–95, for the hermeneutical circle. See the helpful interpretations of Ricoeur in Van Den Hengel, *op. cit.*, pp. 187–208, and David Tracy, *The Analogical Imagination, op. cit.*, pp. 99–153. Needless to say, this is also the approach of Gadamer in his *Truth and Method, op. cit.*

Paul Friedländer, *Plato: An Introduction*, Bollingen Series LIX, I (Princeton, N.J.: Princeton University, 1973), esp. pp. 154–170, gives a helpful view of the Platonic notion of dialogue: "One of the basic principles of the Socratic conversation was to destroy in the pupil his belief that he had knowledge or to awaken him to the realization that he had none—not, by any means, in order to conclude with a skeptical position, but in order to stimulate a continuous mutual quest for the truth" (p. 168).

2. Paul Ricoeur, "Phénoménologie et herméneutique," *Man and World* 7 (1974), 236 (Van Den Hengel's translation, *ibid.*, p. 201). As we noted, the *textual* nature of interpretation is Ricoeur's and Gadamer's special contribution. The same notion, analogously, is found in Voegelin's view of the *symbolic* element in interpretation.

3. *Interpretation Theory, op. cit.*, p. 76. For the notion of conflict in interpretation theories, see his *The Conflict of Interpretations: Essays in Hermeneutics*, ed. Don Ihde (Evanston: Northwestern University, 1974). Gadamer tends to ignore the "explanation" moment, passing directly to comprehension or "application." Voegelin's own theory of consciousness, with its possibilities of differentiation and deformation, through which he strives to interpret the experience and symbolization of cultures, functions effectively as his method of explanation. Cf. his *Anamnesis* (Notre Dame: University of Notre Dame, 1978), for his own view, as well as *Order and History* I (Baton Rouge, Louisiana: Louisiana State University, 1958), pp. ix–xiv, 1–11.

4. This is one of the great themes of Ricoeur, found throughout his entire project. As Van Den Hengel, *op. cit.*, p. 229, puts it, Ricoeur "refuses to start with theological propositions such as a number of Anglo-Saxon theologians have done. He believes that before one can undertake to analyze theological propositions, one must first examine the more originary expressions of these theological propositions. Theological propositions are second-order language in relation to the first-order language of the biblical text. Ricoeur believes that in the hermeneutical quest of the biblical texts one can arrive at the 'most originary expression of a community of faith' " ("Philosophy and Religious Language," *Journal of Religion* 54 [1974], 73).

This is also a constant in Voegelin's work. As Webb, *op. cit.*, p. 67, puts it: "Voegelin, characteristically historical in method, stays as close as possible to the vocabulary developed by earlier philosophers for the articulation of universal experiences." And in Voegelin's work "mythic language . . . remains, despite the possible misleading features intrinsic to the mythic mode, the most adequate language we have for articulating the directional tendency of the tension of existence insofar as this is a longing, an *eros*, for various possibilities of unlimited perfection. It is possible to develop terminology that is less colored by imagined circumstance than is the traditional language of mythology, but to the extent that it becomes abstracted from the sense of *eros* for the concretely desirable it loses its ability to suggest the experience, the actual *eros*, it is being used to explicate" (Webb, *ibid.*, p. 66). See pp. 52–88, "Experience and Language," of Webb's work for Voegelin's attention to originary religious language.

5. David Tracy, *The Analogical Imagination, op. cit.*, p. 276.

6. *Ibid.*, p. 275.

7. *Ibid.*, p. 279.

8. This is part of the importance of his distinction between the text's "sense" and "reference." For Ricoeur's view of historiography, see Van Den Hengel, *op. cit.*, pp. 134–146.

9. See Van Den Hengel, *ibid.*, pp. 147–185, 203–208, for this "critical" moment in Ricoeur. Voegelin analogously works out a theory of the deformation of consciousness and practice, which effectively enables him to incorporate this "critical" moment. Cf Webb, *op. cit.*, "The Loss of Reality," pp. 193–207.

10. Paul Ricoeur, "Biblical Hermeneutics," *art. cit.*, 130–131.

11. *Ibid.*, 131–132.

12. See his *Blessed Rage for Order, op. cit.*, pp. 146–203.

13. Eric Voegelin, *The New Science of Politics: An Introduction* (Chicago: University of Chicago, 1952), pp. 64–65.

14. Van Den Hengel, *op. cit.*, p. 199.

15. For the notion of our present experience as a meaningful text, see Ricoeur, "The Model of the Text: Meaningful Action Considered as a Text," *Hermeneutics and the Human Sciences*, ed. J.B. Thompson (New York: Cambridge University, 1981), pp. 197–221.

16. David Tracy, *The Analogical Imagination, op. cit.*, pp. 62–79. He opts for both a disclosure model and transformational model of truth as distinct but not separate. Perhaps transformational is wide enough to encompass both.

17. The approach I have suggested here in method is broadly "hermeneutical" in the sense of the attempt to interpret and reappropriate both tradition and what is distinct from oneself. For overviews, see: Richard E. Palmer, *Hermeneutics: Interpretation Theory in Schleiermacher, Dilthey, Heidegger, and Gadamer* (Evanston: Northwestern University, 1969); Josef Bleicher, *Contemporary Hermeneutics: Hermeneutics as Method, Philosophy and Critique* (Boston: Routledge and Kegan Paul, 1980); John B. Thompson, *Critical Hermeneutics* (Cambridge, England: Cambridge University, 1981); Frederick Lawrence, "Voegelin and Theology as Hermeneutical and Political," in John Kirby and William M. Thompson, eds., *Voegelin and the Theologian: Ten Studies in Interpretation* (New York: Edwin Mellen, 1983), pp. 314–355; William M. Thompson, "Eric Voegelin: In Ret-

rospect," *Religious Studies Review* 10 (1984), 29–33. Bernard J.F. Lonergan exemplifies the hermeneutical approach in his distinction between mediating and mediated theology (= the dialogue between tradition and contemporary experience); cf his basic study, *Insight: A Study of Human Understanding* (New York: Philosophical Library, 1957), and *Method in Theology* (New York: Herder and Herder, 1972), esp. at p. 135. I also believe that transcendental Thomism can be seen as a further example of hermeneutical theology, inasmuch as it attempts to engage in a critical dialogue between contemporary experience and tradition; cf Karl Rahner, "Reflections on Methodology in Theology," *Theological Investigations*, 11, *op. cit.*, pp. 68–114.

5

Reflections on the Jesus Quest

We have learned that contemporary Christologies emerge from a reciprocal engagement between the Christian tradition and the lessons flowing from contemporary experience. The fruitful tension between these two poles gives rise to the Christological questions which thoughtful Christians must try to explore anew in each age. Probably the most startling way, at least until recently, in which this tension manifested itself for us in our time is the emergence of the famous "quest for the historical Jesus." Actually we will see that there have been several quests in the modern period. It was the emergence of the new historical sciences which began to raise the question of whether the Jesus of the Christian tradition was compatible with our new experience of human historicity. Was the biblical portrait of Jesus incredible in the light of our new historical knowledge? That kind of agitating question seemed to emerge as the historical sciences were applied to the New Testament. We should, then, stop to consider the quest for Jesus, for it raises the issue of whether we can trust the most important text of our tradition. In what follows I will try to survey the history of the quests, what their key results seem to be, and how contemporary Christology must seek to learn from them as it attempts to refashion Christology anew.

A Survey of the Jesus Quests

First Phase: Emergence

Broadly speaking, I think we can delineate four basic phases [1] of the quest(s) for Jesus. The first phase covers the period of the emergence of the quest itself. It begins with the application of the sciences of critical history to the biblical texts themselves. A Catholic priest of the French Oratory, R. Simon (1638–1712), was actually the first to use critical methods. But Hermann Samuel Reimarus (1694–1768) is usually credited with being the initiator of the quest. This German professor of Oriental languages, in his Wolfenbüttel Fragments published posthumously by G.E. Lessing (1774–1778), aruged that the New Testament view of Jesus was an historically improbable interpretation. It "is not controlled by history, but just the opposite," he claimed.[2]

Reimarus viewed his goal as one of recovering the truly "historical" Jesus and exposing the false "dogmatic" interpretation of Jesus as the Christ created by the early disciples and later Church. We already noted in the last chapter how thoroughly he was influenced by the anti-religious trends of the early Enlightenment, and by Deism. Thus Reimarus eliminates the miracles and resurrection from his historical reconstruction of Jesus. These were "created" by the disciples after their disappointment over Jesus' crucifixion. By creating such legends the disciples legitimated their ambitions to preside over a new royal kingdom which they had hoped Jesus would found: "The apostles and all the disciples were induced by ambitious motives, by hopes of future wealth and power, lands and worldly goods, to follow Jesus as their Messiah and King."[3] At the most Reimarus would hold that Jesus was a moral enlightener attempting to improve humanity inwardly through the cultivation of high ideals: love of the Divine and of the neighbor, humility, gentleness, self-denial, etc.[4] It was Jesus' unfortunate belief that he was to be the Messiah of a new kingdom upon earth that brought him into conflict and eventually to his death.

Clearly Reimarus' "historical work" was greatly impeded by his anti-religious prejudices. He mixes uncritical biases and authentic history in a manner difficult to separate. Still he was on to a number of important insights. For example, he distinguished between the historical value of the Synoptics (Matthew, Mark, and Luke) and the highly theological interpretation found in John (although the difference is much less exaggerated today). He grasped that the life of Jesus had undergone a significant process of interpretation by the disciples. He admitted that Jesus was an apocalyptic visionary entertaining hopes of a future Kingdom of the Divine (Reimarus didn't stress this). And he realized that Christology was largely a process set in motion subsequent to Jesus' death. All of these seminal intuitions would become somewhat standard, and refined, among later questers.

David Friedrich Strauss (1808–1874), in his monumental *The Life of Jesus Critically Examined* (four editions, 1825–1840),[5] consolidated what Reimarus began. His major contribution was one of trying to refine the historical criteria to be used in recovering the authentic Jesus of history. For example, he uses a "dialectical method" in which he plays off the traditional "supernaturalistic" and the more recent "rationalistic" interpreta-

tions of the Gospels against one another. As one contemporary interpreter
of Strauss explains it,

> First the supernaturalists are demolished. Then the natural explanation,
> by its own unnaturalness, ever brings us back to the "mythical," upon
> the application of which "the innumerable, and never otherwise to be
> harmonized discrepancies and chronological contradictions in the gos-
> pel histories disappear, as it were, at one stroke."[6]

Over against the supernaturalists and naturalists (or rationalists),
Strauss proposes the category of "myth" as a way of distinguishing true history from false. While a supernaturalist might argue that the resurrection
stories are examples of the divine intervention into history, and a rationalist might attribute them to some form of bodily resuscitation or an hal-
lucination, Strauss opts for myth as an explanation. In their pure form
myths are simply products of the religious imagination. But they can have
an historical incident underlying them in some cases. To this category of
myth he further adds the criterion of the rational laws of nature. An account is not historical but mythical if it contradicts the known laws of nature (such as causality, psychology, etc.), and if it is inconsistent with itself
or contradicts another biblical account.[7]

Actually Strauss' first edition of the *Life* leaves us with a richer historical view of Jesus than is usually thought. Jesus actually lived, he was a
disciple of the Baptist, and he conducted a ministry in Galilee. After coming to regard himself as the Messiah, he called disciples, went to Jerusalem
with his plans for his kingdom, predicted his second coming as the Son of
Man, had premonitions of his death, and was eventually condemned and
crucified. In the *Life*'s third edition he introduced a number of changes,
however. He now omitted the apocalyptic element in Jesus' message. Under the influence of Hegel's philosophy, he recast Jesus: Jesus was not an
apocalyptic visionary believing himself to be the Messiah of a kingdom,
but only a man with an intensive consciousness of the Divine (= Hegel's
"World-Spirit"). But this was balanced by a greater acceptance of the miracles of the Gospels. Insofar as the miraculous could be regarded as an example of nature's unusual powers (namely, cures resulting from hypnotism
and mental telepathy), it could be accepted. Here Strauss displays an
openness to the new science of parapsychology. Still, much of the New
Testament remains as myth. The Messiah-belief was originally implanted
in the disciples' minds by Jesus himself, but it is myth nonetheless, and it
becomes even more highly mythicized as time moves on. The resurrection, of course, blatantly contradicts nature's laws, while the appearances
of the risen Jesus might be explained as subjective hallucinations.

Strauss actually ended his work by maintaining the impossibility of writing a truly historical life of Jesus. Not only do the Gospels refuse to treat Jesus historically; they only leave us with unconnected fragments artificially connected by the Gospel writers. "Nay, if we would be candid with ourselves," he says, "that which was once sacred history for the Christian believer, is, for the enlightened portion of our contemporaries, only fable: the narratives of the supernatural birth of Christ, of his miracles, of his resurrection and ascension, must be rejected by us as at variance with the inductions of our intellect."[8] Liberal Protestant theologians, however, were more optimistic than Strauss, and initiated what has come to be called the "old quest for the historical Jesus."

The "old quest" was stimulated by a number of factors. Liberal theologians partly viewed it as a continuation of the ideals of the Reformation. As Martin Luther freed Protestantism from the later false "dogmas" of medievalism, so the liberals wanted to continue this process all the way back to the New Testament. Not only post-biblical teachings but also New Testament teachings needed purging of their false dogmatic accretions. This reformist program was coupled with the belief that we can gain access to the original Jesus through Mark and a source designated as "Q," the latter being a source of Jesus' sayings ("Q" from the German *Quelle*/source). The acceptance of Mark and Q as the earliest and possible direct links to Jesus (the two-source theory) was becoming common at the turn of the century (see chart at end of this chapter). The result was the spawning of innumerable lives of Jesus in the nineteenth century: from Ernest Renan, from Adolph Harnack, and from a host of others now forgotten.[9] As with Reimarus and Strauss, so with the liberals, we are confronted with a complex mixture of historical intuition and theological bias: Jesus is viewed as the supremely ethical enlightener (Harnack) or the proclaimer of the sweet theology of love which won him all hearts (Renan).

Albert Schweitzer's *The Quest of the Historical Jesus* (1906) is generally considered the end of the old quest. Schweitzer (1875–1965) put his finger on the problem with the quest up to this point: "The historical investigation of the life of Jesus did not take its rise from a purely historical interest; it turned to the Jesus of history as an ally in the struggle against the tyranny of dogma."[10] Thus Reimarus, Strauss, and the liberals share more of the religious skepticism of the Enlightenment than a genuine desire to treat the Bible historically. The Jesus they find looks more like a Deist, a follower of Hegel, or a Protestant liberal than the actual Jesus of history.

That does not mean that real gains weren't realized in the quest. Schweitzer had noted this: "The dogma had first to be shattered before men could once more go out in quest of the historical Jesus, before they could even grasp the thought of His existence."[11] But the historical method had been impeded by uncriticized philosophical and theological presuppositions. We need to allow history to guide our assumptions and views, not our prior presuppositions: "All that can be done is to experiment continually, starting from definite assumptions, and in this experimentation the guiding principle must ultimately rest upon historical intuition."[12]

Schweitzer is the founder of the "consistent eschatological" school of interpretation. Believing, with Johannes Weiss in his *Jesus' Proclamation of the Kingdom of God*,[13] that the apocalyptic mentalilty is the real key to unlocking the historical Jesus, he portrays Jesus at every step along the way as driven by an apocalyptic fever which yearns for the advent of the Kingdom: "Jesus' purpose is to set in motion the eschatological [end-time] development of history, to let loose the final woes, the confusion and strife, from which shall issue the Parousia [second coming], and so to introduce the supra-mundane phase of the eschatological drama."[14] Thus, Jesus' messiahship cannot be written off as unhistorical legend. This is only a small aspect of Jesus' commitment to the apocalyptic Kingdom. Jesus really believes that he is the Kingdom's appointed agent (= Messiah). Jesus truly shares in "the atmosphere of the time [which] was saturated with eschatology."[15]

Jesus, then, in going up to Jerusalem for Passover, comes into contact with the apocalyptic movement of the Baptist; he subsequently appears in Galilee proclaiming the hoped for Kingdom. Early on (from his baptism?) he knows himself to be the Messiah. His ministry is short (perhaps a year, by Mark's reckoning), because the suddenness of "The End" is upon us. Why does Jesus leave Galilee so quickly, despite his success there? Because he is "dominated" by the "dogmatic" idea of the Kingdom, despite the consequences. Jesus is not so much a teacher as the Kingdom's agent: hence his preference for baffling parables and concealing his identity. This Kingdom is thoroughly "supernatural." It cannot be earned. We are predestined to it by the Divine. In fact, Schweitzer holds that Jesus was torn between a more ethical view of salvation (we contribute to our salvation through our deeds of love) and the more predestinarian one.

Schweitzer divides Jesus' life into two great epochs. The non-occurrence of the second coming, which had been promised in Matthew 10:23, is the great break which alters Jesus' self-understanding. Before that he apparently expected the Kingdom's arrival at the annual harvest time. Thus he sent out his disciples to Israel to announce quickly what was about to occur. But this ended in failure (cf Mk 6:6). As a result, Jesus struggled through to a new conviction: if the final tribulation and Kingdom's coming have not yet happened, "that means there is still something to be done, and yet another of the violent must lay violent hands upon the Kingdom of God."[16] The final tribulation will not begin by itself; Jesus must initiate it through his own trial and suffering. This will compel the Kingdom's arrival, as Isaiah foretold in his writings about the suffering servant.

In effect, Jesus identifies his own sufferings with the expected apocalyptic tribulations of the end-time. Schweitzer, in fact, sees this twist which Jesus gives to eschatology as Jesus' and the Baptist's unique contribution: "They themselves set the times in motion by acting, by creating eschatological facts." Unlike the purely artificial character of Jewish apocalyptic, in the Baptist and Jesus "there now enter into the field of eschatology men, living, acting men." This was unique: "It was the only time when that ever happened in Jewish eschatology."[17]

Thus Schweitzer was able to show, against the old questers, that far from being a modern moralist and enlightener, Jesus was thoroughly apocalyptic: a feverish believer in a soon to come supernatural Kingdom. This was enough to bring the old quest to its heels! By almost universal consent today, biblical scholars would agree that this recovery of Jesus' apocalyptic horizon was a genuine step toward the recovery of the original Jesus. Yet Schweitzer seems to exaggerate the other-worldly character of Jesus. He does not bring out the interest in this world so characteristic of Jesus, nor does he recognize how the belief in the Kingdom can itself be interpreted as a vision for the overcoming of oppression in this world. All Schweitzer could do was to admit that the apocalyptic framework of Jesus was outmoded and that we must express in our own way the essential message of Jesus—namely, love. As he explained it in his autobiography:

> . . . the religion of love taught by Jesus has been freed from any dogmatism which clung to it by the disappearance of the late Jewish expectation of the immediate end of the world. The mold in which the casting was made has been broken. We are now at liberty to let the religion of Jesus become a living force in our thought, as its purely spiritual and ethical nature demands.[18]

Perhaps Schweitzer's own presuppositions—a Lutheran spiritualism and an Enlightenment moralism?—blocked him from considering the possible relevancy of the apocalyptic strain in Jesus. As we have indicated before, Jesus' apocalyptic message is not as other-worldly as Schweitzer seems to think, nor as irrelevant. But these were to be the insights of a later day.

Second Phase: Skepticism

Schweitzer's other-worldly Jesus promoted the image of a Jesus of little interest to modernity. During this second phase of the quest a number
of factors converged, all of which indicated that an historical quest was neither possible nor desirable. Already in 1901 Wilhelm Wrede (1859–1906)
had published his important *The Messianic Secret in the Gospels*,[19] in
which he argued that Mark, far from being a direct link with the historical
Jesus, represented an elaborate theological interpretation of Jesus. He illustrates this through an analysis of the "messianic secret" (cf Mk 1:34;
8:30), showing how this is a literary device of Mark's by which he can explain why no one knew who Jesus was during his earthly ministry.
Throughout his Gospel, Wrede contends, Mark presents us with a thoroughly divine, not human, Jesus. However, the original Jesus never made
any such claims to divinity. It was only after the resurrection that the disciples really began to make such high claims for Jesus. They then projected
their later beliefs back into the earthly life of Jesus and created the messianic secret as a way of explaining why Jesus' divinity was unknown to
them and others earlier. Mark took this tradition over in his Gospel.
Wrede's thesis was a serious challenge to the old questers, who invested
greatly in the belief that Mark could link us almost directly with the historical Jesus. However, by bringing out the creative work of an evangelist,
Wrede at least initiated the move of paying greater attention to the original
literary work of the Gospel writers, a field which has come to be known
today as "redaction criticism."

Another factor which seemed to argue against the possibility of a
quest was the emergence of the science of the history of religions. This new
field, which studied the origins and development of Near Eastern and
Mediterranean religions, was being used by biblical scholars as a further
way of throwing light upon the origins and development of Christianity.
Were there any parallels between Christianity and its Near Eastern cousins, were there any borrowings, etc.? For example, as the early Christian
preachers moved into the Greco-Roman world, would they not have come
under the influence of the Greco-Roman official religion of the empire as
well as the more popular mystery religions of the time (the cults of Mithra,
Eleusis, Dionysus, etc.)? Would this not account for some of the New Testament beliefs about Jesus? Was, for example, Paul's belief in Jesus as
dying and rising (cf Rom 6:1–11) an adaptation from the mystery religions:
as the mystery initiates believed themselves to share in the dying and rising of the gods and goddesses, so Paul perhaps refashioned Jesus into similar terms? Perhaps, too, the Gospel miracle stories were adaptations of
Jewish and Greco-Roman miracle legends. Most radically, perhaps the be-

lief in Jesus' divinity was influenced by the general religious tendency of the Greco-Roman orbit to deify holy men. If all of this were true, it would mean that the New Testament through and through represents a rather late religious interpretation of the original Jesus. How could one, with any certainty, peel away these layers of interpretation and recover the Jesus of Nazareth?[20]

Form criticism (see chart at end of this chapter) seemed to complete this offensive against the possibility of a quest. Originally developed in the early 1900's as a technique of interpretation of the Hebrew Scriptures by Herman Gunkel, it was refined by his pupils Martin Dibelius and Rudolf Bultmann and adapted to New Testament study. Form criticism tried to go beyond the two-source theory, which studied the interrelationships between the written Gospels, by exploring the oral process of tradition "behind" the written Gospels. It would dwell upon the process from the period of Jesus up to the actual writing of the Gospels themselves.

This newer form of criticism was governed by two basic postulates. Proposed, first, was the insight that the determinative factor in preserving a particular tradition about Jesus was the needs and interests of the local communities in which catechists and teachers of the early Church worked. For example, Paul would take from the Jesus traditions available to him only what was of relevance for his audience, whether Jewish or Gentile. Were he dealing with Gentiles, he would presumably recast these Jesus traditions into the Greek terms intelligible to his audience. Second, it was proposed that the written Gospels are composed of many smaller units ("pericopes") that originally circulated as separate units or "forms" in the early Christian communities. Dibelius' *From Tradition to Gospel* (1934) is a stellar example of this: it argued that the Synoptics were actually designed for popular consumption, and that they represent more a compilation of pre-existing material ("forms") than true authorship in our modern sense. These "forms" or units of tradition might have been miracle stories, striking pronouncements of Jesus, passion stories, resurrection tales, etc.[21] Again, the evidence was accumulating for the view that the Gospels represent a thoroughly complex end-product of profound interpretation which makes it practically impossible to recover a core of original events stretching back to Jesus.

Rudolf Bultmann (1884–1976) is generally considered the climax of this second, skeptical phase. His work is complex, and assessments of his contribution are varied. Let me hazard a few generalizations. First, he accepts at least as working tools the major insights of Wrede, the history of religions school, form criticism, and Strauss' category of "myth." He uses all of these in his attempts to analyze the New Testament. Thus, he argues that the New Testament represents a complex interpretation of the origi-

nal Jesus, and the only historical reality we find for certain is the bare fact
(the *Dass*) of the existence and death by crucifixion of Jesus. The Jesus of
history is concealed under the "layers" of later beliefs which eventually
went into the making of the New Testament. Bultmann calls these "layers
of belief" the "kerygma," the New Testament proclamation about Jesus as
the risen Christ.

Second, Bultmann is skeptical of the Jesus-search on theological,
rather than simply historical, grounds. His Lutheran belief in justification
by faith alone predisposes him to think that it is a mistake to attempt to
base our faith on historical research. Sufficient for us is the kerygma, the
faith of the early Church which summons us to a similar venture of faith in
our own times. Of course, there is a continuity between the original Jesus
and the kerygma. The kerygma assumes the fact of Jesus' historical existence: for the first disciples the risen one preached in the kerygma was
identical with the earthly Jesus. Further, Jesus' historical career and message "implies" the later Christological belief of the kerygma, for Jesus demands a decision about his person as the proclaimer of the divine word.
But it is not historical research (= "works" in the Lutheran scheme) which
grounds our faith: the kerygma takes the place of the historical Jesus, represents him, and summons us to faith today.

Third, Bultmann is probably most famous for his recognition of the
need to "demythologize" the kerygma of the New Testament. With
Strauss, he holds that much of the New Testament is expressed in the obsolete categories of the world view of the first century A.D., excepting, of
course, the always true belief in the activity of the Divine. We must find a
way to express in our own contemporary terms (= "remythologize") what
was being said in the kerygma. This is similar to what we called earlier the
attempt to engage the tradition with our contemporary experience, issuing
in a fusion of horizons. Bultmann himself uses various forms of philosophical analysis to try to bring home to modernity the futility and emptiness
of living a life without faith and trust in the Divine. "Trust in the Divine"
is, in fact, a fairly good translation of what he regards the message of the
kerygma to be. Arguments with him do not so much center on the need to
reinterpret the kerygma, but on what should be regarded as obsolete
myth. While he tends to place the resurrection and miracle stories in this
category, others disagree. But we will see more of this later.[22]

Assessments of this second phase of the quest must finally hinge on
two questions. The first is historical: Is it true that historical research has
shown that the quest for Jesus is impossible? One might well ask whether
the historical method had, as yet, been really tried. For one gains the
impression that certain prejudices and biases have impeded the researchers up to this point. The governing assumption of this second phase is that

the New Testament was written with no concern for historical authenticity. But that is an assumption, and a later phase of the quest will give us good cause to believe that that assumption is also a bias and prejudice. This connects with a second, more theological question: Is it true, as Bultmann inclines to hold, that Christian faith rules out a genuine interest in the historical Jesus? Is that not an excessively *un*-historical notion of faith which robs faith of its historical origins and foundations? How does the Christian come to faith—immediately through an inspiring act of God, as Bultmann seems to hold, or mediately, through history and tradition?

Third Phase: The Quest's Renewal

Our third phase begins when a number of scholars question Bultmann's tendency to downplay the historical dimensions of the Gospels. Interestingly even Bultmann himself grew less skeptical about the quest toward the end of his career. In a 1959 lecture he said of Jesus: "Characteristic of him are exorcisms, the breach of the Sabbath commandment, the abandonment of ritual purifications, polemic against Jewish legalism, fellowship with outcasts such as publicans and harlots, sympathy for women and children; it can also be seen that Jesus was not an ascetic like John the Baptist, but gladly ate and drank a glass of wine."[23] That is a good deal more than the "bare fact" of Jesus' existence and death, and a number of Bultmann's pupils pursued this interest, eventually giving birth to what has been called the "new quest for the historical Jesus." The Marburg School, embracing scholars like Ernst Käsemann, Ernst Fuchs, and Günther Bornkamm, is perhaps the real origin of this newer phase of the quest.

Ernst Käsemann's programmatic "The Problem of the Historical Jesus"[24] argued that the Synoptic Gospels themselves have an historical interest, for they were written with a twofold aim: not only to make Jesus' life contemporary for later generations, but to guard against false interpretations of Jesus. Without the historical Jesus Christianity runs the danger of becoming an unhistorical myth: "[Primitive Christianity] is not minded to allow myth to take the place of history nor a heavenly being to take the place of the Man of Nazareth."[25] Still, Käsemann argued that it would be difficult to retrieve the historical Jesus through the Gospels: "In only one case do we have more or less safe ground under our feet: when there are no grounds either for deriving a tradition from Judaism or for ascribing it to primitive Christianity, and especially when Jewish Christianity has mitigated or modified the received tradition, as having found it too bold for its taste."[26]

Käsemann has just articulated the famous criterion of dissimilarity,

widely used today in Jesus research, which maintains that a tradition ascribed to Jesus in the New Testament may be considered "authentic" if it
can be shown to be dissimilar to typical emphases of either first century
Judaism or the early Christian Church. The presumption is that such a tradition would then be uniquely Jesus'. But Käsemann goes on to add a qualification: "Certainly [Jesus] was a Jew and made the assumptions of Jewish
piety, but at the same time he shatters this framework with his claim."[27]

Käsemann's program is fairly typical of the new quest. Others have
simply tried to refine it. For example, some think that more attention
should be paid to Jesus' deeds and his inner attitude, not simply to his message. The way he holds table fellowship with outcasts, his sense of authority, his posture toward Jewish groups of his day—all are perhaps "unique"
elements in his ministry, dissimilar to the emphases of his time. Others
have tried to develop further criteria, besides that of dissimilarity. For example, are events or sayings of Jesus, as reported in the New Testament,
multiply attested by several writers? Are they at least consistent with what
we can learn from dissimilarity and multiple attestation? Scholars who use
these criteria are aware of their limitations. They know that Jesus shared
much in common with the Judaism of his times, and that a rigid employ-
ment of these criteria would make Jesus into a first century rarity! They
also know that these criteria must not lead us to think that we know more
about the first century than we actually do. As one scholar put it, "Some of
the judgments we make about historical accuracy on the basis of our criteria may well be defective not because the criteria do not work but because of our ignorance."[28] In the end, new questers are more modest than
those of the old quest; a full biography of Jesus cannot be written. Still,
they would hold that the findings of their search are not inconsiderable. As
the same scholar put it:

> The consensus among scholars who have been applying these criteria to
> the Jesus traditions is that we may recognize authentic reminiscence in
> the large number of stories describing Jesus as proclaiming the inaugu-
> ration of God's kingly rule, in most of the parables and in the group of
> traditions that cluster around the "Abba" and "The Lord's Prayer" tra-
> ditions. They also include main events in the life of Jesus such as his bap-
> tism, his ministry in Galilee, the trip to Jerusalem, his arrest, trial, and
> crucifixion.[29]

New questers have not been alone in their emphasis upon the historical Jesus. Joachim Jeremias shares their interests, and even believes that
we have Jesus' "very words" themselves in many of the "Abba" sayings of
the Gospels. Conservative British scholars have argued that there is a solid

core of historical material recoverable in the Gospels. As one of these, C.H. Dodd, put it: "If we lose hold upon that historical actuality, the Gospels are betrayed into the hands of the Gnostics, and we stand on the verge of a new Docetism [denial of Jesus' humanity]."[30] Conservative Scandinavian scholars, called the "traditio-historical school," have even argued that Jesus taught as a rabbi and that he and his disciples used the methods of oral memorization characteristic of the rabbis. This would involve a highly refined ability to remember, aided by fixed verbal formulae, solemn symbolic actions, and repetition. The apostles, then, developed a skilled corps of reciters of the rabbi Jesus' words, and the Gospels are an edited version of this recital.[31] Finally, the German theologian Wolfhart Pannenberg and his circle have argued, against Bultmann, that divine revelation comes to us only mediately and indirectly, through the events of history. Since history is the site of revelation, the methods of historical scholarship can aid us in verifying this historical dimension of revelation. This was something of a theological defense of the new quest.[32]

Fourth Phase: Catholic Participation in the Quest

We already noted that R. Simon, the Oratorian priest, had used the historical method in the early eighteeenth century. This work was continued by Catholic scholars in the early 1900's: Alfred Loisy, Friedrich von Hügel, and Maurice Blondel come especially to mind.[33] For the most part these thinkers attempted to remain open to the latest findings of historical research and to show how Catholicism could assimilate them. Yet Catholic authorities were generally very critical of the new historical theories, particularly in the era of the early 1900's, the period of the Catholic liberals and modernists. As Raymond Brown puts it, the official Roman congregations of the Curia "made little distinction between the possible intrinsic validity of biblical criticism and the theological misuse of it by the Modernists."[34]

Perhaps the root Catholic difficulty was the refusal to dialogue with modernity and the highly unhistorical nature of the reigning Scholastic brand of philosophy and theology. Thus, the Pontifical Biblical Commission issued decisions between 1905 and 1920 which made it practically impossible for Catholic scholars to participate in the quest(s). For example, it was forbidden to hold (1) that Jesus did not know he was the Messiah, (2) that he did not perform his miracles to prove his Messiahship, (3) that he was mistaken about the timing of the Kingdom's coming, and (4) that he did not enjoy unlimited knowledge (cf CT, nos. 475–488). Needless to say, all of these issues were under debate among the various questers.

Pope Pius XII's encyclical letter Divino Afflante Spiritu (1943) is generally considered the great turning point for Catholic scholars, permitting the "scientific" study of the Bible. This was followed in 1955 by a statement from the Pontifical Biblical Commission which manifested a new openness to biblical study and placed a qualification upon the earlier decrees against the modernists:

> . . . as long as these decrees propose views which are neither immediately nor mediately connected with truths of faith and morals, it goes without saying that the scholar may pursue his research with complete freedom and may utilize the results of his research, provided always that he defers to the supreme teaching authority of the Church.[35]

And this decree rather remarkably adds that there was a "narrowness and constraint which prevailed fifty years ago."

More closely related to the Jesus quest, however, was the important 1964 instruction from the Pontifical Biblical Commission, "The Historical Truth of the Gospels." Issued with the approval of Pope Paul VI, it was an alternative to the conservative document on revelation found unacceptable to the majority at the Second Vatican Council. Interestingly, it begins by maintaining that "the interpreter should pay diligent attention to the three stages of tradition by which the doctrine and life of Jesus have come down to us." Stage one, that of Jesus' ministry, is described as a period in which "he followed the modes of reasoning and of exposition which were in vogue at the time." This means that "he accommodated himself to the mentality of his listeners," although Raymond Brown comments: "Most Catholic scholars would speak more openly of Jesus' own limited knowledge rather than of his accommodating himself to the limited knowledge of his time."[36]

Stage two is that of the period of the oral preaching of the apostles. The instruction holds that "after Jesus rose from the dead . . . his divinity was clearly perceived." In this period the apostles "interpreted his words and deeds according to the needs of their listeners." Here we have a recognition that the Church's Christology is set in motion after the resurrection. Brown's helpful comment is that this "allows for development within the pre-Gospel stage of the Jesus tradition, and is a stage of formation close to what scholars isolate by form-critical analysis."[37]

Stage three moves us into the period of the actual writing of the Gospels. "From the many things handed down," the instruction continues, the Gospel authors "selected some things, reduced others to a synthesis, (still) others they explicated as they kept in mind the situation of the churches." But it carefully adds: "The truth of the story is not at all affected." The authors preserve the "sense" of what Jesus taught. This stage, then, allows considerable scope to the creative work of the evangelists. It recognizes what scholars call redaction criticism. And Brown concludes: "Note that the Roman Catholic Church has gone on record stating that the Gospels are not literal or chronological accounts of the words and deeds of Jesus."[38]

Learning from the Quests

The Jesus quests, as we already indicated in the last chapter, have generated quite a number of questions for Christology. Let us try to grapple with some of the more basic ones that have arisen.

Some Preliminary Confusions

(1) The first confusion that has arisen in the course of the quests is what I would call the attempt to replace the kerygma of the New Testament by the Jesus of history as reconstructed by the Jesus quest. This was particularly true of the early stages of the quest. Reimarus, Strauss, and even Schweitzer to some extent, all sought to use the quest as a means of freeing Christianity from what they perceived to be the false dogmatic overlay of interpretation which the later Church had imposed upon Jesus. Here the quest was being used as a kind of liberating and critical ally of critical natural reason, freeing Christians from an outmoded supernaturalism.

Today the dust has settled to some extent, and the consensus has emerged that the early attempt to shove out the kerygma in favor of an "historical Jesus" was a mistake. A number of arguments have become rather decisive and persuasive in this regard. For example, the "anti-kerygmatists" had a tendency to understress or ignore characteristics of the ministry of Jesus which manifested a high degree of continuity and sometimes identity between the historical Jesus and the New Testament's kerygma. The fact, as Bultmann noted, that Jesus' message implied a claim about himself; the fact that the divine Kingdom, preached by Jesus, was mediated already through Jesus' person—these and more indicated that the kerygma was not a falsification of the historical Jesus, but an explication of what was at least implicit already in the historical career of Jesus. If one were to shove out the kergyma, one would also have to shove out significant facets of Jesus' career which were becoming evident through historical research!

Apparently the anti-kerygmatists were excessively influenced by a rationalistic bias against religious experience and religious "claims" which arise from those experiences. In other words, they were under the influence of the early Enlightenment's bias against religious experience. It is this which ultimately blocked their ability to uncover the continuity and substantial identity between the historical Jesus and the kerygma's "Christ of faith."

Finally, the anti-kerygmatists had a tendency to ignore the implications of the fact that the only source for their "reconstructed" historical Jesus was the kerygma of the New Testament itself. Their "historical Jesus" is not actually the original Jesus, but a reconstruction of salient clues provided them by the New Testament itself. There is a gap between an "original" Jesus and a reconstructed one! Furthermore, the evidence one has to rely upon in one's historical research is provided by the kerygma itself. If the kerygma cannot be trusted, why should a reconstructed Jesus derived from it be so trusted?

(2) The second confusion (which is really another way of stating our first confusion) is the attempt to make a reconstructed historical Jesus the final norm of Christian revelation and theology. This was particularly true of the earlier stages of the quest (the anti-kerygmatists above), but even some contemporary questers seem to imply that this is what they are about. The underlying notion seems to be that if one can uncover through research a sufficient amount of authentic material about Jesus, then this can serve as a norm which tells us what a "true" and "pure" Christianity should be.

It might be too early to speak about a consensus on this issue, but let me hazard a few observations. First, I think that the arguments against our first confusion are equally relevant in this case, at least in the sense that any reconstructed historical Jesus must ultimately rely upon the kerygma of the New Testament for its foundation. But there is a more significant objection to this attempt to make an "historical Jesus" into theology's overriding norm. For a developing religion like Christianity, which believes that the Divine is disclosed not only in the past of the tradition but also in the present of our contemporary experience, the only adequate norm for Christian truth is to be derived from the natural and critical correlation between the tradition and contemporary experience. Put in more experiential terms, humans are bound by both poles of tradition and contemporary experience for their insight into truth. Truth is a prerogative neither of the past nor of the present, but something found only precariously and ambiguously in both. In light of this, the attempt to make an historical Jesus into our norm is another form of the old human tendency to "mythicize" (in the pejorative sense) beginnings at the expense of the present and future. Only the tradition as it is ever actualized anew in each age can function as our norm.

In the light of this, the tradition-actualized-anew is the chief mediating reality of the Jesus event for the Christian tradition. As David Tracy helpfully puts it,

> The Christian tradition, from New Testament kerygmatic [interpretation] to conciliar self-correction and self-clarification to the need for constant reformation as graced and sinful church, is a tradition which lives *as tradition* by ever-new interpretations, ever-new reformations, ever-renewed fidelity to the apostolic witness which originated and sustains the tradition.[39]

Understood in this sense, as an always actualized tradition, it is, as Tracy says, a "constitutive-enveloping" reality for theologians and for participants in the Christian community: it *constitutes* the community of Christians in any given age. Because the tradition must ever renew itself through reinterpretations which attempt to be more and more faithful to the Jesus event, the tradition itself must be open to correction as a sign of its own fidelity. Theologians, through their own critical work, participate in this process of renewing and sometimes even correcting the tradition for the sake of the tradition, but it is the entire Christian community which finally decides what is ultimately a faithful interpretation of the tradition itself.

The Purpose of the Jesus Quest

Following David Tracy's helpful suggestions, a clarification of the role of the historical quest for Jesus will only result from a clear demarcation of the role that the various theological methods play in our theological task of renewing and revitalizing the tradition in each age. Let us recall for a moment that each of our theological methods attempts to perform two functions: (a) either to achieve an "appropriate" interpretation of the tradition's own self-understanding at a given time, or (b) to propose corrections to the tradition in the light of our ongoing experience. Each of these functions of the theological methods corresponds to the two dimensions of the tradition we have mentioned above: (a) the tradition-as-actualized-anew as the "constitutive-enveloping" reality of the Christian community, and (b) the tradition as ever open to new corrections and reformation. An "appropriate" interpretation attempts to uncover what the self-understanding of the tradition in the Christian community actually is, in what way it actually constitutes the community at a given time. A "corrective" interpretation is a challenge to the tradition, to the way Christians are "constituted" by it. In the light of our current understanding, it proposes a new interpretation which removes some inadequacy in the tradition. As Tracy likes to say, it is concerned with modern issues of "intelligibility."

Now, in the light of these basic distinctions, we can perhaps throw some light upon the role that a Jesus quest might play in a contemporary Christology. Tracy helpfully delineates three possibilities.[40] First are those thinkers who would hold that the Jesus quest, with its reconstruction of an "historical Jesus," functions as the norm for Christian theology. We need to engage in the quest, they say, because the historical Jesus is our ultimate norm for Christian truth.

Yet we have already seen that this cannot be true. The only adequate norm is the tradition-as-actualized-anew in its constitutive role of "constituting" the Christian community. This is why Tracy holds that, "on the tradition's own terms," a reconstructed historical Jesus cannot be our norm. "That norm," he continues, "on the tradition's own internal grounds is the apostolic witness *to* Jesus—the actual Jesus remembered by the community and proclaimed as the Christ."[41] In other words, it would be "inappropriate" to the tradition's own self-understanding to erect an historical Jesus into our norm for Christian truth.

Scholars who do this, Tracy thinks, are probably confusing issues of intelligibility (e.g., "I, as a historically conscious person, wish to know what historians on strictly historical grounds can tell me about the 'historical Jesus' "[42]) with issues of appropriateness. They are confusing the need to clarify some confusions in our understanding of the tradition (= intelligibility) with an appropriate understanding of the norm of Christianity itself. At the most, and at the best, a reconstructed "historical Jesus" might serve as a kind of "secondary criterion" of appropriateness for some necessary presuppositions of the constitutive tradition itself. For example, the tradition presupposes the historical Jesus, to which it is itself a response.

Secondly, we have those thinkers for whom the problem of the historical Jesus is "more a problem of intelligibility than a problem of appropriateness."[43] In other words, given our modern historical consciousness, some people want to know just what historians can tell us about Jesus on strictly historical grounds. Historical studies indicate that the Gospels are not historical biographies and seem to be a mixture of fact and fiction. This state of affairs raises questions for many thoughtful people, and the Jesus quest is a way of addressing these issues. In this sense, the Jesus quest to some extent challenges the tradition to admit that the Gospels are not biographies, and it also helps historically conscious people to "retrieve" some relatively solid data about Jesus.

Scholars working within this second option are not making an "historical Jesus" into our norm for Christian truth, but simply trying to correct inadequate understandings of the Scriptures in the light of our current needs for intelligibility. Edward Schillebeeckx, for example, seems to follow this function of the Jesus quest in his remarkable book *Jesus*. He has very much in mind the needs of historically conscious people as he writes. For these, he maintains, it is no longer possible to read the Gospel narratives with a simple innocence. These people first have to pass through an historical detour.[44]

The third approach, and the one that Tracy himself prefers, is to view the Jesus quest "as a contemporary theological way to keep alive and reformulate the 'dangerous' or 'subversive' memory of Jesus for the present community in fidelity to the original Jesus-kerygma and Christ-kerygma of the scriptural communities."[45] In this sense, the Jesus quest serves as a kind of contemporary reformulation of the kerygma itself, if it is done in such a way that it surfaces the substantial identity and continuity between the historical Jesus and the Christ of the New Testament kerygma. Tracy thinks that this is actually the way in which the Jesus quest often functions among theologians today, and in my chapter on the results of the Jesus quest I hope to show how Tracy's judgment is indeed confirmed. This third approach, then, to return to our working categories, would function as an "appropriate" interpretation of the tradition, clarifying and developing what the tradition's own self-understanding really is.

When we come to our critical survey of the results of the quest for Jesus, it will be in the spirit of Tracy's second and third approaches that we do so. Following Ricoeur, the Jesus quest is an important facet of the contribution that historical-critical methods of explanation can offer in a revitalized Christology. The Jesus quest, both as corrective to the tradition and as an appropriate interpretation of the same, is one way in which we can attempt to come to terms with the historical "reference" opened up to us in front of the New Testament text.

**SOME HISTORICAL-CRITICAL METHODS MENTIONED
THROUGHOUT THE CHAPTER**

(1) Two Source Theory

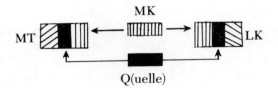

studies the relations between the Synoptics; Mark is thought to be
the oldest (it is shorter and does not seem to know of the destruction
of the Temple in 70 A.D.); Matthew and Luke borrow the narrative
structure of their gospels from Mark, but add the source of Jesus' sayings (= Q); both Mark and Luke have unique material also

(2) Form Criticism-Tradition History

studies the oral process leading up to the writing of the Gospels; believes that original/early traditions about Jesus or from Jesus were
shaped by the needs of local Christian communities and took certain
"forms" in the oral process as a result of catechizing, or teaching, or
worship; some "forms": teachings, miracle stories, sayings of Jesus,
parables, passion stories, resurrection stories, hymns, etc.

(3) Redaction Criticism

tries to explore the unique contributions that each biblical writer (re-
dactor) made:
> Mark created the narrative-story form of the Gospel
> Matthew and Luke added Q to Mark and incorporated their own
> themes
> John drew on traditional materials from his own special com-
> munity and created a highly original Gospel
> Paul created the epistolary/letter form of Christian proclamation

(4) Jesus Research

attempts to reconstruct, not a biography of Jesus, but the basic outlines of Jesus' ministry and teachings; utilizes various criteria to do
this: dissimilarity, multiple attestation, consistency

(5) Some Correctives

(a) Literary-critical analysis would insist that the historian is not re-constructing, through a psychological re-enactment of the author's intentions, events behind the text, but historical references opened up in front of the text

(b) Psychosocial criticism insists on the need to pay attention to the psychological and political dimensions of the text

Notes

1. See John S. Kselman, "Modern New Testament Criticism," *The Jerome Biblical Commentary*, II, Raymond E. Brown *et al.*, eds. (Englewood Cliffs, N.J.: Prentice-Hall, 1968), pp. 7-20.

2. *Reimarus: Fragments, op. cit.*, p. 133.

3. *Ibid.*, pp. 241–242.

4. *Ibid.*, pp. 69–70.

5. (Philadelphia: Fortress, 1972), ed. Peter C. Hodgson.

6. *Ibid.*, p. xxv, citing from the *Life's* first edition.

7. *Ibid.*, p. xxviii, again citing from the first edition.

8. *Ibid.*, p. 776; cf pp. 278–280 on the fragmentary nature of the Gospels.

9. See Schweitzer, *The Quest of the Historical Jesus, op. cit.*, pp. 180–222.

10. *Ibid.*, p. 4.

11. *Ibid.*

12. *Ibid.*, p. 3.

13. (Philadelphia: Fortress, 1971).

14. Schweitzer, *The Quest, op. cit.*, p. 37.

15. *Ibid.*, p. 350.

16. *Ibid.*, p. 389.

17. *Ibid.*, p. 370.

18. *Out of My Life and Thought, op. cit.*, p. 50.

19. (Cambridge: T. and T. Clark, 1971).

20. For an overview of this science, which is considerably more sophisticated and cautious in its judgments today, see Larry W. Hurtado, "New Testament Christology: A Critique of Bousset's Influence," *Theological Studies* 40 (1979), 306–317. The breakthrough study here was Wilhelm Bousset, *Kyrios Christos: A History of the Belief in Christ from the Beginnings of Christianity to Irenaeus* (Nashville: Abingdon, 1970 reissue/originally, 1913).

21. (New York: Charles Scribner's Sons, n.d./originally 1919).

22. Especially helpful on Bultmann: Raymond E. Brown and P. Joseph Cahill, *Biblical Tendencies Today: An Introduction to the Post-Bultmannians* (Washington, D.C. and Cleveland: Corpus, 1969); Schubert Ogden, *Christ without Myth* (New York: Harper, 1961); Ian Henderson, *Rudolf Bultmann* (Richmond,

Virginia: John Knox, 1966). Bultmann's more important studies: *The History of the Synoptic Tradition* (New York: Harper and Row, 1963), for an example of how he analyzes the New Testament; "The New Testament and Mythology," in *Kerygma and Myth*, ed. Hans Werner Bartsch (New York: Harper, 1961), pp. 1–44, 191–211, on demythologization; *Das Verhältnis der urchristlichen Christusbotschaft zum historischen Jesus* (Heidelberg: Carl Winter, 1961), on the continuity between the historical Jesus and the Christ of faith. Martin Kähler's *The So-Called Historical Jesus and the Historic Biblical Christ*, written already in 1892, took a position quite similar to Bultmann's on the issue of the theological unnecessity of a quest.

23. Cited in Brown and Cahill, *ibid.*, p. 30, n. 48.

24. In his *Essays on New Testament Themes* (London: SCM, 1964), pp. 15–47.

25. *Ibid.*, p. 25.

26. *Ibid.*, p. 37.

27. *Ibid.*, p. 38.

28. Keith F. Nickle, *The Synoptic Gospels: An Introduction* (Atlanta: John Knox, 1980), p. 165.

29. *Ibid.*, pp. 165–166. See Brown and Cahill, *op. cit.*, for bibliography on the new questers.

30. Cf, for Jeremias, his *The Prayers of Jesus* (London: SCM, 1967), and "The Present Position in the Controversy Concerning the Problem of the Historical Jesus," *Expository Times* 69 (1958), 338. For British scholars, see the relevant bibliography in Avery Dulles, *Myth, Biblical Revelation and Christ* (Washington, D.C.: Corpus, 1969), pp. 54–60, covering T.W. Manson, Vincent Taylor, and C.H. Dodd. The citation is from Dodd's *History and the Gospel* (New York: Charles Scribner's, 1968), p. 37.

31. Harald Riesenfeld, *The Gospel Tradition and Its Beginnings* (London: A.R. Mowbray, 1961), for a representative example. See, for critical surveys, J.A. Fitzmyer, *Theological Studies* 23 (1962), 442–457, and W.D. Davies, "Reflections on a Scandinavian Approach to 'The Gospel Tradition,'" *Neo-Testamentica et Patristica*, Suppl. to *Novum Testamentum*, 6, Leiden, 1962, 14–34.

32. Wolfhart Pannenberg, ed., *Revelation as History* (London: Macmillan, 1968).

33. See Von Hügel's and Blondel's grappling with the question of whether Jesus was mistaken about the timing of the Kingdom, an issue still heavily debated: John J. Heaney, *The Modernist Crisis: Von Hügel* (Washington, D.C.: Corpus, 1968), pp. 179–190. Loisy tended to accept the latest findings of biblical research, particularly the idea that Jesus was unconscious of his divinity and did not found a Church in the form that it later took. He did, however, regard the Church as a necessary mediator of Jesus to later ages, unlike the Protestant liberals, who tended to regard it as an obstacle to the true Jesus and his message. See Loisy's *The Gospel and the Church* (Philadelphia: Fortress, 1976/originally 1902).

34. Raymond E. Brown, *Biblical Reflections on Crises Facing the Church* (New York: Paulist, 1975), p. 6.

35. *Ibid.*, p. 111. For a complete text, see *Catholic Biblical Quarterly* 18 (1956), 23–29.

36. *Ibid.*, p. 112. I am using Brown's citation. For the complete text, see *Theological Studies* 25 (1964), 386–408.

37. *Ibid.*,

38. *Ibid.* Eastern Orthodox scholarship is also approaching the Scriptures more critically; see John Meyendorff, *Living Tradition, op. cit.,* esp. pp. 7–44.

39. The best and strongest defense of the necessity of the two poles for theological truth is David Tracy, *The Analogical Imagination, op. cit.,* pp. 233–247; this citation, p. 237.

40. Tracy, *ibid.,* remains the best entry into the grappling with this issue. His bibliography is extensive.

41. *Ibid.*, p. 238.

42. *Ibid.*

43. *Ibid.*, p. 239.

44. See Schillebeeckx, *Jesus, op. cit.,* esp. pp. 77–80, "The need is renewed for a post-critical, narrative history."

45. Tracy, *The Analogical Imagination, op. cit.,* p. 239.

PART TWO

Leading Interpretations of New Testament Christology

6

New Testament Christology:
The Literary-Critical Contribution

Our "dialogue" between the Christological tradition and our contemporary experience properly begins with the literary-critical contribution. In this way, as Ricoeur puts it, we are following the natural movement of the tradition's texts: from the "sense" to the "reference(s)" opened up in front of the texts. Of course, Christianity is not a religion of a book, but of a person, Jesus the Risen One. But the Jesus event has left us "traces" of itself in the New Testament, and it is chiefly to this "text" that we must turn for the "normative codification" of the Jesus event. That we go to Jesus *through the biblical text* is finally rooted in our tradition-bound character. Like all other things human, Christianity is an historically-mediated religion.

Paul Ricoeur and David Tracy as Guides

I will take as my chief "representatives" of the literary-critical approach the impressive work of Paul Ricoeur and David Tracy. On any accounting, these two deserve to be considered the most important contributors in this field to date. The two should really be considered together. While Tracy has contributed the most impressive "systematic" view of the biblical Christology, he has relied greatly upon Ricoeur's own seminal work in interpretation theory. It is often hard to know where Ricoeur ends and Tracy begins.

Perhaps it will be well to begin with Ricoeur's observations on the "textuality" of human existence. It is this textuality which provides the "homology" between the Jesus event and its codification into the New Testament. If you will, Ricoeur believes that we humans "participate" in existence through distanciation. Becoming human is not a simple and immediate matter, but requires a kind of detour through self-reflection and language. Our "languagistic" character gives us a means of self-communication, through which we can come to know ourselves or "appropriate" ourselves.[1] In fact, without this "distanciation" of languagistic reflection, self-knowledge would be impossible.

For Ricoeur, the most primordial form of self-communication is the text. He calls it "the paradigm of the distanciation of all communication."[2] This presupposes that our common human existence has a languagistic character, that this sayability of human existence can be inscribed (or textualized), and that therefore human existence resembles (in a very strong sense) a text. ". . . the entirety of human existence is a text to be read," says Ricoeur.[3] Relying upon Max Weber's definition of the object of the human sciences as "meaningfully oriented behavior," Ricoeur proposes that we translate "meaningfully oriented" into "readability characters" as a way of showing how human action can be textually inscribed. Ricoeur also speaks of the capacity of fictive and historical writings to "redescribe" human existence and action.

In his writings, Ricoeur has treated us to a few of the more important homologies between texts and our human existence. For example, human "doing" or "action" finds inscription in language in the latter's ability to cause us to act. Here are some others. Just as a text is distanciated from its author, autonomous from him or her, so our human actions are too: our deeds escape us and have effects we did not intend, says Ricoeur; thus they leave an imprint within human history.[4] As the text is distanciated from the initial situation in which it took place, so our human actions can become ideal paradigms with universal significance. In this way, they open up, like a text, a world of meaningful action. And as a text is distanciated from its original addressee, so our human actions are open to and relevant for anyone who can re-enact them in his or her life. These correspondences between text and life are helpful: they indicate why the "human action" of the Jesus event could find inscription or "codification" (Tracy's term) in our New Testament. If you will, the "readable character" of the Jesus event is opened up to us by the New Testament.

Tracy's Theory of the "Classic"

Tracy has creatively built upon Ricoeur's analysis of meaningful human action as a text. Taking some clues from Gadamer's probing analysis of the classic, he proposes that our human existence finds its most provocative and intense mediation in the form of what we call "the classic." In the most general sense, classics refer to those expressions of the human spirit which disclose a compelling truth about our lives. This is why we cannot deny their authority over us: they "tell" a truth which compels, which finds corroboration from the "text" of our own existence. Here, within and through the classic, we experience a disclosure of reality that we can only call "truth." Tracy likens the experience of the classic to the aesthetic experience of the art work. As the art work confronts one with surprise, impact, even the shock of reality itself, so, too, does the classic. Should the classic, like the art work, capture a paradigmatic experience of the event of truth, it becomes normative. As we have seen, Ricoeur will speak of the text opening up a world of ideal meaning and action. For Tracy, what sets the classic apart is its quality of "intensification": it is not any text, but the text which compels and even shocks. As an artist has undergone the journey of intensification into particularity, so the classic is an homologous journey. This journey, in its intensity, reaches "to the point where an originating sense for the fundamental questions and feelings that impel us all, and a rare response in thought and feeling to these questions, is experienced."[5]

"Religious" classics are specific forms of the classic. Like the latter, religious classics are events of disclosure, too, but this time of specifically religious experience. The shocking truth we encounter in them is the experience of transcendence, where finite lives intersect with infinite boundaries. Tracy likes to say that they give expression to the " 'limit-of,' 'horizon-to,' 'ground-to' side of 'religion.' "[6] Because of their specific nature, they radicalize the intensification process, for religious truth confronts us with the ultimate and most fundamental issue with which we have to do: life's overall meaning and purpose. Ultimately, because they refer to the Transcendent, religious classics cannot find an adequate form. Tracy seems to be saying that they inscribe an experience in search of a form. This searching, pointing-to quality seems characteristic of them. And for their appropriation on the part of the reader, they require certain existential conditions. Perhaps trust, and the struggle with evil and our human finitude, are the most basic of these conditions.

Following Ricoeur, Tracy proposes that there are two basic expressions of the religious classic, and these two are always interrelated. The first typical expression of the religious classic can be called "manifestation." Here the dialectic of the journey of intensification through the particularity of experience releases a radical sense of participating in the Transcendent. Hence Ricoeur calls it "manifestation": one senses that one has met the Ultimate, intersected with it, participated with it, "known" it. Manifestation might be illustrated by the Gospel narratives of the New Testament, which tell a story of Jesus' and his disciples' knowing participation in the Divine Mystery. It might also be illustrated in the writings of the mystics of all religions, who know themselves somehow "oned" with the Divine. Christians should see the sacraments as further examples of manifestation: sacramental encounters are meant to be, at the limit, genuine moments of participation in the Divine.

"Proclamation" is the second typical expression of the religious classic. Now the journey of intensification through particularity releases a radical sense of *non*-participation in the Transcendent. Here the Divine is experienced as "over-against," "radically other than us," a reality we cannot adequately know but must submit ourselves to. The great example here would be the prophetic utterance of the Hebrew Scriptures, "Thus says the Lord. . . ." Here the prophet humbly submits to what he cannot fully comprehend and to what he clearly cannot control. The divine "irruption" from beyond the human comes to the fore: hence Ricoeur's term "proclamation." In the New Testament, Paul perhaps is seen as the outstanding example: "Greetings from Paul, a servant of Christ Jesus . . . set apart to proclaim the gospel of God . . ." (Rom 1:1). In the Protestant tradition, the great emphasis upon the preached word and the doctrine of justification by faith alone are further examples of this typical expression known as Proclamation.

Ultimately, Tracy thinks that both—manifestation and proclamation—belong together and presuppose one another. If I understand him correctly, he is saying that they correspond to the immanence (= manifestation) and the transcendence (= proclamation) of the Divine. In this sense, "Manifestation is always the enveloping presupposition of the emergence and, at the limit, the eruption of the defamiliarizing word of proclamation."[7] Christianity always lives by both, and the "paradigmatic Christ event discloses the religious power of both manifestation and proclamation." As he continues:

> A dialectical sense, not a juxtapositional one nor any relaxed compromise, is present in the entire Christian symbol system to bespeak this need: word and sacrament; the transcendence and immanence of God; operative and cooperative grace; creation and eschatology; prophet-reformer and mystic-sage-priest; incarnation and cross-resurrection; nature-grace and grace-sin; aesthetics and ethics; nature and history; the centering, encoding myth and the decoding, decentering kerygma; epiphany and historical event; analogy and negative dialectics; metaphor and metonymy; ontic event and ontological structure; world-negation and, through the negation, a real release to world-affirmation. What is this always-present "and" in the Christian consciousness? It is, I believe, none other than the radically dialectical, transformative, always-already, not-yet "and" rooted in the classic event and person of Jesus Christ as true word *and* decisive manifestation.[8]

The Christian Classic: The New Testament

Tracy employs Ricoeur's interpretation schema of understanding-explanation-comprehension as his basic hermeneutical guide in interpreting the New Testament. Thus, he is open to the varied methods of explanation which we have surveyed, seeing all of them as provenly effective means of interpreting the Scriptures. But he thinks that the literary-critical approach is especially effective in learning the "sense" of the text in its structure, its forms, and its creative productivity of the referent: "the world of religious and imaginative meaning disclosed by and through the sense of the text."[9] Historical methods, he thinks, in their effort to retrieve an abstract summary of the New Testament, tend to obscure the diversity of the New Testament's expressions, overlooking the power of all the scriptural genres to mediate the Jesus event. If one views diversity, not as a hindrance, but as an aid, then one can discover through the very diversity of scriptural genres an interpretation that is truly "appropriate" to the wide diversity of New Testament Christianity. We need not fear that this diversity will result in meaningless bits and pieces, for all the scriptural genres are united in their one witness to the "text" of the Jesus event.

Taking a clue from Ricoeur's work on genres, Tracy basically advances a genre-oriented interpretation of the New Testament. For Ricoeur, the forms of expression found in the New Testament are not accidental, but flow from the religious experience that the texts seek to open up before us. If you will, the language of faith brings about a specific polyphony of literary expressions, which mutually counterbalance one another. This follows from Ricoeur's view that a literary work, such as the Bible, is a *work* of composition. The idea that the text is a "work" indicates the human sphere of production and labor; literary genres are productive and generative devices, not mere classifications. For this reason, recognizing the genres-forms, as Tracy does, gives us a decisive aid in interpreting the texts, finding out how they "encode" a new message for us. As Ricoeur puts it,

> The "confession of faith" which is expressed in the biblical documents is inseparable from the *forms* of discourse there, by which I mean the narratives, the prophecies, the parables, the hymns, etc. Not only does each form of discourse give rise to a style of confession of faith, but also the confrontation of these forms of discourse gives rise, in the confession of faith itself, to tensions and contrasts which are theologically significant. The opposition between narration and prophecy, so fundamental for the mentality of the Old Testament, is perhaps only one of the pairs of structures whose opposition contributes to engendering the global shape of its meaning.[10]

Thus, for Tracy, the classic which is the New Testament generates the new world of meaning stemming from the journey of intensification through particularity *in* its literary genres. These generative genres are the way in which this new Christian world of meaning is disclosed. In their tensions and contrasts, we experience something of the rich polyphony of meaning found in the Jesus event.

The Corrective Genres

Tracy believes that two genres, which pervade the New Testament, play a subordinate but still essential and corrective role in "opening up" the Jesus event. As Ricoeur indicated, there are tensions and contrasts indicated by the literary genres of the Scriptures themselves. These tensions, signaled by their literary genres, have theological significance: they disclose an essential dimension of the Jesus event. It is in this spirit, I believe, that Tracy speaks of our two "corrective" genres.

(1) *Apocalyptic* is one such corrective genre, characterized by intensification and negations. For Tracy it is a "challenge and reminder of the explosive intensification and negations needed within all other genres" of the New Testament.[11] What Tracy has to say about the apocalyptic presupposes some familiarity with this genre. I would recommend that the reader uninitiated to this area jump ahead to our next chapter, where this topic is treated in a more historical way (pp. 164–168).

What, then, does apocalyptic intensify and negate? It negates all privatism, every tendency to view the divine disclosure in the Jesus event as simply a private message to individuals. The divine disclosure is meant for human peoples as a social collectivity: the Kingdom of the Divine evokes a new kind of community coming into being. At the same time as it negates (privatism), it intensifies the communal aspect of the Jesus event. Negation and intensification coincide; they are obverse sides of the same reality. So, too, apocalyptic intensifies the call to the world's privileged to remember the poor, the oppressed, and the victims of history. Thereby it negates all elitism and aristocratic privilege. The Divine is disclosed in the Jesus event as on the side of the oppressed. So, too, it intensifies the call to remember the hope of a future in the Kingdom for all the dead, thereby negating pessimism and a forgetfulness of history's victims. Above all, it intensifies, through its evocative and rich symbolism, the need to face the *novum*, the really new world of love, justice, and peace that the Divine is working to bring about in the Jesus event.

Thus, through apocalyptic, the world opened up in the Jesus event is seen to be a complex reality; the Divine is disclosed as on the side of humanity as a whole, especially the oppressed and victims of history; the Divine is the bringer of a really new future, which always remains in the future as long as there are victims within history. If we return to our two basic modes of religious expression, manifestation and proclamation, we could say that apocalyptic radicalizes/intensifies the proclamatory aspect of religious expression. It releases and heightens the radical sense of non-participation in the Divine. For the Divine remains ahead of us, as a future promise for history's victims and a future judge for history's tyrants. So, too, it intensifies our non-participation in the Divine as long as our religious life remains purely private and personal, unlinked to the destiny of others, especially the oppressed of history.

Apocalyptic seems best described, not as a central genre of the New Testament, but as a pervasively corrective one. Its intensification and negations act upon the other genres, creating a contrast and tension with them. Thereby they indicate the incompleteness of all genres taken singly and their need to be mutually corrective. Thus, for example, apocalyptic is found, *explosively expressed*, in the "little apocalypse" of Mark 13, throughout all of 1 Thessalonians, and throughout the Book of Revelation. It is found, *transformatively expressed*, throughout Jesus' proclamation of the Kingdom, in his parables, and throughout the deeds of his ministry— transformatively, because it is taken over by Jesus and slanted in the direction of his own, special view of the Kingdom as rooted in the universal love of the Divine. Mark's view of Jesus as the suffering Son of Man and Paul's theology of the crucified Christ present us with yet another apocalyptic genre, which intensifies the divine preference for the oppressed and suffering. The apocalyptic flavor of the Second Letter of Peter presents us with a *somewhat dimly expressed* apocalyptic warning to avoid the dangers of a too settled Christianity, forgetful of the need to expect the new arrival of the Kingdom constantly. This pervasiveness of our apocalyptic genre, throughout the Greek Scriptures, indicates its corrective nature to other genres.

To help the reader unfamiliar with this kind of analysis, let us do a little thought experiment, using as our example the famous "little apocalypse" of Mark 13. In one column (the left), I will present the text; in the other (the right), I will try to highlight some of the intensification and negations Tracy speaks of.

Jesus began his discourse: "Be on your guard. Let no one mislead you. Any number will come attempting to impersonate me. 'I am he,' they will claim, and will lead men astray. When you hear about wars and threats of war, do not

intensifies the need to face the *novum*, the really new future of the Kingdom which the Divine will bring about yield to panic. Such things are bound to happen, but this is not yet the end. Nation will rise against nation, one kingdom against another. There will be earthquakes in various places and there will be famine. This is but the onset of the pains of labor.

Be constantly on your guard. They will hand you over to the courts. You will be beaten in synagogues. You will be arraigned before governors and kings on my account and have to testify to your faith before them. But the good news must first be proclaimed to all the Gentiles.

> intensifies the need to remember the oppressed; negates history's tyrants

When men take you off into custody, do not worry beforehand about what to say. In that hour, say what you are inspired to say. It will not be yourselves speaking but the Holy Spirit.

> intensifies how the Divine sides with the oppressed

Brother will hand over brother for execution and likewise the father his child; children will turn against their parents and have them put to death. Because of my name, you will be hated by everyone. Nonetheless, the man who holds out till the end is the one who will come through safe.

> intensifies the need to remember the oppressed; negates the tyrants and vanquishers

When you see the abominable and destructive presence standing where it should not be—let the reader take note!—those in Judaea must flee to the mountains. If a man is on the roof terrace, he must not come down or enter his house to get anything out of it. If a man is in the field, he must not turn back to pick up his cloak. It will go badly with pregnant and nursing women in those days. Keep praying that none of this happens in winter. Those times will be more distressful than any between God's work of

> intensifies the need to face the *novum;* negates a forgetfulness of the future

creation and now, and for all time to
come. Indeed, had the Lord not shortened the period, not a person would be
saved.

But for the sake of those he has chosen,
he has shortened the days.

intensifies how the Divine sides with
the oppressed

If anyone tells you at that time, 'Look, he
is there!'—do not believe it. False messiahs and false prophets will appear performing signs and wonders to mislead, if
it were possible, even the chosen.

intensifies, thus helping us to remember, the reality of oppression of the innocent

So be constantly on guard! I have told you
about it beforehand!

intensifies the *novum;* negates forgetfulness of it

During that period after trials of every
sort the sun will be darkened, the moon
will not shed its light, stars will fall out of
the skies, and the heavenly hosts will be
shaken. Then men will see the Son of
Man coming in the clouds with great
power and glory. He will dispatch his angels and assemble his chosen from the
four winds, from the farthest bounds of
earth and sky. . . . When you see these
things happening, you will know that he
is near, even at the door. I assure you,
this generation will not pass away until all
these things take place. The heavens and
the earth will pass away but my words
will not pass.

again, the *novum* is intensively highlighted; note the non-privatism: the
Divine will assemble, not just individuals, but the chosen; likewise, the evil
are negated/judged; note how the cosmos is affected

As to the exact day or hour, no one knows
it, neither the angels in heaven nor even
the Son, but only the Father. Be constantly on the watch! Stay awake! You do
not know when the appointed time will
come."

again intensifies the *novum*—it remains truly new and unpredictable

Tracy speaks of "intensification," because the reader can sense the
heightened and exaggerated quality of the metaphors employed. Ricoeur
will call this the device of semantic impertinence: on the ordinary empir-

ical level the language cannot mean what it says. This tips us off that we are being forced to entertain a new world of meaning beyond the normal. The "negations" are implied through the force of the intensifications: if the future Kingdom (= *novum*) is stressed, then forgetfulness of the future is negated; if the oppressed are stressed, then the tyrants of history are negated; if the collectivity of humanity is addressed, then privatism is negated, etc.

(2) *Early Catholicism* is a second phenomenon of the New Testament, giving rise to a second corrective genre, equally pervasive in scope: "doctrinal confession." Now the tension and intensification characteristic of apocalyptic seems relaxed. On the whole, this genre expresses the divine mediation of itself to the ordinary lives of Christians. If you will, it gives expression to the "extraordinariness of the ordinary." If we return to our two major poles of manifestation and proclamation, doctrinal confession highlights the manifestation pole. It voices the sense of participation in the Divine through and in the ordinary fabric of our lives. The Divine is not so much ahead of us as present to us, more immanent than transcendent—not only on the side of the oppressed, but also with the ordinary and established "folk" who must carve out a life for themselves.

Tracy claims that this genre, too, pervades the New Testament. For example, Jesus' table fellowship as inscribed in the Gospels highlights the divine mediation to the everyday reality of people. Jesus frequently appeals to ordinary, everyday realities in his parables and proverbs: these, too, can mediate the Divine presence. "Consider the ravens. . . . Or take the lilies. . . . If God clothes in such splendor the grass of the field, which grows today and is thrown on the fire tomorrow, how much more will he provide for you . . ." (Lk 12:24–28). Unlike the ascetic Baptist, Jesus loves the everyday realities: "The Son of Man came and he both ate and drank, and you say, 'Here is a glutton and a drunkard, a friend of tax collectors and sinners!' " (Lk 7:34).

Of course, "doctrinal confession" is especially characteristic of the relatively late writings of the New Testament stemming from the period of the early Church's institutionalization: the "pastoral epistles" (1 and 2 Timothy, Titus) and the "Catholic epistles" (1 and 2 Peter, James, Jude). Here there is voiced a concern for the ordinary realities of a growing Church and its needs: the poor, widows, heretics, ministers, doctrines, etc. All are seen as legitimate areas of the divine work. Clearly the manifestation pole of our dialectic of manifestation-proclamation is in evidence here.

What world of meaning does this genre open up to us, what dimension of the Jesus event? Surely that the Divine is present and not only future, in the everyday and not simply the horrible or extraordinary, in institutions and not simply the struggles of the oppressed, etc. The Jesus event is not only proclamation (= apocalyptic), but also manifestation. Clearly this genre needs the corrective of apocalyptic, lest it lose the proclamatory dimension of religion. But so, too, does apocalyptic need early Catholicism, lest it lose the manifestation dimension of religion. But, as Tracy notes, doctrinal confession lacks intensity. This would seem to indicate that it is not a central genre of the New Testament, but only a corrective. It is not the "heart," but the periphery.

Proclamation-Narrative-Symbol-Thought: The Central Genres of the New Testament

(1) "Proclamation" is clearly for Tracy one central genre of the New Testament. It has the characteristic of intensity, and it pervades the entire New Testament. Apocalyptic, we have seen, is ultimately dependent upon proclamation, intensifying it and negating its opposites. This indicates that apocalyptic is derivative and corrective, rather than central, in the New Testament. But proclamation finds expression in the kerygma and the kerygmatic elements found throughout all the other New Testament genres: teachings, ethics, apologetic, polemics, narrative, hymns, letters, proverbs, doctrines, theological reflections, etc. It is simply pervasive, intensely felt, and central. Tracy even calls it the "transformative presupposition of all further genres."[12]

We have, in substance, already spoken of this genre in our comments on "proclamation" as one of the two basic forms of religious expression. As we recall, when the journey of intensification through the particularity of experience releases the sense of non-participation in the Divine, then proclamation results as the literary form of this experience. As we have *experienced* "grace," the "divine irruption from beyond," the Transcendent over against us, so the genre of proclamation gives *expression* to this experience. "Proclaiming" or "preaching" expresses this over-againstness: one is addressed, confronted, challenged "from the beyond." Thus, Paul's "I want to remind you of the gospel I preached to you, which you received and in which you stand firm" (1 Cor 15:1). Thus Mark says of Jesus that he "appeared in Galilee proclaiming the good news of God" (Mk 1:14). Thus the many kerygmatic sections throughout Acts (1:14–36; 3:11–26; 4:8–12; 7:2–53; 10:34–43; 13:16–41; 17:22–31, etc.), and indeed throughout all the other New Testament genres.

For Tracy, the genre of proclamation/kerygma is both "event" and "content," both the divine, irrupting address from beyond (= event), and our provoked response to that address in the form of a confession (= content): we proclaim Jesus Christ crucified! As Paul puts it, "I handed on to you first of all what I myself received . . ." (1 Cor 15:3). The world this genre opens up before us is the irruption of the Divine into our history in the form of the crucified Savior, which we can only confess. All other New Testament genres need to be linked with this proclamation, lest they lose their rootedness in the event-character, the divine and gifted character of the Jesus event. Yet, as Tracy so well indicates, proclamation needs the other genres, too, lest it become simply abstract and authoritarian, a kind of esoteric mystery with no "human" meaning.

(2) Clearly a second central genre is that of narrative, as it is found particularly in the four canonical Gospels. As Tracy likes to say, the Gospels share the normal human tendency to want to tell stories. Why is this a normal human tendency? Because human experience is narrable, the unfolding of a "plot," from beginning, through the middle, to an ending. Humans want and need to find a way to order and unify their lived experience. In this way, by disclosing the narrable quality of human life, stories/narratives disclose a "human possibility that might otherwise go unremarked."[13] Thus there is a disclosive and transformative power and meaning in the story.

Here perhaps some observations from Ricoeur's own growing work on narratives may be of some help.[14] For Ricoeur, narrativity is that form of literary expression whose ultimate referent is temporality, humanity's being-in-time. But at the same time this means that human temporality is the kind of existence that finds its proper literary expression in narrativity. For this reason, narrativity is a wide genre in Ricoeur's thought, embracing not only fictional narratives but also historical narratives. Historical writing is also a form of narrativity, and this point will be capital when we move, in our next chapter, to the historical-critical approach to Christology.

Ricoeur introduces the narrative's temporality through an explication of the device of the "plot." It is the plot that transforms events into a story. Van den Hengel, Ricoeur's commentator, will speak of "emplotment" in this regard.[15] What are some of the basic elements of emplotment, this device of craftsmanship used by the story? Of course, every story must be followed and followable. This means that the reader must be able to understand the sequence of characters and events within the story, their interaction, and their conclusion. Following means that the reader is "taken in" or "taken along" by this sequence, challenged by it, and able to grasp the possible conclusions flowing from it. But one must pass through the story to sense the ending.

Ricoeur also distinguishes between episodes/events and their configuration. Emplotment means that these events are crafted into a schema or configuration. This device does not annul the events, but heightens their meaning and power of disclosure. What we are "following" in the story is the story's point, and this is the function of configuration. Configuration also means that there is a certain "closure" to the story. The device of configuration, by imposing a pattern upon the episodes, brings them to a "conclusion." Events which can have multiple meanings are given limited and defined meanings through this device of closure. Thus, emplotment works by means of followability, configuration, and closure.

Now we are in a position to understand why narrativity is connected to temporality. It is the plot/emplotment that connects them. For within the development of the plot there is a certain time orientation. Our curiosity in the possible conclusion of the story draws us along, temporally, through the story. We are thrown into time in the telling and reading of stories. Furthermore, there are semantic indicators of this temporality within stories, "then," "now," "next," "after," "while," etc. The characters are also preoccupied with the things of time: opportunities, a "time to do this," and a "lack of time to do that." But it is especially temporality in its meaning-dimension, not in the ordinary sense of the ticking away of moments by a clock, that is highlighted by the story. Ordinary time is escaped. The time of the story is "now," as Van den Hengel comments,

> Although measurable in terms of days and hours, the emphasis is upon the preoccupation with things, with care, and not upon the abstract, objectifiable time of the clock that can date the preoccupation. The time of the story is "now." It escapes ordinary time in two ways. It is first of all a "now" that is shared each in their own way by the characters of the story in the telling of the story. But secondly, it is as well a "now" that clings to the hearer and reader of the story. The story's saying of "now" is, to use Heidegger's term, a way of "making present" that is more than the "now" of ordinary time.[16]

Narratives, then, give expression to the temporality of our human existence. Emplotment, if you will, "nets" us into the flow of temporality. In this sense, narratives correspond more closely to the manifestation pole of religious expressions. As manifestation refers to the release of our sense of participation in the Divine, so narratives unfold the course of that participation within our temporal existence. If you will, the world which the New Testament narratives open up before us is the world of a human, temporal existence permeated by a divine presence. The apparent lack of concern, within the Gospels, for "factual details" (the world of ordinary time) would seem to indicate that the meaning of the story is on a deeper level. I would suggest, with Tracy, that this deeper level is the sense of participation with the divine presence within temporality.

Tracy underscores the fact that the Gospels are a complex genre, ac-

tually containing several forms of narrative. For example, we have "miniature Gospels" in the form of Jesus' individual sayings: "Q," the source of
Jesus' sayings incorporated in Matthew and Luke; the "Farewell Discourses" of John's Gospel (3:31—17:26); outside our canon, the Cop-
tic/Gnostic Gospel of Thomas comes to mind. We have the parables, which
are stories unto themselves, with rather explosive plots. Jesus' deeds are a
kind of narrative of actions, especially if we keep in mind Ricoeur's view of
meaningful actions as a text. The narratives of Jesus' table-fellowship
should clearly be included here. Finally, Tracy especially highlights the
passion narratives within each of the Gospels. He claims that the heart of
the plot is found here. Beyond these "sub-narratives" we have the Gospels
themselves. Each Gospel finds its own, unique manner of unfolding Jesus'
character in and through the plot of the story. If you will, each sub-nar-
rative and narrative finds its own way of highlighting various facets of
"manifestation," of the way in which the Divine participates in the temporality of Jesus.

For example, Mark seems to develop a narrative that is rather like an
apocalyptic drama. Jesus is the apocalyptic Son of Man who suffers. His
manner of participating in the divine presence is one of suffering love.
Matthew and Luke seem to develop narratives which can serve as "foundation myths" for Christian communities. Jesus' mode of participation in
the divine presence is one of gathering a community of disciples obedient
to a higher righteousness (Matthew), or one of conquering the whole world
on behalf of the Gospel (Luke) through faithful witnesses. Tracy even
speaks of the "more open" Jesus of Matthew and Luke. Presumably he has
in mind a Jesus who is open to gathering followers (Matthew) and even the
world (Luke). John's narrative simply sheerly equates cross and glory,
thereby highlighting the manifestation of the Divine in the very cross of
Jesus.

Tracy's own summary of the world opened up before us in these narratives is especially helpful:

> The authority of this remembered Jesus in both his preaching and his
> deeds is the authority of one who witnesses that the final power is gra-
> cious, that the final power *is* love. The narratives insist that a life lived
> in fidelity to that power is a life like that cruciform life of freedom, con-
> flict, suffering, love, peace, authority confessed as lived by Jesus of Naz-
> areth. Our expectations of God's power are shattered by the preaching
> of the life and words of Jesus. They are transformed into a recognition
> that God's power, the ultimate power at work in the universe, is none
> other than love. Our expectations of life—for happiness, security, com-
> fort, success, justification—shatter against that preaching and that de-
> familiarizing life: a life lived in fidelity to the agapic power of God, a life

meeting rejection and crucifixion from the powers of this world, a life receiving vindication from the final power of God. The community's memory of Jesus remains a dangerous memory endangering it yet. [17]

The danger of the Gospel narratives, of course, is that they will forget the proclamation pole of religious experience, subsuming all into manifestation. The release of the sense of participation in the Divine, expressed in the narratives, will overshadow the sense of our non-participation, the sense that the Divine remains ahead of and beyond us. Temporality and immanence will overshadow transcendence. But the Gospels preserve the dialectic of the tension between proclamation and manifestation, transcendence and immanence. The proclamatory genre (kerygma of Jesus) pervades the narratives. The sheer repetition of the narratives recalls the great theme of the overcoming of chaos through return to our origins in the Divine. In a sense, the narratives do not really end: Mark awaits the second coming, Luke-Acts continues on into an indefinite future. This lack of "closure" indicates the not-yetness of the Divine. The striking paradox of the triumph of cross and resurrection fills us with tension and reminds us that our participation in the Divine is still linked with non-participation (= the cross). The concentration of the narratives upon the single person of Jesus suggests to the reader that one should focus upon one's own individuality as authentic or inauthentic. But the tension of the not-yet throughout the narratives prevents this individual focus from degenerating into narcissistic individualism: until the Divine fully comes; until all, especially the oppressed, are saved; until there are no more crosses—only then can the tension be relaxed.

For Ricoeur, perhaps what most fully preserves this tension between manifestation and proclamation throughout the Gospels is the parables of Jesus. The parables are a kind of conjunction between the narrative form and a metaphorical process. As narratives, they are stories with an obvious surface meaning: ordinary people doing ordinary things, like selling, buying, fishing, sowing, etc. Yet this normal, narrative structure is "invaded" through a metaphorical process. Through this metaphorical process a semantic clash pervades the story, forcing an apparently normal story to deliver another, non-literal, extraordinary meaning. If you will, this semantic clash forces us to entertain the extraordinary.

Ricoeur finds this metaphoricity in the plot of the narrative. Unlike normal narrative, the parables are simply extravagant. Each contains a surprising moment that is simply unexpected: a Samaritan who is good; a mustard seed, the smallest plant of all, becoming the largest plant; the leaving the ninety-nine sheep for simply one, etc. Through this extravagance, the extraordinary invades the ordinary, proclamation invades narrative/manifestation. The plot itself is a metaphorical process, forcing us to entertain a new world of meaning, breaking open the inner "sense" of the narrative to a new "reference." Ricoeur, in shorthand, defines metaphor as "nothing other than the application of a familiar label to a new object which first resists and then surrenders to its application."[18] Our being forced to entertain this new application—the extraordinary in the ordinary—preserves the necessary tension between proclamation and manifestation. This tension is even further heightened by the connection of the parables with Jesus' eschatological sayings which point to the extraordinary Kingdom of God, by their connection with his extraordinary miracles, and simply by their connection with this extraordinary crucified and risen Jesus. All of these connections intensify the extraordinariness within the ordinary, proclamation within manifestation.

(3) "Symbol" and "reflective thought" move us into the final central genres of the New Testament. These genres, too, pervade the New Testament with a striking intensity. Basically the Scriptures turn to certain tensive symbols/images in an effort to disclose the fuller meaning of the manifestation and proclamation of the Jesus event. Symbols, according to Ricoeur, are at the edge of language. They are found at the point where language emerges from its experiential ground. They are the first form of the metaphorical process: the use of literal language to suggest a new, nonliteral meaning. In the New Testament, Tracy finds three of these central symbols which express the originary Christian experience. All three are dialectically interrelated throughout our Testament.

(a) The "cross" is a complex symbol, simultaneously opening up a wide spectrum of "references." It points to the power and pain of the negative, and so opens up to us the paradox of a divine power found in weakness and love for others. It also evokes the sense that the death of the self is the way to a new life. For Tracy it intensifies our focus upon love "as the ultimate, binding, internal relationship of the divine and human."[19] (b) The "resurrection" symbol serves to open up the vision that a life lived in crucified love is vindicated and transformed. It intensifies our focus upon the Divine as the enabling power here and now in our midst, transforming cross into life. (c) "Incarnation" again intensifies the manifestation of the Divine as a reality and power in our midst. As we can see, these three great symbols evoke different dimensions of the Jesus event by intensifying them: our non-participation (= cross) and participation (= resurrection and incarnation) in the divine life simultaneously. The Jesus event releases both a sense of our distance from and nearness to the Divine. In Tracy's words, "The heart of the Christian symbol system is none other than the unbreakable dialectic of cross-resurrection-incarnation disclosing through its own internal tensions the fuller meanings of the event of Jesus Christ."[20]

But these symbols give rise to thought. Thus we find the beginnings of a reflective style of thought (= theology) emerging in the New Testament. Hebrews' liturgical theology and Revelation's apocalyptic theology come to mind. But Tracy singles out Paul and John as the two great theologians of the New Testament. As Ricoeur puts it, the metaphorical nature of symbols, which suggest a new, non-literal meaning-world through ordinary and literal language, creates the tension and energy which drives us to reflection. This is the "ontological vehemence" of the symbols.[21] Thus

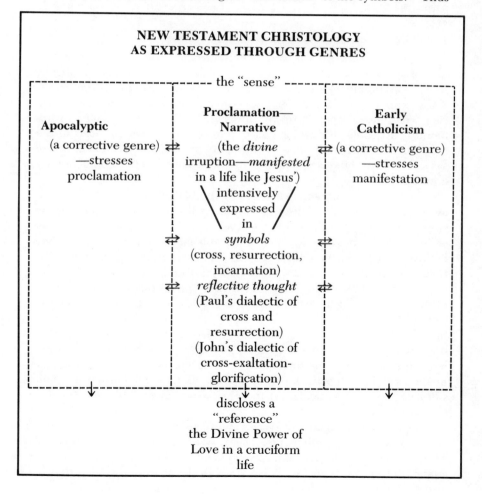

**NEW TESTAMENT CHRISTOLOGY
AS EXPRESSED THROUGH GENRES**

the "sense"

Apocalyptic

(a corrective genre)
—stresses
proclamation

⇄

**Proclamation—
Narrative**

(the *divine*
irruption—*manifested*
in a life like Jesus')
intensively
expressed
in
symbols
(cross, resurrection,
incarnation)
reflective thought
(Paul's dialectic of
cross and
resurrection)
(John's dialectic of
cross-exaltation-
glorification)

⇄

**Early
Catholicism**

(a corrective genre)
—stresses
manifestation

discloses a
"reference"
the Divine Power of
Love in a cruciform
life

Paul and John seem to concentrate the Jesus event into religious tensive symbols which highlight the meaning-world opened up through Jesus. Paul's dialectical juxtaposition of cross-resurrection indicates a deepened penetration of the Jesus event as the dialectic between manifestation and proclamation. "I determined that while I was with you I would speak of nothing but Jesus Christ and him crucified," says Paul (1 Cor 2:2). John's Gospel evidences a similar, more reflective penetration of this same dialectic: the cross is exaltation and glorification and incarnation. There is perhaps a greater stress with Paul on proclamation, and with John on manifestation, but both are present dialectically in each writer.

The Pluralism of Methods of Explanation

A helpful feature of the work of both Ricoeur and Tracy is their awareness of the pluralism of interpretations possible in New Testament literary study. This pluralism is demanded by the very nature of the Testament itself: its varied symbolisms-metaphors-images, its varied genres, and its varied "references" opened up by the sense of the text demand a "community" of scholarship which concentrates on these varied facets of the text. Furthermore, only such a community of scholarship can help insure that our interpretations remain public and "testable" in the light of literary criteria.

Tracy himself argues that the only methods which should be disallowed are those which "disown" the original experience of the literary work and try to replace it with some other experience. A genuine pluralism of "readings" is possible because of the four major elements basic to any literary work. Monistic interpretations stem from an exaggerated concentration upon one of these four elements. Tracy enumerates these four elements in the following way: (1) the artist who creates the work, (2) the work itself, (3) the world the work creates or reveals, and (4) the audience the work affects. "Yet it remains the realized experience which must serve as the first word and the final criterion of relative adequacy in any attempt at both understanding and explanation," says Tracy.[22] What Tracy seems to have in mind is that the final criterion of interpretation is the particular method's ability to enable the interpreter to undergo the journey of intensification through particularity, thereby "experiencing" the classic's disclosure of "truth."

An interesting feature of Tracy's and Ricoeur's work, I think, is that it cuts across these four elements. This is what gives their work a kind of "guiding status" in literary interpretation of the New Testament. For example, both begin their interpretation with the artist's creativity: the realized experience of participation and non-participation in the Divine. In other words, for both our language is rooted in our experience and expressive of our experience. Ricoeur will call this a "discourse" view of language—it is rooted in real speakers who are giving expression to their experience of the world. Further, both Ricoeur and Tracy grapple with how our realized experience finds expression in the literary work itself: participation and non-participation give birth to "manifestation" and "proclamation," with their varied corrective genres and symbolisms-reflective thought. Both then move to a consideration of the "reference" or "world of meaning" opened up in front of the text: the disclosure that the ultimate reality in life is a divine power of love participating with us, explosively in Jesus, less explosively but still effectively in others. Finally, both move to a consideration of how the work affects the audience it creates: the self of the interpreter does not master the text, but the text widens the self, through opening up a new and wider world of meaning and action.

Tracy's enumeration of the four elements constituting the literary work are helpful in another sense. They give us some means of placing in perspective the varied literary currents now being practiced in New Testament studies and Christology. Of course, non-biblical literary analysis is much more advanced than its biblical correlate. Thus we find in literary criticism at large well-developed traditions of interpretation which correspond to the four elements of the work enumerated by Tracy: (1) the artist (= theories of creativity and expression), (2) the work (= formalist theories, like structuralism), (3) the world opened up by the work (= Gadamer's work especially), and (4) the audience (= pragmatic theories and some forms of Marxist analysis). Biblical literary criticism is still in its infancy, having been for well over a century preoccupied with historical and philosophical forms of analysis, in an effort to defend itself against modern secularism.

Let me briefly highlight some of the methods of literary analysis now being practiced in Christology and New Testament studies. If we follow Tracy's suggestion about the four elements of the work, I think we can begin to grasp that these methods are mostly "partial" and tend to corroborate Tracy's and Ricoeur's analysis. Let me say that I put forward the following "schematic analysis" only as a proposal, guided by Ricoeur and Tracy. Some practitioners of the following approaches may not fully agree with what follows.

Artist-Oriented Approaches

Artist-oriented approaches are clearly appropriate to a literary analysis of the New Testament, not in the sense that the interpreter wants to recreate psychologically the artistic experience "behind" the text, but the author in and through the text. Insofar as the author's meaning is a property of the text itself, which shapes and gives "style" to the text, such an artist-oriented interpretation can throw light upon the text itself. A good and recent example of this approach is provided us by Frans Jozef van Beeck's *Christ Proclaimed: Christology as Rhetoric.*[23]

Like Ricoeur and Tracy, Van Beeck bases his work upon a discourse theory of language (the "speech act"). Our language arises from our realized experience (the speech act), and then finds inscription in writing. Especially important is Van Beeck's desire to pay greater attention to what he calls the "non-cognitive" dimensions of language-use. Language primordially expresses our experience of activity, of intersubjectivity (we communicate one with another), and of responding to a gracious and divine presence. Ultimately it is through metaphors, which employ literal language in a non-literal way, that we are able to give expression to this non-cognitive dimension of our experience. Metaphors, if you will, express the richer fabric of our experience in its felt wholeness, prior to its abstract expression in cognitive propositions. Metaphor links the cognitive and non-cognitive in our lives: it permits us an understanding of the rich texture of our existence which is closer to the felt nature of this existence as activity, intersubjectivity, and grace.

Van Beeck proposes that it is this richer kind of discourse which pervades the New Testament. The speech-acts of the authors of the New Testament are powerful "acts of confidence" arising from the felt experience of the Jesus event. These acts of confidence release a triple Christological rhetoric, which we can see inscribed in the New Testament. If you will, New Testament Christology *is* this rhetoric, manifesting "an original non-cognitive element in Christology, namely, the response to the person of Jesus Christ."[24] When the authors of the Scriptures attest that they are speaking "in the Spirit," this is the indication that their rhetoric inscribes this richer, non-cognitive dimension.

The three styles of rhetoric Van Beeck analyzes are those of "inclusion," of "obedience," and of "hope." The rhetoric of inclusion seems to express the experience of Jesus' unconditional acceptance of all things human. All somehow seems "included" in the Jesus event, as this language attests. Van Beeck points to the Christological titles in illustration, for the varied titles are taken from literally all areas of human concern, illustrating Jesus' acceptance of all of these areas. Learning (Rabbi/Teacher), governing (Lord), struggling against evil (Messiah), human sustenance (Shepherd), knowledge (the Truth), life in general (the Way, the Life), our suffering humanity (Son of Man)—all these titles show how Jesus embraces all of these areas. If you will, this rhetoric expresses the fullness of Jesus' humanity and humaneness.

The rhetoric of obedience, also a pervasive reality in the New Testament, seems to express Christ's ability to test, humble, and purify our human concerns. By naming Jesus with all of these titles we attest our willingness to submit ourselves to his paradigmatic example. He is *the* Way in the light of which our own way must be lived and modeled. The rhetoric of hope seems to inscribe what is the foundational speech-act of the New Testament authors, from which the two other rhetorics spring. This foundational speech-act is that of being empowered to speak in this novel manner. This rhetoric of hope is found expressed in the resurrection kerygma, "We have seen the Lord. He lives!" This hopeful rhetoric seems to point to the disciples' meeting with Christ alive and present. It is this experience which "releases the believer's speech." "Bold speaking" attests to its reality. [25]

I would propose that Van Beeck has provided us with an equivalent expression of Ricoeur's and Tracy's proclamation-manifestation dialectic. The rhetoric of hope seems to correspond to the proclamatory pole: the experience of the divine irruption in the Jesus event, over against us, empowering us with "bold speech." The rhetorics of inclusion and obedience would seem to correspond more fully to the manifestation pole: the Divine as participating with us, in the full humanity of Jesus and in our own, humble attempts to pattern our human lives on Jesus.

Work-Oriented Approaches

A possible limitation of the artist-oriented approach is that it does not always account for the difference between the *oral* and the *written* discourse situation. An emphasis upon the speech-act can easily tend to obscure the manner in which the meaning of that speech-act has been "fixed" in writing. Fixation in writing means that the text and its ideal meanings have been distanciated from the original author, the original situation, and the original audience. If you will, the meaning of the speech-act becomes the object of interpretation. But this meaning can only be found through the text, through the way it structures and codifies its major images and symbols. The strength of work-oriented approaches is that they dwell upon the work of the text itself. In this way, they go beyond an analysis of the images, which are perhaps the author's "traces" in the text, to a consideration of the way in which these images are structured and codified, even transformed, by the text. In this way we are brought yet closer to a more appropriate interpretation of the biblical text.

To my knowledge, only Tracy and Ricoeur have provided us with an overall work-oriented literary analysis of the New Testament. As we have seen, they do this through an analysis of the leading images/ symbols in the Scriptures, together with an analysis of the way in which those images are structured and transformed through various literary genres. This kind of analysis provides us with an interpretation of the text's "sense," the ideal meaning immanent in the text itself. Perhaps the crucial insight here is that the literary form of the text is an essential dimension of meaning. As Ricoeur put it above, form cannot be separated from content. The tensions and contrasts between the various forms possess theological significance.

Perhaps Ricoeur's greatest contribution to work-interpretation is his insistence that written discourse appears as a *work*, which implies the categories proper to human production and labor and their extension to the written text. As he puts it, "To impose a form upon a material, to subject a production to specific codes, to produce those unique configurations which assimilate a work to an individual and which we call style, these are ways of considering language as a material to be worked and formed."[26] Thus, grammar and literary genres are "generative codes" ruling the production of a work, not mere devices of classification. In this way, they provide the interpreter with a common ground of interpretation, they preserve the message from distortion, and they insure the survival of the meaning of a literary text.

Perhaps the two best examples of work-interpretation in New Testament study are William A. Beardslee's *Literary Criticism of the New Testament* and Amos N. Wilder's *The Language of the Gospel: Early Christian Rhetoric*.[27] These works demonstrate a profound mastery of the generative, rather than classificatory, nature of New Testament genres. They are basically united with Ricoeur and Tracy on this point and seem to confirm one another's views.

The fact that the text appears as a work using generative devices means that there is a place for structuralist methods of interpretation too. To my knowledge, structuralism has been primarily successful on this level of demonstrating the "deep structures" or "constant devices" employed in various genres, particularly narratives. For example, one can follow V. Propp and attempt to isolate the constant functions found in a narrative (absence, interdiction, violation, fraud, etc.). Or one can follow Algirdas Greimas and search out the constant "actants" of a narrative ("Lord" vs. "sought person," "dispatcher" vs. "addressee," or "helper" vs. "opponent"). All of this simply illustrates that there are certain structures which can be exploited in the generative work of written genres. We have already seen that Ricoeur employs a form of structural analysis in his view of the narrative as an emplotment using followability, configuration, and closure.[28] Dan O. Via, in his *Kerygma and Comedy in the New Testament,* has employed the "actant" model in his analysis of Mark's Christology, attempting to illustrate that we have a classic form of the "hero" vs. "protagonist" structure of the tragicomedy genre.

Via singles out four ways in which his actant model surfaces in Mark's Gospel. There is a contrast between a figure fit for tragedy and a world belonging to comedy in the "normal" tragicomedy. Mark's Jesus, on the other hand, seems to combine both features: his fate qualifies him for tragedy, but some of his actions (a regular human with temptations, associating with sinners, wining and dining, choosing fishermen, etc.) manifest the comic. Instead of the normal contrast between the illusionary (tragic) world of the protagonist and the real world of the audience and other characters (comic), Mark reverses the contrast. It is Jesus' opponents who dwell in an illusionary world. In the remaining two characteristics, Mark seems to follow the normal tragicomedy pattern. For example, the victimization of the tragic figure transforms him into a hero, while the apparent victory of the opponents causes their defeat. This clearly corresponds to Mark's presentation of the death-resurrection motif. Finally, the conflict within a person between intention and fulfillment, self-image and reality, evidences a certain tragicomedy pattern, and this surfaces in Mark. Jesus knows that he is the Messiah, but no one else does; he knows that he acts rightly, but disobeys established piety; Peter confesses Jesus as Messiah, but really does not know its true meaning (8:29–33), etc.[29] Here we seem to have a structuralist confirmation of the Ricoeur/Tracy dialectic of proclamation (= tragedy) and manifestation (= comedy).

World-Oriented Approaches

If Ricoeur and Tracy are correct, the great danger of the work-oriented approach is that it will remain "locked up" within the sense of the text, neglecting the text's "reference." We recall that the "reference" refers to the world of meaning and truth that the text opens up in front of itself to the reader. It is the text's claim to refer to reality, either historical reality in the case of historical references, or the reality of truth, in the case of fiction and non-historical genres.[30] In the latter case, the reference or world of the text seems to refer to our ownmost possibilities as human beings who participate in existence.

For Ricoeur especially, interpretation is not simply or even properly text interpretation. It is rather an attempt to appropriate the reference *on the basis of the* text. As we will see in our next chapter, historical and psychosocial methods are chiefly concerned with the appropriation of the possible historical references of the biblical text. Ricoeur's great contribution,

I think, is in suggesting how the metaphor is the semantic device which discloses a new world of human possibility and existence. Through its semantic impertinence of using ordinary language in an extraordinary way, the metaphor (and its transformation through genres) forces us to entertain a new world of possibilities.[31] If you will, metaphors do not describe ordinary reality. They *re*describe it, and in that way force us to entertain something deeper than surface truth. They open us up to a world richer than sense experience, the world of religious meaning and truth.

So far as I can tell, Rocoeur's work on the metaphor's referential power remains the most significant *literary* analysis of the reference approach to interpretation of the New Testament. Because of the preoccupation with historical questions in biblical research, this area has been chiefly concerned with the appropriation of the historical references of the text. But we will come to that in our next chapter.

Audience-Oriented Approaches

The ability of the text to affect its audience is approached by Ricoeur and Tracy through their notion of appropriation and distanciation. Earlier we spoke of this as the "comprehension" moment of interpretation, following the initial understanding and the movement through "explanation." But elsewhere in his work Ricoeur will speak of "appropriation," from the German *aneignen*, "to make one's own." In effect, appropriation is the dialectical counterpart of distanciation. The text's distanciation from the original writer means that the text becomes a potential source of meaning to any reader. Distanciation creates a potentially universal audience. It also creates the space of a reflective distance through which interpretation can occur. Ricoeur will even speak of "play" as the form in which appropriation occurs. As the author, through the distanciation of the text, submits to the imaginative variations of the text, this then acts as a model offered to the reader's own subjectivity. "The reader as well is invited to undergo an imaginative variation of his *ego*."[32] In appropriation, the reader enters into this playful game of self-divestiture. Here is how Ricoeur puts it:

> Relinquishment is a fundamental moment of appropriation and distinguishes it from any form of "taking possession." Appropriation is also and primarily a "letting-go." Reading is an appropriation-divestiture. How can this letting-go, this relinquishment, be incorporated into appropriation? Essentially by linking appropriation to the revelatory power of the text which we have described as its referential dimension. It is in allowing itself to be carried off towards the reference of the text that the *ego* divests itself of itself. . . .[33]

Thus, for Tracy, New Testament scholars are invited to undergo, playfully, the self-divestiture of the journey of intensification through particularity. If they pursue this journey, they will hopefully experience something of that dialectical tension between proclamation and manifestation, non-participation and participation simultaneously in a Divine presence that comes to expression in the Jesus event.

I would suggest that the approach to Christology by way of a theory of "storytelling" is essentially a variation upon what Tracy and Ricoeur would consider the biblical text's ability to affect its audience. John Navone's recent *The Jesus Story: Our Life as Story in Christ* is a superb example of how the story genre of the New Testament makes "storytellers" of us all. If you will, the biblical narratives/stories transform us into storylisteners first. We are first storylisteners before we become storytellers because we are deeply affected by the stories both lived and told by others that we have encountered. Just as, through our critical reaction to these stories, we are able to begin putting together our own story, so the Jesus story opens up to us the possibility of discovering in our own lives a narrative similar to his.

Stories imply "the belief that we are called to truly meaningful lives in a universe that is essentially benign and comprehensible," says Navone.[34] They imply coherence and meaning, or, otherwise put, the essentially "narrable" quality of existence. Of course, there are fragmented stories, without an ending, but we are always disappointed by them, left wondering where the ending is. This implies our basic thrust toward narrativity. The power of the Jesus story is its disclosure of the narrable quality of life. Through it we can begin to grasp that all "lives are created narrable, and there is no life that is created without the intention of its becoming a truly good story."[35] The special power of the Jesus story, and specifically religious stories, is that they bring to clear expression the ultimately meaningful or narrable quality of life.

Stories, especially autobiographies, also intensify the personal element in the quest for meaning. By stressing, through the characters (in stories) or character (in autobiography), the concrete and personal, the narrable quality and potential of our own concrete and personal life is heightened. They invite us to the *personal* quest for meaning. And yet a personal story is only similar to our own personal character: there is still enough difference to allow us our own free response and personal construction of our own story. As Navone puts it, other selves "come close to home and yet are an invitation to journey. . . . a story engages us because it is both similar and dissimilar."[36] Clearly the Jesus stories of the Gospels function similarly. The explosive concentration upon Jesus, his disciples, and his opponents heightens our own sense of personal authenticity throughout.

Finally, many stories (especially the biblical stories) are community products. Listening to these can free us from our own isolation and fragmented meaning, and link us with a greater and richer plot unfolding within a larger human community. Surely the Jesus story has the capacity to bond us to this larger death-resurrection, proclamation-manifestation story which is unfolding within history.

The Mediation with Contemporary Experience

As we have seen, both Ricoeur and Tracy recognize that the interpretation of the tradition pole of theology requires a mediation with our contemporary experience for its completion. The disclosure and appropriation of the reference(s) through the sense of the text must ordinarily require some form of mediation with our contemporary experience, given the cultural distanciation between ourselves and the "world" of the text. Tracy himself seems to argue that there are three major routes to this mediation available to us today. A possible mediation of the disclosure of "manifestation"—the disclosure of participation in the Divine, explosively in Jesus, less explosively in his followers—can be found in philosophical explorations of the religious dimension in ordinary experience, and in analyses of extraordinary and mystical experiences. Ricoeur himself has primarily followed this route to date.[37] A possible mediation of the disclosure of "proclamation"—the disclosure of non-participation in the Divine, the Divine as truly transcendent and ahead of us, as found explosively in Jesus and less intensively in his followers—can be found in philosophical analyses of human finitude, human brokenness and sinfulness, of human dependency upon the Divine, etc. Here Tracy refers especially to the work of the great neo-Orthodox writers who were so aware of the distance between ourselves and the Divine.

Yet a third route of mediation is that provided us by political and liberation theologians. This style of mediation is new, because it aims, not for a philosophical mediation of the Jesus event in terms of its contemporary *meaning,* but for a practical mediation in terms of its *praxis.* If you will, this mediation represents a new journey of intensification which strives to discover the contemporary practical edge of the Jesus event. It strives to produce, not so much a new theological text-classic, but a classic in the form of "event," action. Characteristic of these theologians is that they begin with some experience of either manifestation or proclamation. For example, the sense of participation with the Divine is released in their participation in the liberation struggles of their own people. This would correspond to the manifestation pole. Liberation becomes an experience of religious participation. Or the sense of non-participation with the Divine (= proclamation) might be released in their experience of the oppression of their people, in their sense of the not-yetness of liberation. In either case, these two very practical experiences are a kind of practical mediation of the dialectic between proclamation and manifestation opened up to us by the Jesus event.

Ultimately Tracy believes that these three contemporary routes of mediation are distinct but not separate, just as manifestation and proclamation reveal distinct but not separate dimensions of our common religious experience. Divine transcendence (= proclamation) and divine immanence (= manifestation) are two sides of our religious experience, requiring an "analogical imagination" capable of grasping unity in difference, similarity within dissimilarity, different foci in one common manifold. As we proceed in this book, I will try to propose my own "mediation" of the Jesus event, but I would like to wait until I have explored some more leading approaches in the field. For the time being, however, I would suggest that Tracy is finally proposing the kind of mediation characteristic of what I have called "centrist" theologians. That is, only a view of experience which is wider than sense experience, which is open to a religious depth in our experience, in both its meaning and praxis modes, holds promise for a relatively adequate mediation of the Jesus event.

Literary-Critical Analysis as Appropriate and Critical

By way of conclusion, what general contribution does this kind of analysis offer to our task of revitalizing Christology today? Let us briefly explore this in the light of what we argued were the two contributions of every method of explanation in theology—namely, in terms of "appropriateness" and in terms of the method's ability to "correct" or "challenge" the tradition.

"Appropriateness," we will recall, is a method's ability to clarify the tradition pole of Christology—in this case, New Testament Christology. What, by way of summary, have we learned in this regard? First and most importantly, we have been "invited" to appropriate an interpretation of New Testament Christology which seems relatively adequate to the *full range* of genres present in the New Testament. Through these genres we have had opened up to us something of the manifold richness of the Jesus event. Through the pervasiveness and intensity of the central genres of proclamation-narrative-symbols-reflective thought we have learned that the heart of New Testament Christology is the disclosure of divine love in the cruciform life of Jesus of Nazareth. There, in that life, was the explosive manifestation of the divine reality of love present within human existence. Transcendence and immanence, divine power and love, grace and freedom, strength and suffering weakness, proclamation and manifestation—all of these are not a simple dichotomy for the New Testament, but dialectical poles of the one same event. Or if one prefers the structuralist's genre of tragicomedy, then we could say that we have been referred to a disclosure of divinity (comedy) through suffering love (tragedy). But these central genres and their disclosure in the explosive life of Jesus need the correction of apocalyptic and doctrine (early Catholicism). Through these corrective genres we learned two crucial dimensions of the Jesus event. First, no matter how explosively the Divine is revealed in Jesus, the Divine still remains ahead of us and truly transcendently "not-yet." In a sense, we must have that experience of non-participation in the Divine: for the Divine is "beyond"; for too many still suffer and are victimized; for too many are still closed in on themselves and refuse to participate in that cruciform love that was Jesus of Nazareth. But, second, the doctrines genre reminds us that the extraordinary is found in the ordinary, in our families, in our institutions, in the many social realities of our lives—perhaps not explosively, as in Jesus, but nonetheless truly and really. The divine disclosure must not be narrowed to Jesus, nor must it be evaporated from the world (apocalyptic). We, too, Jesus' followers, participate in the divine presence. The dialectic of transcendence and immanence is true of us too.

Second, I think we have learned that a contemporary Christology which seeks to be relatively adequate to the New Testament must be attuned to the full range of genres found therein, and must therefore be relatively comfortable with a pluralism of approaches to Christology. The complexity of the Jesus event as disclosed in proclamation-manifestation-apocalyptic-doctrines is quite rich, permitting a manifold of approaches in Christology. Of course, a particular theologian's journey of intensification will have the marks of one's own unique discoveries. One may begin from an existential experience of non-participation in the Divine, and this may cause one to develop a Christology oriented around the cross or apocalyptic. Conversely, one's existential starting point may be the release of the sense of participation in the Divine (= manifestation). This might lead the theologian to develop a Christology oriented toward the resurrection or the incarnation model of the Johannine tradition. But if we are to remain faithful to the full range of New Testament genres, then each of these Christologies must remain open to and in tension with one another for relative adequacy. The only kind of contemporary Christology which would be disallowed is one which is not in continuity with the genres of the New Testament.

Third, I think that the literary-critical approach has helped us restore an appreciation and reverence for the essentially languagistic character of divine revelation. As Ricoeur never tires of arguing, content and form cannot be separated. The originary and metaphorical language of the New Testament, together with its structuration through genres, is not an outmoded form of discourse to be replaced by the theologian's more contemporary analytical discourse. It alone, through its semantic impertinence of using ordinary language in an extraordinary manner, restores to us our capacity to entertain a world of meaning and truth which transcends ordinary sense experience. This, I think, imposes a certain humility upon the work of contemporary Christologians. If they wish to revitalize Christology in a manner appropriate to the New Testament, then the aim must be, not to replace the language of the Scriptures, but to revitalize it. This, I think, is one of the crucial contributions of literary analysis. As Eric Voegelin put it, our aim must be, not only "experiential reactivation," but also "linguistic renewal."[38] Our relatively abstract and second-order theological discourse must always remain linked to the originary discourse of Scripture and in its service. Christologians who too quickly bypass the biblical discourse and attempt to "translate" Christology into historical or philosophical terms betray an insensitivity to the perduring role of symbolic and metaphorical language and are thus less adequately faithful to the New Testament.

Finally, following David Tracy, a Christology which is in continuity with the Scriptures must attempt to be as rich, as concrete, and as existentially powerful as is the New Testament. It must have as its final goal the desire to stimulate that journey of intensification through particularity which releases the dialectic of proclamation and manifestation. Without this, such a Christology would not be adequate to the reference or "world" opened up by the New Testament. In the light of this, modern reductionistic Christologies are clearly inadequate. Christologies of the far right (fundamentalist) collapse manifestation into proclamation. Those of the far left collapse proclamation into manifestation. The tension between the two poles is missing. The literary critical approach offers a certain confirmation that centrist Christologies are relatively adequate to the New Testament.

What, finally, might we say of the literary-critical method's ability to correct and challenge our Christological tradition? First, I would say that it challenges the tendency of the tradition to absolutize one form of Christology as the supposedly normative one. This can happen, for example, when one reads the Johannine incarnation Christology as the supposed "summit" of New Testament revelation, viewing all the others as merely preparatory stages on the way to John's Gospel. Or, perhaps more commonly, the tradition has had a tendency to absolutize the incarnation model of the Council of Chalcedon because of its important status in the early period of the Church. In any case, we have learned that the stress upon the manifestation pole of this incarnation model needs the balance and corrective of proclamation-oriented Christologies for full adequacy to the New Testament.

Second, literary analysis also corrects the tendency to assimilate the writings of the New Testament too quickly to the modern historical biography, with its concern for chronological accuracy of details. In this, literary analysis seems to link up with the findings of historical analysis, as we have seen. A genre-oriented analysis would seem to indicate that the deeper concern of the New Testament is the disclosure of the Divine in human existence. There is a deeper, non-surface story that the Scriptures want to tell. This depth, beyond the ordinary sense experience level, expressed through the symbolism and metaphors and non-linearity of the narratives, highlights the "poetic" nature of the Scriptures. Here I use "poetic" in Ricoeur's sense: poetic language restores our sense of belonging to a "Reality" which transcends ordinary sense experience.[39] This, of course, does not deny that there are possible historical references in the New Testament. It only emphasizes that it is the religious depth of those historical experiences that is of paramount importance.

Finally, I would suggest that literary-critical analysis challenges the hegemony of historical and philosophical approaches in Christology and their near-dominance over the Christian tradition's self-understanding. While there is clearly an important place for both, they need the corrective of the kind of analysis offered in this chapter for full adequacy to the New Testament. Historical analysis runs the danger of being too partial (by abstracting a "summary" of data about the Jesus event), unattuned to the full range of scriptural genres. It also runs the danger of the forgetfulness of the depth dimension in the historical references preserved by the biblical metaphors. Philosophical analysis, if it is done well, will not overlook the depth dimension, but it lacks the existential impact of the biblical "poetic" discourse and symbolism, their attractive "beauty."

Notes

1. See Van den Hengel, *op. cit.*, p. 192, primarily referring to Ricoeur's "The Model of the Text: Meaningful Action Considered as a Text," in John B. Thompson, ed., *Hermeneutics and the Human Sciences* (Cambridge: Cambridge University, 1981), pp. 197–221.

2. Ricoeur, "The Hermeneutical Function of Distanciation," *art. cit.*, 130.

3. Ricoeur, "The Language of Faith," in Charles E. Reagan and David Steward, eds., *The Philosophy of Paul Ricoeur* (Boston: Beacon, 1978), p. 223.

4. Ricoeur, "The Model of the Text: Meaningful Action Considered as a Text," *art. cit.*, 206–207.

5. Tracy, *The Analogical Imagination, op. cit.*, p. 125; for Gadamer's views on the classic, see his *Truth and Method, op. cit.*, pp. 253–258.

6. *Ibid.*, p. 163.

7. *Ibid.*, p. 215.

8. *Ibid.*, p. 218.

9. *Ibid.*, p. 263.

10. Paul Ricoeur, "Philosophical Hermeneutics and Theological Hermeneutics," *Sciences Religieuses* 5 (1975), 22.

11. Tracy, *The Analogical Imagination, op. cit.*, p. 265.

12. *Ibid.*, p. 274.

13. *Ibid.*, p. 275.

14. Cf Paul Ricoeur, "The Narrative Function," in Thompson, *op. cit.*, pp. 274–296.

15. Van den Hengel, *op. cit.*, p. 136.

16. *Ibid.*, p. 139.

17. Tracy, *The Analogical Imagination, op. cit.*, pp. 278–279.

18. Ricoeur, "Biblical Hermeneutics," *art. cit.*, 86. Cf his magisterial *The Rule of Metaphor* (Toronto: University of Toronto, 1977).

19. Tracy, *The Analogical Imagination, op. cit.*, p. 282.

20. *Ibid.*,

21. Cf. Van den Hengel, *op. cit.*, p. 92.

22. Tracy, *The Analogical Imagination, op. cit.*, p. 113.

23. (New York: Paulist, 1979).

24. *Ibid.*, p. 108.

25. *Ibid.*, p. 197.

26. Ricoeur, "Biblical Hermeneutics," *art. cit.*, 68.

27. See Beardslee, *op. cit.*, and Wilder (New York: Harper & Row, 1964).

28. See the reference in note 26 for Ricoeur's treatment of the varied kinds of structuralism, *passim*.

29. Dan O. Via, *Kerygma and Comedy: A Structuralist Approach to Hermeneutic* (Philadelphia: Fortress, 1975), pp. 100–101. Northrop Frye would see the divine comedy genre typical of the Bible as a whole; see his *The Great Code: The Bible and Literature* (New York: Harcourt Brace Jovanovich, 1982).

30. Structuralism is often accused of ignoring the referential power of texts, confining itself to "sense."

31. See his *The Rule of Metaphor, op. cit.* The notion of a "world" is borrowed from Gadamer. See Mary Gerhart, *The Question, op. cit.*, pp. 125–126 on this notion.

32. Ricoeur, "Appropriation," Thompson, *op. cit.*, p. 189.

33. *Ibid.*, p. 191.

34. John Navone, *The Jesus Story: Our Life as Story in Christ* (Collegeville, Minnesota: Liturgical Press, 1979), p. 135.

35. *Ibid.*, p. 132.

36. *Ibid.*, p. 233.

37. See Ricoeur, "Biblical Hermeneutics," *art. cit.*, 107–145, and his *Essays on Biblical Interpretation*, Lewis S. Mudge, ed. (Philadelphia: Fortress, 1980), pp. 95–117; Tracy, *The Analogical Imagination, op. cit.*, pp. 371–456.

38. Eric Voegelin, *Order and History 4, The Ecumenic Age, op. cit.*, p. 56. Cf. also Ricoeur, *Essays on Biblical Interpretation, ibid.*, p. 101.

39. Ricoeur, *ibid.*

7

New Testament Christology from an Historical, Psychosocial, and Philosophical Perspective

An Introduction

Our aim in this lengthy Chapter 7 will be to expose the reader to the rich literature on New Testament Christology from two perspectives primarily—namely, that of historical criticism and that of psychosocial (or practical) criticism. The two belong together, because psychosocial criticism is really a kind of psychological and sociological extension of the historical method. We will also add "philosophical" or "experiential" mediations with our contemporary experience, where that seems demanded by our modern horizon of understanding. It makes little sense to offer reconstructions of historical data which are problematic to the modern mind without attempting some form of contemporary mediation. However, I will offer my own personal "mediation" of the New Testament Christology, hopefully informed by all of these methods of explanation which we have surveyed, at the end of this Part Two. This Chapter 7, because of the enormous range of material it must cover, will be subdivided into four sections: 7/A: The Practical Context of Jesus; 7/B: The Message and Work of Jesus; 7/C: The Easter Experiences; 7/D: From Kerygma to Gospels. Some such division as this seems called for if we are to do justice, even in an introductory way, to the enormous range of materials available to us. The historical-critical method, especially, has a much longer pedigree to it than literary-criticism, and so the range of its contribution is not really too surprising.

This chapter, with its four sub-chapters, will require a certain shift in mentality on the part of the reader. If we take a cue from Paul Ricoeur, we are now moving more fully from the "sense" of the New Testament to the "references" opened up to us in front of the biblical text (and other texts which are of use in this enterprise). Those references, as we have already seen from literary criticism, are of both an historical and a theological nature. That is, the New Testament world discloses to us claims about Jesus and his influence upon followers (historical reference) and claims about the very nature and meaning of reality itself (theological reference). The various methods, with their contributions to Christology, which we are about to survey, can be helpfully looked at as further ways of "thickening" our understanding of these multiple references in a disciplined and critical way.

With Ricoeur, I would suggest that we look at the contributions of these methods as complementary to literary-critical analysis. Ricoeur's interpretation theory, which does not lock itself up into the text by confining interpretation only to the sense, demands of literary criticism that it "graft itself" onto other methods which are helpful for exploring the referential power of the biblical texts. Historical criticism, psychosocial criticism, and philosophical-theological interpretation have all proven themselves to be effective ways of deepening our ability to appropriate the "referential world" of the New Testament.

To some extent the material we are about to survey will seem repetitive of what we have already covered in our last chapter. This should not be surprising, for all of these methods of explanation, like literary-critical analysis, are effective in performing the *same* two tasks. That is, all of them aim to provide us with an "appropriate" understanding of our biblical, Christological tradition. And all of them, in varying degrees, aim to deal with modern issues of "intelligibility," by challenging the tradition or even correcting it in the light of our ongoing experience. I would suggest, however, that the really strong suit of the methods to follow is more in the area of "intelligibility" than of "appropriateness." For example, the historical-critical method helpfully deals with the kinds of questions that modern, historically-conscious people find themselves inevitably asking: What can I know with historical probability about Jesus and his times? Is the New Testament biased or even incorrect in some ways? There are a host of others. So, too, modern psychosocial criticism challenges the tradition to recover the practical and political "punch" of New Testament Christology, as well as to admit some of its shortcomings, perhaps most glaringly its androcentrism and suppression of the liberation of women begun by Jesus.

Perhaps the most controversial section will be my attempted summary of Jesus research to date (chapter 7/B). Let me try to clarify here what I want to do. My first goal is simply to expose the reader to the rich material and views available. It would simply be inexcusable for an introductory survey like this to omit what is, to date, the most voluminous and in many ways most impressive contribution that we have. Readers will never be in a position to make judgments about the effectiveness of these methods unless they are at least exposed to their results! Perhaps the most novel element will be my attempt to combine the results of historical criticism *with* psychosocial and philosophical analysis. Usually scholars employing these various methods operate separately and never get around to attempting an integration with others. I have tried to avoid eclecticism and aimed for integration where that seemed possible. But readers will have to judge for themselves. However, I realize that this kind of integration is somewhat novel and that therefore it only initiates what other scholars will have to refine and correct.

Probably the greatest opposition to this chapter 7/B will come from those who either doubt or deny the validity of any attempted reconstruction of the Jesus of history. On this issue, let me underscore a number of points. First, as we argued in an earlier chapter, our faith does not depend upon a "reconstructed" historical Jesus, but on the Christian tradition as we have it in its ongoing fusion with our contemporary experience. Our norm in Christianity is not a reconstructed "historical Jesus," but the Jesus mediated to us by the Christian tradition. Any other view would seem to be "inappropriate" to the tradition itself. As we argued earlier, the Jesus quest has a modest role to play, in terms of both appropriateness and intelligibility, but it is not our theological norm.

Finally, I tend to agree that exaggerated claims for either certainty or probability are made by scholars for their attempted reconstruction of the "historical" Jesus. Such claims might emanate from their hidden or unconscious feeling that such a reconstructed Jesus must serve as our theological norm in Christology. Perhaps if they were to be freed from such a feeling they might moderate their claims somewhat. In any case, it seems to me that we must learn to be satisfied with relative degrees of probability in this area, which is all that the historical material will permit. Scholars should probably stop speaking about "the very words" of Jesus or his "very deeds," or even of his "authentic words" or an "historical core" in sayings or actions recorded in the biblical tradition. The complex oral tradition, prior to the written biblical texts, calls for a high degree of moderation in our claims.[1]

With David Tracy, I think that a Jesus quest is possible, but that it is also an enormously difficult enterprise. Usually it can supply us with no more than a relatively probable hypothetical reconstruction of Jesus' ministry, which then serves as the basic presupposition of the New Testament kerygma. This is not the same thing as recovering the very words or deeds of Jesus, but it is quite sufficient, if our goal is to come to an understanding of the historical references of the biblical texts.[2]

We should probably begin to speak of historical "probability" as a wide category, a kind of continuum ranging from least probable to more probable. Least probable would be, in my view, reconstructions of the historical Jesus which are based upon attempted psychological re-enactments of Jesus. Plumbing psychological motivations is notoriously difficult to achieve, and practically impossible to verify. In addition, it seems based on the discredited view that text interpretation is a psychological re-enactment of the author's intentions. It seems more plausible to argue with Ricoeur that we are really attempting to uncover the historical references opened up in front of the biblical text. In this view, more probable hypotheses are those which can bring forward textual warrants rather than psychological hunches.[3]

Notes

1. Cf Werner Kelber, *The Oral and the Written Gospel* (Philadelphia: Fortress, 1983), for important reservations about the continuity between the oral and the written phases of the biblical Christology. Oral traditions tend, apparently, to be very fluid and pluralistic, constantly undergoing modification. At the very least, in the light of a work like Kelber's, historians need to rethink their use of such terms as Jesus' "very words," "very deeds," etc. Kelber relies upon Walter J. Ong's important studies on orality versus textuality: *Interfaces of the Word: Studies in the Evolution of Consciousness and Culture* (Ithaca: Cornell University, 1977), and *The Presence of the Word: Some Prolegomena for Cultural and Religious History* (New Haven: Yale University, 1967).

2. Tracy, *The Analogical Imagination, op. cit.*, speaks of the Jesus quest as supplying us, "at best," with "certain necessary assumptions or presuppositions" of the apostolic witness to Jesus (p. 238). Schubert M. Ogden, in his *The Point of Christology* (San Francisco: Harper and Row, 1982), is more agnostic than Tracy and thinks that a Jesus quest can only supply us with the earliest apostolic witness to Jesus, not Jesus himself. But as Schillebeeckx, *Jesus, op. cit.*, indicates, the apostolic witness is a witness *to* Jesus: there is an element of reflectivity of Jesus within it (pp. 17–104).

3. Besides Ricoeur, the best critique of the psychological approach to historical reconstruction is Van A. Harvey, *The Historian and the Believer* (Toronto: Macmillan, 1966).

The Practical Context of Jesus

My own work with students over the years has convinced me that the tendency to mystify Jesus, severing him from his quite practical context, is fairly widespread. This is probably a legacy of our post-biblical dogmatic tradition, and it creates a real obstacle to the students' ability to appreciate realistically the historical references of the New Testament texts.

This sub-chapter seeks to correct that problem by combining the results of research from a wide variety of sources. Historians and historical philosophers like Arnold Toynbee and Eric Voegelin have been used to help us place the Jesus event within the larger context of humanity's struggle for meaning and order. Biblical research on the various parties and movements of Jesus' day helps us focus a little more carefully upon what would seem to be Jesus' immediate context. Perhaps most controversially I have drawn upon some of the work coming from psychosocial critics of the New Testament (Kee, Theissen), in order to uncover the possible social and political dynamics which seem to have stimulated a response from Jesus. My hope is that the student will begin to appreciate that the Jesus event did not simply "drop out of the heavenly skies," but is a real response to quite real human problems.

I have included some helpful charts/materials at the chapter's end, together with some explanations of some of the more important events of Jesus' time.

A Note on Jesus' Existence

As Bultmann noted quite some time ago, the New Testament certainly presupposes the *Dass*, the "bare fact," of Jesus' existence. This seems rather obvious, but for the sake of completeness I would like to say a few things about it. This is certainly the rock-bottom foundation of a Christianity which claims to be a traditional and so historically founded religion. No centrist Christologian denies that an historical person named Je-

sus existed at the beginning of our era and charismatically founded the
Christian movement.

It is true that Jesus never founded Christianity in a strictly "legal"
sense, through a ratified charter or constitution. But none among the centrists doubts that he was the charismatic founder whose teachings and life
inspired the Christian movement. Legal charters are not the only nor the
usual way in which movements emerge.[1] Despite this, from time to time
writers have arisen who question Jesus' existence. Arthur Drews (1865–
1935) in Germany and his American disciple William Benjamin Smith
(1850–1934), for example, argued that Jesus was an unhistorical, mythical
figure created by early Christian propagandists. Why? Because the early
Jewish Christians wanted to bring the Gentiles into the community of Israel. To do this, they presented Jesus as an "idealization of the destiny of
the nation of Israel in its universal inclusiveness."[2] Jesus became the idealized figure spoken of by the prophet Isaiah: the light to the Gentiles. This
claim was further supported by arguing that there already existed in pre-
Christian times a kind of "Christ-cult" celebrating a god or demi-god who
dies and rises again, and that the Christian Gospel is a projection of this
myth onto the fictional creation of Jesus.

While there can be no doubt that Jesus is presented in the Gospels as
open to the inclusion of the Gentiles, this does not prove that he never existed. The existence of a so-called "Christ-cult" has no historical foundations. If it means that there are similarities between some of the early
mystery religions and Jesus, still, where the mystery cults celebrate unhistorical mythical idealizations, the Gospels celebrate an historical figure.
Further, Drews and Smith overlooked the attestations to Jesus found in
the extra-biblical literature. As Günther Bornkamm tells us, it never occurred to anyone, not even Christianity's most bitter opponents, to doubt
Jesus' existence.[3] Thus, the Jewish historian Josephus refers to Jesus'
brother, James as succeeding to the leadership of the Church in Jerusalem, a passage which clearly takes Jesus' existence for granted. A number
of Roman historians also refer to Jesus: Tacitus, writing early in the second
century, speaks of *Christus*, who is a founder; Suetonius, a contemporary
of Pliny, tells us that *Chrestus* inspired Jewish disturbances, and Pliny the
Younger (62–113) reports to the emperor Trajan that Christians worship
Christ as a god. Even the post-biblical Jewish literature, while polemical
in tone to Christianity, never denies Jesus' existence.[4] In the end, Albert
Schweitzer put the entire matter best when he said that writers like Drews
and Smith have to show "how Christianity came into existence without
either Jesus or Paul; how it came, later on, to wish to trace its origins back
to these invented historical personalities; and finally for what reasons it

took the remarkable course of making these two founders members of the Jewish people."[5]

The Psychosocial Context of Jesus' Ministry

As psychological and sociological criticism is increasingly pointing out, we Christians have a tendency to etherealize and mystify Jesus by abstracting him from his quite real and practical context. His work was not a bolt from the heavenly skies unrelated to the real problems and issues of his day. Jesus is inexplicable unless he is understood against the background of the practical struggle against evil, permeating the political, economic, and cultural structures of his time.

The Crisis

Specifically the struggle is set in motion by Pompey. A member, together with Julius Caesar and Crassus, of the first Roman triumvirate, he is given power in 66 B.C. to clear the Mediterranean area of pirates. This brings him to the area of Palestine, where he involves himself in the internal power struggles, siding with Hyrcanus in the latter's squabble with his brother Aristobulus over accession to the high priesthood. In 63 B.C. Rome annexes Palestine, which can serve as a protection against Parthia and a protection of the Egyptian granaries which sustain Rome. Was the annexation also a way of controlling East-West trade? In any case, this conquest is another in a long series of crises for the Jewish people. It takes its place with the Assyrian conquest of Northern Israel and the exile of 721 B.C., with the Babylonian conquest and exile of 587 B.C. which reached down into Jerusalem itself, with the Persian conquest fifty years later, and with the conquest by Alexander the Great and his progeny, beginning in 333 B.C.

What did the conquest mean for the Jewish people? In highly general terms, various scholars have proposed the following. Eric Voegelin speaks of the dialectic between pragmatic conquest and spiritual outburst: the rise of a great universal empire like Rome creates a spiritual void, which in turn gives rise to varied spiritual responses.[6] Similarly, Arnold Toynbee speaks of a dialectic between challenge and response, while Howard Clark Kee speaks variously of the dialectic between differentiation and integration or between adaptation and identity.[7] In the face of the Roman threat, how can we survive? How can we maintain our Jewish identity and yet live within this new total *imperium?* Where is our God, who we Jews believe has specially chosen us? Perhaps in our more differentiated language, we could say that the crisis is at once economic, political, and cultural: how shall we Jews physically survive (economic), how shall we maintain our covenant tradition (political), and how can we maintain our identity as the chosen people (cultural)?

Voegelin and Toynbee are especially helpful here, because they treat the Jesus event against the global backdrop of the human struggle for survival. In this way they help us not to separate artificially the Christian tradition from the larger global tradition of humanity. Apparently all the great spiritual outbursts of the first millennium are associated with "times of trouble." It is in grappling with these struggles that new spiritual energies are released. Buddha (d. 483 B.C.) is responding to the problem of the rise of the Ganges kingdoms and their unsettling of the older aristocracy. His message of "right views, right aspirations, right speech, right conduct, right livelihood, right effort, rightmindedness, right rapture" is an attempt to articulate a more humane alternative to the ethic of violent power sweeping through the Ganges. His struggle to transcend violence helps him discover the human capacity for transcendence in the form of a quest for utter selflessness (nirvana). A similar process occurs in China in the face of the breakdown of the Chou dynasty and the consequent chaos created by feuding princes. Both Confucius (551–479 B.C.) and Taoism discover the human capacity for transcendence in the form of a quest for either order (Confucius) or love and harmony (Taoism). Plato (d. 347 B.C.) and his quest for a true realm of justice and beauty is a similar discovery of our own human capacity to transcend violence in the face of the breakdown of Athenian democracy. In varying ways, as Voegelin puts it, these spiritual outbursts are "leaps in being" or "openings of the soul" to the Transcendent.[8] Voegelin suggests that a similar opening of the soul characterizes the Jewish prophets and Jesus—these, too, discover dimensions of the Transcendent in their struggle to rise above violence.

Let us try to describe the crisis created by the Roman Empire somewhat more fully. Perhaps the greatest expression of the *economic* dimensions of the crisis is found in the taxation system, for the various provinces were expected to sustain the cost of administering the Empire. The Roman tax was of two kinds: direct taxes, collected by Rome itself, involving a land tax amounting to nearly a quarter of what a person's land produced, and a money and property tax, which varied with one's wealth. Indirect taxes were rather more like our modern customs duties. These could include import and export duties of five percent, as well as road tolls and sales taxes on the selling of slaves, produce or articles at market. Every five years the Empire would auction the right to collect these indirect taxes to finance companies, which conscripted local tax collectors for these purposes. Called "publicans" in the Gospels, we are told of Matthew (Levi) collecting at Capernaum (Mk 2:13–14) and of Zacchaeus at Jericho (Lk 19:1–10). It is not hard to believe that frequently these tax collectors demanded more than was their due and kept the difference for themselves. Perhaps they also accepted bribes from the rich, thus placing the greater burden of taxation upon the poor.

Coupled with the heavy Roman taxation were the more "voluntary" taxes expected of every righteous Jewish male over twenty. The annual temple tax, used to maintain the temple and its services, was a half-shekel in Jesus' time (or the equivalent Greek didrachma; cf Mt 17:24). The priests' tithe amounted to one percent of the produce of one's land. The "second tithe" amounted to an obligation to spend a certain amount of money in Jerusalem, thus contributing to Jerusalem's general prosperity.[9] Little doubt exists, from numerous statements in Josephus, that these taxes were felt to be oppressive (*Antiquities*, 17,8,4; 17,11,2; 17,11,4; 18,1,1,etc.). No wonder, then, that the remission of debts became an image of divine grace in the Gospel (Mt 18:23ff).

Gerd Theissen, chiefly basing himself upon Josephus, argues that the economic situation was even further exacerbated. He points to frequent cases of famine and other natural disasters, which even caused Herod to sell his private possessions and remit taxes (*Ant.*, 15,9,1), although there is no mention of Rome's remitting its taxes. There is evidence of overpopulation in Palestine, especially in Galilee (*Jewish Wars*, 3,3,2; *Life*, 45). Agricultural studies indicate that over ninety-seven percent of Palestine's land was under cultivation. This forced Herod to settle Jews outside normal Jewish territory (*Ant.*, 17,2,2). A progressive concentration of possessions seems to have intensified the struggle over the distribution of wealth. Only those with extensive capital were able to buy and especially to export goods. Herod, his descendants, and the Romans were the ones to profit most (*Ant.*, 17,11,2; 17,13,5).

As Theissen comments: "The pessimistic statement at the end of the parable needs no comment: 'To every one who has, more will be given; but from him who has not, even what he has will be taken away' (Luke 19:26)."[10] The rivalry between the Roman and Palestinian elites for controlling the exploitation of the land was, as Theissen thinks, "the decisive reason for the explosive situation in Palestine."[11] Most interestingly he points to the economic friction between Jerusalem and Galilee (the place of Jesus' ministry). As he explains it, practically the entire Jerusalem population had some financial interest in the temple. "This tie brought about a practical community of interest between the upper classes and the lower classes: both profited from the *status quo*."[12] The temple created jobs, brought the pious pilgrims and their money into Jerusalem, and even accorded legal privileges to the city (tax remissions, for example). The people of the country (Galilee), on the other hand, suffered from greater economic pressure. Absentee proprietorship is one indication of this (cf the parables of Lk 16:1ff; 13:6ff; 19:1ff; Mk 12:1ff); the rebellious movements originating in Galilee are another (*Ant.*, 17,10,4).

Politically, as Theissen further notes, the situation in Palestine was explosive. The imbalance and friction between the varied power centers (the Empire, the Hellenistic city states, the Jewish aristocracy, the Herodian puppet monarchy) meant that there was no one legitimated center of power. This, then, created a breeding ground for radical movements, hoping themselves to gain that legitimation. The various *cultural* responses to which I will now turn should be seen as varied attempts to fill this political void and to overcome economic injustices. Recalling Voegelin, they represent "spiritual outbursts" in the face of pragmatic conquest. The recovery of these varied spiritual outbursts[13] is one of the more important finds of current historical research. It further confirms the picture of friction and imbalance which Theissen paints, and forces us to overcome a monolithic view of first century Judaism as a religion with one well defined teaching.

The Zealots

The New Testament tells us that Simon, one of Jesus' disciples, was a "Zealot party member" (Acts 1:13), and Josephus speaks of the Zealots as one of the sects of Jewish philosophy (*Ant.*, 18,1,6). Apparently an underground movement somewhat loosely organized, they could band together with other groups, like the more violent Sicarii, to accomplish their ends. Today they are remembered as the group which in 66 A.D. overthrew the Romans and held out against the Roman siege until about 73, at the fortress of Masada. There it was that about a thousand of them chose suicide rather than submission to Rome. In terms of the crisis created by Rome, the Zealots represent the option of rejection of the Empire through fostering a nationalistic revolt and the re-establishment of the Jewish theocracy. Apart from their violence, Josephus tells us that they agree in all other things with the Pharisees. That probably means that they were religious in orientation, and not merely political revolutionaries. In fact, the modern differentiation between politics and religion simply did not exist at this time.

The Sadducees

The Sadducees (*Ant.*, 18,1,4) appear in the New Testament as a party which does not accept the relatively new belief in the resurrection held by Jesus and the Pharisees (Mk 12:18, 25). So far as we know, they were composed of the older aristocracy of both priests and laity which gradually formed after Alexander the Great's conquest of Palestine. The fact that they did not accept the new belief in the resurrection provides us with a clue for understanding them: they were conservative.

In matters religious, the written revelation of the Pentateuch (the first five books of the Bible) as preserved by the Sadducees constituted the Jewish religion. Hence their name: they were *sadûq*, the "righteous ones" determining authentic piety. In terms of the crisis of Rome, their option represents that of collaboration. Any other course, they felt, would not preserve Jewish identity and hold out hope of an eventual restoration of the theocracy. One of the more interesting finds of contemporary research is that the Sadducees probably constituted, in Roman eyes, the most authoritative body in Jesus' time.

The Essenes

The Essenes,[14] unmentioned in the New Testament, are known to us from Josephus (*Ant.*, 18,1,5) and also from Josephus' older contemporary, Philo of Alexandria. However, it is the discovery of the Dead Sea Scrolls (1947–1967) which has brought them into prominence as the most likely candidate for the sect which preserved those scrolls. Living on the fringes of Jewish society, they were apparently an esoteric community which imposed a lengthy initiation on their candidates. Josephus dates them from the second century B.C. and attests to their existence in his own time. He even tells us that he experimented with their way of life when he was sixteen (he was born 37–38 A.D.; *Life*, 10–11).

Some of their chief characteristics, which conform to the beliefs of the Dead Sea Scrolls (cf. *The Community Rule, The Messianic Rule, The Damascus Rule, The War Rule, The Temple Scroll*), are: a rigorous discipline, entailing a year's probation for candidates, followed by two more years of training; profession of vows as a full member able to be accepted at the common table; grave offenses punishable by excommunication. Evidently they practiced a kind of "communism," handing over their belongings and earnings to a steward. They seemed to shun marriage, although Josephus speaks of a married branch of Essenes.

The Essenes were also known for a certain critical attitude toward the temple, perhaps believing that the Sadducees were corrupted by "foreign" influence. As we shall also see, they seem to swim in the apocalyptic current of the times: their celibacy is like a warrior's training for the great battle of the end time, and their "communism" is a kind of pretaste of the end time Kingdom. In terms of the Roman crisis, their option was one of withdrawal from society. This, they apparently felt, would enable them to pre-

serve Jewish identity as they understood it in the short time remaining
before the divine establishment of the new and pure theocracy which they
expected.

The Pharisees

The Pharisees (*Ant.*, 18,1,3) probably represent for contemporary
Christians the most difficult group to appreciate. For example, an uncritical reading of Matthew's and John's Gospels easily reinforces the typical
stereotype of them as legalists, hypocrites, and crafty types: "All their
works are performed to be seen"; "Their words are bold but their deeds
are few"; "Blind guides"; "You frauds!" (Mt 23:5, 4, 13, 24). To which
John's Gospel adds: "Why do you not understand what I say? It is because
you cannot bear to hear my word. The Father you spring from is the devil,
and willingly you carry out his wishes" (8:43).

Scholars are increasingly agreed that Matthew's and John's Gospels
need to be understood against the background of post-70 Judaism, when
the Pharisees emerged as the dominant party of Judaism in the wake of the
Roman crushing of the Jewish rebellion. It seems clear that the Pharisees
rejected the Christian wing of Judaism, viewing it as an example of that
"messianic activism" which had brought the wrath of Rome down upon
them and destroyed the temple. The point is that both Matthew and John
seem to reflect this later period of the hardening of Jewish-Christian relations. With the destruction of the second temple (for many Jews a crisis
only equaled in import by the Nazi holocaust), it fell to the Pharisees to
salvage Judaism (the Romans had destroyed or neutralized the other parties). This story from the *Talmud* reflects the situation:

> When a disciple of Yohanan ben Zakhai wept at seeing the Temple
> mount in ruins, Yohanan asked him, "Why do you weep, my son?"
> "This place where the sins of Israel were atoned, is in ruins, and should
> I not weep?" the disciple replied.
> "Let it not be grievous to your eyes, my son," Yohanan replied. "For we
> have another means of atonement, as effective as Temple sacrifice. It is
> deeds of loving kindness, as it is said (Hosea 6:6), *For I desire mercy and
> not sacrifice.*"[15]

That rabbinic story faithfully reflects the post-70 Pharisaic view that
"being Jewish" means serving the Divine through prayer, study of Torah,
practice of the commandments, and acts of loving kindness. No clerical

class was required, no temple. The hardening of Jewish-Christian relations is reflected, from the Jewish side, in its critique of Messiah-expectations (thought to be characteristic of Christians). As Jacob Neusner puts it, ". . . what later rabbinic Judaism treats with a considerable measure of reticence and with a clear policy of subordination, is what the messianic Zealots (and in their own way, Jewish Christians) thought most important: the Messiah, the coming of the messianic age, the fighting of the messianic war, and similar concerns."[16] What now counts, for rabbinic Judaism, is adherence to Torah.

As social criticism points out, contemporary Christians must make a real and painful effort to try to understand the Pharisees of Jesus' day. Not only must we learn to read the Gospels critically, trying to assess properly the way in which the hardening of Jewish-Christian relations may have distorted the Gospels. We must also come to terms with our very sad history of anti-Semitism, assessing to what extent this has made the Pharisees easy targets for our vituperations. Keeping this in mind, let me now turn to an attempted summation of the common threads running through current research.[17] There is disagreement, of course, on details. Jacob Neusner, for example, considers the Pharisees to have been a more elitist table-fellowship in Jesus' day, while Ellis Rivkin sees them as more revolutionary and political. These differences in interpretation are mainly accounted for by the fact that we must rely upon the later writings of the rabbis, whose reminiscences are not all equally valid.

All seem agreed that the Pharisees represent a novel and somewhat revolutionary lay movement within Judaism. The heart of this revolution was their belief in oral torah, a belief which enabled them to emancipate themselves from the Sadducees and to remain open to their own experiences as a source of revelation. Originally intended to remain oral, representing the living tradition of experience, it did eventually become written in what is called the *Mishnah*. However the *Mishnah* should not be seen as a commentary on the Pentateuch, but, in accord with its experiential character, as an independent source, extending back to Moses himself. In Rosemary Radford Ruether's words, "Thus it allowed the Pharisees to innovate freely, subject only to that authority which was theirs as the rightful successors of a line of oral tradition that runs back through the *Sopherim* and the prophets to Moses through Joshua (bypassing Aaron!)."[18]

Other novel features of the Pharisaic movement seem related to that belief in oral torah as its consequences, so to speak. A growing personalization in the relationship to the Divine seems evident among the Pharisees. Because the Divine is accessible, not simply at temple, but in

personal acts of mercy, love, prayer, and study, the term "Father" was frequently employed by them. Their belief in the resurrection of the dead is
really a corollary of this new personal view of the Divine: a loving divinity
can be trusted to preserve our personal worth and dignity. A shift occurs,
away from the centrality of the temple, to the synagogue, the "house"
where people strive to realize their prayer, study, and works of justice.
The rabbi, a Pharisaic lay person, gradually replaces the priest as Judaism's
central figure. Liturgy is no longer primarily temple sacrifice, but a
"home-meal setting where the Father of the family or the head of a Pharisaic brotherhood presided."[19] Because being Jewish resides in "mercy,"
Judaism is somewhat spiritualized: it is possible to become a Jew without
being born a Jew. Thus Pharisaism was quite open to proselytes, although
full participation in Judaism would demand a full living out of the Pharisaic
praxis.

In terms of the Roman crisis, the Pharisees seem to represent, like
Jesus and John the Baptist, the option, not of nationalistic revolt or collaboration or withdrawal, but of redefining the divine promises for the Jewish
people. Differences between John, Jesus, and the Pharisees must be
sought here in the respective manners in which they tried to refashion belief in the Divine. The Pharisees seem to have found this in humble at-
tendance to the Pharisaic way of life, or as Ruether puts it, "sober attention
to the path of salvation which God had commanded through his Torah."[20]
This is not legalism, but an attempt to respond as faithfully as possible to
the divine election of the Jewish people.[21] In this way, Jewish identity
could be preserved and renewed.

This emerging view of Pharisaism is terribly helpful for us, inasmuch
as it seems to present us with an insight into the circle which most clearly
resembles Jesus. As John Pawlikowski puts it, "What we can say without
hesitation is that the major ideas of the Pharisaic revolution exercised a
profound influence on his teachings and the shape of his ministry."[22] This
is a strong reason for arguing, as we did earlier, that Matthew's view of the
Pharisees represents, to some extent, a period later than that of Jesus. Perhaps another factor underlies Matthew's view too. The Israeli scholar
David Flusser[23] has pointed out that the Talmud lists seven different kinds
of Pharisees. Five of these are described negatively, and even among the
two positive types (the Pharisees of awe and of love) serious disagreements
existed. Perhaps Jesus identified with the Pharisees of love, and his negative critique of the Pharisees may actually relate to this argument between the varied Pharisaic types. If this is true, then Matthew's portrait,
although exaggerated, may reflect this earlier situation in Jesus' time. Related to this is the view of Ellis Rivkin,[24] who notes that the term "Pharisee" was a negative one, used by the Sadducees with the meaning of

"heretic" or "separated one." The Pharisees themselves preferred being called "scribes" or "wise ones." Now it may be the case that Jesus and/or Matthew used this derogatory term as a way of critiquing what they considered inauthentic Pharisaism.

Without denying possible differences between Jesus and the Pharisees, surely the recovery of Jesus' possible Pharisaic background can go a long way toward sensitizing us to the profound way in which Jesus was related to the context and real crisis of his time. On a rather basic level, it reminds us that Jesus was a Jew. He was probably addressed as "Rabbi Yeshua," as the Gospels indicate (Mk 9:17). He probably wore the "zithzith" (the dangling fringes seen on some Hasidic Jews today), as we are reminded by the story of the woman with the twelve-year flow of blood who touched the fringe of his clothes (Mk 5:27–28). He taught torah, apparently never doubting its validity. But like the Pharisees, he listened equally to the lessons of his own experience (is this oral torah?).

On a rather more hypothetical level, the Pharisaic background of Jesus helps us "fill in" some of the background of Jesus left unexplained by the Gospels. To be sure, the New Testament is silent about what I will have to say now. But it is not a silence which admits of no hypothetical explanations. After all, the New Testament is silent about Jesus' health, but we can safely assume that he fared no better than the rest of us on this score. The point is that there are sound and unsound ways of dealing with the New Testament's silence. A sound way is one which controls hunches through the available evidence. Thus, for example, we are told in rabbinic sources likely reflecting Jesus' own time that a father's duty vis-à-vis his son was to do the following: "He must circumcise him, redeem him, teach him Torah, teach him a trade, and find a wife for him."[25] The New Testament itself gives us good reason to argue that the first four of these duties were fulfilled in Jesus' case. Luke tells us that he was circumcised (2:21) and that he knew torah well (2:46). Luke also implies that Jesus learned his father's trade of carpentry (2:51).

The question of Jesus' possible marriage is a rather more difficult matter, both because of the silence of the sources and the later Church's idealization of the celibate state. Yet the rabbinic tradition is quite clear as reflected in this first century saying: "He who loves his wife as himself, and honors her more than himself; who leads his sons and daughters in the straight path, and marries them near their time of maturity; to his house the words of Job apply: 'Thou shalt know that thy tent is in peace.' "[26]

Some have argued that Jesus was too poor to marry, but poverty rarely stops marriages, and in any case Jesus was very likely a member of the middle, carpenter's class. Some have argued that he followed the Essene practice of celibacy. But Jesus does not seem to share their warrior ethos of sexual abstinence as a preparation for the holy war of the end time.[27] Celibacy was also a characteristic of Buddhism and Hinduism, two religions which like Jesus made the "leap in being" to the awareness of the Transcendent. Celibacy, in this context, is a way of witnessing to the spiritual/transcendent world of values. Perhaps this accounts for the emergence of celibacy in the later Christian tradition, as Christianity came under the influence of Greek spiritual ideals. But Jesus' Father-God is very this-worldly and involved in the human struggle, as we shall see. The dualism reflected in Hindu and Buddhist celibacy (the spiritual-transcendent over against the earthly) seems missing from Jesus.

Some argue that Jesus was probably a celibate because of the enigmatic statement found in Matthew, attributed to Jesus: "Some men are incapable of sexual activity from birth; some have been deliberately made so; and some there are who have freely renounced sex for the sake of God's reign" (19:12). But biblical scholars indicate that this text has nothing to do with celibacy. The "eunuchs for the Kingdom" are those men who, although estranged from their wives for various reasons, will not remarry but will attempt to reunite with them and in this way remain faithful to their marriage covenant. This enigmatic text is apparently related to a rabbinic argument over whether there are grounds for divorce. This is why it is found in Matthew in the context of Jesus' discussion of marriage and divorce.[28]

The upshot of this is that it is possible that Jesus was married. The evidence is too weak to argue for probability. But this means that it is possible (rather than probable) that Jesus was a celibate. We must be open to either view. If one is inclined to stress the Pharisaic background of Jesus, one will probably lean toward the marriage hypothesis. In this case, one could perhaps argue that Jesus grew estranged from his wife as he found himself coming into opposition from the varied Jewish parties. Perhaps this is why she is not mentioned in the New Testament.[29]

On the most important level, Jesus' Pharisaic background helps us to grasp that he, too, represents a spiritual outburst to the pragmatic crisis of his own time. Like the Pharisees, Jesus attempts to redefine the divine purposes for the Jewish people. As I indicated earlier, it is here in the way in which this redefinition is hammered out that we must search for any possible differences between Jesus and the Pharisees. Scholars who have thought about this usually emphasize the following three facets of Jesus' work. First, according to David Flusser, Jesus seems to have radically carried through the emerging Pharisaic belief in the Divine as intimate and loving. Like the other Jewish parties, even the Pharisees have a residue of ethnocentrism: the divine love is especially yoked to Israel, and this is ethically reflected in love for one's fellow Jew. Jesus seems to break through this limitation:

> According to the teaching of Jesus you have to love the sinners, while according to Judaism you have not to hate the wicked. It is important to note the positive love even toward the enemies of Jesus' personal message. We do not find this doctrine in the New Testament outside of the words of Jesus himself. . . . In Judaism hatred is practically forbidden. But love of the enemy is not prescribed.[30]

If that is true, then Jesus brings out more radically in his redefinition of the Divine the universal implications of a loving, divine reality. With the Pharisees, and Judaism generally, Jesus shares the belief in the great commandments of love of the Divine and neighbor (cf Dt 6:5 and Lev 19:18). The Testament of Issachar (5:2) teaches both love of God and of the neighbor. Or as Philo of Alexandria phrased it at a time contemporaneous with Jesus, "And there are . . . two fundamental teachings to which the numberless individual teachings and statements are subordinated: in reference to God the commandment of honoring God and piety, in reference to humanity that of the love of humanity (philanthropy) and justice."[31] But unlike them, he extends this love outward beyond simply the righteous Jew: "Love your enemies, pray for your persecutors. This will prove that you are sons of your heavenly Father, for his sun rises on the bad and the good, he rains on the just and the unjust" (Mt 5:44–45). Apparently, Jesus grasped that the residue of ethnocentrism in Pharisaic piety was an inadequate response to the crisis of his time, which could only perpetuate the conflict rather than resolve it. But more of this later.

A second difference usually pointed to is the reminiscence that Jesus forgave sins (Mk 2:1–12). As Pawlikowski puts it, "For even the 'liberal' Pharisees, it was unthinkable that anyone but the Father could forgive sins."[32] This, too, seems to be related to Jesus' Love-God, who is so intimately near and available that everyone, not only Jesus but also his disciples (Mt 16:19), can experience the forgiveness of sins.

Similarly entailed in Jesus' new universalism is a sensitivity to those who were deemed "unrighteous" for one reason or another. Pawlikowski points to his "continual concern for the 'people of the land' (the 'am ha-arez), the simple and uneducated" who know nothing about the law (cf Jn 7:49). "If the Neusner perspective on the Pharisees as having become a more restricted table fellowship in Jesus' day is validated, then there is a significant contrast here," says Pawlikowski.[33] Actually Jesus seems to break through the contemporary distinctions between righteous and unrighteous. As we will see, there is a radical overcoming of exclusivism in Jesus' work. All of this indicates that a Pharisaic background can only take us part of the way in understanding the kind of spiritual outburst which Jesus represents.

Apocalyptic

In addition to these varied Jewish parties, which Josephus calls "philosophies" and which I, with Eric Voegelin, call "spiritual outbursts," we must turn our attention to the apocalyptic current of Jesus' day. We have already noted Albert Schweitzer's recovery of this element in Jesus' work. Apocalyptic is a "current" rather than a party. As such, some of its emphases run through most of the various parties we have surveyed. To some extent, the Zealots, Essenes, and Pharisees shared aspects of apocalyptic, each giving it their own twist. Each looked forward to a new and restored "kingdom" in which their dreams would find realization. So apparently apocalyptic can function in several ways: to foster nationalistic revolt (Zealots), to legitimate withdrawal (Essenes), and to express the need to rethink the divine promises for the elect (Pharisees, John the Baptist, Jesus).

Scholarship on apocalyptic is complex and continually growing. Here I will hazard only a few observations which seem relatively safe. In general the word "apocalyptic" can carry two references: either to a body of writings (the written apocalypses) or to the beliefs found in those writings. If we seek to characterize these writings from a literary point of view, we could argue that they mostly represent revelatory writings which claim to disclose the secrets of the beyond and particularly of the end time. Some typical literary features: pseudonymity, that is, writing under the name of same famous figure, probably to enhance the authority of one's work; visions and symbolism, perhaps indicating that some religious experience is the foundation of one's work (cf Dn 7; 4 Ezra 11); surveying history as though from the perspective of the past (cf Dn 2:7; 1 Enoch 85–90); an esoteric character, indicating its secret and elitist nature (Dn 8:26; 12:9); ethical exhortations, intended to console the oppressed and call the unrighteous to judgment.

I would particularly single out the "underground character" of apocalyptic. This enables us to grasp why it would have been appealing to the varied spiritual outbursts of the time. Thus, Daniel was written to evoke protest against Antiochus Epiphanes' attempt to impose Hellenistic customs upon the Jews. Thus the War Scroll of the Essenes lists the battle orders for the final conflict between the sons of light and the sons of darkness (1QM). Thus 4 Ezra seems to reflect Israel's crisis after the fall of Jerusalem, and the Christian book of Revelation seems to be a protest against

Domitian's persecution around 95 A.D. It is easy to understand, then, why the Essenes, the Zealots, the Pharisees, John the Baptist, and even Jesus would have seen something of their own protests and aspirations embodied in this literature. The student wishing an insight into this might well turn to Solzhenitsyn's *Gulag Archipelago:* his work is a contemporary example of protest against misery and a yearning for a better future. "The jerkiness of the book, its imperfections, are the true mark of our persecuted literature," says Solzhenitsyn.[34]

Let us now look at some typical theological beliefs of apocalyptic. Commonly we meet the belief in the two ages: ". . . the Most High has made not one age but two" (4 Ezra 7:50). With the prophets, apocalyptic shares a belief in history's movement toward the goal of the divine promises, but it tends to imagine the realization of these promises as a "break" in history, a new and more radical transformation: ". . . and then Satan shall be no more, and sorrow shall depart with him" (Assumption of Moses 10:1).

Allied with the two ages belief is a certain oscillation between pessimism and hope. Toward the present, apocalyptic feels a heightened pessimism, for it is corrupt, under the dominion of Satan, as the unjust suffering of the oppressed righteous indicates. But toward the future it feels hopeful, for the Divine will usher in a new creation: "The earth also shall yield its fruit ten thousandfold and on each vine there shall be a thousand branches, and each branch shall produce a thousand clusters, and each cluster produce a thousand grapes, and each grape produce a cor of wine [= 120 gallons]" (2 Baruch 29:5). We should note that these first two sets of beliefs are linked to apocalyptic's underground character: protest entails criticism of the present (the present age/pessimism) and a yearning for a better future (the second age/hope). Note, too, that apocalyptic modifies pessimism with hope. Unlike Gnosticism, the world is sufficiently good to allow a modicum of hope.

A third typical belief, reflecting the persecuted origins of apocalyptic, is the eschatological climax: as the old age comes to a close, there will be a period of severe distress and suffering, entailing "messianic woes," judgment upon the unrighteous, salvation for the righteous, and resurrection. The student should refer back to our treatment of Mark 13 for an example. A further example: "It shall be a time unsurpassed in distress since nations began until that time. . . .Some shall live forever, others shall be an everlasting horror and disgrace" (Dn 12:1–2). This will be followed by the divine intervention: the establishment of the new age, entailing resurrection for either the righteous alone, or for both righteous and unrighteous.[35]

Because the persecuted sense that they are living in the period of the messianic woes (how else explain their suffering?), we typically meet with a belief in the imminence/nearness of the end. Apocalyptic yearns for this: "How long . . .?" (Dn 8:13; cf 4 Ezra 6:59; 2 Baruch 26, etc.). As James D.G. Dunn explains it,

> . . . typical is the sense of tip-toe expectancy, the conviction that the End itself could not be long delayed. The very fact that these secret revelations which the men of old sealed up for the end of time were now being made known was itself a sure sign that the End was near. The survey of past history in prophetic form arose from the conviction that the final acts of history were about to take place: the stone hewn from the mountain without hands would soon shatter the iron and clay feet of the idol (Dn 2). The present age could be divided into periods because its climax was near—writer and reader, Jew and Gentile together stood already in the final period before the End. God's purpose had first to be fulfilled, of course, but that fulfillment was almost complete. The consummation was at hand (4 Ez 4:33–50).[36]

To return to the Assumption of Moses:

> Then the hands of the angel shall be filled who has been appointed chief, and he shall forthwith avenge them of their enemies. For the Heavenly One will arise from his royal throne, and he will go forth from his holy habitation with indignation and wrath on account of his sons (10:2–3).

We should also note another typical belief: apocalyptic's social-political and even cosmic orientation. While it awaits the vindication of the individual, it does not abstract the individual from his or her social and natural context. It is the whole of humanity and the earth which undergoes the woes, the judgment, and the final transformation. If it is the entirety of creation which is infected by Satan, then it is that same entirety which must undergo transformation. If we read the apocalyptic too individualistically, we will rob it of its political punch as a protest against social misery. As the political theologian Johannes Metz puts it, there is a "sting" in apocalyptic which sensitizes us to "the catastrophic nature of time itself" and forces us "to display a practical solidarity with the least of the brethren."[37]

Typically the present experience of suffering makes the faithful righteous aware of their helplessness in the face of evil (Satan). For this reason they long for the divine intervention, which they typically expect in the form of some "messiah," some "anointed agent" of the Divine. The apocalyptic literally explodes with speculation about the precise form this messiah will take.[38] For some he will be a new King David who will renew the Jewish kingdom, thus reflecting the promises to David's heirs in 2 Samuel

(7:10–14). But there are many possibilities, and scholars are not agreed on how they might all be interrelated: a new prophet like Moses (cf Dt 18:18ff), a new priest who will restore perfect worship to Israel (Essenes), a military leader of the final war (Essenes), a judge mediating the divine judgment (4 Ezra 13), etc. The "Son of Man" figure has almost become the archetype of the messianic expectation, given its prominence in the literature, but it is only one of several possibilities (cf Dn 7:13–14; 1 Enoch 48; 69:26–29; 71:14–17; Mk 13:24–27; Rev 14:14ff).

Finally, underlying the entire apocalyptic message is the belief in the divine sovereignty and control of history. The reason why hope can triumph over pessimism, the reason why apocalyptists enjoy a perspective which enables them to criticize the present, is because of a basic trust in the Divine as able to "wind up" history and inaugurate a new dominion. Thus, history is presented as "foreknown," written down in a scroll (Dn 8:26; Rev 5–8). In a sense, it is "determined," although apocalyptic typically believes in human freedom and doesn't bother to reconcile the possible interrelationship between divine control and human choice.

Thus, apocalyptic is enormously complex. For our purposes it is helpful to remember its origins: it arises as a response to a long history of crises, the Assyrian, Babylonian, Persian, Alexandrine, and Roman conquests of Palestine. This is why it is more "radical" than the earlier Jewish prophets. Thus, Isaiah looked forward to a new future when men would live at peace (Is 2:11). But apocalyptic paints its hopes more boldly: "The discontinuity between old age and age to come is much sharper in apocalyptic than ever we find in prophecy," Dunn tells us.[39] This is why scholars generally distinguish between "eschatology" and "apocalyptic": the first refers to any theological speculation about the future, such as we find it in the prophets. But apocalyptic modifies and even exaggerates eschatology in its more radical fashion, stressing discontinuity within history.

Can we find meaning in apocalyptic from our own contemporary experience? Can the horizons of the apocalyptic tradition "fuse" with our own? Clearly some kind of contemporary mediation seems called for. Writing apocalyptic off as an antique mythology is clearly insufficient, for while it obviously expresses itself in the colorful imagery of myth, we need to ask what experience underlies this symbolism, and to what extent this underlying experience can find an echo within our own experience.[40]

I would suggest that we view apocalyptic as a corollary of our belief in the Divine. It imaginatively probes the implications for our future/ultimate destiny of believing in God. In other words, it extrapolates from the past and present (from what the Divine has done for us in the past and present) into the future. Its belief in the divine sovereignty over history is a corollary of believing in the divine sovereignty over our lives in the present. Because we experience the Divine as a power to protest against and condemn human misery now, we trust that the Divine will so act in the future. Because we experience the Divine as a power of love healing us now, we trust that the Divine will remain this in the future. Because we experience the divine presence as something mediated to us through historical agents and events, we trust that this is the way in which the future, end time events will occur too. We probably will never know whether the original apocalyptic seers thought they were privy to a kind of photographic preview of the future which bows too little to human freedom, the unpredictability of history, and the divine Mystery. But irrespective of this, I think we can find real meaning in the apocalyptic which is still valid, if we approach it in the terms I have suggested here.

Clearly apocalyptic becomes distorted and "sick" when it presumes to read the future literally through complicated time schedules, forgetting its own imaginative and extrapolatory nature. It becomes sick, too, when it is based upon a rather narrow view of the Divine as rigorously wrathful and filled with vengeance. But sick apocalyptic does not negate the importance of all apocalyptic. Most especially, I think, it presents us with a critique of an inadequate view of the Divine and of religious experience. It reminds us of the negative, the social-political dimension of religious experience, which corrects an overly positive and individualistic truncation of religion. It reminds us of the "practical" nature of religion as an attempt to correct social misery. It keeps us from harboring illusions about the present, but without collapsing into sheer pessimism and gnostic negativity. It reminds us that the Divine is ahead of us and beyond us, not simply a present experience, but an objective of future hope and longing which catalyzes an enthusiasm and capacity for protest in our lives. The Divine is transcendent, in other words, and apocalyptic is a powerful witness to that belief.

Apocalyptic, then, is one of the most profound spiritual outbursts of the age of Jesus. Most groups, as we have seen, are to some extent fueled by its hopes, giving it their own particular twist. No wonder, then, that Jesus too swims in its current as he attempts to respond to the crisis of his times. But let us first say something of John the Baptist. Because Jesus seems to identify so closely with John, I think we glimpse a deepened insight into Jesus' work from a consideration of the Baptist. To some extent, John too swims in the current of apocalyptic, giving it a peculiar twist which throws tremendous light upon what Jesus was about.[41]

John the Baptist

Josephus simply mentions John in passing as a preacher whom Herod feared (*Ant.*, 18,5,2), and so we must turn primarily to the Gospels for reminiscences about him. The outstanding view on this matter would seem to be that proposed by Edward Schillebeeckx. He suggests that the Gospels closely intertwine John's preaching and his lifestyle—the one lights up the other—and that this insight should serve as our key of interpretation. We are told that he preached "in the wilderness/wasteland/desert" (Mt 11:7), apparently indicating that the old wilderness spirituality of the Jews governs his work. The desert, for the early Jews, was the place of hope and expectation for the future, and John seems to share this eager longing for a new, divine future. His lifestyle seems to confirm this: he is an ascetic, who is poor, without a profession (Lk 7:33); he lives on the "food" of the wilderness: snails, locusts, honey (Mt 3:4); he wears camel's hair with a rough girdle.

What is this "future" for John? An older "Q" passage gives us a possible clue:

> He would say to the crowds that came out to be baptized by him: "You brood of vipers! Who told you to flee from the wrath to come? Give some evidence that you mean to reform. Do not begin by saying to yourselves, 'Abraham is our father.' I tell you, God can raise up children to Abraham from these stones. Even now the ax is laid to the root of the tree. Every tree that is not fruitful will be cut down and thrown into the fire" (Lk 3:7–9; cf Mt 3:7–12).

As Schillebeeckx explains it, "The future here is God's wrath, his inexorable sentence."[42] It seems related to the Jewish prophetic tradition, which John embraces: like the prophets, many of whom preached in the desert, John calls to repentance. In terms of the crisis of the times, John seems to pick up on the negative dimensions of people's response which call for reform. In this sense he is reinterpreting the divine promises for the people by pointing out that ethnocentric pride ("We are Abraham's children") is inadequate. Perhaps in our own terms we could say that such pride simply legitimates and fosters the kind of violent and dehumanizing power that brings something like the Roman Empire into being. Is John critiquing the residue of ethnocentrism characteristic of our other Jewish sects?

Schillebeeckx sees John as influenced more by the prophets than by the apocalyptic current. The images of the ax, the winnow, and the fire are all typical of the prophets, and nowhere is there a trace of the apocalyptic two ages in John. Yet there is a sharpness to John which is uncommon and somewhat reminiscent of apocalyptic. Perhaps John is aware of apocalyptic and giving it his own special critique. For example, Schillebeeckx maintains that the term "brood of vipers" is especially sharp, inasmuch as John applies this to Israel and not to the pagans, as is the more common approach (cf Mk 7:27; Mt 18:26). He adds, "The divine sentence of annihilation, which according to the ideas, especially the apocalyptic ideas, of the time is to descend upon the heathen, John makes rebound onto the Jewish generation itself; it cannot retreat into the alibi of God's promise to Abraham."[43]

Tied to the critique of ethnocentrism is John's uniquely new summons to baptism. Customarily one baptized oneself to express conversion. But here John himself does the baptizing (cf Mk 1:4; Lk 3:3; Acts 10:37; 13:24). Schillebeeckx reads this as novel and more radical: "Getting oneself baptized by John . . . means letting oneself be changed by God; for a human being cannot do this of himself."[44] Surrendering to another perhaps embodies this realization and expresses how profound the transformation or conversion must be to which the times call. Ethnocentrism is too superficial. It doesn't cut deeply enough. Thus the ax must be laid to the tree (cf Is 43:18–19). This conversion is the reverse side of John's message of judgment.

The final characteristic of John that we find in the Gospels is that his preaching refers to "one to come who is mightier" (cf Lk 3:16; Mt 3:11; Mk 1:7; Acts 13:25). This is possibly a later Christian interpretation of the tradition, giving Jesus the primacy. Yet we have seen the apocalyptic stress on the role of mediators/messiahs, and there is little reason to doubt that John too shares at least the expectation of a "coming one." But here again John gives this figure his peculiar twist by viewing him as "an unmistakably judicial figure."[45] For he comes with the winnow and sickle in hand, preparing the fire of judgment. This seems totally in keeping with the descriptions of the "Son of Man" known to us from the apocalyptic current.

For our purposes John is terribly important because Jesus seems to identify so closely with him. The Gospels tell us that Jesus was baptized by him (Mt 3:13–17; Mk 1:9–11; Lk 3:21–22). The fact that the Gospels record this reminiscence, even though the later Christian community seems to have problems accepting Jesus' humbling himself before John (cf Jn 1:19–34, which omits the baptism), attests to the general authenticity of the Gospel's Baptist traditions. Jesus' baptism would seem to indicate that he identifies with John's proclamation. He seems to accept John's view that ethnocentric pride is an inadequate response to the crisis of the times, calling for repentance and conversion. Jesus seems to take over John's critique of the residue of ethnocentric pride and elitism in apocalyptic. Here I think we gain a real insight into John's importance for Jesus. Perhaps in our own terms we could say that John helped Jesus learn that ethnocentric exclusivism would simply continue the vicious dialectic of oppressors-oppressed which plagued the Palestine of his time. For were the Jews to achieve once again the power, they would then revengefully oppress the Romans and their collaborators. But the oppression would continue, violence and hatred would still exist, the evils would remain the same, only the victims would be different. As we will see, Jesus seems to incorporate this insight into his own message, inasmuch as he also calls for the profound *metanoia*/conversion (Mk 1:15) which challenges the oppressor-oppressed/master-slave dialectic at its root.

But again, so far as we know, John can only take us part of the way in our effort to understand Jesus. The biblical texts as we have them indicate that John only preaches judgment and repentance. Of course, like the prophets, he surely preaches judgment with a view to salvation: the reverse side of repentance is a new life freed from an ethnocentric pride which crushes and oppresses. Thus the prophet Amos preached judgment too: "What will this day of the Lord mean for you? Darkness and not light!" (Am 5:18). But Amos also enunciates the implication of this judgment and reform: "Seek me, that you may live" (Am 5:4).

But the Baptist never enunciates the note of salvation. It may be that this has been lost and/or suppressed by the biblical tradition (to highlight Jesus?), but then why was Jesus' baptism retained? In any case, arguing from what we learn through the texts, John and Jesus have their differences. The Scriptures themselves point to this: "John appeared neither eating nor drinking, and people say, 'He is mad!' The Son of Man appeared eating and drinking, and they say, 'This one is a glutton and drunkard, a lover of tax collectors and those outside the law!'" (Mt 11:18–19). As Schillebeeckx somewhat lyrically puts it, "If John came across to the people as a grim ascetic, in complete harmony with his message of God's approaching and inexorable judgment, as a sort of dirge, therefore, Jesus comes across as a song!"[46] Apparently Jesus' response to the crisis of his time entails not only a critique of that ethnocentrism that seems to infect much of Judaism; it includes a note of joy, carefreeness, and salvation that perhaps saves that serious critique from becoming too serious and fanatic.

THE JEWISH WORLD OF JESUS' TIME

Roman Conquest and Partition of Palestine

Roman conquest under Pompey begins in 63 B.C.; Herod the Great (40 B.C.—4 A.D.) is Rome's puppet monarch, succeeded by three of his sons, on behalf of whom Rome partitions Palestine.

Philip (4 B.C.—34 A.D.) becomes tetrarch of Trachonitis, the area north and east of the Lake of Galilee. Herod Antipas (4 B.C.—39 A.D.), tetrarch of Galilee and Perea, is exiled to France by Caligula. Archelaus (4 B.C.—6 A.D.), ethnarch of Judea, Samaria, and Idumea, is hated by the Jews and deposed in 6 A.D. Rome takes over Judea, where Pontius Pilate rules as prefect under the Syrian Province from 26 to 36 A.D.

Important Jewish Movements

Jews were divided in their response to the Roman occupation, some favoring armed revolt (*Zealots, Sicarii*); some, collaboration (*Sadducees*); some, withdrawal (*Essenes*); some, a more radical redefinition of religious meaning (*Pharisees, John the Baptist,* and *Jesus*). Some were simply too powerless to do anything but suffer oppression (the common *"people of the land"*).

Apocalyptic was a powerful spiritual outburst of protest, making its way into written form. Much of this literature made its first appearance as a result of the sufferings caused by the successors of Alexander the Great, around 200 B.C.

Derived from the Greek "unveiling" or "revelation," apocalyptic records the dreams of the oppressed for their vindication in the future divine Kingdom. Examples of the more important writings and the probable crises to which they are responding are as follows:

1. Assyrian/Babylonian exiles: 721–587 B.C.
   Daniel 1–6
   Epistle of Jeremiah

2. Beginning of Alexander's conquest:
   1 Enoch 72–82
   1 Enoch 1–36

3. Alexander's conquest: 169–64 B.C.
   Book of Jubilees
   Testament of Moses
   Daniel 7–12
   1 Enoch 83–90

4. In response to the Jewish Hasmoneans, who gained control away from Alexander's successors around 164 B.C.
   Qumran (Dead Sea) Scrolls
   Martyrdom of Isaiah
   1 Enoch 92–105

5. Egyptian Exile: 140 B.C.–70 A.D.
   2 Enoch
   3 Maccabees

6. Against the Romans and Herodians:
   Psalms of Solomon
   1 Enoch 37–71 (Parables)
   4 Maccabees

7. A possible apocalypse preserved by or at least influenced by Christianity:
   Testaments of the Twelve Patriarchs

8. In the aftermath of the first Jewish revolt against Rome, c. 69/70 A.D.:
   2 Baruch
   4 Ezra
   Apocalypse of Abraham
   3 Baruch
   During and after the Second Revolt, 74–129 A.D.:
   Paraleipomena of Jeremiah

Josephus, the Jewish Historian

Josephus is perhaps the most important source of information for Jesus' time, apart from the Bible. Born of a priestly family in 37/38 A.D., he carefully studied Judaism and became a Pharisee at nineteen.

Although Josephus wanted to remain neutral during the Jewish-Roman War, he did become a freedom-fighter in Galilee through persuasion. He commanded the fortress of Jotapata, some ten miles from Nazareth, when it fell to the Romans in 67.

Predicting that his captor Vespasian would become emperor, Josephus won Vespasian's trust and was released in 69, the year of Vespasian's accession to the throne. Josephus adopted the emperor's family name, Flavius. He accompanied Titus in the siege of Jerusalem and helped free many Jews. Death took him about 100.

His important writings: *History of the Jewish War*, covering Jewish history from 175 B.C. up to the tragic events of 66–70 A.D. Included also is the famous siege of Masada in 73, shortly after which this book was written. *The Antiquities of the Jews* traces Jewish history from creation to 66 A.D. Written in 93/94, it contains helpful information on the various parties and movements of Jesus' time. He also wrote *Against Apion*, a defense of Judaism against an Alexandrian school teacher, and his *Autobiography (Life)*, in which he defends himself against Justus of Tiberias, another Jewish historian who had accused Josephus of unfair friendliness toward Rome. (Cf. Gerald Hughes and Stephen Travis, *Harper's Introduction to the Bible* [San Francisco: Harper and Row, 1981], p. 111, for information on Josephus.)

174

Greco-Roman Movements

Basically public religion was a complex combination of Greek and indigenous Roman elements. Legitimating the Empire, it extended the Roman cult of the gods and goddesses of the hearth and family into state functions. Greek deities were freely borrowed: Zeus becoming Jupiter; Athena, Minerva, etc.

To some extent, philosophical movements were a reaction to the felt artificiality and meaninglessness of the public cult. Intellectuals, especially, sought an alternative in a less "superstitious" view of life.

Stoics spiritualized and intellectualized the myths. Zeus became the general law of right reason permeating the universe. Basically it was a form of pantheism. Zeno founded Stoicism around 304 B.C. in Athens. It was named after the painted porch (*Stoa Poikile*) in which he taught. Seneca (4 B.C.–65 A.D.) and the emperor Marcus Aurelius (121–180 A.D.) are famous Roman stoics.

Epicureanism employed an even more rational analysis of the universe. Through reason we can learn that death is not fearful, for human experience ends with the decomposition of our atoms. There is no afterlife. The deities are of an atomic nature different from ours—thus they are unconcerned with us. Life's goal is one of harmony with our atomic makeup.

Plato and Aristotle. Plato (427–347 B.C.) established the first "university" in 387 near Athens, the famous Academy. His great discovery was the human search for true transcendent values like truth, beauty, and justice. Through *eros* the human being searches for these and participates in them. The philosophical attempt to analyze them was also his great breakthrough. He initiated a kind of experiential analysis of reason and religious experience.

Plato's early followers tried to systematize him. *Middle Platonism* (first century B.C.—second century A.D.) borrowed from Aristotle and tended to objectify Plato's ideas into objects in the Divine Mind. For Plato they were rather symbols of our transcendent search. *Neoplatonism* (third century—sixth century A.D.) borrowed from Aristotle and Stoicism and systematized Plato even more. The spiritual dimension of humans was exaggerated into a dualism between spirit and matter.

Aristotle (384–322 B.C.) reacted against what he regarded as Plato's idealism and tried to study observable phenomena in the search for truth. Both Plato and Aristotle, according to Eric Voegelin, attempted to explore the questioning mind (*nous*) and its workings in the search for the Transcendent Mystery.

Popular religions are a complex reaction to the times. Finding both the public cult and the more philosophical religions unsatisfying, many turned to these newer religious developments.

Gnosticism offered a belief in deliverance from the alienating powers of the world through a God-given esoteric knowledge (*gnosis*). *Astrology* offered a popular belief in the rule of fate, somewhat typical for troubled times. Belief in the *emperor's divinity* and in *divine miracle workers* was also somewhat typical, manifesting a desire to be "in touch" with the sacred in a more personal manner.

Near Eastern mystery religions had great appeal to the Romans and throughout the Empire generally. Originally indigenous cults, usually fertility cults, they often came to mean the participant's ability to participate in the life-giving powers of the deities. To participate in them was to experience transcendence over evil, suffering, and world. They offered a kind of foretaste of "immortality."

Chief types of mystery religions: Although these cults had a tendency to "mix" in Greco-Roman times, still we can hypothetically outline the main types and their place of origin:

Greece:	Asia Minor:
Eleusis/Dionysos	Cybele-Attis/Mithra
Syria:	Egypt:
Adonis	Isis and Serapis

All of these are roughly similar to the mysteries of Eleusis. This celebrates the story of Kore (or Persephone) who is abducted by Aidoneus. Taken to Hades, she mourns. Finally Zeus allows her to be returned to her mother, but she must also return to Hades for a third of every year. It is her mother Demeter's persistence in withholding the world's fertility which finally persuades Zeus to intervene. The cult seems to be a mythical celebration of the world's fertility (= the period of Kore's return to her mother Demeter) and barrenness (= Kore's return to Hades or the underworld). In Greco-Roman times the cult probably took on a spiritualized meaning, signifying participation in divine immortality.

Dionysos is the god of the vine; participating in his cult probably meant escape from despair and a kind of mystic release or ecstasy. Serapis and his sister Isis, the male sun god Mithra, Cybele and her young lover Attis, the god Adonis—all were probably fertility deities somewhat spiritualized into symbols of divine immortality.

Notes

1. On the notion of the charismatic founder, see Aelred Cody, "The Foundation of the Church: Biblical Criticism for Ecumenical Discussion," *Theological Studies* 34 (1973), 3–18; John Carroll Futrell, "Discovering the Founder's Charism," *The Way*, Supplement 14 (Autumn, 1971), 62–70; Gerd Theissen, *Sociology of Early Palestinian Christianity* (Philadelphia: Fortress, 1978), pp. 8–16; Howard Clark Kee, *Christian Origins in Sociological Perspective: Methods and Resources* (Philadelphia: Westminster, 1980), pp. 54–73.

2. W.B. Smith, *The Birth of the Gospel: A Study of the Origin and Purport of the Primitive Allegory of the Jews* (New York: Philosophical Library, 1957), p. 142. Cf. also Drews, *Die Christusmythe,* 2 vols. (Jena: Diederichs, 1909–1911).

3. Günther Bornkamm, *Jesus of Nazareth* (New York: Harper and Row, 1960), p. 25.

4. Josephus, *Antiquities*, 20, 200; Tacitus, *Annals*, 15, 44; Suetonius, *Lives of the Twelve Caesars*, 25, 4; Pliny the Younger, *Letters*, 10, 94 (see Howard Clark Kee, *Jesus in History: An Approach to the Study of the Gospels* [New York: Harcourt, Brace and World, 1970], pp. 29–43, for detailed citations from the sources and critical references).

5. Schweitzer, *Out of My Life and Thought, op. cit.*, p. 103.

6. See Eric Voegelin, *Order and History*, 4, *The Ecumenic Age, op. cit.*, p. 117: "The carriers of spiritual order tend to separate from the societies of their origin because they sense the unsuitability of the concrete society as a vessel for the universality of the spirit. And the new empires apparently are not organized societies at all, but organizational shells that will expand indefinitely to engulf the former concrete societies. The universality of spiritual order, at this historical epoch, meets with the indefinite expansion of a power shell devoid of substance. From the one side, the universality of spiritual order seems to reach out for the human ecumene rather than a concrete society as the field of its realization. From the other side, the new empires tend to expand over the whole ecumene and to provide an institutional order ready to receive the spiritual substance." The term "spiritual outbursts": *ibid.*, p. 313. See the whole of *Order and History: 1, Israel and Revelation (ibid.*, 1956); 2, *The World of the Polis* and 3, *Plato and Aristotle (ibid.*, 1957); and, of course, volume 4.

7. Cf. Arnold Toynbee, *A Study of History*, 7, *Universal States, Universal Churches* (New York: Oxford, 1979); cf Kee, *Christian Origins, op. cit.*, p. 44.

8. See Eugene Webb, "Eric Voegelin's Theory of Revelation," *The Thomist* 42 (1978), 95–122, for the relevant texts.

9. See Gerald Hughes and Stephen Travis, *Harper's Introduction to the Bible* (New York: Harper and Row, 1981), p. 112, and Edwin Yamauchi, *Harper's World of the New Testament* (New York: Harper and Row, 1981), p. 9.

10. Theissen, *op.cit.*, pp. 41–42; cf pp. 31–95, upon which I rely throughout this section.

11. *Ibid.*, p. 42.

12. *Ibid.*, p. 52.

13. For an overview, see Helmut Koester, *Introduction to the New Testament*, 1, *History, Culture, and Religion of the Hellenistic Age* (Philadelphia: Fortress, 1982), pp. 228–249. Also helpful, Jacob Neusner, *Judaism in the Beginning of Christianity* (Philadelphia: Fortress, 1984), esp. pp. 17–33. I have been influenced by his view of why Rome was interested in occupying Palestine.

14. Cf. Geza Vermes, *The Dead Sea Scrolls: Qumran in Perspective* (Philadelphia: Fortress, 1977), esp. pp. 125–130, and Joseph A. Fitzmyer, "The Dead Sea Scrolls and the New Testament after Thirty Years," *Theology Digest* 29 (1981), 351–367. Their Greek name "Essaioi" apparently derives from the Aramaic *asayya*, "healers," having something to do with their interest in healing. Josephus tells us that they are known for their expert knowledge of the medicinal properties of roots and stones (Vermes, *ibid.*, p. 126).

15. Cited in Jacob Neusner, *The Way of Torah: An Introduction to Judaism* (North Scituate, Mass.: Duxbury, 1979), p. 10. For anti-Judaism in the New Testament, see Rosemary Radford Ruether, *Faith and Fratricide: The Theological Roots of Anti-Semitism* (New York: Seabury, 1974), and the critical but appreciative response, Alan T. Davies, ed., *Anti-Semitism and the Foundations of Christianity* (New York: Paulist, 1979).

16. *Ibid.*, p. 14.

17. Cf John T. Pawlikowski, *What Are They Saying about Christian-Jewish Relations?* (New York: Paulist, 1980), pp. 93–107. The basic studies: Ellis Rivkin, *The Hidden Revolution* (Nashville: Abingdon, 1978) and Jacob Neusner, *From Politics to Piety: The Emergence of Pharisaic Judaism* (Englewood Cliffs, N.J.: Prentice-Hall, 1973). Also helpful: Michael J. Cook, "Jesus and the Pharisees—The Problem As It Stands Today," *Journal of Ecumenical Studies* 15, Supplement, 1978, 441–460; and Ruether, *Faith and Fratricide, op. cit.*, pp. 53–63.

18. Ruether, *ibid.*, p. 54.

19. Pawlikowski, *op. cit.*, pp. 98–99.

20. Ruether, *Faith and Fratricide, op. cit.*, p. 61.

21. See E.P. Sanders, *Paul and Palestinian Judaism: A Comparison of Patterns of Religion* (Philadelphia: Fortress, 1977), p. 100: "The Rabbis did not have the Pauline/Lutheran problem of 'works/righteousness', and so felt no embarrassment at saying that the exodus was earned; yet that it was earned is certainly not a Rabbinic doctrine. It is only an explanatory device. One might have expected the Rabbis to develop a clear doctrine of prevenient grace, but grace and merit did not seem to them to be in contradiction to each other; and doubtless they had good

biblical support here. They could assert the grace of God in bringing Israel out of Egypt, yet at the same time ask by whose *zekut* he did so."

22. Pawlikowski, *op. cit.*, p. 102. Cf Leonard Swidler, "The Jewishness of Jesus: Some Religious Implications for Christians," *Journal of Ecumenical Studies* 18 (1981), 104–113.

23. David Flusser, "A New Sensitivity in Judaism and the Christian Message," *Harvard Theological Review* 61 (1968), 126.

24. Ellis Rivkin, "Defining the Pharisee: The Tannaitic Sources," *Hebrew Union College Annual*, 1970, pp. 205–249.

25. Cf William E. Phipps, *Was Jesus Married? The Distortion of Sexuality in the Christian Tradition* (New York: Harper and Row, 1970), p. 47, upon whom I rely.

26. Cited in *ibid.*

27. Jesus praises the body and marriage; sexual taboos are missing (cf Mt 19:2–9).

28. See *ibid.*, pp. 79–91, for the material. Evidently there were two schools of thought: Shammai, who held for no divorce unless unchastity could be proven of the wife; Hillel, who seems to have liberally permitted divorce by the husband. Jesus apparently opts for no divorce until death. Cf Quentin Quesnell, "Made Themselves Eunuchs for the Kingdom of Heaven," *Catholic Biblical Quarterly* 30 (1968), 357–358.

29. *Ibid.*, pp. 66–68, for the various possibilities.

30. Cited in Pawlikowski, *op. cit.*, p. 104.

31. See Swidler, *art. cit.*, 106, for comments; the Philo reference: "Concerning Individual Commandments," 2, 63. For Jewish views on the Gentiles, see Sanders, *op. cit.*, pp. 206–212.

32. Pawlikowski, *op. cit.*, p. 106.

33. *Ibid.*

34. Solzhenitsyn, *The Gulag Archipelago*, 3, *op. cit.*, p. 527. On apocalyptic, cf James D.G. Dunn, *Unity and Diversity in the New Testament: An Inquiry into the Character of Earliest Christianity* (Philadelphia: Westminster, 1977), pp. 309–340, for an overview upon which I rely throughout this section. Another helpful overview is Nickelsburg, *op. cit.* Highly regarded as seminal is Paul D. Hanson, *The Dawn of Apocalyptic* (Philadelphia: Fortress, 1975); see his succinct article on apocalyptic in *The Interpreter's Dictionary of the Bible*, Supplement (Nashville: Abingdon, 1976), pp. 27–34; for a careful and stimulating overview of the apocalyptic mentality beyond the biblical period, see Bernard McGinn, ed., *Apocalyptic Spirituality* (New York: Paulist, 1979), pp. 1–16, and his more ample "Introduction" in his *Visions of the End: Apocalyptic Traditions in the Middle Ages* (New York: Columbia University, 1979), pp. 1–36. From a social-critical perspective, Metz, *op. cit.*, pp. 175–179, is quite stimulating.

35. The variations are rather countless, indicating no clear consensus on the matter.

36. Dunn, *op. cit.*, p. 314.

37. Metz, *op.cit.*, pp. 175, 177.

38. For a helpful and succinct overview, see Pheme Perkins, *Reading the New Testament: An Introduction* (New York: Paulist, 1978), pp. 50–55.

39. Dunn, *op. cit.*, p. 316.

40. The most succinct overview on the nature of myth I have seen is found in James P. Mackey, *Jesus the Man and the Myth* (New York: Paulist, 1979), pp. 75–82.

41. See Edward Schillebeeckx, *Jesus, op. cit.*, pp. 126–139, upon whom I shall rely.

42. *Ibid.*, p. 127.

43. *Ibid.*, p. 128.

44. *Ibid.*, pp. 129–130.

45. *Ibid.*, p. 132.

46. *Ibid.*, p. 139.

The Message and Work of Jesus

Jesus, as I have suggested, represents, together with the Pharisees and the Baptist, the option of redefining the divine promises for the people. He seems particularly influenced by the Pharisaic current, by apocalyptic, and by the Baptist. But he integrates each of these in his own quite unique way, giving all of them his own "Jesus twist." Let me now, with contemporary research, try to present an overview of Jesus' "spiritual outburst."[1]

A Wandering Charismatic (?)

Scholars influenced by social criticism are increasingly finding Max Weber's analysis of the "charismatic" as a useful tool for indicating just how Jesus may have formed a response to the crisis of his times. The term "charismatic" simply derives from the Greek word for "gifted." Perhaps "persuasive" and "powerful" would be other translations. In his *Sociology of Religion*[2] Weber pointed out that charismatic leadership typically emerges in situations of crisis, in which the tradition is somehow felt to be inadequate as a framework of meaning for at least a segment of the populace. This segment is usually an alienated group, somewhat marginal to the larger society, and deprived of access to power and a sense of destiny and purpose. Weber distinguishes a number of types of charismatics, but the one that throws most light upon Jesus is that of the "ethical prophet."

Persuaded that he or she is the agent of the Transcendent, the ethical prophet's message is the expression of the divine will. His or her charismatic endowment manifests itself in special gifts (namely, healings, special insights) and in persuasive preaching. But it is the latter which especially seems to be the final basis of the charismatic's effectiveness. As Gregory Baum explains it, commenting on Weber, ". . . the charismatic person has power over people because he touches them where they suffer. . . . [He] gives voice to the common suffering; *he articulates the alienation* of the community; he speaks with an authority ultimately derived from the misery or unredemption of the many."3

Charismatics, then, do not derive their position through some legal procedure, such as appointment or ordination. It derives from a charism, which typically seems to entail both a critique of the sufferings of the marginal and a redefinition of the tradition which promises to alleviate those sufferings. We clearly have sufficient evidence to indicate that this style of charismatic leadership was a typical feature within Jesus' time. Certainly the Baptist fits this description. Josephus speaks of unnamed prophets emerging in the wake of the Jewish wars against Rome (*Wars*, 2,4). Both the Jewish and the Greco-Roman traditions know of wandering miracle workers (Elijah, Elisha, Moses [cf 2 Kgs 1:9,11; 4:9] and Apollonius of Tyana [cf Flavius Philostratus' *Life*]).

Gerd Theissen, however, suggests that the itinerant charismatic seems the best description for Jesus. Jesus' call to his disciples to follow him (Mk 1:16–17; Jn 1:35–42) resembles more closely the wandering radicals in the Greco-Roman Cynic tradition than the rabbinic tradition, which focuses more on study. Jesus and his disciples were to be homeless (Mk 1:16; 10:28ff): "The Son of Man has nowhere to lay his head" (Mt 8:20). They often lacked family ties and possessions, having left these behind: "I give you my word . . . no one who has given up home, brothers or sisters, mother or father, children or property, for me and for the gospel . . . will not receive in this present age a hundred times as many" (Mk 10:29–30). They were quite unprotected, having nothing to defend themselves with: hence they do not resist evil, but offer the left cheek if the right is struck (Mt 5:38ff), and they gladly go two miles if someone wants to go only one, as a means of protection (Mt 5:41).

Perhaps this style of itinerant preaching was a concrete way of embodying the desire to touch people where they suffer, for clearly it would be the marginal in society who would see in Jesus' homeless lifestyle their own situation. Perhaps, too, Jesus and his followers followed severer restrictions than the Cynics (no cloaks, knapsacks, staffs) in order to differentiate themselves from the latter. What we can say with some probability is that Jesus' spiritual outburst expressed itself through a wandering form of charismatic leadership which found a welcome among local sympathizers (Peter's home, Mt 8:14; Simon the leper, Mk 14:3ff; Mary and Martha, Lk 10:38ff).4 But what was it that motivated this extreme identification with the alienated? What was the precise nature of Jesus' spiritual outburst?

Commitment to an Alternative Future Community:
Expecting the Divine Kingdom To Come

All three Synoptics tell us that Jesus centered his work on the eager expectation of the Kingdom of God: "Jesus appeared in Galilee proclaiming . . . 'The reign of God is at hand!' " (Mk 1:15); "Jesus . . . proclaimed the good news of the Kingdom" (Mt 4:23); ". . . I must announce the good news of the reign of God, because that is why I was sent" (Lk 4:43). Other New Testament writings usually find other ways of characterizing Jesus' work, probably because their non-Jewish readers would not readily grasp this very Jewish notion of the "Kingdom." But even so, from time to time Jesus' normal proclamation of the Kingdom emerges in even these writings (Jn 3:3, 5; Acts 1:3, 6; 1 Cor 4:20; 1 Thes 2:12; Rev 11:17; 12:10). So an understanding of this "Kingdom" is crucial for grasping the heart and center of what Jesus was about.

Apparently the belief in the divine Kingdom has an extensive historical pedigree. Originally it is found in the ancient Near Eastern myth of divine kingship, which celebrates the god who demonstrates kingly power through creating the world, overcoming the primeval monster of chaos, and through renewing the earth's fertility and sustaining the people. This myth is literally ubiquitous throughout the Near East; only the god's particular name seems to undergo change: in Babylonia, Marduk; in Assyria, Asshur; in Ammon, Milhom; in Tyre, Melkart; in Israel, Yahweh. Very likely Israel received this story from the Canaanites, giving it their own, Israelitish twist.[5]

Israel, like its Near Eastern neighbors, apparently celebrated the myth annually. Each spring was a time for the cultic renewal of Yahweh's overcoming of chaos and "refertilization" of the earth: "Yahweh has become king. . . . The world is established; it shall not be moved . . ." (Ps 93:1–2). But at the same time Israel introduced its own adaptation into the myth from its own history of salvation, from the historical events (namely, the exodus) in which Yahweh acted on behalf of his people: "Yahweh has become king. . . . Righteousness and justice are the foundation of his throne" (Ps 97:1–2). The words "righteousness" and "justice" recall the covenant traditions and the exodus, through which Yahweh displayed his justice in overturning slavery. Eventually these two elements—kingship over nature and kingship through history—were fused. "What happened was that the two myths came together to form one, the myth of the God who created the world and is active on behalf of his people in the history of that world, and the symbol evolved to evoke that myth," says Norman Perrin.[6] For example, "All thy creatures [nature myth] . . . talk of the glory of the kingdom. . . . They proclaim to their fellows how mighty are thy deeds [covenant myth]. . . . Thy dominion stands for all generations" (Ps 145:10–14).

Coming closer now to Jesus' own use of the Kingdom myth, it is important to note some further adaptations of the myth in Jewish history. A first, crucial episode is that of the exiles (under the Assyrians for Northern Israel, 721 B.C.; under the Babylonians for the South, 587 B.C.). It was the prophets who, in the face of the crisis of the exiles, breathed new meaning into the myth by interpreting it futuristically. It now came to symbolize the hope that Yahweh would act anew on his people's behalf, delivering them from captivity: "The Lord our King . . . will save us. . . . The whole world . . . shall see the deliverance of our God. Away from Babylon; come out, come out . . ." (Is 33:22; 52:11). While Israel's brief freedom under Persia brings with it a renewed belief that Yahweh's kingship has again been displayed ("The Lord is among you as King, O Israel": Zeph 3:15), the renewed capturing and persecution of Israel under Alexander's and Rome's empires brings with it a heightened sense of depression and longing for the Kingdom's arrival. This is now the time of apocalyptic, which adapts the myth again by stressing even more intensely the note of persecution and the discontinuity between the present and the hoped for future: "And then his Kingdom shall appear throughout all his creation, and then Satan shall be no more, and sorrow shall depart with him" (Assumption of Moses 10:1). "But *we* hope in God, our deliverer; for the might of our God is forever with mercy, and the Kingdom of our God is forever over the nations, in judgment" (Ps. Sol. 17:3).

Jesus would seem to take over and adapt the Kingdom myth for his own purposes. He, like the apocalyptic, eagerly yearns for and expects the arrival of the divine Kingdom, when God again will display his rulership over history and bring the unrighteous oppressors to judgment. "I assure you, it will go easier for the region of Sodom and Gomorrah on the day of judgment than it will for that town" (Mt 10:15). "The coming of the Son of Man will repeat what happened in Noah's time" (Mt 24:37). "You must be prepared in the same way. The Son of Man is coming at the time you least expect" (Mt 24:44). "But for the sake of those he has chosen, he has shortened the days" (Mk 13:20). Jesus teaches his disciples to pray: ". . . your kingdom come, your will be done on earth as it is in heaven" (Mt 6:10; cf Lk 11:12). He wants them to expect the Kingdom in the same eager fashion. Thus we find the many parables of crisis in Jesus' message, which attempt to sensitize the hearer to an awareness of the Kingdom's arrival with its impending judgment: the absent householder (Mk 13:34–36), the unexpected thief (Mt 24:43–51), the ten virgins (Mt 25:1–12).

Before we go further, let us attempt to express what Jesus hopes for in the terms of our own experience. What he seems to be committed to is an alternative future community for the people, which certainly entails a decisive "no" of judgment upon those who do not live according to the values of this community. The expression "an alternative future community" seems an apt interpretation of the Kingdom symbolism, for that symbolism is derived from the realm of politics and carries a public, social, collective meaning. If we follow this cue from social criticism, we can say that Jesus is committed to a new collective gathering of people, not simply to isolated individuals. This social nature of the Kingdom is further brought out by the collective/social images which Jesus seems to employ: the Kingdom is a wedding feast (Mk 2:18–20), the overcoming of poverty (Mt 5:3–12), a banquet of festivity (Mk 14:25).

It is inadequate to individualize the Kingdom symbolism by viewing it simply as a new kind of relationship between the individual and God. The Kingdom clearly includes individuals, but it relates them into a new network of social relationships. As I indicated earlier, believing in such an alternative community is a corollary of believing in the Divine. It is an implication of our religious experience: because we experience the divine sovereignty and power in our lives now, we trust that the Divine will remain sovereign even in the future. Because we experience the Divine as a power enabling us to protest in judgment against the "anti-divine," we trust that the Divine will remain judge even in the future. But again let us stress the social nature of this trust: apocalyptic underscores the belief that the divine sovereignty and judgment must take a social form to be effective. Human history is a social reality. The "Satanic" expresses itself in complex social relationships. Therefore we trust that the divine sovereignty will manifest itself in a renewal of the social and public, not simply in the private recesses of an individual's heart. I would suggest, then, that Jesus trusts in the arrival of this new community, not simply because he naively swims in the apocalyptic current, but because it is an implication of his own religious experience. We moderns, too, can perhaps find a point of contact with Jesus' experience in our own religious experience of trust in the Divine. Insofar as we experience the Divine as a power over our lives and others' lives, enabling us to trust and to protest the oppressive, we have an experiential correlate to Jesus' own experience enabling us to co-affirm his trust.

What kind of alternative community is this, which Jesus expects and hopes for? A decisive clue is this: Jesus expects not simply any kind of community, but a new community *of the Divine*. It is a community rooted in Jesus' trust in a particular view of the Divine which he expects. Here it is helpful to keep in mind Jesus' typical use of the symbolism "Abba" as an expression for the Divine Mystery. This Aramaic term of endearment and respect occurs some one hundred and seventy times in the Scriptures, and appears to be Jesus' favored way of indicating the kind of God in which he trusts. Just as the child expresses his or her relationship of intimacy with the Father-Abba, so Jesus views himself as in a relationship with an intimate, loving "Daddy." The Hebrew Scriptures, of course, understood the divine fatherhood to imply a relationship of care and authority on the one hand, and love and obedience on the other (cf Dt 1:31; 8:5; 14:1; Is 1:2; Jer 3:19; Mal 1:6). Both of these aspects are present in Jesus' Gethsemane prayer (Mk 14:36) and suggest that he found God's care and authority to be so intimate that he drew from the intimate language of family relationships in order to express this experience. "Abba" should be translated as "Loving Father" or simply "Love," in other words. As James Dunn explains it, it expressed Jesus' "experience of God as one of unusual intimacy." And he continues:

> The divine reality he experienced in those moments of naked aloneness was God as Father. This experience was so vital and creative that it had to find expression in an address to God which would have sounded shockingly familiar to the great majority of his contemporaries. We may presume that this language alone could express the unusual intimacy he found in prayer—the intimacy, trust and obedience of a child with his father.[7]

Thus, Jesus expects a community rooted in divine intimacy and love as the foundation of his hope and trust. It is a community characterized by an unusual intimacy, rather than by blood relationships or prestige or class relationships. Here we should recall how Jesus departs from Pharisaism in his emphasis upon the universalism of God's love. As divine love knows no limits (and so we must love the enemy: Mt 5:44–45), so this new community is rooted in a similar universal love. This is why the poor will be blest (Lk 6:20; Mt 5:3), for they will no longer be marginalized. Because the Kingdom is this new love community, human injustices which result in oppression will be uprooted (Lk 16:19–31). The Japanese novelist Shusaku Endo captured the reality well when he described the Kingdom as "a universe of love based on the presence of a companion to all mankind."[8]

Here we should note how this new community is a saving and liberating reality. If it promises entrance into a community where love rules, then it also promises salvation from those communities where lovelessness rules. Jesus' work on behalf of the Kingdom is an intrinsically saving experience. Undoubtedly this is what attracted both Jesus and what followers he had to this new community. Because it was a saving and liberating reality, it could be an effective response to the crises of the times.

In the end, then, Jesus places his trust in an alternative, future community whose foundation is the intimate and universal love of the Divine Mystery itself. The position of the Love-Pharisees is here radicalized. Like the Baptist, all ethnocentrism is corrected. True, Jesus says he is sent to Israel (Mt 10:6; 15:4). But this sets no limits on the divine love. It indicates the way in which this love will enter history.

The conclusion is that Jesus' experience of trust in the Divine Mystery is an experience of a gracious Mystery. Our own experiences of a gracious power of love present in our lives and luring us toward ever greater depths of love might be a feeble correlate to what Jesus seems to mean. Like the Buddha, the Tao, the prophets, and Plato, Jesus is in search of a new order within history which will overcome injustice, and he finds it in the universal love of his Father-Abba.

Did Jesus expect this new community to arrive within his own generation? Clearly, with the apocalyptic, there is a note of urgency in his expectation. It is as if Jesus views his new community as humanity's last and only hope in the situation of crisis which confronts Judaism. Everything short of universal love will simply prolong the oppression of the time. But there are a relatively few number of texts which go beyond this note of urgency and indicate that Jesus actually expected the Kingdom's arrival within his own lifetime. "I assure you, among those standing here there are some who will not taste death until they see the reign of God established in power" (Mk 9:1); "I assure you, this generation will not pass away until all these things take place" (Mk 13:30); "I solemnly assure you, you will not have covered the towns of Israel before the Son of Man comes" (Mt. 10:23).

No consensus exists among biblical scholars on how best to interpret these enigmatic utterances. A survey of recent literature indicates three different options, each with its own strengths and weaknesses. First are those who would say that Jesus was mistaken. The Kingdom, meaning the actual realization of the new community of universal love, patently did not occur, and still has not occurred. Humanity's continual history of horror, symbolized most powerfully in Guernica, Gulag, Auschwitz, and Hiroshima, ought to be a sufficient proof of this. Jesus' mistake is understandable, though. Caught up as he was in the apocalyptic current, undoubtedly seized by a profound religious experience of trust in the divine sovereignty, this apocalyptic rapture threw him off balance momentarily and convinced him of the Kingdom's nearness. If you will, the Kingdom's soon-arrival within his own mystical experience wrongly leads him to expect its soon-arrival in human history at large.[9] If this is the case, it reminds us of how profoundly Jesus forms a part of his cultural inheritance; it underscores his real humanity, as Von Hügel came to believe.[10]

The difficulty with this view is that it overlooks the reminiscence that Jesus also was aware of apocalyptic's tendency to derail into exact time calculations: "As to the exact day or hour, no one knows it, neither the angels in heaven nor even the Son, but only the Father" (Mk 13:32). Did Jesus momentarily forget his own teaching? This has led some scholars to a second position which argues that the relatively few texts in which Jesus dates the Kingdom's arrival are enthusiastic utterances of the post-Easter Church. As Wilhelm Thüsing puts it, "These logia are probably a transformation of central, original logia of Jesus with a re-apocalypticizing emphasis."[11] Apparently the disciples were caught up in the expectation of the Kingdom's soon-arrival as a result of the Easter experiences, and this apocalyptic fever led them to reinterpret the Jesus tradition on this point. On this view, then, it would be the disciples and not Jesus who were mistaken. While this view is plausible, given the post-Easter enthusiasm of the early Church, it tends to overlook the sense of the presence of the Kingdom, which, as we will see, is also a feature of Jesus' message.

A third position attempts to integrate these various views on the basis of a biblical view of time. Walter Kasper, for example, thinks that the Bible views time not simply quantitatively, as a sequence of days and hours, but qualitatively, by its content. Time is *kairos*, opportunity, rather than simply *chronos*, the passage of minutes. Kasper tells us:

> In the context of this view of time as dependent on its content, Jesus' message of the Kingdom that is now in the future becomes more intelligible. What is being said is that now is the time for the coming of God's Kingdom; that is, the present is modified by the fact that the coming of the Kingdom has begun and faces men with a choice. The Kingdom, in other words, is the power which controls the future. It is now forcing a choice, and in this way is active in the present and totally determines it.[12]

This view preserves the Kingdom's unknowable futurity (Mk 13:32) with its effective presence (Mk 9:1; 13:30; Mt 10:23). Apparently Kasper means that the texts indicating a timing for the Kingdom in Jesus' own generation illustrate how the present is actually being modified by the future sovereignty of the Divine. Yet the Kingdom really remains future (Mk 13:32), for it is the unknowable mystery of God and its offer "is left to man's free choice."[13] In our own terms, perhaps we could say that Jesus' trust in the divine sovereignty modifies his present experience, as our trust modifies our own present experience: from *chronos* to *kairos*, the time of opportunity for sharing in the new community of universal love. In any case, this view has the merit of being biblically grounded (cf Eccl 3:1–8), and of harmonizing with the next trait of Jesus' message (the Kingdom's presence), to which we will shortly turn.

Whichever view we find more plausible—to my mind, the third seems most adequate—does not, I think, essentially call into question the central thrust of Jesus' message. That resides in his trust in an alternative future community based on a universal, divine lover. I think we can co-affirm this from our own experiences of a transcendent power of love operative in our own lives. The validity of what Jesus was about must, I think, be judged on this issue. But the merit of the third approach is that it integrates the various sayings into a coherent view revolving around this basic trust in the divine love: that Love is the new future in which Jesus trusts, a future which changes even the quality of the present by recasting it into the opportunity for participating in the new society of love.

Embodying the Alternative Future Community:
The Kingdom's Presence

Not only does Jesus eagerly trust in the arrival of his new community of love. In some sense it seems to be a present reality in his work. "But blest are your eyes because they see and blest are your ears because they hear" (Mt 13:16; cf Lk 10:23). "The reign of God is already in your midst" (Lk 17:21). The apocalyptic binding of Satan is now taking place: "No one can enter a strong man's house and despoil his property unless he has first put him under restraint" (Mk 3:27). "But if it is by the Spirit of God that I expel demons, then the reign of God has overtaken you" (Mt 12:28).

Note, now, not the many parables of crisis, but the parables of fulfillment, festivity, and joy, seeming to signalize this presence of the Kingdom: the wedding feast (Mk 2:18–20), new patches on old garments/new wine in old wineskins (Mk 2:21–22), the treasure hidden in the field/the pearl of great value (Mt 13:44–46), the metaphor of the end-time as a "harvest" (Mt 9:37–38). Even interpreters who follow Schweitzer's radical apocalyptic view of Jesus end up admitting that there is this note of the Kingdom's presence within the earliest tradition. As Richard Hiers puts it: "One could even argue . . . that Jesus understood the Kingdom of God to be present to the extent that he and his followers, through their exorcisms, were gaining ground, liberating men and recovering territory for the rule of God on earth." And he continues, "Even if in a few sayings Jesus might have hinted that the Kingdom of God was already somehow present, his characteristic orientation was toward . . . future eschatological occurrences and their all-encompassing importance for those who lived in his time."[14] Perhaps if Hiers would include in his range of evidence, not sim-

ply isolated sayings, but more parables and actions of Jesus, his judgment
might even be more "generous."

Just as we may not individualize Jesus' new community, so we may
not etherealize and spiritualize it by simply identifying it with the
"heaven" of the afterlife or the resurrected life. To be sure, Jesus' new
community is life with the Divine, and so it entails a trust in the afterlife
as the experience of fullness of life with God. But it is also a present reality
of experiencing and embodying that new community of love in which Jesus
hopes. In my experience of teaching, some student usually at this point
brings up John 18:36, where Jesus is reported to say to Pilate, "My kingdom does not belong to this world." Perhaps the student can be helped by
being shown that John does not mean a contrast between time and eternity, but between a life based on the anti-divine and a life based on divine
love and life. John's contrast is a "horizontal" rather than a "vertical" one.
Refusing to etherealize the Kingdom in this way also reinforces our view
of the intrinsically saving nature of the Kingdom. It promises, however
fragmentarily, liberation from what oppresses even now.

This Jesus-stress on the Kingdom's presence is one of the ways in
which he modifies apocalyptic's future orientation. Jesus even modifies the
Baptist's future judgment. In a more complex way, Jesus recaptures the
original meaning of the Kingdom as effective now in history: "Yahweh has
become king . . . righteousness and justice are the foundation of his
throne" (Ps 97:1–2). In our own terms, belief in the Kingdom is an implication of Jesus' religious experience of trust in the Divine. Jesus experiences the Divine as a power of protest and trust in the present, enabling
him to effectively mediate the Kingdom now. We can also find an experiential correlate in our own experiences of trust and protest, and in remembering the co-mediated nature of all things human. The community
of love must be mediated through history, through Jesus. It will not happen through magic. Perhaps a similar experience of divine presence characterized the great leaders of the first millennium: Buddha and Plato, for
example, both seem to have had intense experiences of transcendence
which they mediated to others.

Now we are in a position to note, with many scholars, the creative tension in Jesus' message and work between the "already" and the "not yet."
The Kingdom is already: the transcendent power of universal love is establishing a beachhead within history in the form of a community which
breaks through human alienation and oppression. But the Kingdom is not
yet: this new community of love is also an object of future hope, for the
experience of human history and Jesus' own message tell us that it has not
yet fully occurred. Jesus and all of us are caught in the "In-Between," as
Eric Voegelin would put it. This in-betweenness is a creative tension,

avoiding the cul-de-sacs of naive optimism-idealism-utopianism on the one hand, and excessive realism-negativism-pessimism on the other. We are saved from utopianism, because we trust that the Kingdom must yet more fully come. We are saved from negativism, because we trust that the Kingdom is partially and fragmentarily here. Plato seems to have known this too: the category of the in-between, so beloved of Voegelin, comes from Plato's *Symposium*.[15] Plato knew that we live, as yet, within the "cave" of darkness where we see, but not clearly. Did Buddha mean something similar by illusion? This creative tension is simply an implication of all genuine religious experience, it would seem. The Divine is both future and present, a divine Beyond that is within, transcendent and immanent, a power over history and yet a power within history. Jesus lived in the in-between.

Our Response to the Alternative Community: Repent and Believe!

The Gospels summarize the response which Jesus looked for in the two words "repent" and "believe." The importance of repentance is clearly sounded throughout Jesus' preaching: "He began to reproach the towns . . . with their failure to reform . . ." (Mt 11:21); "At the preaching of Jonah they reformed their lives; but you have a greater than Jonah here" (Mt 12:41); "But I tell you, you will all come to the same end unless you reform" (Lk 13:3; cf 13:5; 15:7, 10; 16:30). Jesus intends something quite radical, a turn-around of basic convictions and actions, as is clear, for example, from the parable of the prodigal son (Lk 15:17–18), and from his encounters: with the rich young man (Mk 10:17–31), with Zacchaeus (Lk 19:8), and in his command to become like little children (Mt 18:3; Mk 10:15; Lk 18:17). We especially meet this in his radical call of disciples (Mt 8:19–22), Jesus' special helpers.

Again, it is important for us to appropriate the full depth of what Jesus is about. As we have repeatedly argued with social criticism, we have a tendency to mystify Jesus' message. Repentance is not simply an interior affair of the heart, but a quite radical total change of the person. Repentance stresses the negative and costly side of this change: the painful "no" to attitudes and actions which contradict the new community of universal love. "If a man wishes to come after me, he must deny his very self, take up his cross, and follow in my steps. Whoever would preserve his life will lose it, but whoever loses his life for my sake and the gospel's will preserve it" (Mk 8:34–35; cf Mt 10:38–39; Lk 14:26; Jn 12:25). Jesus aims for the innermost recesses of the heart: the depths of the person, from which all motivations and actions flow, must undergo transformation. To live only at the level of rules and obligations is too superficial, avoiding the painful cost of the transformation that is called for. "Whatever emerges from within a man, that and nothing else is what makes him impure. Wicked designs come from the deep recesses of the heart . . ." (Mk 7:20–21; cf Mt 5:21–32).

By stressing the deep nature of this transformation—it must reach the heart's inner recesses—Jesus indicates that the ultimate source of human oppression is the prideful and loveless heart. This must be changed, or else no adequate solution to the problem of oppression will occur. Without the change of heart, then when the oppressed gain the chance for power, they will become tomorrow's oppressors! Jesus is not interested in inaugurating a new community of oppression, but in rooting out the very source from which oppression comes.

But while Jesus stresses the inner depths which the transformation must reach, he does not individualize and spiritualize repentance.[16] It is not simply "spiritual," because it must find embodiment in action: we must take up our cross and follow in his steps. The verb "follow" also indicates that repentance embraces a lifetime. Neither is it simply "individual": Jesus does not simply summon isolated individuals to reform, but people collectively and wholly, including the power centers of his day. Note how he speaks of Chorazin and Bethsaida (Mt 11:21). Note, too, his cleansing of the temple (Mk 11:15–18). As social criticism would say, there is a social and collective "punch" in Jesus' message of repentance. The only adequate analogy to this note of repentance is our own individual and collective experience of conversion, of opening ourselves to the searing power of a divine and selfless love which cauterizes egocentricity in all its forms, personal and social—what the mystics call the dark night of the senses and mind, or the purgative way, that necessary detachment from the values and actions that are contradictory to the new community of love. But to express the full depth of what Jesus meant, we must complement the individualistic thrust of the mystics with a collective purgation: the social body must undergo the dark night![17]

The other, "positive" side of this repentance is faith. The Synoptics usually associate "faith" with Jesus' miracles: to the woman with a hemorrhage he says, "Daughter, it is your faith that has cured you." And again, "Fear is useless. What is needed is trust" (Mk 5:34, 36). Or to the father of the possessed boy, "Everything is possible to a man who trusts" (Mk 9:23). At times, Jesus will speak of the positive side of our response as "love." Ultimately he reduces our response to *agape* or selfless love: ". . . love your enemies, pray for your persecutors" (Mt 5:44); ". . . you shall love the Lord your God. . . . You shall love your neighbor as yourself" (Mk 12:30–31).

Faith seems to mean a life of trust in and fidelity to the values of the Kingdom. This is why it finds its highest expression in love, for the Kingdom is the community of universal love. Again, as with repentance, so with faith-love, Jesus preaches a radical trust and love, which both penetrates the depths and finds public embodiment in social renewal. Trust changes the person quite radically, from fear to love (Mk 5:36). It is embodied in love of the neighbor and even the enemy (Mt 5:44; Mk 12:31), so that the poor are no longer poor (Lk 6:20), and even the unrighteous are incorporated into the love community (Mt 5:44). Again, the only adequate analogies are our own religious experiences, individually and collectively, of a transcendent power of love freeing us from fear and self-preoccupation, and opening us to the possibility of a new community grounded in love. Perhaps, to carry through the analogy of the mystics, we could say that Jesus has in mind the experiences of "illumination" (trust in the power of the Kingdom) and "union" (embodying the Kingdom through unitive love), as long as we also keep in mind that Jesus finally looks for a collective, public, and social renewal.

This two-sided response of conversion and faith-love is, of course, closely related to the two-sided nature of the new community as not yet and already. Because the Kingdom is not yet, repentance and faith are continual processes, the summons of a lifetime's task. Because the Kingdom is already, we can find the strength and courage to reform and believe, even now. The Kingdom-power is available to us now. The Kingdom's not-yetness saves our repentance and faith from becoming utopian or naively idealistic. The Kingdom's nowness saves them from a crippling pessimism and negativity.

This two-sided conversion and faith is the secret, I think, of Jesus' "ethic," if we feel compelled to use that word. Of course, Jesus does not have an ethics, if we mean by that a systematic system of ethical imperatives and principles. But he clearly has an ethics if we take the term more widely to mean a commitment to the values of the Kingdom and an effort to embody those values personally and collectively. Jesus seems to concentrate especially upon fostering the kind of person and community from which right ethical actions will flow. Faith and repentance are on a more profound level than the merely superficial level of miming each and every one of Jesus' activities. The Kingdom-ethics is on this deeper level, the level of what some would call "character."

If we keep this in mind, we can appreciate how far from the mark are those who have claimed that Jesus proposed a kind of "perfectionistic" ethics or "impossible ideal," as if he wanted to shatter human pride and force us to exert ourselves, even though we could never realistically reach his goals. Jesus is too much of a critical realist for that. Repentance and faith, in his view, are far from impossible: they are the only relevant answers to the dilemma of his time. Jesus' ethics only becomes perfectionistic and im-

possible on a-religious assumptions: truly if there is no transcendent power
of love operative in history, then we are condemned to the impossible.

Similarly, the argument of Schweitzer that Jesus proposes only an "interim" ethics for the supposed time before the end is highly questionable.
There is no textual evidence for this, and it is based on the least possible
of the views about the timing of the Kingdom which we surveyed earlier.
The ethics which we have outlined conforms to the central thrust of Jesus'
message and work. There is no evidence that he regarded it, any more than
he regarded the new community of love, as an interim reality.[18]

Let me end this section by highlighting the intrinsically "salvific" nature of repentance and faith. If these two, interrelated movements bring
about entrance into the Kingdom, they also bring about salvation from the
anti-Kingdom, the realities opposed to justice and love of an individual and
collective nature. Salvation is not a reward "added on" to repentance and
faith. It is their other side, as their intrinsic effect. There always seems to
be a salvific dimension to the work of Jesus, wherever we turn.

The Offer of the New Community

What happens when one risks the challenge of repentance and faith?
One begins to participate in the new community. In the end, this seems
to be the offer held out by Jesus. Perhaps it is symbolized best in his table
fellowship: he dines with all, drunkards, sinners, and tax collectors (Mt
11:19; Lk 15:1), in a fellowship which is a foretaste of the messianic age (Lk
14:13, 16–24). Participation in this community breaks down barriers, integrating the marginalized.

This participation can take many forms in our early Jesus traditions.
We nowhere receive a summary of all its possible forms. All we have are
the remains of experiences in which this participation was especially felt.
Let us, then, dwell upon some representative examples.

The Miracles

The miracles surely deserve mention. No doubt, many experience
difficulties with the extensive miracle traditions of the New Testament, on
both historical and philosophical/theological grounds. And to some extent
these difficulties seem legitimate. After all, critical historical research has
rightly indicated that the Gospel miracles are the end product of a complex
process of development. In some cases the miracles seem to have been
magnified and multiplied: the feeding of four thousand becomes the feeding of five thousand (Mt 14:13–21; 15:32–38), for example. In some cases
there appear to be borrowings from Greco-Roman and rabbinic miracle

stories, which result in placing the miracles into an idealized scenario of request, the disease's nature, the healing, the witnesses, and the confirmation of the cure. Perhaps, too, the post-Easter faith of Christians caused them to magnify the miracle traditions. As Walter Kasper puts it, "The result of all this is that we must describe many of the gospel miracle stories as legendary."[19] They may witness to the early Church's faith, and perhaps have a kind of religious meaning. But historically they are dubious.

The miracle stories also raise significant philosophical and theological questions. The somewhat fashionable notion of miracles as "direct" acts of the Divine beyond nature's powers and apart from nature has greatly hindered their proper evaluation and caused needless skepticism. Such a view is based on a non-theological view of nature as devoid of the Divine presence. Religious experience testifies that the Divine mediates its presence to us through history and nature, not apart from them. A miracle not mediated through our human experience would simply be unintelligible. A properly theological view of miracles would start from the presupposition that the Divine presence permeates the world and humanity. Miracles, then, would be intensive (or extraordinary) manifestations of this Divine presence. Rather than circumventing nature and human causality, they would actualize and liberate it, in accord with the way in which the Divine relates to the world. Walter Kasper, who has presented the most comprehensive view of the miracles among Jesus questers, put it this way:

> The question of . . . miracles . . . turns finally into the question of what the ultimate meaning of reality as a whole is. Is it pure chance, blind fate, a universal regularity which allows no room for freedom, or an all-determining freedom which we call God? If we choose the religious interpretation . . . the question of miracles becomes the problem of correctly defining the relationship between God and the world. [In the biblical perspective God is the one] who in constantly original ways offers his love to human beings in and through the events of the world. This God uses the laws of nature which he created, and which he therefore wills and respects, and in and through them shows men by means of effective signs that he is near to help and hold them. . . . We may therefore postulate as the basic law of the biblical relationship between God and the world that the unity of God and the world and the autonomy of creation are not inversely but directly proportional.[20]

Granting, then, the historical difficulties, as well as the need to reappropriate a more biblical and theological view of the miracles, there is no reason to call into question "a basic stock of historically certain miracles of Jesus," Kasper holds.[21] The miracles are too integral a part of the earliest

traditions, they are linked with Jesus' general proclamation of the Kingdom (cf Mt 12:28), and some have a simplicity and non-tendentiousness
which bespeaks credibility (cf Mk 1:29–31).

The really important element about the miracles for our purposes is
that they are linked to Jesus' ministry on behalf of the Kingdom. Their purpose is not directly to illustrate something about Jesus, but to embody the
presence of the new community of love: "But if it is by the Spirit of God
that I expel demons, then the reign of God has overtaken you" (Mt 12:28).
Here the miracle indicates that participation in Jesus' community brings
healing, health, and a greater wholeness. Further, participation in the new
community is not a purely inner state, but finds embodiment physically
and outwardly. And, as social criticism would argue, there is even a social
and political dimension to the miracles. Jesus' exorcisms and healings are
manifestations that his new community is an alternative to the work of the
apocalyptic "Satan," the symbol of the forces of oppression and evil in society. This is perhaps why Jesus rejects spectacular displays (Mt 12:38–45;
16:1–2; Lk 11:29–32; Mk 8:11–12), for his new community takes the form
of a healing and liberating love, rather than an ostentatious and manipu-
lative display of force (the characteristic of Satan). While all of this illustrates the kind of social embodiment which participation in the Kingdom
takes, something else about the miracles illustrates the note of interior
transformation characteristic of membership in the new community. For
the miracles demand the response of faith for their discernment in the tradition (Mk 9:22–23; Mt 17:20). Apparently only the person open to the values of the Kingdom can penetrate through to the miracle's true meaning.
Inner transformation and social embodiment—these seem to be what the
miracles effect.

There is something more to the miracles, too, which Kasper has very
interestingly noted:

> An important feature of them is the absence of any planned or systematic
> attempt to improve the world. Jesus did not systematically heal all the
> sick or drive out all the demons; he simply gave isolated signs, which
> cannot be separated from the total context of his work, the message of
> the coming Kingdom of God. Jesus is not interested in a better world,
> but in the new world. But according to his message, man and the world
> can only become really human when they have God as their Lord. Any-
> thing else would not be human, but would lead to superhuman efforts
> and very easily to inhuman results.[22]

What Kasper seems to be saying is that the real secret of the miracles, and
therefore the real secret of membership in the Kingdom, is the mystery of

the Divine Itself. It is openness to the Love-Mystery, and not human plans for the betterment of the world, which ultimately heals and liberates from human arrogance and its totalitarian results. The inner transformation and new physical and social being given through the miracles originates in the Divine—that is the really deep lesson of the miracles.

The Preference for the Poor and Oppressed[23]

There can be no doubt that Jesus' offer of membership in the new community is in principle open to all. Yet, the Gospels leave us with the impression that Jesus had a special concern for the poor and oppressed. Albert Nolan, among contemporary Jesus questers, has particularly brought this out in his study of Jesus. He focuses upon how the Gospels characterize Jesus as filled with "compassion" for the marginalized of society:

> The English word "compassion" is far too weak to express the emotion that moved Jesus. The Greek verb *splagchnizomai* used in all the texts is derived from the noun *splagchnon*, which means intestines, bowels, entrails or heart, that is to say, the inward parts from which strong emotions seem to arise. The Greek verb therefore means a movement or impulse that wells up from one's very entrails, a great reaction.[24]

Thus, the Gospels tell us: ". . . his heart was moved with pity, and he cured their sick" (Mt 14:14; cf 9:36); "The Lord was moved with pity upon seeing" the widow of Nain (Lk 7:13; cf Mk 1:41; Mt 20:34; 8:2). Who were these oppressed ones? For Jesus, apparently anyone particularly deprived of full participation in the human community: the beggars; widows and orphans; unskilled laborers, peasants, and slaves; the economically poor; the "sinners," such as prostitutes, tax collectors, robbers, usurers, gamblers; the illiterate, who were deprived of knowledge of torah; the sick. Perhaps Jesus' statement about becoming like children (Mk 10:15; Mt 18:3; Lk 18:17) indicates the oppressed status of children and the need to identify in solidarity with them too. Of course, women occupy an important place on this list.

Jesus does not idealize poverty and oppression, as if these were states which all of us should desire, and as if the poor or disadvantaged were somehow spiritually superior and not in need of conversion. His wandering, charismatic ministry does not seem motivated by an idealization of these states, but rather by an attempt to identify with them and reach out to them in aid. He seems committed to the elimination of poverty and its causes. This is why, in his love community, the poor are especially blessed

(Lk 6:20), for that community is one which seeks to eliminate the forces which foster oppression. The rich and "middle classes" are not excluded from this community, but demonstrate their participation in it by what they do for the poor: "Sell all you have and give to the poor," Jesus says to the rich man (Lk 18:22; cf 16:19–31).

Jesus' approach to the poor particularly illustrates that he is attempting to eliminate what later ages would call the vicious dialectic of the oppressor and the oppressed. He is hard on the rich, to be sure, for their wealth often blinds them to the true values of his love community: ". . . only with difficulty will a rich man enter into the Kingdom of God" (Mt 19:23). But he does not idealize the poor, as if they cannot be driven by hatred, resentment, and the desire for revenge. Jesus not only heals the paralytic at Capernaum; he *forgives* him (Mk 2:1–12). Jesus attempts to get at the root of the causes of oppression, which surely are embodied in social forms, but spring from the deep recesses of the heart: "What emerges from within a man, that and nothing else is what makes him impure" (Mk 7:20). Unless the poor, too, are converted to the values of the love community, then today's oppressed will simply become tomorrow's oppressors, given the opportunity. Perhaps Jesus' own temptations, attested in the Gospels (Mt 4:1–11; Lk 4:1–13; Mk 1:12), are equally an indication that he too needed to root out the deep sources of oppression within himself.[25] Thus, while participation in the Kingdom takes the social form of a preference for the oppressed, it must also take the form of inner conversion on the part of *all* to the values of the Kingdom.

The same attempt to cut through the vicious dialectic of oppressor and oppressed/master and slave seems to characterize Jesus' ministry toward women and men, too. Surely if we pay attention to the rich field of the feminist critique of religion, we must be convinced that women formed an important segment of the oppressed of Jesus' time. Israel shared in the general devaluation of women characteristic of humanity, which seems to have set in particularly in the great urban civilizations of the second millennium. Women's role as the equal partner with men in the early agricultural communities was devalued through urbanization: they remain at home with the garden and children, and men take over the tasks of law, politics, warfare, and public religion. Women begin to symbolize the inferior, the subordinate to the male, the dependent one. Thus, women belong to their male consorts in the Israel of Jesus' day, although they enjoyed some protective rights (Dt 24:1–4). They find their fulfillment in bearing offspring to the male, and barrenness is a legitimate ground for divorce (Dt 24:1–4). They are excluded from the priesthood. The only leadership they might exercise is a charismatic rather than a legal one (like the prophetesses Deborah, Huldah, etc.). In later, post-biblical times, their role was one of enabling their husbands to study torah, while they could not do the same. In the words of the Talmud, "Cursed be the man who lets his wife recite the blessing for him Friday night."[26] As Denise Lardner Carmody sums it up, "The law did command honor for both father and mother, yet it kept women dependent from cradle to grave—literally so, since if a husband died, his male relatives were to take charge of his wife (Gen. 38)."[27]

Jesus apparently attempts to break through this domination of women. We have already noted how, in the story of Martha and Mary (Lk 10:38–42), he elevates the status of Mary to one of equality with the males: Mary has chosen the better part. Consistent with this, he is remembered as having female disciples, some of whom accompanied him on his missionary tours (Mary Magdalene, Joanna, Susanna: cf Lk 8:1–3). He praises the faith of widows and outcast women (Lk 21:1–4. 7. 36–50), performs miracles for them (Mk 1:30–31; Lk 4:38–39; Jn 2:1–11), and even describes himself as a "mother hen" weeping for Jerusalem (Mt 23:37; Lk 13:34). He overcomes the double standard which allows only the male the right of divorce (Mt 5:31–32), and holds out to males the womanly value of service as an apt expression of life in his love community (Mk 10:35–45).

But this "elevation" of women is not meant to result in the equally oppressive subordination of the male. Jesus wants the male to develop the womanly quality of service, not to become the chattel of ladies. Both men and women must transform their inner values in accordance with the Kingdom (Mk 7:20). For women, whose subjugated role has forced them to develop the quality of service, this means developing the sense of true equality, self-worth, and independence. For men, whose power status has enabled them to develop the quality of autonomy, it means developing the capacity for service and mutuality. Service must be modified by autonomy, dependence by independence, self-love by other-love. This keeps autonomy from degenerating into exploitation, and service, from a crippling slavery. Such a modification of values seems to be what Jesus is after. In this way, he undercuts the master-slave dialectic: male mastery is broken through, yet without females simply taking their place.

As Peter Hodgson helpfully put it, participation in the Kingdom seems to entail a form of "critical partisanship" on behalf of the poor and oppressed.[28] It is "partisanship," because it entails a preference for them, a genuine attempt to overcome the social and institutional embodiment of oppression. It is "critical," because it tries to overcome the master-slave dialectic through the transformation of values on the part of all, including the oppressed of today. It is not vengeance Jesus is after, but an effective liberation of all. Because Jesus' partisanship was critical, he refrained from violence, which is perhaps the supreme manifestation of the master-slave dialectic. Violence subverts the possibility of overcoming that dialectic through destroying the people called to undergo transformation. "Instead of keeping history open and moving, it has a deadening, paralyzing effect," says Hodgson.[29] Yet Jesus calls for a genuine partisanship with the oppressed which must find social embodiment, and so Hodgson claims that "Jesus himself practiced *nonviolence* in an *active*, not a passive way."[30] He did not avoid conflict; he mobilized his followers; he confronted the establishment; he knew how to use power (Mt 10:34–36; 11:12; Mk 11:15–19; Lk 22:35–38), yet without resorting to violence (Mt 5:38–42, 43–44). He praises the peacemakers (Mt 5:9).

But the matter is even more complicated than that. For as history shows, and as Jesus himself knew (Mt 10:34–36; 11:12), power, even non-violent power, entails the risk of violence. Again Hodgson points out: "There are certainly occasions when the use of power generates violence, or when violence itself becomes an uncalculated and unavoidable necessity, as for example when conditions grow so inhuman, degrading, or totally threatening that it is better to die than not to resist violently or to act in self-defense."[31] Jesus seems to have been aware of this and took steps to avoid just such a degeneration of his non-violent power. He does not make a fetish out of his critical partisanship, but tries to keep it truly critical through a strategy which seeks to avoid violence. Thus, he not only engages in partisanship, but withdraws, in prayer (Mk 14:35–36) and into the festivity of his table fellowship (Mt 11:19; Lk 15:1). He preaches a radical trust in the Divine Love which tones down the militant fever of the social reformer: "Do not be concerned for your life, what you are to eat, or for your body, what you are to wear. Life is more important than food and the body more than clothing. Consider the ravens. . . . God feeds them. How much more important you are than the birds!" (Lk 12:22–24). Even at the limit, when his non-violence could no longer avoid the risk of the violence of his death, it is surely significant that he does not strike back the oppressor. Even here he tries to keep open the possibility of the transformation of the oppressor, trusting that the Divine can salvage something from the wreck of his own death.

Thus, this little study of Jesus' ministry on behalf of the marginalized teaches us that the offer Jesus holds out is the radical transformation of values into the values of the love community. To be sure, this transformation must find its social embodiment in critical partisanship, but it must equally entail the transformation of the inner self, the ultimate source whence human miseries spring. Given this strong preference for the oppressed in the earliest Jesus traditions, perhaps we should begin to speak of Jesus' community as not only one of love, but also of justice and peace. The strong social and political flavor which punctuates Jesus' new community would seem to demand some such characterization to do it full justice. If we take justice and peace in a rather general sense as what happens when a Jesus-like love becomes public, then it certainly seems appropriate.

Harmony with Nature

Often overlooked in any consideration of Jesus' message is a treatment of his views of creation and nature. Historical scholars have simply not been interested in the issue, and psychosocial critics have focused more on Jesus' political relevance and his approach to the oppressed, as we have just seen. To my knowledge, among Jesus questers the one exception in this regard is Günther Bornkamm.[32] Let me offer some of Bornkamm's insights, as they fittingly form a part of our considerations on the offer of Jesus' new community, inasmuch as a harmonious co-existence with the created world seems one of the results of what Jesus holds out to us.

Although Jesus nowhere speaks of nature or develops a theory of nature, still he continually points his hearers to the world of creation. The parables especially confirm this, but so, too, do many of our early sayings. If you will, the created world is simply an essential presence in his life: the fowls of the air and lilies of the field (Mt 6:26ff), the fig-tree (Mk 13:28), the seed (Mk 4:3ff), the sparrows (Mt 10:29), the sun and rain (Mt 5:45), sunset and the south wind (Lk 12:55), the lightning (Mt 24:27), even the wild dogs (Lk 16:21), the moth and rust (Mt 6:19ff) and the eagles (Mt 24:28).

The world of nature that we find in these sayings is unromanticized and matter-of-fact, something which argues for their historical character. But for our purposes the really significant factor is that Jesus appeals to nature in order to bring home what his message is about. If you will, the created world is a parable of the Kingdom of God. But what does this created world teach? Apparently Jesus finds within it a disclosure of the mystery of love: sun and rain fall on all; they aren't partial and exclusive (Mt 5:45). The imagery of seed, growth, and harvest points to the wonderful promise of God entailed in his love; lightning and storm, to his judgment at the failure to love.

Nature's parable is that we are meant to live in harmony and love. This is why Jesus can point to it in his proclamation of the Kingdom. When we fail to realize this harmonious love, disaster occurs (lightning and storm). Just as sun and rain fall on all, so the true member of Jesus' new community is fueled by a love with equal intensity. It would be too much to argue that Jesus possessed a modern ecological consciousness. But what is significant is his sensitivity to nature, his appeal to it, his inclusion of it into his central proclamation. Participation in the new community entails the harmony of nature itself, and our humility before it and willingness to learn from it. That is as far we can go, but it sounds terribly modern in some ways.

Jesus' Teaching on Prayer

Let me end this survey of the offer Jesus holds out to us by some observations drawn from Jesus' teaching on prayer. Whenever prayer has not degenerated into a purely mechanical and routine observance, it is an especially privileged example of the secret of every religion. Because this is so, we can rightly expect Jesus' teaching on prayer to be a special example of what membership in his new community means: a kind of concentrated expression of that membership. Although this must remain tentative and highly hypothetical (only a few of the prayer traditions are very early), still the biblical texts indicate that Jesus develped his own form of prayer which he shared with his disciples. When those disciples asked, "Lord, teach us to pray" (Lk 11:1), they were probably not asking how to pray as if for the first time. If they were serious Jews, they probably recited the *Shema* in the morning and evening (Dt 6:4, 5–7), and prayed the traditional hymn and benediction known as the *Tephilla* at the accustomed times of morning, afternoon, and evening. Both Acts (3:1; 10:3, 30) and the *Didache* (8:3) indicate that this was still a Christian custom in the first century. Rather, when the disciples asked to be taught to pray, they wanted to know what was the characteristic form of prayer of Jesus' new community. Just as the Pharisees had their distinctive prayer (probably the *Tephilla*), as did the Essenes and the Baptist's disciples (Lk 11:1), so too Jesus' community probably had its own.

Here I would suggest, drawing upon the marvelous studies of Joachim Jeremias especially, that Jesus' prayer manifests that inner transformation of values so characteristic of membership in his new community. The way Jeremias puts this is to say that Jesus goes beyond the Jewish practice of prayer in its time, its language, and its content. The Gospels generally attest that Jesus is remembered as saturating his life with prayer. He does not simply pray thrice daily, but seems to permeate his life with prayer: "Rising early the next morning, he went off to a lonely place in the desert; there he was absorbed in prayer" (Mk 1:35); "When he had taken leave of them, he went off to the mountain to pray" (Mk 6:46); "Then he went out to the mountain to pray, spending the night in communion with God" (Lk 6:12). Likely this tradition of Jesus' solitary prayer has been amplified in the tradition, especially by Luke (cf 5:16; 6:12; 9:18, 28), but this only attests a strong tradition of Jesus in prayer. Particularly significant is the reminiscence that Jesus prays at especially critical moments in his ministry: before curing (Mk 9:29), when he preaches (Mt 11:25), and before his arrest in Gethsemane (Mk 14:35–36).

Jesus' language for prayer is also significant. While the *Shema* and *Tephilla* are prayed in Hebrew, the official liturgical language of the day, Jesus customarily prays in Aramaic, the vernacular language of the time. The address "Abba" to the Divine especially shows this, as well as the first two petitions of the Our Father which echo the *Kaddish*, the one prayer recited in the synagogues in Aramaic. "In so doing, he removes prayer from the liturgical sphere of sacred language and places it right in the midst of everyday life," says Jeremias.[33]

The content of Jesus' prayer, as we might expect, revolves around what he is centrally committed to: the Kingdom as the new community of love, justice and peace. The characteristic address to God as "Abba" shows that Jesus is dedicated to the intimate Source of Love which is the root and foundation of his new community. The Lord's Prayer (Lk 11:2–4; Mt 6:9–13) "is in fact a brief summary of the fundamentals of Jesus' proclamation, with the address 'Father,' the prayer for the final redemption (the two petitions in the second person [the future Kingdom]), the prayer for the present realization, here and now, of that Kingdom (the two petitions in the third person), and the last petition for preservation from apostasy in the last terrible hour of temptation."[34] Interestingly, Jeremias claims that there is a special note of thanksgiving in Jesus' prayer (Mt 11:25; Lk 10:21), perhaps reflecting the belief that the Kingdom's presence is a time above all for thanksgiving: "In the world to come all sacrifices will cease, but the thank-offering will remain for ever; likewise all confessions will cease, but the confession of thanks will remain for ever," runs a Jewish saying.[35]

I don't think we would be doing an injustice to Jeremias' research if we drew the conclusion that the three characteristics which he highlights (timing, language, and content) all indicate that participation in the new community entails the radical transformation of our inner values in accord with that community. The element of timing indicates that our entire life from wake through sleep is to be permeated by the values of the new love, justice and peace community. The transformation called for is total. The element of language indicates the same: Jesus calls for a transformation which reaches into our everyday lives, just as Aramaic does. The worlds of family, profession, play and leisure, politics and war—all are to be lived in accord with the new community of the Kingdom. The element of content indicates the nature of this total transformation: it is love which feeds all that we do, the love expressed in the symbolism of the divine Kingdom rooted in Abba.

While Jeremias captures the note of interior transformation so characteristic of Jesus' prayer, the social critic Jon Sobrino has brought out the social punch of Jesus' teaching on prayer, showing how prayer leads to a new social embodiment of the Kingdom's values. Prayer leads, not only to inner conversion, but also to social renewal and critique. To be sure, the element of inner transformation is particularly strong in Jesus' prayer, as we have it in the tradition. It is through the withdrawal of prayer that he purifies himself of that inner temptation to continue the master-slave dialectic. But still there is a note of critical partisanship and social critique in the prayer tradition.[36]

Some of the petitions of the Our Father express the note of critical partisanship: one does not simply pray to Abba, but also for the Kingdom's arrival, for bread right now, and for deliverance from the evil of the anti-Kingdom. Authentic Jesus-prayer is not a simple aloneness with the Divine, but a sensitivity to our unjust human plight right now and a greater commitment to struggle against that. Latin American theologian Jon Sobrino points to Jesus' remarkable criticism of the prayer tradition of his day.

Inauthentic prayer fosters a "numbness" to the need for critical partisanship. It can take the form of a mechanism which blinds us to our own evil and contribution to human misery: "I give you thanks, O God, that I am not like the rest of men—grasping, crooked, adulterous—or even like this tax collector," says the Pharisee (Lk 18:11)—to which Jesus responds that prayer should make us self-critical: "For everyone who exalts himself shall be humbled while he who humbles himself shall be exalted" (Lk 18:14). Similarly, inauthentic prayer blinds us to the need for action within society. It spiritualizes and individualizes religion and prayer, robbing them of their critical punch: "None of those who cry out, 'Lord, Lord,' will enter the kingdom of God, but only the one who does the will of my Father in heaven" (Mt 7:21; cf 6:7–8). Similarly, inauthentic prayer can actually oppress people; a numbness to our own perversion can turn our prayer into a tool for the perversion of others: "Be on guard against the scribes, who like to parade around. . . . These men devour the savings of widows and recite long prayers for appearance's sake; it is they who will receive the severest sentence" (Mk 12:38–40).

All of these representative examples, then, help us to grasp what membership in the new love, justice and peace community entails. Repentance and faith lead both to the profound transformation of values in line with the new community, and to the public and social embodiment of those same values. Inner change and social embodiment, inner self-critique and social critique—through these the vicious dialectic of master and slave can be cut through.

Again, all of this is intimately related to Jesus' central commitment to the Kingdom as both a future and a somewhat present reality. The Kingdom's presence makes our inner renewal and social critique a present possibility within history, saving us from a negative pessimism that blocks any effective change. The Kingdom's futurity reminds us that inner conversion and social renewal need constant critique, constant salvation from a utopianism which blinds us to human misery and our own need for renewal. Again, a possible correlate to this is our own experience, personal and social, of the presence of the Divine in our lives, gifting us with the present capacity to transcend ourselves in love, justice and peace, and yet saving them from idolatrous pretensions and utopianism.

Salvation the "Reverse Side" of the Offer of Jesus

These few examples of Jesus' offer to us show how impossible it is to sever the gift of salvation from Jesus' work on behalf of the Kingdom. If Jesus heals through his miracles, then he is setting us free from what chains and oppresses us. If he has a preference for the poor and oppressed, it is because there is a vicious poverty and oppression from which we must be released. If he critiques inauthentic prayer, it is because we are in need of liberation from those forces which cause us to use prayer in a destructive way. Everything he does in his ministry seems permeated by a saving dimension. In the end, the offer Jesus holds out is a participation in a community which brings, as its reverse effect, salvation from the lack of authentic community.

Passion, Death, and Abandonment

Universally attested in the New Testament is the passion, death, and abandonment of Jesus. The historical details, as we shall see, are blurred. But the substance of the matter is secure. As we approach this issue, it would probably be best to try to clear up some misunderstandings which usually surface. One perennial tendency which we have inherited is that of the "wrathful God syndrome," which looks at Jesus' passion as the price he had to pay in order to appease his angry Father. Connected with this is a kind of "cult of bodily masochism," which views the Christian life, really quite unbiblically, as a cult of pain and bodily degradation, the cross becoming the supreme manifestation of this anti-body asceticism. There is no doubt that the New Testament views Jesus' death as the expression of the divine will (cf Mk 14:36; Mt 26:39; Lk 22:42), but to read this as the appeasement of a wrathful God contradicts Jesus' belief in the intimate and loving Abba. Similarly, the cult of bodily pain contradicts the biblical teaching that God created the body good (Gn 1:31) and that we should glorify God through our bodies, for they are the Spirit's temples (1 Cor 6:19–

20). In the light of this, we should rather read Jesus' death as an act of commitment to his Father's work: not an appeasement, nor masochistic heroics, but an expression of his solidarity with the Divine justice love, and peace. The death is an expression—a supreme one—of love, in other words.

A further perennial difficulty is that of comprehending why this utterly good man Jesus had to die. Why did his solidarity with the Divine love, justice and peace entail death? Part of our problem comes from abstracting Jesus from his historical context and projecting our own, later Christian hindsight onto his times. We Christians believe that Jesus was utterly good, but this may have by no means been obvious to those caught up in the highly volatile conflicts of his time. Another portion of our difficulty stems from excessively depoliticizing Jesus' death. We tend to forget that he did not die a "private" death, from old age, or sickness, or even from suicide. Jesus was put to death, by public authorities. This indicates that his life and work met with a rather stubborn opposition. Something about him was a nuisance, perhaps even a threat, to the powers of the time.

If we keep these "clarifications" in mind, I think that we can arrive at a reasonable assessment of this very difficult matter. First, if we view Jesus' death an an act of solidarity with the Divine love, then we can better understand why he goes to Jerusalem. This is not motivated by a morbid desire to die. In fact, Jesus also prays at Gethsemane that the cup pass him by (Mk 14:36). Rather, we should connect his visit to Jerusalem with his ministry on behalf of the Kingdom, as he himself does: "Today and tomorrow I cast out devils and perform cures, and on the third day my purpose is accomplished. For all that, I must proceed on course today, tomorrow, and the day after, since no prophet can be allowed to die anywhere except in Jerusalem" (Lk 13:32–33; cf Mk 14:25). His trip to Jerusalem is an attempt to issue his summons to the new community at the very center of Judaism. Like the prophets who called for the reformation of Jerusalem, so Jesus takes on the prophetic role of summoning Jerusalem to change (Is 56:7; Jer 7:11). Perhaps the temple's cleansing forms a part of this summons, a kind of prophetic enactment of what it entails (Mk 11:15–25). In our own terms, we could say that if one wanted to renew America, he or she would eventually have to carry the message of renewal out of Helena and into the power centers of the country (perhaps New York, Los Angeles, Dallas, Chicago, and Washington, D.C.!).

Second, if we keep in mind the public/political nature of his death, then we can appreciate somewhat more fully why Jesus' preaching and work in Jerusalem brought him to his death. His work led him into opposition from the powers of his day. The biblical texts indicate opposition from two fronts. On the one hand, he meets with opposition from some powerful figures within Judaism, possibly the Sadducees, given their status of power at the time. The charge of blasphemy (Mk 14:64) and the threat of punishment by stoning from earlier in his ministry (Jn 8:59; 10:31–33; 11:8; Lk 4:28–30) would seem to echo this opposition from some Jewish sectors. On the other hand, he meets with opposition from the Empire. Jesus is crucified, which is the normal Roman punishment for slaves and rebels. He is not stoned, which was the normal form of Jewish punishment. The texts clearly implicate Pilate (Mk 15:15).

Why this opposition? From the side of the Sadducees (?) we are on safest ground if we view them as in opposition to Jesus' new universal community of love, justice, and peace. This would surely be perceived by some as a threat to Jewish identity and ethnocentrism. But more than that, Jesus threatens the very *raison d'être* of particularism. Like the Love Pharisees, but apparently even more radically, Jesus challenges all pretensions to control access to the Divine. From the Roman side, while Jesus was probably more of a nuisance than a threat, he meets with opposition too. Some have argued that he was perceived as a rebellious Zealot, but the differences between Jesus and the Zealots are rather glaring. At the very least, we can say that the Romans intuited a contradiction between their own values and those embodied in Jesus. It is perhaps the friction which occurs when an empire based on violent power meets with a community and its leader grounded in universal love, justice and peace.

Arguments as to whether Jesus was crucified for political or for religious reasons are really anachronistic. Both the Jewish and the Roman cultures were based on polities which knew no separation between politics and religion. A religious claim would *ipso facto* entail political claims, and vice versa. Jesus was probably perceived as both religiously and politically problematic. And this corresponds with what we have learned of Jesus, too: after all, he dedicates himself to a new public community within history (political), a community which is rooted in religious beliefs (religion).

There is, beyond the above minimum, much that we do not know with any degree of probability. The traditions of the various trials are contradictory (and there were apparently no Christian witnesses). Was it in the night and morning (Mt and Mk)? Only in the morning (Lk)? Before the full high council (Mk, Mt, Lk), or only before Annas and Caiaphas (Jn)? Scholars even debate whether the council could have lawfully met. The texts are somewhat idealized, and we cannot be even relatively sure about how much is post-factum interpretation and how much historically probable (note the extensive citations from Ps 22, Ps 69, Ps 41, and Zech 9—13). The date, too, is ambiguous: was it the day before Passover (Jn 19:14), or the day of the feast itself (as the Synoptics indicate)? Even Jesus' declaration before the Sanhedrin (Mk 14:61–62), in which he seems to declare himself "Messiah," must remain exceedingly ambiguous. This is the only time in the Gospels that Jesus accepts this title clearly, and so it may be a post-Easter interpretation. Yet the Gospels do indicate that Jesus was condemned as "King of the Jews" (Mk 15:26). Jews could possibly have had in mind the prophetic tradition of messiahship rather than the Davidic. He, like the prophets, is a suffering agent of God. Perhaps now his impending death would make it clear which tradition of messiahship he identifies with.[37] But this must remain highly conjectural.

In any case, Jesus' commitment to his new community brought him down, to death. In our own experiential terms, we might view this as a supreme embodiment of that universal peace, love and justice to which Jesus was dedicated. Just as the transcendent presence of Love in our own lives can lead us to heroic levels of selflessness, so Jesus' death leads him down that same path known to many of the righteous victims of history. Again, we should note how this death interconnects with the Kingdom-message. It embodies the presence and actuality of the Kingdom as a reality which enters history in the form of negativity: a struggling and protesting "no" to the powers of dehumanization. Most of all, it is the cross which forces us to de-etherealize and de-individualize our groping understanding of Jesus' new community. We must de-etherealize it, because it entails the cross of the passage from egocentricity to selflessness. We must de-individualize it, as social criticism emphasizes, because it entails opposition to the quite public powers of oppression within history.

Precisely because the cross comes to us in the form of the negative, it also points to the Kingdom's futurity, its not-yetness within history. As long as someone can say, with the slave in Plautus' comedy, "I know that the cross will be my grave,"[38] we will know that the Kingdom is yet to arrive. Yet it is this difficult "in-betweenness" of the already and not yet which empowers Jesus with the courage to undergo the cross willingly. Because the Kingdom is present, he can find the courage to trust and commit himself in solidarity with the Father and us. Because it remains future, that trust will often take the negative form of the degrading crucifixion.

The later New Testament considers Jesus' death to be salvific in a special way (Mk 14:22–25). Through his blood all of us are saved. What could possibly be salvific in the disaster of the shedding of one's blood? It is quite possible that Jesus linked his death with his work on behalf of the Kingdom (Mk 14:25). At least this gives us a clue: the death can be seen as an act, indeed the climax, of Jesus' work on behalf of the Kingdom. As such, it is an act of love, justice, and peace. It is the love, justice, and peace which takes the supreme form of suffering. As this love, justice and peace has acted throughout Jesus' ministry to save people from oppression, we are invited to contemplate the possibility that they have the same saving power, even more intensively so, in the moment of the passion and crucifixion. Evidently the later Christian community was brought to just this conviction.

The New Testament texts end their story of Jesus' passion with the sad news of Jesus' abandonment: upon his arrest "all deserted him and fled" (Mk 14:50). All the Gospels are quite explicit about this (Mt 26:31–35; Lk 22:21–23, 54–62; Jn 16.32). In fact, the Gospels seem somewhat embarrassed by the disciples' infidelity. Jesus' harsh rebuke of them in Mark (14:37–38) is somewhat softened in Luke, who says they were "exhausted with grief" (22:45). This failure to stand by Jesus was aggravated, of course, by a more general rejection of Jesus on the part of many throughout his life: people find offense at him and his work (Lk 7:18–23; Mk 3:6; 11:18). According to Mark, it was only some women disciples who remained with him to the end (15:40). Luke says that the disciples did eventually show up at the cross (23:49), but perhaps this is in accord with his tendency to modify Mark's harsh picture. Luke certainly admits Peter's infidelity (22:32). As Edward Schillebeeckx puts it, "Historically speaking, the hard core of the tradition is that all the disciples somehow or other let Jesus down."[39]

We might conjecture that the general failure to stand by Jesus stems from the nature of the commitment he embodies. Jesus is not trying to be "hard" to understand; nor is he an esoteric teacher of secrets and mysteries. Rather, he is committed to a community of peace, justice and love. And in the context of his time and place, this was a quite novel and unexpected event. Jesus was let down because a call to universal love came up against hearts still trapped in partial and narrow loves and concerns. Is this perhaps why some women disciples (the one possible exception to Schillebeeckx' view) remained faithful? Was their "double bind"—oppressed and women—the factor which enabled them not to let Jesus down? We cannot know with high probability, but the remarkable tradition of womanly fidelity in an androcentric culture bespeaks credibility.

Pointing Ahead

If we take a kind of "backward glance" over the message and work of Jesus, many scholars suggest that we can plausibly find striking threads of continuity with the later, post-Easter faith of original Christianity. This is an important proposal, because it argues that the faith of the New Testament, while admittedly later than Jesus, is still rooted in Jesus. Such threads of continuity would aid us in grasping the New Testament's conviction that the risen Jesus is substantially identical with the Jesus who worked in Galilee and Jerusalem. Because of these threads, scholars use various terms to describe the transition from the Jesus of the ministry to the Jesus proclaimed in the New Testament: they speak of a transition from the "implicit" to the "explicit" or from the "hidden" to the "manifest." What they are trying to say is that there is a "depth dimension" to Jesus, pointed to by these threads of continuity, which somehow became clearer in the later Church.

We should not misunderstand this kind of language. These scholars do not mean that the transition to an explicit or manifest Christology (as we have it in the New Testament) was simply the deduction from a syllogism. The adandonment by the disciples, the general incomprehension of Jesus on the part of many, and the complex events of Easter all point to the fact that we are dealing with something much more complex than merely syllogistic reasoning. As we will see, it apparently took the events of Easter to begin the process of fully removing the ambiguity surrounding Jesus. But these threads of continuity indicate that there was already some preparation within Jesus' own ministry for what was to come. Probably we should think of a kind of dialectical process, a to-and-fro movement between looking back at this Jesus and the events of Easter as the way in which Christianity's later Christological beliefs emerged.

Probably the most plausible of these threads of continuity is this. It is a safe generalization to say that there is wide agreement about Jesus' experience of the Kingdom as pointing to real continuity with the post-Easter faith of the Church. We have noted, in our sketch, that Jesus experiences the Kingdom as a present reality entering history through him (cf Mt 12:28). His healings and exorcisms, his table fellowship, his acts of forgiveness, his parables, his intimacy with Abba, his call to repentance and faith, his bringing about a new community of justice and love—all of these are expressions of the divine presence and work flowing through him. This is a real thread of continuity with the New Testament's faith, for all of the proclamations of the Testament are saying in varied ways that the divine work and presence are found in Jesus. Naming Jesus the Messiah, or the Lord, or God's Son, even saying he is risen—all of these imply that somehow God is at work within him. But the point is that these later beliefs are not a kind of bolt from the sky—there was already some preparation for them in the ministry of Jesus.

Aided by the above, which is admittedly rather general, some scholars extend their lines of inquiry further, and find further threads of continuity. James Dunn has particularly pointed to "Jesus' expectation of vindication" as a probable thread of continuity.[40] It is, he thinks, very probable that Jesus knew that suffering and death would be the outcome of his ministry. The Gospels seem to indicate this (cf Mk 10:32–45). He was aware of mounting opposition, and there is no reason to doubt that he regarded martyrdom as a possible consequence of his prophetic actions (Mk 12:1–9; Mt 23:29–36; Lk 13:33–34). Jesus may have been influenced by the tradition of the vindication of the suffering righteous (cf Wis 2–5) and/or by the martyr theology which viewed the martyr's death as efficacious for Israel and something to be vindicated by resurrection (cf 2 Mac 7:14, 23, 37–38). Dunn even adds, "It is even possible that Jesus expressed his hope of vindication in terms of *resurrection* (cf. 2 Mac 7:11, 23; 14:46)—that is, the general resurrection when the kingdom came in its fullness, beginning the final judgment. . . . Such a hope is certainly implied in Mark 10:37–40, 12:25, 14:25, Matthew 19:28, Luke 22:28–30."[41]

Dunn's proposal is strengthened by the Gospel reminiscence that Jesus did not view his death as a calamity to be avoided, but as related to his work on behalf of the Kingdom: he regards his death as the possible outcome of his healings (Lk 13:32–33) on behalf of the Kingdom and links it with the future reign of God (Mk 14:25). If so, then it is not implausible that Jesus trusted, beyond his death, in the divine vindication of his ministry and death. In Dunn's words:

> The precise character of the vindication he expected is no longer clear to us; in our sources it is couched too much in terms of what actually transpired; and we should not exclude the possibility that Jesus himself was not clear about what would happen (cf. Mark 13:32; Luke 11:29–32/Matt. 12:39–42; 16:4). But at least one can say that in this expectation of Jesus we have a substantial line of continuity between Jesus' own message and the kerygma about the risen Christ—that *the resurrection of Jesus was in a very real sense the fulfillment of Jesus' own expectation,* that however different or not it was from his own expectation *it provided in the event the vindication that Jesus had looked for.*[42]

What Dunn seems to be saying is little else than that Jesus probably trusted in the Divine Mystery of Love, as did the suffering martyrs before him. This trust enabled him to expect vindication (or resurrection) in the future, although he probably did not know the precise form that this vindication would take.

Further threads of continuity can be plausibly discovered in some of the Christological and soteriological titles applied to Jesus by the New Testament. Even if Jesus did not use these titles himself, they do not seem to be bolts from the sky, but are somewhat rooted within his own work and ministry. Thus, for example, there is widespread agreement that Jesus did not use the title "Son of God" of himself. Such a thing remains unmentioned in the New Testament. But the title was not unprecedented. Israel could be called God's son (Ex 4:22; Hos 11:1; Jer 31:9), or the king (Ps 2:7;

Ps 89:27–28), or even a messiah (2 Sam 7:14). Sometimes, even all the
pious could be so called (Ps 73:15; Wis 5:5). It seems perfectly natural,
then, that the later Church might appropriate this title, despite Jesus' non-
use of it. For this title manifests continuity with Jesus' own filial relationship to his Abba-Father and his work as the mediator on behalf of the King-
dom-community. So, too, the title "messiah," although not probably used
by Jesus, is at least rooted in his work as the mediator of the new community.[43]

Of all the Christological titles, the one to receive the most emphasis
among contemporary Christologians is that of "prophet." Walter Kasper
simply states: "The best description for [Jesus] is 'prophet' . . . not just one
in the line of the prophets, but the eschatological one: the last, definitive,
all-transcending prophet."[44] Reginald Fuller, a prominent British scholar,
held a similar view even earlier: "Take the implied self-understanding of
his role in terms of the eschatological prophet away, and the whole ministry falls into a series of unrelated, if not meaningless fragments."[45] But it
is Edward Schillebeeckx who has especially renewed our attention to this
designation. He argues that the crucial link "between the earthly Jesus and
the kerygmatic Christ is the recognition . . . of the earthly Jesus as the eschatological prophet (who does, it is true, surpass all expectations) and that
this identification (at least as question and surmise) was most likely made
prior to Easter. . . ."[46] This points to a considerable element of continuity,
and Schillebeeckx even thinks that this title was the "matrix" or basis out
of which all the Church's later kerygmata flow. In line with this, he castigates exegetes for either ignoring this title or bringing it up at the "end" of
their considerations: "One may well ask . . . whether one is not simply
evacuating Jesus' self-understanding of all content or even filling the vac-
uum with later Christological insights. . . . [Thus] the matrix of all other
honorific titles and credal strands is entirely overlooked."[47] In a later work
Schillebeeckx adds a comment which links up with the concerns of social
criticism. By ignoring this title "Christ can be made into a heavenly icon,
moved so far on the side of God, who himself has already vanished from
the world of men, that as a prophet he loses all critical force in our
world."[48]

Clearly the New Testament witnesses that during his ministry Jesus
made the impression (as "question and surmise") of being a prophet. He is
regarded as "one of the prophets" (Mk 8:28; cf 6:15), a Semitism for belonging to the prophetic type. This coheres with our comments earlier on
Jesus as a wandering charismatic prophet who touches people where they
suffer. The resurrection story in Luke of the party making their way to Em-
maus reflects this memory too. As the risen Jesus asks them "What are you
discussing?" they respond, "Are you the only resident of Jerusalem who

does not know the things that went on . . .? All those that had to do with Jesus of Nazareth, a prophet powerful in word and deed. . . . We were hoping that he was the one who would set Israel free" (Lk 24:17–21).

Another series of passages, perhaps somewhat influenced by the post-Easter situation, seem to reflect the tradition that Jesus was an "eschatological prophet," the "final" one awaited by Israel. At least some wondered whether he were such. Is he Elijah returned to us (*redivivus*), or the revived John the Baptist, or even Jeremiah *redivivus* (cf Lk 9:8; Mk 6:15; Lk 9:19; Mk 8:28; Mt 16:14; Jn 6:14–15)? Schillebeeckx thinks it is difficult to argue that this memory is entirely post-Easter, for it seems that after Easter John the Baptist was considered the revived Elijah (Mk 9:13; Lk 7:25–27) who is the *forerunner* of the eschatological prophet.

Speculation about the eschatological prophet is something characteristic of the intertestamental period. Apparently it goes back to Deuteronomy and circles influenced by that work: "A prophet like me [viz., Moses] will the Lord, your God, raise up for you from among your own kinsmen; to him you shall listen" (Dt 18:15; cf 30:1–3; Ex 23:20–22). Originally this was not connected with the expectation of an Elijah *redivivus*. His expectation was a later addition to this tradition (cf Mal 3:1, 23; Sir 48:1–14). Eventually in Jewish circles Elijah came to be seen as a forerunner of the final prophet (namely, in Qumran[49]), and the New Testament seems to reflect this in calling the Baptist this Elijah *redivivus* (cf Mt 3:1–17; 17: 9–13), since he precedes Jesus.

This final Moses-like prophet takes on the characteristics of Moses: he mediates between God and humanity (Dt 5:5), he suffers on behalf of the people (Dt 1:37; 4:21–22). There is a finality about him, as with Moses: "Should there be a prophet among you, in visions will I reveal myself to him, in dreams will I speak to him; not so with my servant Moses! Throughout my house he bears my trust; face to face I speak to him, plainly and not in riddles. The presence of the Lord he beholds" (Nm 12:6–8; cf Ex 33:11). The suffering servant of Isaiah bears resemblances to this prophetic Moses (Is 42:1–4; 49:1–6; 50:4–11; 52:13–53:12), which argues for a mutual influence between this Moses tradition and the Isaiah tradition. Particularly in the Essene and Samaritan traditions does Schillebeeckx find the expectation of this Moses-like prophet. But the amazing thing is that the Gospels witness that already during his ministry people wondered whether Jesus might not be this one (Lk 9:8). Clearly the post-Easter kerygmata consider Jesus to be this prophet. This is why John becomes the forerunner (Mk 1:2; 9:11–13) and Jesus becomes the prophet to whom one should listen (Mk 9:2–9). Here we have considerable continuity, as Schillebeeckx claims, between the earthly and kerygmatic Jesus.

Some further traits of Jesus also seem to confirm this prophetic view of the ministry. Indeed, these further traits seem to indicate that Jesus himself considered himself in the line of the prophets. "Jesus admittedly never identifies himself with the eschatological prophet; but he does nevertheless interpret his mission and course of action in terms of latter-day prophecy," says Schillebeeckx.[50] Jesus compares his destiny to that of the prophets (Mk 6:4; Lk 13:33), "especially in his prophetic, nay, more-than-prophetic siding with humble and lowly people and the socially and religiously 'disinherited.' "[51] Reginald Fuller finds a number of prophetic traits surfacing in Jesus' career: he uses the prophetic "I came" and "I was sent" (Lk 12:49; Mk 2:17); his sense of authority; his critiques as recorded in Matthew (23), whose finality "indicates that Jesus thought of his mission not only as belonging to the same class as that of the Old Testament prophets, but as representing the final prophetic mission to Israel, and of his own rejection (and possible martyrdom) as the culmination of Israel's rejection of the word of Yahweh."[52]

That Jesus could have raised such questions, and possibly entertained them himself, points to something remarkable in his career, a "remarkable something" that with some fair degree of plausibility we can call the depth dimension of his life which the later Church would more fully come to accept. But, as Schillebeeckx so nicely puts it, this remains a question and surmise, apparently even for his women disciples, until the events of Easter.

Finally, let me mention the difficult title of "the Son of Man." This is perhaps the most controverted of the titles in biblical scholarship, but some are convinced that it is one of the strongest threads of continuity between the pre-Easter and post-Easter Churches. The remarkable fact is that this title almost always occurs as a usage of Jesus in the Bible, with the exception of Acts 7:56. If some of these usages go back to Jesus himself, then we have another strong thread of continuity between the earthly Jesus and the later Church, which very likely applied the title quite commonly to him.

Unfortunately, opinions are quite varied: some argue that none of the occurrences of the Son of Man go back to Jesus; others, that some do; others, that all do. What we have are three series of usages: a present, earthly Son of Man (Mk 2:10, 28; Lk 7:34; 9:58; 19:10); a suffering Son of Man (Mk 8:31; 10:45; 14:21, 41); and a future Son of Man (Mk 8:38; 13:26; 14:62; Lk 12:8-12, 40; 17:22-30; 18:8; Mt 10:23; 19:28). If this was a title in circulation among apocalyptic circles, is it possible that Jesus took it over and used it as an expression for his own mediation of the Kingdom? There is a strong likelihood that at least the third series may have been used by Jesus as a symbol of the future vindication that he expected: his work would somehow be vindicated by the coming of the future Son of Man. This third series is in our earliest sources (Mark and Q). If this is likely, then it is possible that he used the other series, too, for they all cohere with what we know of the earthly Jesus. But these latter usages must remain only a possibility, given the present state of research. The difficulty with these other two series is that the present Son of Man is unknown to apocalyptic circles, while the suffering Son of Man series is not in our earliest source (namely, Q).[53]

Let me end this section on possible threads of continuity between the earthly Jesus and the later New Testament with the issue of soteriology. Clearly the later Church professes belief in the saving work of Jesus, his ability to set us free from sin and evil. This motif of Jesus' saving work is certainly rooted in the earthly Jesus; it is not a sheer fabrication of later Christianity. Whether we look to Jesus' own probable view of his death as a saving act on behalf of others, or whether we look more generally to his work on behalf of the Kingdom as itself a salvific deed, in either case there is the note of working to save others which bridges the earthly Jesus with the later Church. As we have seen, saving humanity from evil is always the other side of Jesus' work on behalf of the community of love, justice, and peace. This surely points us ahead to the later New Testament's explicit soteriological beliefs. But first we must turn to the Easter experiences for the major catalyst of this later development.

Notes

1. What I have presented is an overview of Jesus research which seems to reflect views *held in common* among the various questers, except in the cases of some views which seem likely to win acceptance (viz., Schillebeeckx on the eschatological prophet). I have then added to this the seeming consensus among psychosocial critics. For an author's departure from the above "shared view," one will have to consult the particular works.

Representative works I have consulted: American: Norman Perrin, *Rediscovering the Teaching of Jesus* (New York: Harper and Row, 1967), *The New Testament: An Introduction* (New York: Harcourt Brace Jovanovich, 1974), *Jesus and the Language of the Kingdom: Symbol and Metaphor in New Testament Interpretation* (Philadelphia: Fortress, 1976); John Reumann, *Jesus in the Church's Gospels: Modern Scholarship and the Earliest Sources* (Philadelphia: Fortress, 1968); Joseph A. Fitzmyer, *What We Know about Jesus from the New Testament* (New York: Paulist, 1982); James P. Mackey, *Jesus the Man and the Myth* (New York: Paulist, 1979); Michael L. Cook, *The Jesus of Faith: A Study in Christology* (New York: Paulist, 1981); Reginald H. Fuller and Pheme Perkins, *Who Is This Christ?: Gospel Christology and Contemporary Faith* (Philadelphia: Fortress, 1983).

British: Reginald H. Fuller, *The Foundations of New Testament Christology* (New York: Charles Scribner's, 1965) and *A Critical Introduction to the New Tes-*

tament (London: Duckworth, 1971); James D.G. Dunn, *Jesus and the Spirit. A Study of the Religious and Charismatic Experience of Jesus and the First Christians as Reflected in the New Testament* (Philadelphia: Westminster, 1975), *Unity and Diversity in the New Testament, op. cit.*, and *Christology in the Making: A New Testament Inquiry into the Origins of the Doctrine of the Incarnation* (Philadelphia: Westminster, 1980); I. Howard Marshall, *The Origins of New Testament Christology* (Downers Grove, Ill.: InterVarsity Press, 1976).

Continental: Bornkamm, *Jesus of Nazareth, op. cit.*; Ferdinand Hahn, *The Titles of Jesus in Christology* (London: Lutterworth, 1969); Hans Conzelmann, *Jesus* (Philadelphia: Fortress, 1973); Eduard Schweizer, *Jesus* (Richmond, Virginia: Knox, 1971); Edward Schillebeeckx, *Jesus, op. cit.*, and *Interim Report on the Books Jesus and Christ* (New York: Crossroad, 1981); Hans Küng, *On Being a Christian, op. cit.*; Karl Rahner and Wilhelm Thüsing, *A New Christology* (New York: Seabury, 1980).

Psychosocial critical approaches: South American: Jon Sobrino, *Christology at the Crossroads* (Maryknoll: Orbis, 1978). Continental: Metz, *op. cit.*; Jürgen Moltmann, *The Crucified God: The Cross of Christ as the Foundation and Criticism of Christian Theology* (New York: Harper and Row, 1974). South African: Albert Nolan, *Jesus before Christianity* (Maryknoll: Orbis, 1976). American (United States): Kee, *Christian Origins, op. cit.*; Rosemary Radford Ruether, *To Change the World: Christology and Cultural Criticism* (New York: Crossroad, 1981); Tyrrell, *Christotherapy*, I and II, *op. cit.*; Peter C. Hodgson, *New Birth of Freedom: A Theology of Bondage and Liberation* (Philadelphia: Fortress, 1976).

2. (Boston: Beacon, 1963), esp. pp. 46–59.

3. Gregory Baum, *op. cit.*, p. 170; cf pp. 162–192 (on Weber).

4. For all of this, see Kee, *Christian Origins, op. cit.*, pp. 54–73, and Theissen, *op. cit.*, pp. 7–30.

5. Especially helpful on the origins of the Kingdom myth: Perrin, *Jesus and the Language of the Kingdom, op. cit.*, pp. 15–88, and Rudolf Schnackenburg, *God's Rule and Kingdom* (Edinburgh: Nelson, 1963).

6. Perrin, *ibid.*, pp. 20–21.

7. Dunn, *Jesus and the Spirit, op. cit.*, pp. 24–25. The classic here is Joachim Jeremias, *The Prayers of Jesus, op. cit.*, esp. pp. 11–65, 108–115. According to Dunn, perhaps Sirach 23:1, 4 addresses the Divine as "Abba." Otherwise, the usage is unprecedented.

8. Endo, *op. cit.*, p. 87.

9. An example of the mistake thesis: Richard H. Hiers, *Jesus and the Future: Unresolved Questions for Understanding and Faith* (Atlanta: John Knox, 1981). It is possible that the religious experience of Jesus in this case was so turbulent that it impeded a proper exegetical interpretation. On the dynamics of the interplay between experiential depth (in religious/theophanic experiences) and exegetical, surface interpretation, see Voegelin, *Order and History*, 4, *op. cit.*, p. 252.

10. Baron Friedrich von Hügel, "The Apocalyptic Element in the Teaching of Jesus: Its Ultimate Significance and Its Abiding Function," in *Essays and Ad-*

dresses on the Philosophy of Religion, First Series (London: J.M. Dent and Sons, 1949), pp. 119–143.

11. Rahner and Thüsing, *A New Christology, op. cit.*, p. 134.

12. Kasper, *op. cit.*, p. 77; cf pp. 76–78 for an overview.

13. *Ibid.*, p. 78.

14. Hiers, *op. cit.*, pp. 70, 88.

15. *Symposium*, 202–204. See Voegelin, *Order and History*, 4, *The Ecumenic Age, op. cit.*, pp. 183–187.

16. Cf Walter E. Conn, ed., *Conversion: Perspectives on Personal and Social Transformation* (New York: Alba House, 1978).

17. See Richard Woods, "Mysticism and Social Action," in his *Mysterion: An Approach to Mystical Spirituality* (Chicago: Thomas More, 1981), pp. 159–173, and Baum, *op. cit.*, pp. 72–76.

18. Cf. Pheme Perkins, *Reading the New Testament: An Introduction* (New York: Paulist, 1978), pp. 95–99, for an overview of approaches to Jesus' ethics. Apparently Schweitzer, who did argue for an interim ethics, has been widely misunderstood: Jesus' "individual ethic does not perish with the collapse of eschatology, but thereby loses only the idea of reward and its eudaemonistic conditionality. The powerful demands of world-denial and inner perfection thereby lose nothing of their significance" (Hiers, *op. cit.*, p. 55).

19. Kasper, *op. cit.*, p. 90. I rely mainly on his helpful overview, pp. 89–99. Also helpful and representative: R.H. Fuller, *Interpreting the Miracles* (London: SCM, 1963), for the historical data; Louis Monden, *Signs and Wonders: A Study of the Miraculous Element in Religion* (New York: Desclee, 1966), and Bela Weissmahr, *Gottes Wirken in der Welt: Ein Diskussionsbeitrag zur Frage der Evolution und des Wunders* (Frankfurt am Main: Josef Knecht, 1973), for a theological-philosophical interpretation similar to Kasper's.

20. Kasper, *ibid.*, p. 94.

21. *Ibid.*, p. 90.

22. *Ibid.*, p. 96. To my knowledge, Kasper is the only one to notice this important datum.

23. Especially helpful here is Nolan, *op. cit.*, pp. 21–29, 56 (on children). For a sensitivity to children's oppression, see Lloyd de Mause, ed., *The History of Childhood* (New York: Harper Torchbooks, 1975).

24. *Ibid.*, p. 28.

25. See Ruether, *To Change the World, op. cit.*, pp. 29–30: ". . . the real point of danger comes when victory becomes possible. How can one avoid the temptation of the victorious poor to become the avengers? Is it possible to dethrone the mighty and still redeem them as brothers and sisters? How does one really root out a system of oppression and yet still exercise forgiveness and reconciliation towards those who have tortured and murdered the people? Here is where the Christian character of the struggle is really tested. The Christian begins to understand Jesus' own struggle against messianic temptation. Here the Church learns to pray with Jesus, 'Lead us not into temptation, but deliver us from evil.' " Very good on the master-slave dialectic is Hodgson, *op. cit.*, pp. 265–321.

26. Cited in Denise Lardner Carmody, *Women and World Religions* (Nashville: Abingdon, 1979), p. 103.

27. *Ibid.*, p. 98. For the history of the denigration of women, see Ruether, *New Woman/New Earth: Sexist Ideologies and Human Liberation, op. cit.*, pp. 3–35. For Jesus and women, cf. Elizabeth Schüssler Fiorenza, *In Memory of Her: A Feminist Theological Reconstruction of Christian Origins* (New York: Crossroad, 1983), pp. 105–159.

28. Hodgson, *op. cit.*, p. 320; cf pp. 319–321 for the best treatment of Jesus and violence that I have seen.

29. *Ibid.*, p. 320.

30. *Ibid.*, p. 319.

31. *Ibid.*, p. 321.

32. See Bornkamm, *op. cit.*, pp. 117–120.

33. Jeremias, *The Prayers of Jesus, op. cit.*, p. 76; cf pp. 66–81. Dunn, *Jesus and the Spirit, op. cit.*, pp. 15–21, is also helpful. For the general significance of prayer in religion, see the classic work of Friedrich Heiler, *Prayer: A Study in the History and Psychology of Religion* (London: Oxford, 1932).

34. Jeremias, *Ibid.*, p. 77.

35. Cited in *ibid.*, p. 78.

36. So far only indicated by Sobrino, *op. cit.*, pp. 146–178.

37. Most helpful on all these questions: Hans-Ruedi Weber, *The Cross: Tradition and Interpretation* (Grand Rapids, Mich.: William B. Eerdmans, 1979); Martin Hengel, *Crucifixion: In the Ancient World and the Folly of the Message of the Cross* (Philadelphia: Fortress, 1977); Douglas John Hall, *Lighten Our Darkness: Toward an Indigenous Theology of the Cross* (Philadelphia: Westminster, 1976). For the theories on the trials, see Gerard S. Sloyan, *Jesus on Trial. The Development of the Passion Narratives and Their Historical and Ecumenical Implications* (Philadelphia: Fortress, 1973). Kasper regards as "fairly probable" Jesus' use of the title "messiah" in this one instance of the trial. Cf Kasper, *op. cit.*, p. 106.

38. Weber, *ibid.*, p. 5.

39. See Schillebeeckx, *Jesus, op. cit.*, p. 325; cf pp. 320–327.

40. Dunn, *Unity and Diversity, op cit.*, pp. 210–211.

41. *Ibid.*, p. 211.

42. *Ibid.*

43. Generally this title is never used by Jesus himself in the Gospels; rather, the disciples apply it to him (Mk 8:27–33; 14:61–65). Perhaps, as many questers hold, this is because of its ambiguity. Clearly it means an "anointed agent" of the Divine, but what kind of agent? Is it a king (1 Sam 10:1), the king's heirs (Am 9:11; Is 9:6–7; Jer 33:15–17), the suffering servant (Is 42:1–7), Daniel's apocalyptic Son of Man (7:13), or even the two messiahs of the Essenes (the warrior-king and the new high priest)? It is possible that Jesus did use this title once, at his trial (Mk 14:61–62): there the ambiguity is removed; it is clear that he is a suffering agent of the Lord.

44. Kasper, *op. cit.*, p. 69.

45. Fuller, *Foundations, op, cit.*, p. 130; cf pp. 125–131.

46. Schillebeeckx, *Jesus, op. cit.*, p. 479.

47. *Ibid.*

48. Schillebeeckx, *Interim Report, op. cit.*, p. 66; cf pp. 64–74, and *Jesus, ibid.*, pp. 475–499, and *Christ, op. cit.*, pp. 309–321, for what follows.

49. Schillebeeckx, *Jesus, ibid.*, p. 449. This literature apparently displaces both Elijah and the Moses-like prophet to the status of forerunners of their final messiah(s).

50. *Ibid.*, p. 477.

51. *Ibid.*

52. Fuller, *Foundations, op, cit.*, p. 129.

53. A good survey of the controversy is found in I. Howard Marshall, *op. cit.*, pp. 63–82. The "Son of Man" Christology of Q is often regarded as the earliest Christology of the New Testament. For this, cf Michael L. Cook, *op. cit.*, pp. 103–110.

7C

The Easter Experiences

My goal in this sub-chapter is to expose the reader to what seem to be the most important and typical issues discussed and debated by scholars relative to the Easter experiences. Most biblical scholars and Jesus questers are convinced that the Easter experiences were the crucial factor bringing the early Church to faith in Jesus. But, as we shall see, they are not agreed on precisely what happened. That the Easter experiences were the crucial factor has good textual warrant: "If Christ was not raised, your faith is worthless," says St. Paul (1 Cor 15:17). Many, apparently very early kerygmata recorded in the New Testament likewise underscore the resurrection as the central and pivotal factor in the faith of the early Church (Lk 24:34; 1 Cor 15:3–5; Rom 1:3–4; 10:9; Phil 2:6–11; 1 Pt 3:18–22; 4:6; Acts 2:23–24; 3:15; 5:30–32). But beyond this, ambiguity begins to surface as to precisely what occurred.

What Was the Original Model?

Probably the first question we should tackle—one that has surfaced in the writings of Helmut Koester and Edward Schillebeeckx[1]—is whether the "resurrection-belief" was the original form and expression (or model) of the Easter experience. Is it possible to maintain, as Koester and Schillebeeckx apparently do, that various routes were originally traveled on the way to belief in Jesus, and that the model of the resurrection belief (or resurrection symbolism) was only one of these, and probably not the first one at that? It might be helpful to bear in mind that there can be no such thing as a purely non-linguistic or non-symbolic experience of anything, given the essentially linguistic structure of human cognition. To know is to know through symbolism, and our question here is whether the "death-resurrection" symbolism was the original and primary one.[2] It seems that purely theoretically there can be no objection to raising this question. Other symbolic routes may indeed have been traversed by the early Church. As we will see, there were symbolisms other than the death-resurrection model available in the Jewish and Greco-Roman traditions. The issue can only be whether Koester's and Schillebeeckx' views adequately reconstruct the textual evidence. But this is more than a matter of historical curiosity. Given the essentially linguistic texture of human and religious experience, the language symbolism of an experience is our only access to that experience, to its varied dimensions. That language may never be totally adequate, but it is all that we have. A needless change in that symbolism can easily lead to distortion or to a forgetfulness of the full dimensions of an experience.

What is the state of the evidence on this question? First, it would appear that the resurrection kerygmata are very old. If we distinguish between the resurrection kerygmata and the more elaborate resurrection stories of the Gospels, we can say that the former appear to be much more primitive, stemming from the earliest, pre-Gospel liturgical and missionary traditions which took shape in the crucial period of 30 to 50 A.D. Crucial here is the fact that these early kerygmata firmly proclaim the resurrection (Lk 24:34; 1 Cor 15:3–5), without any further elaboration, such as we find it in the Gospel resurrection stories. This could argue for their very early age.[3]

Second, there were various symbolisms ready to hand, which could have been used by the early Church to give expression to its remarkable origins in the Easter experiences.[4] Hebrews speaks of Jesus as the heavenly high priest (9:11–12); Paul will sometimes speak of the exaltation (Phil 2:9) and even of Jesus as "living" (Rom 14:9; 2 Cor 13:4); Luke uses both "resurrection" and "ascension" (a kind of rapture model) in his writings (Lk 24:46, 51; Acts 1:1–10); John speaks of Jesus as entering into his glory (17:1–5), or as "going away for a while" (15:28) and going back "to him who sent me" (16:5). But as Raymond Brown put it, ". . . it is not really clear that any of the 'alternative' language for Jesus' victory over death existed in Christianity independently of a belief in Jesus' resurrection from the dead."[5] Brown's view has good textual warrants. Hebrews seems to know something like the death-resurrection tradition (13:20; 11:19). Exaltation, ascension, and glory language may simply be ways of expressing the belief that the resurrection transformed Jesus into a new (eternal) life; we possess not textual evidence that they were independent of the resurrection tradition. Saying Jesus "lives" simply seems another way of saying "was raised" (compare 2 Cor 13:4 with Acts 2:23–24). Schillebeeckx argues for the priority of a conversion model, but again there is no textual evidence in the New Testament for this.[6]

Third, there is the problem of the "Q" source, which the reader will remember as the hypothetical sayings source, which was integrated in Matthew and Luke. What puzzles scholars is that this early source, as hy-

pothetically reconstructed,[7] nowhere mentions the kerygma of Jesus'
death and resurrection. Given the antiquity of this source, we would seem
to have here an argument in favor of Koester and Schillebeeckx. But on a
further look, "Q" seems much more ambiguous. As H.E. Tödt has argued,
it seems to presuppose Jesus' death and resurrection. It alludes to the kill-
ing of the prophets as their typical fate (Lk 11:51), thus implying that Jesus,
too, will undergo death. Furthermore, Jesus' proclamation as the final divine messenger—Q's great belief—had been radically called into question
by his death. The Church community of Q could only continue to hand
down Jesus' final, eschatological proclamation if indeed Jesus had been
vindicated in some way. As Reginald Fuller put it, ". . . side by side with
the continuation of Jesus' eschatological proclamation Q also contains a
Christological kerygma—not the kerygma of the saving significance of the
passion, to which the circles from which Q emanates had not yet arrived,
but the kerygma of Jesus who in his earthly ministry spoke with the authority of the Son of Man vindicated in face of the rejection of men (Lk
7:34; 9:58), and who will come again in order finally to vindicate the authority of his word (Lk 11:30; 12:8–10, 40; 17:24–30)."[8]

What Fuller is suggesting is that there must have been some pivotal
event which lies behind the Christological belief of Q. It does not clearly
express what this event was; it is mainly a sayings, not a narrative, source.
But the reference to Jesus' death (as implied in the slaying of the prophets)
indicates that it knew of the passion. It also knew of the vindication by God
of his suffering prophets. And the typical vindication for suffering martyrs
was believed to be some form of resurrection.

Koester and Schillebeeckx build a somewhat strong case on the fact
that there are some apparently quite early kerygmata which do not mention Jesus' death and resurrection. Jesus is proclaimed, in these, as (1) the
coming Lord of the future (1 Cor 16:22; Rev 22:20; 1 Cor 15:51–52; Lk
17:24), as (2) the divine miracle worker (Acts 2:22; 2 Cor 3:1; 5:12; 4:5), as
(3) Holy Wisdom's envoy/Wisdom itself (Lk 11:49–51; Mt 11:27; Phil 2:6–
11; Jn 1:1–16). Like the resurrection kerygmata, these, too, are unelabor-
ated and seemingly very early. This could mean that there existed in the
early Church other models for expressing the Easter faith. But again the
matter is ambiguous. What was it, for example, that shocked the disciples
out of their unbelief and enabled them to believe all the things that these
kerygmata proclaim? Like Q, these kerygmata plausibly require some pivotal event making them meaningful. Once belief in Jesus emerged, one
could argue that these creeds could begin to flourish. One could even see
why they do not mention Jesus' death, given the rather exalted Christology which characterizes them.

None of the above proves Koester and Schillebeeckx wrong and the "opponents" right. The question is too ambiguous. The most anyone can argue for is relative probablility, and in the light of that I would be inclined to go along with the "opponents." Too many "hunches," too much psychological guessing, and too few textual warrants lie behind Koester and Schillebeeckx on this point. If readers are inclined toward the view that no side has relative probability in its favor, then I would suggest that they simply look at the resurrection model as "representative" of the Easter experiences rather than as the originary model of those experiences.

But let me mention a personal view which inclines me even more strongly to dissent from Koester and Schillebeeckx on this issue. Why has later Christianity (including the New Testament) shown such a preference for the death-resurrection model, supposing that this was only one of a number of alternative models available to it? It clearly did not have to, and yet it did. Partially we might argue that the death-resurrection model brings out well the continuity between the earthly Jesus and the risen one: one who rises dies first. The alternative symbolisms (exaltation/ascension/glory) lack any clear reference to the earthly and crucified Jesus. This may account for the later Church's preference, at least to some extent.

But, perhaps more importantly, death-resurrection symbolism was not really one of several symbolisms available to early Christianity. What was believed in some Jewish circles was the resurrection of the dead in the last times, not the resurrection of an individual prior to the general resurrection. It is this surprising fact that needs explanation. Something caused the early Christians to alter the general resurrection belief of the times. Perhaps the most plausible explanation is that the pivotal Easter experiences were first symbolized in the death-resurrection model known to us in the early kerygmata. We will, of course, never know for sure. But great and profound experiences co-originate their own symbolisms. They also, if they are profound enough, alter ready-to-hand symbolisms in a peculiar manner. Perhaps something of this occurred to the death-resurrection model of the times.[9]

The Easter Event as the Transformation of Jesus

If we use the various symbolisms that are available to us, what can we say about what really happened? The cumulative thrust of contemporary scholarship would seem to hold that early Christianity believed that Jesus underwent an experience of "personal transformation" which enabled him to "live" beyond death. This belief was coupled with another: this personally transformed Jesus somehow manifested himself to various of his early disciples (male and female) through a series of actual, historical, revelatory encounters, which were variously expressed as "appearances," "revelations," or "conversion" experiences. We then have two elements needing clarification: (1) the event of Jesus' personal transformation, enabling him to live beyond death, and (2) Jesus' manifestation through encounter episodes to his disciples.[10] Let us dwell upon the first in this section.

Despite discrepancies in historical details, there is a marvelous agreement throughout the New Testament that Jesus has undergone a transforming experience which enables him to live even beyond death. Scholars usually highlight some or all of the following. We should not overlook the fact that no one actually witnessed the Easter event. This would seem to indicate that we are dealing with something other than the resuscitation of a corpse, the return back to one's former life. Jesus is "new," living a life which transcends our normal, earthly existence. It cannot, as such, be witnessed.[11] The biblical accounts carefully distinguish Jesus' resurrection from a bodily resuscitation through their language symbolism and presentation of Jesus' actions. Paul uses the apocalyptic language "was raised" (egēgertai), which suggests the definitive transformation of the end-time (1 Cor 15:4; cf Is 26:19; Dn 12:3; Enoch 92:3). He apparently invents the symbolism of the "spiritual body" to describe this transformed Jesus: "A natural body is put down and a spiritual body comes up" (1 Cor 15:44). But the Gospels, too, underscore this transformation of Jesus. They, too, use the apocalyptic language of "being raised" (Mk 16:6–7; Lk 24:34). Jesus is not immediately recognizable to those who stand before him; he is "different" (Lk 24:16; Jn 20:14; 21:4); some even doubt that it could be he (Mt 28:17; Lk 24:41). As Mark sums it up: ". . . he was revealed to them completely changed in appearance" (16:12). Further, Jesus comes and goes in a way impossible to an ordinary earthly being (Lk 24:31; Jn 20:19, 26).

We should particularly note the symbolism of the "third day." Apart from the issue of whether this is an historical reminiscence (is it linked with the popular idea that the soul finally leaves the body after the traditional day of decomposition?), the phrase "in accordance with the Scriptures" (1 Cor 15:4) indicates that we are dealing with a motif of the Hebrew tradition. In Exodus, it is the day of Yahweh's theophany to Moses (Ex 19); in Genesis, Isaac is spared through Abraham's faith on the third day (Gn 22); in the prophet Hosea (6:1–2) it is the hoped for day of deliverance and liberation. Thus, the "third day" symbolism seems to underscore Jesus' transformation as one of a religious transformation entailing knowing the Divine, liberation, and ultimate victory.

The alternative symbolisms sometimes used in the New Testament also underscore the transforming nature of the Easter event. "Exaltation" language, for example, highlights slightly different elements than resurrection language. The image is more vertical—Jesus is lifted up to divine glory—while resurrection language necessarily implies that Jesus has first

died, thus implying a more earthbound reference. The former brings out
Jesus' entry into a new mode of existence. Gerald O'Collins even thinks
that this exaltation symbolism was a later attempt to keep believers from
imagining the resurrection as a merely bodily resuscitation. Originally, he
suggests, the two symbolisms of resurrection and exaltation developed
somewhat independently, only eventually becoming interchangeable. He
outlines the following possible course of development: (1) death followed
by resurrection (1 Cor 15; Mk 9:31), (2) death followed by exaltation (Phil
2:8–11; Mk 14:62) or glory (Lk 24:26), (3) death followed by both a resurrection and exaltation (Rom 8:34; Acts 2:32–33) or enthronement (Rom
1:4), and (4) resurrection and exaltation as finally interchangeable (Lk
24:26–46; Mt 28:16–20).[12] The deeply theological interests of John, in
which Jesus is viewed as dwelling in the Father's glory, explains his preference for exaltation terminology (3:14; 6:62; 8:28; 12:32). In fact, for John
the death of Jesus *is* the exaltation. Luke even adds the symbolism of "ascension" (a rapture model) which further gives a note of completion and
finality to the transformation of Jesus (Acts 1:9–11). In the end, all of these
symbolisms bring home the belief, as O'Collins puts it, "that the resurrection was no return to earthly life and transcended any mere resuscitation
of a corpse."[13]

There are, to be sure, conflicts in historical details in the various Gospel stories. The early belief in Jesus' resurrection from the dead was incorporated into the Gospels only quite late. Details blur over time. In
part, too, the evangelists are motivated by different theological concerns.
Mark seems to place a great stress upon the passion. Perhaps he is attempting to combat the tendency to make Jesus into a splendidly royal
messiah or miracle worker. In any case, he is carefully circumspect in what
he says about the resurrection, omitting any reference to appearances.
Perhaps the appearances would understress the suffering humanity of the
messiah?[14] Matthew is apparently written at a time when Christianity was
encountering great hostility from Judaism. Perhaps he wants to address
Jewish attacks on the resurrection as a fable, and so he has the story of the
guards and elders, who clearly admit that the resurrection has occurred
(28:1–15).[15]

Luke and John "are obviously at pains to establish the indubitable
physical reality of the risen Christ," says O'Collins.[16] In Luke, the risen
Jesus walks, talks, and eats: "Look at my hands and my feet; it is really I.
Touch me, and see that a ghost does not have flesh and bones as I do"
(24:39). In John he similarly invites his disciples to see/touch him (20:20–
27). Although we have seen above that Luke and John also stress how
much Jesus has been transformed—resurrection is no mere resuscitation—still their stress upon Jesus' physicality is quite in contrast to the

other scriptural writers. O'Collins thinks that they want to counter views
which would excessively spiritualize the resurrection, robbing the Risen
One of his continuity with the earthly Jesus. In the light of the Greco-Roman context of Luke and John, such a possibility seems probable. For
there was a tendency among the Greeks to denigrate the physical in favor
of the spiritual. Luke is also the one who distinguishes between the period
of the appearances and the ascension. Scholars think that he makes this
distinction in order to highlight the end of the originating period of revelation. Ascension ends the period of Jesus and inaugurates the period of
the Church.

There are other conflictual details too. There seem to be two separate
appearance traditions: a series occurring in Galilee (Mt 28; Jn 21; Mk 16:1–
8), and a series which occurs in Jerusalem (Lk 24; Jn 20; Mk 16:9–20). Was
Jesus' body anointed immediately after his death (Jn 19), or only after three
days (Lk 23:56; 24:1; Mk 16:1)? Did three women visit the tomb (Mk 16:1),
or only two (Mt 28:1)? Upon their visit, was the tomb already open (Mk
16:4; Jn 20:1), or did an angel first have to open it (Mt 28)? Was one young
man "in a white robe" present there (Mk 16:5), or two (Lk 24:4)? Did some
women actually see the Risen Lord (Mt 28:9; Jn 20:14–18), or apparently
not (Lk 24:22–24)? And when was the Spirit outpoured: immediately after
the resurrection (Jn 20:19–23), or only after the ascension (Lk 24:49; Acts
1:5)? Again, very likely we are dealing with conflicts that arise from a combination of theological interests and the lateness of the reports. As Dermot
Lane explains it, it is more realistic to view these discrepancies as "inevitable in view of the lateness of the reports and the nature of the events they
are trying to relate. It is a fact of life that reporters and witnesses are notorious for providing conflicting evidence, especially when it concerns
something new and different."[17]

We should not let these conflicts, however, overshadow the amazing
substantial agreement in our sources on the belief that Jesus has undergone a transforming experience which enables him still to live beyond
death. As we have said, the New Testament wants to proclaim that its belief in a still and really "living" Jesus is the basis of the Easter experiences.
Our temptation at this point is to leave the matter at that: we are before a
mystery which transcends empirical verification. Yet, if we do this, we run
the danger of robbing the resurrection of any real meaning for us. If there
are simply no analogies or correlates to the resurrection belief within our
own experience, then we can simply have no appreciation of it, not even a
partial appreciation. We would also run the danger of reducing the resurrection to an unreal myth. Unlike the dying and rising myths of the mystery religions, the New Testament proclaims an actual victory beyond
death by a quite real historical person.[18] Biblical scholars, particularly,

have a tendency to be satisfied with simply reconstructing the historical evidence, without pursuing this further issue of the possible meaning for our experience of the resurrection belief. For this reason, the student needs to complement historical research with a more philosophical-theological form of analysis which tries to tackle these experiential questions. Even some theologians needlessly ignore the possibility of exploring possible experiential correlates to the resurrection belief, thus passing over its significance for us today.[19]

As we know by now, the resurrection belief was a latecomer to Judaism. Apparently the result of a slow evolution among the Persians, Greeks, and Jews, it is only in the apocalyptic literature that it clearly surfaces (cf Dn 12:1–3). The belief that the Divine is characterized by justice, by life, and by fidelity to humanity, along with the belief in the dignity of the individual human person among the prophets (cf Ez 37; Is 53), seems to lie at the basis of resurrection belief. In the late Jewish period speculation about resurrection seems to flourish. Will it occur only for the righteous Jew (1 Enoch 83—90), for both the righteous and unrighteous (1 Enoch 6—36), or even for all humanity (2 Esdras)? Will it include the body, what will be the body's nature, and will there be continuity with our "old" body? We remember that both the Pharisees (Mk 12:18) and even Jesus (Mk 12:25; cf Mt 8:11–12; 24:30–31; 25:31–32) adhered to some form of resurrection belief. And Paul, too, had apparently accepted it: "If there is no resurrection of the dead, Christ himself has not been raised" (1 Cor 15:13).

The best we can do, I think, is to argue with Gerald O'Collins and others that resurrection belief is "a corollary of theism." It means that "God would vindicate himself in the face of death and concomitant evils."[20] As such, it does not arise from a presumptuous attempt to know the ultimate future, but from our own present experience of trust in the Divine as a giver of life, justice, joy, love, and peace. Because we truly experience the Divine in this way, so we trust that the Divine will remain this way even into the final future. If we think along these lines, then resurrection belief becomes an "extrapolation" from our own present religious experience into the future. It is not the resurrection life itself which is available to us; we only "know" it in part through our own present experience of God as a giver and sustainer of life for us. This partial knowledge, however, supplies the experiential basis we need in order to appreciate this belief. Insofar as we now experience the divine gift of life, we are truly experiencing something of the resurrection life to come, which is basically life's fulfillment.

If we follow the lead of what these scholars are suggesting, I think we can find many possible "foretastes" of the resurrection within our experience. Our ability to survive and to keep trusting, even after the death of a loved one or after some psychological scar we have received, is a partial experience of the transition from death to resurrection. At such moments we seem to discover the transcendent power of life and love, which sustains our trust and gives us the capacity to "rise" above these deaths. The passage from ignorance, bias, bigotry, and intellectual closure to greater insight, less bias, and more openness is also a kind of death-resurrection passage. Here the transcendent power of life and love manifests itself through that greater openness and overcoming of closure. Our human capacity to hope against defeatism and to protest human misery is also a foretaste of the resurrection victory over human degradation and destruction. Hoping and protesting, so stressed by psychosocial criticism, are echoes of the divine gift of life sustaining and renewing us. Even whole social movements can be gripped by this kind of partial resurrection experience. Perhaps the human experience of love is the best analogy and correlate to resurrection belief. If we describe love as the constant passage from egocentricity to other-centeredness, then we could say that love is the echo of the divine love within us, enabling us to rise above narcissism and "one" ourselves with others. Supreme acts of heroism, justice, and peace for others are other forms of this partial, resurrection love found within our experience. All of these experiences are only partial pointers to and analogies for the resurrection, but they do enable us to give some real meaning to that fullness of life, meaning, and love which Christians believe was the transforming experience that Jesus himself shared in at Easter.[21]

The upshot of this is that we can say, with the New Testament, that Jesus still "lives." All of the varied symbolisms found in the texts are attempting to point to this. But they can only point, for we only know this in part, fragmentarily. Our language must be imaginative, evocative, symbolic, and analogical. The failure to appreciate this results from an unjustified and arrogant forgetfulness of the partial and extrapolatory "faith knowledge" that we are permitted in this realm. But if we keep this in mind, I think we can say with Walter Kasper:

> Resurrection and Exaltation mean: Jesus lives wholly and for ever in God (Rom 6:9f). Raising up to the right hand of God does not therefore imply being spirited away to another-worldly empyrean, but Jesus' being with God, his being in the dimension of God, of his power and glory. It does not mean distance from the world, but a new way of being with us; Jesus is now with us from God and in God's way; expressed in imagery: he is with God as our advocate: *semper interpellans pro nobis* [always interceding for us] (Heb 7:25).[22]

In some real sense, Jesus still "lives" with God, with a God who is present within the world and human history, gifting them with life. God, world, and humanity can never be separated. Now if we trust that Jesus still "lives" with the Divine Mystery, then we can also trust that he still "lives" with us. If you will, Jesus has made the final death-resurrection passage from egocentricity to other-centeredness. He is still with us, but in God's way: as a risen power of love, justice and peace. At least this seems to be the thrust of what O'Collins, Kasper, and other scholars who have tackled this issue seem to be saying.

The Easter Event as the Transformation of Early Christians

Let us move now to the second element of the Easter event discussed in the literature, namely, the belief that the risen Jesus manifested himself to some early Christians through a series of actual, historical, and revelatory "encounters." There is a certain amount of ambiguity within the texts as to the precise form that these revelatory encounters took. The primitive resurrection kerygmata do speak of a tradition of "appearances" of the risen Jesus (Lk 24:34; 1 Cor 15:3–5). But the appearance model may have only been one model, for some of the resurrection kerygmata omit any reference to appearances (Rom 1:3–4; 10:9; Phil 2:6–11; 1 Pt 3:18–22; 4:6; Acts 2:23–24; 3:15; 5:30–32), and Paul will speak of a "revelation" from the Lord (Gal 2:1–3) and of "seeing the Lord" (1 Cor 9:1). Thus, I prefer to speak of "encounters," leaving open the question of the precise model being used. As we also saw earlier, Acts will even employ a "conversion" model when describing Paul's encounters with the risen Jesus, something which Schillebeeckx thinks was the earliest model for the resurrection.

The crucial element in these episodes is probably given us in Paul's use of the verb "he appeared" (*ophthe*). In the light of this verb's use in the Greek Scriptures (Septuagint), where it describes theophanies, we can say that it carries two meanings: an objectively real initiative on the part of the Divine to become manifest, and a personal, subjective response in faith on the part of those who claim to undergo this experience. Despite their amplified nature, the Gospel appearance stories underscore these same two elements, for they, too, are based upon Jewish theophany stories of a divine appearance (cf Gn 18; Ex 3; Jdt 6:13; 1 Sam 3; Tb 5:12; Test. of Abraham).[23] In other words, the encounter texts point to an experience of the divine initiative, through which the disciples, through their personal receptivity, actually encounter the risen Jesus. The objectivity of these episodes is particularly stressed in the form of the verb, which highlights the divine initiative: "he appeared" (to them); this objectivity is also brought out by the listing of various eye-witnesses (cf esp. 1 Cor 15:6).

Dermot Lane, who has surveyed the literature, notes two extreme interpretations which do not seem warranted by the biblical texts. On the one hand, we can speak of a subjectivistic reduction of these revelatory encounters. On such a view these encounters are explained as a kind of outward projection of the interior beliefs of the disciples themselves. For some, this mechanism of projection is triggered by the conviction that the "cause" of Jesus remains valid; for others, it is triggered by the fact that the life of Jesus was contagiously inspiring, despite his death.[24] The difficulty, however, is that this view fails adequately to explain the texts.

Why is that? Let me list some of the typical objections to the subjectivistic thesis. The prophets, for example, knew well the distinction between merely illusory and subjective fancies and divinely initiated or authentic inspirations (cf Jer 23:25–29), a distinction clearly recognized in the New Testament (cf Gal 5:16–26; 1 Jn 4:1–3). This distinction is not simply a modern discovery of depth psychology. In the light of this, we must be cautious in arguing that the disciples were duped, albeit sincerely, by their own subjective whims. Further, how does one adequately explain the dramatic change in the disciples, from abandoners to followers of Jesus? It does strain the imagination to think that disciples would follow Jesus even unto martyrdom for a projection, unless one could prove mental illness. But the authors of the Scriptures evidence a down-to-earthness which argues against mental instability.

But there are even more serious difficulties. How, for example, does one explain the fact that the resurrection belief, which was quite peripheral in Judaism, moves to the center in Christianity?[25] This was really quite novel and unexpected. Coupled with this is the difficulty that the subjectivist thesis does not really explain the source of the disciples' "projection." It won't do to say that the source was readily available in Pharisaism or apocalyptic belief patterns. For what was commonly expected was the resurrection of the dead at the end time, not an individual's resurrection before the end. As Wolfhart Pannenberg put it, "The primitive Christian news about the eschatological resurrection of Jesus—with a temporal interval separating it from the universal resurrection of the dead—is, considered from the point of view of the history of religions, something new."[26] Perhaps what most profoundly lies behind the subjectivistic thesis is an overly impersonal view of the Divine, quite out of keeping with Jesus' intimate Abba who graciously initiates personal encounters with his own.

On the other end of the spectrum is what Lane calls the "overly objectivist" outlook. Perhaps we could call it "naive realism or objectivism." Typically this approach "oversimplifies the New Testament in a way that loses sight of the complex character and historical formation of the gospel material."[27] It does not allow for the theological overlay of interpretation pervading the Gospel appearance stories, which clearly borrow the symbolic language of the Hebrew theophany traditions. It literalizes what can only be pointed to partially and analogically—we do not experience the fullness of resurrection life but only its partial foretaste. Ultimately, it tends to reduce the resurrection to the revivification of a corpse, failing to appreciate the novelty of the transformed Jesus. Even the New Testament avoids literalism, particularly by allowing a certain amount of freedom in its expression of the encounters.

These extremes teach us, many think, that we need to move to a critically realist approach on this issue of the encounters. It should be "realist," for it should recognize that we are confronting a truly religious experience in which the divine initiative is offering itself to human beings. This is not a subjective illusion, but an objectively real moment of grace. However, it should also be "critical," for it must recognize that we can only analogically and symbolically point to this experience on the basis of our limited experiences or foretastes of the resurrection life. The critical approach also recognizes that the divine initiative does not violate the subjective capacities of the disciples involved in these encounters, but works through their dispositions, openness, and degrees of theological perceptivity. It is not by accident that only those "with faith" undergo these encounters.

The only experiential correlates to these encounter episodes we can point to are those religious experiences mentioned earlier, in which we truly experience some foretaste of the life, peace, hope, justice, and love which we believe characterize the risen life. In these encounters, we can suggest, the risen love and life that Jesus shares in impinges upon the disciples and revitalizes and renews them through that love and life. But because it is love, it does not violate them and rob them of their subjectivity. They must respond in freedom and love, and struggle through to an awareness of this love present in their midst. The texts indicate that this was a gradual process of recognition (at first they do not recognize him). Luke's description of Paul's encounter is apt here: Paul is blinded (Acts 9:1–9). Only slowly as he responds to this risen love and life and lets them permeate him does he begin to "see."

Apparently, then, we can plausibly hold that these encounters can be partially understood on the basis of the model of our religious experiences in which we "taste beforehand" the promise of resurrection life. Through similar and analogous experiences the disciples "knew" that love and life and justice which the risen Jesus now shares in. Because they knew the earthly Jesus whose life was one of justice, love, and peace they were prepared for these encounters and could recognize them as the confirmation and fulfillment of who Jesus was. It was their experience of justice, love, and peace in these encounters which enabled them to grasp the substantial identity between Jesus earthly and risen. What Jesus had been in his life was now profoundly experienced by them and "confirmed" for them within their own experience.

The texts seem to indicate what we are suggesting in a number of ways. For example, the risen Jesus enables some to experience a new sense of fellowship and at-one-ment (Lk 24:13–25; Jn 21:1–14), a new solidarity in the Spirit (Mt 28:16–20; Jn 20:22), a new experience of forgiveness (Jn 20:21–23), and peace (Jn 20:19). I would interpret this analogically on the model of our foretastes of resurrection life: the disciples experienced the risen reality of love in their lives, a love-power enabling them to transcend their fear and guilt (at abandoning Jesus) and uniting them within a new sense of fellowship, solidarity, and peace. The texts also speak of the risen Jesus "commissioning" them for the apostolate of continuing Jesus' work on behalf of justice, peace, and love: "But the time came when he who had set me apart . . . chose to reveal his Son to me, that I might spread among the Gentiles the good tidings concerning him" (Gal 1:15–16; cf Lk 24:47, 53; Mt 28:16–20; Jn 20:21–23; 21:5–7). This suggests an analogy with our own experience of yearning for that justice and life which we believe characterize the risen life. Just as our own experiences of protesting human misery, hoping for a better future, and being impelled to struggle for that future are foretastes of resurrection life, so the disciples were similarly impelled, as their commissioning indicates.

The dimension of "justice" present in these encounters surfaces in another way, too. John's Gospel reports that it was Mary Magdalene to whom the Lord first appeared, and who in turn brought the good news to the disciples: "I have seen the Lord," she says (Jn 20:18). Matthew recounts something similar: it is Mary Magdalene and "the other Mary" who first met Jesus as they returned from the empty tomb (Mt 28:9–10). Similarly, although they do not "see" the Lord, Mary Magdalene and two other women visit the tomb and are the first to learn that Jesus is risen (Mk 16:16). This striking role of women is a strong tradition in the texts which contains an important lesson for us.

I know it is fashionable among biblical scholars to hold that women are unofficial witnesses of the resurrection, while male disciples, especially Peter, are considered official heralds of the good news.[28] Clearly Peter enjoys a primary role as witness throughout the texts (1 Cor 15:5; Lk 24:34; Mk 16:7; Jn 20:1–10), and undoubtedly in the misogynist culture of that time only a male's word would really count for much. But the point is still secure: in the tradition women are the first witnesses, regardless of any role that Peter may play or may have come to play in the Church. Gerald

O'Collins, who is sensitive to this surprising role of women, argues: "Women enclose the paschal mystery. . . . To know this mystery we need to know it in a feminine way."[29] Unfortunately, by "feminine," he seems to mean the typical qualities of passivity and receptivity which are supposed to characterize women. He seems to imply that because women are by nature receptive and open, they were in a position of openness to the resurrection encounters. But there is no evidence that Jesus viewed women as foreordained to this passive feminine stereotype. Quite the contrary, if we recall the Martha and Mary episode. Furthermore, there is evidence that this entire stereotypical symbolism of "masculine-active" and "feminine-passive" characteristics—the sexual archetypes—is really a nineteenth century legitimation of the passive role that women were forced to play in society, and still are forced to play.[30]

Influenced by the feminist critique of Christology, I would suggest a different interpretation. These revelatory encounters were, in part, experiences of that life and justice which we believe characterize the risen life. They should be understood on the basis of the analogy with our own partial experiences of resurrection life, our own resurrection foretastes. In this case, the specific analogy I have in mind is our own death-resurrection passage from contributing to human oppression to struggling to overturn that oppression. We genuinely experience something of the resurrection in our struggle against oppression and injustice—the divine gift of life and love is truly at work in such experiences. The surprising place of women in the resurrection traditions symbolizes, I suggest, the fact that these resurrection encounters were ones in which the disciples discovered the resurrection gift of being able to transcend oppression. They (the disciples) "tasted" a new (risen) way of being and living, which in this case cut right through misogynism and, for a time at least, transcended it. The women were freed from a merely passive role forced on them by an androcentric culture—they found the courage to witness, and to do so first. The males had to listen to them—without giving up their developed quality of action, they had to discover the capacity to receive. In each case, for the women and the men, it was a partial experience of that fullness of life which we call "resurrection." The key to this dimension of the encounters is not some unreal "feminine archetype," but justice and freedom from oppression.

This once again illustrates that we cannot separate Jesus from the gift of salvation. These encounters were not only moments of recognition of what Jesus positively is, was, and works for. They were also moments of liberation from what was opposed to him, and still is so opposed. They were free-ing moments, moments of recognition of how Jesus acts to save us from oppression and sin. With Schillebeeckx, we can say that they were moments of forgiveness at abandoning Jesus, refusing to open ourselves to his saving work on our behalf. The link between Jesus and the gift of salvation (salvation as the reverse side of Jesus' work for the Kingdom) is an obvious dimension of the Easter encounters.

Thus, along with many writers today, I would suggest that we interpret the resurrection encounters on the model of our own religious experiences, in which we "learn" something, however partially, of what resurrection life is. Like us, in these encounters early Christian disciples experienced a foretaste of what resurrection life is. Our own experiences of love and justice, hope, peace, and meaning, and so on, are a kind of key for us, helping us to connect with what the disciples experienced. By drawing upon these analogies from our own experiences I do not mean to imply a simple identity between our own religious experiences and those of the female and male disciples. Analogy is not identity, but similarity in difference. Clearly the disciples are unique, in the sense that only they knew the earthly Jesus and could grasp the substantial identity between Jesus earthly and risen. In that sense, their experience is irrepeatable. Furthermore, their witness to the risen Jesus (their "mission") is the foundation of our own. They are the mothers and fathers of the Church, upon whose witness we all depend. Paraphrasing John, they have seen and believed; we have not seen and believed (Jn 20:29). This is a further irrepeatable dimension of their experience.[31] So while we cannot identify our own experiences with theirs, we can at least point to similarities and analogies. This is in keeping with the experiential character of Christian revelation, which is not an unhistorical myth, but a revelation which occurs through real, historical experiences. If you will, for an historical religion like Christianity, the Divine works through our human experience, not apart from it. Thus, the religious nature of our own experience serves as a kind of bridge to the religious experience of the early disciples.[32]

Finally, by drawing upon analogies from our own experience I do not imply that there were not some rather extraordinary features which accompanied the original encounter episodes of the disciples. The appearance stories of the Gospels, and even Paul (in 1 Cor 15), point to visual elements which accompanied these encounters. The very notion of an appearance implies some kind of visualization. There are also auditory elements—hearing the Lord, speaking with him. We even have tasting and touching, if we think of the meals with the risen Jesus and the doubting Thomas story. In other words, the entire sensorium of the human senses seems involved in these complex events. This need not mean, like the naive realists/objectivists, that we should literalize the accounts, forgetting their necessarily analogical and symbolic nature. Jesus remains transformed: his resurrected existence cannot be reduced to a bodily revivification. I would suggest, drawing on analogies from mystical literature

especially, in which visions and auditions play a great role, that these encounters were *total* experiences. They were not simply cognitive moments
of new insight, but also physical and affective-psychic experiences which
gripped the disciples totally. The senses equally responded to the "inrush"
of resurrection love and life! But they responded in the manner appropriate to them: through visualization, audition, touching, tasting, etc. Particularly would this be the case for a more oral culture, which is more in tune
with the full range of the human senses.

Among Jesus questers, perhaps Edward Schillebeeckx deals with this
sensorial issue best. In response to some of his critics, he clarified his own
position:

> . . . it does not seem to me at all necessary to deny visual elements in
> the Easter experience of the first Christians. Easter grace seized their
> heart and senses, and their senses through heart and spirit. It would in-
> deed be a mark of one-sided rationality if we were to remove all emo-
> tional aspects from this particular experience. Concomitant, even visual
> effects seem to me to have been ready at hand for these men [and
> women!] within their culture, while the existing model [the theophany
> traditions] itself already points to them; in other words, even the models
> usually come into being only on the basis of particular historical expe-
> riences. [33]

We have enough analogies to such sensorial experiences in the mystical literature to justify what Schillebeeckx is saying. We need not deny the legitimate place of such "extraordinary" phenomena, nor fall into a crude
form of theological magic which denies their human origins and our ability
to explain them experientially. Thus, the senses, too, form a part of the encounter episodes: they sensorially are vehicles for expressing that foretaste
of resurrection life in which Jesus now shares. But, still, they are only partial experiences of resurrection life, not its fullness. Is that why John has
Jesus respond to Mary Magdalene, "Do not cling to me, for I have not yet
ascended to the Father" (Jn 20:17)? Is this a way of symbolizing that even
the power of a sensory foretaste of resurrection life is only partial and fragmentary—only a pointer toward our resurrection destiny?

Empty Tomb Tradition

This is the appropriate place to offer some observations on the empty
tomb tradition, which also forms a part of the resurrection narratives as we
have them. Scholars are quite divided on this matter, on both historical
and philosophical-theological grounds. Historically this tradition is absent

from Paul, our earliest witness to the resurrection. The accounts are literally studded with discrepancies: all the Gospels mention women's experiences at the tomb, but was it three women (Mk 16:1; Lk 24:10), two
(Mt 28:1), or one (Jn 20:1)? Why did these women go to the tomb: to anoint
the body (Mark and Luke), or simply to see the tomb (Matthew)? Mark
claims that the women told no one afterward (16:8), but Matthew and Luke
have them running to tell the disciples. Were there two angels (Lk 24:4;
Jn 20:12) or only one (Mt 28:2–5; Mk 16:5)? Mark 16:1–8 is probably the
oldest account, but even it has some imponderables. To want to anoint a
body which has lain dead in a shroud for three days makes little sense in
Palestine's climate. And why are the women silent, after they are told to
announce their news to the disciples?

It is probably safest to say that historians rather neatly divide on the
historicity of this tradition into two camps. On the one hand, we have those
who would see in the tradition a reflection of the customary cult of honoring the tomb of significant figures. Schillebeeckx would seem to take this
approach. As Walter Kasper explains this, ". . . the primitive Christian
community in Jerusalem may well have honored Jesus' tomb and have as-
sembled yearly at or in the empty tomb on the anniversary of the Resurrection for a cultic ceremony, during which the joyful message of the
Resurrection would be proclaimed and the empty tomb used as a symbol."[34] Without denying that, others more conservatively argue that there
are persuasive grounds for accepting the historical credibility of an actual
empty tomb. They ask, for example, how this tradition could have been
sustained in the face of Jewish and Roman opposition, unless the tomb
were actually empty. More strongly, they point to the significance of
women witnesses. Legend-makers would probably have chosen male witnesses in an androcentric society. The presence of women, these scholars
hold, has a ring of historical authenticity to it.

There is also strong disagreement on philosophical and theological
grounds. Some argue that this tradition presupposes a crudely physicalist
understanding of the resurrection: ". . . it was only natural that most of the
unsophisticated early Christians understood the resurrection to have been
of Jesus' physical body—and the obvious conclusion to be drawn from this
was that the tomb where that body had been laid was now empty," says
Gordon Kaufman.[35] Others, on the other hand, suggest that this tradition
points to the continuity between the earthly and risen Jesus. It is the full
earthly Jesus-with-a-body who has been raised into eternal life. They add
that even Paul, who avoids a crudely physicalist view of the resurrection
and omits any mention of an empty tomb, still implies that our mortal bodies are transformed, not that they are simply replaced by completely different ("spiritual") bodies.[36]

From a survey of writers, so far as I can tell Walter Kasper has proposed an alternative which would seem to be compatible with all parties concerned. What Kasper has attempted to do is to think through anew the possible meaning of believing in the "resurrection of the body" in the light of sound biblical and anthropological underpinnings. Let us look at the main lines of Kasper's approach.

Biblically, Kasper suggests, the body (*soma*) is viewed as a co-constitutive dimension of the human being: we do not "have" a body but we are "embodied spirits." We are created as embodied creatures and we live out our lives, even religiously, through the body (Gn 1:27; 2:7, 23). Paul reflects this biblical orientation when he says, ". . . offer your bodies as a living sacrifice holy and acceptable to God" (Rom 12:1). Thus, in the biblical understanding, which seems to conform to the insights of modern anthropology, the human being must be seen holistically. The body highlights the reality of the whole person as an embodied spirit. Through the body we are inserted into the world and enabled to engage in communication with others. The body is the vehicle for the communication of our spirit. Unlike some strands of Greco-Roman thought, the Scriptures do not denigrate the body: we are not souls trapped in bodies. The body can be perverted, of course, and used for egocentric ends. But it can also give glory to the Divine. When it is treated in this latter sense, as a vehicle of our deepest and best spirit, it is a spiritualized body, a body in tune with the Divine (1 Cor 6:13). Perhaps this is what Paul has in mind when he speaks of the "spiritual body": the whole person is in tune with and lives with the Divine. What we have been and done in our bodies, our life of communication with others through our body—all that is now taken up with the Divine in the risen life.

In the light of these biblical and philosophical orientations, Kasper draws an important distinction between the merely "material" nature of the body and the more profound "spiritualized body" spoken of in the Scriptures. Clearly our "material" makeup is subject to constant metabolic change and, at least in our experience, undergoes decomposition at death. If this is true, Kasper thinks that we do not need to engage in unfounded speculations about the material nature of the resurrection body. "What will it look like? What age will it have?"—such questions seem to be on the level of the merely material, and even Paul considers them foolish questions (cf 1 Cor 15:35–44). On the other hand, we can maintain belief in the spiritualized body spoken of by Paul. What this latter seems to mean is that all that we have been and done through our bodies in our relations with others and the world is now, in resurrection life, "completely penetrated by the love of God," as Kasper expresses it.[37] What this seems to come to, then, is that the risen life, so we may trust, is our total fulfillment as creatures of intercommunication with one another and our world. Of course, we do not and cannot know what this fully means. We only partially know this now through our experiences of bodily intercommunication. But these partial experiences may at least serve as experiential pointers to what is being affirmed in the tradition of the body's resurrection.

Kasper's view is attractive for a number of reasons. Most importantly it penetrates through to the important role that our bodies play in our experience as vehicles of intercommunication and solidarity and proposes that this is fulfilled in the resurrection life. This nicely coheres with what we said earlier about the resurrection as an experience of solidarity. Furthermore, Kasper's view would seem to be compatible with either side of the historical evidence. Kasper's thesis of actual material decomposition (as distinct from the spiritualized body) can get along quite well with either the cult-legend hypothesis or the actual empty tomb hypothesis. Kasper's thesis also steers a middle ground between the two main philosophical-theological positions. He argues against a crudely physicalist approach, without denying the important element of meaning in a spiritualized or transformed body.

But in any case, in and of itself, the empty tomb tradition is a theologically ambiguous reality. Finding an empty tomb need not necessarily mean that Jesus has been raised. The body could have been stolen, misplaced, or decomposed. This ambiguity is reflected in the texts, too: Luke says that "the story seemed like nonsense" (24:11), and John says that Mary Magdalene simply opined: "The Lord has been taken from the tomb! We don't know where they have put him" (20:2, 13). Apparently it could only have been in the light of the Easter faith that the disciples could have drawn the right conclusions about an empty tomb. Given this faith first, probably mediated through some encounter experience, the empty tomb could then take on real theological significance as a further sign of resurrection life. For this reason, most scholars do not place the same significance upon the empty tomb tradition that they place upon the encounter episodes.

A Note on the Shroud of Turin

Recently a good deal of interest has been shown in the Shroud of Turin, the cloth piously believed to be the burial cloth of Jesus. Now venerated in Turin, Italy, the cloth's origins are still wrapped in historical obscurity. There is a tradition that a disciple of Jesus, Thaddaeus, brought a miracle-working cloth with him on his travels to Edessa, bearing the image of a man's face. But from the first to the sixth century, there is no written evidence of the cloth's whereabouts, nor again from 1204 through 1357. Its existence in the intervening period only rests on the slender hypothesis of the existence of a "Mandylion" (cloth) venerated in Constantinople and somehow received by the De Charny family of France in the fourteenth century. Be that as it may, a surprising number of "scientific" tests have been given the Shroud from 1969 to the present, thus catapulting it into some prominence.

To my knowledge, theologians have said little about the Shroud. Before the scientific testing, the Anglican scholar C.F.D. Moule probably spoke for most when he called it "patently ridiculous."[38] Now, however, there is an apparent shift in some theological circles. The ever surprising biblical scholar and Anglican bishop John Robinson called the Shroud a "trigger of faith" during a BBC television discussion, and the respected Roman Catholic scholar Gerald O'Collins has written a persuasive article in its favor.[39] My interest in raising the issue is to explore the Shroud's possible connection to the Easter events.

If I read O'Collins correctly, he considers the scientific and the biblical evidence quite forceful. The cloth's material and pattern is said to match that of products in common use in the Middle East in the first century A.D. Prevailing standards of the fourteenth century would not have allowed naked images of Jesus, yet this nudity is what the Shroud shows. Would a forger have dared to attempt that? It is said that no medieval forger could have anticipated modern science by making the image on the Shroud a negative. Yet Secondo Pia discovered that it was precisely a negative when he photographed it in 1898. Pollen samples from the cloth appear to be similar to pollen taken from plants which grow only in Palestine, and found especially in layers of sediment in the Lake of Galilee from the time of Jesus. "At some point in its history the shroud was exposed to the air in Palestine," says O'Collins.[40] Some argue that the cloth cannot be a painting, for pigmentation samplings are inconclusive as a result of chemimicroanalytical work. Red blood stains are argued to be present, because of appreciable amounts of iron, protein, and porphyrinic material. Analysis of coins from Jesus' time indicates that only Jews were depicted with beards and hair falling to the shoulders, something the Shroud portrays. Some even think that the Shroud influenced the way painters depicted Christ, for from the sixth century Christ is always portrayed as a mature man with a forked beard and long hair. Before that he was customarily portrayed as young and beardless.

Biblically the Shroud strikingly matches the particular details of Jesus' passion as recorded in the Gospels. The markings correspond anatomically to what we would expect from a crucified man and from the biblical record:

the crowning with thorns (Synoptics) and the piercing of the side (John). The "linen cloths" (*othonia,* plural) said to have been on Jesus (Jn 20:6) can be interpreted, we are told, as a generic-plural for grave cloths, thus rendering *othonia* compatible with a single cloth like the Shroud. Because of this, some argue that we cannot rule out the possibility that the cloth actually depicts Jesus.

Apparently some of the scientists working on the Shroud project have concluded that the Shroud image is a scorch formed by a burst of radiation emitted by the corpse. Here it is important to note that the Shroud bears no indications of a possible tearing, as if it were pulled from the corpse. If we are dealing with such a scorch, one scientist notes: "Not only would the source of the radiation be unprecedented, but the radiation emanating vertically from every element of the body surface would somehow have to be collinated to project an image and would have to fall off to zero intensity at about two inches—properties totally unknown to science."[41]

While this kind of evidence is remarkable, still I think a heavy dose of caution is in order. We now know that there is wide disagreement among the scientists working on the project as to the validity of the scorch hypothesis. Tests with lasers of diverse wave-lengths and pulse-widths have not been able to duplicate the Shroud image through scorching linen. Further, the evidence for blood stains is inconclusive: porphyrins are common in plants and animals; old blood stains are always brown or black, not red (as on the Shroud). The stains could actually emanate from an artist's pigment composed of iron oxide. Most importantly, there is some evidence that artists' pigments are present—namely, iron oxide (red ochre or hematite), which was widely used in the Middle Ages. "All that would be necessary . . . to form the Shroud image is to postulate that the rubbing was done using a semi-solid, presumably colored (so the artist could see what he was doing) medium that, over the six centuries or in the 1532 fire, has virtually disappeared, leaving behind only cellulose fibrils discolored by dehydration."[42]

In other words, a rubbing process by an artist is also a possible explanation for the Shroud's origin. At least that is the view of the Shroud critic Marvin Mueller, from whom much of the above is taken. More recently, the Jesuit Robert Wild, in a critical review of Shroud publications, has raised some further difficulties. He is convinced that the alleged blood stains are clearly not proven to be first century stains (they may be from a later period). More independent testing needs to be done on these stains before relatively safe conclusions can be drawn. Wild's biggest problem with these "stains" is their clear and precise outline (surely real blood would have smeared in the process of moving Jesus' body) and the fact that the "blood" flows in the wrong direction if it happened while Jesus lay in the tomb.

Wild surfaces some supporting problems too. The fact that the face and hands stand out so clearly is quite typical of painting, which emphasizes these features. The artistic "modesty" (the covering of the genitals by the joined hands) seems odd, requiring an unrelaxed body and some elongation of fingers and the right forearm. The way the face is depicted is typical of medieval portraits. We should probably also be suspicious about the claim that the Shroud matches the biblical data quite well. This might be an instance of a medieval attempt to harmonize artificially data from four quite different Gospels. Particularly troubling is the plural for cloths (*othonia*) in John's Gospel (cf 20:5–7). It is by no means proven that this Gospel intends the term as a generic plural. Finally, Wild thinks that the lack of any convincing history prior to the fourteenth century is also a serious problem which challenges the cloth's authenticity.

In the absence of carbon dating, the critical person should be cautious, I think. Wild believes that an artist probably scorched a linen cloth by means of a heated statue or pair of bas-reliefs, also using blood to create stains. This would explain the three-dimensionality of the image, its photographic negative nature, and the lack of paintbrush marks. As we have seen, Mueller inclines toward a rubbing process. The advantage of this latter hypothesis over scorching is that it would not burn the cloth, while one would think that heating a statue to scorch a cloth would. In any event, the issue is far from settled, and the evidence inclines me to a verdict of "no" on the question of historical authenticity. One might do well to listen to Bishop Pierre d'Arcis' fourteenth century verdict on the Shroud, recorded in his letter to Pope Clement VII: "Eventually, after diligent inquiry and examination, Henry of Poitiers [another bishop] discovered the fraud and how the said cloth had been cunningly painted, the truth being attested by the artist who had painted it, to wit, that it was a work of human skill and not miraculously wrought or bestowed."[43]

Quite clearly the Shroud is an ambiguous phenomenon. Even were the scorch hypothesis (from miraculous radiation) sustained, this would still be true. For scorching does not necessarily imply resurrection, and believers would still need to open themselves in faith to the resurrection reality on other grounds. I would suggest that the Shroud is somewhat similar to the empty tomb tradition. Perhaps, like that tomb tradition, it might enable some people to give themselves a kind of "scientific underpinning" to their faith, an empirical foundation for faith. But the present evidence inclines me to regard it as even more ambiguous than that. At the best I would regard it as a pious reminder, not of the resurrection, but of the pas-

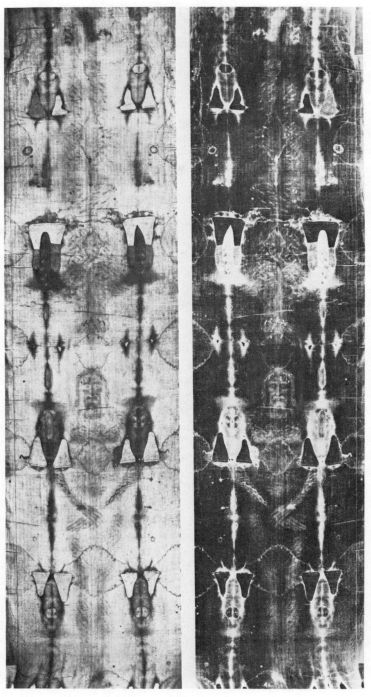

242

sion of Jesus. In fact, this is precisely the significance Gerald O'Collins finds in it:

> What we have . . . in the Shroud is a pictorial counterpart to St. Paul's message about Christ who "was crucified in weakness, but lives by the power of God" (2 Cor. 13:4). "Vulnerability" catches better what the apostle means by "weakness." Who is more vulnerable than a crucified man? And yet through the crucifixion of Jesus, the divine power comes to heal and help us. By its impact on viewers, the Shroud of Turin illustrates and re-enacts the mystery of the passion. In his utter vulnerability and seeming powerlessness, the man on the Shroud acts to save us.[44]

Summing Up: Easter as Confirmation and Transformation

If we briefly try to sum up what the Easter events contribute to our growing understanding of Jesus, I think the two words of "confirmation" and "transformation" can serve us well in our efforts. On the one hand, it would appear that the Easter experiences served as a catalyst of confirmation for the early Christians, convincing them in faith that the power of peace, love and justice was the true depth dimension of Jesus, the deeper story behind, in, and through the surface story of his earthly life. By proclaiming that *God* had raised Jesus from the dead, the early disciples were implying that somehow the Divine Mystery itself was at work in Jesus. This points us ahead to our next chapter, in which we will survey the biblical development of Christology, the emergence of the proclamation of this deeper dimension of who Jesus was.

But on the other hand, the Easter experiences did more than simply clarify and confirm who Jesus was. They actually introduced something novel, too. For they convinced the early Christians that Jesus still "lives" with the Divine. Not only *was* Jesus' earthly life a deeper story of the divine work of love, justice, and peace; he *is* still right now the effective presence of that divine love, justice, and peace. Jesus, the Risen One, still shares in this divine work—Jesus' work on behalf of the new community continues on today. This is why I have chosen the word "transformation," for in his transformed risen existence Jesus becomes a partner with the world and with the Divine Mystery at work in that world. This, too, points us ahead to our next chapter, for we will see that the emerging biblical Christology proclaims the deeper dimension not only of what Jesus was, but of what he continues still to be on our behalf. It also points us ahead to the emerging biblical soteriology, the belief that Jesus is the Savior. Jesus was and remains, not simply the mystery of divine love, justice, and peace, but a mystery which sets us free from injustice, lovelessness, and war.

This, too, was confirmed in the Easter experiences, and continued, as the early Church's ability to know forgiveness, to rise above disunion, and to oppose injustice illustrates.

Notes

1. See Helmut Koester, "The Structure of Early Christian Beliefs," in James M. Robinson and Helmut Koester, eds., *Trajectories through Early Christianity* (Philadelphia: Fortress, 1971), pp. 205–231, esp. pp. 223–229; and his *Introduction to the New Testament*, 2, *History and Literature of Early Christianity* (Philadelphia: Fortress, 1982), pp. 1–5, 160–177; and Schillebeeckx, *Jesus, op. cit.*, pp. 403–515, and *Interim, op. cit.*, pp. 74–93.

2. See Avery Dulles, *Models of Revelation* (Garden City, N.Y.: Doubleday, 1983), pp. 131–154, on the symbolic nature of revelation.

3. See Reginald H. Fuller and Pheme Perkins, *Who Is This Christ? op. cit.*, pp. 28–40, for a succinct critique of Schillebeeckx.

4. Especially helpful here: Ulrich Wilckens, *Resurrection: Biblical Testimony to the Resurrection: An Historical Examination and Explanation* (Atlanta: John Knox, 1978). Less accessible: Klaus Berger, *Die Auferstehung des Propheten und die Erhöhung des Menschensohnes: Traditionsgeschichtliche Untersuchungen zur Deutung des Geschiches Jesu in früchristlichen Texten* (Göttingen: Vandenhoeck und Ruprecht, 1976).

5. Raymond E. Brown, *The Virginal Conception and Bodily Resurrection of Jesus* (New York: Paulist, 1973), p. 75.

6. See Fuller and Perkins, *op. cit.*, pp. 32–34.

7. For a helpful reconstruction and survey of the literature, see Kee, *Jesus in History, op. cit.*, pp. 62–103.

8. Fuller, *Critical Introduction to the New Testament, op. cit.*, p. 74, relying upon H.E.Tödt, *The Son of Man in the Synoptic Tradition* (Philadelphia: Westminster, 1965).

9. This is a cardinal principle of Voegelin's project; cf his *Order and History*, 1, *Israel and Revelation, op. cit.*, pp. 1–11.

10. Representative works I am summarizing: Gerald O'Collins, *The Resurrection of Jesus Christ* (Valley Forge, Pa.: Judson, 1973), and *What Are They Saying About the Resurrection?* (New York: Paulist, 1978), and his helpful "Thomas Aquinas and Christ's Resurrection," *Theological Studies* 31 (1970), 512–522; Brown, *The Virginal Conception, op. cit.;* Edouard Pousset, "La resurrection," *Nouvelle Revue Théologique* 91 (1968), 1009–1044, and "Croire en la resurrection," *ibid.*, 96 (1974), 147–166, 366–388; C.F. Evans, *Resurrection and the New Testament* (London: SCM, 1970); Reginald H. Fuller, *The Formation of the Resurrection Narratives* (New York: Macmillan, 1971); Paul de Surgy, ed., *The Resurrection and Modern Biblical Thought* (New York: Corpus, 1970); Norman Perrin, *The Resurrection according to Matthew, Mark, and Luke* (Philadelphia: Fortress, 1977); Wilckens, *op. cit.;* Krister Stendahl, ed., *Immortality and Resurrection* (New York: Macmillan, 1965); Willi Marxsen, *The Resurrection of Jesus of Nazareth* (London: SCM, 1970).

11. To my knowledge, only the non-canonical Gospel of Peter claims to witness the event: the soldiers "saw again three men come out from the sepulchre, and two of them sustaining the other, and a cross following them, and the heads of the two reaching to heaven, but that of him who was led by the hand overpassing the heavens." Cited in Fuller, *The Formation, ibid.*, p. 190: Gospel of Peter, 8:39–40.

12. O'Collins, *The Resurrection of Jesus Christ, op. cit.*, p. 51.

13. *Ibid.*, p. 52. This was Aquinas' position too: "Christus resurgens non rediit ad vitam communiter omnibus notam, sed ad vitam quandam immortalem et Deo conformem" ("The risen Christ did not return to the life commonly known by all of us, but entered into a life which was in some way immortal and conformed to the divine life"); cf *Summ. theol.*, 3, 55, 2.

14. See Jack Dean Kingsbury, "The Gospel of Mark in Current Research," *Religious Studies Review* 5 (1979), 101–107. Mk 16:9–20 is an interpolation.

15. See John P. Meier, *The Vision of Matthew* (New York: Paulist, 1979), esp. p. 207.

16. O'Collins, *The Resurrection of Jesus Christ, op. cit.*, p. 83.

17. Dermot A. Lane, *The Reality of Jesus* (New York: Paulist, 1975), p. 51.

18. On the resurrection beliefs of unhistorical myths, see Pierre Grelot, "The Resurrection of Jesus: Its Biblical and Jewish Background," in De Surgy, *The Resurrection and Modern Biblical Thought, op. cit.*, pp. 1–29, esp. pp. 2–6, 7, 13–16.

19. James P. Mackey, *op. cit.*, refuses to explore possible experiential correlates to the resurrection belief, and relies wholly on the earthly Jesus as the catalyst of the disciples' faith. He thinks that the historical Jesus' life was contagiously inspirational. A similar view is found in Rudolf Pesch, "Zur Enstehung des Glaubens an die Auferstehung Jesu," *Theologische Quartalschrift* 153 (1973), 201–228. This is a minority opinion among biblical scholars. Most feel that rooting faith simply in the earthly Jesus does not come to terms with the tradition of Jesus' abandonment by the early disciples, nor does it face the clear textual evidence found in the New Testament about the role of the resurrection. Could we say that this is a case of history as psychological guesswork rather than an exploration of the historical references opened up before the text itself? For a survey, see John P. Galvin, "Resurrection as *Theologia Crucis Jesu:* The Foundational Christology of Rudolf Pesch," *Theological Studies* 38 (1977), 513–525.

20. O'Collins, *The Resurrection of Jesus Christ, op. cit.*, p. 104.

21. Representative of those exploring experiential correlates: O'Collins, *The Resurrection of Jesus Christ, op. cit.*, pp. 69–73, and *What Are They Saying About the Resurrection? op. cit.*, pp. 68–86; H.A. Williams, *True Resurrection* (New York: Harper and Row, 1972); William Johnston, *Silent Music: The Science of Meditation* (New York: Harper and Row, 1974), esp. pp. 160–161; Karl Rahner, "The Hermeneutics of Eschatological Assertions," *Theological Investigations*, 4, *op. cit.*, pp. 323–346; Eric Voegelin, "Immortality: Experience and Symbol," *Harvard Theological Review* 60 (1967), 235–279; Louis Dupré, *Transcendent Selfhood: The Rediscovery of the Inner Life* (New York: Seabury, 1976), pp. 79–104; Peter J. Riga, "The Resurrection and Mystical Experience," *The Bible Today* (April 1971), 351–356. Less accessible: G. Martelet, *L'au-delà retrouvé: Christologie des fins*

dernieres (Paris: Desclee, 1975), esp. pp. 159–162; Leo Scheffczyk, *Auferstehung: Prinzip des christlichen Glaubens* (Einsiedeln: Johannes, 1976). Still enormously fruitful is Friedrich von Hügel, *Eternal Life: A Study of Its Implications and Applications* (Edinburgh: T and T Clark, 1912/1948).

22. Kasper, *op. cit.*, p. 149.

23. The standard work on the influence of the theophany traditions upon the resurrection stories is John E. Alsup, *The Post-Resurrection Appearance Stories of the Gospel-Tradition: A History-of-Tradition Analysis with Text-Synopsis* (London: SPCK/Stuttgart: Calwer, 1975), esp. pp. 214–265.

24. This is Marxsen's view; cf. note 10. Another form of the same view is Hugh Jackson, "The Resurrection Belief of the Earliest Church: A Response to the Failure of Prophecy?" *Journal of Religion* 55 (1975), 415–425.

25. Emphasized by Evans, *op. cit.*, pp. 11–40, and O'Collins, *The Resurrection of Jesus Christ, op. cit.*, pp. 106–107.

26. Pannenberg, *Jesus—God and Man, op. cit.*, p. 96; cf O'Collins, *ibid.*, pp. 30–34.

27. Lane, *op. cit.*, p. 59; cf pp. 57–60 for his helpful overview of the positions.

28. Cf O'Collins, *What Are They Saying About the Resurrection? op. cit.*, pp. 89–95. Cf E. Fiorenza, *op. cit.*, pp. 139–140, for the view underlying the text's.

29. *Ibid.*, p. 98.

30. See Rosemary Radford Ruether and Eleanor McLaughlin, eds., *Women of Spirit: Female Leadership in the Jewish and Christian Traditions* (New York: Simon and Schuster, 1979), esp. the introduction.

31. O'Collins, *What Are They Saying About the Resurrection? op. cit.*, pp. 58–60.

32. See the helpful study of William P. Loewe, "The Appearances of the Risen Lord: Faith, Fact, and Objectivity," *Horizons* 6 (1979), 177–192, which argues for the rightfulness of analogies with our own experience. Similar in this respect is Béla Weissmahr, "Kann Gott die Auferstehung Jesu durch innerweltliche Kräfte bewirkt Haben?," *Zeitschrift für Katholische Theologie* 100 (1978), 441–469. In other words, these writers simply extend the experiential approach to the appearances, like the authors in note 21. For an interesting, but non-reductionistic, Jungian approach, see Margaret E. Thrall, "Resurrection Traditions and Christian Apologetic," *The Thomist* 43 (1979), 197–216.

33. Schillebeeckx, *Interim, op. cit.*, pp. 80–81. See, for the mystics: Friedrich von Hügel, *The Mystical Element of Religion as Studied in Saint Catherine of Genoa and Her Friends* (London: J.M. Dent/James Clarke, 1961), 1, pp. 3–82; 2, pp. 3–61; William Johnston, *op cit.*, pp. 45–103. For texts, see "Voices and Visions," in Evelyn Underhill, *Mysticism: A Study in the Nature and Development of Man's Spiritual Consciousness* (New York: World, 1972), pp. 266–297. Her helpful definition of mystical sensoria: "They are the automatic expressions of intense subliminal activity: not merely the *media* by which the self's awareness of the Absolute is strengthened and enriched, but the outward and visible signs of its movement towards new levels of consciousness" (p. 290). On the role

of the sensorium in an oral culture, see Walter J. Ong, *The Presence of the Word, op. cit.*

34. Kasper, *op. cit.*, p. 127.

35. Gordon Kaufman, *op. cit.*, pp. 419–420, n. 16.

36. O'Collins, *The Resurrection of Jesus Christ, op. cit.*, p. 44; Brown, *The Virginal Conception, op. cit.*, pp. 113–125.

37. Kasper, *op. cit.*, p. 152; cf pp. 150–153, esp. p. 152: "All the attributes [offered by the Scholastic theologians], incapability of suffering (*impassibilitas*) and imperishability (*immortalitas*), finesse (*subtilitas*) and dexterity (*agilitas*): that is, intellectual formation and complete control and mastery over the body through the spirit, the overcoming of all alienation in man, and finally clearness (*claritas*), transfiguration by the glory of God: all these could be undertood basically as the effect of the final validation of the whole man in the glory of God—in spite of all the problems of such speculations individually." Plato, contrary to common stereotypes, reversed his body-negativism of the earlier dialogues in his later *Republic* and *Philebus*. Cf G.M.A. Grube, *Plato's Thought* (Boston: Beacon, 1968), pp. 51–86. The post-Plato Greek dualism is sometimes called the *soma-sema* view; that is, the body (= *soma*) trapped in the tomb (= *sema*).

38. C.F.D. Moule, *The Phenomenon of the New Testament* (London: SCM, 1967), p. 2.

39. Gerald O'Collins, "Theological Trends: The Shroud of Turin," *The Way* 20 (1980), 140–147.

40. *Ibid.*, 141.

41. Marvin M. Mueller, "The Shroud of Turin: A Critical Appraisal," *The Skeptical Inquirer* 6 (1982), 17.

42. *Ibid.*, 28.

43. Cited in *ibid.*, 18. For complete texts of the critiques used here, see *ibid.*, 14–34, and Robert A. Wild, "The Shroud of Turin," *Biblical Archaeology Review* 10 (1984), 30–46. Raymond E. Brown is also quite cautious; cf his *Recent Discoveries and the Biblical World* (Wilmington, Delaware: Michael Glazier, 1983), pp. 81–83. Wild admits that his scorching theory cannot yet explain how the cloth would not be burned nor why the body image did not fluoresce when subjected to ultraviolet light, while the portions scorched in the 1532 fire did. The rubbing process, proposed by Mueller and greatly based on Joe Nickell's suggestions, would seem to overcome these difficulties. Would a rubbing process leave such clear and precise stains? Perhaps. Cf also Joe Nickell, *Inquest on the Shroud of Turin* (Buffalo, N.Y.: Prometheus Books, 1983).

44. O'Collins, "Theological Trends," *art. cit.*, 147. Other, more positive, literature on the Shroud: Ian Wilson, *The Shroud of Turin* (New York: Doubleday, 1978), still fine, although it does not incorporate the findings of the Shroud of Turin Research Project (= STURP), composed of scientists (physicists, chemists, computer specialists, etc.) from various scientific establishments; John H. Heller, *Report on the Shroud of Turin* (Boston: Houghton Mifflin, 1983); Frank C. Tribbe, *Portrait of Jesus?* (Briarcliff Manor, New York: Stein and Day, 1983); Kenneth E. Stevenson and Gary R. Habermas, *Verdict on the Shroud* (Ann Arbor, Michigan: Servant Books, 1981).

7D

From Kerygma to Gospels

Most biblical scholars are convinced that the dialectical process of reflection back on the earthly Jesus and the Easter experiences eventually gave birth to what we can call "Christology." But they are somewhat divided on the actual course this development took. Widely accepted has been the view that we can rather neatly delineate an early Palestinian, a later Jewish-Hellenistic, and a quite late Hellenistic form of Christological and soteriological speculation. This theory is based on the hypothesis that the first proclaimers were chiefly Palestinian. As the Christian movement spread into the Hellenistic world, it increasingly took on a Hellenistic form, first from the Jews of the diaspora (Jewish-Hellenistic), and finally from the Gentiles themselves (Hellenistic). However, a number of scholars are now telling us that many of the earliest Christians were Hellenists from the beginning (cf Acts 6:1). Furthermore, there had been a constant interpenetration between Judaism and Hellenism from the days of Alexander the Great. As James D.G. Dunn expresses it, we cannot "readily divide the New Testament writings into such clearly distinct pigeon-holes; in a very real and important sense all the New Testament writings are Jewish and Christian documents."[1] It seems prudent, then, not to attempt an implausible chronological differentiation, from an earliest Palestinian to a late Hellenistic Christology. We should rather imagine a constant interpenetration between the Jewish and Hellenistic traditions as the early Christians attempted to clarify their apprehension of Jesus.

Early Developments: An Historical Sketch

We have already seen how there is a kind of "Christology" already present in the earthly Jesus, at least in the basic sense that he is the Kingdom's "agent" who probably expects some form of resurrection-vindication, and who knows himself to be one in the line of prophets, and perhaps the final prophet at that. With Reginald Fuller, we should probably call this a "theology of Jesus" rather than a Christology in the proper sense.[2]

248

Yet the point is crucial, because it indicates that the post-Easter developments we are about to survey were a clarification of who Jesus was, not a fabrication with no roots in the earthly Jesus. The New Testament, in other words, does not appear to be a falsification of the earthly Jesus, but a deeper penetration, under the impact of the Easter experiences.

The Earliest Development: A "Two Stage" Christology

Scholars think that in the earliest, post-Easter period, there was a tendency to attribute different titles and descriptions to the two phases of Jesus' career, his earthly and risen lives. Thus the title "two stage" Christology. Therefore, for his earthly career we find the texts designating Jesus as a "servant" (Acts 3:13, 26; 4:27, 30), as the "holy" and "righteous" one (Acts 3:14), and possibly even as the eschatological, Moses-like prophet (note the use of the citation from Deuteronomy 18:15 in Acts 3: 22–23).

In the second phase of his career, Jesus is now taken up into heaven, waiting to return (Acts 3:21), but he is exalted and reigning with God (Acts 2:33). In this respect he is designated as *Christos* (or *Messiah*) and *Kyrios* (Lord), as we learn from Acts (2:36; cf Phil 2:11). By the application of Psalm 2:7 to the risen Jesus, it appears that he is also designated as "Son of God" (cf Rom 1:4). The thrust of this early two stage Christology does not seem to be to imply that Jesus is somehow a radically different person in the two phases of his career, as if he went from being a mere man to being somehow divine. As Reginald Fuller explains it, "Rather, the formulas are saying that at his resurrection or exaltation Jesus embarked on a new role in salvation history."[3] If he was the earthly, eschatological prophet in his first phase, now he is the risen Christ and Lord who directs the Christian community from heaven. In other words, both phases of Jesus' career are given a Christological significance. We are not dealing with two radically different Jesuses but with one Jesus in various phases of his career and saving work. If this is true, then this two stage Christology should not be called "adoptionist" in the sense that that term carries in the later disputes of the Church. That is, Jesus is not somehow "adopted" by the Divine at the resurrection. Throughout his total career he is the one through whom the divine work happens.

Some Examples of "Later" Developments

According to Raymond Brown, and most biblical scholars along with him, the key development after the two stage Christology is the "retrojection" onto Jesus' earthly life of Christological titles originally reserved for his post-resurrection phase of existence.[4] "Perhaps the easiest title to retroject into the earthly life of Jesus was *Christos*, or Messiah," says Fuller.[5] We have already seen the important role that "messiahs" played in the expectations of apocalyptic circles. It is not implausible to think that Jesus raised messianic expectations already during his life by his message of the Kingdom. People possibly already thought (as question and surmise, to use Schillebeeckx' helpful phrase) that he was a messiah. In any case, we find Paul saying that he died as *Christos*, as the Messiah (1 Cor 15:3). Here the title Messiah has moved from being a designation of his risen existence to being one for his earthly death. Fuller thinks that this probably means "Messiah-designate," for Jesus must return to complete his messianic work (cf Acts 2:36). But beyond even this, there was a tendency to push the Messiah-title even further back into Jesus' earthly career. In Paul "Christ" simply becomes part of Jesus' name, designating his whole career (Rom 1:8). Fuller suggests that this could easily happen, for already in the earliest period Jesus was believed to have been "anointed" ("christ-ened") by the Spirit early in his career (at his baptism?: cf Acts 4:27;10:38). Thus, the title Messiah became an apt expression for his whole life, from the beginning of his ministry on through to his resurrection existence.

The title *Kyrios* (Lord) is apparently another central example of retrojection. Paul uses it frequently as a designation, like Christ/Messiah, for Jesus in his total person (Rom 10:9; 1 Cor 12:3; 8:6, etc.). The title has a wide range of meanings, from simply "Sir" on to some kind of implied "divine" status, for it was used in the imperial cult and in the Septuagint as a designation for the Divine. Apparently the Easter experiences convinced the early Christians that the divine authority or "lordship" was something that Jesus exercised, in both his risen and his earthly life. Authority, in fact, seems to be the chief notion behind this title's use.[6]

The title "Son of God" is apparently another early example of retrojection. Originally this title emanates from Israel's royal ideology: the kings and their heirs are "God's sons." In this way it is also associated with the Messiah-title, for one of the messianic expectations was precisely an heir of King David, as we have seen. We noted above how this title was first applied to Jesus in his risen life, under the influence of applying to him Psalm 2:7. Now, Fuller goes on to say, "There is fairly clear-cut evidence that Ps. 2:7 projected backward into the earthly life of Jesus to his baptism, to his transfiguration (it is unclear whether Son of God was first retrojected to the transfiguration and thence to baptism or vice versa), and finally to his conception/birth."[7] In any case, Luke's infancy story (Lk 1) has clearly pushed the title of divine sonship back to Jesus' very birth itself.

Fuller points to the "sending-of-the-son" pattern as another distinctive development, which probably pushed "Christological concern to the birth of Jesus."[8] This pattern, found in various sections of the New Testament (Mk 12:1–12; Mt 21:33–46; Lk 20:9–19; Gal 4:4; Rom 8:3; Jn 3:17), describes Jesus as one "sent by God" to perform the divine work. It probably has nothing to do with the sending down of a pre-existent divine being, but indicates "the historical mission of key figures in Israel's history."[9] The prophets, after all, were likewise sent by God for their special tasks. But the important point is that this pattern very likely caused interest to arise in Jesus' birth and its Christological significance, thus causing "exalted" titles to be pushed back to the moment of Jesus' conception. For it is characteristic of the prophets that they trace the origin of their call back to their very origins and birth (Jer 1:5, 7; Is 49:1). Fuller helpfully comments on this:

> Birth or conception is the moment when God predestines and elects a prophet in preparation for a concrete role in salvation history. It would probably be wrong to say that it is the actual moment of sending, for alongside the conception/birth motif we also have in the prophetic tradition the call story (*Berufungsgeschichte*). At the birth the call is planned and announced; at the call it is set in motion. Here, perhaps, we see the factors that led to the retrojection of the Son of God christology to the moment of Jesus' birth, as has happened in the infancy narratives. The Matthean and Lukan annunciations express this retrojected christology in narrative form.[10]

Finally, I should say something about the "wisdom Christology" which apparently took root rather early in some Christian circles. The series of "Q" sayings, found in Matthew and Luke, clearly identify Jesus as Holy Wisdom herself speaking (Mt 11:19/Lk 7:35; Mt 11:25–30/Lk 10:21–22; Mt 23:34/Lk 11:49; Mt 23:37–39/Lk 13:34–35). The location of these sayings in "Q" argues for their antiquity. Pheme Perkins even goes further: ". . . the ubiquity of wisdom materials in the teaching of Jesus makes it difficult to suppose that all such sayings were later accretions."[11] Jesus preached a feminine *Sophia*-God(?). Most scholars think that the wisdom tradition, as found for example in Proverbs, lies behind this early wisdom Christology (8:1–6). That is, Jesus is being depicted as God's holy Wisdom, a kind of street preacher, calling out to humanity. In the wisdom tradition, there is no indication of divine pre-existence; wisdom is God's firstborn, but still she is a creature!

Many scholars think that originally it was the risen Jesus who was identified with holy Wisdom; only later was this retrojected back onto the earthly Jesus. Some early "wisdom hymns" would seem to indicate as much (Phil 2:6–11; Heb 1:3–4). In these hymns, the focus is upon the exalted Jesus as exercising the functions of divine wisdom. But Pheme Perkins seems to suggest that Jesus may have been seen as Wisdom throughout his earthly career. She points to the tradition in which Wisdom withdraws from the humanity that refuses to receive her (cf Prv 1:28; 1 Enoch 42:1–2; 4 Ezra 5:10). So, too, the rejected Jesus withdraws, especially in his death; wisdom will send no more messengers (Mt 23:38–39/Lk 13:35). In any case, there is an evident application of this title to Jesus in the New Testament as a description for his entire career (1 Cor 8:6; Col 1:15–20). This wisdom Christology is rather significant, because it associates the rather "high" functions of divine wisdom with Jesus: co-creating, planning, and directing the universe itself. For this reason, Pheme Perkins says that the wisdom hymns "represent . . . a crucial stage in the development of christology, since these hymns begin to articulate the special relationship that exists between Jesus and God."[12]

A Tentative Evaluation

A number of older hypotheses have been brought forward from the more "radical" days of biblical scholarship as a way of explaining this rather remarkable development of Christology. A rather common one was the *Hellenization thesis*, according to which the early Christians borrowed freely from the Greco-Roman religious ideologies, thus in effect creating Christology. The "weak" form of this thesis raises no objections from scholars today—namely, that early Christianity was indeed influenced by Greco-Roman patterns of thought. The titles "Lord" and "Son of God" were used by the Hellenistic culture for their religious heroes. The Gnostics of the second century A.D. even had a Wisdom-myth, whereby divine Wisdom descends to earth. This may reflect an earlier wisdom tradition that could have influenced the wisdom Christology we noted above.

The "strong" form of the Hellenization thesis, however, has failed to win many adherents. This would argue that Christology is simply a falsification of the earthly Jesus, a kind of unfounded projection onto Jesus of Greco-Roman religious titles. There are many problems with this "projection" thesis in this bald form. Probably most fundamentally, it fails to come to terms with the substantial elements of continuity between the earthly and the risen Jesus, and ignores the significance of the Easter events. One gains the impression that this earlier thesis was unduly influenced by the rationalism and a-religiousness of the historical sciences as they were being practiced in the nineteenth century. Furthermore, the parallels between the early Christian Christology and the Greco-Roman ideology are never completely identical. Christians profess belief in a crucified human being who has been raised. The Christian stress on crucifixion and Jesus' humanity is somewhat different from the stress on the prodigious and suprahuman character of the heroes of the Greco-Roman cults. Finally, there is a kind of "hidden" denigration of the Greco-Roman cults in the strong Hellenization thesis. Implicit is the view that the religious belief of the Hellenists is simply crude, primitive, and false. Thus, to show lines of borrowing from this is, *ipso facto*, to discredit Christology. But this rests on the unwarranted and "unecumenical" presupposition that divine revelation could not also be present within the Greco-Roman world. If one were to think more ecumenically, one might argue that the early Christians saw many of the religious dreams of the Greco-Roman world illustrated in the remarkable career of their own Jesus from Nazareth. [13]

Others, without denying the validity of Christology, have proposed that what we are witnessing is a kind of cognitive development among the early Christians, from the more practical/functional categories of thought on to the more sophisticated and ontological modes of speculation. That is, the earliest Christologies are focused upon what Jesus does for people— his saving deeds. As we move on toward the wisdom Christology and the pushing of the Christological titles back into the entire career of Jesus we can notice a more ontological attempt to describe Jesus' very being itself. In the cognitive realm, speculation on being follows acquaintance with action, so it is said. But it can be asked whether this is not to impose back onto the texts a kind of alien metaphysics, which looks at being in abstract, static, and unrelational terms. Whether the scriptural authors ever separated being and action, Christology and salvation is highly questionable. It might be more realistic to speak, not of a simple shift from action to being (or from "practical" thought to "speculative" thought), but of a constant dialectic between action and thought, practice and theory, as psychosocial criticism is recommending. [14]

It is probably best to argue, with the majority of biblical scholars, that early Christianity's Christology represents the clarification of the meaning and significance of who Jesus was and is. It is the explicitation of what was to a great extent implicit in the career of Jesus; a sort of "depth" dimension of Jesus is gradually brought to light. Thus, the messiah-Christology clarifies Jesus' role as the advocate and mediator of the divine Kingdom, the new community of justice, love and peace. It does not project onto Jesus what he was not, but clarifies what he was and remains. So, too, the *Kyrios*-Christology clarifies the element of divine authority present in the man Jesus as earthly and risen. As he spoke and acted under the inspiration of the Divine Mystery, so he continues so to "speak" and "act." The Son of God, sending-of-the-son-pattern, and wisdom Christologies also clarify the presence of the Divine Mystery in Jesus—he is a man through whom the Divine works on our behalf. Christology did not transmute Jesus, either from a mere man into a God, or, worse, from a mere man into a kind of demi-god. It clarified aspects of what he was as earthly and remains as risen.

A Note on the Virginal Conception Stories

We have alluded to these stories above, and this is the appropriate place to offer some more observations on this rather difficult problem. As the reader will likely know, these stories are found only in Matthew (1:18–25) and Luke (1:31–35). The Christological intent behind them appears to be similar to some of the Christologies we have already surveyed: by proclaiming that Jesus was conceived by the Holy Spirit they want to show that Jesus was regarded as and was Son of God throughout the entirety of his earthly career. They witness, then, to early Christianity's belief in the Divine Presence throughout Jesus' life. In this sense, the virginal conception stories are equivalent to the Son of God Christology above. Through the genealogy and the angel's message to Joseph, Matthew expresses Jesus' Davidic descent (his messianic role) and the Spirit's role in his conception. Luke expresses the same two themes in the message of Gabriel to Mary. Thus, Matthew and Luke appear to be dramatically expressing the early kerygma proclaimed by Paul: "descended from David according to the flesh . . . made Son of God in power according to the Spirit of holiness" (Rom 1:3–4).

The difficult question of the historicity of these stories is another matter. As Raymond Brown wisely puts it, "The scientifically controllable evidence leaves an unresolved problem."[15] The arguments for and against seem to balance if not cancel one another. For example, on the negative side first, it is now agreed that the citation from Isaiah (7:14) means little historically: it does not historically refer to Jesus, but to a descendant of David; it may also not envision a virginal conception at all, but rather a woman, now a virgin, who will later normally conceive. The earlier sections of the New Testament, moreover, know nothing of a virginal conception and some sections even seem to presuppose a natural conception (namely, the genealogies). Some Christian writers prior to the second century even argue for a normal conception, making no mention of a virginal conception. Post-second century authors, however, do assume a virginal interpretation, but they are heavily influenced by a late Hellenistic antagonism to the flesh, pitting it against the beauty of the "spirit." Perhaps most basically, Joseph Fitzmyer has argued that these stories concern "what has been called Mary's *virginitas ante partum* [virginity before birth]; nothing is said in them about the mode of her giving birth to Jesus (= *in partu*)."[16] This leaves the door open to an interpretation which proposes that Mary was a virgin only prior to her conception of Jesus.

Let us move to the positive arguments. We appear to have old traditions in these stories, taken over by both Matthew and Luke, for the two agree on little else. The parallels with the pagan religions are not very close: the New Testament does not speak of actual physical descent by God or physical insemination. This means that we cannot simply trace the stories to Hellenistic sources. Further, the New Testament seems to record a tradition of Jesus' "illegitimate birth" (cf Mk 6:3; Jn 8:41; Mt 1:18). Raymond Brown comments on this: "Irregularity of conception may have been rumored all along; and the virginal conception may represent not only a development in Christology but also an attempt to explain the irregularity in light of two fixed attitudes, namely, a respect for the image of the blameless, pious parents (Matt. 1:19; Luke 1:35, 42) and an insistence on Jesus' freedom from sin (II Cor. 5:21; I Pet. 2:22; Heb. 4:15; John 8:46)—a freedom which may have been judged irreconcilable with sinful conception."[17] Perhaps, too, Brown wonders, there was a family tradition on this matter which supported this "explanation" of the charge of illegitimacy.

In matters such as this, where the historical evidence can be argued either way, the interpreter will normally fall back upon larger philosophical and theological assumptions to arrive at a tentative "resolution." On the "positive" side we could propose, like Karl Rahner, that the virginal conception illustrates the radical novelty of the Jesus event, the departure from the normal mode of human reproduction being a dramatic "sign" that history is now taking a new turn in Jesus. Rahner's proposal takes the postbiblical tradition very seriously, which from the second century is virtually unanimous in its belief in a literal virginal conception and virgin birth, Mary remaining a virgin throughout her life.

On the negative side, however, we might propose that the novelty of the Jesus event does not need a virginal conception to support it, and to the extent that a virginal conception legitimates taboos about sexuality, it would seem to contradict Jesus' God, who loves all created realities. The real novelty in Jesus is love, justice, and peace. Only by a rather uncompelling logic can one show how they require virginal conception. A loving conception and birth for the sake of justice and peace—these would seem quite coherent with the thrust of the Jesus event. We could add to this the well documented fact that the later Church's emphasis upon a virgin birth seems to reflect a late Hellenistic bias against sexuality, rather than a carefully thought out biblical view of celibacy, at least in part.

I would suggest we seem to lack any human experiential analogy to a literal virgin birth. Our own experience has no way of even partially grasping what such a reality might mean, and so the "doctrine" runs the danger of disclosing no really saving meaning for us. This does not mean that I am denying the miraculous, the divine penetration of reality which can restore

and renew all things created. But I would view the miraculous, with many
scholars today, as occurring through and intensifying our human and created processes, not as negating them (which a virginal conception seems to
suggest). We are clearly at a crossroads of interpretation, on both historical
and more fundamental theological grounds. For this reason I think we can
be justified in holding, with Joseph Fitzmyer, that the virginal conception
is a *Glaubensaussage* (affirmation of faith in the theological-Christological
meaning) whose historicity is, for now, in need of more study.[18]

Some Observations "Prompted" by Psychosocial Criticism

This is the appropriate place to offer some further observations on the
development we have surveyed from the point of view of psychosocial criticism. Up to this point we have followed an historical approach, chiefly because only biblical scholars who pursue an historical approach seem to
have concerned themselves with this area of Christological development.
But my reading of psychosocial criticism, particularly the South American
Jon Sobrino and the American feminist theologian Rosemary Radford
Ruether, has at least "stimulated" the comments which follow.[19]

Possibly the first thing that psychosocial criticism suggests is that we
need to de-privatize our understanding of the early Christological development. Just as the earthly Jesus did not simply preach God, but the *King-
dom/community* of God, so we might fruitfully ask whether early
Christology simply shrank the Jesus event to a proclamation of Jesus himself, forgetting the community to which he was committed. Paraphrasing
Bultmann, did only the Proclaimer become the Proclaimed, or did his new
community for justice, love and peace continue to be proclaimed too?
Here I would suggest that we need to rethink creatively the collective
punch implicit in many of the early Christological titles.

For example, the title "messiah" makes little sense without a "Kingdom" or "community" for which the messiah works to perform God's work
of justice, love and peace. For a messiah is the Kingdom's advocate and
mediator, the one through whom it makes a beachhead within history. If
this is true, then by proclaiming Jesus the Messiah, earthly and risen, early
Christianity is proclaiming its belief in the community of justice, peace and
love, to which Jesus was committed and which still continues now through
Jesus' risen advocacy. Paradoxically enough, if this is accurate, then early
Christology does not simply shrink its belief to Jesus alone. The Jesus community is also a crucial part of this belief.

We might fruitfully apply a similar de-privatization to the other Christological titles too. "Lord," for example, connotes authority, it is true. But
in the normal sense of the Jewish and Greco-Roman worlds, it connotes

either God's or the ruler's authority over a kingdom. If early Christianity proclaims Jesus the "Lord," it would seem to be affirming belief in the community of justice, love and peace over which he "reigns." Jesus' lordship and Jesus' community must be critically thought together. The connection of the title "Son of God" with the royal messiah ideology would seem to mean that there is a social and collective punch to this title too. One's sonship is demonstrated by one's care for the community over which one rules. As Son of God, Jesus' community of justice, love and peace is believed by early Christians to be one in which a filial obedience to God holds sway. Likewise, the "sending-of-the-son-pattern," with its connections to the prophets, indicates a social punch to this Christological description too. As the prophets were sent on behalf of the community of Israel, so early Christians believed that Jesus was sent on behalf of God's new community of justice, love, and peace. The wisdom Christology, with its rather cosmic implications, captures this collective punch to Christology even more radically. As Holy Wisdom, God's outreach to the world at large is occurring through Jesus. This de-privatization of the early Christology helps us grasp that Christology is not a myopic shrinking of the Jesus event to the individual Jesus himself, forgetting his work on behalf of the Kingdom of justice, love and peace and on behalf of the world itself. Here we have substantial continuity, not only between the earthly Jesus and the kerygmata, but between the Kingdom and the kerygmata.

A second lesson suggested by psychosocial criticism is that we need to recapture rather creatively the "critical edge" that may be hidden in the early Christology. To have recaptured the collective punch of the Christological titles, to have de-privatized them, is already to recapture anew the early Christology's critical edge. Christology is Kingdom-ology, community-building on behalf of justice, love, and peace. It is attempting to create (or better: co-create) a community where the messiah and lord of the kingdom can reign. But we also glimpse something of this critical edge at work in the process of "retrojecting" the titles back into the ministry of the earthly Jesus. This was an important and even crucial step in the history of Christianity, for it meant that these exalted titles—from whatever source they may have come: the royal messiah ideology, the Greco-Roman cults, etc.—were now qualified by their reference to the earthly and crucified Jesus of Nazareth. Whatever else a messiah might have meant, it now meant for Christians the one who suffers on behalf of justice, love, and peace. Lordship was now a peculiar kind of lordship: not paternalistic and arbitrary power, but the power of service as reflected in the life of the crucified one. In other words, these titles are now critical and liberating tools, at least to some extent.

But this brings us to a third lesson suggested by psychosocial criti-

cism. The development of Christology must be seen as an ambiguous phenomenon. The application of exalted titles to Jesus, whether earthly or
risen, runs the danger of assimilating him too neatly to the religious and
secular powers who name themselves with similar titles. The novelty of
the Jesus event—as a disclosure of justice, love, and peace—can become
toned down, turned into a kind of legitimation of the *status quo*. This is an
especially acute problem when the original Jesus followers, many of whom
are of the oppressed classes, are succeeded by more "successful" Christians. Then the Christological titles, which could function in a liberating
way, can become tools of oppression in their turn. We at least need to be
aware of this ambiguity. Later Christian history confirms its danger, and
there are even some indications of its presence in the New Testament. Already in the two stage Christology, the precious title of "servant," which
is so evocative of what Jesus was about (Acts 3:13, 26; 4:27, 30), is confined
only to the first phase of his career and found inappropriate for his risen
existence. Why is this? Is the loss of the critical edge of the Jesus event
beginning already this early? Some feminist scholars point out, in this regard, that John's Gospel substitutes the more masculine *Logos* for the
feminine *Sophia*/Wisdom of the early wisdom Christologies (cf John's prologue). Is this substitution a mere curiosity, or does it reflect a loss of Jesus'
radical stance toward the liberation of women, a kind of repatriarchaliza-
tion of the Jesus event?

Finally, psychosocial criticism has a word of criticism for historically-
oriented biblical scholars, too. It suggests that the search for the earliest
Christology and the lines of continuity between the earthly and the risen
Christ has been conducted too narrowly, as a search for exalted titles and
their retrojection back onto Jesus. Without denying the validity of this hypothesis, we might also search for the development of Christology in the
emergence of the Jesus movement itself, as a movement on behalf of justice, love, and peace. The relative success of the Jesus movement in carrying this forward is perhaps a deeper thread of continuity between the
pre-Easter and post-Easter Church, and is perhaps the real matrix of the
emergence of Christology itself. Howard Clark Kee, among biblical scholars, has pointed to this thread of continuity by way of the strong note of
inclusiveness which cuts across the pre-Easter and post-Easter strands of
the New Testament. As he expresses it, "The open attitude toward persons
considered outsiders by Jewish standards permeates both the Gospels and
the letters of Paul, and it is a central theme in Acts as well."[20] And this inclusiveness links up with the picture of Jesus which we sketched in an earlier chapter, as one who admits all into the new community. The
continuing belief in the availability of the divine power of justice, love, and
peace, which makes such inclusiveness possible, is perhaps the real thread

of continuity between the earthly and the risen Jesus, between Jesus' Kingdom and post-Easter Christianity.

The Soteriological Dimension

Until relatively recently, historical-critical studies have paid scant attention to the soteriological dimension of the Jesus event. Attention has been focused rather narrowly on the "exalted" titles which were attributed to Jesus, ignoring his "saving" work on behalf of others. Yet we know that there developed in the early Christian communities a belief in Jesus as the Savior, the one who sets people free. It would appear that Christology (penetrating what the Jesus event means) and soteriology (penetrating how that event sets us "free") developed alongside one another in the early tradition. For example, it seems clear that the early titles we have surveyed carried a saving meaning. "Messiah," "Son of God," etc., connoted Jesus' saving action on behalf of others, if we pay heed to our earlier observations from psychosocial criticism. Messiahship is integrally linked to work on behalf of the Kingdom, as are the other titles. Further, the Easter experiences themselves were saving events: through these moments of grace early disciples were revitalized, experienced forgiveness, and "tasted" something of the healing power of the Jesus event.

It would also appear that in the earliest stages the Christian community turned to the Psalms and wisdom literature, where the pattern of suffering and vindication is regularly featured (cf Pss 22 and 69). As with the suffering righteous, so Jesus' cross was seen as an act on behalf of others, from which Christians could derive comfort, for God vindicates the righteous (cf 1 Cor 15:3). Eventually early Christians turned to the suffering servant theology of Isaiah (cf 53:10–11), seeing Jesus' cross as an atoning death on behalf of others (cf Mk 14:24; 10:45; 1 Cor 11:24). Very clearly these latter texts express a belief in Jesus' cross as a saving act which is effective for others.

Most biblical scholars treat this emergent soteriology in the same way that they treat Christology: as a shift from the largely implicit saving work of the earthly Jesus to the more explicit soteriology of the post-Easter community. Like Christology, it is not an unfounded projection onto the Jesus event, but a clarification of what he was and is. Some scholars think that the earthly Jesus explicitly pointed to the saving significance of his death in an early saying in which he links his dying with the saving work of the Kingdom (Mk 14:25). Others rather more generally think that the thrust of Jesus' later ministry illustrates that Jesus attached a saving meaning to his work and death. He very likely knew that prophets die on behalf of their work; he very likely was aware of the suffering righteous tradition of the

Psalms and wisdom literature. But most importantly, his work for the
Kingdom is through and through a saving work for others. This is clearly
enough evidence to indicate that the later explicit soteriology is rooted in
the earthly Jesus. Apparently the Easter experiences, coupled with reflection on Jesus' life and cross, enabled some to grasp more clearly this soteriological dimension: they became convinced that the divine saving work
was and is a dimension of the Jesus event.

All of this illustrates that we cannot separate Christology from soteriology, just as we cannot separate the earthly Jesus from his saving work.
The two dimensions need to be seen as interpenetrating and dialectically
related. As the earthly Jesus worked on behalf of the Kingdom, so he acted
to save and liberate from sin and oppression. So, too, the risen Christ was
not only inaugurating the Kingdom now as Messiah, but also setting people free from their sins. Christology and soteriology are the right and left
hands of the one same event.

As we can see from the above, special attention was paid to Jesus'
cross as the saving event *par excellence*. But as we can also see from the
above, it was the entire Jesus event that was seen to be salvific. Perhaps
this teaches us that we should view the cross as the dramatic climax of the
work of suffering love on behalf of others that Jesus did. This seems to be
the intent behind the suffering righteous and suffering servant traditions.

What does the Jesus event save us from? A very early formula says
that he "died for our sins" (1 Cor 15:3). Very likely we should take the word
"sin" in the Jewish sense as a collective one for any kind of transgression of
the covenant. In this sense, anything that blocks our relationship with the
Divine and with one another is sin. If this is true, then the saving power
of the Jesus event is a healing of our disordered relationships.[21]

Paul's Contribution to Christology

Anyone who has wrestled with the enormous amount of literature on
Paul put out by biblical scholars will quickly know that it is hazardous to
try to summarize his contribution to the forward movement of Christology.
Paul is a practical, pastoral person, with enormous theological insight. He
is "on the move," clarifying and working out his positions as he confronts
various pastoral problems in his ministry. It is probably this almost diz-
zying movement and shifting in Paul which makes it difficult for scholars
to attempt anything like a "synthesis" of his work. What follows here is not
in any sense a "synthesis." Paul very likely didn't have one. I will rather
try to present three "foci" or themes, which seem to be central, cutting
across much or all of what he wrote. I think these three foci will be readily

apparent to anyone who has worked through both Paul's letters themselves, and the scholarly literature.

Paul as Continuator of Early Christology

In an earlier day of biblical scholarship it was fashionable to view Paul
as the Hellenist who distorted the humble, earthly Jesus, turning him into
another one of the many Greco-Roman "divine men." But as we have seen,
the extreme form of the Hellenization thesis suffers from too many difficulties to be really credible. No, Paul does not distort Jesus, but basically
continues the thrust of the Christology of the earliest disciples. This continuation of the early Christ-proclamation is, in fact, a constant focus running throughout his project.

Paul only gives us the barest details of Jesus' earthly career (his birth,
Davidic descent, and betrayal: Gal 4:4; Rom 1:3; 1 Cor 11:23–25). He
speaks most often of the crucified and risen one, using this as a designation
for who Jesus was and is. The crucified and risen one—this is the center of
Paul's theology, as it was for the earliest Christology. Note the prominence
of this designation of Jesus in his kerygmatic formulae (Rom 1:3f; 4:24f;
8:34; 10:9; 1 Cor 15:3–11; 1 Thes 1:10), and his favored use of the title
"Lord" to designate both the crucified and risen one throughout his writings (some two hundred and thirty occurrences in all: cf especially 2 Cor
4:5; 1 Cor 12:3; Phil 2:11). Apparently his own conversion experience (Gal
1:11–20) existentially convinced him of the truth of the early Lord-Christology we surveyed above. He knew the "authority" of Jesus, the one now
living but who also lived and died, as a matter of personal experience.

Albert Schweitzer's great contribution to Pauline studies was to show
that Paul was not dominated by a relatively modern and late "Protestant"
fascination over the question of his own salvation, which can lead to an undue emphasis upon Paul's doctrine of justification by faith alone. Rather,
like the early Christologies, Paul moves within the apocalyptic-eschatolog-
ical framework of early Christianity. The Jesus event has inaugurated the
shift of the aeons. Jesus' resurrection "confirms" that the Divine is now
really establishing the Kingdom within history. As Schweitzer put it, "If
Jesus has risen, that means, for those who dare to think consistently, that
it is now already the supernatural age."[22] The divine and the human are
now "interpenetrating" as a result of the Jesus event. Schweitzer argued
that this divine-human interpenetration has given birth to a "Christ-mysticism": "The fundamental thought of Pauline mysticism runs thus: 'I am
in Christ; in Him I know myself as a being who is raised above this sensuous, sinful, and transient world and already belongs to the transcendent;

in Him I am assured of resurrection; in Him I am a child of God.' "[23] We don't need to go along with Schweitzer's needless denigration of this world. But his fundamental insight—that the Divine has radically acted in Jesus to renew the world—is capital. This is but another way of saying that Paul proclaims the early Lord-Christology we spoke of before. In the end, Paul agrees with and continues the early Christology of the Church.

Rediscovering the "Agape" of the Jesus Event

One of the fronts against which Paul had to struggle was that of the "Judaizing" trend within early Christianity. The term "Judaizer" is perhaps not very felicitous. It is a scholarly neologism, and so I will use it here, but we must be careful to weed out any implicit anti-Semitism in the term. After all, Jesus was a Jew and he preached many of the great themes of Judaism. The scholarly term refers to those Jewish Christians (perhaps non-Christians too?) who attempted to impose customs and theologies which were deemed incompatible with the Jesus event in Paul's mind. Paul apparently clashes with different kinds of Judaizers, as we learn from his correspondence. In Galatians, it is Jewish Christian missionaries who stress ritual prescriptions as still binding on Christians, whether Jew or Gentile: circumcision, dietary regulations, sabbath and festival observance, etc. (cf Gal 3:6–18; 4:8–11). In Philippians, the Judaizers preach the binding character of circumcision and the law, and the need to strive for perfection with their aid (3:2—4:3). In 2 Corinthians, these Judaizers do not stress the law as binding, but the Jewish covenant and Judaism's role in God's plan of salvation (11:22; 12:11f; 12:1–9; 3:4–18).[24]

Schweitzer had noted long ago that it was when Paul was confronting the Judaizers that he hammered out what has come to be known as his "doctrine of justification by faith." Some, therefore, have called this doctrine a "corollary" of his thought. It is a corollary, because it is genuinely rooted in his Christology. But it is only corollary, so some say, because it is not his normal way of describing the Jesus event.[25] In any case, I would suggest that this "doctrine" enshrines a crucial rediscovery of Paul's, a genuinely capital insight into the Jesus event as we have come to know it so far.

Basically, what Paul seems to be arguing (and that is, unfortunately, the right word!) is this. Against those who would limit God's gracious love in some manner (God only loves the faithful follower of torah, God only loves the circumcised, etc.), Paul is convinced that God's love is universal, gratuitous, and therefore unconditional. What saves is faith in this, not attachment to torah and certain prescriptions. This note of universalism surfaces most clearly in Paul's use of an early baptismal formula: "There does not exist among you Jew or Greek, slave or freeman, male or female. All are one in Christ Jesus" (Gal 3:28). In his own way, Paul has recaptured Jesus' insight: the Father's "sun" rises on all, the bad and the good, the just and the unjust (Mt 5:45). The crucified and risen Lord is one who now reigns on behalf of this universal love, not on behalf of elitism and conditional love.

We can only guess at how Paul arrived at this insight. Perhaps the unmerited character of his own conversion convinced him of God's unconditional/unmerited love. He probably knew, too, that according to the law a crucified man is accursed (cf Dt 21:23), and yet Jesus the crucified is now the Lord. Did this mean that the law was in some way annulled? In any case, Paul's struggle with the Judaizers illustrates that early Christianity was struggling with the radical implications of the Love-God disclosed in the Jesus event. Basically, Paul remained faithful to the thrust of the Jesus event in this regard.

This was apparently an enormously difficult insight to come to and stick with. The same insight killed Jesus, and very likely it killed Paul too.[26] Unfortunately, too, in most of his anti-Judaizing letters (Galatians, Philippians, 2 Corinthians) he is not really fair to Judaism, for he fails to distinguish between those elements of torah which are compatible with Jesus' God and those which are not. He seems to modify his position somewhat in his later Letter to the Romans. There he is fairer to Jewish tradition and to the Jewish-Christian wing of the Christian movement. He argues that the law in its unperverted state is good and God's gift (cf Rom 7). He also argues that God's unmerited love does not mean that Christians are antinomian, "doing their own thing." There is a form of law-keeping for Christians, too (3:31). This last caution would indicate that some Christians were drawing the wrong conclusions from their belief in God's unconditional love. Just as Jesus called for repentance and faith (not "doing your own thing-ism"), so Paul would seem to have worked through to an equivalent position in fidelity to Jesus.[27]

Rediscovering the Cross: Agape as Cruciform Agape

It is chiefly in his struggle with the "enthusiasts," found mainly in his 1 Corinthians (cf also Rom 12–15), that Paul hammers out the characteristic emphases of his Christology. "Enthusiasm" literally means "being in God," and both Paul and his Corinthian disciples quite literally believe that they are "in God" as a result of the Jesus event. The crucified and risen Lord, through whom God's justice, love and peace has entered history, has "unleashed" the Spirit and grace, Paul's favorite terms for the inbreaking of the Kingdom through Jesus (Rom 5:5; 6:1f; 8:9, 14; 5:21; 6:14; 2 Cor

12:9). We seem to owe the term "charism" to Paul (it is found only in 1 Peter 4:10 apart from Paul), the term he employs to describe the innumerable ways in which the Divine is now impinging upon human beings.[28]

In other words, the force of the Jesus event leads Paul to a basically charismatic understanding of the Christian life: "To each person the manifestation of the Spirit is given for the common good" (1 Cor 12:7). In Jewish tradition, the unleashing of the Spirit was associated with the Kingdom's arrival.[29] But apparently the great danger of the Corinthian community was the forgetfulness of the Jesus-like nature of Paul's charismatic Christianity. For Paul, as for the early Christology, it is the *crucified* Jesus who reigns as Lord: "I determined that while I was with you I would speak of nothing but Jesus Christ and him crucified" (1 Cor 2:2).

While Paul praises the Corinthians for their many charisms ("richly endowed with every gift of speech and knowledge": 1 Cor 1:5), he castigates them for ignoring the earthly Jesus (they say, "cursed be Jesus": 1 Cor 12:3), thereby tearing apart the earthly from the risen one. Ernst Käsemann suggests that what was occurring "was analogous to the mystery religions' preaching of the dying god restored to life, who brings along a new world in which his own people are to share."[30] Rather than viewing the resurrection as confirmation and continuation of the earthly Jesus, the Corinthians read it as a marvelous display of divine power and suprahuman gifts. Resurrection becomes the cancellation of the life and cross, not its confirmation and continuation. Rather than stretching their egos toward love, justice and peace, their egos are becoming inflated, Paul seems to be saying. In his struggle to avoid this common danger of enthusiasm, Paul hammers out the Jesus-like characteristics of authentic charismatic Christianity. In doing so, I think he creatively rediscovers the cruciform kind of agape which was disclosed in the Jesus event.

How does Paul do this? Primarily he develops a Jesus- or Christ-mysticism, according to which authentic charismatic Christianity must "reflect" the characteristics of Jesus himself. He will say that our Spirit is the Spirit of Jesus (Rom 8:9). We must reproduce Jesus' own Abba-relationship through the Spirit (Rom 8:14f). Thus, the authentic Christian takes on the character of Christ himself (1 Cor 15:45–49; 2 Cor 3:18; 4:16–5:15). As James D.G. Dunn well put it:

> The character of the experience in which Christ speaks through a man is determined by the character of the Christ who speaks. And the key fact here is that Christ remains the crucified even though he now lives by the power of God (cf. 2 Cor. 13:4). To experience the exalted Christ therefore is to experience not merely new life but new life which is life through death, life out of death, and which always retains that character.

As soon as the exalted Christ is separated from the crucified Jesus, charismatic experience loses its distinctive Christian yardstick.[31]

Union with Christ, in Paul's sense, does not so much result in lofty
peaks of spiritual excitement, but more commonly in self-giving love
through the cross of suffering on behalf of others. Union with Christ is
union with Jesus in his self-giving death (Rom 6:3–6). This is why Paul says
that he wants to share in Christ's sufferings (2 Cor 1:5). So, too, in his struggle to discern authentic charismatic phenomena, he will employ a "Jesus-
test": Do these experiences correspond to the earthly Jesus (1 Cor 9:21)?
Do they embody the love of Jesus (1 Cor 13:1–13)? Do they build up community, as Jesus' love built it up (1 Cor 14:3–5, 12, 17, 26)?

Fascinatingly, Paul's Jesus mysticism not only rediscovers the crucified nature of the love disclosed in Jesus. It also rediscovers the typical
tension in Jesus' message between the already and the not yet of
the Kingdom. Perhaps this means that when love must take the form of the
cross, then the Kingdom is not yet fully here. In any case, this tension between the Kingdom's inauguration in the Jesus event and its futurity is remarkably preserved by Paul. The typical Pauline metaphors illustrate this:
justification is already (Rom 5:1) but not yet (Gal 5:5); we are adopted as
God's children (Rom 8:15), but we still await the full adoption (Rom 8:23);
redemption is both now (Rom 3:24) and in the future (Rom 8:23); resurrection is experienced now in some way and yet its fullness will only come
at the end (Rom 6:5; 8:11, 23). Although we enjoy the Spirit now, this is
but the down payment and first installment (2 Cor 1:22; 5:5). Like Jesus,
who followed the way of the cross, we are caught in warfare between the
Spirit and the flesh, between the evil and imperfection of the present and
the groaning emergence of something wholly better (Rom 8:9; 6:19; 7:14–
18; Gal 5:6). If you will, the Corinthians had slackened this creative tension, naively forgetting the not yet, fragile, and incomplete character of
the Jesus event.

Observations Prompted by Psychosocial Criticism

In terms of the forward movement of Christology, Paul chiefly continues the Lord-Christology, as we have seen. But his creative contribution was to have qualified that Lord-Christology in two ways. Jesus reigns
as Lord, yes. But his lordship is an unfamiliar one of universal love and cruciform self-giving on behalf of others. Paul preaches a Lord-Christology
modified by agape and the cross. Here we can easily note Paul's fidelity to
the thrust of the Jesus event as a disclosure of universal love through loving
self-giving.

But, again "prompted" by psychosocial criticism, we should recognize that Paul's contribution is an ambiguous one. We must question whether he, or at least his followers, always consistently followed out the implications of his rather radical Lord-Christology. I do not think it is fair to hold that Paul tolerated slavery, as is rather commonly thought. I think that Helmut Koester has rather convincingly shown that Paul wanted Onesimus the slave "freed" by his master Philemon, not only "in the Lord" (in the spiritual realm), but also in the practical, worldly realm ("in the flesh": cf Phlm 16).[32] On this score I think Paul was consistent with the kind of love Christology in which he believed. Furthermore, Paul does not preach a privatized Christology, which shrinks the Jesus event to Jesus himself. Jesus' lordship is very much of a community and even cosmic affair: in Jesus God has inaugurated the Kingdom of justice, love and peace. This is why Paul is so concerned with love, with overcoming bitterness between the Jewish and Gentile wings of Christianity. One of Paul's favorite terms is "community" or "fellowship" (1 Cor 1:9)—this is apparently his term for what Jesus meant by the Kingdom. In the Jesus event, God has acted to revitalize our community-making powers. After all, Paul speaks of and founds "churches" (1 Cor 10:17, etc.).

It is on the issue of women that Paul seems inconsistent with his love Christology. We have already noted the great liberation text of Galatians 3:28: "There does not exist among you Jew or Greek, slave or freeman, male or female. All are one in Christ Jesus." This text is clearly consistent with Paul's love Christology, and seems to indicate that the Jesus event calls for the abolition of all structures of oppression and domination, even that of patriarchalism. Consistent with this is Paul's usual tendency to accord women the same freedom and dignity that he accords men (cf 1 Cor 7:3–4, 17–24). Furthermore, Elisabeth Schüssler Fiorenza finds strong evidence for the existence of the emancipation of women in the Pauline letters: women are Paul's co-workers, not his subordinates (Rom 16:6, 12); they are leaders of the urban house-churches in which Paul works (Phlm 2; 1 Cor 16:19); Junia is even called an "apostle" by Paul (Rom 16:7), and Phoebe (Rom 16:1f) is a "deacon" for the whole church. As Fiorenza sums up her research:

> Paul's letters indicate that women were among the most prominent missionaries and leaders of the early Christian communities. They were co-workers with Paul but did not stand under his authority. They were teachers, preachers and prophets. As leaders of house-churches they had great influence and probably presided also at the worship celebrations. If we compare their leadership with the ministry of the later dea-

conesses it is striking that their authority was *not* restricted to the ministry for women nor to specific feminine functions.[33]

Two series of texts, however, indicate that Paul (or his disciples, if these are interpolations) drew back from this emancipation of women so in keeping with his Christology (cf 1 Cor 11:2–16 and 14:33–36). The first text tells women to keep their hair covered, and to respect the differences between men and women: woman reflects man, man reflects God. The woman's covered hair reflects her "submission" to the man. Perhaps Paul does not want to offend the Jewish-Christians: in Jewish tradition loosened hair is a sign of sinfulness or uncleanness (cf Nm 4:18; Lev 13:45 *LXX*). In this case, this change on Paul's part would be of a piece with his later, more ameliorated stance toward the Jewish-Christian wing of the Jesus movement. Perhaps, too, Paul wants to distinguish Christians from the Greco-Romans: women devotees of the Isis cult wore long hair to symbolize their liberation from the dictates of official Roman society.

The second text, which is probably addressed solely to wives, tells them not to speak in the worship assemblies of the Church. Apparently Paul thinks that married women can ask their husbands for spiritual "food." Unmarried women, presumably, can still speak in the Churches. The same text seems to exalt the unmarried woman because of her "celibate" status. Perhaps something of Paul's own preference for the unmarried state lies under the surface here.

It would appear that in these cases Paul is more concerned about the Christian movement's acceptance by the wider world than he is about the love Christology which he so beautifully preaches. We have no way of knowing whether the women accepted his injunctions. We do know that these texts became an important stage on the way toward the fuller patriarchalization of the Christian movement. In this sense, the radicality of Paul's love Christology was greatly diminished.

The Soteriological Dimension

Paul's soteriology is always the other side of his Christology. As he probes the Jesus event (Christology), he increasingly discovers its power to set us free from sin and evil (soteriology). We find the earlier soteriological tradition repeated by Paul: Jesus' death is an atoning one for us (Rom 5:6, 8; 8:32; 14:15; 2 Cor 5:15, 21; Gal 1:4; 2:20; 3:13; 1 Thes 5:10). But, as Reginald Fuller suggests, there are some central images which Paul uses to describe the saving power of the Jesus event.[34]

"Redemption," an image borrowed from the manumission of slaves, stresses the note of liberation and freedom in the Jesus event. The Jesus event unleashes an experience of freedom from sin and the perverted use of the law (Rom 3:24). Using a similar manumission imagery, Paul will speak of Christ "buying us back" from sin and slavery. This seems to refer to the cost involved in the shedding of blood (1 Cor 6:19–20; 7:23)[35] and to the pain ("curse") Jesus suffered from the perverted use of the law (Gal 3:10).

"Justification," which we have already seen, can be viewed as one of Paul's soteriological images. Apparently it means that the Jesus event unleashes a universal agape, freeing us from barriers and divisions, such as Jew and Gentile. For Paul, justification is a dimension of the eschatological breakthrough of the Jesus event (cf Rom 3—11). Paul's final great image is that of "reconciliation," which has given rise to the modern word "atonement" (at-one-ment). Apparently this is derived from battle imagery: two opposing sides are in warfare and are now brought together. Again, Paul is thinking of the universal agape of the Jesus event, which has united Jew and Gentile in a new way (cf 2 Cor 5:19; Rom 5:10).

What is important here is to grasp the linkage between Paul's Christology and his soteriology as two sides of a dialectic. If Jesus' breakthrough is a lordship of universal love, then it frees us from lovelessness and injustice. If that lordship is one of a cruciform love, then it is costly and painful. The Jesus event is both an entrance into a new sphere of love (Christology), and freedom from an old sphere of lovelessnes (soteriology).

Gospel Christology

Mark

Mark, like Paul, stresses the *crucified* character of the risen one. Apparently, as the cases of both Paul and Mark illustrate, there was a very real danger within the early stages of the Christian movement of forgetting and annulling the cross, the dimension of suffering for justice, peace and love, in the Jesus event. Jesus was being understood in the terms of "power" and "force" so typical of the political and religious thinking of the time. Whether Mark's problem comes from Jewish-Christian circles, wanting to make Jesus into a royal Messiah, or from Greek Christians who want to make him into a "divine" and "powerful" hero, we cannot tell.[36] In any case, Mark attempts to narrate a different story about the manner in which the Divine comes to us in Jesus.

The first chapters of Mark, filled with miracle stories, clearly express the belief that the divine power is at work within Jesus. But beginning with the eighth chapter, and then throughout, the divine power begins to be understood in a radically new way. Jesus indicates to Peter that his mission is to suffer: he is a suffering Messiah, not a royal, kingly one (8:27–33). His divine "sonship," revealed at the transfiguration (9:7), is finally clarified when the centurion sees Jesus on the cross and confesses: "Clearly this man was the Son of God!" (15:39). The theme of divine sonship, which begins the Gospel at Jesus' baptism (1:1–16) and links the two major parts of the Gospel together (1—7, 8—16), is really the theme of a suffering messiahship. Even as a miracle worker, this is the messianic secret that runs under the surface. The resurrection event does not annul this suffering messiahship: the Gospel ends by omitting any resurrection appearances, thus warding off the tendency to identify the Divine disclosed in Jesus with royal and flashy power, rather than suffering love.

Matthew

Matthew (like Luke) does not dwell upon Christology in the narrow sense, as a telling of the story of the individual Jesus himself. In Matthew (and Luke), something of the fuller ramifications of the Jesus event come more fully to the surface. That is, the Jesus event is not only the breakthrough of God into the life of the individual man Jesus. It is also the breakthrough of a new possibility of community-making, through living a life rooted in the justice, love, and peace now made available to us through Jesus. As Jesus was, as earthly, and remains, as risen, the advocate of the Kingdom, so Matthew (like Luke) seems fascinated by the community-making implications of the Jesus event. A new power of love in the community-forming sense has occurred through the Jesus event—this is Matthew's (and Luke's) central intuition, an intuition that is rather more subterranean in Mark (note his stress on discipleship, chapters 9—10). Note a new use of the word "Church" in these writings (Mt 16:18; Acts 15:1; 15:22, etc.).

Matthew shows his interest in the community-making power of the Jesus event by using, not Jesus' death, but his ministry of teaching as the central issue in the Gospel. Note how he places Jesus' teaching ministry in the center, framed by the birth at the beginning and the death and resurrection at the end. The frame is just that, a frame. The real center is Jesus the teacher of a new community. Jesus' birth presages the teaching ministry; the death and resurrection confirms it and continues it. The core of this teaching ministry is the five discourses (Mt 5—26), which detail the new kind of community or "Church" made possible by Jesus. Basically

Matthew pictures Jesus as calling for a new, perfect righteousness (5:48), which keeps the law through radical, selfless love (5:43–48). Behind this is probably Matthew's attempt to distinguish the Christian movement from the Judaism from which Christians were probably recently expelled.

The image of Jesus which emerges here is quite special. Because he founds the community which keeps the law perfectly, Jesus is the fulfillment of the Jewish prophecies (Mt 1:22; 2:15; 4:14–16; 8:17; 12:17–21, etc.). He is not a new Moses (what Moses founded is now being "replaced"), but a new embodiment of God's Holy Wisdom preaching the higher righteousness. Like Holy Wisdom, he invites people to take upon themselves her easy burden (11:28–30; cf Sir 24:18). Like the wise and righteous ones of old, he will suffer the fate of the suffering righteous (cf Sir 22). But through his resurrection he breaks the cycle of the wise servants of God being crushed (27:51–53). His "higher way" still continues now to be a possibility for all (25:31–46; 28:20).[37]

Luke-Acts

Luke-Acts continues this "wider" kind of Christology typical of Matthew, but again in a unique way. This writing emerges from the Christian movement taking root in Asia Minor, the Greco-Roman wing of early Christianity. Matthew appears to come from Syria, where Jewish-Christian relations were still a very strong issue (perhaps Mark too?). In any case, Luke-Acts represents a new turning toward the Roman world, a new openness to it. It wants to illustrate how Christianity is an integral part of the world of the time (= Roman Empire). Thus, together, Luke and Acts describe the unfolding of God's plan as it gradually reaches out and embraces Jerusalem (Luke) and moves on to embrace the Empire (Acts). The work of God is announced in the Old Testament, proclaimed by John the Baptist, founded in history through Jesus, and slowly moves on from Jerusalem to Rome to "conquer" the world.

Luke's Gospel, then, should be read as focusing upon Jesus as the founder of "God's new movement" within history. The birth narrative announces this movement (1:5—2:51). The center of the Gospel portrays Jesus as the "center" of human history, the new axis upon which it turns. The famous Lucan travel narrative (Lk 9:51—18:15) depicts the Jesus movement slowly moving toward Jerusalem—if you will, slowly "conquering" the world. Throughout, Jesus is the "divine man" attested by his marvelous deeds and his many witnesses. He dies a "hero's death" in the Greco-Roman sense, and his resurrection appearances clearly confirm for his followers that he is the new center of time. In the idealized picture of early Christianity that we find in Acts, Luke shows how Peter and Paul are the great Christian heroes, imbued with the spirit of Jesus, who carry the Jesus movement to Rome.

The Jesus event, for Luke-Acts, is clearly the inauguration of a new, divine, and universal movement within history. Jesus, earthly and risen, is preeminently the founder, whose powerful spirit and presence continues in the work of his followers. Scholars will usually characterize Luke-Acts as imbued with the "universalism" of the Jesus event. If by this they mean that the Jesus event is seen as an event in which God is at work to revitalize the entire world, then it seems appropriate.[38]

The Johannine Community

John's Gospel seems to represent the attempt to integrate the special traditions of the Johannine communities, as they were developing in Syria, with the larger traditions of the Syrian Christian Church in general (as represented, for example, by Matthew). What is the Johannine Christology? Perhaps we can take our clue from the structure of the Gospel itself. The central focus of the Gospel is the "signs source," which recounts the seven crucial miracles worked by Jesus (2—11), and the passion narrative (12—20), which recounts Jesus' "farewell discourses" (13:31—17:26) and his death. This is clearly the central focus, for it is framed by the prologue which announces what is to come, and the resurrection appearances, which confirm and continue it.

In the signs or miracles source, John wants to portray Jesus as more than any ordinary human. His works are "from God" (8:47) and "from the truth" (8:37). There is this deeper, divine dimension to him, which his opponents cannot grasp. Jesus remains a human being, and he works his miracles to heal real human needs, not to display some arbitrary power. But still there is this deeper dimension. This same "double" story (of divinity in humanity) continues in the passion narrative. There Jesus speaks to his disciples of his coming exaltation, but the exaltation will come through the path of the cross. In fact, the cross is the exaltation. And Jesus' disciples will be like him: they, too, are not "from the world" (17:14), but yet they must labor in the world and likewise suffer (cf chapters 13, 15, 16, and 17).

In the light of this, we can grasp why the prologue is a true prologue: an announcement of what we have said above.[39] This hymn, probably sung in the Johannine communities, announces what the Gospel unfolds: the Divine has become flesh, Divinity has entered into humanity. Here we have the one text in the New Testament which clearly claims that the Divine which dwells in Jesus "pre-exists" in God's very own being. Pheme Perkins calls this a "quantum leap," inasmuch as it identifies God with a particular human being.[40] Certainly it does this more clearly and radically than any of the other Christologies we have surveyed. Perhaps the famous "I am" sayings, found later in the Gospel, linking Jesus with the "I am" of Moses' theophany, most clearly echo the prologue's proclamation of incarnation (cf 6:35; 8:12; 10:7, 11; 11:25; 14:6; 15:11). It is no accident, then, that two of the three New Testament texts declaring Jesus "God" are found in John (1:1; 20:28).[41] But even here, in the atmosphere of this exalted Christology, John continues his double theme of divinity in humanity. Jesus remains human, for he must be obedient to the Father (4:34), and he will suffer and die.

The pre-existence Christology probably accounts for John's unfair antagonism toward Judaism. In Jewish eyes this would seem to amount to a denial of monotheism (cf 8:44). It could also give birth to a forgetfulness of Jesus' humanity, and a kind of elitism (we are the ones who have the deepest knowledge of Jesus), two problems reflected in the Johannine letters. In fact, it seems clear that some Johannine Christians did in fact secede from the larger Christian movement (cf 1 Jn 3:10; 4:5). It is not accidental that John's Gospel was enormously popular with the later Gnostics, some of whom denied Jesus' actual humanity.[42]

Observations Prompted by Psychosocial Criticism

Clearly the central thrust of the Jesus event, as the divine disclosure in the life, death, and resurrection of Jesus, surfaces in the Gospel Christologies in a powerful and relevant manner. But again there are ambiguities and discordances which we must not hide. Let me suggest two such "ambiguities" which seem to make themselves felt.

There are the beginnings of the loss of the critical, liberating edge of the Jesus event. This surfaces in a number of ways. In Matthew, with his depiction of Christianity as the perfect righteousness, we can see the beginnings of the tendency to project outward onto outsiders the imperfections that are necessarily a part of all things human. In his case, it is the Pharisees, as representatives of Judaism, who become the scapegoats of evil. This can easily reinforce the loss of self-critique, and lead to a new oppressor-oppressed relationship. And the later history of Christian anti-Semitism confirms this. Luke rather too nicely stresses the agreement between Rome and the Jesus movement, fashioning a Christian morality which is little more than a legitimation of the morality of the Roman Empire. He absolves Rome of any guilt in Jesus' death (Lk 23), and presents the Christian movement as imbued with the piety typical of the Empire (Lk 11:1–13). In Acts, Peter's and Paul's martyrdoms by Rome are too nicely ignored. This adjustment of the Jesus event to the Empire too quickly ignores the radical conversion from all master-slave relationships entailed in the Jesus event. The elitism of the Johannine community, coupled with its tendency to lose sight of Jesus' crucified humanity, leads to a similar danger. And underlying all the Gospels is the gradual institutionalization of the Christian movement as it shifts from being a charismatic movement to being a more "organized" and structured movement. This entailed the danger of copying the structures of organization typical of the day, structures still imbued with the master-slave dialectic.

The second problem I would underscore is the gradual loss of the eschatological tension of the Jesus event. Jesus himself, as we saw, was caught in the in-between of the fragmentarily present and still awaited Kingdom. As long as the master-slave dialectic continues, so the Kingdom remains ahead of us as an unrealized dream rooted in faith in the Divine. In the earliest Christology to develop after the resurrection, this unrealized character of the Jesus event was not lost. The resurrection confirmed that the Kingdom was happening, true. But Jesus must still come in the future to complete his messianic work (cf Acts 2:36). Paul never loses this tension, as we have seen.

We can trace, under the surface of the Gospels, the beginning of the loss of this eschatological tension. The tension is still present in Mark and Matthew, but the latter's tendency to speak of Jesus as the fulfillment of the Old Testament prophecies introduces the dangerous tendency to think that the Jesus event has "completed" the work of the Kingdom. Luke likewise de-emphasizes the eager expectation of the coming of the Kingdom's fullness. The Spirit is not the sign of the last days, as for Paul, but a proof that God's work is continuing now in the Christian movement. The resurrection is not the sign of the Kingdom's breakthrough, but the proof of Jesus' messiahship. Bearing one's cross (Lk 9:23) is not a sign of the eschatological tension, but simply a daily struggle in the life of the Christian.[43] For the Johannine community, the world is already "conquered" (Jn 16:33). There is still some tension, because the Christian must suffer and labor (Jn 17) and Jesus must still work on our behalf as risen (14:12–14). But still, as Helmut Koester has suggested, it is as if the second coming (*parousia*) has already come in the death (= exaltation) of Jesus.[44]

Later New Testament Christology

I think we can characterize the later thrust of the New Testament as the attempt to hold on to and rediscover the full contours of the Jesus event. The later story is one of a struggle, a dialectic between partial and simplistic views of the Jesus event and their attempted corrections by other views and movements. On the one hand, we have the renewal of the eschatological edge of the Jesus event, as a struggle against the master-slave oppressiveness of the Empire in the Book of Revelation. This work was not without its problems, for it too quickly assimilates Jesus to a victorious and almost ruthless field marshal crushing his opponents (cf Rev 6:1–8). But it does represent a reaction to the kind of assimilation to the Empire typical of Luke-Acts. Hebrews, too, represents something of a renewal of the eschatological tension, by stressing the sufferings of the Savior (4:15; 5:7–8), and our need to await the Kingdom's coming (10:27). There is something of an attack on making Christianity into a sacral cult, too, which overlooks the role of struggle and warfare in the Christian life (9:15–17).[45]

On the other hand, we have the gradual transformation of the Jesus movement into an institutionalized organization, which is not without its legitimacy, although it is fraught with dangerous tendencies. An emphasis upon Church order, doctrine, and a bourgeois morality too assimilated to the ethics of the Empire characterize most of the remaining New Testament literature (Colossians, Ephesians, 1 and 2 Peter, 1 and 2 Timothy, and Titus). Characteristic of this is the adoption of the "house codes" or ethics typical of the day (cf 1 Tm 2:8, for men; 2:9–15, for women; 6:1–2, for slaves, etc.). Here the emancipation of women and slaves is no longer a concern. The emancipatory thrust of the Jesus event, while never denied, becomes subterranean. 1 Peter does somewhat recapture the eschatological tension of the Jesus event, together with an antagonism toward the powers of oppression. It is not by accident that this precious letter describes Jesus as a "servant" suffering on our behalf (2:22–24). Equally precious are the texts which uphold Jesus' mother Mary as a privileged focus of fidelity, truly a challenge to an androcentric culture (Lk 1:46–55; Rev 12; Jn 19:27, etc.).[46]

Soteriological Developments

Given the dialectical interplay between Christology and soteriology, it is not surprising that we find some further soteriological developments in the Gospels and later New Testament writings. The Synoptic Gospels chiefly continue the earlier soteriological reflection of the Church: they recognize that Jesus' work for the Kingdom is a saving from evil and sin (Mt 1:21; Lk 19:10), and repeat the early Church's belief that Jesus' death is an atoning act on behalf of all (Mk 14:22–25). Work for the Kingdom and salvation can never be separated for these Gospels. Interestingly, too, Luke is the first Gospel to employ the Greco-Roman term "Savior" as a title for Jesus (Lk 2:11; Acts 5:31; 13:23), a usage which occurs now and then in other writings (Eph 5:23; Phil 3:20; 2 Pt 1:1).

Perhaps one rather important soteriological development is the tendency to view death as a consequence of sin, and to confess that the Jesus event has overcome this last "enemy" of humanity. Our earliest references to this special interest in death are found in Paul (cf Rom 5:12–19; 1 Cor 15:25–28), but also show up occasionally elsewhere (2 Tm 1:10; Heb 2:14; Jn 11:26, etc.). Perhaps this reflection upon death as redeemed by Jesus represents simply another attempt in the New Testament to probe the furthest implications of Jesus' saving work. Apparently the New Testament does not mean that death is abolished by Jesus, but that it is transformed: death is no longer a consequence of sin and alienation from the Divine. The divine love flowing through the Jesus event enables us to trust that this love even transforms death, as the resurrection indicates.

In general, one gains the impression that the later soteriology of the New Testament is not particularly creative, but continues what has gone before. We do find some new imagery: in John, eternal life and light (5:24; 1:5), which is to know Jesus (Jn 17:3). "Descent to hell" imagery surfaces Jesus' solidarity with the dead (1 Pt 3:19). Later soteriology continues to witness to the belief that the Jesus event is a liberation from sin and evil, but it shares in the ambiguities of the New Testament's later Christology. The loss of the eschatological tension, the too-easy adaptation to imperial mores, the growing elitism and anti-Semitism and androcentrism—all blunted the critical edge of the redemption initiated in the Jesus event.[47]

Notes

1. Fuller, *Foundations, op. cit.*, and Hahn, *op. cit.*, represent the earlier view. Fuller has clarified his position: "I never thought of them as a straight-line, consistent development; the three types continue alongside each other, even in the same communities and in the same writers. But the three types must have emerged in that order" (Fuller and Perkins, *Who Is This Christ? op. cit.*, p. 51, n. 5). Marshall, *op. cit.*, pp. 32–42, gives a good summary of the issue. The breakthrough work pointing out the interpenetration between Judaism and Hellenism was Martin Hengel, *Judaism and Hellenism*, 2 vols. (Philadelphia: Fortress, 1974). Cf Louis H. Feldman, "Hengel's *Judaism and Hellenism* in Retrospect," *Journal of Biblical Literature* 96 (1977), 371–382. This citation is from Dunn, *Unity and Diversity, op. cit.*, p. 34.

2. Fuller and Perkins, *Who Is This Christ? ibid.*, p. 42. I will follow Fuller's helpful overview, *ibid.*, pp. 41–52, and Perkins, *ibid.*, pp. 53–66. I am only taking representative examples of early Christological developments, hoping in this way to give the reader a sense of the movement. Others take other examples. See Schillebeeckx, *Jesus, op. cit.*, pp. 403–438, for some different early Christologies.

3. *Ibid.*, p. 43.

4. Raymond E. Brown, *The Birth of the Messiah* (New York: Doubleday, 1977) pp. 29–32, 311–316. Also employed by Fuller, *ibid.*, p. 43, who refers to Brown.

5. Fuller and Perkins, *Who Is This Christ?* *op. cit.*, p. 44. See Gershom Scholem, *Sabbatai Sevi: The Mystical Messiah*, Bollingen Series XCIII (Princeton, N.J.: Princeton University, 1973), esp. pp. 8–15, 795–802, for a masterful comparison between the retrojection of "Messiah" onto Jesus and a similar retrojection onto Sabbatai in the seventeenth century. Cf also Scholem's *The Messianic Idea in Judaism and Other Essays in Jewish Spirituality* (New York: Schocken, 1971), pp. 1–36.

6. Its use in the emperor cult indicates this. When it is used in the Septuagint, it regularly refers to God's authority over his creatures. Cf Joseph A. Fitzmyer, "The Contribution of Qumran Aramaic to the Study of the New Testament," *New Testament Studies* 20 (1973–74), 386–391. Marshall, *op. cit.*, gives a good historical survey, pp. 97–110.

7. Fuller and Perkins, *Who Is This Christ?* *op. cit.*, p. 45.

8. *Ibid.*, p. 47.

9. *Ibid.*, pp. 46–47.

10. *Ibid.*, pp. 47–48.

11. *Ibid.*, p. 55. Cf E. Fiorenza, *op. cit.*, pp. 130–140, for the possibility that Jesus preached a *Sophia*-God.

12. *Ibid.*, p. 63. There is some debate in the scholarly literature whether the earliest Christologies originally referred only to the Jesus who was to come again to fulfill the Kingdom, or whether they also referred to the risen Jesus reigning now among his followers. In other words, was Jesus Messiah and Lord now as risen, or will he only be these in the end? Marshall, *op cit.*, comments on this: "While it is true that references to his parousia are more explicit than references to his present exaltation, the two aspects of his work hang together, and the attempt to discover an earliest stage at which Jesus' activity was confined to the future is a failure. It was the resurrection appearances and the continued heavenly activity of Jesus which fanned the flame of hope in the parousia" (p. 104). Cf the important study on this by Wilhelm Thüsing. "Erhöhungsvorstellung und Parusieerwartung in der ältesten nachösterlichen Christologie," *Biblische Zeitschrift* 11 (1967), 95–108, 205–222; 12 (1968), 223–240.

13. Voegelin's *Order and History*, *op. cit.*, is a stellar example of this renewed appreciation of the Greco-Roman inheritance.

14. Kasper, *op. cit.*, pp. 165–166, represents a creative rethinking of the ontic vs. the functional issue, made popular by Oscar Cullmann's *The Christology of the New Testament* (London: SCM, 1959).

15. Brown, *The Virginal Conception*, *op. cit.*, p. 66.

16. Joseph A. Fitzmyer, "Jesus the Lord," *Chicago Studies* 17 (1978), 92.

17. Raymond E. Brown, "Virgin Birth," *Interpreter's Dictionary of the Bible*, Supplement, *op. cit.*, p. 941. See also his magisterial *The Birth of the Messiah*, *op. cit.*

18. Cf Karl Rahner, "Virginitas in Partu," *Theological Investigations*, 4, *op.*

cit., pp. 143–162. There is a strong New Testament tradition of Mary's having more children than Jesus. Cf Rosemary Radford Ruether, "The Brothers of Jesus and the Virginity of Mary," *Continuum* (Spring 1969), 93–105, and F.V. Wilson, "Brothers of the Lord," *Interpreter's Dictionary of the Bible,* 1 (Nashville: Abingdon, 1962), pp. 470–472. It was Jerome who first translated Jesus' "brothers" and "sisters" into "cousins." In the Scriptures, Jesus' brothers are James, Joses/Joseph, Judas, and Simon (Mk 6:3; Mt 13:55). The texts also speak of Jesus' sisters (Mk 6:3; Mt 13:56).

19. Sobrino, *op. cit.*, has comments similar to what follows in the text. Ruether has influenced me more generally.

20. Kee, *Christian Origins, op. cit.*, pp. 91–92.

21. For an overview of the positions, see Gerald O'Collins, *What Are They Saying About Jesus?* (New York: Paulist, 1983 revision), pp. 27–39. Kasper, *op. cit.*, *passim*, represents a fine interrelation between Christology and soteriology, and espouses the positions put forth here.

22. Albert Schweitzer, *The Mysticism of Paul the Apostle* (New York: Seabury, 1968), p. 98.

23. *Ibid.*, p. 3.

24. A helpful overview of Paul's problems is in Koester, *Introduction to the New Testament,* 2, op. cit., pp. 97–145.

25. The strongest defender of the corollary thesis is E.P. Sanders, *Paul and Palestinian Judaism* (Philadelphia: Fortress, 1977). See his helpful overview of Pauline scholarship, and critical retrieval of Schweitzer, pp. 431–556. The following also somewhat displace the centrality of justification: Krister Stendahl, *Paul among Jews and Gentiles* (Philadelphia: Fortress, 1976), and Ernst Käsemann, *Perspectives on Paul* (Philadelphia: Fortress, 1971).

26. Raymond Brown has recently suggested that it was opposition from Jewish-Christians that brought about Paul's death, and Peter's. Cf Brown and John P. Meier, *Antioch and Rome: New Testament Cradles of Catholic Christianity* (New York: Paulist, 1983), pp. 122–127.

27. See Brown and Meier, *ibid.*, pp. 105–127, for evidence on Paul's change of his position in Romans.

28. The best overview of Paul's charismatic view of Christianity is Dunn, *Jesus and the Spirit, op. cit.*, pp. 199–342.

29. See W.D. Davies, *Paul and Rabbinic Judaism* (New York: Harper Torchbooks, 1965), pp. 177–226.

30. Ernst Käsemann, "For and Against a Theology of Resurrection," *Jesus Means Freedom* (Philadelphia: Fortress, 1970), p.66.

31. Dunn, *Jesus and the Spirit, op. cit.*, p. 331.

32. Koester, *Introduction,* 2, *op. cit.*, pp. 134–135.

33. Elisabeth Schüssler Fiorenza, "Women in the Pre-Pauline and Pauline Churches," *Union Seminary Quarterly Review* 33 (1978), 158; cf 153–166, for the whole. Also cf her most recent *In Memory of Her: A Feminist Theological Reconstruction of Christian Origins, op. cit.*, pp. 205–241.

34. Cf Reginald H. Fuller, "Jesus Christ as Savior in the New Testament, "

Interpretation 35 (1981), 151–154. The entire study, 145–156, is the best current overview of biblical soteriology by a leading biblical scholar.

35. For a helpful study on the soteriological significance of blood imagery, see Gerald O'Collins, "Our Peace and Reconciliation," *The Way* 22 (1982) 112–121. O'Collins is especially surprised that it does not play more of a role in the writings of liberation theology. Jesus' shedding of blood certainly underscores the opposition from oppression involved in the Jesus event, and the painful cost of his saving work.

36. For an overview, see Paul J. Achtemeier, *Mark* (Philadelphia: Fortress, 1975), and Jack Dean Kingsbury, *art. cit.*

37. I have relied on Koester, *Introduction*, 2, *op. cit.*, pp. 171–177. A fine, in-depth analysis is John P. Meier, *The Vision of Matthew: Christ, Church and Morality in the First Gospel* (New York: Paulist, 1979).

38. Cf Koester, *ibid.*, pp. 308–323. Pheme Perkins, *Reading the New Testament, op. cit.*, pp. 221–233, is quite helpful also.

39. I rely on Koester, *ibid.*, pp. 178–198. For a reconstruction of John's community in its origins and development, see the marvelous work of Raymond E. Brown, *The Community of the Beloved Disciple: The Life, Loves, and Hates of an Individual Church in New Testament Times* (New York: Paulist, 1979).

40. Fuller and Perkins, *Who Is This Christ? op. cit.*, p. 99. The important study here is James D.G. Dunn, *Christology in the Making, op. cit.* This incarnation doctrine should not be read physically, as if the Divine changes into a physical man. It rather points to the personal nature of the Divine as an outpourer of its personal being in Jesus. Cf Dunn, *ibid.*, p. 249. For the debate on this issue, which moves beween those who view the doctrine as a crude, physicalist myth and those espousing the position here, see now Michael Goulder, ed., *The Debate Continued: Incarnation and Myth* (Grand Rapids, Michigan: William B. Eerdmans, 1979).

41. The basic study is Raymond E. Brown, "Does the New Testament Call Jesus God?" *Jesus: God and Man* (Milwaukee: Bruce, 1967), pp. 1–38. The other text: Hebrews 1:9. Texts which "probably" call Jesus "God": Jn 1:18; Tit 2:13; 1 Jn 5:20; Rom 9:5; 2 Pt 1:1. Less probable: Gal 2:20; Acts 20:28; 2 Thes 1:12.

42. See Brown, *The Community, op. cit.*, for the Gnostic development in the Johannine community, pp. 145–164. Also helpful: Elaine H. Pagels, *The Johannine Gospel in Gnostic Exegesis* (Nashville: Abingdon, 1973), and M.F. Wiles, *The Spiritual Gospel: The Interpretation of the Fourth Gospel in the Early Church* (Cambridge: University Press, 1960).

43. I have relied on Koester, *Introduction*, 2, *op. cit.*, pp. 272–276, and Perkins, *Reading, op. cit.*, p. 228.

44. Koester, *ibid.*, pp. 192–193.

45. Cf Adela Yarbro Collins, *The Apocalypse* (Wilmington, Delaware: Michael Glazier, 1979), and Elisabeth Schüssler Fiorenza, *Invitation to the Book of Revelation* (Garden City, N.Y.: Doubleday, 1981), for Revelation. For Hebrews, see Koester, *ibid.*, pp. 272–276, and pp. 147–347 (for all later New Testament literature).

46. For I Peter cf Sobrino, *op. cit.*, p. 186; on the household codes, Fiorenza, *op. cit.*, pp. 245–342; for Mary, Anthony J. Tambasco, *What Are They Saying About Mary?* (New York: Paulist, 1984).

47. I have greatly relied on Fuller, "Jesus Christ as Savior in the New Testament," *art. cit.* Cf Schillebeeckx, *Christ, op. cit.*, his giant reinterpretation of New Testament soteriology, esp. pp. 463–514. Also Hans Urs von Balthasar, "The Descent into Hell," *Chicago Studies* 23 (1984), 223–236.

8

New Testament Christology: A Contemporary Summary

What follows is a personal interpretation of the Jesus event, which is informed by the major routes of interpretation covered above. Ultimately, all the routes we have covered would seem to converge in their interpretation of Jesus as a simple story of divine love, justice, and peace, disclosing itself in Jesus and through his fragmentary movement within history. But the routes do this in different ways. Literary-critical analysis dwells more upon the language and genres through which the Jesus event has been mediated to us. It stresses how New Testament language and genres "refer" us to a world of new meaning: the heart of the matter is the intensive disclosure of divine love (= proclamation) in the life and ministry of the crucified Jesus of Nazareth (= manifestation). This explosive disclosure in Jesus, is, however, qualified in two ways: there are still the cries of the innocent victims of history, still the untold sufferings of millions who do not enjoy Jesus' justice, love, and peace. The Divine, then, still remains beyond us and ahead of us, a future hope and not a present enjoyment (= apocalyptic). And yet the Divine has entered into our lives, inspiring us and renewing us, guiding us in our daily affairs and institutions (= early Catholicism).

Literary-critical analysis, then, is an entirely appropriate interpretation of our New Testament Christological tradition. It pays attention to the whole of the New Testament legacy, and its special strength is in not bypassing the languagistic character of our historical revelation. It presumes the historical character of the Jesus event (the historical references opened up in front of the text), but dwells more upon the theological meaning or the "world" disclosed to us in the text.

Our other routes of interpretation (historical, psychosocial, and philosophical) likewise provide us with an appropriate interpretation of our New Testament legacy. If their tendency is perhaps to bypass too quickly the languagistic character of revelation, their strength is to dwell upon the historical and theological references opened up to us by the biblical texts.

In this way, they complement the literary-critical approach, and deepen our appreciation of the world disclosed to us by the New Testament. In a critical age like our own, these methods are in fact essential. They aid the historically critical person in assimilating our biblical heritage. They help us discover the limitations and fallenness of our heritage. They help us mediate our heritage to our contemporary experience. This is why literary-critical analysts like Ricoeur and Tracy always try to fuse their own approach with these other methods. And so do we. The future in Christology, it seems, lies in some kind of critical fusion between all of these methods of explanation. As we have seen, all *can* appropriately mediate our heritage to us; all can do so in that critical manner which helps us to revise our estimate of the tradition.

What follows, then, is a kind of contemporary statement of New Testament Christology, based upon a "fusion" of all of the approaches we have surveyed. Hopefully this will help the readers achieve their own personal fusion. I am employing as my basic model of exposition the fourfold or "quaternion" structure of our human existence: God, self, society, and nature/world.[1] Simple experience tells us that our lives are constituted by relationships to these various "poles." On a Christian view of experience, we are in some kind of relationship to the Divine, the transcendent dimension of our existence. This is either repressed or affirmed by us, but in any case it is a pervading dimension to what we are. Likewise we are all involved in "carving out" ourselves. Selfhood is not a simple possession, but more of a process of person-making. We either develop our capacities for human development, or we stunt them. But in either case there is this self-pole in our human existence, in which we are inextricably involved. Similarly we are social creatures, inevitably intertwined with our societies. These "societies" can take many shapes, from the interpersonal relationships we enjoy with our relatives, friends, and loved ones, to the more impersonal relationships we have with our culture, our government, our economy, even other cultures. We know that our social relationships can either help us or hinder us, nourish our potential or weaken and destroy it. But in either case, society is there as a pervading dimension of what we are and become. Finally, we are bodily and earth creatures. We are related to nature and to the cosmos or world. We know how important our body is, as the sacrament of our "spirit" and the means of our communication with one another, verbally and non-verbally. We know we are localized in some space, and how that "space" can either dampen or delight our spirits. Sometimes we have to become sick to notice our body. Or the atmosphere must become polluted before we pay it any heed. But body and world (= nature) are always there, pervading us constantly.

Simple experience also tells us that these four poles are interrelated.

We are involved in a kind of oscillation between them constantly. Von Hügel would say that there is a constant "friction" between them, and that
through that friction we become the persons that we are. We develop in
our relationship with God through our person-making, through our social
relationships, and through our bodies and natural world. Likewise, all the
other poles influence one another. Our complex relationships toward God
and self, society and nature, interpenetrate and co-determine the quality
of our lives—for better or worse. Our fourfold relationships are usually ambiguous: some may nourish, some may destroy.

I propose, then, to explore what the Jesus event discloses about the
fourfold character of our common human existence, informed by all the
methods we have surveyed. This might be a contemporary way to mediate, in summary form, our New Testament heritage. A kind of "synthetic
simplicity" is what motivates this approach. It is "synthetic," because it
seems to embrace the major dimensions of our contemporary existence.
Yet it is "simple," affording a rather easy way of "fusing" the combined contributions of the various, rather technical methods we have surveyed up to
this point.

God

The heart of New Testament Christology is a novel disclosure of the
Divine, which introduces a new vision and praxis of our human relationship to God. With literary-criticism, we can speak of the divine irruption
of *agape*, most intensively in Jesus, less intensively in his followers. Or,
with our other routes of explanation, we can speak of the mediation of divine justice, love, and peace, through the earthly and crucified Jesus, and
through the risen Christ today. In either case, it is a disclosure of a love-,
justice-, and peace-Divinity that comes to us through the Jesus event.

This Jesus-like disclosure of the Divine confronts us with nothing less
than a quite radical alteration of both our thinking about God, and our living in the light of that God (our praxis). Basically, we might call this a
love-, justice-, and peace-oriented view of the Divine, which seems to owe
a good deal to the Jewish heritage, but somewhat modified by Jesus and
his followers. It continues that strand in Jewish tradition which knows the
Divine as a "dialogical God" who exists in a relationship of openness and
fidelity toward humanity. Israel's God, in this tradition, is not an isolated,
self-inclosed Being, but a relational and interrelational Reality, ec-static or
"standing outside" itself to and for others. Essentially, the prophets—the
great "carriers" of this God-tradition—maintained a love-justice-peace experience of the Divine.

Thus, the God of the prophets was primarily a God-of-relationships, giving guidance and life in human history. The mysterious revelation of Yahweh's name in the theophany to Moses (cf Ex 3:14), while expressing Yahweh's transcendence, wants to indicate that this transcendence is not a world-absence, but a promise of involvement in Israel's misery and enslavement. The entire context of this theophany indicates that Yahweh reveals the divine name because this God wants his people to know that "I will be with you" (Ex 3:12; 4:12, 15; 6:7). For this reason, too, the revelation of Yahweh's name does not "lift" Moses out of the world, but deepens his sense of mission to his people (cf Ex 3:10). Of course, we do find a profound experience of Yahweh's eternity and transcendence in the Hebrew Scriptures, particularly among the prophets. But this should be understood as a *transcendence modified by never failing fidelity to humans*, rather than in some aloof and uninvolving sense. Thus, for Hosea, Yahweh is "the Holy One in your midst" (Hos 11:9), and Amos calls God "Immanuel," the God who is "with us" (Am 5:14–15). Even Jeremiah, who stresses against the false prophets that God is "afar off" and not to be assimilated to our whims, proclaims that there is no hiding place from this God (Jer 21:23–32).

To turn the image around, the prophetic tradition experienced God as undergoing an "inner exodus," opening the divine reality to relationships with the Jewish people, through which affliction is truly heard and overcome through guidance (cf Ex 3:7–8). In this light we can grasp that the contemporary Jewish philosopher Abraham Heschel was being more than hyperbolic when he suggested the category of "pathos" as a kind of summary of the prophets' God-experience. In his own words:

> The essential meaning of pathos is therefore not to be seen in its psychological denotation as standing for a state of the soul, but in its theological connotation, signifying God as involved in history. He is engaged to Israel—and has a stake in its destiny.[2]

Heschel does not intend to downplay the prophets' awareness of the divine transcendence, but wants to stress that it is a covenantal transcendence, a "transcendent relatedness, a divine claim and demand."[3] The metaphor chosen by Heschel—"pathos"—does not annul the difference between the Divine and the human, but brings out the interconnection between them. Unlike apathy, which connotes indifference and the negation of genuine relationships, pathos symbolizes the intensity of relationships. Thus we find in Deuteronomy: "Think! The heavens, even the highest heavens, belong to the Lord your God, as well as the earth and everything on it [= divine transcendence]. Yet in his love for your fathers the Lord was so attached to them as to choose you, their descendants, in preference to all other peoples, as indeed he has now done" [= pathos, covenantal relatedness] (Dt 10:14–15). And we find in the Psalter, Israel's prayer book: "Clouds and darkness are round about him [= divine transcendence], justice and judgment are the foundation of his throne" [= pathos] (Ps 97:2). Pathos symbolizes Heschel's view that the prophets knew no gulf between the Divine and the human: it is a "form of relation."[4]

Heschel thinks that the prophetic experience of God presupposes an ontology or philosophy of Being-as-Involvement, which refuses to separate Being from its actions and movement. He tries to bring this home by saying that the prophets do not concentrate on "Being" (= "what is"), but on the "surprise of Being" (= "what can happen through the divine pathos").[5] Thus, for example, Heschel interprets Hosea's marriage to a prostitute (Hos 2–3), not only as a symbol of Israel's betrayal of God, but as the divine pedagogy itself, one of the ways in which the Divine relates to Hosea and educates him "in the understanding of divine sensibility."[6] So, too, Heschel takes seriously the biblical tradition of the "wrath of God" (cf Jer 10:10). Instead of treating this as an outmoded view of the Divine to be replaced by more sophisticated analogies, he views it as an expression of the highly involving and pathic God of the prophets.

Only if the Divine is unrelated and immobile should the category of divine wrath be ignored. As an expression of pathos, it points to the divine refusal to be neutral to human evil: "Its meaning is . . . instrumental: to bring about repentance; its purpose and consummation is its own disappearance."[7] And so we find that the divine wrath is always temporary (Mi 7:18–20; Is 26:20; 54:7–8; 57:16–19; Jer 3:5, 12). Of course, like all categories for the Divine, that of pathos is analogical and anthropomorphic. But Heschel thinks that it is an analogy rooted in the prophets' genuine experience, and so to be taken more seriously than we have. "It is an oversimplification to assume that the prophets, who were so deeply aware of the grandeur and transcendence of the Creator of heaven and earth as well as the failure and frailty of human nature, should have sought to invest God with human qualities."[8] Pathos, rather, refuses excessively to humanize or anesthetize God: God is not neutral to evil, but working against it through an authentic concern and involvement. This is why Heschel can put forward the startling view: a God of pathos creates a sym-pathetic prophet. As he explains it, "An analysis of prophetic utterances shows that the fundamental experience of the prophet is a fellowship with the feelings of God, a sympathy with the divine pathos, a communion with the divine consciousness which comes about through the prophets' reflection of, or participation in, the divine pathos."[9]

The disclosure of the Divine in the Jesus event seems to move within the horizon of this dialogical experience of God found within late, prophetic Judaism. As the biblical scholar Wilhelm Thüsing understands it, "The Christ-belief is not a lessening, but a qualitatively new radicalizing of the Old Testament Yahweh-monotheism and its justly intense and emphatic confession, 'Hear, O Israel, Yahweh, your God, is one.' " Thüsing suggests that we can fail to recognize this if we move from an "all too individualistic concept of the God-relation" in which the "theological and sociological" presupposition for knowing God is overlooked—namely, history and our fellow brothers and sisters. We only know God through the way in which God relates to us within history, through persons and events. The Christ-belief of New Testament Christology, then, is "not a surrender of the dynamic dialogical character of the Old Testament Covenant, but its maintenance, its 'setting in power' (Rom 15:8)." Through the human being Jesus, so the New Testament wants to say, God continues the divine dialogue with humanity. This is why the literature of the Johannine community could take the step of saying, "God is love" (1 Jn 4:8, 16). For in the Jesus event God reveals himself as outgoing and dialogical for humanity. Thüsing concludes with an observation which seems highly significant for our appreciation of Judaism: "The promises of the Father through Jesus are not simply fulfilled or exhausted, but irreversibly placed in motion."[10] This is the meaning he draws from Romans 15:8: "Yes, I affirm that Christ became the servant of the Jews because of God's faithfulness in fulfilling the promises to the patriarchs."

But Thüsing observes that the Christ-belief to some extent represents a radicalization of Judaism's dialogical God. He singles out the overcoming of any "lofty paternalism" in Jesus' disclosure of God. This may be true for some Jewish circles, but I would single out the unconditional nature of the divine love as expressed through Jesus. This would seem to be the really radical dimension. I am referring to Jesus' stress upon the universal availability of the divine love, justice, and peace, apart from any prior limitations, even that of being a faithful follower of the covenant. The cross, to a great extent, epitomizes this unconditionality, illustrating the far reaches to which the divine love extends itself. As Paul puts it, "It is rare that anyone should lay down his life for a just man, though it is barely possible that for a good man someone may have courage to die. It is precisely in this that God proves his love for us: That while we were still sinners, Christ died for us" (Rom 5:7–10). Let me add here that it is Jesus who represents this radicalization of Israel's dialogical divinity. In this sense, through its own son Rabbi Yeshua, Judaism broke through to an unconditional Love-God Who Struggles for Justice and Peace. It is important for Christians to remember that. Contemporary Jews, too, are beginning to reclaim Jesus as they discover how faithful he was to their heritage.[11]

Something which gets in the way of this interpretation of the divine

disclosure through Jesus is an inadequate view of the resurrection as somehow cancelling out or annulling the importance of the death (and even the
earthly life) of Jesus for our faith. The Jesus event is interpreted in a linear
fashion, as a progressive movement toward resurrection, a movement
which annuls all that went before. Yet the thrust of New Testament Christology is to proclaim the resurrection *of the earthly and crucified one.* Resurrection is the divine confirmation and continuation of the life of justice,
love, and peace embodied in Jesus and epitomized in his death, not the
cancellation.

In other terms, the New Testament believes that God, and thus divine transcendence, has manifested itself in Jesus. But it is a transcendence modified by suffering justice, love, and peace (= the crucified one).
What continues through Jesus' risen life is the saving and ultimately victorious power of suffering justice, love, and peace. If the resurrection is
severed from the cross, we run the danger of missing the distinctive kind
of transcendence which emerges in Jesus. Without the life and cross of Jesus, divine transcendence can too easily be conceived as some suprahuman
and supraterrestrial power. The really novel element in Jesus is that divine
transcendence and divine immanence, divine otherness and divine relatedness, are not a simple dichotomy. Because transcendence is modified by
love, justice, and peace, it never becomes tyrannical and exploitative. Because love, justice, and peace are modified by transcendence, they are
never merely tragic and sentimental, but victorious. It is a *transcendence
through the pathos of the cross* that is revealed in Jesus: "I determined that
while I was with you I would speak of nothing but Jesus Christ and him
crucified," says Paul (1 Cor 2:2).

The Jesus event, then, can be viewed as a radicalization and intensification of Israel's dialogical and relational God. *Through the sym-pathetic
man Jesus God is disclosed as radically pathos.* Jesus, the earthly, crucified, and risen one, is an aspect of the Divine Mystery. Through him that
Mystery manifested that it was and still is a dialogical presence of justice,
love, and peace on behalf of humanity. Jesus, crucified and risen, is one of
the ways in which the Divine remains a dialogical partner with humanity.
Somehow the Divine Presence is a "Christoform" presence, a transcendence that bears the crucified wounds of genuine pathos.

I would suggest that it is only in the light of our own experiences of a
transcendent power of justice, love, and peace at work within us that we
can co-confirm what the New Testament is attempting to proclaim. If we
"know" this experience in our own lives, and if we experience it quite practically as a reality moving us in the direction of that struggle on behalf of
justice, love, and peace which characterized Jesus, then perhaps the belief
of the New Testament will sound like more than pious chatter. The expe-

rience may take a primarily positive form: we sense ourselves as "carried" by a gracious presence which fills us with courage, with a desire to go outside ourselves in love, justice, and peace, to spend ourselves with genuine pathos on behalf of others. Or that experience may take the "negative" form of protesting against human misery, our own and that of others, of struggling to rectify the force of dehumanization in history and to eliminate war. In either case, we are genuinely experiencing something of the transcendent pathos which was disclosed in the Jesus event.

This disclosure of transcendent pathos in Jesus was and still remains enormously novel and liberating. We have seen how the earthly Jesus was not understood, how he was abandoned, except perhaps by his women followers. Were Jesus' disciples looking for a different kind of divinity in Jesus, and not the pathic one he was manifesting? We have seen, too, that Paul (or his followers) failed to apply consistently the lessons which flow from the radical Love-Divinity disclosed in Jesus; inconsistently he holds that only men are the image of God, women being men's image. How is this consistent with a Divinity whose love unconditionally relates to all? Ours is a fallen tradition which has not fully and faithfully transmitted the radicality of the Jesus event. Apparently even the earthly Jesus himself, through his use of masculine terms for the Divine, did not fully free himself of that patriarchalism which is inconsistent with the divine disclosure going forward through him. So, too, we ended our study of the New Testament with the struggle between the recovery of the eschatological tension of the Jesus event and its near-loss through the gradual institutionalization and too-settled life of "successful" Christianity. What is this but another way of saying that the pathos on behalf of the world's miserable, on behalf of which Jesus struggled, was disappearing from sight? As we will see, as we move forward in this book, the disappearance of divine pathos is still our problem today.

Self

New Testament Christology is not only a new disclosure of the Divine Mystery. It is also a new disclosure of what it is to be a human being. A new vision and praxis of human-making or person-making comes to us through the Jesus event. With literary criticism we can speak of the agape, intensively present in Jesus and less intensively in his followers. Person-making is found through the path of love. Or with our other routes of interpretation we can say that person-making is achieved through the path of repentance and faith, through conversion from a me-centered form of existence to an existence rooted in the values of the new community or Kingdom of justice, peace, and love, as embodied in Jesus and his disciples. In either case we are saying that New Testament Christology proclaims a new model of the human self. This is a part of the Jesus event. As Paul put it, our spirit must be the Spirit of Jesus (Rom 8:9). Reproducing Jesus' own Abba-relationship, our lives must take on the crucified character of Jesus himself (1 Cor 15:45–49).

I would suggest that just as New Testament Christology works out of a covenantal experience of the Divine, so it works from a covenantal vision and praxis of the human self. Particularly for the prophets, selfhood or person-making is not an isolated and autonomous achievement, but a sharing in and commitment to the covenant. This is why they castigate Israel's sinfulness, for it expresses a failure to live out the values of the covenant. Israel's sin, for the prophets, is a kind of regression to narcissism: the elders and princes are "grinding down the poor when they look to you" (Is 3:15; cf Jer 5; Hos 4–8; Am 1–8). To return to Abraham Heschel's imagery, authentic selfhood is *sym*-pathy, a feeling with the divine pathos, an embodiment of it in one's own life. This is a love-, justice-, and peace-oriented vision and praxis of self-making, which calls for the achievement of personhood through the purgation of narcissism and fidelity to the covenant.

New Testament Christology moves within the horizon of this "covenantal self" of the prophets, of this "sym-pathetic self." Like the prophets, Jesus and his followers must actively commit themselves to the struggle against social misery. Christian sym-pathy takes on the active form of struggle and protest: selfhood is realized through that. This is especially epitomized in the cross of Jesus, and in the cross that his disciples must bear as they meet with opposition to this new vision and praxis of justice, love, and peace. Clearly here we can see how the Christian model of the self prolongs the covenantal self of the prophets.

But just as the Jesus event radicalizes the covenantal God of Judaism, so it radicalizes the covenantal self of the prophets. The most important radicalization is the unqualified nature of justice, love and peace to which the Jesus event summons us. As the divine justice, love, and peace is universal, beyond distinctions of class and race, so must our own be. In Paul's great liberating terms, "There does not exist among you Jew or Greek, slave or freeman, male or female" (Gal 3:28).

This new model of personhood which is intensively embodied in Jesus and less intensively in his followers illustrates the interpenetrating oscillation between the divine pole and the self pole of our common human existence. A divinity of pathos creates a sym-pathetic person, said Heschel. The flow of divine justice, love, and peace creates the overflow of a Jesus and his followers working on behalf of justice, love, and peace. For today's person, this new model of the self represents a decisive break from individualism and egocentricity. These latter lifestyles "block" the overflow of divine pathos: instead of feeling with the divine pathos, they feel against it. And the result is injustice and lovelessness.

Just as this new model of selfhood is a great challenge to us today, so apparently was it one for earliest Christianity too. Our fallen Christological tradition was not always equally faithful to this new vision and praxis. Already in the earliest Christology we noted the "demotion" of the title of servant as expressive of the deepest meaning of what Jesus was about. Insofar as servanthood was demoted in Christian consciousness, so, too, was the model of the sym-pathetic self. Paul's stirring mysticism of the crucified Jesus is a creative re-expression of the sympathetic self, but his blindness to the liberation of women is an equally stirring failure to live out the implications of the new self. Matthew, Mark, and Luke all creatively describe the new kind of suffering love embodied by Jesus and his disciples, but there is also a tendency toward elitism (Matthew) and complacent acceptance of imperial morality (Luke). John dazzles us with the symbol of the cross as the key to what Jesus was about, but he also lapses into elitism, Jewish defamation, and a tendency to forget the work of the Kingdom which yet needs to be done on behalf of the world's miserable. This fidelity and near-infidelity to the new model of the self disclosed in Jesus is, as we have seen, a constant struggle in the later writings of the New Testament. Christian person-making is not a once-for-all achievement: it must be constantly proven in our struggle on behalf of justice, love, and peace. This is why Tracy speaks of the apocalyptic genre as a corrective one: the miseries of the many must be continually matched by a sympathetic self willing to work for their experience of justice, love and peace.

Society

The Jesus event also initiates a novel experiment in human, social relations. The oscillating interpenetration between the divine pathos and sympathetic human beings brings about a new possibility of community-making too. The Jesus event involves a transformation in our vision and praxis of society too. Literary analysis has surfaced this social punch to the Jesus event: the dialectic between proclamation and manifestation is the dialectic between divine agape and its embodiment as a shared life for others in Jesus and his followers. The doctrines genre refers us to the shared life of agape in the daily and ordinary lives of Christians. And the apocalyptic genre puts some "sting" into this by reminding us that shared agape remains fragile and incomplete as long as there are victims in history. Our other routes of interpretation surface a similar message. The earthly Jesus commits himself to working on behalf of the new community of justice, love, and peace (= Kingdom), and his followers believe that this Kingdom has made a decisive breakthrough in history through Jesus, taking root now in a fragile yet effective way. Paul will speak of a community rooted in fellowship; Mark, of a new kind of discipleship; Matthew, of the Kingdom of the higher righteousness; John, of doing the works of Jesus. In each case, New Testament Christology witnesses to the unleashing of a new community-making dynamic in the Jesus event.

Again, I would suggest that New Testament Christology moves from a covenantal vision and praxis of human, social relations. As the prophets never entertained an atomistic view of the individual as separated from the covenant, so the New Testament thinks within a similar horizon, and acts accordingly. Person-making is simultaneously society-making. As the covenant is a collective-social reality within which individuals exist, and through commitment to which they find salvation, so the new covenant or community of the Jesus event is the same. But there is a radicalization of prophetic community-making unleashed by the Jesus event. For this new community is the building up of the unqualified nature of that love, justice, and peace disclosed in Jesus. It is an attempt to realize the apocalyptic dream of a community devoid of human misery and exploitation (cf Mt 5:3–12).

This emphasis upon the social "edge" of the Jesus event is an insight we especially owe to psychosocial criticism. It is a difficult insight, for as sociologist John Coleman pointed out, "the human mind . . . typically thinks in terms of persons rather than structures."[12] Yet it is crucial that we appropriate this insight, for as every sociologist knows, every effective idea must have "carriers" or social groups which introduce that idea into the social network and render it effective. So, too, the breakthrough of the Jesus event would remain mere theory without its carriers. But the good news of New Testament Christology is that such carriers of new justice, love and peace exist within history. The divine pathos has overflown into sympathetic disciples who actually create a new possibility of communal love and justice within history.

In some sense the story of the New Testament is the story of the near-loss and creative recapturing of this liberating community-making dynamic unleashed in Jesus. All of the "ambiguities" in New Testament Christology which we have surveyed up to this point (in the sections on the self and on God) apply here. To the extent that the divine pathos and its correlative, the sympathetic self, were lost from view, to that extent the community-making power of the Jesus event was diminished. However, nowhere is this dialectic between near-loss and recapturing more palpably illustrated than in the struggle to remain faithful to the fragile and incomplete nature of the community begun through Jesus.

The political theologian Johann Baptist Metz creatively comments on this "incomplete" nature of the Jesus event:

> It would be false to think that in the Christ-Event the future is entirely behind us, as if the future of the history after Christ only plays itself out, but does not *realize* itself. On the contrary, the Christ-Event intensifies this orientation toward the not yet realized future. The proclamation of the resurrection of Jesus, which can never be separated from the message of the crucifixion, is essentially a proclamation of promise which initiates the Christian mission. This mission achieves its future in so far as the Christian alters and "innovates" the world toward that future of God which is definitely promised to us in the resurrection of Jesus Christ. The New Testament is therefore centered on hope—a creative expectancy—as the very essence of Christian existence. [13]

The critical sentence is this: "The Christ-Event intensifies this orientation toward the not yet realized future." How? The Jesus event discloses that the divine community on behalf of justice, love, and peace will only effectively enter history through the Jesus-like struggle of the carriers of this community on behalf of justice, love, and peace. The Jesus event discloses that pessimism is unwarranted: despite human misery and exploitation (= the cross), the Divine is at work salvaging life from death (= resurrection). That event also discloses that utopianism is unwarranted: victory (= resurrection) comes only through the struggle (= cross). That difficult stretch of road between pessimism and utopianism is what the Jesus event empowers. In this sense, the creative tension between the already and the not yet is implied in the Jesus event. As Von Hügel saw so well, this is but a corollary of believing in a present yet transcendent Divine Mystery, who empowers us now for the struggle on behalf of the Kingdom, and in so doing moves us closer to that Kingdom itself. The Jesus event does not annul the future: it empowers us to move toward a better future through the path of sympathetic community-building.

One of the constant threads running throughout the New Testament is the struggle to maintain this creative tension of the Jesus event. Literary criticism speaks of the apocalyptic genre as a necessary corrective to the other genres. Our other routes of explanation say something similar. The New Testament was never apparently tempted by the pessimistic vision, but it did struggle with the utopian one in several guises. As we have seen, earliest post-Easter Christianity was fueled by apocalyptic expectations. The breakthrough of the resurrection convinced some that the end-time was now beginning; Jesus' resurrection was its first installment (Rom 1:3f;

1 Cor 15: 20, 23; Mt 27:52f). They were living in the "last days" (Acts 2:17).
They daily expected the second coming (1 Cor 16:22; Jas 5:7f; Rev 22:20),
and some even gave up their goods in anticipation of the soon-to-come end
(Acts 2:44f; 4:32–37). While this expectation represents a thread in the
New Testament, an opposite thread shows a tendency to restrain this near-
utopianism. Paul has to argue that there will be an interval before the end
(2 Thes 1–2), and life's business must be carried on (2 Thes 3:10). This
trend, as we have seen, is carried further in Luke-Acts and John, in which
the feverish expectation of the end is considerably "cooled." A new form
of near-utopianism begins to emerge with the phenomenon of early Catholicism, the gradual institutionalization of the Christian community.
This tends to bring with it another near-slide into utopianism and a too-
easy alignment with the moral ethos of the empire.

As James Dunn put it, the problem with this expectancy is how both
to "retain it and to restrain it"[14]—to hold on to the tension of the in-between, without sliding into either pessimism or utopianism. These varied
strands—near-utopianism and its correlative cooling—seem to be mutually corrective attempts to preserve the fragile, in-between character of
the Jesus event.

Nature

The nearly forgotten member of our human quaternity is nature. To
my knowledge, literary criticism has not surfaced this dimension of the Jesus event, although it is quite capable of doing so. As we have seen, among
Jesus questers it is only Günther Bornkamm who offers a few comments
about the matter. Some few contemporary theologians are paying attention to the issue, but not precisely from the point of view of the Jesus
event.[15] Fascinated as we are, almost egocentrically, upon ourselves and
our interrelations with one another, we are apt to miss the potential implications for our relationship with nature which are implied in the Jesus
event.

I would suggest that the real ecological originality of the Jesus event
resides in the vision and praxis of the new community (or Kingdom) as the
end of exploitation, the overcoming of the oppressor-oppressed dialectic.
Divine justice, love, and peace, as carried in sympathetic followers, refuses to exploit and harm, but promotes a covenantal harmony between all
peoples and things. This covenantal harmony, radicalized to a universal
love, justice, and peace in the Jesus event, flows from that continual conversion from self-aggrandizement to the values and praxis of the Kingdom.
Nature is meant to participate in this harmony, and that is why Jesus can
appeal to it in his parables to illustrate what life in his new community is

about. The ecological originality of the Jesus event resides in the praxis of self-limitation and the corresponding vision of harmony among all creatures. It is true that there is little explicit attention in the New Testament to nature and the land. But there is much attention to this vision of harmony which could be revolutionary in its consequences for our relationship with nature and our ecological habitat.[16]

My suggestion here is that again there is this interpenetrating oscillation between the various poles of our common human existence. The overflow of the divine pathos into sympathetic selves and communities should extend into our relationship with nature. Jesus' rootedness in nature, his frequent allusions to it in his parables, illustrates not only his agricultural background but this "flow of pathos" toward all realities. His remarkable freedom from taboos about the body and sexuality is perhaps an indication of this. There are a few indications that post-Easter Christianity glimpsed this new harmony with nature present in the Jesus event. The belief in the resurrection of Jesus' body would seem to indicate a "high view" of nature and the role that it plays in our person-making. But perhaps the most remarkable text is found in Paul: "Creation was made subject to futility, not of its own accord but by him who once subjected it; yet not without hope, because the world itself will be freed from its slavery to corruption and share in the glorious freedom of the children of God" (Rom 8:20–21; cf 2 Pt 3:12–13 and Rev 21:1). Here the ecological ramifications of the Jesus event intriguingly poke themselves out at us. But, on the whole, an ecologically developed Christology barely surfaces in the New Testament. This must be part of our story to come.

The Soteriological Dimension

We have noted earlier that the New Testament never separates Christology from soteriology. So far as I can tell, this soteriological dimension remains rather subdued and implicit in literary criticism of the New Testament. It is implied in the notion that the New Testament genres disclose a world of divine agape empowering Jesus and his followers to live with that same agape. But this needs much more development. It was primarily our other routes of explanation which uncovered the soteriological dimensions of the earthly Jesus and their later development in New Testament Christology. In the end, the New Testament believes that Jesus was and is the Savior, the one who sets us free from all forms of sin and evil. Although I will speak about this more fully in a later chapter, I would like to make some observations here on how this soteriological dimension of the Jesus event links up with the quaternion structure of our common human existence.

I have interpreted the Jesus event as the disclosure of a novel vision and praxis in our four, interrelated dimensions: we are related to a Divine Mystery that is "pathos"; we are empowered to become sympathetic selves; we are equally empowered to create a community rooted in divine pathos; and we are empowered to build up a sympathetic/harmonious relationship with our bodies and their further extension, nature. If you will, this is my suggested reinterpretation of Christology, as we find it in the New Testament.

The Jesus event, then, can be seen as the disclosure of a novel experiment in our relationships with God, with ourselves, with our societies, and with our world. But the reverse side of this is that it is also the healing or liberating or redeeming of our four relations from their brokenness, their distortions, their "blockages." The Jesus event is an empowerment to a new kind of relationship with our four dimensions. But it is also a freeing from and healing of what stands in the way of this new kind of relationship. I would suggest that it is along these lines that we might fruitfully reinterpret soteriology for our times. Soteriology is, if you will, the reverse side of Christology.

There is not simply one melody playing in our common human existence: the interpenetrating oscillation between a divine pathos, a sympathetic self, a sympathetic community, and a sympathetic harmony between humanity and nature. There is another melody which is less harmonious and more discordant: our inability to trust in a divine justice, love, and peace, our consequent lapse into a-pathetic selfhood, the further extension of this apathy into our social relations, and the further pollution of nature and our body through our un-sympathetic lifestyles. Our quaternion structure is somehow diseased, rather pervasively so. This is why the New Testament piles up one image after another of our common human bondage: we are ruled by sin, by principalities and powers, by Satan, by the law and death, we are without peace and unreconciled, etc. These images virtually range over the entire area of our common human existence, and well they might. For it is the totality of our existence in its fourfold structure which is in need of healing.

The basic thrust of New Testament soteriology, if I understand it correctly, is to proclaim that there is a counter-power to the destructive "powers" that pollute our quaternion structure. That counter-power is that of a divine justice, love, and peace—which, with Heschel, we metaphorically name the "Divine Pathos"—disclosed by the Jesus event as an empowering reality present within our history, overflowing into us and transforming us into sympathetic selves, sympathetic communities, and harmonizers with nature. On this view, the only real evil or sin from which we must be redeemed is the failure to open ourselves to love, justice, and peace. Whatever blocks this—and this can take many forms in history—is *the* reality from which the Divine Pathos redeems us. But we are not redeemed tyrannically: it is a redemption which comes to us in the form of a sympathetic, cruciform love, justice, and peace. We know from our experience the healing power of such love, justice, and peace. It is truly effective, but not violently so. Like the Jesus event as a whole, the promise of redemption is fragmentary, in-between, a truly effective counter-power which avoids both pessimism and utopianism, but nonetheless effectively heals. A new vision and praxis of love, justice, and peace is the therapeutic power of the Jesus event. But we will continue this story in a later chapter.

Notes

1. Readers of Voegelin's *Order and History* will note that he employs this quaternion structure throughout in his analysis of human experience and symbolization; cf 1, *Israel and Revelation, op. cit.*, p. 1.

2. Abraham J. Heschel, *The Prophets* (New York: Harper Torchbooks, 1971), 2, p. 6. Cf. Maurice Friedman, "Abraham Heschel among Contemporary Philosophers: From Divine Pathos to Prophetic Action," *Philosophy Today* 18 (1974), 293–305. Moltmann, *The Crucified God, op. cit.*, pp. 270–272, has creatively used Heschel in his Christology. I also have used him in my *Jesus, Lord and Savior, op. cit.*, esp. pp. 113–161. For an overview of Judaism's God-experience, see Denis Baly, *God and History in the Old Testament: The Encounter with the Absolutely Other in Ancient Israel* (New York: Harper and Row, 1976), and Voegelin's *Order and History*, 1, *Israel and Revelation, op. cit.*

3. *Ibid.*, p. 7.

4. *Ibid.*, p. 11.

5. *Ibid.*, p. 43.

6. *Ibid.*, 1, p. 56.

7. *Ibid.*, 2, p. 66.

8. *Ibid.*, p. 49.

9. *Ibid.*, 1, p. 26.

10. See Karl Rahner and Wilhelm Thüsing, *Christologie: systematisch und exegetisch* (Freiburg: Herder, 1972), pp. 227–233 (my translation).

11. Cf John T. Pawlikowski, *op. cit.;* see Pinchas Lapide, *Israelis, Jews and Jesus* (Garden City, N.Y.: Doubleday, 1979).

12. John A. Coleman, *An American Strategic Theology* (New York: Paulist, 1982), p. 278.

13. Metz, *op. cit.*, p. 89.

14. Dunn, *Unity and Diversity, op. cit.*, p. 340.

15. See John B. Cobb, Jr., *Process Theology as Political Theology* (Philadelphia: Westminster, 1982), pp. 111–134; Rosemary Radford Ruether, *Sexism and*

God-Talk: Toward a Feminist Theology (Boston: Beacon, 1983), pp. 72–92; and Richard Woods, *Symbion: Spirituality for a Possible Future* (Santa Fe, N.M.: Bear and Co., 1982), esp. pp. 114–128, for creative theological thinking on ecology.

16. See the helpful book by W.D. Davies, *The Gospel and the Land: Early Christianity and Jewish Territorial Doctrine* (Berkeley: University of California, 1974), esp. pp. 336–376, for some helpful insights.

PART THREE

Jesus in Thought and Practice
after the New Testament

9

Jesus and the Exploration of the Divine in Later Christianity

As we have seen reason to believe, the Jesus event is an enormous one, entailing profound consequences for our vision and praxis of human life. Jesus quite literally alters our fourfold makeup as humans related to God, to self, to society, and to world. The Jesus event has become not only a story about Jesus himself as a private individual, but about ourselves in all of our central dimensions.

Now our temptation at this point is to jump immediately into the present, to explore the ramifications of the Jesus event for today. But this would be a mistake, I think. It is terribly important that an introductory book like this one acquaint the reader with at least the basic highlights of the tremendous effort and contribution of the post-biblical period up until contemporary times. For it is simply artificial, even naively uncritical, to think that one can jump directly from the biblical inheritance into the modern period. The tradition-bound nature of our humanity and faith means that the way we experience Christianity today is, in theory and practice, at least partially the result of the entire tradition from which we spring. The questions we ask of the Jesus event, even the way in which we have so far interpreted the biblical heritage, are to a great degree determined by our post-biblical history.

R.P.C. Hanson made the point: "Our Christology is basically the Christology of early Christian tradition or, to put it in a simpler and more straightforward way, what the Fathers made of the Bible." Thus, he goes on, "Consciously or unconsciously, the vast majority of believing Christians of all traditions look at God and at Jesus Christ through the spectacles of Nicaea, and probably through those of Chalcedon as well."[1] This is but another way of saying that we are anamnetic (from *anamnesis*, remembering) or tradition-bound people, for better or worse. It is better not to ignore this fact, but to face it critically, learning from the tradition's strengths and shedding its errors.

In this spirit, then, we will be exploring some of the more important currents of the full story of Jesus in the post-biblical tradition. Our approach will be the same used throughout: constantly moving to and from the tradition through our varied methods of explanation, where they are available, seeking a contemporary restatement. Borrowing an insight from Hanson, in a sense the work of our post-biblical elders serves as a paradigm for us. "They first encountered the problems, made the mistakes, felt their way round the pitfalls, explored the blind alleys, drew the conclusions, which to a large extent we all meet and must meet if we are true to original Christianity and can use right reason."[2] They are an experience for us which we must try to re-enact.

What follows here ought to be regarded as only a brief "guide" seeking to alert the reader to an enormous range of material. I will dwell only upon some highlights, hoping in that way to inspire readers to launch out further on their own. There is the difficult question of how to arrange what is literally a mountain of material. My own proposal will be to stay with our fourfold structure (God, self, society, and nature) as a kind of unifying center by which we can move through the material. If the story of Jesus is really the story of how he alters our vision and praxis in the four relations of our common existence, then it seems sensible to query the tradition in this way. Thus, I will be exploring representative moments within the post-biblical tradition when Christianity's experience of Jesus has been especially important for our groping vision and praxis with respect to our relations to the Divine, to ourselves, to our societies, and to our world. As I have done before, I will consider soteriology the "reverse side" of the Jesus event, treating it more extensively in a later chapter.

Jesus and the Divine:
Reconciling Transcendence with Justice, Love, and Peace

As we have seen, the Jesus event entails a quite radical alteration in the way we imagine God and practically relate to this Divine Mystery. By proclaiming that the Divine was manifest in Jesus, the New Testament was taking the step of saying that divine transcendence appears in the humiliated form of justice, love, and peace. Perhaps the clearest expression of this is found in the Johannine literature: "Love is of God"; "God is love"; "God's love was revealed in our midst in this way: he sent his only Son to the world that we might have life through him" (1 Jn 4:7, 8, 9). Under the pressure of Jesus, divine transcendence needed to be modified in the experience of Christians. It had become a dialogical or "pathos-like" transcendence—in a word, a transcendence that appears in the form of human justice, love, and peace.

Taking the broad view, one of the first tasks to confront the early

Church was the need to clarify its experience of God in the light of Jesus. The New Testament had already taken the decisive step in naming God love. This implied a radicalization of Jewish monotheism: Jewish belief in divine oneness and transcendence was not denied, but freed from ethnocentrism. Divine love had become universal for Christian experience, at least in principle. But this was also something novel in the Hellenistic world of experience.

To a great extent, the Greco-Roman world was still polytheistic. It had not yet differentiated the one transcendent One beyond its many manifestations in nature and society. To be sure, there were steps in this direction. The search among the Greek philosophers for a transcendent order beyond the finite gods and goddesses of Homer; the Socratic search for order within the depths of one's own soul; the search of the mystery religions for divine ecstasy—all were signs within Hellenism of the discovery of divine transcendence. As Eric Voegelin has especially noted, both Plato and Aristotle underwent the leap in being which was an opening of their souls to the Divine: "Both Plato's eroticism of the search (*zetesis*) and Aristotle's intellectually more aggressive *aporein* recognize in 'man the questioner' the man moved by God to ask the questions that will lead him toward the cause of being." Voegelin even has a more daring formulation: "Plato was just as conscious of the revelatory component in the truth of his *logos* as the prophets of Israel or the authors of the New Testament writings."[3]

What Voegelin means is that the great philosophers had discovered the divine power of transcendence within them. Their search for order and justice in response to the breakdown of Athenian democracy was an echo of the Transcendent Presence within their lives. Now this kind of teaching on divine transcendence was further developed in the Platonic schools and reached a kind of climax in Plotinus' doctrine of the One or the Good (third century A.D.). This "One" was a transcendent source of being beyond being and thought, to whom we can only point in thought and language, without ever attaining.[4]

But accompanying the progressive consciousness within Hellenism of divine transcendence was another trend, that of the teaching on divine power, immutability, and apathy. The identification of the divine with power has ancient roots, probably reaching back to archaic humanity's tendency to view the sacred as that which controls. Thus nature is frequently sacred, because it exercises power. In any case, Homer's deities characteristically are known for their power: "they live at ease" (*rheia zoontes*). Speaking of one of the gods in his *Works and Days*, Hesiod describes him thus: "For easily (*rheia*) he makes strong, and easily (*rheia*) he brings the strong man low; easily (*rheia*) he humbles the proud and raises the ob-

scure, and easily (*rheia*) straightens the crooked and blasts the proud."[5]
Here the sacred is an hypostatization of power. Homer's deities in the *Iliad*
and the *Odyssey* are especially known as powerful, possibly reflecting the
old warrior ethos of the Dorians (1100–650 B.C.).

Gradually the notion of the divine power became fused with the notion of divine immutability/unchangeability. Partially this is the result of
the poets' and philosophers' efforts to improve upon the earlier deities,
making them less irrational and arbitrary. We can see this in the sixth century Xenophanes, for example: "Always he [God] remains in the same
place, moving not at all, for it is not fitting for him to rush about to different
places at different times." And he adds: ". . . for utterly without effort he
makes to tremble all things by the thought of his mind."[6] The older, more
arbitrary power of Homer's deities is here refined and rationalized. The
Greek discovery of mind as a spiritual capacity has led to the spiritualization of divine power. It now is utterly immune from human limitations.
Whereas ordinary mortals must expend effort, the gods dwell in a sphere
beyond such limits. They are immutable.

Both Plato and Aristotle take up this teaching. Plato already teaches
that "God neither changes himself nor deceives others. . . ." Perhaps we
should say that his own discovery of mind as a spiritual power lies behind
this highly spiritual notion of God as beyond the sphere of human change.
Plato's thinking about God is an extrapolation from his own spiritual experience. But Plato is quite complex, for he knows that if one removes God
entirely from the world of change, he cannot account for the created world
of flux and change. To answer this question, he proposes his myth in the
Timaeus of the demiurge, a sort of divine-created artist at work in creation,
serving the immutable one on whom it depends. Today we might say that
Plato is on to the outgoing, creative aspect of the Divine, but he nowhere
fully integrates this into his thinking. One senses that he was close to the
covenantal God of Judaism and Christianity. But he was only close. The
covenantal God is a transcendence in the form of love, justice and peace.
Plato leaves us with an immutable One *somehow* related to the world
(through the demiurge).

Aristotle emphasizes unchanging divinity. He reconciles divine immutability and created change through his celebrated notion of the Un-
moved Mover: it moves by being loved. As Geddes MacGregor explains,
"Deity is totally immutable, radically impassible; but it draws everything
to itself through the longing that everything has for God."[7] The post-
Aristotelian schools (Epicureanism, Stoicism, Middle and Neo-Platonism)
will eventually develop a doctrine of divine apathy as the radical consequence of this entire trend. Happiness becomes *ataraxia*, a state of mental
calm, which issues from *apatheia* (some kind of freedom over the passions)

and *autarkeia* (self-sufficiency). However, scholars debate the actual extent of the critique of the passions among the Stoics. There is a growing tendency to hold that the important Stoic thinkers condemned only inordinate passions, not all passions.

The ideal of the apathetic and self-sufficient individual is a reflection of the immutable deity of the later Greco-Roman tradition. As the Divine is free from all passion, so the apathetic person imitates the Divine through calming (if not denigrating) the passions. Plato, as we saw, never went this far. He maintained an uneasy tension between an immutable God and a changing creation, as well as between reason and passion. He argues that none of us would choose to live "without an atom of pleasure, or indeed of pain, in a condition of utter insensibility. . . ."[8]

Now these reflections on the Hellenistic tradition enable us to grasp how difficult it was for the early Greek-influenced theologians of Christianity to come to terms with the New Testament heritage. That the Divine could somehow be linked to the messiness and changeability of human history—could somehow really be present in the crucified life of Jesus—demanded a creative revision of the doctrine of divine transcendence. Transcendence and pathos needed reconciling. Plato's uneasy tension between perfection and change needed resolution.

It is important that we grasp the practical contours of the issue too. As psychosocial criticism reminds us, our theory is always co-determined by our praxis. The Greeks did not evolve their impressive tradition on the gods through purely speculative reason. Clearly the harsh military and warrior experience of the Dorians contributed to the exaltation of power in the Greek experience. This was only reinforced by the later experience under the empires of Alexander and the Romans. Practical experience confirmed, if you will, that power works. Power brings with it servitude, and freedom from expending effort. It renders its possessor "immutable," unaffected by the problems of the ordinary mortal.

I would suggest that we look at the early Christological struggles as varied attempts, in thought and practice, to move from a power-immutable experience of the Divine to a view around the axis of love, peace and justice. The so-called early docetists (from *doketai*, "to seem") argued, for example, that Jesus only appeared or seemed to suffer and die. He only seemed to indwell a body. Underlying this is the belief that Jesus' divinity must remain immutable, unaffected by human limits. As the second century Acts of John has it: ". . . I saw that he was not . . . in any wise as a man. . . . And oftentimes when I walked with him, I desired to see the print of his foot, whether it appeared on the earth; for I saw him as it were lifting himself up from the earth: and I never saw it."[9]

A related but more complicated phenomenon is that of gnosticism

(from *gnosis*, "knowledge"). The standard view of this ethos is to characterize it as a broad movement of personal and social alienation occurring in
the first millennium, traceable to the intense political disorder of the
times. The experience of disorder and alienation is the real key to gnosticism's rich mythic imagery, its chief tenets, and its ethics/praxis. As Hans
Jonas has shown, its imagery revolves around the themes of man/woman
as alien in the world. The psychological mood is one of dispersal, sinking,
forlornness, dread, homesickness, numbness, intoxication. Salvation becomes a release from this world. There is also a strong element of protest
against the world's corruption. Thus gnosticism inverts the great symbols
of the tradition: the serpent, not Eve, brings gnosis; Cain, not Abel, is the
great gnostic; Prometheus, not Zeus, is the one who points the saving way.
The use of mythical imagery is not accidental: it expresses the primarily
affective and dramatic tone of the gnostic's protesting alienation. "My soul
became afflicted for the sons of men, because they are blind in their hearts
and do not have sight," says the gnostic Gospel of Thomas (2,2,28,
NH:121/second century A.D.).

Gnosticism's characteristic tenet, radical dualism, is also traceable to
its protesting alienation. God is absolutely transmundane, not only separate from but alien to the cosmos. Hence its dualism: God over against the
world. God's relation to the world is not simply one of indifference, but of
antagonism. This seems to be a psychological state of alienation projected
into a speculative, religious system. The ethical praxis likewise expresses
alienation, but in two possible modes. The ascetical posture simply lives
out the ethos of denigration of the bodily and the world. The libertinist
posture, apparently less common, by doing what one will with the body,
expresses the underlying scorn of the body, its fundamental unimport-
ance. Both postures, however, are antinomian, actively antagonistic toward the cosmos, seeking its ruin. The Book of Thomas the Contender
gives voice to some of these themes. Jesus says,

> Watch and pray that you not come to be in the flesh, but rather that you
> come forth from the bondage of the bitterness of this life. And as you
> pray, you will find rest, for you have left behind the suffering and the
> disgrace. For when you come forth from the sufferings and passion of the
> body, you will receive rest from the Good One, and you will reign with
> the king, you joined with him and he with you, from now on, for ever
> and ever. Amen (2,7, *NH*:194).

Christologically it is not too difficult to grasp what the gnostics of the
Christian variety will do with Jesus. Usually there will be a tendency to
treat him as an envoy of the transmundane deity who awakens the spark of

saving gnosis in the potential gnostic. Jesus triggers, as it were, the dynamic awareness of one's lostness. This awakens one's ability to protest against the mundane, and opens one to the return journey to the God beyond the world. This portrait of Jesus is often accompanied by a denigration of his humanity or earthrootedness. Perhaps the most extreme statement of this is found in the Apocalypse of Peter, which seems to argue that the "real" (= gnostic) Jesus does not suffer:

> And I said, "What do I see, O Lord, that it is you yourself whom they take, and that you are grasping me? Or who is this one, glad and laughing on the tree? And is it another one whose feet and hands they are striking?"
> The Savior said to me, "He whom you saw on the tree, glad and laughing, this is the living Jesus. But this one into whose hands and feet they drive the nails is his fleshly part, which is the substitute being put to shame, the one who came into being in his likeness" (7,3,81, *NH*:344).

Scholars generally tend to link gnosticism with the Greco-Roman world. All the examples of it we possess come from that sphere of influence. Certainly its highly transmundane God resembles the immutable and apathetic deity characteristic of late Hellenism. When this gets translated into a Christological key, we find Jesus' humanity denigrated in favor of the divine element within him. Like docetism, only more intensively, it can only make sense of the biblical heritage about Jesus by sacrificing the human dimension of Jesus to the divine. If he is truly divine, then his humanity must be a ruse. Perhaps we can argue that the experience of world-alienation has intensified and exaggerated the transmundane character of the Divine. God is not simply immune from the contamination of the cosmos, but antagonistic toward it: Jesus laughs, after all, at his crucified body!

While the above represents a fair view of what most scholars are saying about gnosticism, still the phenomenon is far from settled in scholarly circles.[10] Some propose that the "carriers" of this movement stem from the broad group of peoples in between the relatively affluent and the miserably poor and uneducated. The affluent would not experience intense alienation; the poor would be incapable of the rich mythical and quasi-rational thought of the gnostics and powerless to do anything about their plight. The emerging merchants, business people, and recently freed people, however, would be capable of this experience of alienation and mixture of mythical-rational thought. Other scholars go beyond this and propose a kind of revisionist view of the gnostics. They stress the liberationist elements in the gnostic writings. Gnostics unmask the evils and inequities in the society surrounding them. If they are alienated from their world, they are not interiorly alienated. They value inner, mystical experience (gnosis) as an alternative to the bankrupt world in which they live. Gnosticism's highly transmundane God is a cipher of the new world freed from alienation for which they long. For Christian gnostics, Jesus becomes the envoy of this new world of liberation for which the gnostic longs.

The revisionist view of gnosticism cautions us against being too glib and simplistic in our evaluation of this phenomenon. Perhaps its Christology is a precious source which continues something of Jesus' own protest against the alienating and dehumanizing powers of his own time. Something of the longing for justice, love, and peace perhaps surfaces here. But surely, too, the gnostic approach is a dead end. For it does not attempt to transform the world sickened by alienation, but to flee it into another, inner world of mystical solace. It takes over Hellenism's immutable deity and uses it, not to legitimate the apathetic *status quo,* but to legitimate its own inner world of freedom from the terrors of this world. The Divine that surfaces in the Jesus event, however, fosters a much more active and "aggressive" involvement in the transformation of this world. The Jesus of the New Testament does not laugh at his cross, but carries it.

Docetism and gnosticism follow the route of downplaying Jesus' real humanity in an effort to preserve what they consider his divine character: to be truly divine, he must be immune from human limitations and imperfections. An opposite tendency is to downplay his divine character in favor of his humanity: if he is truly human, then he cannot be truly divine in the full sense, for the Divine remains immune and immutable. For example, some would argue that Jesus was a good man inspiring others (moralism). "Adoptionism" would hold that this good man Jesus was somehow "adopted" by God, used by God, rather than truly being divine himself. "Subordinationism" would hold that Jesus was a kind of "third-entity" between the Divine and humanity. A kind of power or energy separated itself from God and appeared in the man Jesus. Using the favored Greek terminology, it was said that the *Logos* (Word/Expression) of God in Jesus was a kind of subordinate divine reality.

Origen (d. 253 A.D.) and Tertullian (d. 222 A.D.) seem to have been subordinationists. The latter even developed the language of two conjoined substances in Jesus, the human and the *Logos.* Paul of Samosata (third century) tried to move beyond subordinationism, with its tendency to dehumanize Jesus by transforming him into a *tertium quid.* He will call Jesus "of one substance" (*homoousios*) with the Father, meaning that Jesus somehow manifests the Father but is not the very presence of the Father. The Synod of Antioch (268 A.D.) would condemn his views. Subordinationism was a kind of symptom that something was inadequate in the in-

herited manner of imagining the Divine. The Jesus event required
something other than an immune and immutable deity.

It was the priest from Alexandria by the name of Arius (d. 336 A.D.)
who finally brought this phase of the Church's Christological development
to a climax. In Arius' thought, the divine *Logos* of Jesus is a creature, made
from nothing. There was a time when the *Logos* in Jesus did not exist. But
this *Logos* is prior to our temporal existence. Again, Jesus becomes a kind
of third-entity: a semi-divine power resides in him, making him utterly unlike the Divine, and even utterly unlike any human being. Apparently Arius' denial of Jesus' divinity did not stem from any proto-modern brand of
secularism, but rather from a very Hellenized conception of the deity. His
God was "the only unbegotten, the only eternal, the only one without beginning, the only true, the only one who has immortality, the only wise,
the only good, the only potentate."[11] This God was really a "Monad"—a
being severed from all else. The theological historian Jaroslav Pelikan calls
this an "uncompromising view of divine transcendence." As he explains it,
"Such a total transcendence was necessary not only for the sake of the utter
oneness of God, but also because of the fragility of creatures, which could
not endure to be made by the absolute hand of the Unoriginate."[12]

The famous Council of Nicaea (325) condemned Arius and his sup-
porters. In opposition to him, it asserted that Jesus Christ is of one substance with the Father (*homoousios*). Here Paul of Samosata's term is
taken over, but given a new meaning. For the Divine in Jesus is now said
to be the truly Divine One, equal to the Father. And it also condemned
anyone holding the Arian belief that there was a time when the *Logos* was
not (cf. *DS* 125–126).[13] The basic point was to assert that Jesus Christ is
fully divine. If you will, the Divine within him (the *Logos*) is not some subordinate or unknown entity, but the very reality of the Holy Mystery itself.

How do scholars assess the settlement of Nicaea? Usually they maintain that Athanasius and Nicaea saved Christianity from an "extreme form"
of Hellenization. If you will, under the pressure of the disputes emerging
in the Hellenistic world, the Nicene theologians attempted to remain true
to the biblical heritage. They essentially transposed into Hellenistic terms
the Christian belief in the dialogical Divine One of Jesus. We might summarize Nicaea's intuition in this way: precisely because the Divine is outgoing and dialogical, and not immune from humanity, this Holy Mystery
could be fully present in the man Jesus. This was not a wholesale rejection
of Hellenism. Both Christianity and Hellenism shared a common belief in
a Holy Mystery. It was a creative adaptation of Hellenism, a "Christifying"
of it, so to speak. There was also a profound soteriological dimension to the
Nicene settlement. For it was the divine outpouring into the Jesus event
which undergirded the belief that the Divine had truly embraced human-

ity in Jesus and liberated it from evil and sin. This was also a "Christifying" of Hellenistic forms of soteriology: salvation becomes, not flight from the world into a spiritual sphere of immutability, but a healing of the world, a world-renewal.

Ultimately the settlement of Nicaea would lead to the articulation of the Trinitarian doctrine. Although this was not definitively clarified until the First Council of Constantinople (381) defined the Spirit's divinity, still the ingredients of the Trinitarian belief were already present at Nicaea. For our purposes, what is crucial is to grasp how the Trinitarian doctrine is linked to the Jesus event. As that event called for the reconciliation between divine transcendence and human justice, peace and love in the earthly life of Jesus, so the Trinitarian doctrine attempts to express this Christian intuition in adapted Hellenistic terms.

To put the matter succinctly, the "Father" is divine transcendence; the "Son" is the modification or expression of that transcendence through self-giving justice, love and peace; this double pulsation is one single act of generous love or "Spirit."[14] When transcendence (= Father) self-limits itself through justice, love and peace (= Son), generous, outpouring love (= Spirit) results. Here we are very far from an immutable deity closed up in itself. We are much closer to the God of pathos so typical of the prophets and radically expressed in Jesus.

To be sure, Nicaea did not express itself in this way. What it did was to inject into Hellenistic terminology a deeper, biblical meaning. The great Cappadocian theologians (Basil, Gregory Nazianzus, and Gregory of Nyssa) would later crystallize this entire development. They proposed a distinction between *ousia*, the one divine nature, and *hypostasis*, a term which they quite originally understood to mean the concrete manner in which the divine nature expresses itself. *Ousia* was thought to be modified by *hypostasis*, or by justice, love and peace. *Hypostasis* was a quite original way in which the Cappadocians broke through to the personal and dialogical view of the Divine characteristic of the New Testament. If you will, the Trinity, understood as the symbol for the dialogical Holy Mystery disclosed in Jesus, is the condition of the possibility of the Jesus event. Christian Trinitarianism, then, was not a denial of monotheism, but its "Christifying." Under the pressure of the Jesus event, the Church was able to clarify the precise kind of monotheism in which it believed. With Judaism and Hellenism, it clearly affirmed the one transcendent reality (*ousia*/monotheism). But from its own experience of Jesus, it had discovered that this transcendence self-limits itself through a self-giving justice, love and peace for humanity (*hypostasis*/Trinitarianism).

However the Nicene settlement was an ambiguous phenomenon. To be sure, the impressive construction of a noetic theology[15] with the aid of

Hellenistic philosophy was a gain in the sense of promoting a greater differentiation in the Christian understanding of the Divine and our practical relationship to the Divine. The Jesus event does, after all, raise important questions about the nature of the Divine, the most fundamental reality with which we have to do. The New Testament was clearly on to this, and the debates culminating in Nicaea brought this kind of probing to a climax. Because we stand on Nicaea's shoulders, we are able to see this more clearly now ourselves.

But a differentiation can also result in a "contraction" of the full contours of an event, and something like this seemed to occur at and after Nicaea. Borrowing an insight from literary criticism, contraction is one of the deficits of the doctrine-genre. Recalling Ricoeur's and Tracy's dialectic between "proclamation" and "manifestation," the doctrine-genre gives intensive expression to the manifestation pole of our religious experience. It expresses our ability to lay hold of the Divine, to know it and participate in it. In a sense, it witnesses to our ability to somewhat "domesticate" it. But the danger in this is that we will accommodate the Divine too easily to our experience and pre-conceptions, forgetting its "proclamation pole," its over-againstness and its ever surprising nature. Just as the biblical doctrine genre needs the corrective of the apocalyptic genre, so Nicaea's doctrine demands a corrective too.

Why is this? The Nicene stress on Jesus' divinity—*homoousios*, after all, was its novel contribution—tended to overshadow the other dimensions of the Jesus event. The appearance of the divine *Logos* in Jesus' flesh could now be thought to be the full expression of the Jesus event. But what happens to the ministry, the death, and the resurrection of Jesus? This could quickly lead to an unhistorical view of the Divine who can get along quite well without the Jesus of real history. The biblical view is, after all, the belief that the entire life of Jesus is revelatory of the Divine. If one detaches that entire life from the belief in the Divine—contracting the entire Jesus event into the birth of the *Logos*—then the door is open to a view of the Holy Mystery no longer governed by the Jesus event. This was clearly not Nicaea's intention, but the very "sense" of Nicaea's doctrine genre as well as the later history of Christology bears witness to this tendency. As one commentator put it, after Nicaea "the Christ of dogma cast a shadow over the discussion, eclipsing the problems of historical revelation and the concrete actions of Jesus which the evangelists had reported and which Paul had considered so important (cf Rom 6:19; 12:1; Phil 2:12f; 4:7)."[16] This has important consequences for soteriology too: an eclipsing of Jesus' humanity can lead to an eclipsing of the very human world which he entered to save us.

Furthermore, this entire discussion of the Nicene settlement needs

to be complemented by the more practical kind of analysis used by psychosocial criticism and even deconstruction. Nicaea was an event not simply in the history of meaning, but also in the history of praxis. Practical
factors of a cultural and political kind influenced it and necessarily delim-
ited the implications of its contribution. In this perspective, Nicaea needs
to be understood against the background of Emperor Constantine and his
invitation to the Christian movement "to play a role similar to that which
the old State religion of Rome had played."[17] This development fostered
the tendency to politicize the Christian view of Jesus after the manner of
the Roman emperors. Imperial functions and powers were increasingly attributed to Jesus. As Hans Schmidt put it, "No longer is the 'political
Christ' seen as the consoler of an oppressed and downtrodden Church. He
is the Commander, Lawgiver, and Judge of a triumphant, conquering
Church." In attestation of this, Schmidt refers to Eusebius' *In Praise of
Constantine*. This work pictures God from above as extending his power
down to the emperor, assuring the latter of victory over opponents and
enemies.[18]

The politicization of Jesus tended to create a sort of Christian ideology
of the Empire. As the emperor rules in the name of Christ, so the emper-
or's success bears witness to Christ's lordship. Something similar to the
Hellenistic idealization of power and success now becomes projected onto
Christ. Here we can see how this political backdrop can further reinforce
Nicaea's tendency to sever Jesus' divinity from his concrete life. Schmidt
puts it this way: "Whereas the earthly Christ endured the humiliations of
life and resigned himself to the power of the sword, the heavenly Christ
and his representatives on earth ruled over God's enemies in power and
glory."[19] The Jesus of the ministry who sides with the alienated and is
brought down by the cross is now obscured. What Christians mean by the
Divine is detached from the event which can tell us about the Divine Mystery and replaced by a new, imperial ideology. The practical result is that
Christology no longer fosters the end of exploitation, but legitimates a new
and imperial war machine. What has happened to the Jesus-like Divinity
of love, peace and justice? The implications for soteriology are perverse
too. Rather than spelling the end of human exploitation, Christian soteriology becomes a cult of conquering the masses, piling up conversions, and
demonstrating the imperial hegemony of an imperial Christ.

But there were countervailing trends, often of a subterranean kind,
which to some extent balance and correct the Nicene-Constantinian "two-
edged" contribution to our Christian experience of the Divine. The first
trend I would point to is the appropriation of the Jesus event in the experience and writings of the martyrs, the saints, and the great mystics of the

Church. Running through these men and women is a constant stress upon the humiliated and suffering Jesus of the Gospels which corrects the imperial Christology of the Constantinian era. Insofar as these followers of Jesus derived their experience of the Divine from their Jesus-centered Christology, to that extent they expressed for their own times the love, justice and peace Divinity characteristic of the Jesus event.

It is well known, for example, that the literature of early Christian martyrdom presents us with a Christology of the humiliated Jesus. The very genre of the martyrology is a kind of "proclamation" genre suggesting the surprising and paradoxical way in which the Divine irrupts into the martyr's life and shatters our expectations. "My search is for Him who died for us; my love is for Him who rose for our salvation. The pangs of new birth are upon me. Do nothing to prevent this new life," says Ignatius in his letter to the Romans.[20] In this remarkable text Ignatius indicates that the cross produces glory, that it was through his cross that Jesus revealed the Divine, for he speaks of the cross as a "birth." And he links this experience of humiliation with the Divine, indicating that the Holy Mystery as revealed in Jesus is one of suffering love for us: "As there are two currencies, the one of God, and the other of the world, each stamped in its own way, so the unbelieving have the stamp of the world; those who, in charity, believe have the stamp of God. . . . And, unless it is our choice to die, through Him, unto His passion, His life is not in us."[21]

It is not surprising that women, too, the subjugated of the subjugated, even in Christianity, have left us precious accounts of martyrdom and their own recovery of the humiliated Jesus. Perpetua (c. 202–203) says that the "prison became my palace." The courage she experienced during her moment of trial makes her exclaim, "Suddenly I was a man," perhaps indicating the oppressed status of the women of her day. Only "men" have courageous power in the ideology of an androcentric culture. Her martyrdom is an imitation and re-expression of the humiliated Jesus: "Now it is I who suffer, but then another shall be in me to bear the pain for me, since I am suffering for him." This suffering is a true disclosure of the Divine: Perpetua was "a true spouse of Christ, the darling of God," says the account of her martyrdom.[22]

The Christology of the humiliated Jesus and its richness as a source for our experience of God is one of the major stimulants for the emergence of early monasticism. But it surfaces with particular power and clarity in the writings of the Jesus mystics. Like the Gospels, these mystical writings are usually narratives, expressing the manifestation of the Divine in the very life and struggles of the mystic. In a sense, mystical autobiographies prolong the Gospels, narrating a Gospel-like disclosure of the Divine in the earthly and struggling mystical "ascent." One finds the Divine, so these writings suggest, there in the humiliated life of the mystic, as it was found in the humiliated life of Jesus.

Let me single out two contributions of these mystics that seem especially fecund for our Christian experience of God. First, the mystical teaching on the "dark night" or the so-called "purgative way" seems rich in potential meaning. It is well known that all the mystics, from Jesus and Paul on through to our own times, teach and live some form of purgation as a necessary and always present dimension on the path to union with God. On one level, the dark-purgative night is a metaphor with which to describe what Jesus meant by repentance—the progressive purging of exploitative narcissism which blocks the mystic from participating in the justice, love, and peace characteristic of the Kingdom of God preached by Jesus. On another and even more profound level, the dark night is a participation in and pointer to the Divinity of love, justice, and peace disclosed to us in the Jesus event.

Look, for example, at what the thirteenth century Henry Suso has to say:

> None can come to the sublime heights of the divinity . . . or taste its ineffable sweetness, if first they have not experienced the bitterness and lowliness of My humanity. The higher they climb without passing by My humanity, the lower afterward shall be their fall. My humanity is the road which all must tread who would come to that which thou seekest: My sufferings are the door by which all must come in.[23]

In this vision and revelation from Christ Henry Suso tells us that we only learn what divinity is—in the Christian sense—if we "pass through" the sufferings of the humiliated Jesus. Somehow the true nature of divinity is disclosed in the love, peace and justice of Jesus which brought him down to the cross. Clearly this is a very different perspective from that fostered by the imperial and royal Christology of the Constantinian settlement. It does not deny Nicaea, but corrects it: the transcendence that manifested itself in Jesus came in the form of pathos, the night, the costliness of justice, love, and peace. Similarly the Spanish mystic John of the Cross spoke of the "mystical night" as a participation in and embodiment of a "loving transcendence": "This renovation is . . . an informing of the will with love of God so that it is no longer less than divine and loves in no other way than divinely, united and made one with the divine will and love."[24]

Intimately related to this discussion of the dark night is the Jesus mystics' teaching on the role of the humanity of Jesus in the Christian spiritual life. This theme of the continuing role of Jesus' humanity is again, like that of the dark night, a nearly constant thread in the mystical tradition. What I would suggest here is that, underlying this rich mystical theme, is a view of the Divine Mystery itself. By stressing the Jesus-like and Jesus-mediated nature of our access to God, the mystics are giving witness in their own experiences to the kind of divinity disclosed to us in the Jesus event: a Mystery whose transcendence takes the form of a pathos-like relatedness to humanity in the person of Jesus.

Interestingly, the mystical tradition indicates a certain struggle over this matter which illustrates how difficult to comprehend and how novel is the new form of transcendence disclosed in Jesus. One trend suggests that Jesus' humanity is an obstacle on the path to spiritual growth. Meister Eckhart, for example, in commenting upon John 16:7 ("It is good for you that I go away"), states,

> By that [Jesus] meant to speak not only to his disciples of that time but to all who want to be his disciples now and to follow him to higher perfection. His humanity is a hindrance to them in the pleasure with which they depend on him. If they are to follow God in all his ways, they must not follow the ways of any human being, for these will put them off the road to God.[25]

Here Eckhart does not deny the mediatorial role of Jesus' humanity, but tends to view it as a necessary but still lesser means of access to divine union. One senses that the full novelty of the Jesus event as a revelation of the Divine in suffering love, peace and justice is somewhat overshadowed by an excessively transcendent view of the deity. In commenting upon the same text, Thomas Aquinas to some extent balances and even corrects Eckhart:

> Matters concerning the Godhead are, in themselves, the strongest incentive to love and consequently to devotion, because God is supremely lovable. Yet such is the weakness of the human mind that it needs a guiding hand, not only to the knowledge, but also to the love of Divine things by means of certain sensible objects known to us. Chief among these is the humanity of Christ, according to the words of the Preface [for Christmas], *that through knowing God visibly,* we may be caught up to the love of things invisible. Wherefore matters relating to Christ's humanity are the chief incentive to devotion, leading us thither as a guiding hand, although devotion itself has for its object matters concerning the Godhead.[26]

Here Thomas puts forward a somewhat more favorable view of Jesus' humanity: through it the Divine is encountered. This implies the Christian experience of transcendence as one in the form of love embodied in Jesus. But still there are negative overtones: "Such is the weakness of the human mind that it needs a guiding hand."

To my knowledge it is primarily in the writings of Teresa of Avila, the courageous Spanish mystic and foundress, and, following her, of those of Pierre de Bérulle, the founder of the French Oratory, that we find a fully positive appreciation of the enduring role of Jesus' humanity in the spiritual life. In her autobiography, *The Book of Her Life* (c. 1562), Teresa tells us that she cannot agree with those spiritual teachers who would counsel bypassing Jesus' humanity:

> [Some books] say that in the case of those who are advancing . . . corporeal images, even when referring to the humanity of Jesus, are an obstacle or impediment to the most perfect contemplation. . . . but to withdraw completely from Christ or that this divine Body be counted in a balance with our own miseries or with all creation, I cannot endure.
>
> . . . But if I should have kept to that practice, I believe I would never have arrived at where I am now because in my opinion the practice is a mistaken one.[27]

Teresa goes on to tell us that in this area she listens to the lessons of her own experience: "There was nothing I understood until His Majesty gave me understanding through experience." In so doing she discovered three key reasons for contemplating Jesus' humanity. First, it teaches us humility, if we remain "at the foot of the cross with St. John." Second, it conforms to our human natures, for "we are not angels but we have a body." And most profoundly, it teaches us divine love: "As often as we think of Christ we should recall the love with which He bestowed on us so many favors and what great love God showed us in giving us a pledge like this of his love, for love begets love."

Here it seems that Teresa is on to the incarnational kind of transcendence revealed in the Jesus event: a transcendence in the form of humiliation, conformed to our humanity, and supremely expressed in love. Thus, she continues: "God is very pleased to see a soul that humbly takes His Son as mediator. . . . Such has been my experience; it's the way God has led my soul." Teresa is not denying a wordless, conceptless form of contemplation. There are times when Jesus' "presence is taken away," but this seems replaced by a new kind of presence of Jesus: "Blessed be such a loss that enables us to enjoy more that which it seems is lost." A Jesus-mediated experience of the Divine remains even in the heights of contemplation, even when this new presence is imageless. Apparently even the apophatic tradition of mysticism (= imageless contemplation) is quite congenial to a Jesus-mediated experience of the Divine. Perhaps the apophatic way stresses, in part, the transcendent element even in a Jesus-mediated experience of the Divine: the Divine remains truly Divine and "beyond" the finite. Perhaps, too, the apophatic way stresses the negative dimension of purification from egocentricity involved in a truly Jesus-like experience of the Divine. This purification extends even to our concepts of the Divine. The more affirmative (kataphatic) form of mysticism, which uses images and concepts even in the highest stages of contemplation, perhaps stresses the joyful presence of a Divinity which has entered into our human drama.

Teresa's work of spiritual maturity, *The Interior Castle*, continues to teach that in the highest stages of contemplation the risen Jesus remains present: "The Lord appears in this center of the soul, not in an imaginative vision but in an intellectual one, although more delicate than those mentioned, as He appeared to the apostles without entering through the door when He said to them *pax vobis.*" Interestingly she connects this highest stage of contemplation with a vision of the Trinity, too, and indicates that its effects issue forth in "a forgetfulness of self" and "a great desire to suffer . . . that the will of God be done."[28] Again, I think that Teresa has discovered the novel experience of the Divine revealed in Jesus: a Holy Mystery taking the form of self-forgetful and suffering love. Jesus cannot be severed from the experience of the Divine, because divine transcendence can never be severed from Jesus' love, justice, and peace. Teresa, we know, was a woman, a Jew (?), and a reformer who met with intense opposition. Surely this has a lot to do with her identification with the humiliated Jesus of the Gospels.

Pierre de Bérulle would echo Teresa's teaching in a later context: "If we regard his humanity, it is still a life and source of life . . . emanating from and dependent upon the mystery of the Incarnation, which unites the human and divine natures in one person, and makes this human nature alive and vivifying, by the spirit of the divinity which reposes and dwells in it as a primordial life."[29] Bérulle, too, despite his aristocratic and cardinalatial status, was a reformer who met with intense opposition. Why are reformers attracted to the humble humanity of Jesus?

Jesus mystics, it would seem, are echoing and even enriching Nicaea's teaching that Jesus somehow is taken up into and discloses actual Divinity itself. Divinity has linked itself to Jesus and thereby the Holy Mystery takes the self-limiting form of suffering love. Teresa's stress on humility, self-forgetfulness, love, and even the desire to suffer in imitation of Jesus' passion[30] to some extent corrects any tendency to read Nicaea in the "imperial Christological" sense.

Of course, we need to balance these observations on the martyrs and mystics with a more practical (psychosocial) kind of analysis. What praxis do they inspire, and does this praxis bring out the full force of the Jesus event? Clearly their witness and teaching furnishes a corrective to the imperial Christology: the dark night of suffering and Jesus' humble humanity necessarily remind us of the humiliated Gospel Jesus who sides with the exploited. Curiously, too, it is from the rather marginal martyrs and mystics, and not from the ruling elite of the Church, that this teaching and witness comes. Still, the practical danger of the martyr, and even more of the mystic, is to individualize and interiorize the path of humiliation as a route of access to divinity, as if a "spiritual" and "private" dying with Christ becomes a substitute for the more public path of social humiliation which Jesus walked.[31] The full power of the Jesus event, biblically conceived, demands a recognition of the social and collective protest against human misery which Jesus embodied. This especially is the "locus" of divine presence. The example of the martyrs embodies this "social sting" somewhat more forcefully than the mystics we have surveyed. Still, the intent of the mystics was never simply to privatize the humiliated Jesus. Each tried to embody this social punch of the Jesus event through ecclesial and societal reform.

A final, countervailing trend to the imperial Christology deserving of mention is that of "kenoticism." The word comes from Philippians 2:11, the *kenosis* or self-emptying of God in Jesus. Here I will use the term widely to refer to that strain within the post-biblical tradition which wrestled with the new form of self-limiting transcendence disclosed in Jesus and opposed to any tendency to sever that transcendence from Jesus' humiliated life.

Clearly the Jesus-like disclosure of the Divine raises difficult philosophical and theological questions. It raises equal challenges to our praxis of human living. This was already intuited by the early "Fathers," who often tried to hold in tension the two poles of divine transcendence and human humiliation in the Jesus event. Ignatius of Antioch, the martyr we met earlier, speaks of this tension: "The timeless, the invisible, who was made visible for our sake; impalpable, beyond suffering, who for our sake was subject to suffering." Irenaeus substantially repeats the same tradition, and the best Tertullian can do is to say that he believes this "because it is absurd."[32] Origen goes a little further: "The Father himself is not impassible. If he is asked, he takes pity and experiences grief, he suffers something of love and he comes to be in a situation in which, because of the greatness of his nature, he cannot be and for our sake he experiences human emotion."[33] Origen's disciple Gregory Thaumaturgos will even hold that God voluntarily suffers in the Jesus event, but in such a way that he remains master of his fate and even experiences a secret joy.

Those few statements are enough to indicate that the early Christian thinkers were struggling with the altered form of divinity disclosed in Jesus. The problem was especially acute for them, given the Hellenistic heritage of apathy and divine immutability. Nicaea fostered a certain closure to the discussion by holding that God is not changeable, failing to probe whether we need to distinguish different forms of change in order to come to terms with Jesus' God. Nicaea, too, was apparently only a partial Christifying of Hellenism.

So far as I can tell, Martin Luther is the first to break new ground with his highly fascinating theology of the cross (*theologia crucis*). The remarkable thing about Luther, as Walter Kasper put it, is that "he tries constantly to see, not the cross in the light of a philosophical concept of God, but God in the light of the cross."[34] Thus, in his famous Heidelberg thesis number 20, Luther proposes:

> But he is rightly called a theologian who understands that part of God's being which is visible and directed towards the world to be presented in suffering and in the cross. That part of God's being which is visible and directed towards the world is opposed to what is invisible, his humanity, his weakness, his foolishness. . . . Thus true theology and true knowledge of God lie in Christ the crucified one.[35]

From this angle, Luther refashions Christology, while accepting the teachings of the great councils. If we only know God through Jesus, especially in the cross, then all statements about the majesty of God are transferred to Jesus' humanity, and all statements of Jesus' humanity are transferred to the divine majesty. While this raises intellectual difficulties—if the divine majesty is present in the cross, does he suffer?—still Luther was addressing the novelty of the Jesus event for our understanding of God.

Luther drew practical implications from his suffering "theology" too. The one who "knows" God is the one who is crucified:

> Through the regime of his humanity and his flesh . . . he makes us of the same form as himself and crucifies us by making us true men instead of unhappy and proud gods. . . . That is the Kingdom of faith in which the cross of Christ holds sway, which sets at naught the divinity for which we perversely strive. . . .[36]

While Luther still leaves us with the tension and paradox characteristic of the earlier "Fathers," still he represents something of a more radical development. Unlike the Fathers, he goes from Jesus' cross to the

Divine, not from a prior philosophical viewpoint. What led Luther to the cross? He, like Teresa of Avila, was a reformer too. This link between protesting reformation and the humiliated Jesus is a rather remarkable "undercurrent" in the Christological tradition.

Until our contemporary period, the last great fertile period of kenoticist speculation occurred in the early nineteenth century. It was stimulated by the new psychological studies of the human being as a center of finite consciousness, expressed in the human will, reason, and feelings. Psychology no longer defined the human person in terms of an abstract "nature," but in terms of psychological functions. Some theologians saw in this a new challenge for Christology: how to reconcile a limited human consciousness with Jesus' divine status?

The general trend of these early kenoticists was to suggest that God in some way divested himself, so that the divine presence in Jesus would not "harm" his real human constitution. "Kenosis was to mean a literal loss or diminution of certain aspects of the divine being."[37] Unlike the Fathers and even Luther, who held divine transcendence and human kenosis in a kind of tension, these thinkers more radically argued for a diminishment on God's part. For example, Gottfried Thomasius suggested that God divested himself of certain attributes in the Jesus event. Omniscience, omnipresence, and omnipotence (the "relational attributes") were supposedly shed by God in uniting himself with Jesus. Some wanted to eliminate all divine attributes from Jesus, while others (most famously, Charles Gore) suggested that Jesus was both limited and unlimited. August Ebrard proposed that the divine attributes were somehow "transformed" in Jesus, so as to render them compatible with his humanity. On this view, omniscience would be mutated into a kind of "super" knowledge of events and persons, something rather extraordinary but still compatible with human limits (ESP?).

Each of these early kenoticist theologians was struggling with the novel shape of transcendence taken in the Jesus experience. By hindsight we can perhaps suggest that each was not radical enough. They could not penetrate their problem deeply enough, because they all assumed a certain view of the Divine as basically immutable and impassible. They asked: How is kenosis possible in the light of God's immutable nature? But the Jesus experience forces us to ask: What is the divine nature in the light of kenosis?[38] What the tradition seemed to be struggling with is the need to rethink the Divine in such a way that "we perceive that self-emptying does not mean a loss of divinity," but is the way that divinity discloses itself in Jesus.[39]

Somehow in the Jesus experience divine self-limitation is not a divestiture of divinity, but a revelation of it by peace, justice and love. For

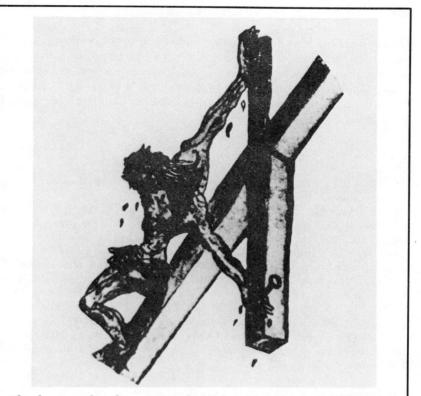

This drawing is based on a vision which John of the Cross had in Avila at the Convent of the Encarnación sometime between September 1572 and December 1577. We know now, from an examination under ultraviolet rays performed in 1969, that this drawing was tampered with. Apparently some later painter "touched up" the upper part of the right forearm and the right hand, as well as the legs. In doing so, this painter obscured the twisted, distorted lines typical of John's drawing.

The remarkable fact about this drawing is that it is unique in the history of crucifixional representation. Note that the cross is seen, not from a spectator's point of view, but from above. This suggests that John views the cross from the divine perspective, as a disclosure of the divine kenosis on our behalf. This drawing expresses, in artistic medium, the thrust of this entire chapter. It is also not without importance that John knew great suffering and persecution in response to his reforming attempts in Spain.

(Cf. José C. Nieto, *Mystic, Rebel, Saint: A Study of St. John of the Cross* [Geneva: Droz, 1979], pp. 101–107)

319

the further story we will have to move into the contemporary period. Still, the kenoticist tradition shows that the Nicene-Constantinian inheritance was not an entirely adequate one. From a practical viewpoint, kenoticism fostered kenosis as a model of the Christian life, a model which undercut Christian imperialism and brought people closer to the suffering Jesus of the Gospels.

Notes

1. R.P.C. Hanson, "The Age of the Fathers: Its Significance and Limits," *Eastern Churches Review* 2 (1968), 131.

2. *Ibid.*, 137. In what follows I will be mainly using an historical-critical and psychosocial approach, since these approaches have made the most substantial contributions thus far. I will inject literary-critical observations when I feel able to do so. We should begin to speak, not only of the Fathers, but also of the Mothers of the Church. Because writings by our founding Mothers are often examples of persecuted literature, they are especially fruitful for Christology. Cf. Patricia Wilson-Kastner *et al.*, *A Lost Tradition: Women Writers of the Early Church* (Washington, D.C.: University Press of America, 1981), and her "Macrina: Virgin and Teacher," *Andrews University Seminary Studies* 17 (1979), 105–117.

3. Eric Voegelin, "The Gospel and Culture," in Donald G. Miller and Dikran Y. Hadidian, eds., *Jesus and Man's Hope*, 2 (Pittsburgh: Pittsburgh Theological Seminary, 1971), p. 62, p. 75.

4. For a helpful overview, see A.H. Armstrong and R.A. Markus, *Christian Faith and Greek Philosophy* (New York: Sheed and Ward, 1960).

5. Lines 5–7, as cited in Geddes MacGregor, *He Who Lets Us Be: A Theology of Love* (New York: Seabury, 1975), p. 23. See his helpful overview, "The Ancient Greek Tradition of Immutability," pp. 23–42. The basic study is Wilhelm Maas, *Unveränderlichkeit Gottes: zum Verhältnis von griechisch-philosophischen und christliches Gotteslehre* (München: Ferdinand Schöningh, 1974). Also helpful: Wolfhart Pannenberg, "The Appropriation of the Philosophical Concept of God as a Dogmatic Problem of Early Christian Theology," *Basic Questions in Theology*, 2 (Philadelphia: Fortress, 1971), pp. 119–183.

6. Fragments 26 and 25, as cited in *ibid.*, p. 25.

7. *Ibid.*, p. .37. The references: Plato, *Republic*, 382e (*The Collected Dialogues of Plato, op. cit.*, p. 630); Aristotle, *Metaphysics*, Lambda 1072b.

8. For the Stoics, cf Heschel, 2, *op. cit.*, esp. p. 33, and J.M. Rist, *Stoic Philosophy* (Cambridge: University Press, 1969), esp. pp. 22–36, 37–53 (for the revisionist view). Eric Voegelin, *Anamnesis, op. cit.*, pp. 97–103, presents the most convincing analysis I have seen. The citation from Plato: *Philebus*, 21e (*The Collected Dialogues of Plato, ibid.*, p. 1098).

9. Acts of John, 90 and 93, Montague Rhodes James, ed., *The Apocryphal New Testament* (Oxford: Clarendon, 1969), pp. 252–253. Cf Aloys Grillmeier, *Christ in Christian Tradition*, 1, *From the Apostolic Age to Chalcedon* (Atlanta: John Knox, 1975²), p. 71.

10. For the standard view set forth here: Hans Jonas, *The Gnostic Religion: the Message of the Alien God and the Beginnings of Christianity* (Boston: Beacon, 1963); Eric Voegelin, *Science, Politics and Gnosticism* (Chicago: Henry Regnery, 1968), and *Order and History*, 4, *The Ecumenic Age, op. cit.*, pp. 20–27; Gregor Sebba, "History, Modernity and Gnosticism," in Peter J. Opitz and Sebba, eds. *The Philosophy of Order: Essays on History, Consciousness and Politics*, Voegelin *Festschrift* (Stuttgart: Klett-Cotta, 1981), pp. 190–241; James M. Robinson, ed., *The Nag Hammadi Library* (New York: Harper and Row, 1977), esp. pp. 1–25; and Kurt Rudolph, *Gnosis: The Nature and History of Gnosticism* (San Francisco: Harper and Row, 1983). Somewhat critical of the standard view: Pheme Perkins, *The Gnostic Dialogue* (New York: Paulist, 1980). Revisionist: Elaine Pagels, *The Gnostic Gospels* (New York: Herder and Herder, 1979).

11. Jaroslav Pelikan, *The Christian Tradition*, 1, *The Emergence of the Catholic Tradition* (Chicago: University of Chicago, 1971), p. 194, citing *Ep. Alex.*, 2. Other overviews: Grillmeier, *op. cit.*; Piet Smulders, *The Fathers on Christology* (De Pere, Wis.: St. Norbert Abbey Press, 1968); and Frances M. Young, *From Nicaea to Chalcedon: A Guide to the Literature and Its Background* (Philadelphia: Fortress, 1983), especially good on Arius and Athanasius, pp. 57–83. Also see the challenging view of Bernard J.F. Lonergan, *The Way to Nicaea* (Philadelphia: Westminster, 1977).

12. *Ibid.*, pp. 194–195, citing *The Letter of Athanasius to Arius*, 2, 24. A new study has recently brought out how Arius was struggling to preserve the authentic humanity of Jesus in the Hellenistic context: cf. Robert C. Gregg and Dennis E. Groh, *Early Arianism: A View of Salvation* (Philadelphia: Fortress, 1981), and the review of this study in *Proceedings of the Catholic Theological Society of America* 36 (1981), 178–182.

13. See Smulders, *op. cit.*, pp. 68–79.

14. I owe this formulation to Simone Weil: "The Father is creation of being, the Son is renunciation of being; this double pulsation is one single act which is Love or Spirit. When humility gives us a part in it, the Trinity is in us. This exchange of love between the Father and the Son passes through creation. All we are asked to do is to consent to its passing through. We are nothing else but this consent" (*First and Last Notebooks* [London: Oxford, 1970], p. 102). For the patristic material on the trinitarian debates, see Pelikan, *op. cit.*, pp. 211–225. For some contemporary analyses, see Joseph A. Bracken, *What Are They Saying About the Trinity?* (New York: Paulist, 1979).

15. I borrow this term from Voegelin, *Conversations with Eric Voegelin* (Montreal: Thomas More Institute, 1980), p. 44. The view of Nicaea as a Christianization of Hellenism is now standard: see Grillmeier, *op. cit.*, p. 267: "Christian monotheism is preserved from Arian Hellenization." Also cf Werner Jaeger, *Early Christianity and Greek Paideia* (Cambridge, Mass.: Harvard University, 1965); E.P. Meijering, *Orthodoxy and Platonism in Athanasius: Synthesis or Antithesis?* (Leiden: Brill, 1968); and F. Ricken, "Nikaia als Krisis des altchristlichen Platonismus," *Theologie und Philosophie* 44 (1969), 321–341.

16. Hans Schmidt, "Politics and Christology: Historical Background," *Concilium* 36 (1968), 79.

17. *Ibid.*, 80.

18. *Ibid.*, 81. Cf. *In Praise of Constantine: A Historical Study and New Translation of Eusebius' Tricennial Orations*, H.A. Drake, trans. (Berkeley: University of California, 1976).

19. *Ibid.* Cf Peter Brown, *The Making of Late Antiquity* (Cambridge, Mass.: Harvard University, 1978), esp. "An Age of Ambition," pp. 27–53, and "The Rise of the Friends of God," pp. 54–80, for a further confirmation of this imperial ideology.

20. *To the Romans*, 6 (*The Fathers of the Church*, 1 [New York: Christian Heritage, Inc.], 1948, p. 110).

21. *To the Magnesians*, 5 (*ibid.*, p. 97).

22. Wilson-Kastner, *op. cit.*, pp. 19–30, for the references.

23. Cited in Underhill, *op. cit.*, p. 409, from *Buchlein von der ewigen Weisheit*, chapter 2.

24. *The Dark Night*, 2,13,11, (*The Collected Works of St. John of the Cross, op. cit.*, p. 361).

25. Cf the comments of Jean Dagens, *Bérulle et les origines de la restauration catholique (1575–1611)* (Paris: Desclée de Brouwer, 1952), pp. 307–308. This citation: *Meister Eckhart: A Modern Translation*, Raymond Blackney, trans. (New York: Harper Torchbook, 1941), p. 199. Cf Dagens' whole chapter, "L'Humanité de Jésus," pp. 301–321, for a helpful overview of the role of Jesus' humanity among the mystics. Also helpful on this: Irenee Noye *et al.*, *Jesus in Christian Devotion and Contemplation* (St. Meinrad, Indiana: Abbey Press, 1974), and George H. Tavard, "The Christology of the Mystics," *Theological Studies* 42 (1981), 561–579. See also Karl Rahner's great essay, "The Eternal Significance of the Humanity of Jesus for Our Relationship with God," *Theological Investigations*, 3 (Baltimore: Helicon, 1967), pp. 35–46.

26. *Summ. theol.*, 2-2, 82, 3, 2 (English trans.: New York: Benziger, 1947, 2, p. 1536).

27. *The Book of Her Life*, 22,1,2 (*The Collected Works of St. Teresa of Avila*, 1, Kieran Kavanaugh and Otilio Rodriguez, trans. [Washington, D.C.: Institute of Carmelite Studies, 1976], pp. 144–145). All references from her *Life* are to this edition, pp. 144–152 at 22, 5, 10, and 14.

28. *The Interior Castle*, 7,1,6; 7,2,3; 7,3,2 (Kanavaugh and Rodriguez, trans. [New York: Paulist, 1979], p. 178, 175, 183). Cf for helpful studies: Joseph Glynn, *The Eternal Mystic: St. Teresa of Avila, the First Woman Doctor of the Church* (New York: Vantage, 1982); Antonio Moreno, "St. Teresa, Contemplation and the Humanity of Jesus," *Review for Religious* 38 (1979), 912–923; and the magisterial work by Secundino Castro, *Cristologia Teresiana* (Madrid: Editorial de Espiritualidad, 1978). A helpful literary study: Mary C. Sullivan, "From Narrative to Proclamation: A Rhetorical Analysis of the Autobiography of Teresa of Avila," *Thought* 58 (1983), 453–471.

29. Bérulle, *Oeuvres de Pieté* (my translation), 29, 3–4. For full references see my *Jesus, Lord and Savior, op. cit.*, "A Study of Bérulle's Christic Spirituality," pp. 226–249. The best brief study is Fernando Guillèn Preckler, *Bérulle Aujourd'hui: Pour une spiritualité de l'humanité du Christ* (Paris: Beauchesne, 1978).

30. See Castro, *op. cit.*, pp. 308–319, for the role of Jesus' passion in Teresa's spirituality.

31. On this danger see Jürgen Moltmann, "Theology of Mystical Experience," *Scottish Journal of Theology* 32 (1979), 501–520.

32. Ignatius of Antioch, *To Polycarp*, 3 (*The Fathers of the Church*, 1 *op. cit.*, p. 125); Irenaeus, *Against Heresies*, 4,20,4; Tertullian, *On the Flesh of Christ*, 5 (*The Ante-Nicene Fathers*, 3, *op. cit.*, p. 525).

33. *Homily on Ezekiel*, 6,6, cited by Robert M. Grant, *The Early Christian Doctrine of God* (Charlottesville: University Press of Virginia, 1966), p. 30. See pp. 111–114, "The Impassibility of God."

34. Kasper, *op. cit.*, p. 180.

35. Cited in Moltmann, *op. cit.*, p. 211 (See Martin Luther, *Werke: Kritische Gesamtausgabe* [Weimar: Herman Böhlau and Nachfolger, 1883ff.] 1, 355). The key work here is Walther von Loewenich, *Luther's Theology of the Cross* (Minneapolis: Augsburg, 1976), esp. pp. 28–31, 112–143.

36. Cited in *ibid.*, pp. 212–213 (*Werke, ibid.*).

37. Donald G. Dawe, "A Fresh Look at the Kenotic Christologies," *Scottish Journal of Theology* 15 (1962), 343; 337–349 for the whole.

38. Cf *ibid.*, 348.

39. *Ibid.* Cf MacGregor, *op. cit.*, and Lucien J. Richard, *A Kenotic Christology: In the Humanity of Jesus the Christ, the Compassion of Our God* (Washington, D.C.: University Press of America, 1982), for studies of the history of kenoticism and its creative applications to a contemporary theology and Christology.

10

Jesus and the Exploration of the Self, Church, Society, and Nature in Later Christianity

Jesus and the Self: Toward a
Jesus-Centered Model of the Self

We have already noted, in our summary of New Testament Christology, how a new model of the self flows from the Jesus event. To borrow Rabbi Heschel's helpful formulation, the God of pathos fosters a sympathetic person. Jesus embodies the lifestyle of repentance and faith, he makes the movement from egocentricity to other-centeredness and the values of the Kingdom. And this Jesus summons us to make the same movement. All of this presents us with the model of a covenantal self, who engages in person-making through the path of commitment to the love, justice, and peace of the new community. Person-making becomes, if you will, a relational project, for one becomes a self through spending oneself in the service of others.

As the early Church had to struggle over the pathos-like divinity disclosed in Jesus, so it had to struggle over the new "sympathetic" humanity disclosed there too. Because of the interrelatedness of the four poles of our existence (God, self, society, nature), oscillations within one of the poles eventually or simultaneously introduce oscillations in all of the others. The history of the Christian tradition is really a history of these oscillations and the Christian community's attempt to understand them and live them out. So it is not surprising that we find a fresh outbreak in thought and praxis of the new self disclosed in Jesus.

One of the ways in which this new interest in the self surfaced in the Fathers' works was in the crucial debates over the "personhood" of Jesus. From Nicaea to Chalcedon primarily, but also extending beyond this point into the rather abstract speculations of the medieval theologians, the

Church struggled with what has been called the "Christological problem proper." What kind of person is this Jesus who bodies forth both humanity and divinity?—that was the constant question. Simultaneously there was speculation on Christian anthropology and Mariology, probing the nature of self-making on the part of ordinary Christians. In the works of the Fathers this gave birth to the great theme of humanity as the image of God, which bodies forth in a Jesus-like way the divine presence too. The two traditions of thought, Christology and anthropology, cannot really be separated. Both were attempts to penetrate the new model of the self disclosed in Jesus. As we will see, each tradition illuminates the other. But for now let me dwell upon the Christological development.

The story begins with Athanasius, who, we recall, used the crucial term *homoousios* (of Nicaea), thus defending the divine presence in Jesus as one identical to the Father. But in his efforts to defend orthodoxy against Arius, he had a tendency to pay very little attention to whether Jesus possessed a real human "soul" (intellect and will). He seems to forget completely the human soul of Jesus. Apollinaris (d. c. 390) goes even further than Athanasius. He not only overlooks Jesus' human soul; he denies it. In this way he thinks he can preserve the divinity of Jesus, avoiding any Arius-like reduction of Jesus to a mere man. He suggested that in the composite of the God-man Jesus, the *Logos* takes the place which the soul occupies in ordinary people. As Piet Smulders explains,

> Or at least—in a sense Apollinaris wavered, conceivably under pressure from his adversaries—the Word takes the place of the higher soul, which in us is the seat of understanding and freedom, the chief principle of our human life, the *nous*. Christ has no human *nous* but in him its function is fulfilled by the Word himself.[1]

Apollinaris is a hinge figure in the history of Christology because he had explicitly raised the question of whether Jesus possessed a truly human soul. Eventually this led the early theologians to a recognition of the inadequacy of the old framework out of which Arius, even Athanasius, and Apollinaris worked—namely, the so called "*Logos-sarx*" (Word-flesh) model of the person of Jesus. There were basically two ways of coping with Apollinaris. One was to remain within the older *Logos-sarx* model, Jesus being modeled forth as a composite of the divine *Logos* and the human flesh. Athanasius apparently took this route. He did not deny Jesus' human soul, but he didn't give that soul any role either. The second manner of coping was to challenge the model itself, suggesting that we should begin to speak, not of a Word-flesh, but of a Word-human ("*Logos-anthropos*") model. On this view, introduced by Theodore of Mopsuestia (d. c. 428), Jesus becomes a composite of divine Word and full humanity (flesh and

soul), rather than the truncated human of Apollinaris. The First Council of
Constantinople (381) condemned Apollinaris and paved the way for the acceptance of this newer, more complete model of the biblical Jesus.[2]

The next stage of the discussion was dominated by the question of the
nature of the union between the divine and human in Jesus. Two key figures in the debate were Nestorius, the patriarch of Constantinople (428–
431) and Cyril, the bishop of Alexandria. Nestorius primarily stressed the
distinction between Jesus' divinity and humanity, without, however, apparently denying their unity (although he was commonly understood as so
denying it). On the other hand, Cyril emphasized the oneness of Jesus'
person, and apparently was unable to clarify the distinction between the
divine and the human to his opponents' satisfaction. At this stage of the discussion, we can begin to speak of two distinct geographical schools of
Christology emerging. Antioch, represented by Nestorius and his followers, takes up the legacy of the "*Logos-anthropos*" model, stressing the
fully distinct natures of Jesus' humanity and divinity. Alexandria, represented by Cyril and the home of the older "*Logos-sarx*" model, tends to
stress Jesus' unity of personhood as the divine Word.

The Council of Ephesus (431) condemned Nestorius, for it thought
that he denied the unity of Jesus' person. It felt that he taught only a kind
of moral or psychological union between the divinity and humanity, the
kind of union found between husband and wife or God and the soul
through grace. A further interesting development was Ephesus' confession of Mary as *Theotokos*, the "Bearer" or Mother of God. The Council's
reasoning was that if Jesus were truly divine and human in one person,
then Mary was birthing God while she was birthing Jesus' humanity. Nestorius had suggested that Mary was only *Christotokos*, the birther of the
humanity.

The Antiochene theologians responded negatively to Ephesus for its
condemnation of their leader, and it was the ensuing debate between the
Antiochenes and Alexandrines that eventually resulted in the "middle
way" of the Council of Chalcedon (451). Just prior to this Council, Eutyches, the archimandrite (abbot) of the monks at Constantinople, had
emerged as a radical Alexandrine. He was popularly thought to stress the
unity of Jesus' person in the divine Word so greatly that he endangered
Jesus' full humanity. Eutyches' teaching came to be called "Monophysitism" (or "Eutychianism"), the reduction of Jesus to one nature, that of the
divine Word. A synod at Constantinople (448) condemned Eutyches, and
Pope Leo the Great, the bishop of Rome and patriarch of the West, accepted this condemnation in his famous "Tome" of 449. In this same Tome,
the Pope proposed the crucial terminology of Jesus' dual natures, human
and divine. Flavian, the patriarch of Constantinople, contributed the no-

tion of Jesus' being one person with his terminology of "one *hypostasis*" and "one *prosopon.*"

Building upon the terminological contributions of Flavian and Leo (person and natures), Chalcedon was able to propose its middle way. With the Antiochenes, it confessed Jesus' dual natures, fully divine and fully human (Leo's contribution). With the Alexandrines, it confessed Jesus' single personhood (Flavian's contribution). The extremes of Monphysitism (the denial of the two natures) and Nestorianism (the supposed denial of a single personhood) were ruled out. The Second Council of Constantinople (553) later clarified Chalcedon by making it clear that the one person (or *hypostasis*) in which the two natures reside is that of the divine Word itself. If you will, the two natures "indwell" the "Logos" (this is called *enhypostasia*). The Third Council of Constantinople (680–681) followed by confessing that Jesus possesses two wills, human and divine, in conformity with his human and divine natures. Apparently there was some debate as to whether Jesus' divine nature robbed him of the exercise of his human freedom (will). This later Council said no, proposing instead that his human will would always act in conformity with his divine will, but it would do so freely.

THE CHRISTOLOGICAL COUNCILS

1. **Nicaea** (325)—debate with Arius over Jesus' divinity; Jesus proclaimed *homoousios* with God

2. **First Constantinople** (381)—upholds against Apollinaris Jesus' human soul/intellect; Trinity defined

3. **Ephesus** (431) —upholds, against Nestorius, that Jesus is one person, although divine and human; Mary proclaimed the *Theotokos*

4. **Chalcedon** (451)—upholds, against Eutyches and Nestorius, that Jesus is two natures in one person—a middle way between extreme Alexandrines and extreme Antiochenes

5. **Second Constantinople** (553)—confesses that the divine Word in Jesus is the foundation of his person in which dwells his divine and human natures; this is called *enhypostasia* (= in the *hypostasis* or person of the Word dwell the natures)

6. **Third Constantinople** (680–681)—confesses that Jesus possesses two fully functioning wills, divine and human

---

CHALCEDON'S DECREE

Following therefore the holy Fathers, we confess
(1) *one and the same* our Lord Jesus Christ, and we all
teach harmoniously [that he is] the same (2) *perfect in
Godhead,* the same (3) *perfect in manhood,* truly God
and truly man, the same of a reasonable soul and body;
(4) *consubstantial with the Father in Godhead,* and
the same (5) *consubstantial with us in manhood, like
us in all things except sin;* begotten before ages of the
Father in Godhead, the same in the last days for us;
and for our salvation [born] of Mary (6) *the virgin theotokos* in manhood, one and the same Christ, Son,
Lord, unique; (7) *acknowledged in two natures without confusion, without change,* (8) *without division,
without separation*—the difference of the natures
being by no means taken away because of the union,
but rather (9) *the distinctive character of each nature
being preserved,* (10) *and [each] combining in one Person and hypostasis—not divided or separated into two
Persons, but one and the same Son and only-begotten
God, Word, Lord Jesus Christ:* as the prophets of old
and the Lord Jesus Christ himself taught us about him,
and the symbol of the Fathers has handed down to us.
[This citation is from Vincent Zamoyta, *The Theology
of Christ: Sources* (Milwaukee: Bruce, 1967), p. 70.]

This decree is a second draft. The first was rejected because it had
lacked any mention of Leo's Tome and because it had the problematic phrase "out of the two natures," which might be given a Mono-
physite sense (out of two natures, Jesus then becomes a third,
singular being). The present draft reads "in two natures" (#7). The
full decree includes (1) a preamble, (2) the creeds of Nicaea and First
Constantinople, (3) the Chalcedonian "symbol" or decree (as above),
and (4) a conclusion. For a detailed analysis, see Ignacio de Urbina,
"Das Symbol von Chalkedon: Sein Text, sein Werden, seine dog-
matische Bedeutung," in Aloys Grillmeier and Heinrich Bacht, eds.,
Das Konzil von Chalkedon: Geschichte und Gegenwart, 1 (Würz-
burg: Echter, 1951), pp. 389–418.

Key to the above: anti-Arian, #4; anti-Apollinarian, #5; anti-Nesto-
rian, ##1, 6, 8, 10; anti-Monophysite, ##2, 3, 4, 5, 7, 9; Flavian's
contribution, #10; Leo's contribution, ##7 and 9.

How do today's scholars evaluate Chalcedon? On the most general level there is widespread agreement that it simply prolongs Nicaea: it is a part of Christianity's defense against an extreme form of Hellenization, which would deny the ability of the Divine to fully unite with the human man Jesus. Apollinaris and Eutyches seem particularly influenced by late Hellenism's immutable deity. The first denies to Jesus a human soul, so that the Divine can fully "govern" Jesus and not be "polluted" by an imperfect human intellect and will. The latter virtually allows the Divine to overpower the human in Jesus, thus preserving divine immutability and impassibility. The Antiochenes, too, are influenced by late Hellenism, even if the Jewish heritage was a strong one in Antioch. One senses that their inability to clarify the union of the divine and human in Jesus can be traced to the legacy of late Hellenism's transmundane and immutable deity.

On another level, that of the clarification of what it is to be a "self" or "person," a growing number of scholars now think that a relational or covenantal model was struggling through to expression, despite the enormously complex language. The crucial point to note is that Chalcedon borrows the term *hypostasis* for its notion of "person," a term which was used earlier in the Trinitarian speculations of the Cappadocians. *Hypostasis* carried the meaning of "relationship," the relationship between Father, Son, and Spirit. Thus, *hypostasis* means that personhood is essentially relational. Now Chalcedon goes further and holds that Jesus' personhood is bipolar: it is a relational reality co-constituted by the two poles of humanity and divinity. If you will, Chalcedon is saying that Jesus is a living relationship with Divinity and humanity. Person-making for Jesus is a relational project, a unity (= person) through duality (= through relating to Divinity and humanity).

Contemporary theologians try to mediate this in contemporary terms in a number of ways. Pannenberg will say that Jesus' person is a living relationship of obedience to the Father. Rahner will say that it is a life of openness to the supreme Mystery that we call God. Von Balthasar, more aesthetically, suggests that Jesus' life is an ecstatic and loving openness to the outgoing Love of God. All of these thinkers view the self of Jesus in relational terms: one becomes a human person through relating to the Divine Mystery. Growth in humanity goes along together with growth in Divinity. Full personhood for Jesus is a divine-human unity and project.

Building on these thinkers, Walter Kasper has perhaps proposed the most balanced mediation of Chalcedon. He suggests the following relational model as implicit in Chalcedon's teaching. Vertically, we can speak of the self's relation to God. This would be the all-encompassing relation, both grounding the self's identity (God calls each unique self into being) and supporting its growth (God is the Mystery toward which we are drawn). Horizontally, we can speak of the self's human pole: its relation to its own psychic history, to other human selves, and even to the world at large. Here we mean that the self comes to self-realization through its varied human and created interrelationships. On this view, "person" means relationality in a dual sense: vertically, to the Divine; horizontally, to the human and created. I would suggest the following diagram of Kasper's "relational model":

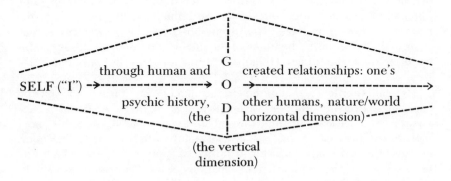

Interestingly, Kasper's model connects with the original meaning of the word "person." Derived from the Latin *per* and *sonare*, it means "to sound through." Kasper is suggesting that one becomes a person through allowing both the vertical and horizontal dimensions of one's existence to "sound through" one. Both planes of relationship are dialectical: they develop or misdevelop together. Some writers speak of this as a "union through differentiation": in the process of person-making, one's self is not annihilated but differentiated (enriched) through openness to the poles of one's existence.

In the light of the above, Chalcedon seems to be saying that Jesus is *persona:* the Divine and the human sound through him in the most complete manner. Second Constantinople was correct to argue that the Divine *Logos* (Word) was the all-encompassing ground of his person, but this needs to be complemented by the horizontal dimension (Jesus' human will and action), which was Third Constantinople's contribution. Jesus relates to the Divine, or it fully sounds through him, in and through his humanity and its various relationships.

In brief, if I might use my own formulation, selfhood is sym-pathy: one-ing with the pathos of the Divine and of humanity. Self-making is the very opposite of apathy![3] Here we see how the sympathetic self disclosed in Jesus corresponds to the Divine pathos likewise disclosed in Jesus. A pathos-like divinity creates a sympathetic humanity. This removes us quite far from the Stoic ideal of the self-sufficient person dwelling in a state of *apatheia*. In this sense, Chalcedon continued the critique of late Hellenism by remaining true to our biblical heritage.

But like Nicaea, Chalcedon and its further aftermath was an ambiguous phenomenon. It represented a greater differentiation of the Jesus event, a kind of noetic clarification of the kind of self implied in the Jesus event. But differentiations tend to become contractions, as we have suggested. The very genre of doctrine lends itself to this. Stressing the manifestation pole of our proclamation-manifestation dialectic, it tends to obscure the challenging and surprising way in which the Divine refuses to allow us to domesticate it. Thus, for example, Chalcedon tends to contract into an abstract formula about the inner constitution of Jesus the whole concrete and dynamic life of relationships characteristic of the biblical Jesus. The formula also fails to clarify the key differences between the ways in which the Divine and human each contributes to the singular unity which Jesus is. They do not simply co-exist, but the Divine is the supporting ground of the human. The salvific significance of the entire Chalcedonian effort is hardly touched upon either. There is a brief mention that the Jesus event is for our salvation, but nothing more.

The dissatisfaction with Chalcedon becomes even greater when we complement our analysis with the concerns which flow from praxis and psychosocial/deconstructive criticism. This dissatisfaction would even apply to the views of the contemporary theologians we have mentioned above (Rahner, Von Balthasar, Pannenberg, and Kasper), which are not sufficiently informed by praxis on this issue. Again, Chalcedon was an event in the history not simply of meaning, but also of praxis. Its desire was to promote not only right understanding, but right living. Both Monophysitism and Nestorianism, influenced as they are by late Hellenism's apathetic deity, foster an ethics of apathy. An excessively transmundane deity fosters an excessively low view of humanity, and this leads to human callousness and apathy. This praxis-dimension of Chalcedon is missing in our modern theological interpretations, and in Chalcedon.

But psychosocial criticism would go even further and suggest that Chalcedon, together with many contemporary, rather idealistic theological theories, fails to bring out the full critical and social "punch" of the self disclosed in the experience of Jesus. Jesus did indeed embody the "relational self" implied by Chalcedon, and so helpfully elaborated by contemporary theologians. But he spent himself in the humiliated service of others through solidarity with the victims of history, and through risking the crushing opposition of oppressive powers. His network of relations was not simply of the peaceful, serene, bourgeois type (family, intimates, and

affirming disciples), he was in relation with the harsh powers of the society
of his time. He was in relationship with the powerful institutions of his day,
struggling to bring about the new community of justice and love. By failing
to bring this out, Chalcedon and its contemporary commentators play into
the hands of the dogmatic-imperial Christ fostered by the Nicene-Constantinian settlement, and subtly rob the self of Jesus of its full critical and
practical punch.

Fortunately there were countervailing and corrective trends to the
Chalcedonian settlement within the tradition. These are found, not primarily in the history of Christology in the narrow theological sense, but in
the history of Christian spirituality and theological anthropology. For reflection upon the kind of self or person-making disclosed in the Jesus experience also occurred, not in grappling simply over the person of Jesus,
but in grappling over the person-making to which all Christians are called
by Jesus. While the post-biblical tradition clearly thinks, like the Scriptures, that the "self" of Jesus is in some real sense special and unique, that
same tradition recognizes an analogous similarity between Jesus' self and
that of every other Christian. Others are his disciples who imitate him.
Their experience, too, can serve as an index of the new self disclosed in
Jesus.

In this regard, I would single out as particularly important the contribution of the great Christian mystics. In many of them we find the Jesus-
like model of the relational self embodied and reflected upon. For them,
person-making is not a narcissistic project, but a painful passage from egocentricity to the other-centeredness of the Divine pathos and human sym-
pathy. The so-called "purgative way" is a metaphor for this painful passage
from the negative side: slowly transforming one's life from its islands of
egocentricity and exploitativeness. The "illuminative" and "unitive" ways
of the mystics are metaphors of this passage from the positive side: as one
moves from narcissism, one grows in commitment to justice, peace and
love. One commits oneself to the values of the Kingdom (= "illumination"), and in so doing, one is united with the God disclosed in Jesus (=
"union").

The Jesus mystics view their person-making as an imitation (better: a
reflection) of the self disclosed in Jesus: "First, have a habitual desire to
imitate Christ in all your deeds by bringing your life into conformity with
His. You must then study His life in order to know how to imitate Him and
behave in all events as He would," says John of the Cross.[4] We clearly find
Kasper's "vertical pole," the Godward pole, of our self-making in the mystics: "What God seeks, He being Himself God by nature, is to make us
gods through participation, just as fire converts all things into fire."[5] And,
as well, the "horizontal pole": "Always be more disposed toward giving to

others than giving to yourself, and thus you will not be envious of nor self-ish toward your neighbor."[6] One senses in the mystics, represented here by John of the Cross, a somewhat fuller appropriation of the Jesus-self than that put forward by Chalcedon. If you will, Jesus' path of humiliation and struggle comes through somewhat more powerfully here. The narrative genre of the mystics' autobiography underscores this: in the drama of their struggling lives, with the ups and downs, we find the "manifestation" of the new self of Jesus.

There are, of course, other precious examples of Christian anthropology within the tradition which we could use for insights about the new Jesus-like self of Christianity. The brilliant speculations of the Fathers on humanity and Jesus' mother Mary especially as the *imago Dei*, imag-ing forth divine agape, likewise point to the new self.[7] But something of the actual struggle of person-making, its unserene and non-bourgeois charac-ter, surfaces rather more effectively in the narrative-autobiographies of the Jesus mystics. And again it is not unimportant that these mystics represent a rather marginalized and critical element within the Church. The pull and attraction of these kinds of persons to the humiliated Jesus-self of the Gos-pels deserves more careful consideration.

To be sure, as psychosocial criticism would insist, there is among the mystics the typical danger of interiorizing and individualizing the Jesus-like process of self-formation. Spiritual oneing with the Divine and the neighbor can be substituted for the kind of involvement in social and po-litical renewal to which Jesus calls us. This would fail to bring out the full pathos of the self of Jesus with its sympathy for the oppressed. But mys-ticism is a developing reality, and as mystics are found more and more, not among the relatively elite and privileged, but among the ordinary, this so-cial punch of Christian self-making surfaces ever more clearly. Gladly some recent scholars in spirituality, like Matthew Fox and Richard Woods, under the influence often of political/liberation theology, are correcting the privatization of the spiritual life.[8]

Jesus and Society:
Toward a Covenantal Community

We recall that for the New Testament the Jesus experience inaugu-rated a new experiment in human and social relations. Not only was the Jesus event a disclosure of the divine pole of human existence, and the re-sponse to that pole on the part of the self. If you will, a pathos-like God and a sympathetic self were seen to co-implicate one another. It was also an event with a collective and social punch. A pathos-like God generates a sympathetic community too. The self and God are not isolated "monads":

they exist within human societies and create social reverberations. The transcendent power of justice, peace and love, revealed in Jesus, is a community-making power, transforming interhuman relationships within history.

In a kind of shorthand way, I described this new social experiment as a "radicalized covenantal community." By this I meant, staying close to the biblical symbolism, that the new community of Jesus was a covenant-making one, through the overcoming of all master-slave relationships. Although tempted by utopianism and pessimism from time to time, this community remains a fragile but nonetheless effective force for social transformation in human history.

In regard to this, and again taking a broad view of later developments, we can note two rather dangerous tendencies within the post-biblical tradition. One is a utopian tendency which reduces the Jesus-like community of justice, peace and love to the Church or to particular political and cultural movements within history, forgetting its fragmentary, in-between character. This characterized the Constantinian epoch (which clearly extends in some way up through the Middle Ages) and much of the subsequent history of the Roman Church. As we noted, the dogmatic Christ of Nicaea could function as a political legitimation of the Roman-Christian Empire: the emperor becoming the earthly reflection of the Lordship of Christ, vanquishing all foes. We end up with the famous trilogy of Eusebius of Caesarea: "One God, one *Logos*, one Empire." Rather than being Jesus' new community on behalf of justice, peace and love, the Kingdom gets reduced to a political empire.

The Roman Church, especially in the important medieval disputes about its freedom from the state, argued that the Church's charge was to witness to the power of the transcendent within history. While this was an important segment of the struggle to appropriate the transcendent character of Jesus' new community, fueled as it is by *divine* love, still the Church fell into the tendency to identify itself in simple terms with the Kingdom of Jesus. A triumphalism of the Church tended to replace the triumphalism of the Empire.[9] A similar reduction of the Kingdom occurred in the liberal theology of the nineteenth century, which tended to identify the Kingdom with progressive liberal movements for reform within Western society. All of these examples illustrate the tendency toward utopianism, the failure to preserve the peculiar in-between and fragmentary character of the Kingdom inaugurated by Jesus.

And there are practical effects from such utopianism. For it tends to overlook the unfinished character of the new Jesus-community. It masks the incompleteness of either the Church or the Empire. It mutes the call to work for the overcoming of all master-slave relationships, and fosters a loss of self-critique. It also fosters arrogance, dogmatism, intolerance, and even a form of totalitarianism in the name of the Divine. For if one is perfect, then one doesn't need to look at failures.

The second and opposite tendency is that of excessively opposing the reality of the Kingdom to both the Church and social movements within history. This is the pessimistic, rather than the utopian, temptation. There is a recurring tendency on the part of spiritual movements to be fueled by an excessively negative attitude toward Church and world, viewing both as simply corrupt and headed for self-destruction. The Lutheran "two kingdoms" doctrine can be read in this way, as well as the spiritual protests of many fundamentalists down through the ages. This tendency overlooks the present efficacy of Jesus' community of love, peace and justice in history. The thrust of the Jesus event is to disclose that the Kingdom has indeed made a breakthrough, however tenuous, within history: the transcendent power of justice, love, and peace is operative now, moving us toward a better future. Fidelity to Jesus means being in-between utopianism and pessimism. The first tendency overlooks the fragmentary and not-yet character of Jesus' new community, reducing it to empire (or its equivalents) and Church. This second one overlooks the community's present effectiveness, drowning itself in an apocalyptic pessimism.

And there are practical consequences which flow from pessimism too. For the spiritual carriers of such sentiments are frequently elitist and moralistic. They are the ones who know the secret meaning of the world, and this shields them from any self-critique. This also fosters a kind of fanaticism, a pressing urgency to bring others around to their infallible point of view. Curiously, too, pessimism leaves the world unchanged. Its waiting until the Kingdom comes leaves the world's oppressed as victimized and as miserable as they were before the *illuminati* had their great revelations.

So far as I can tell, on the theoretical level it was St. Augustine who faithfully interpreted the Jesus event, when he suggested that the "City of God" (= Jesus' Kingdom) and the "City of Man" (= the anti-kingdom of lovelessness) are in a kind of perpetual conflict and cut across both the Church and society at large. That is, either or both Church and wider society can embody the City of God through works of love, or the City of Man through works of exploitative narcissism and power-grabbing (the lust for power). Augustine grasped the peculiarly in-between character of Jesus' new community. Church and society can be fueled by the City of Man, by lovelessness. They can also be fueled by the City of God, by love. They are an ambiguous mix, for the new community of Jesus is in the in-between of the present and the not-yet.

Somewhat missing from Augustine's powerful and still relevant mediation of the Jesus-like community is the social edge of the Jesus event,

as one which actively works for the overcoming of all master-slave relationships. He tends to identify the Kingdom with love, understood in a
more neighborly and bourgeois sense, and forgets too easily about justice
and the actual confrontation with societal powers implied in the new community of Jesus. He also tends, one-sidedly, to limit this love to the
Church, forgetting that it is a community-making power which can spill
over beyond the frontiers of the Church itself.[10]

But our tradition is rich and complex, and again we find corrective, if
marginal, tendencies which offset both utopianism and pessimism. I would
point within Roman Catholicism to the continual emergence of the religious orders; within Eastern Orthodoxy, to the renewing power of monasticism; within Protestantism, to the critical "Protestant principle" and
the work of the Reformers; and even to the radical, Free Church wing of
the Reformation. All of these movements were attempts to re-express what
Jesus meant by his community of justice, peace and love. First of all, they
were all movements: not isolated individuals, but attempts to give social
embodiment to the community-making power of the Jesus event. In this
sense, they were timely reminders and confirmations of the social punch
of the Jesus event. They point to the inadequacy of a purely interior and
privatized interpretation of the Kingdom. Second, they were all fueled by
a commitment to the concrete Jesus of the Gospels, rather than an imperial
Christology. They remain close to the biblical Jesus who walked the path
of humiliation in the service of his work. Staying close to the humiliated
Jesus is a way, if you will, of remaining in that in-between space of Jesus
which avoids utopianism without lapsing into pessimism.

The evangelical counsels of poverty, chastity, and obedience, embraced by Catholicism's religious orders, have been a creative way of re-
embodying the values of the Kingdom. At their best, these counsels fostered an identification with Jesus' solidarity with the poor (poverty), his
own non-narcissistic commitment to justice, love, and peace (chastity),
and his openness to the God of love, justice, and peace upon whom the
new community is founded (obedience). Of course, as psychosocial criticism reminds us, there has always been a tendency to spiritualize and privatize these counsels, robbing them of their critical and liberating punch
for Church and society. But despite this tendency, one still senses that Jesus' new community often comes through more powerfully within the orders than within the larger, more formalized Church itself.[11]

The Eastern Orthodox tried to re-express Jesus' vision of a new community through the development of a communal monastic life out of the
earlier, more solitary eremiticism of the desert Fathers and Mothers. This
was primarily the ground-breaking work of Pachomius (d. 348) and Basil.
"The Basilian community was an expression of the charity of Christ, which

cannot be shut up in itself, and its atmosphere was that of a family ruled by the Gospel above all," says M.J. Le Guillou.[12] This monastic community attempted, fragmentarily, to embody the Kingdom. It strove to realize the "paradise" of the Kingdom through the way of the cross and death, in unceasing conflict with the Satanic powers of the anti-kingdom. Especially important in Orthodox monasticism is its wholly cross-centered asceticism: it cultivates humbleness, obedience, brotherly and sisterly charity, work, and communal prayer. Interestingly, the Orthodox believe that communal commitment to the cross opens the way to true "transfiguration": "Those who have lifted their mind to God and exalted their soul by his passion see their flesh, too, transformed and exalted, sharing the divine fellowship and becoming God's dwelling place; for the body is no longer a centre of opposition to him, it has ceased to have desires that are contrary to the Spirit."[13] Despite the tendency to spiritualize and idealize their in-between paradise, something of the true Jesus-community surfaces here. As Isaac the Syrian put it, monasticism should produce "a heart that burns with love for every creature, for men, animals, birds, evil spirits, for all creation."[14]

Protestantism, too, has spawned its communal embodiments of Jesus' new community of justice, love, and peace. The great Reformers, of course, from Luther to Calvin and on through to Wesley, attempted to renew the Church by freeing it of triumphalism and returning to the values of the Gospel. Like the reformist religious orders, however, these Reformers were gradualists in their attempts to reform the Church. If you will, they were somewhat radical in doctrine but conservative in Church polity, if I might borrow from Rosemary Ruether's interpretation.

In England, for example, the Anglican Church was simply nationalized. In Lutheran territories, the older Catholic parish structure was retained, but brought under the rule of the princes. Presbyterians in Scotland and Puritans in England also established their ruling councils and "assumed a single territorial church in an established relationship with the state."[15] In this way, the older Constantinian settlement, whereby the Church relies on the state to coerce dissenters, was maintained by the Reformers. If you will, this was the thread of utopianism in the Reformation: reducing the Kingdom to a particular political and religious force within history.

The Radical Reformation went further in its attempts to renew the Church. It recovered the older apocalyptic symbol of the Kingdom as a reality which transcends the world in anticipation of a better age to come. Free Churches rejected the alliance of Church and state, and viewed themselves as a body over against both Church and society. They advanced a radical doctrine of the "fall" of the Church and looked toward

God's restitution of a more perfect Church. In accord with this spirit, they formed "free" communities, accepted no support from the state, adopted a simple lifestyle, and practiced a communal ethic of sharing—all in an attempt to embody the Kingdom.

Of course, the great danger of the Radical Reformation is that of pessimism, a forgetfulness of the ability of the Jesus event to change Church and society effectively now. Still, one can see struggling for expression many of the authentic dimensions of the Jesus-community, particularly the stinging critique of all triumphalism.

To this brief survey we should add any of the other explicitly Christian and even social movements which have been primarily fueled by a spirit of opposition to exploitation and trying to further the work of justice, love, and peace. As Augustine put it, the City of God cuts across both Church and society, and we should not be afraid to recognize non-churchly variants of the presence, even if fragmentary, of the Kingdom. In our Western world, a good case could be made that the City of God finds at least partial realization in the gradual development of democracy, with its various attempts to extend the liberal values of freedom, equality, and justice to a wide assortment of peoples. Of course, this has now spilled over into more radical movements—a kind of secular equivalent of the Radical Reformation—which are trying to correct the inequities still present in the major Western democracies: the feminist movement, the overcoming of racism, ecological movements, etc. These, too, from a Christian perspective, are pointers to the community-making power and dynamic of the Jesus event.

Jesus and Nature:
Appropriating an Ethics of Self-Limitation

As we have proposed throughout, the fourfold structure of our common existence is an interpenetrating whole: oscillations in one of the poles entail oscillations in all of them. Thus, the pathos-like God and the sympathetic self and society disclosed in Jesus' experience are three dimensions of the one, same reality. Now I want to turn to the final member of our quaternity, the world/nature. I proposed earlier that Jesus links the Kingdom together with nature. Nature is the place and space of the Kingdom, and it plays a role in Jesus' dreams for our better future. Jesus' real and special originality seems to reside in his ethics of self-limitation, that is, in his refusal to exploit and harm anyone or anything. In this way, nature is a true partner with us in our quest for justice, peace and love. How has this dimension of the Jesus event fared in the post-biblical tradition?

Taking the broad view again, which is all that this survey will allow, we can notice two dangerous tendencies at work. One is the attitude and embodiment of distrust toward the world and nature. Just how this creeps into the Christian tradition is a complex and still ambiguous issue. On a very basic level it perhaps has something to do with a primal fear of the body and of nature. After all, we do not completely control our bodies, or nature for that matter. They (bodies) get sick, embody uncontrollable rage, become involuntarily stimulated, master us quite frequently (we must eat, defecate, and reproduce), and they grow old. Nature, too, of which our body is a part, is an ambiguous phenomenon. It not only nourishes and protects, but harms and kills. It, too, is unpredictable. We notice this primal fear of nature/ body in taboos about sexuality, and in the awe of nature as a sacred power which overwhelms us (it is awe-ful).

Other attitudes also play their part. Sometimes we blame the body for our faults and sin, when in fact it is our disoriented desires that are the cause. Alcoholism or sexual license is our body's fault, so we think, when in fact the fault lies much deeper. The body becomes the victim of a projection. An important factor is a kind of philosophical and theological dualism, which opposes the material to the spiritual. To some extent, the twin discoveries of mind and transcendence in Greece tended to foster a denigration of the material.[16] The trans-material power of the spiritual was set over against a supposedly inferior matter. This dualism can reinforce and legitimate our primal fears and taboos about nature and body, giving them a pseudo-justification. The enormous influence of the Greek world of thought and experience over the early Christian thinkers not surprisingly allowed this denigration of matter to enter our orbit. But this was probably not simply a matter of a one-way influence from Greece, but of a mutual attraction by both parties. After all, the primal fears of nature and body were not limited to the Greeks.

In any case, it is not difficult to illustrate, through the texts of our tradition, the distrust and denigration of matter. Most blatantly, Ambrose will argue: ". . . it is not possible to be at home with God and with the flesh at the same time."[17] Origen, in his *Commentary on the Song of Songs*, says of the person reading it "only after the flesh": he "will twist the whole manner of his hearing it away from the inner spiritual man on to the outward and carnal; and he will be turned away from the spirit to the flesh. . . ."[18] All of this comes close to a gnostic alienation from matter. Generally, the early thinkers combine a late Hellenistic distrust of the body with a Christian and biblical appreciation of it as a good gift. But they do so in an unintegrated manner. One can find in Augustine and Thomas Aquinas, for example, both negative and affirmative statements on matter. Augustine, for example, knows that the body is good—a divine creation—and yet he will argue that conjugal intercourse "is effected in such a way as to be accompanied by a feeling of shame, by way of punishment."[19] Meister Eckhart can likewise argue: "There is no physical or fleshly pleasure without some spiritual harm."[20]

The second dangerous tendency is that of exploiting and abusing the world of nature and body. Historically this has taken several forms. Libertinism or sheer sensualism does with the body what it will. Irenaeus accused some gnostics of this tendency: they "yield themselves up to the lusts of the flesh with the utmost greediness, maintaining that carnal things should be allowed to the carnal nature, while spiritual things are provided for the spiritual."[21] Sensualism regards the body as a mere tool to be used as one wishes. Exploitation often takes the form of a raping of nature for one's own material and technological ends, without regard for what this does to nature itself. A dualism of preference for the spiritual over the material can often reinforce this posture of exploitation. In any case, our history of the abuse of nature hardly needs much more proof today.

What is crucial is to grasp the connection between our two postures, that of distrust and that of exploitation. Both are fueled by a "low view" of matter. Instead of seeing it as a divine gift and partner with us, it is viewed as essentially valueless. It is "neuter"—neutral, to be used and abused as one wishes. From this same spring, our two postures draw opposite conclusions. If the material is valueless, the distrusters argue that we must either avoid it or control it, in order to give free scope to the spirit. Asceticism becomes a technique of avoidance of matter or bodily punishment and control. The exploiter, on the other hand, seeing no value in matter, sees no harm in doing anything with it, even abusing it. Sexual libertinism and the exploitation of nature are two forms of the one and same reality: rape. Here asceticism yields to hedonism.

Generally the Christian tradition has struggled to avoid these two extremes. The biblical view of a divine creation and the Jesus-view of matter as the space of the Kingdom have found expression in post-biblical Christianity in a sacramental approach to nature and body, regarding them as mediators of the Divine. This is the ethos lying behind the sacraments of the Churches, behind the mystics' celebration of nature, and behind the Christian artist's paintings and architecture. Here the estimate of the material is not "low," but "high": matter can mediate the Divine.[22] Perhaps this reached its consummate expression in Francis of Assisi's hymn to Brother Sun and Sister Moon. This Christian celebration of the material spawns its own asceticism, too; however it is not one of distrust, but of vigilance over the egoistic self which can misuse nature for its own greedy ends. At its best the tradition's teaching on detachment and asceticism was motivated by a desire to overcome the "inordinate" misuse of the body and matter through egoism. And at this point—that of detachment—the post-biblical tradition links up with and appropriates in its own way Jesus' ethic of self-limitation.

But let me complement this brief sketch with some observations motivated by psychosocial criticism. The latter would sensitize us, first, to the fact that an ethics of self-limitation has a tendency to be viewed too privatistically. This is true among the mystics and spiritual writers in general. The social and collective punch of Jesus' ethic of self-limitation needs greater development and stress. Not only personal detachment from egoism, but collective detachment is our summons. Only in this way can an effective antidote to the raping of nature be set in motion. Only in this way can we effectively cut through the many ways in which society reinforces our fears and taboos of matter, helping us to project on matter what really stems from our inward misorientation. The postures of distrust and exploitation of nature are rooted within the social fabric too, and require a social remedy.

Finally, I think that psychosocial criticism alerts us to the systematic linkage between self-exploitation, societal exploitation, the exploitation of matter, and even our disoriented relation to the Divine. Paying attention to praxis helps us grasp that exploitation in any one of these areas wears a similar "practical" face in all of the other areas, namely, exploitation. An effective, practical therapy must penetrate our entire quaternion structure. But with these final observations, we are already moving toward our consideration of soteriology and some of the concerns of our contemporary scene. So let us end our brief sketch of the post-biblical tradition here.

Notes

1. Smulders, op.cit., p. 82.

2. I am summarizing Grillmeier, op. cit. Young, op. cit., pp. 178–289 is also helpful, esp. p. 180, where she shows that the two Christologies tend to overlap (*Logos-sarx* and *Logos-anthropos*); The question was: Who was the subject of the incarnate experiences of Jesus? Alexandrines stressed the Word as the subject. On the other hand, the Antiochenes felt that the teaching of Nicaea made it impossible to attribute human actions to the Word.

3. For an overview of the various theories, see my *Jesus, Lord and Savior*, op. cit., pp. 162–192, esp. pp. 188–191, notes 51 and 52. A good study of the medieval development is Philipp Kaiser, *Die Gott-menschliche Einigung in Christus als Problem der spekulativen Theologie seit der Scholastik*, Münchener Theologische Studien, No. 36 (München: Max Hueber, 1968).

4. *The Ascent of Mt. Carmel*, 1,13,3 (*The Collected Works of St. John of the Cross, op. cit.*, p. 102).

5. *Maxims on Love*, 28 (*ibid.*, p. 676).

6. *Degrees of Perfection,* 17 (*ibid.,* p. 681).

7. For this, see John Meyendorff, *Byzantine Theology: Historical Trends and Doctrinal Themes* (New York: Fordham, 1974), pp. 138–150, and Tambasco, *op. cit.*

8. Cf Richard Woods, *Mysterion, op. cit.,* and Matthew Fox, *On Becoming a Musical Mystical Bear* (New York: Paulist, 1976²) and *A Spirituality Named Compassion* (Minneapolis: Winston, 1979).

9. Cf Kasper, *op. cit.,* pp. 264–265, for a helpful sketch. On the triumphalist Church, see Avery Dulles, *Models of the Church* (Garden City, N.Y.: Doubleday, 1974), pp. 31–42; on the Byzantine equivalent, see Meyendorff, *Living Tradition, op. cit.,* pp. 187–202.

10. Cf Augustine, *City of God,* ed. David Knowles (Baltimore: Penguin, 1972), and Charles N.R. McCoy, "St. Augustine," in Leo Strauss and Joseph Cropsey, eds., *History of Political Philosophy* (Chicago: Rand McNally, 1963), pp. 151–159 (for a good summary).

11. Cf Lawrence Cada *et al., Shaping the Coming Age of Religious Life* (New York: Seabury, 1979), and Johannes B. Metz, *Followers of Christ* (New York: Paulist, 1978). Extremely helpful is Raymond Hostie, *Vie et Mort des Ordres Religieux* (Paris: Desclee de Brouwer, 1972), for a psychosocial analysis of the religious orders.

12. M.J. Le Guillou, *The Spirit of Eastern Orthodoxy* (New York: Hawthorn, 1962), p. 64; cf pp. 63–72, for an overview.

13. *Ibid.,* p. 69.

14. *Ibid.,* p. 72.

15. Ruether, *The Radical Kingdom: The Western Experience of Messianic Hope* (New York: Harper and Row, 1970), p. 22; pp. 21–35, for an overview. Also cf her *The Church Against Itself, op. cit.*

16. For an overview, see Armstrong and Markus, *op. cit.,* pp. 30–58.

17. *De Isaac,* 54, cited by Margaret R. Miles, *Augustine on the Body* (Missoula, Mt.: Scholars Press, 1979), p. 59.

18. *Ancient Christian Writers,* 26 (Westminster, Md.: Newman, 1957), pp. 22–23.

19. *City of God,* 14, 18, *op. cit.,* p. 580.

20. *Meister Eckhart, op. cit.,* p. 90.

21. *Against Heresies,* 1, 6, 3 (*The Ante-Nicene Fathers,* 1 [Grand Rapids, Michigan: Wm. B. Eerdmans, 1956], p. 324).

22. A helpful study on this is Charles Davis, *Body as Spirit: The Nature of Religious Feeling* (New York: Seabury, 1976).

11

Salvation and Spirituality in the Light of Jesus: A Suggestion

Throughout this work I have tried to emphasize the intimate bond between Christology and soteriology, Jesus as the Christ and as the Savior. A balanced study must never really separate these twin dimensions of the Jesus event. As we saw in our survey of New Testament Christology, the Jesus event is at once a new disclosure of our common fourfold structure, and a promised rectification of its misorientation. The New Testament believes that somehow our relations to God, to self, to society, and to nature are out of sorts. The fresh start of peace, love and justice unleashed in Jesus works to rectify this. That is what the New Testament means by salvation. It uses a dazzling assortment of images, but underlying them all is the realist conviction that we are out of sorts and equally liberated by the Jesus event.

Sadly a tendency toward isolating soteriology from Christology took root in the post-biblical tradition. To some extent, the great Christological councils contributed to this tendency, forced as they were by heresy to consider only isolated elements of the Jesus event. While these councils always prefaced their work with the observation that Jesus was "for our salvation," still their greater emphasis was upon the "inner constitution" of Christ. The enormous influence of these councils meant that the Church would take its chief clues from them, thus pushing soteriology to the background.

The more speculative and rational theologies inspired by Hellenism's entrance into Christianity also furthered the tendency. The rational mind likes to dissect, and such dissection can lead to the separation of realities that should be united. In the East, we can see this analytical mentality at work in John Damascene's *On the Orthodox Faith* (eighth century). In presenting a synthesis of the early Fathers' teachings, he separates the Trinity from creation and sin, and even from Christology. In the West, this same separation is typical of the most important authors: Honorius of Autun, Anselm, Peter Lombard. Thomas Aquinas tries to hold Christology

343

and soteriology together, but in a somewhat artificial way. He builds his great *Summa* on the famous *exitus-reditus* pattern of Neo-Platonism: God outgoes himself in creation (= *exitus*), and creation returns to him through salvation (= *reditus*). Thus, the *Summa* begins with God, moves to a consideration of creation, and ends up with a study of Christ and the sacraments, which are the saving means of return to God. But one may well ask whether Christology and soteriology do not come rather late in this schema.[1]

We should probably add some further factors in this regard. At the top of the list should be the gradual loss of the emphasis upon the humiliated Christ of the Gospels. The rather "high" Christ of Nicaea fostered a forgetfulness of the evil powers which brought Jesus down to his death. As we saw, Christianity was threatened by an imperial Christology which masked the real horrors from which we are in need of salvation. Scholars often point to the growing subjectivism and individualism of the West as another factor to be considered. This did foster a kind of interest in soteriology by focusing upon what the Jesus event has done "for me." This "for me" emphasis is typical of Luther, for example. This privatism, however, tends to rob the Jesus event of its collective and critical punch toward societal evils and sin, thus obscuring the social dimension of soteriology.[2]

Spirituality fared no better than soteriology. The narrowness of focus of the Christological councils hardly enabled them to surface the new "spiritual lifestyle" implied in the Jesus event. Theology's increasingly rational mode drove the study of spirituality into the religious orders, and Scholastic theology paid it little attention. Subjectivism tended to create a kind of privatistic spirituality, divorced from the great social themes of Jesus. In brief, spirituality was severed from Christology and soteriology, and that is why most books on Christology, even today, ignore the great intuitions of the mystics and saints.[3]

Most scholars today now recognize that we need to correct the fracturing of the Jesus event which has corroded our Christological work. This means that we must make a continual effort to unite Christology and soteriology, and even spirituality, if we are to be faithful to the full contours of the Jesus event. In what follows, I would like to retrieve some of the post-biblical insights that seem most fruitful in this regard. I will range rather widely through the tradition, and then attempt a possible synthesis at the chapter's end.

Taking the broad view, I would suggest that two key intuitions emerged from the biblical soteriology. First, the New Testament is "critically realist": implied in its rich soteriological imagery is the conviction that humanity is in bondage or plighted—"out of sorts," as we suggested.

Second, it implies that the Divine has acted in the Jesus event to overturn our human bondage and initiate a process of salvation. In a kind of abbreviated formula, we could say, the breakthrough of divine justice, peace and love is the therapy of the Jesus event to be applied to our human bondage. Let us now see how these two intuitions have fared in the post-biblical tradition, and then attempt our own contemporary restatement.

Some Insights from the Later Tradition

Salvation-Imagery in the Age of the Fathers and Mothers

This early period almost assaults us with a dazzling variety of images for the soteriological mystery of Jesus. Joseph Mitros[4] suggests that soteriology was never really challenged in this early period; hence, the lack of unified theories. The Fathers and Mothers are still relatively close to the Jesus event, and the wholeness of that event as both a Christological and a soteriological mystery, with profound consequences for spiritual praxis, was kept in focus. Typical is the statement from Clement, which we have seen before: "The Word of God speaks, having become man, that such as you may learn from man how it is even possible for man to become a god." Here we see how Jesus and the mystery of salvation are linked. As the Fathers put it, "theology" (God's disclosure in Christ)' and "economy" (God's saving work) form one whole reality.

Apparently the early theologians sought to correlate the biblical heritage with their own experience in a creative way. They struggled to bring to expression the two great biblical intuitions of soteriology: our plighted character, and the divine rectification of that bondage through Christ. Mitros has helpfully noted six major salvation-images among the Fathers. Let us see how these images surface our two great biblical intuitions.

We dwell in darkness, or ignorance, and Jesus the teacher has brought us new knowledge. Christ is "God's husbandman . . . making men divine by heavenly doctrine," said Clement of Alexandria.[5] This pedagogical imagery is a favorite one for the Hellenistic and philosophical fathers, and "knowledge" here seems to carry a fuller meaning than we are accustomed to. This knowledge is a deification which puts God's laws "into our minds" and "onto our hearts."

Satanic imagery is also used by the early writers. Our plight is one of captivity to demonic powers, darkness and evil, and the Christ event does battle with the Satanic, breaking its hold on humanity. Just as pedagogical imagery has its biblical source in Jesus the teacher (cf Jn 1:1–18; 17:21–26; Mt 11:25–29), so this imagery goes back to Jesus the exorciser (Mt 12:28).

This imagery is much more dramatic than the former, because it portrays Jesus as engaged in battle, and uses the colorful and dreadful imagery of the Satanic.

In some ways, the Satanic model is a very balanced presentation of the biblical soteriology. The "demonic" seems to be a holistic image which covers all sources of human evil and oppression, individual (Mt 4:1–11), and social and cosmic (cf Rom 8:38; 1 Cor 15:24; Col 1:16, etc.). Thus, evil and sin are not privatized or intellectualized as mere lack of knowledge. This imagery also powerfully expresses a dimension of human evil which more abstract language misses. As Langdon Gilkey put it, it brings out evil's "blind fanaticism, its unlimited destruction, its infinite cruelty."[6] The demonic is what happens when evil becomes the ultimate center of a people's loyalty, elevating evil to the position of the absolute. The imagery also highlights Jesus' saving solidarity with the oppressed, and his struggle against the personal and collective powers of alienation. The battle imagery captures the brokenness and the pain involved in Jesus' redemptive work on our behalf.

Of course, this Satanic imagery could degenerate. As Mitros explains it, some Fathers (Origen, Gregory of Nyssa, Ambrose, and Augustine) "introduced into their mythological theory the idea of deception of Satan by God."[7] For example, Jesus was thought to have tricked the devil into thinking he could defeat Jesus, but the Devil later found Jesus' hidden power cloaked under his humanity. So Gregory of Nyssa:

> For he who first deceived man by the bait of pleasure is himself deceived by the camouflage of human nature. But the purpose of the action changes it into something good. . . . For when death came into contact with life, darkness with light, corruption with incorruption, the worse of these things disappeared into a state of non-existence, to the profit of him who was freed from these evils.[8]

The notion of this trickery on God's part was rejected by Gregory of Nazianzus; he maintained that it is wrong to think that God must pay any ransom to the devil, even Jesus' humanity. God would not demand the blood of his own Son, and he could more openly use force against Satan.[9]

Irenaeus developed a somewhat complex "recapitulation symbolism," according to which Christ corrected the pride and disobedience introduced into humanity by Adam. Apparently Irenaeus was influenced by Paul's notion of corporate solidarity: just as all humanity shares in Adam's corruption, so all humanity shares in Christ's regeneration (cf Rom 5:18–19). In this way, Christ recapitulates or sums up what will happen to humanity as a whole. Close to Irenaeus is the imagery of a more Neo-Platonic sort. According to this symbolism, our human nature has been corrupted, and the incarnation introduces the divinization of our common human nature into history. This was an especially popular model among the Greek Fathers, and our earlier citation from Gregory Nazianzen illustrates it well. Both of these models bring out our real human solidarity, in sin and salvation. They are far removed from a privatized conception of human existence: sin is a social event, and so, too, is the Jesus event.

Sacrificial imagery represents a fifth, typical symbolism for salvation. Mitros calls this the "most commonly adopted conception of salvation among the fathers."[10] Here our plight is one of sin, a rupturing in our relationship with God. "For to this end had Christ come, that, being Himself pure from sin . . . He might undergo death on behalf of sinners," said Tertullian.[11] In this sense, Christ was "sent to die" (missus mori). Underlying this is the biblical intuition that Jesus' death was a saving act of love, an outpouring of love on our behalf.

Mitros considers "satisfaction" imagery the sixth typical symbolism among the Fathers. Here Christ's death is imagined as an act of reparation for the sin of withholding from God the honor owed him by his creatures. Many of the early writers employed this symbolism, and usually combined it in some way with the sacrificial imagery. This was true of Cyril of Alexandria, Origen, Eusebius of Caesarea, Basil, Hilary, Ambrose, and Augustine. But since it is the key symbolism employed by Anselm, I will wait until our consideration of him for a further explanation.

On the whole, the early period attempted to preserve the full contours of the Jesus event as both a Christological and a soteriological mystery. Our human plight and the divine rectification of that plight through Jesus both surface repeatedly in a way that was helpful to the age. Through their rich imagery, the early thinkers were trying to say that every dimension of our common human existence, even though "darkened" and "sinful," is now redeemed. Death was often the great symbol, representing and summing up all the evil and sin broken through in the Jesus event. Jesus' victory over his own death symbolizes all Christians' victories over their own deaths. This is a constant motif in the early soteriology. Sometimes our plight is conceived too narrowly: mere ignorance, or only a rupturing of our relationship with God (What about other humans and nature?). Helpfully the Satanic imagery focuses the collective dimensions of our plight: we are in battle with larger social and cosmic powers of dehumanization. Does the more intellectual and narrow view of our plight reflect the more serene and established situation of the Church?

Sometimes, too, the divine rectification of our plight through Jesus is too narrowly conceived. Jesus' saving act is too narrowly reduced to his birth (incarnation), for the Neo-Platonists, or to his death, for the users of sacrificial imagery. The outpouring of divine justice, peace and love in the entirety of the Jesus event, from birth to resurrection, is sometimes missing. Especially missing is Jesus' saving solidarity with the oppressed, probably because of the influence of the Nicene-Constantinian settlement. Linked with this is the fact that the fragmentary nature of Jesus' redemptive work hardly surfaces at all. Perhaps the Church felt that it had really conquered evil in winning the empire.

Anselm and Abelard: The Struggle Between Justice and Love

Anselm especially deserves our attention, for until relatively recently his contribution has been dominant in the Western Church. Just as the incarnation model became the dominant one for the Church's Christology, so Anselm's satisfaction model became the dominant form of soteriology in the West. The Churches of Eastern Christianity, more rooted in the heritage of the Fathers, have continued to maintain a more pluralistic approach. It is not logical that a satisfaction model should have become so influential. One would rather imagine that the Neo-Platonic model, with its notion of the deification of our humanity through the *Logos'* assumption of a human nature, would have complemented the Chalcedonian Christology. Yet this is not what happened. And this illustrates, to some extent, the growing separation between Christology and soteriology.

Jaroslav Pelikan suggests that, although historians have looked for the origins of the satisfaction model in the Germanic "wergild," "whereby a crime against a person must be atoned for in accordance with the station of that person, or in feudal law, the most obvious and immediate source of the idea would appear to be the penitential system of the church, which was developing just at this time."[12] Penance was considered a way of "making satisfaction"; satisfaction was a standard term in the penitential practice of the age. Still, throughout his magisterial three-volume (so far) series on Christian doctrine, Pelikan has a tendency to slight social and cultural factors as an influence upon doctrinal thinking. There is much in Anselm's thought which coheres with the feudal structure of eleventh century Europe, as we will see.

Anselm was dissatisfied with the Satanic imagery of the Fathers, especially the notion of a ruse worked by God: "The devil had no justice on his side against man." The key problem, our human plight, was essentially that of the perverted relationship between men and the sovereign Lord of the universe. This, and not Satan's power, is the issue. Here we see, I think, how the feudal background comes into force. Humans (= serfs) have violated God's holy will: a serf has defied his sovereign Lord. This creates an intolerable situation, for God must assert his righteous sovereignty through punishing the sinners. "One who does not render . . . honor to God takes away from God what belongs to him, and dishonors God, and to do this is sin." "Therefore, if it is not fitting for God to do anything unjustly or without due order, it does not belong to his freedom or kindness or will to forgive unpunished the sinner who does not repay to God what he took away."

But God is merciful, and wishes to re-establish harmony with the sinner: "I do not deny that God is merciful." The problem is one of reconciling divine mercy with divine justice, "since God cannot be in opposition to himself." But how can God's proper honor and the demands of justice be maintained on the one side, while we humans are forgiven, and the demands of mercy (love) be served on the other? The problem seems totally insoluble from our side. First of all, "a sinner cannot justify a sinner." Only corrupt acts flow from a corrupt nature. Further, God is the Infinite Being, and even the slightest acts against him are of immeasurable and infinite weight: ". . . when I see how it is against God's will, I recognize that it is of the greatest weight, and cannot be compared with any loss." Here we see how Anselm seems to reflect the Germanic wergild: "God requires satisfaction according to the greatness of the sin: . . . you do not make satisfaction unless you repay something greater than that for the sake of which you were obliged not to commit the sin."

If it is impossible for the finite creature to satisfy for disobedience, this brings us to the answer to our question, "Why did God become man?" Though innocent of sin, by offering himself up on the cross, the God-man Jesus was able to make an infinite act of reparation, thus satisfying God's honor. In virtue of this, God could then show mercy through remitting to others as a reward what Jesus had wished bestowed upon them. ". . . the person who is to make this satisfaction must be both perfect God and perfect man, because none but true God can make it, and none but true man owes it." Once this God-man accomplishes this act, in justice he deserves a reward: ". . . it is both just and necessary for the Father to pay it to anyone to whom the Son wills to give it, because the Son has a right to give what belongs to him, and the Father can only give what he owes him to someone else."[13]

As a number of scholars are now suggesting, we need to view Anselm's theory against the circle of ideas characteristic of feudalism. Accordingly, the Lord's honor is not simply a personal privilege, but a social status, whereby he preserves and guarantees public order and peace. Estrangement from the feudal lord signifies a social regression toward lawlessness, chaos, disorder. The entire medieval collective order and social sense of solidarity lies behind Anselm's thought. Thus, the need to restore honor to God is a restoration of the order of society, a return to order, har-

mony, fidelity, justice, and even love. Jesus' act of satisfaction, then, is not
the placating of an angry God, but an attempt to restore the harmony of
society. Jesus introduces into the world a new order, where God's honor
is truly acknowledged. Our modern sense of individualism, with its accompanying loss of the medieval sense of solidarity, makes it very difficult for
us to appreciate what Anselm is getting at.

Against the above backdrop, Anselm's satisfaction theory is fairly harmonious with the biblical soteriology. Just as the human plight is seen, in
the Bible, holistically as a personal and social experience of bondage, so
Anselm packs the social and personal dimensions of our plight into the medieval experience of order's regression into chaos. Anselm apparently considers our suffering of death one such example of chaos, which wouldn't
have happened, had it not been for sin. He sees the divine rectification of
our plight through Jesus as really an act of solidarity with humanity,
whereby Jesus attempts to introduce into history a new order of harmony,
at-one-ment, and the overcoming of death.[14]

What does not surface in Anselm are some of the dimensions of the
biblical soteriology emphasized by psychosocial criticism. For example,
what of the plight of the alienated and oppressed, with which the humiliated Jesus of the Gospels identified so strongly? The Jesus event is not simply one in which God is on the side of order and harmony. Some forms of
order mask enormous suffering and injustice: "order" can be a part of our
plight. In acting to restore order, Jesus introduces an authentic justice,
love, and peace, not a feudalistic master-slave arrangement. Furthermore,
the New Testament does not indicate a struggle on God's part between
mercy and justice. Mercy, rather, takes the form of justice when it is extended into society with its injustices. Anselm's opposition between these
two reflects more of feudalism than of Jesus.

Anselm's younger contemporary, Abelard, can be read as a corrective
to the more harsh aspects of the satisfaction theory. Unlike Anselm, Abelard's diagnosis of our plight is chiefly one of not disorder and lawlessness,
but lovelessness. In his famous *Exposition of the Epistle to the Romans,* he
proposes that "our redemption through Christ's suffering is that deeper af-
fection in us which not only frees us from slavery to sin, but also wins for
us the true liberty of sons of God, so that we do all things out of love rather
than fear. . . ."

Lovelessness—a collective symbolism embracing the suffering of
death and sin—is our plight, says Abelard. And God's rectification of that
plight comes through Jesus' act of love: Jesus "came for the express purpose of spreading this true liberty of love amongst men." Although there
are texts from Abelard which seem to reduce Jesus only to an "example"

for the rest of us ("By the faith which we hold concerning Christ love is increased in us"), still Abelard seems to hold that Jesus really and effectively saves us. For example, our justification is "by the grace of him—that is God—who 'first hath loved us.' " Or, "We have been justified by the blood of Christ and reconciled to God in this way: through this unique act of grace manifested to us—in that his Son has taken upon himself our nature and persevered therein in teaching us by word and example even unto death—he has more fully bound us to himself by love; with the result that our hearts should be enkindled by such a gift of divine grace, and true charity should not now shrink from enduring anything for him."[15]

With Abelard, one senses that one is rather close to the biblical soteriology. The description of our plight as one of lovelessness, and the divine rectification of that plight through Jesus' infusion of love, capture the compassionate God disclosed in the Jesus event. Abelard's danger is that lovelessness and its corrective through love will be read privatistically and mystically, thus obscuring the social dimensions of our common plight. This would foster a spirituality of personal love, rather than one of solidarity with the oppressed.

One final observation. Both Anselm and Abelard fail to bring out the fragmentary and in-between character of the saving act of Jesus. Both allow, of course, for our personal response to the Jesus event. But one gains the impression that Jesus has already conquered the world, as if our personal response were only a kind of inevitable play-acting of what is already foreordained. Perhaps the power of medieval Christendom lies behind this near-utopianism. The non-utopian character of salvation needs more emphasis in the medieval theories.

Toward a Contemporary Restatement of Soteriology

We continually need to do in our own time what the tradition was struggling to do in its own. Drawing upon the above, trying to be faithful to the tradition and yet to the lessons of our own experience, let us try to draw forth some guiding principles for a future soteriology.

(1) *An adequate soteriology demands an adequate diagnosis of the human experience of bondage.* Surely one of the great constants of the soteriological tradition is its realism, its awareness that we are indeed a plighted humanity in need of liberation and salvation. This is not the whole picture of course. There is the other "melody" playing in the tradition, namely our goodness and capacity for love, peace and justice. Still, there is this counter-movement into evil and sin. This was something rather taken for granted by the tradition. As Reinhold Niebuhr suggested, human evil and

sin is an empirically proven doctrine! Being a "fool for Christ's sake" doesn't mean that we are just "plain, damn fools," as Niebuhr also suggested!

In our own times, there is perhaps a greater need to clarify and critically legitimate our plighted character. Our relatively modern stress on the liberating power of human reason and technology tends to foster an excessive optimism. It also fosters a creed of self-salvation, whereby we think we can "save ourselves" from almost any problem that comes our way. Oftentimes it is not obvious to modern people that we are deeply plighted and in need of salvation from God.

I would suggest that the most promising sources for a contemporary restatement of our human plight are to be found among the Neo-Orthodox theologians, such as Reinhold Niebuhr and Gordon Kaufman, who have attempted to retrieve for our own time Augustine's great diagnosis of human perversity in *The City of God*, Books 13 and 14. It is no accident that this kind of contribution emanates from Neo-Orthodox circles. The reader will remember that the Neo-Orthodox were critical of nineteenth century liberal theology's too easy accommodation to modernity. The liberals, they maintained, had forgotten about human depravity, and thus the Otherness of the Holy Mystery whose transcendence cannot simply be identified with any human movement, even apparently good ones, like reason and technology. This was the key defect in the liberal soteriology: a naive grasp of human corruption and a too close identification of God with supposed human movements of advance and progress.

Building upon the Neo-Orthodox contribution,[16] we can begin by proposing what is the major thesis of Christianity with respect to our plighted character—namely, that to the degree that we humans find ourselves unable to trust in an ultimate, divinely-given meaning and love, to that degree we sink into ever greater forms of bondage and self-destruction. As Gordon Kaufman explains it, this bondage will take either of two forms. Either (1) we will attempt to treat something we know, something which lies close at hand, as our true and proper source of meaning and love, or (2) we will seek to deaden our own sensibility and consciousness.

The first option interestingly corresponds to the majority of the "seven deadly sins": pride, covetousness, lust, gluttony. All these sins describe inordinate attachments to finite realities, hoping to find in them ultimate satisfaction. The second option corresponds to the traditional sin of "sloth," a kind of retreat from life, a sinking into stupor. The result of either of these two choices is an ever expanding experience of bondage and self-captivity—and this is what the soteriological tradition is pointing to when it speaks of our plighted character.

It is easiest to see how the first option plunges us into ever greater forms of bondage. Let us listen to Kaufman:

> . . . the immediate consequence of this step is the very opposite of what was intended: instead of salvation from meaninglessness one is enslaved to a merciless master. This can most easily be seen with the passions. The more one seeks meaning through satisfaction of, for example, drives for food or sex, the more he becomes enslaved to gluttony and lust and thus plunged deeper into the search for genuine meaning and satisfaction. The reason, as Augustine long ago saw, is quite simple: no finite object can satisfy man's craving for God. 'Our hearts are restless till they find their rest in Thee' (*Confessions*, 1, 1). Seeking gratification in the finite object only increases the craving, thus plunging one deeper in enslavement to the passion. Moreover such meaning as he originally found in eating and sexual activity begins to grow flat and cloy upon him as he becomes satiated but still unsatisfied, and it becomes obvious that this was in fact not what was needed. But this only makes him more desperate in the search for meaning and salvation, and so he plunges yet more blindly into deeper bondage.[17]

The issue here is that of idolatry, not the concrete examples Kaufman gives. It would perhaps be more relevant to speak of the attempt to find full meaning through prestige, exploitative power, profession, and other "power-trip" strategies. But regardless of the particular example, the result is the same: "In every idolatrous movement, one gradually but increasingly is dominated by the passion to which he has given himself."[18] But the second option (of sloth) also plunges us into bondage. For if we seek to withdraw from the tension of life, giving up on the quest for meaning, we lose "the very power to act, retiring finally, in extreme cases, into a kind of catatonic stupor."[19] Enslavement to inaction and meaninglessness is the result.

Now I would suggest that this basic mechanism of bondage, briefly described by Kaufman, gradually pollutes and perverts the fourfold structure of reality which constitutes us as human beings. Our relation to God, to self, to society, and to nature gradually sinks into ever greater and expanding circles of bondage, meaninglessness and lovelessness.

Let us begin with our relation to the Divine. The inability to trust in the ultimacy of a divine love, justice, and peace, and to act on its basis, means that we replace our "hunger" for the Divine with surrogate deities, which we hope will bring us our desired meaning and fulfillment. Either that, or slothful ennui will result. We humans can idolatrize just about anything, from sex to wealth to power to nature, etc. Regardless, as we deliver ourselves over to these pseudo-deities, we discover their inability to grant us the satisfaction we desire. This experience breeds anxiety, fear, hatred, anger, the inability to trust, and other disorders that rock the self and make it a prey to yet worse disorders. Often, too, as Kaufman explains it, most of us are not "monotheistic" idolators, but "polytheistic": we deliver ourselves over to multiple pseudo-deities. This threatens our personality with disintegration, for we find ourselves divided, caught between competing allegiances. This only intensifies our fear and distrust, and allows rage and hatred to surface all the more.

As our divine pole of existence plunges into bondage, so, too, does our self-identity. The human self is gradually and ever more viciously enslaved, either to finite realities which cannot deliver what we think they promise, or to crippling sloth. This breeds the fear, anger, rage, etc., of which we have spoken. Should our bondage be polytheistic, the personality becomes even more split and torn, and this in turn intensifies our anger. As this process continues, it grows and intensifies, making it increasingly hard to turn back. Perhaps we begin to blame God for bringing this misery upon us. Perhaps we even deny a divine source of grace in our lives. We begin to experience guilt, too, for we suspect our own complicity. But this guilt only intensifies our sense of distrust and fear. As Kaufman put it, "The vicious cycle moves ever deeper."[20]

Increasingly, the self finds it difficult to be honest and preserve its integrity. One begins to lie to himself/herself and to others, in an effort to legitimate and justify one's unsatisfying allegiances. Or one falls victim to what Freud called defense mechanisms: unconsciously justifying one's actions, or projecting onto others the blame for one's plight. But this process of rationalization only splits the self further: there is a residue of "self A" which suspects one is lying. Self A now is at war with "self B," which is doing the lying. All of this further intensifies the anger, rage, hatred, and just plain meanness that has been taking root all along.

In biblical terms, our "heart" has become perverted. And it is from such perversion that lovelessness spreads outward into society as a whole. This is clearly Jesus' diagnosis of our plight: "What emerges from within a man, that and nothing else is what makes him impure" (Mk 7:20). It is also Paul's diagnosis: "I do not do what I want to do but what I hate. . . . the desire to do right is there but not the power. What happens is that I do, not the good I will to do, but the evil I do not intend" (Rom 8:15–19). It is also Augustine's in *The City of God:* ". . . it was not the corruptible flesh that made the soul sinful; it was the sinful soul that made the flesh corruptible." Or, in the words of his *Confessions:*

> . . . but I was held fast, not in fetters clamped upon me by another, but by my own will, which had the strength of iron chains. The enemy held

my will in his power and from it he had made a chain and shackled me.
For my will was perverse and lust had grown from it, and when I gave
in to lust habit was born, and when I did not resist the habit it became
a necessity. These were the links which together formed what I have
called my chain, and it held me fast in the duress of servitude.

As our divine pole, and together with it our self-pole, plunge into enslavement, so, too, does our social pole. The oscillating dimensions of our
existence are simultaneous. Society itself in all of its complex dimensions—from interpersonal relations to the more impersonal, institutional
network of relationships—falls into bondage. Jesus was aware of this, confronting societal bondage from the resisting power centers of his day. Augustine perhaps captured much of what we mean in his image of the "City
of Man," which is at war with the "City of God." He says:

> We see then that the two cities were created by two kinds of love: the
> earthly city was created by self-love reaching the point of contempt for
> God, the Heavenly City by the love of God carried as far as contempt of
> self. In fact, the earthly city glories in itself, the heavenly City glories in
> the Lord. The former looks for glory from men, the latter finds its high-
> est glory in God, the witness of a good conscience. The earthly lifts up
> its head in its own glory, the Heavenly City says to its God: "My glory;
> you lift up my head." In the former, the lust for domination lords it over
> its princes as over the nations it subjugates; in the other both those put
> in authority and those subject to them serve one another in love, the rul-
> ers by their counsel, the subjects by obedience. The one city loves its
> own strength shown in its powerful leaders; the other says to its God, "I
> will love you, my Lord, my strength."

It is the special merit of political and liberation theology to have given
renewed attention to the social sources of human depravity. Our analysis
would strongly agree with them that our human bondage is not only a
disorientation in our inner selves, but also within society at large. It is also
not simply a perversion of values, but a perversion of praxis, individually
and collectively, even within institutions.

Let me hazard a brief description of our social bondage. Following
Kaufman, we can say that society will follow the path of the diseased self,
only now on the collective level. As Plato called society the "soul writ
large" (meaning, by the "soul," not a modern, individualistic self, but a self
inherently social), so perverted society is the perverted soul writ large. On
the one hand, society in search of meaning (either a Church or otherwise)
can fall into the path of idolatry by elevating to the level of the ultimate
some finite reality. Candidates for such pseudo-deities might be: science,

technology, human reason, various political or cultural institutions, etc. On the other hand, a society might fall into an ennui or sloth. In this case, a society's very existence is threatened.

Should society follow the path of idolatry, various forms of bondage typically ensue. What seems to happen is that, should society follow the path of "monotheistic idolatry," elevating one finite reality to the level of the ultimate, a "demonic one-sidedness"[21] results. In the cultural sphere, for example, the idolization of reason, technology, or prestige can crush all other relative values which may be struggling for recognition. In the political sphere, a particular polity can be idolized, issuing forth in the loss of a critical sense, the collapse of all political dissent, and the emergence of tyranny. In the economic sphere, the same rigidity and loss of critique can result: capitalism can become "laissez-faire-ism," socialism can become totalitarian statism, etc.

Should society pursue, as most individuals do, a form of "polytheistic idolatry," it will find itself torn by competing loyalties in its various spheres, gradually disintegrating into chaos, for lack of an overall meaningful goal. As this bondage hardens, societies will find it ever more difficult to reverse these destructive trends, and this will only intensify the bondage. As the individual experiences a residue of guilt from the haunting suspicion of complicity, so societies can suffer a form of collective guilt. At the limit, they will try to deceive themselves, seeking to legitimate their perverted goals. Thus, destructive ideologies emerge, which mask the real horrors going on. And in the wake of these we find societal hate, fear, rage, exploitation, war, greedy competition, imperialism, etc. Traditionally we sum up forms of social bondage in the powerful phrase "the lust for power."

The gradual enslavement of our divine pole, self-pole, and social pole also reverberates upon our relation to nature and the bodily cosmos. As Paul put it, "Creation was made subject to futility, not of its own accord but by him who once subjected it. . . . Yes, we know that all creation groans and is in agony even until now" (Rom 8:20–22). Augustine was on to this too in *The City of God:* "And so we are weighed down by the corruptible body." He finds the source of this corruption in the perverted heart: ". . . and yet we know that the cause of our being weighed down is not the true nature and substance of our body but its corruption. . . . And it was not the corruptible flesh that made the soul sinful; it was the sinful soul that made the flesh corruptible."[22]

If we follow the path of idolatry, our body and bodily world become the victim of a fetish. The more we try to take from them what they cannot offer, the more we are driven to plunder and rape them. Exploitation is the inevitable result. And the greater is our history of this exploitation, the harder is it to turn back. And yet the greater is our guilt, too, because we hauntingly suspect that somehow we are exploitative creatures. We must, of course, lie to ourselves to justify our actions—"Nature is for our use"; "My body belongs to me"—and so we sink into even further self-and societal-deception. Anger, resentment, hatred—all these and more are spawned. Death, that last gift of nature to us, becomes increasingly something to be resented and dreaded. How can we calmly let go of our body and bodily habitat, when we have fetishized them? Now death takes on another image: it is a result of sin.

Should we sink into the path of sloth, the world and nature increasingly become more meaningless. No longer the possible site of meaning, nature loses its value and becomes one more thing which we must endure. We find ourselves unable to revere the world; it cannot give us what we sought. Death, nature's final act, becomes either the great meaningless climax of an empty life, or at last the cessation of a horrible boredom.

This is only one possible account of our plighted nature, but I believe that it is wide enough to account for the myriads of evil and sin from which humanity and nature suffers. The key, of course, is the mechanism of idolatry or sloth. Idolization leads to all the forms of the master-slave dialectic only too well known to history. Sloth leads to that crippling loss of meaning which paralyzes all possibility of meaningful living.

(2) *Since the ultimate cause of human and natural bondage is the inability to trust in a divine source of meaning and love, an adequate soteriology must show that only the infusion into history of a divine source of meaning and love is really adequate to the human plight.* By its very nature, the corrupted self and society cannot extricate themselves from their plight, for the mark of the corrupted self and society is to seek solutions from the finite, and this will only plunge them further into bondage. In other words, the human experience of bondage requires a "Divine Therapy," and this is the second great constant of the soteriological tradition. For that tradition maintains that the Divine has acted in the Jesus event to rectify our plight. Underlying all the diverse imagery of the soteriological tradition is the constant conviction that the divine power of justice, love and peace disclosed itself in Jesus and initiated a process of cosmic therapy. Let us try to appropriate this faith conviction of our tradition through considering how the divine therapy heals the quaternion structure of our common human existence.

First, with respect to our divine pole, the Jesus event discloses that God works in history to reverse our tendency toward either sloth or the idolization of pseudo-deities through the therapeutic power of justice, love, and peace. There is available to us, within history, a transcendent power of justice, love, and peace which does not violate our freedom, but

grants us the capacity to use that freedom properly, in the service of justice, love, and peace. This enables us to trust in the Divine, and thus to
rise above sloth and its crippling inactivism. It also frees us, not to idolize
the finite realities of our world, but to allow them to be vehicles of a more
freeing justice, love and peace within the world as a whole. The Jesus-like
love, peace, and justice of God does not mean that we negate and ignore
the finite: it liberates us to allow the finite to be the authentic space of a
more just and loving life.

With respect to our self-pole, the divine therapy of justice, love, and
peace gives us the capacity to live out what we earlier called the "covenantal self." By this I mean the divinely given ability to rise above narcissism, or the clinging to the finite which results from the fetish of the finite.
We are freed to trust that justice, love and peace in solidarity with others
is the true road to human fulfillment. This does not reduce other humans
to things to be possessed and mastered, but frees them, too, for life and
fulfillment within the world. Sloth becomes unthinkable.

We find ourselves (our "hearts") reoriented: they revolve around the
trust in justice, love and peace. This is their new axis, which breaks
through the ultimate source of all master-slave dialectics.

All of this enables us to reverse the destructive trends within the social body itself, whether that of the Churches or otherwise. We experience
the ability to build up the covenantal community of justice, love and
peace. For the divine therapy of justice, love, and peace is a true community-making dynamic and power. It breaks down the narcissism and ennui which makes true community impossible. Ultimately love, justice, and
peace are the real foundations of any true community in which genuine solidarity exists. Where trust in these is lacking, community-making becomes
impossible. These provide the transcendent ground and context within
which genuine community can be established, and through which the alienated and dispossessed can be reintegrated within the social bonds. In
this sense, Jesus is our "Representative," not in the sense that he takes our
place in this world of ours, but in the sense that the divine justice, love,
and peace which flowed through him and in which he still participates
makes it possible for others to experience authentic justice, love, and
peace. Jesus is the "medium," if you will, of a new power of solidarity
within history.[23]

Finally, the dynamic of love, justice, and peace disclosed in Jesus
works toward the re-establishment of humanity's harmony with the body
and with nature. For this "divine therapy" fosters that reverential self-limitation which does not violate the material, but embraces it with an attitude and praxis of justice and love. It provides the transcendent ground
within which the horrible misuse of nature can be curtailed and the earth

can truly become the space of the divine Kingdom. While death, nature's final act for the individual, is clearly not abolished, yet we can trust that it is transvalued by a Loving Transcendence. We are enabled to trust that death is not cessation, but passage to a deeper and richer form of communion with the Divine. The death which the Bible calls the result of sin becomes, through a divine therapy, a death which the mystics call sweet.

(3) *An adequate soteriology will need to bring out the in-between character of Jesus' saving work, if it is to avoid a naive utopianism on the one hand, and a too hard-nosed crippling pessimism on the other.* Clearly one of the constants of the biblical tradition is this "in-between" character, whereby the gift of salvation is both a present experience of the believer (Rom 5:1, 9), and yet something whose fullness we still await (Rom 6:22). The tradition does know the attractive pull of utopianism, to be sure. The early Christian expectation that the Kingdom was right around the corner, the too-easy identification of the Kingdom with empire and Church—all of these brought Christianity perilously close to the utopian derailment. The Lutheran "two kingdoms" doctrine, whereby the powers of this world are simply perverse, and the sectarian castigation of this world as simply corrupt—all these came perilously close to the pessimistic derailment. I have suggested that we view these two strains as correctives to the mainline tradition: the utopian highlighting the present effectiveness of the power of justice, love, and peace; the pessimistic, that of the not-yetness of the Kingdom to come. Each strain captures, intensifies, and perhaps even exaggerates one pole of a dialectical, two-edged reality.

I have the impression that the soteriological tradition of post-biblical Christianity has rather tended to downplay the necessarily in-between character of the salvation process. It is not that it is denied, for mainline Christianity has always professed and awaited the second coming. It is rather that the tension of the in-between (to use Voegelin's helpful idiom) has somehow faded. Tension has relaxed into waiting and near-forgetfulness of the hoped-for future.

In any case, a contemporary soteriology, to be faithful to the main thrust of the tradition and to the lessons of our contemporary experience, must revitalize the in-between character of salvation. This does not mean that we do not trust in the ultimate power of divine justice, love, and peace disclosed in Jesus. There is a legitimate eschatology which we can imaginatively extrapolate from the Jesus event. But this most ultimate of trusts does not magically take away the in-between in which we live, and either our responsive or our perverted freedom as it reacts to the divine therapy in our midst.

The great danger of utopianism is that it will blind us to the massive reality of bondage within ourselves, our societies, our Churches, and our cosmos. If you will, utopianism is itself an experience of bondage, for it is a defense mechanism and ideology which enslaves us to illusion. It is but another form of idolizing the finite. The great danger of pessimism is that it will cripple and defeat our capacity to struggle on behalf of justice, peace, and love. Pessimism, too, is an experience of bondage, corresponding to what we earlier named the sin of sloth. Only a soteriology of the in-between can do justice to the kind of saving power released in the Jesus event.

(4) *The unity between Christology and soteriology must be reasserted by contemporary theology. This requires paying attention to the Jesus event holistically.* The separation (not distinction) between Christology and soteriology has harmful consequences in two directions. Christology becomes abstract and utopian, severed from its real relevance to humanity's plight. This distorts Christology, making the story of Jesus esoteric and unreal. It becomes difficult to understand why anyone is really attracted to Jesus. Soteriology suffers too. By severing it from its Christological roots, the belief in Jesus the Savior becomes unrealistic: either it becomes a mythological belief (in the pejorative sense) which cannot explain how Jesus really saves us now as the medium of peace, justice and love, or Jesus is reduced to a mere "example" which we ought to imitate.

In my view, we need to keep the contours of the *whole* Jesus event in focus, as the Scriptures usually do. We need to combine in our own way the *theologia* and *economia* of the works of the Fathers. I would suggest that we can accomplish this by taking a cue from psychosocial criticism. That is, we must constantly de-privatize the Jesus event by grasping its implications for the fourfold structure of our common human existence. It is the privatistic focus of our Christologies, which perhaps corresponds to the individualism of the scholarly community, that greatly impedes the expression of the intrinsic unity between Christology and soteriology.

That means that we need to view Christology, not as the study of the inner constitution of Jesus himself, but as the disclosure through this man of a new way of relating to our God, to ourselves, to our societies, and to our material cosmos. This way of explaining Christology does not de-personalize Jesus, but de-privatizes him, surfacing his interconnection with the Divine and the rest of humanity and indeed the cosmos. But the other side of Christology is soteriology: the new breakthrough of divine justice, love, and peace in him is simultaneously the liberation and salvation from injustice and lovelessness. The Jesus-event, now de-privatized, becomes the disclosure of a divine therapy at work in our world: it reorients our relation to the Divine, saving it from idolatry and sloth; it renews our self around the axis of justice, love, and peace; it founds the possibility of authentic community in solidarity; it relinks us with the cosmos through an ethics of stewardship and self-limitation. In this way, Christology and soteriology are distinct, but not separate. They are distinct, because they give expression to the two sides of the Jesus event, as both the disclosure of a new manner of human existence and as the healing of that existence. They are not separate, because they are the two sides of the one and same reality.

(5) *Christian spirituality needs to be linked with Christology and soteriology, so that it is seen as our human response, in a total way, to the Jesus event.* A spirituality rooted in the Jesus event becomes our total response to the offer that event holds out to us, as a Christological and soteriological mystery.

Concretely, this would seem to mean that spirituality becomes our *spirit*-ed response to the God of justice, love, and peace disclosed in Jesus. That response is as much a matter of values as of praxis. For as we open ourselves to this pathos-like God through commitment to unconditional love, justice, and peace, we find ourselves struggling on behalf of that love, peace and justice within history. Simultaneously, spirituality becomes a reorientation of our inward self, directing it to the values of justice, peace, and love, and moving it to embody those values within society as a whole. Spirituality is not only inner-directed or privatistic, but also collective and social. As such it becomes the growing embodiment of Jesus' new community of peace, justice and love. For a response to the Jesus event brings with it a call to social renovation. Finally, spirituality inevitably has its bodily and material dimension. This finds expression in an ethics of stewardship and self-limitation, which frees the body and the material cosmos from exploitation, enabling them to be the site of the new community of justice, peace and love. In brief, a spirituality which responds to the Jesus event is one which embodies the new fourfold structure of our common human existence disclosed in Jesus.

As psychosocial criticism reminds us, spirituality is as much a matter of vision/values as it is of praxis. This means that there will always be a contemplative movement in spirituality, an ongoing attempt to open ourselves to the values of justice, peace, and love, through prayer, meditation, contemplation, learning, questioning, etc. Contemplation of whatever sort is really the attempt to align our vision of the Divine, of ourselves, of our society, and of our world with the Jesus experience.

But there will also be the simultaneous practical movement, whereby our praxis, too, is aligned with the Jesus experience. We not only envision Jesus' pathos-like God; we practice this vision through justice, peace, and love. We not only envision our deepest self as made for justice, love, and peace; we actually act more lovingly, justly, and peace-fully. We not only contemplate a new covenantal community; we actually struggle on its be-

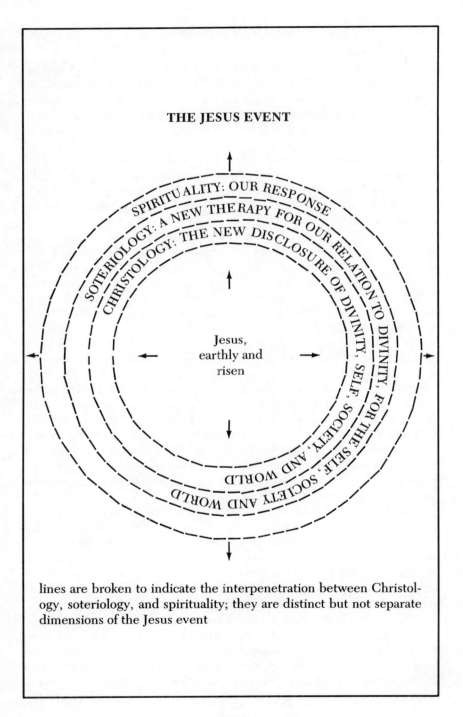

THE JESUS EVENT

SPIRITUALITY: OUR RESPONSE

SOTERIOLOGY: A NEW THERAPY FOR OUR RELATION TO DIVINITY, FOR THE SELF, SOCIETY AND WORLD

CHRISTOLOGY: THE NEW DISCLOSURE OF DIVINITY, SELF, SOCIETY AND WORLD

Jesus,
earthly and
risen

lines are broken to indicate the interpenetration between Christology, soteriology, and spirituality; they are distinct but not separate dimensions of the Jesus event half. We not only think of our bodies and nature in a less rapacious manner; we actually embody that in wholesome bodily habits and in struggling against the victimizers of nature.

By linking spirituality with soteriology, we are also able to comprehend that there is a necessarily ascetical dimension to our fourfold spiritual movement. *Ascesis* in the full sense of that word is involved. For spirituality is not only growth toward the God of Jesus, toward the Jesus-oriented self and society, and toward his ethics for nature. It is also a *struggle against* human bondage in all of its forms. There is a purgative dimension involved in breaking free from pseudo-deities and overcoming the constant tendency toward narcissism and exploitation, all of which so easily and powerfully pollute our fourfold human existence. But there is a "secret joy" in all authentic spirituality, a joy which flows from the transcendent power of justice, love, and peace. This Jesus-like joy does not derail us into utopianism, but neither does it drown us in the ocean of pessimism. It is the peculiar joy of the in-between—a "holy" or "sweet" tension.

The Jesus event as a Christological and soteriological mystery inevitably overflows into a spirituality. They cannot be separated. For our spirituality, as it takes hold of us, is the "sign" and experiential confirmation that a new disclosure of our fourfold human existence is coming to be within history through Jesus (= Christology), a disclosure that is also a liberating from the disorientation of that existence (= soteriology).[24]

Notes

1. See Alois Grillmeier, "Christology," *Sacramentum Mundi*, 3 (New York: Herder and Herder, 1969), pp. 186–188. Again in this chapter I employ an historical-critical and psychosocial approach. A literary-critical approach could equally well be applied to the soteriological tradition, but none exists to my knowledge.

2. Helpful on Luther's soteriology is Pannenberg, *Jesus, op. cit.*, pp. 43–44. The beginnings of a psychosocial approach to soteriology, which overcomes its privatism, is by Francis Schüssler Fiorenza, "Critical Social Theory and Christology: Toward an Understanding of Atonement and Redemption as Emancipatory Solidarity," *Proceedings of the Catholic Theological Society of America* 30 (1975), 63–110.

3. Some helpful beginnings: Sobrino, *op. cit.*, "The Christ of the Ignatian Exercises," pp. 396–424; Robert L. Schmitt, "The Christ-Experience and Relationship Fostered in the Spiritual Exercises of St. Ignatius of Loyola," *Studies in the Spirituality of Jesuits* 6 (1974); John Meyendorff, *Christ in Eastern Christian Thought* (Washington: Corpus, 1969), pp. 85–98; of course, the great work of Von Balthasar: see his *The Von Balthasar Reader, op. cit.*, "Saints in the Church," pp. 376–407; my own *Jesus, op, cit.*, pp. 195–276. Also see Castro's work on Teresa of Avila's Christology, and Tavard's article on the mystics' Christology *supra*. Tavard

is now working on a full study of John of the Cross' Christology. Finally see Harvey D. Egan, *What Are They Saying About Mysticism?* (New York: Paulist, 1982), and his more lengthy *Christian Mysticism: The Future of a Tradition* (New York: Pueblo, 1984). This latter work especially sees the mystics as correctives to theology and Church, and nicely, for Americans, points out the significance of Thomas Merton (pp. 215–259). Cf also John Higgins, *Merton's Theology of Prayer* (Spencer, Mass.: Cistercian Publications, 1971).

4. Joseph F. Mitros, "Patristic Views of Christ's Salvific Work," *Thought* 42 (1967), 415–447. This is the handiest study for the beginning student, in some ways surpassing the more book-length treatments. Standard studies: Louis Richard, *The Mystery of the Redemption* (Baltimore: Helicon, 1965); H.E.W. Turner, *The Patristic Doctrine of Redemption* (London: Mowbray, 1952); and Emile Mersch, *The Whole Christ* (London: Dennis Dobson, 1962).

5. *The Exhortation to the Greeks*, 11, 88–89 (Butterworth, trans., *op. cit.*, p. 245).

6. Langdon Gilkey, *Message and Existence: An Introduction to Christian Theology* (New York: Seabury, 1979), p. 147. On the demonic, see the helpful study of Trevor Ling, *The Significance of Satan*, *op. cit.*, and Davis, *op. cit.*, pp. 109–124 (a very fine and provocative study of the Satanic).

7. Mitros, *art. cit.*, 424.

8. *An Address on Religious Instruction*, 26 (*Christology of the Later Fathers*, The Library of Christian Classics, 3, Edward Rochie Hardy, ed. [Philadelphia: Westminster, 1954], p. 303).

9. See Mitros, *art. cit.*, 425, referring to *The Homilies on the Psalms*, 7, 2 and 48, 3.

10. *Ibid.*, 430. In various forms, this cuts across both Eastern and Western early thinkers. "Because the sacrificial theory of salvation was built on scriptural foundations and its substance was based on the traditional creed, it could not but have been commonly accepted by the Fathers. However, it was not always the preferred interpretation of the salvific work of Christ," says Mitros (431).

11. *On Modesty*, 22 (*The Ante-Nicene Fathers*, 4 [Grand Rapids, Michigan: Wm. B. Eerdmans, 1956], p. 100).

12. See his *The Christian Tradition: A History of the Development of Doctrine*, 3, *The Growth of Medieval Theology (600–1300)* (Chicago: University of Chicago, 1978), p. 143. See pp. 106–157 for medieval soteriology as a whole.

13. I am citing from Eugene R. Fairweather's translation, in his *A Scholastic Miscellany: From Anselm to Ockham* (New York: Macmillan, 1970), "Why God Became Man," pp. 100–183, at pp. 107, 119, 121, 144, 143, 141, 138, 139, 152, 180. I have also been helped by Kaufman, *op. cit.*, pp. 395–396, note 5.

14. Kasper, *op. cit.*, pp. 219–221, has brought this out, relying on G. Greshake, "Erlösung und Freiheit. Zur Neuinterpretation der Erlösungslehre Anselms von Canterbury," *Theologische Quartalschrift* 153 (1973), 323–345. Cf also John McIntyre, *St. Anselm and His Critics: A Reinterpretation of the "Cur Deus Homo"* (Edinburgh: Oliver and Boyd, 1954). Cf Bk. 1, ch. 9, ch. 22; Bk 2, ch. 2 and ch. 11 of "Why God Became Man" for the view of salvation from death.

15. Text in Fairweather, *op. cit.*, pp. 276–287, at pp. 284, 278, 279, 283. An important study is Richard Ernest Weingart, *The Logic of Divine Love: A Critical Examination of the Soteriology of Peter Abailard* (London: Clarendon, 1970). An older study by Gustaf Aulén, *Christus Victor: An Historical Study of the Three Main Types of the Idea of the Atonement* (London: SPCK, 1931), has some helpful ideas on the biblical and patristic soteriology, but it is one-sided on Anselm, as well as on Abelard.

16. I rely upon Kaufman, *op. cit.*, pp. 352–377. Also important is Reinhold Niebuhr, *The Nature and Destiny of Man*, 2 vols. (New York: Charles Scribner's, 1941–1943). Some Niebuhr scholars hold that his most succinct views are set forth in his *Man's Nature and His Communities* (New York: Charles Scribner's, 1965). A helpful entry into Niebuhr is Nathan A. Scott, Jr., ed., *The Legacy of Reinhold Niebuhr* (Chicago: University of Chicago, 1975). Kaufman has been deeply influenced by Niebuhr, as well as by Augustine's *City of God*, Books 13 and 14. An equivalent analysis of human bondage, given from a global and not only a Christian perspective, is to be found throughout Voegelin's *Order and History*. See Webb, *Eric Voegelin, op. cit.*, "The Loss of Reality," pp. 193–207.

17. *Ibid.*, p. 369.

18. *Ibid.*

19. *Ibid.*, p. 368.

20. *Ibid.*, p. 373.

21. *Ibid.*, p. 371.

22. Citations: Augustine, *City of God*, 14, 3; 14, 28 (Knowles, ed., *op. cit.*, p. 551, p. 593); *Confessions*, 8, 5 (R.S. Pine-Coffin, trans. [Baltimore: Penguin, 1974], p. 164). The phrase "lust for power": *City of God*, 1, 30 (*ibid.*, p. 42); cf. Thucydides, *The Peloponnesian War*, 3, 82, with Voegelin's commentary, *Order and History*, 2, *The World of the Polis, op. cit.*, pp. 349–373.

23. To my knowledge, the only Christologian who has attempted anything like a careful integration of soteriology with Christology is Kasper, *op. cit.*, pp. 252–268, 185–192, 215–225. I have borrowed the notion of Christ "the Representative" from him, esp. pp. 215–225. For Kasper, the bond uniting Christology and soteriology is the unconditional love of God which creates solidarity among humans. Through the medium of Jesus, earthly and risen, this unconditional love enters history as an effective force. I clearly agree with Kasper, but try also to relate Christology to soteriology by seeing the link not only in the disclosure of God, but in that of the self, society, and nature.

Not only is soteriology hardly touched upon by Christologians; their analyses of our human plight (what we are saved from) is similarly rudimentary. Helpful ideas can be found in Kasper, Moltmann, Küng, Schillebeeckx, Lamb, etc., but nothing approaching what we yet need. Hopefully this little study here will help.

Some further new sources on soteriology, which still need integrating with Christology, are: "The Salvation Event," *Chicago Studies* 22 (1983), No. 1 (articles on Jesus as a Savior, on Old Testament soteriology, on salvation in Paul and Luke, on the post-biblical tradition, on the American experience of salvation, salvation and liberation, and salvation in the non-Christian religions); Carl F. Braaten, "The

Christian Doctrine of Salvation," and Donald G. Bloesch, "Soteriology in Contemporary Christian Thought," *Interpretation* 35 (1981), 117–131, 132–144; and the brilliant psychological interpretation of soteriology by Sebastian Moore, *The Fire and the Rose Are One* (New York: Seabury, 1980). For Moore, Jesus' voluntary death is the disclosure that we need not be afraid of dying in any form. The power of God, in which Jesus trusted, freed him from the death-fear, and the resurrection experience was the acceptance of this freeing power by the disciples. Salvation, here closely linked to the cross (perhaps too narrowly), becomes the release from the fear of death (understood widely as any crippling experience). Peter C. Hodgson's *New Birth of Freedom, op. cit.*, is a brilliant interpretation of "bondage" from the Christian perspective, and an insightful analysis of how Jesus liberates from this. It especially applies this to the American scene.

24. See the works of Fox and Woods, referred to earlier. Cf Henri J.M. Nouwen, *Pray To Live: Thomas Merton: Contemplative Critic* (Notre Dame, Indiana: Fides, 1972), for a fine analysis of this American mystic, who combines the personal, social, and global in a startling way. It has an extensive bibliography of Merton's key writings.

12

Jesus and the Divine in the Contemporary Debate

We have defined a "centrist" mediation of the Jesus event as one which flows from a to-and-fro dialogue between the Christological tradition and the lessons of our contemporary experience. For the most part I have dealt with the tradition, seeking, with the help of centrist scholars, to mediate it in terms of our modern experience. Now I would like to turn to some special challenges to our Christological tradition which flow from our contemporary experience. What follows are only "representative" issues, but they will give the reader some inkling of the kinds of issues now being debated in the present problematic. Other writers might choose other challenges as being more representative and critical. I must simply acknowledge that I am writing from a centrist perspective *within the American tradition*, and for that reason I have chosen issues of particular interest to the American reader. Each theology is culture-specific, but I believe that the Divine Mystery is somehow at work in our American experience, with a possible message for Christianity as a whole. At the same time I recognize that this American perspective needs to be complemented and corrected by other perspectives. I hope that the reader will recognize this too.

Jesus and the Divine in Contemporary Thought and Practice

It is fitting that I begin with some contemporary challenges to the disclosure of the Divine in the Jesus event. This is the heart and foundation of the Jesus event, from which all else follows. But for the contemporary person, there are as yet some unresolved issues in this area. Let me concentrate upon two which seem to be particularly pressing.

The Problem of Whether the Divine
Suffers and Changes in the Light of Jesus

Clearly the most remarkable element of the Jesus event is the new disclosure of divine transcendence in the form of justice, peace and love.

This is the startling revelation implied in the belief in Jesus' divinity: the Divine is Jesus-like. The Holy Mystery, while remaining the Transcendent One, manifests that transcendence through working to bring peace, justice and love within the human family and the cosmos as a whole. Such a view of the Divine necessarily involves God quite fully in the human drama, and it is just at this point that contemporary experience locks horns with the tradition.

The problem is, in part, a theoretical one. For example, we noted that side by side with the kenoticist trend of the tradition (which is more of an undercurrent), there runs the major current which apparently denies too close an involvement between the Divine and human history. Even though our world is characterized by change and even suffering, this latter current would say that the Divine is not. God is, as the First Vatican Council put it, "completely simple and unchangeable . . . distinct in reality and in essence from the world, perfectly happy in Himself, and inexpressibly exalted above all things other than Himself that exist or that can be conceived."[1] Vatican I's teaching simply echoes a constant theme throughout the tradition: Pope Leo I in 449 described God as "simple and unchangeable"; the Fourth Lateran Council (1215) repeated Leo's teaching, and, even earlier, Athanasius interpreted Nicaea as holding that there is no change in the *Logos.*[2]

But, the contemporary mind responds, how can the Divine be involved in human misery and history and not in some way be subject to these realities? Doesn't this compromise the novelty of the Jesus event and contradict our contemporary experience of the world? And there are further intellectual puzzles. If the Divine is simply unchangeable, does this mean that we have no impact upon it: our pains and sufferings, our insights—do none of these really affect it? Does this also mean that there is no divine response to our free will—is our free will a ruse, as far as the Divine is concerned? And finally, what about evil? Does this make no difference to the Divine Mystery?

This problem is also a practical one. I am referring here to the powerful conviction of a number of recent writers that our God-thinking simply must be different once we pass through the horrors of the twentieth century: Guernica, Auschwitz, the Gulag, Hiroshima, Cambodia, etc. Probably the most powerful case for this conviction is found in Arthur Cohen's *The Tremendum*, a passionate but careful rethinking of God in the darkness (not "light") of the Jewish holocaust. As he puts it, "The way for thought about God and God's world must be made vastly more difficult and treacherous than I imagined a generation ago."[3] The thrust of his argument is that the traditional belief in God's omnipotence, which lets God off the hook for responsibility for evil by saying "God permits it," is simply rendered too problematic by our contemporary horrors. These horrors both call that supposed omnipotence into question and cry out for a God who does more than simply permit the horrible sufferings of the innocent. The practical edge in this theodicy is that it fosters a stance of passivity in the face of evil. Instead of a God who actively struggles against human misery, we have a divine neutrality toward it, which the faithful believer is supposed to accept.

Interestingly, the problem is also posed in an intensive way through what I earlier called our experience of globalization. Christianity's growing relationship with the great Far Eastern religions of Buddhism and Hinduism is causing us to ask whether the traditional stress on divine transcendence and "otherness" is an adequate expression of humanity's global religious experience. Hinduism has its "dualistic" current, which preserves God's "personal" otherness from creatures: the *Vishishtadvaita* typical of the *Bhagavad Gita*. But it also has its monistic current, which holds that on the deepest level it is not possible to separate the creature from the Absolute. Here Brahman (the ultimate) is purely undifferentiated consciousness, beyond all limits and distinctions. This is the *Advaita* tradition typical of the Vedantic Scriptures, and synthesized by Shankara (788–820 A.D.).

Buddhism, too, in its "no soul" doctrine (*anatta*) clearly teaches a form of monism, whereby the distinction between the creature and the Absolute is transcended in a state of undifferentiated unity (*nirvana*). This, as well as Hindu monism, presupposes a much greater emphasis upon the divine immanence than is traditionally accepted by Christianity. Interestingly, some Buddhists manifest a high interest in the kenotic trend of our faith, viewing it as an intuition comparable to the Hindu and Buddhist stress on the non-differentiation of the Divine. As Heinrich Dumoulin puts it, in commenting upon Masao Abe, a Buddhist scholar:

> Abe, proceeding from Barth's Christological theology, extends the idea of the *kenosis* or emptying of Christ (Phil. 2:7f) to God the Creator, and sees a kind of divine self-emptying in his creative work. The impelling force, as Abe sees it, is God's love; but thereby God assumes a negativity. Thus, "The Christian God should not be understood as a God aloof from non-being and negativity, but as taking on non-being and negating himself of his own free will. . . . Because of his love, God, self-sufficient though he is, negates himself and creates the world which is different from himself." Since this self-renunciation is grounded in the divine essence, namely in God's *agape*, it precedes the self-renunciation of God in the act of creation. Self-renunciation, Abe concludes, is not a motive external to God, but rather is of his very essence.[4]

The question of the Divine involvement in the world curiously might aid us in affirming some of the secrets of the Far East much more wholeheartedly.

As I understand the matter, there appear to be three competing views about the Divine in our tradition. What is called by some "classical theism" would hold that the Divine is simply unchangeable and unable to suffer. To attribute such qualities to the Divine is to compromise divine transcendence, rendering it subject to the imperfections of creaturely existence. At the other end of the spectrum we have "classical pantheism," which in various ways identifies the Divine with the creaturely processes of the world. Pantheism clearly makes the Divine subject to change and even suffering, but at the price of the truncation of transcendence. Transcendence here is merely finite: the ongoing change and development of the finite cosmos itself. Some have argued that classical theism tends to generate pantheism. For, if the Divine remains immune from change and suffering, pantheism argues that we have little need for such a deity. Its deity, pantheism thinks, is much more relevant to a finite world like ours.

Is there a way beyond these two extremes? Some think that panentheism represents a genuine middle way.[5] As I will use this term, it signifies that the Divine is truly within the world and that the world is truly within the Divine, so that there is a reciprocal relationship between them. Hence, "panen-theism": the "all" is "in" God. But what distinguishes panentheism from pantheism is that the divine transcendence truly remains transcendent: involved with the world, but also more than the world. Let us diagram our three options as follows:

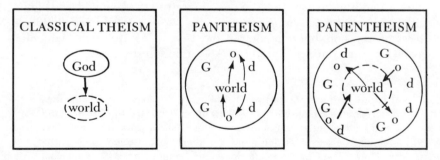

On first sight, the panentheistic approach would seem to have the merit of being a more adequate rendering of the divine disclosure in the Jesus event: it surfaces the divine bondedness and involvement with the world. It also coheres with our contemporary experience of change, process, and even suffering. This is not denied of God. Yet, panentheism does not sacrifice divine transcendence: this truly remains more than the world, a power of revitalization which can alter the world itself. This also coheres with our global religious experience, and with our own experiences of the transcendent within our lives.

As we hazard the risk of entering into the arena of panentheism, however, we find that there are many who brand themselves such, yet who are not in agreement on the fundamental questions involved: What precisely is divine transcendence, and what are the varied forms of divine involvement within the world? So far as I can tell, on the continuum of panentheism, we have on the extreme left those influenced by the process philosophy of Alfred North Whitehead and Charles Hartshorne. The key difficulty here is that many non-process commentators are not convinced that this school truly advocates a doctrine of divine transcendence. It appears to many that process thinkers regard God as one component, although the "supreme" one, within the creative process of the world. Rather than being the Creator, God is subject to and limited by that wordly creative process. If you will, the Divine seems "caught" in the vortex of finite creativity. This leaves the origins of the world unexplained, and reduces God to being one finite element within the world who supplies, process thinkers say, the "initial aim" to our creaturely transactions.

For many it is doubtful that process theology does justice to the experience of divine transcendence, and even more doubtful that it coheres with the God mediated to us in the Scriptures.[6] While its strength is to be clear about the fact that God really changes and suffers, its weakness is its ambiguity on whether it truly accepts a transcendent deity. To be sure, process theologians regard themselves as "dipolar" in their thought: God is absolute in one pole, and relative in the other whereby he is related to the world. But the ambiguity is over what is meant by "absolute." Does this refer to a transcendent reality which is more than, and greater than, the creative vortex of the world itself?

On the "right" end of the continuum are professed panentheists who seem unclear about whether the Divine actually undergoes the change and even suffering characteristic of our world. Unlike process thinkers, these latter are not unclear on divine transcendence: the Divine is variously described as "sovereign," "more than the world," "the absolute Creator and Sustainer of all," etc. But they seem rather vague on whether and how what really transpires in our world affects the Divine. Some say that God does not change in his "inner being," but only in the "otherness" of creatures. Others hold that God changes in "consciousness," but not in "being." These expressions are enormously ambiguous, and do not correspond to our experience. Just as we cannot artificially dichotomize inner and outer, consciousness and being, so it is extremely difficult to grasp how these distinctions throw any light upon our problem, even allowing for analogy.[7]

To avoid these ambiguities, I would suggest that we present a form of panentheism that seems relatively clear on these matters. This will enable us to query a bit more precisely in just what sense panentheism might cohere, both with the Jesus event, and with our contemporary experience. I personally have found the work of Geddes MacGregor to be helpful in this regard.[8] Let me try to set forth his leading themes. Readers can then judge for themselves whether I have been fair to our panentheists of the "left" and the "right," by studying them a little more carefully.

MacGregor begins by clearly affirming the sovereignty and transcendence of God, in the traditional sense of that term. "If the term 'God' is to be intelligible, God must be sovereign and independent." Later he adds that God is "absolutely sovereign." But he goes on to qualify this transcendence, by suggesting that its nature is one of "self-limitation" or "love" (*agape*):

> . . . there is plainly no conceivable way in which God, being absolutely sovereign and independent, could possibly be ambitious or self-seeking. There is nothing for him to seek for himself, nothing toward which he could extend ambition, nothing for him to achieve, for *ex hypothesi* he is complete, perfect, self-subsistent. In choosing to engage in a creative purpose there is, so to speak, only one way for his power to go: it must be in some measure abdicated. It cannot go to a plus side, for there is no plus side to perfection; so if it is to go anywhere it must be to the minus side, that is, to the side of voluntary self-renunciation. God, in creating the universe, to that extent empties himself, letting the beings go free that he has created.

MacGregor is influenced by Simone Weil's view of divine creation as an act, not of self-expansion, but of restraint and renunciation. But more importantly, he suggests that his view coheres both with our contemporary experience, and with the great lessons of the Jesus event. Just as all acts of human creativity involve giving something of myself away, so, correlatively, the creative acts of an infinite being would involve a "giving away" of infinite proportions.

For these reasons, MacGregor considers *kenosis* or self-limitation the "root principle of Being." Calling God "kenotic" is a way of specifying what we mean by saying "God is love." This would mean that God does not "increase" or "expand" in performing any creative acts. Such self-expansion tends to be narcissistic or destructive in the long run, and, in any case, as

the Infinite Being "there would be nowhere into which an infinitely powerful Being could expand." It is not the path of self-expansion, but that of
self-limiting love that God has available for the divine purposes.

Here it seems important to grasp the difference between this form of
kenoticism and the older views we surveyed earlier. Whereas the older
views urged that God ceases to be the infinite one in the incarnation (God
holds infinity back, so to speak), MacGregor holds that agapeistic self-limitation *is* the form which divine transcendence takes.

MacGregor thinks that his kenoticist interpretation of God provides
us with a new perspective upon human freedom and human evil. The divine self-limitation makes room for our genuine human freedom: "To provide room for human freedom of choice, or indeed for any kind of freedom
within a theistic system, God must not only occasionally restrain himself
in the exercise of his power; he must never exercise it at all except in support of love, and love without freedom is impossible." Here, I think, we
glimpse a key difference between MacGregor's panentheism and that of
process thought. Process theology views God as one agent among many
who contributes to our person-making, although he is the "highest" agent
supplying our "initial aim." The God of process theology does not coerce;
he "persuades," but as one persuasive force among others. MacGregor, on
the other hand, suggests that God's agapeistic self-limitation actually creates and sustains our freedom, yet without violating it. If you will, God is
a sovereign love force, creating and moving our freedom, yet without violence, toward love.

So, too, God's self-limitation, in taking the risk of creating our freedom, has also taken the risk of the possible misuse of our freedom through
evil and sin. Evil is "the price of the risk that God assumes when, in sending his creatures forth, he refrains from restricting them." Yet the divine
agape does not simply "sit back" in indifference to the massive evil of the
creaturely process. Because that *agape* is the power at work creating and
sustaining the universe, we can in some real sense speak of "the anguish
of God." Because "he is so completely He-who-loves his anguish at the
lovelessness of his creatures must be all the more poignant."

MacGregor seems to mean, not that God passively views the human
spectacle and agonizes in that sense, but that the divine agony unleashes
a power of self-sacrificial love, which is capable of defeating evil, yet without violating our human freedom. He continues,

> In no way is God either unconcerned as is a rock or immutable as we like
> to take a rock to be. God, far from being impassible, is ever-agonizing in
> his self-emptying. Yet these old models were not by any means wholly
> false, for such is God's creative love that it is, as we might say, not only

"as impregnable as a rock," but, rather, infinitely more so, since no dy-
namite or even atomic blast could ever touch it. And if by impassibility
we mean that God's love cannot be undermined by anything outside itself, we may accept the notion without protest.

And he adds a clarifying gloss: "The divine power should be conceived as
. . . the infinite power that springs from creative love." It is an "unlimited
capacity . . . so that not only does he bring creatures into being to let them
be; he creatively restores whatever seeks such restoration."

Finally, MacGregor suggests that "God" cannot be exhausted in the
category of self-emptying. Not only is God the fullness of Being which is
more than self-emptying. God's creative letting be presupposes a fullness
of Being that transcends creation, and from which creation comes. For this
reason, while there is truly anguish in God, there is also a deep joy and
happiness: "We may say . . . that God as Being is also ever-joyous in his
self-emptying."9 This is MacGregor's form of dipolarity: divine fullness
and divine self-emptying, a Mystery of deep joy and a mystery of self-renunciation, letting be, risking human freedom, and agonizing with human
failure.

MacGregor calls his approach "panentheistic," for while it tries to acknowledge divine transcendence, it also clearly bonds God with the creaturely drama. Relations here are two-way. The really novel element is the
proposal, clearly derived from the Jesus event, of self-limitation or *agape*.
God cannot become "more," but can "spend freely" of the divine fullness.
This helps us to see, I think, that there is a form of "change" which is compatible with a divine being. The difficulty, hitherto, in all views which attributed change to God is that they implied that God is somehow
defective, becoming something "more" through change. MacGregor professes that God remains sovereign, not becoming something more.
Through self-limitation, God truly changes, but the change is not a passage
to something more, but a giving and risking of what God already is. This is
what is meant by a voluntary self-renunciation. Our own acts of self-renunciation, and the change that brings to us, are the proper experiential
ground for this kind of God-thinking.

So, too, is there a form of "suffering" that seems compatible with a
sovereign God. But, again, it is the suffering that comes not from imperfection, but from the perfection of love. This is, of course, a special kind of
suffering, typified by Jesus' cross and perhaps somewhat by the mystical
"dark night." But it is a true form of suffering nonetheless. It is a selfless
form of suffering. Teresa of Avila's "I die because I do not die" (*Muero por-
que no muero*) perhaps comes close: she selflessly desires to suffer with the
suffering Christ. Baron Friedrich von Hügel suggested that we should

speak of the "compassion of God" rather than the suffering of God, for God's suffering is transmuted by love and love's ultimate victory. "The religious sense," said Von Hügel, "at its deepest and in the long run, will not, must not, be restricted to the Self-limited Creative God, or (worse still) to the persuasion that the whole of the Absolute—that God in and for himself—has been and is absorbed in God as creator." For at the deepest, God is "joy, pure joy, an ocean of it, unplumbed, unplumbable."[10] "Com-passion" does perhaps capture MacGregor's suggestion. It suggests true agony on the part of the Divine, but it also brings out its qualitatively unique nature.

The American Feminist Critique of the Divine Presence

The second challenge to our contemporary Christology which seems highly representative is that coming from American feminist theology. As is increasingly well known, feminist theologians regard the male image of God, characteristic of Western Christianity, not as a trivial issue that can be blinked aside through semantic games, but as a destructive development reflecting the subjugation and even "slavery" of women. The male-God serves as a primary symbol, perhaps *the* primary symbol, which reinforces the inferior status of women. One of the ways in which this is reflected in the religious sphere is to regard the male as the primary spokesperson for God, while the woman derives her God-knowledge only derivatively from the male. We already noted that some of Paul's writings reflect this current: "I want you to know that the head of every man is Christ; the head of a woman is her husband; and the head of Christ is the Father. . . . A man ought not to cover his head, because he is the image of God and the reflection of his glory. Woman, in turn, is the reflection of man's glory" (1 Cor 11:3, 7).

I raise this issue here in the context of Christology, because it is deeply related to the kind of divine disclosure which flows from the Jesus event. We have suggested that Jesus reveals a Divinity that is on the side of justice, love, and peace. If it is the case that a male-God reinforces feminine inferiority and subjugation, then the thrust of the Jesus event would seem to call for a revision of our symbolism for the Divine.

It is true that Jesus uses the male image "Abba" when he prays. But it is also true that he constantly acts to liberate women, and indeed all oppressed persons, from inferiority. I am inclined to believe that the thrust of Jesus' God-image is not sexist, although he possibly did not carry this so far as to speak of the Divine in terms taken from women's experience. Certainly we can argue that one of the major effects of Jesus' use of "Abba"-language was to deprive the patriarchy of its absolute power, as Robert

THE TWO CHRISTS OF MIGUEL DE UNAMUNO[11]

A good case could be made that a vision and praxis of the Divine Presence that is panentheistic in tone was put forward by the Basque philosopher Miguel de Unamuno at the turn of the century. In his writings he indicates that the Spanish tradition has given birth to two quite different "Christs."

The one Unamuno calls the "Recumbent Christ of Palencia" is an utterly dead Christ. Here the gruesome image is of a Christ taken down from the cross, gory and pallid. Unamuno says that this expresses "death's eternity," the "immortalization of death." "This Christ will never rise again." Playing upon the Spanish word *tierra,* meaning both "land" and "earth," he says: *El Cristo de mi tierra es tierra/*"The Christ of my land is the earth." And he adds, "O Christ of heaven, deliver us from the Christ of earth."

The Christ of Palencia fosters the "coalman's faith" (*la fe del carbonero*). This is a dead faith which stifles all inquiry and struggle. It generates passivity and does not forward peace, justice and love. Clearly the image of God flowing from the Palencian Christ is one of indifference to the human struggle, one allowing the struggle to end in death's "eternity."

But Unamuno also speaks of the "Crucified Christ of Velazquez," a Christ who never ceases to agonize. This Christ is not dead, but in agony. This is the Christ who "saved earth" and "made death our mother." Here we have a poet's intuition which is close to the panentheistic insight that God voluntarily agonizes for and with creation. However this agony of God is but one side of a divine love.

LINES FROM UNAMUNO'S THE CHRIST OF VELAZQUEZ

. . . the Man eternal that makes of us new men (1,1)

. . . our minds have been forged, as in furnace of thy bowels, and we
see the universe through thine eyes (1,3)

. . . the sun is the wound that was opened by the flame rending the
deep darkness of God thy Father, that sun that burning gives light
by thy breast, thy breast that is wounded by seething love (1,7)

. . . neither does love bear fruit without blood (1,9)

Thy sleep is the peace that is given by war, and thy life is the war that
gives us peace (1,10)

Thou wast alone with thy Father—and He
face to face with Thee—, glances intermingled
—the blue of heaven and the blue of Thine eyes—,
at the sob of immensity, his breast,
the limitless sea of the spirit trembled,
and God, feeling Himself to be a man,
tasted death, solitude divine, Thy Father
desired to feel what it is to die,
He saw Himself for a moment alone
without his Creation, when bowing thy head,
Thou didst give thy human breath to the 'breathing'
of God. To thy last groan responded only
in the far distance the pitying sea! (2,2)

Will the Father be deaf, not being dumb?
. . . The Word, only for being
the Word, cannot be deaf, for it exists
by words, and Thou by prayers that are words! (3,8)

Hamerton-Kelly suggests. The Abba who is on the side of justice and love necessarily breaks through patriarchy, with its master-slave relationships. It may also be true, as Hamerton-Kelly suggests, "that Jesus chose the father symbol precisely to humanize the patriarchy, but that must remain a conjecture."[12] In effect, what we seem to have in Jesus' God-imagery and praxis is the beginnings, not the completion, of a turn-about in our vision and praxis of the Divine Presence. This incompleteness and ambiguity goes a long way in explaining the later ambivalence of Paul (or his followers) and the domestic codes of the later New Testament. An ambiguity in Jesus with respect to women left an open hole, into which patriarchy could easily jump.

The challenge raised by the feminist critique of our God-symbolism is both a theoretical and a practical issue, as are all issues in theology. Not only does the meaning of the Jesus event seem to call for a careful reconsideration of this matter. Jesus' praxis does too.[13] A fully consistent thinking through of Jesus' liberating Divinity on both the theoretical and the practical plains demands this revision.

It also seems that we should unashamedly regard our awareness of the feminist issue as a particularly American contribution to Christology. It is true that misogynism as a "human fall into the bondage of male idolatry" goes back at least as far as the urban "civilizations" of the second millennium B.C. with their separation between hearth (where the woman stayed: because of constant pregnancy?) and society (the new male province of political, social, and religious power). Perhaps there was even misogynism in the pre-urban period, given the likely inability of the pregnant women to engage in the important tasks of hunting and survival-fighting. It is also likely that the emergence of the universal religions in the first millennium was a mixed blessing for women, given their stress upon spirituality and transcendence, and the simultaneous identification of women with the lower biological-material functions.[14] But it is in America that the misogynism of the ages has been especially felt and revolted against. This feminine revolt may be one of America's greatest contributions to our new global development.

The rise of industrialization from the Civil War period on brought with it the disruption of the predominantly agricultural character of the American economy. In the agricultural context, women to some extent participated with their husbands in the economic power and decisions of the farm/ranch. Stability and sustenance on the farm were a co-contribution of the women. With industrialization we have an intensification of what occurred earlier in the urbanization of the second millennium: hearth is severed from society and industry, and thus women are deprived of access to the real sources of power and wealth. The older roles of women were disrupted, and at least the "founding" American feminists found their new subjugated status dissatisfying. This was the real beginning of American feminism.

Women had also been very active in the struggle for the liberation of the blacks, beginning around the Civil War period and extending into the civil rights struggles of the 1960's. Their experience in the abolitionist movements both gave them a sense of their own capacity to act in the political realm, and also made them aware of their own enslavement in a male society. As Sarah Grimke, one of the great abolitionists, put it: "I ask no favors for my sex. . . . All I ask of our brethren is that they take their feet off our necks and permit us to stand upright."[15] What Sarah and her sister Angelina grasped was that the logic which led to the subjugation of the blacks was the same logic which leads to all forms of oppression, that of women included.[16]

What are the choices that face us as we seek to revise our God-symbolism in a way which is sensitive to the feminist critique (woman's experience) and to the liberating thrust of the Jesus experience? Here I would single out Rosemary Radford Ruether as someone who has thought through the possible options and provided us with clues which might move us in the right direction.[17] Her writings are enormously helpful for the beginner, because she carves out her approach in dialogue with the major options that seem to be surfacing. The breadth of her writings makes her very appropriate for a survey book like this one.

Ruether thinks that some theologians, awake to the feminist challenge, have suggested that patriarchalism is not the whole story of the Jewish and Christian traditions. They have tried to recover the subterranean current of the "feminine" in patriarchal theology—Ruether calls it the "suppressed feminine"—as a corrective to our predominantly misogynistic God-symbolism. For example, there are some biblical texts which do describe God in female images. One series of these texts stresses the "motherly" characteristics of women as especially appropriate images for God: a mother's anguish, her birthing, her unconditional love for her children, etc. "But now, I cry out as a woman in labor, gasping and panting," says Yahweh (Is 42:14). Or, "But Zion said, 'The Lord has forsaken me; the Lord has forgotten me.' Can a mother forget her infant, be without tenderness for the child of her womb? Even should she forget, I will never forget you," says Yahweh (Is 49:14–15). Something of the same imagery, I might add, surfaces in the Jesus tradition. "How often have I wanted to gather your children together as a mother bird collects her young under her wings, and you refused me!" says Jesus of Jerusalem (Lk 13:34).

A second series of texts describes the mediation of God to humans in feminine terms. In the wisdom tradition, Holy Wisdom is the way God

mediates the gift of creation and revelation: "My son, if you receive my
words and treasure my commands, turning your ear to wisdom . . . if you
seek her like silver . . . then you will understand the fear of the Lord" (Prv
2:1–5; cf 8:23–31; Wis 8:2–9, etc.).

Ruether thinks that behind the imagery of Holy Wisdom are rem-
nants of the ancient Near Eastern goddesses (Isis and Astarte), who were
imagined as creators and redeemers. Goddesses like this were projections
of cultures which valued female experience, seeing in women's attributes
something of the sacred. In this case, social justice and the harmony of nature, and its lack of chaos, were qualities found in women and considered
sacred. Occasionally the Wisdom/*Sophia* tradition also surfaces in Christianity. Ruether refers to the somewhat marginal orthodox theologian Ser-
gius Bulgakov, who developed a somewhat esoteric view of God as male-
female: "Sophia is the matrix or ground of Being of the three (male) persons
of God!"[18] Joan Chamberlain Engelsman cites some texts from the early
Fathers in which this *Sophia*-symbolism surfaces. For instance, because
Clement of Alexandria identifies Christ with Wisdom, he does not hesitate
to endow him with breasts flowing with the milk of wisdom:

> Milk of the bride,
> Given of heaven,
> Pressed from sweet breasts—
> Gifts of Thy Wisdom—
> These Thy little ones
> Draw for their nourishment;
> With infancy lips
> Filling their soul
> With spiritual savor
> From breasts of the Word.[19]

But in general the male *Logos*-symbolism of the Greeks supplanted the *Sophia*-symbolism. Jesus was more commonly identified with the male *Logos*.[20]

Ruether's problem, and I share it with her, is that "these suppressed
feminine aspects of God . . . still remain fundamentally within the context
of the male-dominant structure of patriarchal relationships."[21] The element to note here is that the feminine always exists in a subordinate status
to the male: nurturing, supporting, faithful, but always subordinate to the
male God-Father and the male *Logos*. This should not be surprising in a
patriarchal culture which cannot view the woman as autonomous, equal,
self-initiating, etc. The difficulty here is that the feminine always means a
truncated women's experience, that of the subjugated female, reinforcing

the "feminine archetype" of woman as passive and receptive. This archetype is more the creation of a misogynistic culture than an expression of woman's real potential as a human being.

Ruether's second option is the revolt against the biblical and patriarchal God, through the return to "pagan feminism." Some of the trends within this movement would be: substituting a goddess and nature religion for the patriarchal God of the West; returning to the original cults of what are believed to have been matriarchal societies preexisting the rise of patriarchy; an imitation of the witches of the European Middle Ages, who preserved the earlier goddess religion, etc.

While this revolt is surely understandable, given the history of misogynism, still Ruether thinks that it suffers from a number of important "immaturities." For example, its idealization of supposed matriarchal societies is based on questionable research. It repudiates the male in the favor of the female, thus cutting off the possibility of a truly new and mutual form of human existence; it reverses the master-slave relationship. Very importantly, it accepts the concept of the "feminine," without asking whether that concept might not be a patriarchal creation. Judith Ochshorn[22] has recently shown that the goddesses of earlier pre-urban and urban cultures simply do not fit the supposed feminine stereotypes—these deities represented a greater fullness of attributes, ranging from sovereignty, power, and autonomy, on through to nurturing and fidelity. Women's experience, it seems, cannot be limited to the passive and secondary characteristics typical of an "eternal feminine."

The first two options, if you will, seem to be dead ends. This is true from at least two points of view. In terms of our contemporary experience, they are inadequate to the full range of women's experience, seeking to lock women into the limited stereotype of the feminine archetype. This not only has deleterious consequences for women, robbing them of their full potential and actuality. It also hurts men, for it locks them into a master-slave relationship with women, reinforcing their own oppressive tendencies, and blocking the possibility of a more mutual interrelationship between men and women. From the point of view of Christology, these two options do not forward the liberating thrust of the Jesus event. Instead of fostering justice, peace, and love, they foster injustice, lovelessness, and aggression.

In the light of all of this, the only choice left to us is to revise our God-symbolism in such a way that both men's and women's experiences are equally (better: mutually) seen as pointers to the Divine Presence. Only this would seem to be adequate to the liberating Divinity of justice, peace, and love found in Jesus, whose presence flows unconditionally through all humans, irrespective of gender. Just how this can be practically implemented is another matter. Clearly it will involve a transformation of both human individuals and human societies. But we will come to that in time. For the moment, let us dwell upon this single issue of our God-symbolism.

Ruether seems to suggest that we should draw our imagery/analogies for the Divine from the experiences of both women and men. God is also Goddess. In an earlier piece, she created the neologism "God(ess)." In her more recent book she has changed to "God/ess." This can only be written, not said. We will have to experiment with terms appropriate for worship: Holy Presence, Divine Mystery, etc. The important point is to symbolize our belief that the Divine Mystery flows through all humans. The experiences of all are appropriate pointers to the deepest Mystery. Ruether does not say so, but this implies that we need a feminist revision of our Trinitarian symbolism too, if this is to remain a viable symbol for all. Father, Son, and Spirit needs complementing and correcting: by Mother, Daughter, and Love?

But Ruether recognizes that these analogies are quite limited. For God/ess is always more than our experience. God/ess does not simply "embrace these experiences and validate them in their traditional historical form."[23] For God/ess points to a fullness of justice, peace, and love "who is both male and female, and neither male nor female, [pointing] us to an unrealized new humanity."[24]

Ruether's contribution, at this point, seems enormously appealing, on both experiential and Christological grounds. Surely one of the great tests for any future Christology will be its ability to confront the hidden and destructive misogynism at the center of our Christian symbol system.

Notes

1. Cited in John F. Broderick, *Documents of Vatican Council I* (Collegeville, Minnesota: Liturgical Press, 1971), p. 40.

2. See Maas, *op. cit.*, p. 20, pp. 142–143, referring to *DS* 297, 800, and 805, and Athanasius, *Letter To Serapion*, 1,16; 2,3; and other references.

3. Arthur A. Cohen, *The Tremendum: A Theological Interpretation of the Holocaust* (New York: Crossroad, 1981), p. 34.

4. Heinrich Dumoulin, *Christianity Meets Buddhism* (LaSalle, Ill.: Open Court, 1974), p. 180. For Hinduism, the best entry is John Hick, *Death and Eternal Life* (New York: Harper and Row, 1976), pp. 311–331, 425–449 (overviews of Hinduism).

5. See Woods, *Mysterion, op. cit.*, pp. 93–108, for a succinct introduction to panentheism. He traces the term to Baron Friedrich von Hügel; cf Whelan, *op. cit.*, p. 274, note 135, for the appropriate sources in Von Hügel.

6. See John B. Cobb, Jr. and David Ray Griffin, *Process Theology: An Introductory Exposition* (Philadelphia: Westminster, 1976). For a critique repre-

sentative of the one in the text, see Langdon Gilkey, *Reaping the Whirlwind: A Christian Interpretation of History* (New York: Seabury, 1976), pp. 306–318.

7. Typical of these two approaches respectively are Joseph F. Donceel, *The Searching Mind: An Introduction to a Philosophy of God* (Notre Dame: University of Notre Dame, 1979), pp. 164–201, and W. Norris Clarke, *The Philosophical Approach to God: A Neo-Thomist Perspective* (Winston-Salem, N.C.: Wake Forest University, 1979).

8. See his *He Who Lets Us Be, op. cit.*

9. Citations are from *ibid.*, pp. 97, 98, 107, 109, 120, 136, 149, 184, 15, 187.

10. Freidrich von Hügel, "Suffering and God," *Essays and Addresses on the Philosophy of Religion*, Second Series (London: J.M. Dent and Sons, 1926/1939), pp. 167–213, at pp. 206, 212. The citation from Teresa of Avila, *Complete Works of St. Teresa*, 3, E. Allison Peers, trans. and ed. (London: Sheed and Ward, 1975), pp. 277–279, from her poem *Vivo sin vivir en mi. . . .*

11. On Unamuno, see his *The Tragic Sense of Life* (New York: Macmillan, 1921); *The Christ of Velazquez*, Eleanor L. Turnbull, trans. (Baltimore: Johns Hopkins University, 1951)—citations are from this; "The Spanish Christ," in *Perplexities and Paradoxes* (New York: Philosophical Library, 1945), pp. 75–80. For a helpful interpretation of this Basque panentheist, see John A. Mackey, "Miguel de Unamuno," in Carl Michalson, ed., *Christianity and the Existentialists* (New York: Charles Scribner's Sons, 1956), pp. 43–58.

12. Robert Hamerton-Kelly, *God the Father: Theology and Patriarchy in the Teaching of Jesus* (Philadelphia: Fortress, 1979), pp. 102, 103.

13. A very helpful practical analysis: Anne Wilson Schaef, *Women's Reality: An Emerging Female System in the White Male Society* (Minneapolis: Winston, 1981).

14. For an historical overview of misogynism, see Ruether, "The Descent of Woman: Symbol and Social Condition," *New Woman/New Earth, op, cit.*, pp. 3–35. On pre-urban times, she comments: "Feminism should not idealize the tribal period as a 'golden age' for women's autonomy and power. . . . the sex-linked complementarity of work roles established at that time became the basis for an increasingly repressed role and image of women" (p. 9). Cf also Denise Lardner Carmody, *Women and World Religions* (Nashville: Abingdon, 1979), and E. and F. Stagg, *Woman in the World of Jesus* (Philadelphia: Westminster, 1978).

15. From her *The Equality of the Sexes and the Condition of Women* (Boston, 1838), p. 10, cited in E. Flexner, *Century of Struggle* (New York: Atheneum, 1974), p. 47.

16. For other American liberation movements which have grasped this lesson, see James H. Cone, *A Black Theology of Liberation* (Philadelphia: Lippincott, 1970); Vine Deloria, *God Is Red* (New York: Grosset and Dunlap, 1973); Virgilio Elizondo, *Galilean Journey: The Mexican American Promise* (Maryknoll: Orbis, 1983).

17. I am following her succinct "The Female Nature of God: A Problem in Contemporary Religious Life," *Concilium* 143 (1981), 61–66, more amply treated in her *Sexism and God-Talk, op. cit.*, pp. 47–71.

18. *Ibid.*, 63.

19. From "Hymn to the Educator," *The Fathers of the Church*, 23 (New York: Fathers of the Church, Inc., 1954), p. 277, as cited in Joan Chamberlain Engelsman, *The Feminine Dimension of the Divine* (Philadelphia: Westminster, 1979), p. 144.

20. *Ibid.*, pp. 74–120, 139–148, for a good overview of the replacement of *Sophia* by *Logos* in Christology.

21. Ruether, "The Female Nature of God," *art. cit.*, 63.

22. Judith Ochshorn, *The Female Experience and the Nature of the Divine* (Bloomington: Indiana University, 1981).

23. Ruether, "The Female Nature of God," *art. cit.*, 66.

24. *Ibid.*

13

Jesus and the Self
in the Contemporary Debate

In this chapter I would like to turn to the second member of our great
quaternity, the "self," and explore some issues that are surfacing in the
current debate. We noted that the Jesus event disclosed a new model of
person-making. The human self, as embodied in Jesus explosively, and in
his followers less explosively, was imaged forth as a relational project of
growth in all of our relations through justice, love, and peace. The Jesus-
like model of the self is anything but an individualistic and egocentric project. I preferred the phrase "the covenantal self," in order to stay close to
the concrete life of Jesus as a project of solidarity with God, with other humans (especially the oppressed), and with nature. Person-making, in other
words, becomes justice- and love- and peace-making, and to the extent
that this is realized in us, we become "images of the Divine." Person-making is a divine-human (theandric) project, an allowing of divine pathos to
create in us human sympathy. Linking up with our last chapter, we might
say that panentheism should lead to panenhumanism, whereby every human builds up and supports every other human. Two current debates, I
suggest, are helping us to discover some further ramifications of this new
kind of Jesus-like self.

The Uniqueness of Jesus

Different dimensions of our contemporary experience are pressing in
on the traditional belief in the unique self of Jesus. But first let me say
something about that "unique self" that we Christians believe Jesus images forth. Traditional Christianity clearly considers Jesus to be special.
The New Testament attributes the various titles of Lord, Son of God, even
God and Savior, only to him. Paul speaks of Jesus as inaugurating the "fullness of time" (Gal 4:4), indicating by this that Jesus brings a radical break
in human history, something unknown before. For Hebrews, he is the
only and sinless mediator (4:15; 7:24–25; 10:12–13, etc.). John echoes He-

brews: no one comes to the Father except through Jesus (Jn 14:6; 15:4, 6).
The Council of Chalcedon, too, thought that Jesus was unique: his "hy-
postatic" union with the Divine was not the same as the relation between
the Divine and other creatures. There can be no doubt, then, that the specialness of Jesus is deeply rooted in our tradition. He uniquely models
forth our covenantal self, going before us as the image and model of what
person-making is. "He is . . . the first-born of all creatures" (Col 1:15), says
the Pauline school.

And yet the pressures of our contemporary experience raise questions. Some of these are of a more theoretical kind. Have we perhaps
exaggerated the differences between Jesus and ourselves? Is it not historically common for exceptional people in history to be credited with qualities that are true of the rest of us? Just as the "rights" of monarchs are now
more widely democratized, should not exceptional religious qualities, attributed to people like Jesus, be seen as possiblities for the rest of us? After
all, the Jesus event calls us to become aware of the divine dimension of
every human being. All of us are called to be covenantal selves, just like
Jesus, who embody a living relationship to the Divine and to other human
beings. All of us are in some sense "theandric," divine-human unities. As
John of the Cross put it, "We are 'gods' by participation." All of these questions make us query whether we might not have exaggerated the differences between Jesus and ourselves. As we become aware of these issues
and grow in solidarity with God and others, we find ourselves saying anew,
with Paul, "The life I live now is not my own; Christ is living in me" (Gal
2:20).

Practical issues exert their pressure too. What is the practical punch
of the Jesus event, if Jesus is so qualitatively different from the rest of us?
If we cannot model forth in some analogous but real way the life he lived,
then why bother to profess belief in him? By making him into a kind of
"metaphysical exception," are we not robbing him of his salvific power to
chart and empower a path for the rest of us to pursue?

But there are larger practical issues. Is there a link, however difficult
to trace, between believing in Jesus' specialness and Christian arrogance
and intolerance of outsiders, even the persecution of them? Has Jesus' specialness provided us with an ideology for the Constantinian Empire and its
medieval continuation in Christendom, for anti-Semitism and the horrible
Christian contribution to the holocaust, and for the denigration of the
world's non-Christian religions? Does Jesus' specialness forever block the
ability of Christians to admit the possible worth and excellence, religiously, of others in history? These are terribly complex waters, for there
is no simple correlation between beliefs and behavior. Yet we do know that

theory and praxis co-condition one another. At the very least the sad history of Christian praxis forces us to probe Jesus' uniqueness anew.

Finally, it is the reality of globalization that most intensively forces us to query Jesus' uniqueness. A number of factors seem to be at work simultaneously. First, the Jesus event discloses a God who is panentheistically available to all within the universe. It seems impossible to limit the divine self-disclosure to the Western orbit of the globe. Furthermore, our own experience convinces us that the Divine is available to us within the depths of our own experience, and within those movements within history which seem to be carrying forward the liberating thrust of the Jesus event. On these grounds, too, the religious experiences of the sages and mystics of the Far East must be accorded a significance similar to that which we accord Christianity.

As if to confirm the above, one contemporary scholar speaks of an emerging new consensus among scholars about the similarity between Jesus and the Buddha.[1] "The missions of both consisted basically in *revealing* something and in *modeling* what was revealed," says Paul Knitter.[2] Both preached an urgent message of liberation (the Dharma, the Gospel). Both were recognized for their "authority," which flowed from their extraordinary religious experience (Nirvana, Abba). Both embodied the reality of their revelation: Buddha was called the *Tathagata*/"He who has arrived"; Jesus, the "Messiah." Both likewise animated a sense of the universality of their message. The Buddhist scholar Richard Drummond says that Buddha's universal message "has no parallel in the previous history of India."[3] Their messages are similar too: for Jesus, it is the conversion to peace, justice and love; for Buddha, from the limited ego to universal compassion. Knitter also claims that Buddhism has undergone a development similar to Christology. Just as Christians gradually came to an awareness of Jesus' divine presence, so the Mahayanist tradition developed "the nearly complete deification of the Buddha." He comments: "Intrinsic to this interpretation is what Amore terms 'an ancient, legendary pattern' of descent— the Ultimate descends to humanity to become part of it."[4]

How are today's theologians responding to those insights? One group argues for "exclusivism." This means that this group in some way limits the Divine self-disclosure to the Jesus event. Sometimes writers within this approach will employ the distinction between prophetic/revealed religions and natural religions, holding that divine revelation is confined to the former. The latter are merely human aspirations for the Divine, as distinct from the Divine's own self-response. Sometimes the categories of the sacred and the profane are also used. The major problem is that this option contradicts both the Jesus event and our own experience. The distinction between a revealed and a natural religion breaks down in the face of a universal God known to us from experience and from Jesus. On the practical level, exclusivism breeds arrogance and elitism.

A second group espouses some form of "relativism." This option surfaces in such statements as: "All religions teach the same thing"; "All religions are equally good"; "There are no absolute religious truths," etc. As the appeal of exclusivity in a global age is its clarity and decisiveness, so the appeal of relativism is its openness and freedom. Yet the Jesus event clearly rejects relativism: not all forms of supposedly religious piety are consistent with the peace, justice and love preached by Jesus. Relativism would reduce Jesus' arguments with the religions of his day to mere "misunderstandings" that need never have happened. Our own experience also teaches us that we need to be discriminating about religious claims: not all of them are founded upon equally sound views of human experience. I might add that one of the great problems with relativism is that it leaves only raw power as an arbitrator between competing claims—either that, or indifference.

Most centrist theologians are dissatisfied with exclusivism and relativism, and are struggling to give birth to a third alternative. This "third" alternative would be "inclusive," open to affirming the religious worth of non-Christian religions, yet without denying the central importance of the Jesus event. In what follows, I would like to build upon the insights of the "inclusivists," but in a way that is consistent with the entire thrust of the Christology which we have developed throughout these chapters.[5] In a kind of shorthand way, we can call the approach given here a "kenotic approach to Jesus' uniqueness." Such a kenoticist inclusiveness gives birth to the hypothesis of "complementary and critical uniqueness" as a way of describing the interrelationships between the religions in a global age. What does this mean?

First, we can affirm the complementary uniqueness of each of the religions, of their founders and of their tenets. The complementary nature of the religions is entailed in our belief in a panentheistic, kenotic God who is intimately present throughout the breadth and depth of the cosmos. This belief enables us Christians to accord a measure of validity to all the religions and religious figures of global history. It is the commonality of the one God which finally undergirds the complementarity of the religions. If you will, the Divine does not work against itself.

But the uniqueness of each of the religions also flows from belief in the one, universal God. Their uniqueness flows from the belief that the Divine has kenotically self-limited itself and disclosed itself within the necessarily limited, cultural forms of the varied religions and their founders. No one religion and no one religious "sage" is identical to others in all respects, simply because of the unique cultural and historical way in which each realizes its responsiveness to the divine presence. Thus, it is ultimately the divine kenosis of self-emptying into the finite, unique, and limited cultural forms manifest within history which undergirds the uniqueness—the specialness—of each of the religions and religious figures. We should note that uniqueness follows from the nature of the Divine itself as a kenotic mystery of self-emptying into the diverse and limited vessels of human history.

In a real sense, this approach is a kenoticist reinterpretation of the older, patristic *Logos*-doctrine. The strength of that tradition was to suggest the universal presence of the Divine (= the *Logos*) and thus the potential validity of all the religions. This is why most inclusivists today favor some form of the *Logos*-theory. Its weakness was its inability to account positively for the uniqueness of each of the religions. A kenoticist reinterpretation views the Divine as also committed to the unique elements of each of the religions, seeing them positively as reflections of the divine kenosis, rather than negatively as hindrances to an appreciation of the one, true *Logos*. Whereas the patristic *Logos*-model would suggest that the Divine is present partially in all and supremely in Jesus, its kenoticist variant would propose that the Divine is common to all, but always under the form of kenosis and limitation and particularity, even in Jesus.

Let us try to unravel some of the implications of our approach so far. First, I think it helps us grasp why there are so many striking similarities among the religions (= complementarity), and yet these similarities are wedded to unique, historical, and cultural differences (= uniqueness). The one God of all always appears under the form of particularity. Voegelin will speak of a common structure of human experience shared by all the religions, but uniquely differentiated in varying manners.[6] Thus, Hinduism, Buddhism, Taoism, Islam, Judaism, and Christianity all know the Ultimate/Absolute, but each knows this Absolute in uniquely irreducible ways. The undifferentiated All or Nothing of Hinduism and Buddhism is not identical with the highly personal Allah of Islam who calls supremely for obedience, or with the highly personal Father and Abba of the Jewish and Christian orbits. The cosmic numen of the oral cultures is likewise not identical with the transcendent God of the world religions.

So, too, many religions recognize that the Absolute discloses itself in history through mediators. All the varied religions in some way recognize this mediatorial nature of revelation: the mediator may be a person, an entire historical process, sacred scriptures, liturgies, fellowship, etc. But again this commonality of the religions is wedded to historical particularity. There are unique differences between the divine Buddha of the Mahayana who realizes nirvana, the Hindu avatars (Vishnu, Krishna) who incarnate Brahman, and the divine-human Jesus who takes the form of solidarity with the oppressed.

Our kenoticist approach also seems to avoid some of the well-known problems entailed in other views of the religions.[7] It seems more adequate than the notion of a "common essence" or "common core," because it recognizes that such a common core is actually a reified abstraction which does not exist in the concrete. The latter overlooks the diverse and kenotic forms which the Divine takes throughout history. The common core thesis (the legacy of the *Logos*-model) overlooks and denigrates historical and cultural particularity. In the hands of some thinkers (Radhakrishnan, Toynbee) it promotes the supposed goal of establishing a sort of meta-religion which has distilled this common core to the fullest extent. Distinguishing between the "inner" (faith) and "outer" (doctrines, rituals, etc.) elements of a religion seems to be another variant of the common core thesis, sharing in its liabilities.

From the Christian point of view, perhaps the most important facet of our approach is that it does not undermine the decisiveness of the Jesus event. Pointing this out has been Howard Burkle's important contribution to our problem. In a highly suggestive study, he proposed that the complementarity of the religions "does not destroy the decisiveness of Christianity." Christians can still affirm that their religion, centered on Jesus, makes an essential contribution to humanity's salvation. "For one thing, it is through Jesus that God redeems that segment of humanity who are Christian." Christianity even offers elements to non-Christians, "which certain human beings need, find congenial, and can obtain from no other religion." But on the deepest level, we can affirm that what occurred and still occurs through Jesus is "absolutely decisive for the whole world." What Burkle means is that the Jesus event is of salvific importance for all of humanity. Some inclusivists tend to overlook this:

> What is often overlooked about the Christian salvation events is the power of their objectivity. What God has done in Jesus has been *done* and, whether it is accepted or not, it has consequences. God *has* become one with humanity and understood us from within. God *has* suffered with us and forgiven us. God *has* conquered death and sin. And because these things happened in a human life, they are not just concealed within the privacy of God's heart but live on as a part of human history.

But what needs simultaneous affirmation is the possible decisiveness of the other religions:

> What I have been saying about Christianity's decisiveness for others may have a converse. It may be as necessary for Christians to hear of

Gautama as it is for Buddhists to hear of Jesus. Gautama's enlightenment at the Bo-tree may also be a salvation event for all people. Perhaps no Christian's salvation is complete until she/he breaks through the wall of the ego, extinguishes wrong desires, and attains that detachment from the world which gives peace. It is possible that the salvation event called Gautama Buddha influences the consciousness of Christians far more profoundly than they realize.[8]

In line with this, our kenoticist approach does not undermine the self-identity of the religions, together with their possible missionary thrust. It remains the vocation of the religions to value and witness to the unique but complementary disclosures of the Divine that are their foundation. To surrender this conviction would be to surrender the unique decisiveness that each represents as an act of God. But simultaneously, "conversion" as the traditional goal of missionary witness requires a wider, more global meaning. There is still room for speaking of conversion in the negative sense as a "giving up" of error and sin. But what our approach calls for is the notion of conversion as also a widening or expanding of consciousness and praxis. Rather than forfeiting one's religion, perhaps in our global age conversion will increasingly take the form of expanding one's religious horizon to embrace the grandeur of others.

Finally, our kenoticist approach seems to correspond to our experience. Our own experience seems to teach us that complementarity and uniqueness can bear a direct rather than inverse relation to one another. Often it is through the mutual enrichment of our relationships with one another that we discover and refine our unique potential. Others complement us in various respects, and, rather than robbing us of our potential, stimulate and catalyze it, helping us to carve out our unique identities. Complementarity and uniqueness can advance together in our experience. Perhaps the same can be true on the global level of the religions. Our approach would suggest that the mutual complementarity that we experience in life is a reflection of the creative and salvific God who grounds our human commonality. Likewise, our discovery of uniqueness reflects the divine kenosis which uniquely summons each of us into being and self-limits itself in such a way that our unique potential can thrive.

Our approach, however, goes beyond simply affirming the complementary uniqueness of each of the religions. It wants to introduce a "critical" note, proposing that religions must also be critical of one another. If "complementary uniqueness" avoids exclusivity, this critical dimension strives to avoid relativism. At least in principle we don't need to hold that all religions are always equal in all respects, representing equally adequate expressions of humanity's religious experience. Religions can be complementary without being equally adequate. This is true within our own experience, and there seems no reason to doubt its truth on a global level. This inequality of the religions seems to be a part of the kenotic mystery of history too: the Divine is wedded to our historical limits!

We know, for example, that all religions are tempted by sin and self-idolatry. They can become fanatic and harmful. They are also incomplete. The religions of oral cultures, for example, strongly emphasize the divine presence throughout the material cosmos, but they commonly underemphasize the divine transcendence. Turning it around, a typical danger of transcendence-affirming religions is dualism: denigrating the cosmos or overshadowing divine immanence with divine transcendence. Islam's rigorous stress on obedience might be helpfully balanced by Christians schooled in Jesus' love ethic and his intimacy with *Abba*. Judaism's covenantal religion sharply criticizes Christian lapses into individualism. Buddhism's mystical nirvana criticizes religions which ignore the mystical dimension. Jesus' active stress on solidarity with the suffering challenges the social lethargy of all religions. In short, religions know inadequacies and need mutual correction. A desire to be open to the world's religions need not make us naive.

The same critical sensitivity holds for individuals within the various religions too. Complementary uniqueness is just that: complementarity, not equality and identity. We need not hold, nor should we hold, that all individuals are equal in the way in which they body forth the divine presence. Christians can surely maintain that Jesus uniquely and consummately bodies forth the divine presence in his life, death, and resurrection in a way that no one else does. So, too, there are no texts which would lead us to believe that Jesus is simply equal with or identical to any other religious sage of history. To pursue another example, Buddha's own unique and decisive realization of nirvana is not simply paralleled anywhere else. A critical use of our complementary uniqueness model need not land us in untenable views about equality and identity.

Does this approach do full justice to what Christians have traditionally affirmed about Jesus? Is arguing for the unique decisiveness of Jesus, while being open to the unique decisiveness of other religions, enough for Christians? Some theologians would argue that we need to go beyond affirming simply Jesus' unique decisiveness to affirming that he is the "highest" and "supreme" mediator in humanity's religious history. Only this, they say, can do justice to that part of the Christian tradition which makes Jesus somehow different from every other mediator in religious history.

But there is an alternative possibility, suggested by a kenoticist approach to the matter. With the Christian tradition, we can and must hold that the Ultimate, the Highest, has appeared in Jesus and saved humanity, but under the form of kenosis and self-limitation, subject to the partial and fragmentary limits of human history. We Christians, after all, still await the full arrival of the hoped-for Kingdom. Under kenoticist presuppositions, it is possible to say that the Highest has arrived. This the tradition has always emphasized—but, we must add, under the form of kenosis. I would suggest that the tradition has been rightly fascinated by the first element: the Highest has come. However the kenoticist proviso has generally been either suppressed by the tradition or remained subterranean: under the form of kenosis. It is this latter element which our global age is perhaps helping us to re-emphasize. But let me emphasize that I put this forward only as a hypothesis needing to be tested by the religious sensitivities of the Christian and non-Christian faithful. In the long run only they can tell whether we have short-circuited something essential in humanity's religious heritage.

Perhaps an immediate, urgent, and yet quite difficult test-case of our approach suggested above is that of Jewish-Christian relations. For most Christians, the global dialogue seems a bit distant. Few of us know, in any significant way, a Buddhist, a Hindu, or a Moslem. But many of us have known and do know Jews. For us, perhaps the most immediate and practical way in which we enter into the global dialogue is through our Jewish contacts. Furthermore, contemporary Judaism and Christianity are sisters: we were both birthed by first century Judaism. Our common parent and our common heritage gives a kind of traditional priority to the Jewish-Christian dialogue. And, if we add to all that our sad history of anti-Semitism, there is a great urgency in our need to heal and transform our relationship to our fellow Jews. For all of these reasons, the Jewish-Christian dialogue is probably the most dramatic example, currently, of our global dialogue. On traditional and existential grounds, this dialogue has priority.

Some of the issues involved in the dialogue we have already treated in earlier chapters: the modern reassessment of the Pharisees, the "Jewishness" of the rabbi Jesus, the anti-Semitic aspects of the New Testament, the falsity of the charge of deicide against the Jews, the "Jewish" character of the God revealed by and in Jesus. Here let me highlight some further facets suggested by our approach to the global dialogue, which I would summarize under the two words "covenant" and "Messiah."

If we truly take seriously the disclosure of the Divine in Judaism—the *kenosis* of God into Israel—then we should be willing to reverence the unique decisiveness of the holy covenant with Israel. A Divinity that kenotically weds itself to many cultures and individuals is a God of many covenants. Christians must learn to think in terms of multiple covenants which are in varying ways both complementary and yet in a kind of critical tension with one another. Bearing this in mind, Christians can begin to affirm some of the unique features of the Jewish covenant: its stress on a communal form of religious piety, its stress on an activist God involved in human history, its stress on the land and reverence for it, its appreciation for suffering and negative religious experiences. I would say that these are especially characteristic features of the Jewish covenant which are truly complementary to Christianity and capable of critically revitalizing these dimensions in our own faith. Above all, our approach calls for a new theology of the covenant, one less insular and willing to entertain a divine kenosis into many covenants—but under the kenotic proviso. Every covenant, including that with Jesus and Christianity, is subject to the fragmentary limitations of time. No covenant abolishes the limitations of history and simply transcends every other covenant.

Furthermore, I suspect that our kenoticist revision of the Logos (or Messiah) doctrine might help us make a fresh start in this dialogue. So far as I can tell, the deepest theological stumbling block between Jews and Christians has been Christology. Traditionally Jews have considered our claims for Jesus' messiahship unreal and unfounded: the Kingdom has not fully come, evil and suffering still abounds, the Messiah has not yet come. A kenotic Messiah might remove many of these objections, for such a messiahship does not remove the scars and inevitable limitations of history. Not the royal, Davidic Messiah, but the prophetic, suffering Messiah— that is what our approach suggests. Clearly this would seem to be something that Jewish theologians could affirm as a unique disclosure of the Divine in history. But on the Christian side this would mean abandoning Christologies which try to abolish the in-between of history. While contemporary scholarship would not generally argue that all Christologies are inherently anti-Semitic, still one could argue that non-kenotic Christologies tend to be triumphalistic and to foster the inherent inferiority of others.[9]

Let me end with a speculative possibility. The current and painful globalization through which we are now passing is enormously difficult. In Christian terms, it is a living out of the death-resurrection mystery on a global scale; in Jewish terms, a global exodus; in Buddhist, a global nirvana. Such a process is finally a global experience of transcendence (one of the great signals of transcendence in our times) which requires the ultimately Transcendent One to ground and sustain it. Perhaps a Transcendence self-limited to kenosis, a kenotic *Logos*, offers us an analogous model of what our Holy God is up to. For only the truly Transcendent could globally unify in solidarity the entire race and cosmos. But only a kenotic One could do so in such a way that our unique particularities are not destroyed in the process.

Can a Male Savior Save Women?

A second, representative question which has festered over the unique self of Jesus has to do with his character as a male. Recently American feminist theologians have begun to query, not only the androcentric character of the Divine, but the male character of Jesus' self and the possible consequences that should be drawn from that. Like all issues, this one has both a theoretical and practical edge to it. Mary Daly has raised the theoretical issue clearly: she argues that women must reject Jesus as a liberating model for women, because his maleness reinforces an androcentrism which forever blocks women from the full realization of their potential. In effect, a male Savior holds up a male model for women to emulate, and thus reinforces patriarchalism.[10] The practical edge to this issue is that, if Christology is inherently androcentric, it will forever bar women from any mutual status with males within the Christian religion. Christianity would then be doomed to foster the sore of misogynism whenever it proclaimed the disclosure of the Divine in the male Jesus from Nazareth!

Again I would like to turn to Rosemary Radford Ruether as representative of feminist theologians who are grappling with this difficult issue. Quite helpfully she outlines three major options which seem to be emerging among those who are paying attention to women's experience.[11] The first she calls the model of "the imperial Christ," which for all practical purposes is a blatantly patriarchal approach to the self of Jesus. What Ruether means is that the Christological heritage stemming from the biblical and Chalcedonian settlements was androcentric in its formulation and meaning. It was essentially a fusion between Hebrew messianism and Greek philosophy. From the Hebrew tradition Jesus was proclaimed as the Messiah, a male figure who was believed to mediate the divine Kingdom. From the Greeks, Christianity borrowed the *Logos*-speculation, the belief in a divine principle of rationality and order through which the Divine governs the universe. In traditional Greek thought, the male most fully represented the working of this *Logos:* male rationality was set over against female bodiliness and concern for the natural, fleshly elements. So, too, in the Jewish heritage messiahship was a male prerogative: only the male could be the warrior-envoy of God who could establish the royal kingdom in history. The upshot of this dual heritage was that Jesus, as the Messiah and *Logos*, had to be a male if he were to body forth the messianic dreams of the Hebrews and the Greek belief in an order of rationality and meaning. In other words, the saving work of Jesus was tied to his maleness.

The difficulty here is that Christology seems to sanction patriarchy and the subjugation of women. Of course, we saw how Christianity in some

respects creatively rethought Jewish messianism and Greek *Logos* speculation. But the historical record does not indicate that Christianity broke
through the patriarchal underpinnings of the Greek and Hebrew traditions. Even as late as 1976 the "Vatican Declaration Against the Ordination
of Women" could argue that there must be a "physical resemblance" between the priest and Christ, thus linking Jesus' status as saving Messiah
and *Logos* with his maleness.[12] The Vatican's declaration simply repeats a
long line of historical patriarchalism. Even Augustine and Aquinas considered women to be "defective" humans, only males representing the fullness of humanity.[13]

A second approach, which Reuther has fascinatingly uncovered, is
that of "androgynous Christologies." Essentially these Christologies represent an attempt to break the strict linkage between Jesus' saving work
and his maleness by identifying him somewhat more closely with females.
It is instructive that these approaches surface only among the somewhat
more radical, less acceptable currents in the tradition, or at least among
figures with little cultural and political clout. For example, we find them
among the early gnostics, among some medieval mystics, and in some
nineteenth century American sects (namely, the Shakers). Not surprisingly, it seems characteristic of somewhat underground currents to be
somewhat freer and equalitarian in their thought and practice, as a kind of
protest against the perceived evils of the dominant powers.

Let us look at but two of the many androgynous Christologies which
Ruether unearths. Julian of Norwich, for example, is a medieval mystic
who takes over some androgynous themes already developed in the
twelfth century by Cistercian authors, incorporating them into her remarkable journal, *Showings*. Some typical and startling statements:

> And so Jesus is our true Mother in nature by our first creation, and he
> is our true Mother in grace by his taking our created nature. All the
> lovely works and all the sweet loving offices of beloved motherhood are
> appropriated to the second person, for in him we have this godly will,
> whole and safe forever, both in nature and grace, from his own goodness
> proper to him.

> The mother can lay her child tenderly to her breast, but our tender
> Mother Jesus can lead us easily into his blessed breast through his sweet
> open side, and show us there a part of the godhead and of the joys of
> heaven, with inner certainty of endless bliss.

Julian continues by suggesting that Jesus is the true paradigm of motherhood: "This fair lovely word 'mother' is so sweet and so kind in itself that
it cannot truly be said of anyone or to anyone except of him." And what

does motherhood mean? "To the property of motherhood belong nature, love, wisdom and knowledge, and this is God," says Julian.[14]

The Shakers are a somewhat more radical example of the androgynous type, insofar as they seem to believe in a dual Christ, both male and female, who reflects an androgynous Father-Mother God. Redemption, they hold, remains incomplete so long as it has taken place only in the male form of Jesus. Some Shakers believed that their foundress, Mother Ann Lee, was in fact the female messiah, the necessary androgynous complement to the male Jesus.

For the androgynous types, Jesus' saving work is not tied to his maleness, but to his androgynous (male-female) nature. Julian does this more conservatively by transforming Jesus himself into an androgyne; the Shakers, more radically, by uniting the male Savior Jesus with a female counterpart. This clearly represents a certain liberation for women, inasmuch as their femaleness can image forth the saving work of the Divine. Participation in salvation is a matter not only of maleness, but of androgyny.

But the great difficulty with androgynous thought and imagery is its equation of femaleness with the supposed feminine qualities of nurturing, mothering, and loving. This tends to foster a truncated view of women and of men: women nurture; men are nurtured to. In this light, Mariology especially needs a critique.[15] It is easy enough to grasp why women might define themselves in such a way: mothering and nurturing are the key roles open to women in a patriarchal culture. But it is still questionable as to whether this represents full liberation for women. On these terms, they still remain derivative from the male and in a dependent relationship with him.

Ruether calls her third and own option the "prophetic, iconoclastic Christ," but perhaps I may be permitted to call it the model of the liberating Jesus. In this approach, Jesus is imaged forth as one who is in solidarity with God, humans, and nature, embodying the work of justice, love, and peace. Jesus acts to overcome master-slave relationships, wherever they may occur. As we have seen, for men this means that he holds out to them the ideal of service (Mk 10:35–45); for women, the ideal of dignity and full participation in the new community (Lk 10:38–42). As Ruether explains it, in this model the saving work of Jesus does not consist in his maleness, nor in his supposedly androgynous makeup, but in his ability to liberate from injustice and lovelessness. As she goes on to explain:

> He speaks especially to outcast women, not as representatives of the 'feminine', but because they are at the bottom of this network of oppression. His ability to be liberator does not reside in his maleness, but, on

the contrary, in the fact that he has renounced this system of domination and seeks to embody in his person the new humanity of service and mutual empowerment.[16]

Males should reflect for a moment on what it means to tie Jesus' saving work to sexual gender. If we say that only males fully image forth Jesus' redemptive work, then we forever bar women from mutual participation in the Jesus event. But, correlatively, if we turn the table around and say that salvation can only come by way of the female, then we bar males from mutual participation in salvation. The mistake, even the tragedy, of this "sexual" and "genital" reading of the Jesus event is that by linking salvation with sex it inevitably truncates the renewal of life which should flow from the Jesus event.[17] Just why our Christian Savior came in the form of a male rather than a female, while unessential to Jesus' saving work, is probably best understood as part of that kenotic, self-emptying mystery which the Divine disclosed in Jesus. The Divine has limited itself to the cultural limitations of a given epoch. But perhaps there is more to it, too. A male proclaiming and embodying the overturning of injustice was a kind of "slap" to the males of the time, a sort of contradiction to the inherited prejudices and bigotry of the androcentric culture. Something of the transvaluation or renewal of life flowing through Jesus seems to surface here, a transvaluation which doesn't simply reverse, but overcomes all master-slave relationships.

Notes

1. Paul F. Knitter, "Horizons on Christianity's New Dialogue with Buddhism," *Horizons* 8 (1981), 40–61.

2. *Ibid.*, 56.

3. Richard H. Drummond, *Gautama the Buddha: An Essay in Religious Understanding* (Grand Rapids: Eerdmans, 1974), p. 44; cf p. 80.

4. Knitter, "Horizons," *art. cit.*, 57, referring to Roy C. Amore, *Two Masters, One Message: The Lives and Teachings of Gautama and Jesus* (Nashville: Abingdon, 1978), pp. 51, 16, 57. Cf Paul F. Knitter, "Jesus—Buddha—Krishna: Still Present?" *Journal of Ecumenical Studies* 16 (1979), 651–671. Thomas Merton, of course, is important for opening Christianity up to the transcultural dialogue; see his *Zen and the Birds of Appetite* (New York: New Directions, 1968) and *The Asian Journal of Thomas Merton* (New York: New Directions, 1975); cf William M. Thompson, "Merton's Contribution to a Transcultural Consciousness," in Donald Grayston and Michael W. Higgins, eds., *Thomas Merton: Pilgrim in Process* (Toronto: Griffin House, 1983), pp. 147–169.

5. For examples of exclusivists and relativists, see Charles Davis, *Christ and the World Religions* (London: Hodder and Stoughton, 1970). I first came

across the designation of an "inclusivist Christology" in Tracy, *Blessed Rage for Order, op. cit.*, p. 206. For examples of modern inclusivists, who usually employ some form of the patristic *Logos* speculation, see Richard, *What Are They Saying About Christ and World Religions? op. cit.*, and Michael B. McGarry, *Christology After Auschwitz* (New York: Paulist, 1977), for a fine application to the Jewish-Christian dialogue. Voegelin is a further modern inclusivist: "I am indeed attempting to 'identify' . . . the God who reveals himself, not only in the Prophets, in Christ, and in the Apostles, but wherever his reality is experienced as present in the cosmos and in the soul of man. One can no longer use the medieval distinction between the theologian's supernatural revelation and the philosopher's natural reason, when any number of texts will attest the revelatory consciousness of the Greek poets and philosophers; nor can one let revelation begin with the Israelite and Christian experiences, when the mystery of divine presence in reality is attested as experienced by man, as far back as ca. 20,000 B.C., by the petroglyphic symbols of the Palaeolithicum. The modern enlargement of the ecumenic horizon to globality, and of the temporal horizon by the archaeological millennia, has made a revision of the traditional 'common language' indeed ineluctable. . . . In practice this means that one has to recognize, and make intelligible, the presence of Christ in a Babylonian hymn, or a Taoist speculation, or a Platonic dialogue, just as much as in a Gospel" ("Response to Professor Altizer's 'A New History and a New But Ancient God?' "*Journal of the American Academy of Religion* 43 [1975], 765–772 at 766–767). Of course, Raimundo Panikkar is one of the best known inclusivists; see his *The Intrareligious Dialogue* (New York: Paulist, 1978); *Myth, Faith and Hermeneutics: Cross-Cultural Studies* (New York: Paulist, 1979); and his newly revised *The Unknown Christ of Hinduism: Towards an Ecumenical Christophany* (Maryknoll, N.Y.: Orbis, 1981).

6. See his *Order and History, op cit.*

7. See, for the references, Howard R. Burkle, "Jesus Christ and Religious Pluralism," *Journal of Ecumenical Studies* 16 (1979), 457–471.

8. *Ibid.*, 464–466, for the citations.

9. This would be my reformulation of Rosemary Ruether's more radical (but, I think, unsubstantiated) view that anti-Semitism is an inherent result of the emergence of Christology in general. Somewhat baldly put, Ruether thinks that as the earliest Christians "defied" Jesus, so they vilified the Jews in partial legitimation of the emerging Christology (= it is because they are "vile" that they cannot accept the Christ). So far as I can tell, the scholarly consensus would seem to point in the direction of my proposed reformulation. After all, Christology can be said to result from Jesus, from his implicit Christological and soteriological dimensions, and from the Easter experiences. It is not necessarily the result of Jewish vilification. Thus, there are Christologies that are not anti-Jewish or anti-Semitic in the New Testament. On all of this, see Ruether, *Faith and Fratricide, op. cit.*, and the response edited by Alan T. Davies, *AntiSemitism and the Foundations of Christianity, op. cit.* Very helpful on the state of the Jewish-Christian dialogue: "From Holocaust to Dialogue," *Journal of Ecumenical Studies* 18 (1981), Number 1; Pawlikowski, *What Are They Saying About Christian-Jewish Relations? op. cit.*

10. See Mary Daly, *Beyond God the Father* (Boston: Beacon, 1973), p. 19.

11. Cf her "Christology and Feminism: Can a Male Savior Save Women?" *To Change the World, op. cit.*, pp. 45–56, substantially repeated in her *Sexism and God-Talk, op. cit.*, pp. 116–138.

12. See No. 27 (the decree was issued 15 October 1976).

13. Cf. *Summ. theol.*, 1,92,1 and 2; 3,39,1; and *De Trin.*, 7,7,10.

14. Citations are from *Julian of Norwich: Showings* (New York: Paulist, 1978), pp. 296, 298, 299.

15. This holds true, even if one introjects these qualities into every person, instead of simply projecting masculine qualities onto males, and feminine qualities onto females. Cf Ruether, *New Woman/New Earth, op. cit.*, pp. 36–62.

16. Ruether, *To Change the World, op. cit.*, p. 56.

17. The silence of Jesus regarding matters of sexuality needs to be remembered here. It would appear that he rather consistently overcame all sexual taboos in matters of religion.

14

Jesus, Church, and Society in the Contemporary Debate

Let us now move into the third member of our quaternity. As we have seen, the Jesus event gives birth to a novel community within history, caught in the in-between of our incomplete present and the greater future. We have called this the "covenantal community": a community where true solidarity with the Divine, with our fellow human partners, and with nature is the overriding basis and commitment. We have also seen how the community-creating power of the Jesus event cuts across both the Churches and the larger society: it is a bonding power that flows where it will. What, now, are some key challenges from our contemporary experience to the vision and praxis of this novel Jesus-like community?

The Churches

The community-empowering reality of the Jesus event does not exist in the abstract. It takes place within the world, among communities of women and men within the Churches and out who respond to the summons to struggle for the peace, justice and love that is rooted in the peace, justice and love of Jesus' God. It has "carriers" (träger was the German sociologist Max Weber's term), in other words, who must make it a reality. Here our focus will not be upon individual carriers of the Jesus event—the saints and mystics, known and mostly unknown, who are empowered by the Jesus event—but upon the "social" *träger*.

It seems that a number of contemporary sensitivities are forcing us to probe this issue a little more carefully these days. The theoretical issue can be put quite bluntly: Where should we Christians recognize the community-empowering work of Jesus as most apparently taking shape today? I say "most apparently," because we cannot simply identify Jesus' work with any earthly community: in our experience love, justice, and peace are always mixed with the bondage of lovelessness, injustice, and aggression. The practical edge of this question is this: Should we Christians not practically align ourselves with those movements within history which seem to be most responsive to the community-empowering work of Jesus? Would not those movements hold out promise for the most effective continuation of Jesus' work: the revitalization of our vision and praxis in a Jesus-oriented way? From the global perspective, would it not be our alignment with such movements which would be our greatest contribution to the forging of a new transcultural solidarity among women and men?

Most of us will probably want to continue to align ourselves with the various Christian Churches. Despite their sinfulness, we see them as attempting to remain faithful to the basic thrust of the Jesus event. If we are honest with ourselves, we realize that our own appropriation of the Jesus event has largely been the Churches' gift to us. They have, however falteringly, mediated it to us. Where would we be, where will our children be, without this mediation of the Churches?

Perhaps an increasingly new development today is that many of us find ourselves aligning ourselves with the Churches in a novel and critical manner. As we wake up to the basic thrust of the Jesus event and the lessons of our contemporary experience, we sense many glaring inconsistencies within the Churches. This gnawing sense of inconsistency is a kind of ecclesial conversion for us: we find ourselves undergoing a shift, from being simply a cultural Christian to becoming a more deeply committed and critical one.

What are some of these inconsistencies within the Churches that many of us experience today? Let me briefly highlight some of them under three headings.

(1) *Mission*. Many of us, under the twin pressures of the Jesus event and contemporary experience, view the Churches' mission as one of responding to and embodying the community of peace, justice and love, where all master-slave relationships are overcome. Yet we cannot help wondering whether the Churches do not often take this mission too lightly, or, perhaps worse, think that they have some other mandate in human history. In the experience of many of us, reintegrating the marginalized of society into the womb of the ecclesial family seems to be a kind of "added on" job, a sort of extra to be accomplished after all the more "properly" churchy tasks have been accomplished. This reduces and even mutilates Jesus' solidarity with the oppressed into a kind of charitable almsgiving. In this way, many Churches remain relatively comfortable, wealthy, and shielded from conflict with those societal powers that are most responsible for the marginalization of the oppressed in the first place. The Churches are also able to shield themselves from asking about the degree of their own responsibility in the plight of the oppressed.

In America, perhaps the "inconsistency" that links up with all the other inconsistencies and symbolizes them is the androcentric character of many of the Churches. Ministers still blithely recite the misogynistic texts of Scripture as if we have learned nothing about women's oppression. We still train our children in the male-language of prayer, cementing them in androcentrism from very early on. Predominantly or exclusively male clerics control the Churches, institutionalizing in an ecclesial context the very master-slave relationship they are supposedly committed to uprooting. Androcentrism is but a symbol of our ecclesial cancers. But if this most obvious one cannot be confronted, what shall we think of the many other more concealed inconsistencies which surely are present within the Churches?

(2) *Ministry*. All effective social carriers of the Jesus event are in need of ministers, those persons who especially provide for the welfare of the entire ecclesial community, fostering and catalyzing its growth and development. Jesus had his disciples, male and female, and so must we today, if we are truly to build community. But again many of us sense horrible inconsistencies with the ministry of Churches. Hierarchicalism or clericalism, which is but an ecclesial form of the master-slave relationship, is built rather tightly into most Churches today. The very language of "clergy" and "laity" lends itself to a demeaning of most of the people in a Church, cementing the so called "laity" into a passive posture which keeps them at the bottom of the hierarchical pit. One can even have clericalism in Churches without clergy: in this case, the "elders" become the paternalistic power-brokers who keep people (= the laity) in their places. Clergy are also pedestalized by special garb and dress, which also creates class structures within the Churches. There is a place, of course, for festival garments meant to symbolize the community's highest aspirations and joys. But a class garb which creates hierarachicalism needs a thorough cleaning out.

Hierarchicalism/clericalism is systematically linked, of course, with misogynism. It is not accidental that Churches which downplay the mandate to transform master-slave relationships fall into both hierarchicalism and sexism. For both are a form of the master-slave vicious circle. In a Jesus-centered Church this must go. The systematic exclusion of women from all types of ministries is simply an inexcusable cancer in the womb of the Church. Either the entire thrust of the Christology presented in these papers is wrong, or sexism of whatever stripe is wrong.

(3) *Ritual*. The problems we have but touched on spill over into the ritual life of the Churches and find symbolic expression and reinforcement there. None of us should call into question the extremely important role

that ritual plays in the life of the Churches and in our human lives generally. Just as Jesus had his table fellowship, so must the Churches today, if
they are to nourish the community and build it up. The issue is not
whether there should be ritual, but what kind of ritual is most promising
for carrying forward the thrust of the Jesus event.

All too often, ritual is but an embodiment of the hierarchicalism we
have spoken of earlier. Laity do not gather to celebrate and develop their
talents for the work of the Kingdom. They do not gather to be rocked out
of their lethargy and made to feel uncomfortable about the plight of the
marginalized. All too often they gather to reinforce the system of domination that holds sway in society at large. All or mostly male ministers proclaim the word and celebrate the Eucharist: the people listen and attend.
They are systematically excluded from the most important parts of the liturgical service, as if their mutual participation would make a difference to
the "validity" of what occurs.

The above is but a suggestive smattering of the glaring inconsistencies
that face many of today's critical Christians as they seek to align themselves
more effectively with the thrust of the Jesus event. What can they do about
them? One possible option is to borrow a clue from the religious orders of
Catholicism. Originally—and to some extent still today—members of the
religious orders were people, common people often, who were fueled by
the values of the Jesus-like community. They maintained tight links with
the dominant Church, even seeking its official approval. But their relationship was often an uneasy, dialectical one with the larger Church. They
would nourish their own members and celebrate their own deeply cher-
ished values, and then seek to revitalize and critique the larger Church in
a kind of gradualist, ongoing way. I would suggest that this is still a viable
model for many critical Christians today. Christian women committed to
the uprooting of misogynism; Christians in general committed to the uprooting of hierarchicalism and all master-slave relationships; the daring
"prophets" who risk themselves on behalf of the oppressed—all these
groups can and should seek one another out, nourish one another on the
values and praxis of the Jesus event, and seek an uneasy but persistent relationship with the larger Church, hoping to be an effective voice in its
gradual renewal and a humble disciple of its wisdom.

A second, more radical option is for Christians to find their primary,
challenging and nourishing group outside the official boundaries of the
Christian Churches. In the case of women, for example, this may take the
form of being linked with women's groups, such as ERA. Here one finds
the strength and courage to work for society's renewal, and the challenge
which comes from this difficult task. Or one might be closely linked with

groups whose primary focus is civil rights (Native Americans, Mexican Americans, the blacks, etc.), or some form of peace and disarmament, etc. Professionals of various types might find their primary nourishment in various critical groupings of their own kind. In any case, these Christians might then try to maintain a critical and dialectical relationship with their own larger parent Churches, seeking to be a voice in their renewal. Being linked with the parent Churches is especially important for those pursuing this second option, lest they lose their "Jesus-focus" and the peculiar strength that flows from it. It will save them from either utopianism or pessimism, exposing them to the tradition's wisdom.

At times, too, quite radical renewal can come from the leadership of the official-institutional Church itself. The prophetic leadership of the American Roman Catholic bishops on behalf of peace is a stunning example. Likewise, the leadership of the Pope and Protestant leaders on behalf of peace stands out glowingly.

There are, of course, many other issues relative to the Churches which could and should be treated in a study of ecclesiology. I have only tried to suggest those problems that seem most "pressing" from the Christological perspective of this book.[1]

The Great Debate Beyond the Churches

We Christians believe that the community-making power of the Jesus experience flows out beyond the borders of the Churches and takes root wherever the master-slave dialectic is effectively confronted, resisted, and sometimes even abolished. But where is this occurring most effectively today? The answer to that question would enable Christians to align themselves with those movements which seem to be empowered, whether knowingly or not, with the dynamic power of the Kingdom. Currently, the issue is under intensive debate.

In general terms, we can say that some opt for socialism. An increasing number of theologians, especially from the third world, have clearly expressed a preference for some form of socialism as a polity which seems most compatible with Christian goals and aspirations. This is true of Jürgen Moltmann, Gustavo Gutierrez, Peter Hodgson, John Coleman, and Gregory Baum, to name but a smattering of influential "critical" theologians.[2] On the other hand, some opt for what they call democratic capitalism. Those espousing this position are not as numerous, but they do exist, and Michael Novak has become perhaps their most influential representative.[3]

We inevitably encounter a certain amount of ambiguity about just what socialism and democratic capitalism are. Peter Berger, the influential sociologist, is probably correct when he suggests: "Everything is in some kind of continuum, in which it is very difficult to make clear-cut divisions." And he continues:

> . . . the terms "capitalism" and "socialism," if defined with any degree of intellectual elegance, refer to two phenomena which, as such, do not exist in the empirical world today. A pure capitalist system would be one in which the basic goods available in the society are distributed solely by means of market mechanisms. A socialist system would be one in which the same goods are distributed through a system of political allocation.[4]

If Berger's distinction is correct, then socialism would be a system which preponderantly inclines in the direction of the political allocation of goods, while democratic capitalism inclines in the direction of the free market mechanism. Hybrids would seem possible: democratic socialism might be a polity with capitalistic elements; welfare capitalism might combine capitalism with some degree of the political allocation of goods. But if words are to mean anything, we should speak of the preponderant tendency as the distinguishing characteristic of the system.

Why are so many theologians and Christians attracted to some form of socialism? The answer surely lies in its attractive moral vision and powerful critique of capitalism. Morally, socialism is fueled by the dream of human solidarity, which strives to overcome alienation and exploitation and truly promote the common good. It has a powerful moral ethos, claiming that the promotion of human and humane values is more important to it than material success or the profit motive. It is based upon a somewhat optimistic view of history, according to which human tragedy can be overcome and true justice achieved. Historically, it is an outgrowth of the Enlightenment: it wants to fulfill the Enlightenment dream of human perfection, through the creation of human community and solidarity. Obviously the resonances of socialism with Christianity are quite striking.

Socialism usually combines its moral vision with a critique of the destructive trends of capitalism, particularly as that is practiced in the United States. Different versions of this critique can be found among socialists, but it usually includes both a "spiritual" and an "economic" dimension to it. Spiritually, capitalism is accused of fostering materialism, narcissism, excessive individualism, and consumerism. These "spiritual" emphases of capitalism lead it to give priority to profit, even at the expense of human alienation and exploitation. Thus, factory workers may experience intense frustration from their routinized and technologized work, but because assembly lines are more cost efficient, no matter. Thus, too, the profit motive may lead capitalists to go after contracts wherever they may be found—namely, military contracts, regardless of whether this is healthy for the human community.

Capitalists, it is argued, are able to amass huge fortunes through accumulating property and controlling the work of others, thus making it difficult for the poor and less advantaged to climb the economic ladder. Because the capitalist ethos and economy dominate the state, laws tend to favor the wealthy (namely, through tax loopholes), and the economic sector exercises undue influence over the state: government protects big business, and many of the elected officials are drawn from the wealthiest sector of the population.[5] Socialism, then, wants to break through the destructive effects of capitalism, both through transforming the reigning values of society and through a more equitable distribution of goods, usually thought to be achievable through a more collective form of ownership.

On the other hand, democratic capitalism is equally fueled by its own moral vision and simultaneous critique of socialism. Like socialism, democratic capitalism is an outgrowth of the Enlightenment dream of human betterment too. The Enlightenment ideals of liberty, justice, freedom, and happiness all lie at its basis. But historically it comes, not from the more radical French wing of the Enlightenment (which birthed socialism), but from the more conservative Anglo-Scottish wing, with its distrust of ruling classes.

Michael Novak plausibly argues that the ultimate foundation of democratic capitalism is "pluralism":

> A pluralistic spirit decisively distinguishes democratic capitalism from either traditionalist or socialist societies. Every other form of society the world has ever known imposes a collective sense of what is good and true. In all other systems, every decisive economic, political, and moral-cultural power is exercised by one set of authorities. Democratic capitalism is unique among all forms of political economy by reason of its pluralism.[6]

This pluralistic spirit and polity is thought to be the embodiment in concrete reality of the ideals of freedom, liberty, equality of access to human betterment, and justice for all. Thus, democratic capitalism is really "three systems in one: a predominantly market economy; a polity respectful of the rights of the individual to life, liberty, and the pursuit of happiness; and a system of cultural institutions moved by ideals of liberty and justice for all."[7] The differentiation of spheres (= pluralism) gives scope to the freedom and creativity of the citizens of a democratic polity. Economically, a free market economy gives scope to freedom and ingenuity; a limited government tries to serve the common good of its citizens without violating

their freedom; and the relative freedom of the citizens in the moral-cultural sphere enables their values to serve as a check and balance on the
other spheres of the society.

Novak argues that while democratic capitalism has been relatively
successful in the economic and political spheres, through sustained economic growth and the survival of democratic forms of government, it has
been less successful in the moral-cultural sphere. It has failed to bring out
the real moral values undergirding its existence. But he is convinced that
it possesses real values, which do and can correct the "underside" of capitalism.

For example, Novak views the differentiation of spheres as a means of
building human community without damaging human individuality. As
the political/economic/moral spheres are distinct but not separate, so
democratic capitalism tries to foster regard for the distinction and non-
separation of the individual and the society. It is not really hyper-individ-
ualistic: the many mediating structures it has birthed attest to that
(families, Churches, voluntary associations, unions, corporations, neigh-
borhoods, etc.). It gives birth to a different kind of social grouping, "less
. . . rooted in kith and kin, blood and status, propinquity and immobility
. . . more voluntary, fluid, mobile . . . nonetheless communities for
that."[8]

This regard for individuality-within-community to some extent reflects a God who builds community through equal love for all, Novak suggests. Democratic capitalism is also very "incarnational": "One of the most
difficult lessons of the Incarnation is the difficult teaching that one must
learn to be humble, think concretely, face facts, train oneself to realism."[9]
Thus, democratic capitalism tries to avoid utopianism, designing institutions appropriate not for saints but for sinners. Hence its checks and balances, differentiation of spheres, and respect for the freedom of its
citizenry. The capitalist stress on "competition" likewise needs rethinking:
it can degenerate, but it can also be "the natural play of the free person."[10]
It literally means "to seek together" and need not enshrine a hedonistic
individualism. Democratic capitalism also takes the doctrine of sin seriously: hence it is devised against tyranny through a system of checks and
balances. But it is not pessimistic: "Belief in original sin is consistent with
guarded trust in the better side of human nature."[11] Novak sums up his
vision in the Christian ideal of *caritas:* "To look upon human history as
love-infused by a Creator who values others, who sees in those originating
sources of insight and choice which we have come to know as 'persons' the
purpose of his creation; and who in loving each as an individual creates of
the contrarious many an unseen, hidden, but powerful community, is to

glimpse a world in which the political economy of democratic capitalism makes sense."[12]

Throughout his writings, Novak tries to build the case for the underside of socialism. Let me try to capture the important elements. Socialism tends to foster the view, he claims, that all evil has its source in social structures and systems, rather than the perverted heart of the self. Thus, it tends to overlook the imperfections of every system, including its own, which come from the perverted heart. It also tends to take the direct route to economic planning, through imposing a certain vision of the economic order upon others. Hence its unease with the "free market" mechanism, and the great role it gives to planners, the vanguard elite, and state bureaucrats. It also tends to be a "zero-sum economy." Instead of increasing productivity, goods, and resources, it is more static in its view of economics. If you will, instead of increasing the size of the "economic pie," it takes the same pie and slices it in many different ways. This creates large scale dissatisfaction, for inevitably there isn't enough to go around.

Most importantly, socialism tends to be a system of no compromise, no partial solutions. It does not allow free play to interest groups and checks and balances. In other words, it tends to concentrate all powers in the hands of the vanguard government. This is often accompanied by a moralistic spirit—the sense that it is the true and future goal of humanity. This fuels its revolutionary spirit and its often coercive behavior. It teaches individuals to loathe any society which is short of the more perfect socialistic vision. It fosters the mentality of placing one's trust in the hands of a bureaucracy, thus intensifying the power of the state and patterns of dependency. It ultimately confuses brotherhood and sisterhood with collectivism.

One of the more interesting facets of Novak's work is his claim that we can now assess socialism as it actually has existed within history. The Soviet orbit provides us with an empirical source for the testing of socialism, rather than a simply idealized version of it. Capitalism, he claims, has usually fared unfavorably with socialism, because scholars tended to compare the rugged history of an actual capitalism with an idealized version of socialism. Novak adds, too, that scholars and clergy are perhaps excessively attracted to socialism because it enables them to exercise moral control over the masses, a temptation not unknown to the clerical and scholarly world.

What are Christians to do as they face these two apparently contradictory options which are emerging within human society and competing for one's affections? With which should one align oneself in the attempt to contribute toward the building of Jesus' novel community within history?

Let me try to suggest some principles of discernment which flow both from the Jesus event and from our experience.

First, neither socialism nor democratic capitalism is simply identical with Jesus' new community, which is a divinely-created and community-empowering force of peace, justice and love. To my knowledge no theologian claims this for either option. But, second, today's Christians must make concrete choices about the options available to them. Ultimately, these choices must be rooted in the belief that a particular option seems most promising for carrying forward the thrust of the Jesus event. That, for the Christian, is the ultimate principle of discernment. If we base ourselves upon the Jesus event, then I think we can say that the stance of critical partisanship is what the in-between character of the Jesus event calls for when making concrete political choices. What does that mean?

We might recall that Jesus' community is in-between utopianism and pessimism; it is critically realist. Hence, the Christian should be a partisan of those concrete movements which seem to be open to the ideals and the praxis of the Jesus event, or at least capable of being influenced by it. This is the "realist" dimension. But the Christian should also be a "critical" partisan, refusing to slide over into utopianism. This means, in the case of democratic capitalism, that he or she must strive to make Christian values and praxis a "soul force" within the moral-cultural sphere of democratic polities, which can serve as a check and balance that pressures those polities to live up to their high ideals, avoiding the oppression of others in the name of an "American profit." This means, in the case of socialist and democratic socialist polities, that the Christian must act as a "soul force" correcting and opposing any regression into state tyranny or simple collectivism. Under these provisos, the Christian ethos would seem to be at least compatible with either of these two options.[13] In other words, a Jesus-inspired approach to either democratic capitalism or socialism fosters a critical stance of partisanship. In this sense, a "revisionist" socialism and democratic capitalism seem to be viable Christian alternatives.

Perhaps we can go further too. Personally I think the "soul force" which is the Jesus event (and, in a complementary way, the "soul force" of the other great religions) might work in such a manner that it could enable the two major currents of socialism and democratic capitalism to transcend and sublimate their differences. Many partisans of both sides seem to be trying to find a way to preserve the values of welfare and social solidarity, without lapsing into bureaucratic collectivism and tyranny. So, too, they are trying to preserve the ability of capitalism to provide economic growth and opportunity, without regressing into materialistic hedonism and individualism. Practically this would mean fostering the notion that the state should function, not as the ultimate controller doing all through its offices, but as the empowerer or servant of its people, supporting and empowering individuals and voluntary associations as they struggle to meet the needs of the citizenry. Christian sensitivity to peace, justice and love, its heightened abhorrence of all master-slave relationships—these would seem to be the kind of womb which could nourish and foster such a sublimation of the differences between capitalism and democratic socialism.

This debate between capitalism and socialism is singled out here because it is truly one of the *great* debates of our time. Many nations are currently making choices about their future between those two options. Christian participation in those choices will have an important contribution to make in the debate. An equally *great* issue "beyond the Churches" which should at least be noted here is that of the issue of nuclear warfare and nuclear deterrence. Quite clearly the future of any revised capitalism or socialism—indeed, the future of the planet—rests upon a serious and successful grappling with the nuclear threat.

Christians should want to be involved in the nuclear debate. They should see this as a moral imperative flowing directly out of the Jesus event and fidelity to it. The summons of the Jesus event to work for the establishment of peace, justice and love seems to entail a basic commitment to work against trends and movements which make a nuclear holocaust of the human planet likely. In other words, the same Christological imperative which calls for Christian participation in the capitalism-socialism debate also calls for Christian participation in the nuclear debate. Avoiding a nuclear holocaust, and allowing Hiroshima and Nagasaki to inform our Christological theory and praxis, is a crucial way of being faithful to the Jesus event today.

Let me mention a useful primer in this regard, a work by David Hollenbach called *Nuclear Ethics*.[14] This work is terribly helpful for our purposes because it diligently attempts, in a "centrist" manner, to root our thinking about warfare in the tradition of Jesus. In this way, Hollenbach's work is a kind of model of the way a centrist would integrate nuclear ethics and Christology. For Hollenbach, the two major traditions of the ethics of war—the pacifist and the just war theory—are constant trends within the Christian tradition, extending continuously from Jesus to the present. Of course, the complete rejection of violence (= pacifism) quite clearly has roots within the Jesus tradition, as we have seen before (cf Mt 5:9; Jn 20:19). What is not so well known is that this tradition continued in Christianity even after Christians began to enter into military service. Whatever the motives for pacifism before the Constantinian epoch (avoiding the emperor worship of the military, the notorious sexual license of the military, a genuine belief in the ethics of Jesus, etc.), pacifism continued within the monastic and mystical-contemplative traditions even after Constantine.

Even Thomas Aquinas, who thought military service moral in some cases, believed that the clergy should be pacifists. Although this tends to feed into a problematic hierarchicalism, still it recognizes the importance of the pacifist tradition as a part of the heritage of Jesus.

On the other hand, the just war tradition, although only formulated in Augustine's time and later, appeals to the Hebrew Scriptures, to biblical texts supporting obedience to political authorities (Rom 13:1–2; Mt 22:21), and in general to the belief that Jesus' coming has not abolished the "in-between" character of human history as a legitimation for its posture (Mk 13:32–33). It, too, feels that it has genuine roots in the Jesus tradition, especially when one remembers that it, too, abhors violence as immoral, resorting to violence only as the least immoral of the choices available.

The startling persistence of the above two trends within the tradition would seem to argue that both should have a role to play in any decision about nuclear warfare and deterrence to be reached by Christians. The temptation of pacifism is to accept injustice too quickly, refusing to come to terms with the in-between character of human existence. The temptation of the just war tradition is to accept violence too easily, not exhausting every strategy short of violence in pursuit of justice. Each tradition needs the other and seems to be rooted in the in-between character of Jesus' own message and work itself. In other words, if I read Hollenbach correctly, he would root the value of peace (= pacifism) in the future Kingdom proclaimed by Jesus. The just war tradition, which tries to grapple with the contingencies and evils of history, he would root in the fragmentary, only imperfectly realized actualization of the Kingdom. As the tension between the two avoids both pessimism and utopianism, so perhaps this gives us our best chance of making an effective Christian contribution to the Christian debate. A critical partisanship on behalf of peace, humbly aware of the in-between character of the human drama—that would seem to be a Jesus-inspired foundation for a nuclear ethics.

Where does all this practically leave Christians as they struggle with the nuclear issue? For Hollenbach the relation between peace (pacifism) and justice (the just war theory) is a complex one, entailing a practical, prudential judgment in every instance. Sometimes it would seem that a war is justified (= justice) precisely to protect peace, sometimes not. One cannot predict this judgment *a priori*, but must attempt to discern how best to live out the summons of the Kingdom under the conditions of this imperfect world. Hollenbach himself would argue that nuclear warfare can never be justified, even in an imperfect world, given its totalistic destructive consequences. It cannot accomplish what the just war tradition says it must to be just: namely, present us with the best chance of preserving more life than destruction. A similar judgment has been registered by the American Roman Catholic bishops in their enormously prophetic and brave pastoral letter on war and peace, *The Challenge of Peace: God's Promise and Our Response,* which condemns counter-population (civilian) nuclear warfare and the initiation of nuclear warfare, and is highly skeptical about the possibility of limited nuclear warfare.

So far as I can tell, Hollenbach registers a somewhat novel contribution to the deterrence debate. For him, the existence of nuclear deterrence is a glowing example of the in-between character of human existence. If we lived in a perfect world where threats to human and national dignity did not arise from the lust for domination, deterrence would not be necessary. The real challenge for a Jesus-inspired morality is to foster a policy of deterrence which best promotes peace. Given our world, our choice is not deterrence or no deterrence. It is rather a matter of opting for a deterrence policy which will actually make the world progressively more secure from nuclear warfare. In other words, the intention behind deterrence must be the firm resolve to act always in such a way that war becomes less likely. Thus, we should avoid the kinds of deterrence which actually seem to foster the likelihood of war by threatening the opponent in an inequitable manner or forcing the opponent to a "launch on warning" position, etc. Again, Hollenbach has suggestively rooted his proposals in a fine analysis of the Jesus event as a vision and praxis of the tension-filled space of the in-between.

Hollenbach's views on deterrence seem rather similar to the proposals put forward by the American bishops in their peace pastoral. Hollenbach would seem to agree with the bishops that deterrence is not "adequate as a long-term basis for peace," and must be linked with a policy of progressive disarmament. As the bishops powerfully put it, "We are living in a global age with problems and conflicts on a global scale. Either we shall learn to resolve these problems together, or we shall destroy one another." Both political disarmament and "disarmament of the human heart" (to use the bishops' haunting phrase) are required. The World Council of Churches, at its 1983 meeting, argued against the use of all deterrence. The issue needs careful study.

Because of the massiveness of the nuclear issue, we would do well to turn to prayer, as the bishops recommend. Such "contemplative prayer," they say, "is especially valuable for advancing harmony and peace in the world." Such prayer "bridges temporarily the 'already' and 'not yet,' this world and God's Kingdom of peace." Because we Americans were the first and only ones to use the atomic bomb in war, perhaps ours is the greatest responsibility to struggle on behalf of peace.[14]

Lessons from the Feminist Critique

Another important example of the struggle to revitalize Church and society through attunement to the Jesus event is provided us by women's struggles against social sexism. Again, this issue has a theoretical, a practical, and even a global edge to it. Just as sexism requires us to revise our image and praxis of the Divine Presence and of the self, so it requires a similar adjustment in our social relations. Because of the quaternion and interlocking structure of all things human, we cannot preach the overcoming of sexism with respect to the Divine and to the self, and expect society within and outside the Church to remain as before. Our social theory and praxis must adjust accordingly. This may be a decisive contribution which the West can make to the overcoming of sexism on a global scale. A non-sexist Western society could act as a powerful "soul force" within the global dialogue as it is currently taking shape.

What would a non-sexist renewal of society and Church—a renewal rooted in the lessons of the Jesus event and women's experience—entail? While Rosemary Radford Ruether has developed some possible answers to this question, it is primarily the theologian Mary Buckley who has concisely faced this issue. Let me outline her proposals, and then take up a concrete question of some relevance. Particularly important with Buckley is her attention to the public and political sphere, and the need to correlate changes in models of the person with changes in the social fabric as a whole. As she puts it, "In the feminist movement it is often said, 'The personal is the political,' but the deep interrelation of these two is not easily probed in depth."[15] What she suggests is that different models of the role of women are linked with and supported by corresponding societal/ecclesial structures.

For example, a blatantly patriarchal model of women—woman as inferior to man—seems to correspond to an "hierarchic-elitist" society and Church, in which roles are carefully defined and stratified, with women occupying a position at the bottom or close to the bottom of the social hierarchy. The "order" might run this way: men - women - children - slaves - property. It is probably this kind of society and Church which has existed for much of human history, particularly since the rise of urbanization in the second millennium. To some extent, Christianity represented a break with elitism, but it was an incomplete break, certainly as far as women were concerned. One could also say that the Enlightenment and the French and American Revolutions also constituted a break with hierarchicalism. But men alone were the full recipients of the new freedoms.

Probably the model of society and Church highly characteristic of the

West today is the "one-dimensional society," which corresponds to the androgynous model of women. This largely seems to be the product of modern democracies, which have abolished the nobility and aristocracy to some extent, proclaiming the great ideals of freedom, justice, equality, and brotherhood. Much is attractive in this vision, but it was an incomplete one for women. "Under the cloak of democracy, the real ruling groups have been hidden," says Buckley.[16] In pre-revolutionary eras, the privileged—kings, nobility, aristocracy—were much more visible, while the real powers today are much less evident. For example, blacks, Indians, and women often have no voice, or at the most a "muted" one. The upper elite and wealthy males actually predominate, but in a concealed way, for the official ideology proclaims the equality of all.

To some extent, one-dimensionalism is a continuation of the older patriarchal societies. In other respects it is a transformation. With the emergence of industrialization, power in society began to shift from the home/farm to the public marketplace, as well as to the increasingly bureaucratized state. Women largely were segregated from the spheres of power (remaining at home), and yet they were told that they are equal. A new conception of women developed: they nurture, mother, support; they represent the pure, the clean, and the domestic virtues; they are not meant to dirty themselves by entering into the economic and political worlds. In other words, it is the androgynous model that surfaces.

The feminine archetype embodied and institutionalized in one-dimensional societies does not really represent the full range of women's capacities. It corresponds, rather, to the role forced upon women by a powerful male elite. For example, women are expected to be the ones who stay at home. If they choose or need to work, they suffer from the double bind of having to do the domestic work and the hired work. It is well documented, too, that their salaries are consistently lower than those of males. This same kind of thinking and praxis surfaces in Churches, which regard women as suitable for certain domestic tasks—secretarial, cleaning, cooking, etc.—but exclude them from the real positions of power.

A third model is struggling to emerge, one which might hold out promise of a fuller liberation for women. This model would correspond to the full range of women's potential, and be much more consistent with Jesus' vision of a community of justice, peace and love. Buckley calls this the "transformative model," for it attempts to transform the earlier patriarchalism and androgyny into a full liberation for all. In this model, autonomy and power would not be viewed as simply male, while nurturing and love fall on the female side of the ledger. Autonomy and power, and nurturing and love—all together are human possibilities and needs for all.

Full humanity demands both. When autonomy is split from love, tyranny results. But when love is split from autonomy, it becomes dependency and slavery.

Many people fear this kind of transformative vision for society. Its full practical implications remain unknown. But more importantly, it will be costly, demanding a profound change in the way we perceive one another and structure our societies and Churches. Perhaps something that may allay our fears somewhat is that this third model is not an argument for a "unisex" society, which tries to abolish physiological differences between the sexes. Women and men are clearly different in this regard, but the characteristic of humans is that their physiology is meant to be integrated with their psychic-spiritual potential. Women will still give birth in transformative societies; however birthing will not be an experience of dependency upon the male, but an act involving both power and love, autonomy and nurturing simultaneously.

An important test case for our new model will be that of the family. There are innumerable factors within the present climate of opinion which work against the family. Industrialized societies put a high premium upon the professional person who has broken free from family bonds. Careers often replace families in the public eye as the crucial component in society. Professionals often reinforce the myth that parents are unsophisticated and incapable of properly raising their children. Radical groups argue that the traditional family is out of date. And now, along comes the feminist critique, which seems to pull the mother away from the home, making her, too, one of society's "professionals."

But there is another possibility, another imaginable scenario. The family need not, and should not, be denigrated within a truly transformative model of society. Common sense and historical experience combine to tell us that the family is the foundational community within any society which nourishes the basic values and skills needed throughout all of life. It is the seedbed of economic skills, it is the protection against alienation and despair, it is the *ecclesiola* ("little Church") where Christian values are learned, it is the school of spirituality where narcissism is first broken through and love, justice, and peace are lived. The family is also politically crucial: one learns social solidarity there, and yet within the enclave of the family one is protected against the domination of the state. A strong family, a society full of strong families, is a tremendously crucial counterpoise to the state and its possible domination. It is also a strong counterpoise to the image of the narcissistic individual, whose highest value is his or her own inflated egoism. In religious terms, the family is meant to be the foundational covenantal community, where peace, justice and love are learned and lived.

I suggest that Buckley's transformative model looks not to the denigration of the family, but to its transformation and its strengthening. Through fostering a more just and loving experience of familial community, families would be enriched. Within a transformative family, motherhood would not mean simply nurturing; fatherhood would not be simply autonomy. Parenting would foster and promote a more complete realization of human capacities for all. How this can happen in societies which want only males in the work place and females at home requires creative ingenuity and a constant uphill battle. Working for laws and tax benefits for the family, making it possible for women to work and develop their career potential through tax supported (and business-supported) day care centers, creating jobs and professions which make it possible for both parents to be at home and to work equally in a shared manner, fostering sports open to males and females simultaneously, etc.—all of these and more are the challenges that lie before us.

Notes

1. I have been greatly stimulated by Ruether's *Sexism and God-Talk, op. cit.*, pp. 193–213, throughout this section on the Churches. For more standard treatments of ecclesiology, see the works of Avery Dulles and Richard P. McBrien, for example. On the question of the division between the Christian Churches, I share the optimism that the theological differences between us can be bridged in principle; what is lacking is the institutional will. In terms of Christology, I would suggest that the major divisions represent the creative recovery of different dimensions of the Jesus event, each needing to be dialectically interrelated: Jesus' new community as universal and international in scope (Catholicism); that community as embracing the richness of the entire Christian tradition down through the ages (Orthodoxy); that community as a radical, Gospel-like critique of injustice and lovelessness (Protestantism). Cf. McBrien, *Catholicism* (Minneapolis: Winston, 1981), pp. 567–901.

2. See Moltmann, *op. cit.*; Gutierrez, *op. cit.*; Hodgson, *op. cit.*; Coleman, *op. cit.*; Gregory Baum and Duncan Cameron, *Ethics and Economics: Canada's Catholic Bishops on the Economic Crisis* (Toronto: James Lorimer, 1984).

3. See his *The Spirit of Democratic Capitalism* (New York: American Enterprise Institute/Simon and Schuster, 1982), and, more briefly, *The American Vision: An Essay on the Future of Democratic Capitalism* (Washington, D.C.: American Enterprise Institute, 1978). Cf also Robert Benne, *The Ethic of Democratic Capitalism: A Moral Reassessment* (Philadelphia: Fortress, 1981).

4. Peter Berger, "Capitalism and Socialism: Empirical Facts," in Michael Novak, ed., *Capitalism and Socialism: A Theological Inquiry* (Washington, D.C.: American Enterprise Institute, 1979), p. 85.

5. I have followed the socialist critique of capitalism given in Arthur F. McGovern, *Marxism: An American Christian Perspective* (Maryknoll: Orbis, 1981), esp. pp. 135–171.

6. Novak, *The Spirit, op. cit.*, p. 49.

7. *Ibid.*, p. 14.

8. *Ibid.*, p. 339.

9. *Ibid.*, p. 340.

10. *Ibid.*, p. 347.

11. *Ibid.*, p. 351.

12. *Ibid.*, p. 355. See the Vatican's "Instructions on Certain Aspects of the Theology of Liberation," *National Catholic Reporter* 20 (Sept. 21, 1984) 11–14, for another critique of primarily Marxist socialism, stressing the dangers of a class analysis which opposes the saved proletariat to the unregenerate.

13. Papal teaching would appear to agree; Cf David Hollenbach, *Claims in Conflict: Retrieving and Renewing the Catholic Human Rights Tradition* (New York: Paulist, 1979). Also helpful, Peter L. Berger and Richard John Neuhaus, *To Empower People: The Role of Mediating Structures in Public Policy* (Washington, D.C.: American Enterprise Institute, 1977).

14. The full title of Hollenbach's work: *Nuclear Ethics: A Christian Moral Argument* (New York: Paulist, 1983). The Roman Catholic American bishops' pastoral letter: *The Challenge of Peace: God's Promise and Our Response* (Washington, D.C.: United States Catholic Conference, 1983), the citations at p. 58 (#186), p.76 (#244), p. 88 (#284), and p. 90 (#294). Also helpful: Richard A. McCormick, "The Challenge of Peace," in his "Notes on Moral Theology: 1983," *Theological Studies* 45 (1984), 122–138, esp. 129–130, where he explains the position of the World Council of Churches (rejects any and every use of nuclear arms, including deterrence). McCormick gives a fine overview of the critical literature on the issue. My references to the World Council of Churches are to McCormick's citations.

15. Mary J. Buckley, "The Rising of the Woman Is the Rising of the Race," *Proceedings of the Catholic Theological Society of America* 34 (1979), 48–63 at 56.

16. *Ibid.*, 59. Cf Joann Wolski Conn, "Women's Spirituality: Restriction and Reconstruction," *Cross Currents* 30 (1980) 293–308.

15

Jesus and Ecology
in the Contemporary Debate

One of the promising new developments in theology today is the growing sensitivity to ecology. Let us try to probe this final member of our human quaternity, focusing upon its intersection with the Christological and soteriological concerns of this book. Our ecological interwovenness with nature, body, and matter is just now coming into heightened focus as an object of concern, despite the fact that we humans have always been biological creatures. What accounts for this new interest?

Our new ecological awareness primarily stems from our growing sensitivity to the destructive consequences of industrialization. The huge amounts of toxic wastes that are polluting the air, waters, and soil seem to be threatening the biosphere. Some argue that the basic resources on which industry depends—fossil fuels, metals, and minerals—are limited, and that industry is hopelessly raping these resources in such a way, that the "non-industrialized" sector of humanity will forever be robbed of the possibility of a better way of life. Finally, population is expanding at such a rapid pace that food production cannot keep apace, famine is inevitably spreading, and there is an increasingly aggressive competition between the nation-states for the food of the earth. One of the really new elements is the fact that these problematic features of industrialization are affecting the relatively affluent and well-developed nations themselves, thus forcing them to query the possible bases for this state of affairs. At the same time, this awareness of the affluent can stimulate a frenzied march to hoard even more of the earth's resources, thus worsening the problem even more.

Another factor heightening our ecological sensitivity is the increasing sophistication of human technology. This both highlights our human dependency upon matter and yet our inability to deal adequately with some of its destructive consequences. Human technology has achieved remarkable results in some ways: one thinks of the advances in medical technology, such as prosthetics of all kinds (artificial hearts, kidneys and aortic valves, heart regulating transistors), immunizations, etc. One thinks, too, of the mass production of food and of the harnessing of energy, of computers, of space travel and technology, and so on. And yet at the same time, technology confronts us with dangers of an unparalleled sort: one thinks of human experimentation, especially with sperm banks, and the possible genetic mutation of the human species. One thinks of a cadre of scientific elite, controlling the course of future human development in a kind of "Walden II." One thinks especially of a possible nuclear holocaust of the race, resulting from a technology hopelessly severed from human and humane values.

I would add that the increasing "materialism" of the West also promotes a new and troubled sensitivity to the bodily, organic nature of our humanity. The extended life-expectancy of humans curiously fosters a cult of youthfulness and yet simultaneously creates an extensive class of elderly who are shunned as reminders of the senescence of all things created. What is valued is to think and feel (more importantly) young. Advertising celebrates this cult of youth—one rarely sees old or "out of shape" (by youthful standards) bodies. Does this neo-materialism represent an acceptance of matter and the body, or an uneasy attempt to disown it, cover it up, and flee from it? The same could be said about our attitude toward death, the great and final reminder of our materiality. Has our neo-materialism fostered a greater acceptance of death, or the reverse?[1]

Under these pressures, the West, and increasingly the globe, are looking for an ecological consciousness and praxis that is respectful of the gains provided humanity through industry and technology, and yet critical of their destructive consequences. This new consciousness and praxis would, at once, have to be a new vision of ecological responsibility, and a new praxis of ecological right living. It would have to promote a global harmony, protecting the biosphere and the legitimate biological needs of humanity as a whole.

To achieve this, some walk down the path of a kind of "mysticism of science and technology," seeking the answer in an ever-refined science itself. Perhaps Carl Sagan's celebration of science might serve as the symbolic focus of this orientation. Thus, for example, the destructive consequences of industrialization can progressively be solved by means of technological advances. What are needed are better safety devices and standards, pollution control, exploring alternative energy resources, medical prosthetics on a global scale, space technology and energy, etc. Technology can be refined so that only the "best" genes are transmitted, so that nuclear waste is safely stored, so that an effective balance of power is maintained among the nuclear powers, etc. Finally, senescence and the dying process can be mollified through better drugs and physical panacea which ease the pain of human mortality.

Others walk down the path of an anti-industrial and anti-technological revolt. They tend to idealize nature and the primitive, seeking to withdraw from contemporary urbanized and industrialized society. Radical nature groups, some radical alternative living communes, perhaps some Native American groups, would typify this approach. This option is highly sensitive to our biological rootedness.

But one can rightly question whether either of these approaches is adequate to the ecological challenge awaiting the human community. Each seems sensitive to an element of truth: the first, to the possible benefits of technology; the second, to our biological rootedness. But each inevitably leaves the final problem unsolved. For what ultimately lies at the basis of our contemporary dilemmas is a perverted heart which finds public embodiment in domination of all sorts, whether over humans or over matter and nature, a perverted heart which has no regard for the welfare of the human community as a whole. More technology or less technology fails to come to grips with this deeper issue.

It is at this point that ecology seems to intersect with Christology, in the sense that Jesus' ethics of self-limitation perhaps offers us the possibility of combining scientific progress with religious wisdom. Such an ethics neither denigrates technology nor flees from it, but recognizes that it is in the service of the community of peace, justice and love. This ethics tries to respect nature as the possible site of the new community, the "place" and "space" where peace, justice and love can be realized. This view promotes ecological "harmony," in the sense that each part of the universe is recognized as vital to the remaining parts. As Rosemary Radford Ruether expresses it, "We must start thinking of reality as the connecting links of a dance in which each part is equally vital to the whole."[2]

Jesus' ethics of self-limitation calls for a new form of asceticism for the future which must find social and even global embodiment: an asceticism of care for the body and bodily and ecological health. In other words, a Jesus-inspired ethics seeks to build up the true covenant intended for us by God, a covenant of harmony in which exploitation no longer reigns. The peculiar originality of Jesus lies in his tracing of the sources of disharmony to the perverted heart itself. Only a "conversion" of the heart can move us in the direction of a proper use of technology and at-one-ment with nature. Without this conversion, there can be no even probable guarantee that a mysticism of science and technology cannot be perverted toward destructive ends. And without this conversion, who is to say that the tribal revolt against technology won't regress into a crude barbarism and primitivism?

An important link exists between this new ecological awareness struggling to emerge and the feminist critique of religion and society. As many feminist theologians have pointed out, the exploitative abuse of nature and body has gone hand in hand with the exploitative abuse of women.[3] The early emergence of urbanization brought with it an increasing subjugation of women, we recall: they remained "tied" to the home and its maternal duties of pregnancy and child rearing, while males entered into the new urban spheres of politics, business, religion, and warfare. Women became symbols of "the inferior," and, along with them, the body and its maternal functions became denigrated. Woman-body-nature, along with children and slaves—these were the inferior ones set over against males-society-culture-religion-the affairs of the spirit.

The later dualism of late Greek philosophy, with its great stress upon rationality and "spirit," further intensified the dualism between body-matter-women on the one hand, and males-reason-spirit on the other. Judaism and Christianity represented only a partial break from this dualism, showing strong tendencies to regress back toward it. Like women, nature was to be dominated and controlled by superior male rationality and spirituality. This is probably best symbolized in the many menstrual taboos, which closely link women with nature's processes. A demonic uncleanness is ascribed to women's sexual fluids, and this belief is in turn "used to segregate adult women for most of their lives and forbid them access to male precincts of sacerdotal, political, and educational power."[4]

The much later feminine "ideal of pure womanhood," developing in the modern industrial period, seems to have been a kind of compensation for women's harsh and continued segregation from the centers of power. She is too pure to be dirtied by politics and industry. But this "compensation" still did not remove the inferior status of women: they were most suitable for houses of prostitution and for the sweatshops. Female carnality and inferiority still continued as the underside to female "purity."

The ultimate issue here is the pattern of exploitation and domination, legitimated by a projection of inferiority and servility upon women and nature. This is why the emergence of an ecological awareness must go along with the overcoming of misogynism and all other forms of exploitation. The hidden link between misogynism and ecological imbalance is the heart perverted by exploitation, which then finds embodiment in abusive social and natural interrelations. As Ruether puts it,

> Our model and relationships must cease to be hierarchical and become mutually supportive, a cooperative model of fellowship of life systems. As Vine Deloria says, in his Indian liberation theology, *God is Red*, we must believe, not just in the brotherhood of man, but in the fellowship of life. Or, as Mary Daly declares, we must seek, not just the new social covenant, but the new cosmic covenant as well.[5]

It would seem that Ruether is calling for what I would call a revitalization of Jesus' ethics of self-limitation.

I would also suggest that one of the real contributions of the Native American critique of American values and religion is its disclosure of the hidden link between ecological imbalance and an exploitative system of values and praxis. Just as the feminist critique has its origins in women's attention to their own history of subjugation, so we have a similar origin for the Native American critique. In Vine Deloria's words: "The one common thing that each tribe experienced was its invasion of its homeland by Western European white men." What distinguishes theologian Deloria from many tribalists is his attempt to uncover the deeper roots of the exploitativeness that has characterized white-red relations and white attitudes toward the eco-system. He particularly singles out the "temporal" perspective of the West as one opposed to the "spatial" imagination of the Indians. "American Indians hold their lands-places as having the highest possible meaning, and all their statements are made with this reference point in mind."[6]

The perspective of the Indians is naturally rooted in their nature-based origins as oral and agricultural cultures. Divine revelation is found in space, in nature, and in the tribal community that is intertwined with that space and living symbiotically with it. This consciousness promotes a greater sensitivity to the land and to the tribe's needs as dependent upon that land. "Tribal religions find a great affinity among species of living creatures, and it is at this point that the brotherhood of life is a strong part of the Indian way."[7] Characteristic of the West, according to Deloria, is a time-orientation which stresses the movement of peoples through history to some awaited goal. This desensitizes people to their lands, and enforces a narcissistic individualism which destroys the brotherhood of the whole cosmic system.

As a Christian theologian I read Deloria as a critical partner and corrective to the debasement of Christianity which is indeed a sad part of our heritage (even now). What he seems to be attacking is what Ruether calls "the Western dream of infinitely expanding power and wealth which defies the actual finitude of ourselves and the world and conceals the exploitative use of other people's resources."[8]

Actually there are many points of contact between Deloria and the vision of Christianity typified throughout these pages. It is true that Christianity stresses time, for, like Judaism, it believes that the Divine is revealed in ever new historical events. But the difference between the Jewish-Christian heritages and the nature-based religions of oral cultures has been exaggerated. Both Judaism and Christianity believe, not only in the transcendent God, but in the kenotic one panentheistically present throughout the cosmos. Creation is good, and the Divine is "found" there. Like the Indians, Judaism and Christianity espouse a covenantal or "tribal" form of life which interlocks humans and nature together. Christianity did not precisely debase the value of the land, but relativized it, by acknowledging that the Divine transcends any one space and person and can be encountered in all spaces and persons. What Deloria seems to be attacking is the relatively more recent Western cult of the inflated individual fired by the dream of his or her expanding power. This "cult" has some roots in Christianity's high reverence for the person, but more properly it is an outgrowth of one trend of the Enlightenment. Still, we Christians need the critical partisanship of a theologian like Deloria to help us uncover the way in which we have distorted our own tradition.

Toward a New Ecological Praxis
Inspired by Jesus and Our Experience

Working out a Jesus-inspired ethics is a complex question requiring that today's Christian be guided by a dialectical interplay between Jesus' ethical vision and praxis and the lessons of our own contemporary experience. We have already stroked the broad contours of what we are seeking: a new, covenantal vision and praxis of the Divine Presence, according to which the divine power of self-limiting love, justice, and peace empowers us to act with that same love, justice, and peace; a covenantal self, whereby person-making is a project of solidarity with others in the entire human family, with nature, and with God; the embodiment of this new covenantal self within a transformed society which promotes the full liberation of all— the "self writ large"; and now, finally, the translation of this covenantal vision and praxis into a biological/ecological key through the establishment of an ecology of harmony and mutual linkage. In short, the broad outlines are a reverence for the quaternion structure of human and material existence itself.

Perhaps on a more practical level, I can hazard the following as possible "ecological" translations for our time of a Jesus-inspired ethics. On a personal level, the self needs to undergo a conversion to a vision and praxis of ecological harmony. This would involve both repentance and faith: repentance from a narcissistic lifestyle that cannot limit an exploitative relationship to the body and the environment, and faith in the alternative of a restored and harmonious cosmos.

The most immediate way in which the self experiences the eco-system is through the body. Bodiliness is the most obvious thing about us, the way in which we are present to one another and our world, and they to us. It is the "space" in which we present ourselves to one another. Our bodies share in the whole history of matter—we are spirited matter. Conversion to ecological harmony, then, must start here with our bodies. In a sense, we must be able to do what Jesus did in his own way: just as he could appeal to bodily and natural images as metaphors or mediators of his Kingdom, so we must come to experience our bodies as Kingdom-mediators too. This would involve repentance: we must repent the sin of making our bodies the scapegoat of our own narcissism, which lets us off the hook from our real sinfulness. This would also involve faith in the value of the harmony promised us by Jesus' Kingdom: seeking to treat our bodies with respect, refusing to hurt them and pollute them through better eating habits, athletic discipline, general physical hygiene, but doing this in a manner calculated to restore our bodily harmony. One cannot jump from too much drink and food to crash diets without harm!

Basically we must seek a careful, holistic, and integrative approach to our bodies if we are to promote bodily and spiritual harmony. We should make an effort to be in tune with our bodies, listening to their rhythmic cycles and respecting them. We are generally insensitive to these. As theologian Richard Woods puts it, "We are even embarrassed by 'body signals' such as when our stomach is suddenly heard 'growling' or when we sneeze or cough, for all of which, and many other bodily sounds, we automatically apologize."[9] There is also no reason why biofeedback techniques should not be used. These can enable us to monitor our various bodily systems and "feed back" that information. Dishabituation exercises, too, like depriving ourselves temporarily of food, drink, sleep, sex, and work, can break us out of our usual insensitivity to the body and heighten our care for it.

A particularly fascinating topic treated by the mystical theologian Richard Woods is that of pets. Pets, like house plants, are another primary source of contact with nature for most of us. They can help restore our needed harmony with nature, for they relate us inescapably to the world of nature and matter. Interestingly, too, because they cannot fully satisfy us, they also point us in the direction of our need for fellow humans and even for the Transcendent One. The way we treat our pets is a fair index of the way we treat our bodies, and, indeed, nature generally. Further, the pet's allegiance to us can teach us much about devotion and fidelity to all realities, including God. Nature, if you will, is a great teacher of fidelity and care. And, as many researchers are pointing out, pets can heal us, restoring our broken harmony: "The pet becomes," says Woods, "a medium of human (and, I believe, divine) love and trust at a time when the recovering patient is too vulnerable and weak to endure the full effort and risk of reaching out to other persons."[10] Who of us has not been such a "vulnerable patient"?

On a societal level, the translation of a Jesus-oriented vision and praxis into an ecological key is much more difficult. I am convinced that we will have gone a long way, though, if we persevere on the personal level. If Jesus is right, it is the perverted heart which is the ultimate source of our problems. Still, social embodiment of ecological harmony is the necessary complement to its personal embodiment. Certainly here the key task is the humanization and spiritualization of our industry and technology, in such a way that its destructive dimensions are minimized, and its creative potential maximized. Ways must be found to more justly care for and distribute the world's resources. Efforts must be made to seek alternative forms of energy that are less polluting, equally available for all and inexpensive, and renewable (sun, wind, water especially). Greater efforts should be made in urban renewal to respect nature and provide easy access to natural parks. We need much less addiction to the concrete which smothers our earth, and to the mighty automobile, which now demands about three times as much space as humans do. Should society embody values and practices such as these, this would act as a real soul force upon the technological and industrial sector, forcing them to operate for the common good. One of the real tests for the survival of industrialized, capitalistic economies is whether they will be willing and able to meet these challenges that are upon us. Can the moral-cultural sphere exercise enough courage and restraint upon the economic and political spheres to see these changes through? That is the challenge now confronting us.

It is somehow fitting that we end our book on an ecological note. *Divine* nature is the holy womb from which all creatures come and to which they return. It is our final link with one another and with the Divine. As we pass through it and "fertilize" it, it in turn fertilizes us, moving us into our final destiny. We end where we begin: with the Divine.

Notes

1. The best theological overview of the ecological issue is to be found in Woods, *Symbion, op. cit.*, esp. pp. 114–220. Cf also his *Mysterion, op. cit.*, pp. 75–107, 325–371. Also cf now John Carmody, *Ecology and Religion: Toward a New Christian Theology of Nature* (New York: Paulist, 1983).

2. Ruether, *To Change the World, op. cit.*, p.67; pp. 57–70, "Ecology and Human Liberation: A Conflict Between the Theology of History and the Theology of Nature?" for the entire essay. R. Woods is consistently critical of Sagan as a scientist who ignores religious values. For an alternative view which finds an "im-

plicit" religious sense in Sagan, see William Frost, "Sagan's 'Cosmos': Secular or Religious?" *The Ecumenist* 20 (1982), 43–46.

    3. See Ruether, *New Woman/New Earth, op. cit.*, pp. 13–31, and her more recent *Sexism and God-Talk, op. cit.*, pp. 72–92. See also John B. Cobb, Jr., *Process Theology as Political Theology, op. cit.*, pp. 111–134, "Sociological Theology or Ecological Theology," for a fine process-oriented appreciation of the importance of ecology in theology and its linkage with feminism. Note the comment: ". . . the emancipation of women for the sake of justice is the key to the stabilisation of global population" (p. 131).

    4. *Ibid.*, p. 16.

    5. *Ibid.*, p. 31.

    6. Deloria, *op. cit.*, p. 75.

    7. *Ibid.*, p. 103. On Deloria, see P. Joseph Cahill, "Vine Deloria: An Essay in Comparison of Christianity and Amerindian Religions," *Journal of the American Academy of Religion* 45 (Supplement, June 1977), 419–446. Also very helpful from a Christian perspective: Carl F. Starkloff, *The People of the Center: American Indian Religion and Christianity* (New York: Seabury, 1974).

    8. Ruether, *To Change the World, op. cit.*, p. 66.

    9. Woods, *Mysterion, op. cit.*, p. 84.

    10. *Ibid.*, p. 105.

Index of Subjects

Index of Names

431